A PLATO READER

A PLATO READER

Eight Essential Dialogues

EUTHYPHRO
APOLOGY
CRITO
MENO
PHAEDO
SYMPOSIUM
PHAEDRUS
REPUBLIC

Edited by

C. D. C. Reeve

Hackett Publishing Company, Inc.
Indianapolis/Cambridge

Printed in the United States of America

17   16   15   14   13   2   3   4   5   6   7   8

For further information, please address:

Hackett Publishing Company, Inc.
P.O. Box 44937
Indianapolis, IN 46244-0937

www.hackettpublishing.com

Cover design by Brian Rak
Text design by Meera Dash
Composition by William Hartman

Library of Congress Cataloging-in-Publication Data
Plato.
    [Dialogues. English. Selections]
    A Plato reader : eight essential dialogues / edited by
C.D.C. Reeve.
       p. cm.
    Includes bibliographical references (p.   ).
    ISBN 978-1-60384-811-4 (pbk.) —
    ISBN 978-1-60384-812-1 (cloth)
    I. Reeve, C. D. C., 1948– II. Title.
B358.R45 2012
184—dc23
                                                    2012013057

The paper used in this publication meets the minimum requirements of American National Standard for Information Sciences—Permanence of Paper for Printed Library Materials, ANSI Z39.48–1984.

Contents

Introduction

Plato was born in Athens in 429 BCE and died there in 348–347. His father, Ariston, traced his ancestry to Codrus, who was supposedly king of Athens in the eleventh century BCE; his mother, Perictione, was related to Solon, architect of the Athenian constitution (594–593). While Plato was still a boy, his father died and his mother married Pyrilampes, a friend of the great Athenian statesman Pericles. Plato was thus familiar with Athenian politics from childhood and was expected to enter it himself. Partly in reaction to the execution of his mentor and teacher Socrates in 399, he turned instead to philosophy, thinking that only it could bring true justice to human beings and put an end to civil war and political upheaval.

Few ancient authors have been as lucky as Plato. His works, which are predominantly dialogues, all seem to have survived. They are customarily divided into four chronological groups, though the precise ordering (especially within groups) is controversial:

Early: *Apology, Charmides, Crito, Euthyphro, Hippias Minor, Hippias Major, Ion, Laches, Lysis, Menexenus*

Transitional: *Euthydemus, Gorgias, Meno, Protagoras*

Middle: *Cratylus, Phaedo, Symposium, Republic, Phaedrus, Parmenides, Theaetetus*

Late: *Timaeus, Critias, Sophist, Statesman, Philebus, Laws*

This volume presents eight of the most widely read of these dialogues, drawn from every group except the last.

Plato also contributed to philosophy by founding the Academy, arguably the first university. It was a center of research and teaching both in theoretical subjects and also in more practical ones. Eudoxus, who gave a geometrical explanation of the presumed revolutions of the sun, moon, and planets around the earth, brought his own students with him to join Plato, and studied and taught in the Academy; Theaetetus developed solid geometry there. But cities also invited members of the Academy to help them in the practical task of developing new political constitutions.

The Academy lasted for some two-and-a-half centuries after Plato died, ending around 80 BCE. Its early leaders, including his own nephew

This Introduction has been adapted from *Introductory Readings in Ancient Greek and Roman Philosophy*, edited by C. D. C. Reeve and Patrick Lee Miller. Copyright © 2006, Hackett Publishing Co.

Speusippus, who succeeded him as head, all modified his teachings in various ways. Later, influenced by the early dialogues, which end in puzzlement
(*aporia*), the Academy, under Arcesilaus, Carneades, and other philosophers,
practiced Skepticism; later still, influenced by different dialogues, Platonists
were more dogmatic. Platonism of one sort or another—Middle or Neo- or
something else—remained the dominant philosophy in the pagan world
of late antiquity, influencing St. Augustine, among others. Much of what
passed for Plato's thought until the nineteenth century, when German
scholars pioneered a return to Plato's writings themselves, was a mixture
of these different Platonisms.

Given the vast span and diversity of Plato's writings and the fact that
they are dialogues, not treatises, it is little wonder that they were read in
many different ways even by Plato's ancient followers. In this respect nothing has changed: different schools of philosophy and textual interpretation
continue to find profoundly different messages and different methods in
Plato. Doctrinal continuities, discontinuities, and outright contradictions
of one sort or another are discovered, disputed, rediscovered, and disputed afresh. Neglected dialogues are taken up, old favorites reinterpreted.
New questions are raised, old ones resurrected and reformulated: Is Plato's
Socrates really the great ironist of philosophy, or a largely non-ironic figure? Is Plato a systematic philosopher with answers to give, or an explorer
of philosophical ideas only? Is he primarily a theorist about universals, a
moralist, or a mystic with an otherworldly view about the nature of reality
and the place of the human soul in it? Or is he all of these at once? Does the
dramatic structure of the dialogues undermine their apparent philosophical
arguments? Should Plato's negative remarks about the efficacy of written
philosophy (*Phaedrus* 274b–278b) lead us to look behind his dialogues for
what Plato's student Aristotle refers to as the "so-called unwritten doctrines" (*Physics* 209b14–15)?

Aside from this continued engagement with Plato's writings, there is,
of course, the not entirely separate engagement with the problems Plato
brought to philosophy, the methods he invented to address them, and
the solutions he suggested and explored. So many and various are these,
however, that they constitute not just Plato's philosophy, but much of philosophy proper. Part of his legacy, they are also what we inevitably bring
to our reading of him.

SOCRATES

Socrates is the central figure in most of Plato's works. In some dialogues
this central figure is thought to be—and probably is—based to some extent
on the historical Socrates. As a result, these are often called "Socratic" dialogues. In the so-called transitional, middle, and late dialogues, however,

the central figure is thought to be a mouthpiece for ideas that go well beyond Plato's Socratic heritage.

In the Socratic dialogues, philosophy consists almost exclusively in philosophically pointed questioning of people about conventionally recognized moral virtues. What is piety? Socrates asks, or courage? or temperance? He seems to take for granted that there are correct answers to these questions—that piety, courage, and temperance are each some definite characteristic or form (*eidos,* idea). He does not discuss the nature of these forms, however, or develop any explicit theory of them or our knowledge of them. He does not, for that matter, explain his interest in definitions, or justify his claim that if we do not know what, for example, justice is, we cannot know whether it is a virtue, whether it makes its possessor happy, or anything else of significance about it (*Republic* 354b–c).

Despite this silence on Socrates' part, there is nonetheless ample evidence that he sought definitions of forms because he thought of them as epistemic first principles, and that he did so because his model of genuine or expert knowledge was that of craft (*technē*). As a shoemaker, for instance, treats a well-made shoe as a pattern or paradigm in making another, so the moral expert, if he existed, would look to the form of piety (or courage or temperance, and so on) in order to decide what actions or people were pious and what it was that made them so (*Euthyphro* 6d–e). In the *Phaedrus,* with its attempt to define what a properly scientific rhetoric would look like, we see these ideas being developed.

Socrates' style of questioning is called (by us, not him) an *elenchus*—from a Greek verb meaning "to examine or refute": he asks what justice is; his interlocutor puts forward a definition he sincerely believes to be correct, at least for the moment; and he refutes this definition by showing that it conflicts with other beliefs the interlocutor sincerely holds and doesn't think he can reasonably abandon. In the ideal situation, which is never actually portrayed in the Socratic dialogues, this process continues until a satisfactory definition emerges—one that is not inconsistent with other sincerely held beliefs, and so can withstand elenctic scrutiny.

The goal of an elenchus is not just to reach adequate definitions of the virtues, however. Its primary aim is *moral reform.* Socrates believes that, by curing people of the arrogance of thinking they know something when they do not, leading the elenctically examined life will make them happier and more virtuous than will anything else. Socrates believed that philosophizing is so important for human welfare that he was willing to accept execution rather than give it up (*Apology*).

PLATONIC PHILOSOPHY

In a number of dialogues, Plato connects the relativist doctrines he attributes to some of the Sophists with the metaphysical theory of Heraclitus, according to which the perceptible things or characteristics we see around us are in constant flux or change—always *becoming,* never *being.* Plato seems to accept some version of this theory himself. In the *Symposium,* for example, Diotima argues that "everything mortal is preserved, not, like the divine, by always being the same in every way, but because what is departing and aging leaves behind something new, something such as it had been" (208a–b).

The theory of flux has clear repercussions for the Socratic elenchus. If perceptible things and characteristics are always in flux, how can justice or love be stable forms? How can there be stable definitions of them to serve as correct answers to Socrates' questions? And if there are no stable definitions, how can there be such a thing as knowledge of them? More generally, if perceptible things and characteristics are always in flux, always *becoming,* how can anything *be* anything? How can one know or say what anything is? Aristotle tells us that it was reflection on these fundamental questions that led Plato to "separate" the forms from perceptible things and characteristics (*Metaphysics* 987a29–b1). The famous ladder of love in the *Symposium* seems to reflect this separation (210a–212b).

Conceived in this way, forms seemed to Plato to offer solutions to the metaphysical and epistemological problems to which the elenchus and flux give rise. As intelligible objects, set apart from the perceptible world, they are above the sway of flux, and so are available as stable objects of knowledge, constant meanings or referents for words. As real, stable, and mind-independent entities, they provide the basis for the definitions Socrates seeks.

Like many proposed solutions to philosophical problems, however, Plato's solution raises new problems of its own. If forms really are separate from the world of flux our senses reveal to us, how can we know them? How can our words connect with them? If items in the perceptible world really are separate from forms, how can they owe what share of being they have to forms? In the *Meno, Phaedo,* and *Phaedrus,* Plato answers the first of these questions by appeal to the doctrine of recollection (*anamnēsis*). We have knowledge of forms through our soul's direct prenatal contact with them; we forget this knowledge when our souls become embodied at birth; then we "recollect" it in this life when our memories are appropriately jogged. Plato answers the second question by saying that items in the world of flux "participate" in forms by resembling them. Thus, perceptible objects possess the characteristic of beauty because they resemble the form of beauty, which is itself beautiful in a special and basic way (*Symposium* 210b–211e).

The doctrine of recollection presupposes the immortality of the soul—something Plato argues for in the *Phaedrus* (245c ff.) and elsewhere (*Phaedo* 69e ff.; *Republic,* Book x). It also presupposes some method of jogging our memories in a reliable way. This method is dialectic, which is a descendant of the Socratic elenchus. The "method of division," discussed in the *Phaedrus* (265d–266b) is part of dialectic, since it explains how correct definition must proceed.

Once acquired, such correct definitions are available as first principles or starting points for the various sciences. But if these are treated as "absolute," that is, to be accepted without argument, there is a problem: if the starting points are false, the entire system collapses (*Republic* 510c–d). It is here that dialectic comes in again. It defends these starting points—it renders them "unhypothetical"—not by deriving them from something more primitive (which is impossible, since they are "starting" points) but by defending them against all objections, by solving all the *aporiai,* or problems, to which they give rise (534b–c, 437a). With the objections solved, our intellectual vision is cleared and we are able then to see the forms as we did before our souls became embodied (540a–b).

In the process of their dialectical defense, the definitions themselves undergo conceptual revamping, so that their consistency with one another—and hence their immunity to dialectical (elenctic) refutation—is revealed and ensured. This enables the philosopher (to whom the craft of dialectic belongs) to knit them together into a single unified science of everything and so to see things as a whole (*Republic* 557c; cf. *Symposium* 210d–e). It is this unified science that provides the philosopher—and the philosopher alone—with genuine knowledge (533d–534a).

The editor gratefully acknowledges the cooperation of the translators and the publisher in allowing minor alterations to be made to the translations of *Phaedo, Symposium,* and *Phaedrus* for the sake of consistency with other dialogues reprinted in this volume.

Euthyphro, Apology, Crito, Meno, and Phaedo

Socrates was born in Athens in 470/69 BCE and died in 399. He was the son of Phaenarete (a midwife) and Sophroniscus (a stone-carver), husband of Xanthippe (and later, or perhaps earlier, of Myrto), and father of three sons, two of whom were still infants at the time of his death. In the *Euthyphro* (11c), he traces his ancestry to the mythical sculptor Daedalus, so it may be that he, too, practiced his father's craft early in life. He served as a hoplite (heavily armored infantryman) in the Athenian army during the Peloponnesian War with Sparta (*Apology* 28e), where he gained attention for his courage; his capacity to tolerate hunger, thirst, and cold; and for powers of concentration that could keep him rooted to the spot for hours on end (*Symposium* 219e–221d). Because hoplites had to own property and provide their own weapons, Socrates cannot always have been poor. Still, he seems to have been exceptionally frugal in his habits. He often went barefoot, seldom bathed, and wore the same thin cloak winter and summer (*Symposium* 174a, 219b).

In 406 BCE, Socrates served on the steering committee of the Athenian Assembly, where he alone voted against an illegal motion to try as a group the generals who had failed to pick up the bodies of the dead after the sea-battle at Arginusae (*Apology* 32a–c). Later, risking his own life, he disobeyed the unjust order of the Thirty Tyrants to bring in Leon of Salamis for execution (*Apology* 32c–d). It is with these events in mind, we may imagine, that in the closing lines of the *Phaedo,* Plato describes him as "a man who, we would say, was of all those we have known the best, and also the wisest and the most upright" (118a).

In 399 BCE, Socrates was brought to trial on a charge of corrupting the youth of Athens by teaching them to not believe in the gods. He was found guilty and condemned, by a close vote, to death by hemlock poisoning. Central—it seems—to the prosecution's case was one of the most puzzling aspects of Socrates—his *daimonion* or familiar spiritual voice, which held him back whenever he was about to do something wrong. Though this may, in fact, have been no different from other acceptable forms of religious practice, in someone already suspected of being an atheistic sophist, it no doubt seemed—or could be made to seem—much more sinister and subversive.

In the *Euthyphro,* we meet Socrates on his way to a preliminary hearing at which he will hear Meletus' formal charges for the first time. There the official in charge of impiety cases—the King Archon—will determine whether there is a case to answer. Appropriately enough, the topic of the dialogue is the nature of piety.

The *Apology* is (or purports to be) the speech of defense given at the trial itself. Under examination by Socrates, Meletus identifies his charges as these: Socrates is an atheist who believes in strange daimonic activities, in the visitations of a *daimonion,* or divine voice; he corrupts the youth by teaching these beliefs to them. A majority of the jurors found Socrates guilty of these charges. Athenian law allowed him to propose a counter-penalty to the death penalty demanded by Meletus and required the jury to choose which of the options to impose. A yet larger majority of them voted for the death penalty.

In the *Crito,* Socrates is in prison awaiting death by hemlock poisoning. Crito wants him to escape; Socrates explains why he cannot. The topic is legal or political obligation.

The *Meno* and *Phaedo* are linked by the emergence and development within them of Plato's famous theory of forms. The *Meno* begins with the question of whether virtue can be taught. This leads to an inquiry into virtue: what is the one form shared in common by all the virtues that makes each of them a virtue (72c–d)? Various answers are proposed and rejected. Then Meno introduces a general problem for the inquiry: if neither he nor Socrates knows what virtue is, how will they recognize it if they find it (80d)? Socrates answers with the theory of recollection, which he attempts to underwrite by the examination of the slave boy (82a–86c). The dialogue ends with a return to the original topic of whether virtue can be taught. The theory of recollection presupposes that the soul is immortal.

In the *Phaedo,* explicit arguments are given in favor of this presupposition, the theory of recollection is modified and enriched, and we learn more about the nature of forms and about the role of forms not just in ethics but in science and cosmology. The *Phaedo,* which—like the *Crito*—is set in the prison where Socrates spends his last days, ends with an account of his death.

EUTHYPHRO

EUTHYPHRO:[1] What's new, Socrates, to make you leave the Lyceum,[2] where 2a
you usually spend your time, to spend it here today at the court of the King
Archon?[3] Surely, *you* don't have some sort of lawsuit before the King, as
I do.

SOCRATES: *Athenians* don't call it a lawsuit, Euthyphro, but an indictment.

EUTHYPHRO: What? Someone has indicted you, apparently, for I'm not 2b
going to accuse you of indicting someone else!

SOCRATES: No, I certainly haven't.

EUTHYPHRO: But someone else has indicted you?

SOCRATES: Exactly.

EUTHYPHRO: Who is he?

SOCRATES: I hardly know the man myself, Euthyphro. He's young and
unknown, it seems. But I believe his name's Meletus. He belongs to the
Pitthean deme—if you recall a Meletus from that deme,[4] with straight hair,
not much of a beard, and a slightly hooked nose?

EUTHYPHRO: No, I don't recall him, Socrates. But tell me, what indictment
has he brought against you? 2c

SOCRATES: What indictment? Not a trivial one, it seems to me. I mean, it's
no small thing for a young man to have come to know such an important
matter. You see, according to him, he knows how the young men are
being corrupted, and who's corrupting them. He's probably a wise man,

---

The text of *Euthyphro,* translated by C. D. C. Reeve, is reprinted from *The Trials of Socrates: Six Classic Texts,* edited by C. D. C. Reeve. Copyright © 2002, Hackett Publishing Co.

[1] Euthyphro was a *mantis,* or prophet (3b–c, 3e), a self-proclaimed authority on Greek religion (4e–5a), who takes very literally the stories embodied in its myths (5e–6b).

[2] The Lyceum was one of three great gymnasia outside the city walls of Athens.

[3] The nine archons, chosen annually, were the chief public officials in Athens: one was civilian head of state, one was head of the army (*polemarchos*), and six had judicial roles (*thesmothetai*). The King Archon dealt with important religious matters (such as the indictment against Socrates for impiety) and also with homicide (the subject of Euthyphro's indictment). The king's court, or porch (*stoa*), was in the marketplace (*agora*).

[4] A deme was a relatively independent administrative unit rather like a village or township. Athens consisted of 139 of them.

who's seen that my own ignorance is corrupting his contemporaries, and is coming to accuse me to their mother the city, so to speak. In fact, he seems to me to be the only one who's starting up in politics correctly. For it is correct to take care of the young first, to make them the best possible, just as it's reasonable for a good farmer to take care of the young plants first and all the others afterward. And so Meletus, too, is presumably first weeding out those of us who corrupt the young shoots, as he claims. Then, after that, he'll clearly take care of the older people and bring about the greatest goods, both in number and in quality, for the city. That, at any rate, is the likely outcome of such a start.

EUTHYPHRO: I hope it happens, Socrates, but I'm terribly afraid the opposite may result. You see, by attempting to do an injustice to you, it seems to me he's simply starting out by wronging the city at its very hearth.[5] Tell me, what on earth does he say you're doing that corrupts the young?

SOCRATES: Strange things, my excellent friend, at any rate on first hearing: he says I'm an inventor of gods. And because I invent new gods, and don't acknowledge the old ones, he's indicted me for the latter's sake, so he says.

EUTHYPHRO: I understand, Socrates. That's no doubt because you say your daimonic sign comes to you on each occasion. So he has written this indictment against you for making innovations in religious matters and comes before the court to slander you, knowing that such things are easy to misrepresent to the majority of people.[6] Why, they even mock me as if I were crazy, when I speak in the Assembly on religious matters and predict the future for them! And yet not one of my predictions has failed to come true. But all the same, they envy anyone like ourselves.[7] We mustn't give them a thought, though. Just meet them head on.

SOCRATES: Yes, my dear Euthyphro, but being mocked is presumably nothing to worry about. Athenians, it seems to me, aren't much concerned if they think someone's clever, so long as he doesn't teach his own wisdom. But if they think he's making other people wise like himself, they get angry, whether out of envy, as you say, or for some other reason.

EUTHYPHRO: As to that, I certainly have no desire to test their attitude toward *me*.

SOCRATES: Don't worry. They probably think you rarely put yourself at other people's disposal, and aren't willing to teach your own wisdom. But

---

[5] The reference is to the communal hearth in the Prytaneum, which was the symbolic center of Athens.

[6] Five hundred (or 501) of whom will serve on the jury that will eventually try Socrates.

[7] That is, people who have the gift of prophecy. Socrates' sign is mantic, or prophetic (*Apology* 40a).

I'm afraid they think my love of people makes me tell whatever little I know unreservedly to any man, not only without charging a fee, but even glad to lose money, so long as someone cares to listen to me. So, as I was just saying, if they were going to mock me, as you say they do you, there'd be nothing unpleasant about their spending time in the law court playing around and laughing. But if they're going to be serious, the outcome's unclear, except to you prophets. 3e

EUTHYPHRO: Well, it will probably come to nothing, Socrates, and you'll fight your case satisfactorily, as I think I'll fight mine.

SOCRATES: But now, Euthyphro, what is this case of yours? Are you defending or prosecuting?

EUTHYPHRO: Prosecuting.

SOCRATES: Whom?

EUTHYPHRO: Someone I'm again thought to be crazy for prosecuting. 4a

SOCRATES: What's that? Is your prosecution a wild-goose chase?

EUTHYPHRO: The goose is long past chasing: he's quite old.

SOCRATES: Who is he?

EUTHYPHRO: My father.

SOCRATES: My good man! Your own *father*?

EUTHYPHRO: Yes, indeed.

SOCRATES: But what's the charge? What's the lawsuit about?

EUTHYPHRO: Murder, Socrates.

SOCRATES: In the name of Heracles![8] Well, Euthyphro, I suppose most people don't know how it can be correct to do this. I mean, I can't imagine any ordinary person taking that action correctly, but only someone who's already far advanced in wisdom. 4b

EUTHYPHRO: Yes, by Zeus, Socrates, far advanced indeed.

SOCRATES: Is the man your father killed one of your relatives then? Of course he must be, mustn't he? You'd hardly be prosecuting him for murder on behalf of a stranger.[9]

EUTHYPHRO: It's ridiculous, Socrates, for you to think it makes any difference whether the dead man's a stranger or a relative. It's ridiculous not to see that the sole consideration should be whether the killer killed justly or not. If he did, let him go, if he didn't, prosecute—if, that is to say, the

---

[8] Heracles (Hercules) was a hero of legendary strength. His famous labors—twelve extraordinarily difficult tasks—are alluded to at *Apology* 22a.

[9] Normally, the close relatives of the victim took responsibility for prosecuting the murderer.

4c   killer shares your own hearth and table.[10] For the pollution's the same if you knowingly associate with such a person and don't cleanse yourself and him by bringing him to justice.

In point of fact, though, the victim was a day laborer of mine, and when we were farming on Naxos, he worked the land there for us. Well, he got drunk, became enraged with one of our household slaves, and cut his throat. So my father tied him hand and foot, threw him in a ditch, and sent a man here to find out from the official interpreter what should be

4d   done. In the meantime, he ignored and neglected his captive as a murderer, thinking it mattered nothing if he did die. And that's just what happened: hunger, cold, and being tied up caused his death before the messenger got back from the interpreter.

That's precisely why my father and my other relatives are angry with me: because I'm prosecuting my father for murder on the murderer's behalf, when my father didn't even kill him, so they claim, and when, even if he definitely did kill him, it's wrong—since the dead man was a murderer—to concern yourself with the victim in that case. You see, it's impious, they say,

4e   for a son to prosecute his father for murder. Little do they know, Socrates, about the gods' position on the pious and the impious!

SOCRATES: But, in the name of Zeus, Euthyphro, do you think *you* have such exact knowledge about the positions the gods take, and about the pious and the impious, that in the face of these events, you've no fear of acting impiously yourself in bringing your father to trial?

EUTHYPHRO: I'd be no use at all, Socrates, and Euthyphro would be no

5a   different from the majority of people, if I didn't have exact knowledge of all such things.

SOCRATES: So, my excellent Euthyphro, the best thing, it seems, is for me to become your student, and to challenge Meletus on this very point before his case comes to trial, telling him that even in the past I always considered it of great importance to know about religious matters, and that now, when he says I've done wrong through improvising and innovating concerning the gods, I've become your student. Shouldn't I say to him, "Meletus, if you agree that Euthyphro is wise about the gods, you should also regard

5b   me as correctly acknowledging them and drop the charge. But if you don't agree, prosecute this teacher of mine rather than me, for corrupting the old men—myself and his own father, me by his teaching, and his father by admonishment and punishment." If he isn't convinced by me, and doesn't

---

[10] It is because Euthyphro shares hearth and table with his father—and so risks being contaminated by the pollution (*miasma*) thought to adhere to murderers—that he feels especially obliged to prosecute him.

drop the charge or prosecute you instead of me, shouldn't I say the same things in court as in my challenge to him?

EUTHYPHRO: Yes, by Zeus, Socrates, and if he tried bringing an indictment against *me,* I think I'd soon find his weak spots, and the question in court 5c
would very quickly be about him rather than about me.

SOCRATES: I realize that as well as you do, my dear friend, and that's why I'm eager to become your student. I know that this Meletus, as well as others no doubt, pretends not to notice *you* at all, whereas he has seen *me* so sharply and so easily that he has indicted me for impiety.

Now then, in the name of Zeus, tell me what you were just claiming to know so clearly. What sort of thing would you say the holy and the unholy are, whether in cases of murder or of anything else? Or isn't the pious itself 5d
the same as itself in every action? And conversely, isn't the impious entirely the opposite of the pious? And whatever's going to count as impious, isn't it itself similar to itself—doesn't it, as regards impiety, possess one single characteristic?

EUTHYPHRO: Absolutely, Socrates.

SOCRATES: Tell me, then, what do you say the pious and the impious are?

EUTHYPHRO: Very well, I say that what's pious is precisely what I'm doing now: prosecuting those who commit an injustice, such as murder or temple robbery, or those who've done some other such wrong, regardless of whether they're one's father or one's mother or anyone else whatever. Not prosecuting them, on the other hand, is what's impious. 5e

Why, Socrates, look at the powerful evidence I have that the law requires this—evidence I've already offered to show other people that such actions are right, that one must not let an impious person go, no matter who he may happen to be. You see, those very people acknowledge Zeus as the best and most just of the gods, and yet they agree that he put his own father 6a
in fetters because he unjustly swallowed down his children, and that *he,* in his turn, castrated his father because of other similar injustices.[11] Yet they're extremely angry with *me,* because I'm prosecuting my father for his injustice. And so they contradict themselves in what they say about the gods and about me.

SOCRATES: Could this be the reason, Euthyphro, I face indictment, that when people say such things about the gods, I find them somehow hard to accept? That, it seems, is why some people will say I'm a wrongdoer. But now if you, who know so much about such matters, share these views,

---

[11] Cronus mutilated his father, Uranus (Sky), by cutting off his genitals when he was copulating with Gaea (Earth). He ate the children he had with his sister Rhea. Aided by her, however, their son Zeus escaped, overthrew Cronus, and fettered him.

6b it seems that the rest of us must assent to them too. I mean, what can we possibly say in reply, when we admit ourselves that we know nothing about them? But tell me, by the god of friendship, do you really believe those stories are true?

EUTHYPHRO: Yes, and still more amazing things, Socrates, that the majority of people don't know.

SOCRATES: And do you believe that there really is war among the gods? And terrible hostilities and battles, and other such things of the sort the poets relate, and that the good painters embroider on our sacred objects—I'm

6c thinking particularly of the robe covered with embroideries of such scenes that's carried up to the Acropolis at the Great Panathenaean festival?[12] Are we to say that these are true, Euthyphro?

EUTHYPHRO: Not only those, Socrates, but as I mentioned just now, I will, if you like, tell you lots of other things about religious matters that I'm sure you'll be amazed to hear.

SOCRATES: I wouldn't be surprised. But tell me about them some other time, when we've the leisure. Now, however, try to answer more clearly

6d the very question I asked before. You see, my friend, you didn't teach me adequately earlier when I asked what the pious was, but you told me that what you're now doing is pious, prosecuting your father for murder.

EUTHYPHRO: Yes, and what I said was true, Socrates.

SOCRATES: Perhaps. But surely, Euthyphro, there are also many other things you call pious.

EUTHYPHRO: Yes, indeed.

SOCRATES: Do you remember, then, that what I urged you to do wasn't to teach me about one or two of the many pieties, but rather about the form itself, by virtue of which all the pieties are pious? You see, you said, I believe, that it was by virtue of one characteristic that the impieties are

6e impious, and the pieties pious. Or don't you remember?

EUTHYPHRO: I do indeed.

SOCRATES: Then teach me what that characteristic itself is, in order that by concentrating on it and using it as a model, I may call pious any action of yours or anyone else's that is such as it, and may deny to be pious whatever isn't such as it.

---

[12] The Acropolis, set on the steep rocky hill that dominates Athens, was the central fortress and principal sanctuary of the goddess Athena. It was the site of the Parthenon, as well as of other temples. The Great Panathenaean festival took place every four years and was a more elaborate version of the yearly festival that marked Athena's birthday. At it, her statue in the Parthenon received a new robe embroidered with scenes from the mythical battle of the gods and the giants.

EUTHYPHRO: If that's what you want, Socrates, that's what I'll tell you.

SOCRATES: That *is* what I want.

EUTHYPHRO: In that case: what's loved by the gods is pious, and what's not loved by the gods is impious. **7a**

SOCRATES: Excellent, Euthyphro! You've now given the sort of answer I was looking for. Whether it's true, however, that I don't know. But clearly you'll go on to demonstrate fully that what you say is true.

EUTHYPHRO: Yes, indeed.

SOCRATES: Come on, then, let's examine what it is we're saying. A god-loved thing or a god-loved person is pious, whereas a god-hated thing or a god-hated person is impious. And the pious isn't the same as the impious, but its exact opposite. Isn't that what we're saying?

EUTHYPHRO: It is indeed.

SOCRATES: And does it seem to be true?

EUTHYPHRO: It does seem so, Socrates. **7b**

SOCRATES: And haven't we also said that the gods quarrel and differ with one another, and that there's mutual hostility among them?

EUTHYPHRO: Indeed, we did say that.

SOCRATES: But what are the issues, my good friend, on which differences produce hostility and anger? Let's examine it this way. If you and I differed about which of two groups was more numerous, would our differences on this issue make us hostile and angry toward one another? Or would we turn to calculation and quickly resolve our differences? **7c**

EUTHYPHRO: Of course.

SOCRATES: Again, if we differed about which was larger or smaller, we'd turn to measurement and quickly put a stop to our difference.

EUTHYPHRO: That's right.

SOCRATES: And we'd turn to weighing, I imagine, to settle a dispute about which was heavier or lighter?

EUTHYPHRO: Certainly.

SOCRATES: Then what sorts of issues *would* make us angry and hostile toward one another if we disagreed about them and were unable to reach a settlement? Perhaps you can't say just offhand. But examine, while I'm speaking, whether they're issues about the just and unjust, fine and shame- **7d** ful, good and bad. Whenever we become enemies, aren't these the issues on which disagreement and an inability to reach a settlement make enemies of us—both you and I and all other human beings?

EUTHYPHRO: That is the difference, Socrates, and those are the things it has to do with.

SOCRATES: And what about the *gods,* Euthyphro? If indeed they differ, mustn't it be about those same things?

EUTHYPHRO: Absolutely.

7e SOCRATES: Then, according to your account, my noble Euthyphro, different sets of gods, too, consider different things to be just, or fine or shameful, or good or bad. For if they didn't differ about these, they wouldn't quarrel, would they?

EUTHYPHRO: That's right.

SOCRATES: Then are the very things that each group of them regards as fine, good, and just also the ones they love, and are the opposites of these the ones they hate?

EUTHYPHRO: Of course.

SOCRATES: But the very same things, so you say, that some gods consider
8a to be just and others unjust are also the ones that lead them to quarrel and war with one another when they have disputes about them. Isn't that right?

EUTHYPHRO: It is.

SOCRATES: Then the same things, it seems, are both hated and loved by the gods, and so the same things would be both god-hated and god-loved.

EUTHYPHRO: It seems that way.

SOCRATES: So, on your account, Euthyphro, the same things would be both pious and impious.

EUTHYPHRO: Apparently.

SOCRATES: So, you haven't answered my question, my excellent friend. You see, I wasn't asking you what the selfsame thing is that's both pious and impious. But a thing that's god-loved is, it seems, also god-hated. It follows,
8b Euthyphro, that it wouldn't be at all surprising if what you're now doing in prosecuting your father was something pleasing to Zeus but displeasing to Cronus and Uranus, or lovable to Hephaestus and displeasing to Hera,[13] and similarly for any other gods who may differ from one another on the matter.

EUTHYPHRO: But, Socrates, I think that on this point, at least, none of the gods do differ—that anyone who has unjustly killed another should be punished.

---

[13] Hephaestus, the god of fire and of blacksmithing, was armor maker to the gods. His mother, Hera, the wife and sister of Zeus, threw Hephaestus off Olympus because he was lame and deformed. This act pleased her, not him. In revenge, Hephaestus made her a throne that held her captive when she sat on it. This act pleased him, not her. Similarly, Cronus cannot have been pleased at being fettered by Zeus.

SOCRATES: Is that so? Well, what about men, Euthyphro? Have you never heard them arguing that someone who has killed unjustly or done anything else unjustly should *not* be punished? 8c

EUTHYPHRO: Why yes, they never stop arguing like that, whether in the law courts or in other places. For people who've committed all sorts of injustices will do or say anything to escape punishment.

SOCRATES: But do they agree, Euthyphro, that they've committed injustice, and, in spite of agreeing, do they still say that they shouldn't be punished?

EUTHYPHRO: No, they certainly don't say that.

SOCRATES: So it isn't just anything that they'll do or say. You see, I don't think they'd dare to say or argue that if they act *unjustly,* they should not be punished. Instead, I think they deny acting unjustly, don't they? 8d

EUTHYPHRO: That's true, they do.

SOCRATES: So they don't argue that someone who acts unjustly should not be punished, though they do, perhaps, argue about *who* acted unjustly, *what* his unjust action consisted of, and *when* he did it.

EUTHYPHRO: That's true.

SOCRATES: Then doesn't the very same thing happen to the gods as well—if indeed they do quarrel about just and unjust actions, as on your account they do, and if one lot says that others have done wrong, and another lot denies it? For surely no one, my excellent friend, whether god or human being, dares to say that one who acts unjustly should not be punished. 8e

EUTHYPHRO: Yes, what you say is true, Socrates, at least the main point.

SOCRATES: I think that men and gods who argue, Euthyphro, if indeed gods really do argue, argue instead about *actions*. It's about some action that they differ, some of them saying that it was done justly, others unjustly. Isn't that so?

EUTHYPHRO: Of course.

SOCRATES: Come then, my dear Euthyphro, and teach me, too, that I may become wiser. A man committed murder while employed as a day laborer and died as a result of being tied up before the master who tied him up found out from the proper authorities what to do about him. What evidence do you have that all the gods consider this man to have been killed unjustly, and that it's right for a *son* to prosecute and denounce his *father* for murder on behalf of such a man? Come, try to give me a clear proof that all gods undoubtedly consider this action to be right. If you can give me adequate proof of that, I'll never stop praising your wisdom. 9a 9b

EUTHYPHRO: But presumably that's no small task, Socrates, though I could of course prove it to you very clearly.

SOCRATES: I understand. You think I'm a slower learner than the jury, since it's clear that you'll prove to *them* that those actions of your father's were unjust and that the gods all hate them.

EUTHYPHRO: I'll prove it to them very clearly, Socrates, provided they'll listen to what I say.

9c SOCRATES: They'll listen all right, provided you seem to speak well. But a thought occurred to me while you were speaking, and I'm still examining it in my own mind: "Suppose Euthyphro so taught me that I became thoroughly convinced that all the gods do consider a death like that to be unjust. What more would I have learned from Euthyphro about what the pious and the impious are? *That action* would indeed be god-hated, so it seems. Yet it became evident just now that the pious and the impious aren't defined by that fact, since it became evident that what's god-hated is also god-loved. So I'll let you off on that point, Euthyphro. If you like,

9d let's suppose that all the gods consider the action unjust, and that they all hate it. Is that, then, the correction we're now making in the account, that what *all* the gods hate is impious while what they *all* love is pious, and that whatever some love and others hate is neither or both? Is that how you'd now like us to define the pious and the impious?

EUTHYPHRO: What's to prevent it, Socrates?

SOCRATES: Nothing on my part, Euthyphro. But you examine your own view, and whether by assuming it you'll most easily teach me what you promised.

9e EUTHYPHRO: All right, I'd say that the pious is what all the gods love, and its opposite, what all the gods hate, is the impious.

SOCRATES: Then aren't we going to examine that in turn, Euthyphro, to see whether what we said is true? Or are we going to let it alone and accept it from ourselves and from others just as it stands? And if someone merely asserts that something is so, are we going to concede that it's so? Or are we going to examine what the speaker says?

EUTHYPHRO: We're going to examine it. However, I for my part think that this time what we said *is* true.

10a SOCRATES: Soon, my good friend, we'll be better able to tell. Consider the following: is the pious loved by the gods because it's pious? Or is it pious because it's loved?

EUTHYPHRO: I don't know what you mean, Socrates.

SOCRATES: All right, I'll try to put it more clearly. We speak of a thing's being carried or carrying, and of its being led or leading, and of being seen or seeing. And you understand that these things are all different from one another and how they differ?

EUTHYPHRO: I think I understand, at any rate.

SOCRATES: Then is there also something that's loved, and is it different from something that's loving?

EUTHYPHRO: Certainly.

SOCRATES: Then tell me whether the carried thing is a carried thing because   10b
it's carried or because of something else.

EUTHYPHRO: No, it's because of that.

SOCRATES: Again, the led thing is so, then, because it's led and the seen thing because it's seen?

EUTHYPHRO: Of course.

SOCRATES: So it's not seen because it's a seen thing; on the contrary, it's a seen thing because it's seen; nor is it because it's a led thing that it's led, rather it's because it's led that it's a led thing; nor is something carried because it's a carried thing, rather it's a carried thing because it's carried. So is what I mean completely clear, Euthyphro? I mean this: if something's changed in some way or affected in some way, it's not changed because it's   10c
a changed thing; rather, it's a changed thing because it's changed. Nor is it affected because it's an affected thing; rather, it's an affected thing because it's affected. Or don't you agree with that?

EUTHYPHRO: I do.

SOCRATES: Then isn't a loved thing, too, either a thing changed or a thing affected by something?

EUTHYPHRO: Of course.

SOCRATES: And so the same holds of it as of our earlier examples: it's not because it's a loved thing that it's loved by those who love it; rather it's because it's loved that it's a loved thing?

EUTHYPHRO: Necessarily.

SOCRATES: Now what are we saying about the pious, Euthyphro? On your   10d
account, isn't it loved by all the gods?

EUTHYPHRO: Yes.

SOCRATES: So is that because it's pious or because of something else?

EUTHYPHRO: No, it's because it's pious.

SOCRATES: So it's loved because it's pious, not pious because it's loved?

EUTHYPHRO: Apparently.

SOCRATES: On the other hand, what's god-loved is loved—that is to say, god-loved—because the gods love it?

EUTHYPHRO: Certainly.

SOCRATES: Then the god-loved is not what's pious, Euthyphro, nor is the pious what's god-loved, as you claim, but one differs from the other.

EUTHYPHRO: How so, Socrates?   10e

SOCRATES: Because we agreed that the pious is loved because it's pious, not pious because it's loved. Didn't we?

EUTHYPHRO: Yes.

SOCRATES: The god-loved, on the other hand, is so because it is loved by the gods; it's god-loved by the very fact of being loved. But it's not because it's god-loved that it's being loved.

EUTHYPHRO: That's true.

SOCRATES: But if the god-loved and the pious were really the same thing, my dear Euthyphro, then, if the pious were loved because it's pious, what's
11a god-loved would in turn be loved because it's god-loved; and if what's god-loved were god-loved because it was loved by the gods, the pious would in turn be pious because it was loved by them. But, as it is, you can see that the two are related in the opposite way, as things entirely different from one another. For one of them is lovable because it's loved, whereas the other is loved because it's lovable.

And so, Euthyphro, when you're asked what the pious is, it looks as though you don't want to reveal its being to me, but rather to tell me one of its affections—that this happens to the pious, that it's loved by all the gods. What explains its being loved, however, you still haven't said. So please
11b don't keep it hidden from me, but rather say again from the beginning what it is that explains the pious's being loved by the gods or having some other affection—for we won't disagree about which ones it has. Summon up your enthusiasm, then, and tell me what the pious and the impious are.

EUTHYPHRO: But Socrates, I have no way of telling you what I have in mind. For whatever proposals we put forward keep somehow moving around and won't stay put.

SOCRATES: Your proposals, Euthyphro, seem to be the work of my ancestor,
11c Daedalus! Indeed, if I were to state them and put them forward myself, you might perhaps make a joke of me, and say that it's because of my kinship with him that my works of art in words run away and won't stay put.[14] But, as it is, the proposals are your own. So you need a different joke, since it's for you that they won't stay put, as you can see yourself.

EUTHYPHRO: But it seems to me, Socrates, that pretty much the same joke does apply in the case of our definitions. You see, I'm not the one who makes them move around and not stay put. Rather, you seem to me to be
11d the Daedalus, since as far as I'm concerned they would have stayed put.

---

[14] Daedalus was a legendary sculptor of great skill. His statues were so lifelike that they moved around by themselves just like living things. Socrates' father, Sophroniscus, is alleged to have been a sculptor or stone-carver, and some of the statues on the Acropolis may have been attributed to Socrates himself.

SOCRATES: Then, my friend, it looks as though I've grown cleverer in my area of expertise than my venerated ancestor, in that he made only his own works not stay put, whereas I do this to my own, it seems, and also to other people's. And the most subtle thing about my area of expertise is that I'm wise in it without wanting to be. You see, I'd prefer to have accounts stay put and be immovably established for me than to acquire the wealth of Tantalus[15] and the wisdom of Daedalus combined. But enough of this. 11e Since you seem to me to be getting sated, I'll do my best to help you teach me about the pious—and don't you give up before you do. See whether you don't think that the pious as a whole must be just.

EUTHYPHRO: Yes, I do.

SOCRATES: Then is the just as a whole also pious? Or while the pious as a whole is just, is the just as a whole not pious, but part of it pious and part 12a of it something else?

EUTHYPHRO: I don't follow what you're saying, Socrates.

SOCRATES: And yet you're as much younger as wiser than I. But as I say, your wealth of wisdom has weakened you. Well, pull yourself together, my dear fellow. What I'm saying isn't hard to understand. You see, what I'm saying is just the opposite of what the poet said, who wrote:

> With Zeus the maker, who caused all these things to come about,
> You will not quarrel, since where there's dread there's shame too.[16]   12b

I disagree with this poet. Shall I tell you where?

EUTHYPHRO: Of course.

SOCRATES: It doesn't seem to me that "where there's dread there's shame too." For many people seem to me to dread disease and poverty and many other things of that sort, but though they dread them, they feel no shame at what they dread. Or don't you agree?

EUTHYPHRO: Of course.

SOCRATES: But where there's shame, there is also dread. For if anyone feels shame at a certain action—if he's ashamed of it—doesn't he fear, doesn't he dread, a reputation for wickedness at the same time?   12c

EUTHYPHRO: He certainly does dread it.

---

[15] Tantalus, son of Zeus, was a legendary king proverbial for his wealth, who enjoyed the privilege of dining with the gods. He killed and cooked his son Pelops, and mixed pieces of his flesh in with the gods' food to see whether they could detect it. He was punished in Hades by being "tantalized"—any food or water he reached for always eluded his grasp.

[16] Author unknown.

SOCRATES: Then it isn't right to say that "where there's dread, there's shame too." But where there's shame there's also dread, even though shame isn't found everywhere there's dread. You see, dread is broader than shame, I think. For shame is a part of fear, just as odd is of number. Hence where there's a number, there isn't something odd too, but where there's something odd there is also a number. Do you follow me now at least?

EUTHYPHRO: Of course.

12d SOCRATES: Well, that's the sort of thing I was asking just now: whenever there's something just, is there also something pious? Or is something just whenever it's pious, but not pious whenever it's just, because the pious is part of the just? Is that what we're to say, or do you disagree?

EUTHYPHRO: No, let's say that, since it seems to me you're right.

SOCRATES: Then consider the next point. If the pious is a part of what's just, we must, it seems, find out what part of the just the pious is. Now if you asked me about one of the things we just mentioned, for example, which part of number is the even—that is to say, what sort of number it is—I'd say that it's any number not indivisible by two, but divisible by it. Or don't you agree?

EUTHYPHRO: Yes, I do.

12e SOCRATES: Then you try to teach me in the same fashion what part of the just is pious. Then we can tell Meletus not to treat us unjustly any longer or indict us for impiety, since I've now been sufficiently instructed by you about what things are holy or pious and what aren't.

EUTHYPHRO: Well then, it seems to me, Socrates, that the part of the just that's holy or pious is the one concerned with tending to the gods, while the remaining part of the just is concerned with tending to human beings.

SOCRATES: You seem to me to have put that very well, Euthyphro. But I'm
13a still lacking one small piece of information. You see, I don't yet understand this tending you're talking about. You surely don't mean that in just the way that there's tending to other things, there's tending to the gods too. We do speak this way, don't we? We say, for example, that not everyone knows how to tend to horses, but only horse trainers. Isn't that right?

EUTHYPHRO: Of course.

SOCRATES: Because horse training is expertise in tending to horses?
13b EUTHYPHRO: Yes.

SOCRATES: Nor does everyone know how to tend to dogs, but only dog trainers.

EUTHYPHRO: That's right.

SOCRATES: Because dog training is expertise in tending to dogs.

EUTHYPHRO: Yes.

SOCRATES: And cattle breeding is expertise in tending to cattle.

EUTHYPHRO: Of course.

SOCRATES: Well, but piety or holiness is tending to the gods, Euthyphro? That's what you're saying?

EUTHYPHRO: It is.

SOCRATES: But doesn't all tending accomplish the same end? I mean something like some good or benefit for what's being tended to—as you see that horses tended to by horse trainers are benefited and made better. Or don't you agree that they are?

EUTHYPHRO: Yes, I do.

SOCRATES: And so dogs, of course, are benefited by dog training and cattle by cattle breeding, and similarly for all the others. Or do you think that tending aims to harm what's being tended? 13c

EUTHYPHRO: No, by Zeus, I don't.

SOCRATES: Rather, it aims to benefit it?

EUTHYPHRO: Certainly.

SOCRATES: Then if piety is tending to the gods, does it benefit the gods and make the gods better? Would you concede that whenever you do something pious, you're making some god better?

EUTHYPHRO: No, by Zeus, I wouldn't.

SOCRATES: No, I didn't think that that was what you meant, Euthyphro—far from it. But it is why I asked what you did mean by tending to the gods, because I didn't think you meant that sort of tending. 13d

EUTHYPHRO: And you were right, Socrates, since that's not the sort I meant.

SOCRATES: All right. But then what sort of tending to the gods would the pious be?

EUTHYPHRO: The very sort of tending, Socrates, that slaves provide to their masters.

SOCRATES: I understand. Then it would seem to be some sort of service to the gods.

EUTHYPHRO: It is indeed.

SOCRATES: Now could you tell me about service to doctors? What result does that service—insofar as it is service—aim to produce? Don't you think it aims at health?

EUTHYPHRO: I do.

SOCRATES: What about service to shipbuilders? What result does the service aim to produce? 13e

EUTHYPHRO: Clearly, Socrates, its aim is a ship.

SOCRATES: And in the case of service to builders, I suppose, the aim is a house?

EUTHYPHRO: Yes.

SOCRATES: Then tell me, my good friend, at what result does service to the gods aim? Clearly, you know, since you say you've a finer knowledge of religious matters than any other human being.

EUTHYPHRO: Yes, and what I say is true, Socrates.

SOCRATES: Then tell me, in the name of Zeus, what is that supremely fine result that the gods produce by using our services?

EUTHYPHRO: They produce many fine ones, Socrates.

14a SOCRATES: So too do generals, my friend. Nonetheless, you could easily tell me the main one, which is to produce victory in war, is it not?

EUTHYPHRO: Certainly.

SOCRATES: And farmers, too, I think, produce many fine results. Nonetheless, the main one is to produce food from the earth.

EUTHYPHRO: Of course.

SOCRATES: What, then, about the many fine results that the gods produce? Which is the main one they produce?

EUTHYPHRO: I told you a moment ago, Socrates, that it's a pretty difficult
14b task to learn the exact truth about all these matters. But to put it simply: if a person knows how to do and say the things that are pleasing to the gods in prayer and sacrifice—those are the ones that are pious. And actions like them preserve both the private welfare of households and the common welfare of the city, whereas those that are the opposite of pleasing are unholy, and they, of course, overturn and destroy everything.

SOCRATES: If you'd wanted to, Euthyphro, you could have put the main point I asked about much more briefly. But you're not eager to teach me—
14c that's clear. You see, when you were just now on the point of answering you turned away. If you had given the answer, I'd already have been adequately instructed by you about piety. But as it is, the questioner must follow the one being questioned wherever he leads. Once again, then, what are you saying that the pious, or piety, is? Didn't you say that it was some sort of knowledge of sacrificing and praying?

EUTHYPHRO: Yes, I did.

SOCRATES: And sacrificing is giving to the gods, and praying is asking from them?

EUTHYPHRO: Yes, indeed, Socrates.

14d SOCRATES: So, on that account, piety would be knowing how to ask from the gods and how to give to them.

EUTHYPHRO: You've grasped my meaning perfectly, Socrates.

SOCRATES: Yes, my friend, that's because I really desire your wisdom and apply my mind to it, so that what you say won't fall on barren ground. But tell me, what is this service to the gods? You say it's asking for things from them and giving things to them?

EUTHYPHRO: I do.

SOCRATES: Well then, wouldn't asking in the right way consist of asking for the things we need from them?

EUTHYPHRO: What else could it be?

SOCRATES: And, conversely, giving in the right way would consist of giving 14e them, in turn, the things they need from us? For surely giving someone what he didn't at all need isn't something that an expert in the art of giving would do.

EUTHYPHRO: That's true, Socrates.

SOCRATES: Then piety, Euthyphro, would be a sort of expertise in mutual trading between gods and men.

EUTHYPHRO: Yes, trading, if that's what you prefer to call it.

SOCRATES: I don't prefer anything, if it isn't true. But tell me, what benefit do the gods get from the gifts they receive from us? I mean, what they give is clear to everyone, since we possess nothing good that they don't give us. 15a But how are they benefited by what they receive from us? Or do we get so much the better of them in the trade that we receive all our good things from them while they receive nothing from us?

EUTHYPHRO: But Socrates, do you really think gods are benefited by what they receive from us?

SOCRATES: If not, Euthyphro, what could those gifts of ours to gods possibly be?

EUTHYPHRO: What else do you think but honor and reverence and—as I said just now—what's pleasing to them.

SOCRATES: So is the pious pleasing to the gods, Euthyphro, but not benefi- 15b cial to them or loved by them?

EUTHYPHRO: No, I think that it's in fact the most loved of all.

SOCRATES: So, once again, it seems, the pious is what's loved by the gods.

EUTHYPHRO: Absolutely.

SOCRATES: Well, if you say that, can you wonder that your accounts seem not to stay put but to move around? And will you accuse me of being the Daedalus who makes them move, when you yourself are far more expert than Daedalus in the art of making them move in a circle? Or don't you see that our account has circled back again to the same place? For surely you remember that earlier we discovered the pious and the god-loved are 15c not the same, but different from one another. Or don't you remember that?

EUTHYPHRO: Yes, I do.

SOCRATES: Then don't you realize that you're now saying the pious is what the gods love? And that's the same, isn't it, as what's god-loved? Or is that not so?

EUTHYPHRO: Of course, it is.

SOCRATES: Then either we weren't right to agree before, or, if we were right, our present suggestion is wrong.

EUTHYPHRO: So it seems.

SOCRATES: So we must examine again from the beginning what the pious is, since I won't willingly give up until I learn this. Don't scorn me, but apply your mind to the matter in as many ways and as fully as you can, and then tell me the truth—for you must know it, if indeed any human being does, and, like Proteus,[17] you mustn't be let go until you tell it. For if you didn't know with full clarity what the pious and the impious are, you'd never have ventured to prosecute your old father for murder on behalf of a day laborer. On the contrary, you wouldn't have risked acting wrongly because you'd have been afraid before the gods and ashamed before men. As things stand, however, I well know that you think you have fully clear knowledge of what's pious and what isn't. So tell me what you think it is, my excellent Euthyphro, and don't conceal it.

EUTHYPHRO: Some other time, Socrates. You see, I'm in a hurry to get somewhere, and it's time for me to be off.

SOCRATES: What a way to treat me, my friend! Going off like that and dashing the high hopes I had that I'd learn from you what things are pious and what aren't. Then I'd escape Meletus' indictment by showing him that Euthyphro had now made me wise in religious matters, and ignorance would no longer cause me to improvise and innovate about them. What's more, I'd live a better way for the rest of my life.

---

[17] Proteus, the Old Man of the Sea, was a god who could change himself into any shape he wished. In this way, he avoided being captured, until his daughter, Eidothea, revealed this secret: keep tight hold of him, no matter what he changes into.

APOLOGY

I don't know, men of Athens, how you were affected by my accusers. As 17a
for me, I was almost carried away by them, they spoke so persuasively.
And yet almost nothing they said is true. Among their many falsehoods,
however, one especially amazed me: that you must be careful not to be
deceived by me, since I'm a dangerously clever speaker. That they aren't
ashamed at being immediately refuted by the facts, once it becomes appar- 17b
ent that I'm not a clever speaker at all, that seems to me most shameless
of them. Unless, of course, the one they call "clever" is the one who tells
the truth. If that's what they mean, I'd agree that I'm an orator—although
not one of their sort. No, indeed. Rather, just as I claimed, they have said
little or nothing true, whereas from me you'll hear the whole truth. But
not, by Zeus, men of Athens, expressed in elegant language like theirs, 17c
arranged in fine words and phrases. Instead, what you hear will be spoken
extemporaneously in whatever words come to mind, and let none of you
expect me to do otherwise—for I put my trust in the justice of what I say.
After all, it wouldn't be appropriate at my age, gentlemen, to come before
you speaking in polished, artificial language like a young man.

Indeed, men of Athens, this I positively entreat of you: if you hear me
making my defense using the same sort of language that I'm accustomed
to use both in the marketplace next to the bankers' tables—where many
of you have heard me—and also in other places, please don't be surprised
or create an uproar on that account. For the fact is that this is the first 17d
time I've appeared before a law court, although I'm seventy years old. So
the language of this place is totally foreign to me. Now, if I were really a
foreigner, you'd certainly forgive me if I spoke in the accents and manner
in which I'd been raised. So now, too, I'm asking you, justly it seems to me, 18a
to overlook my manner of speaking (maybe it will be less good, maybe it
will be better), but consider and apply your mind to this alone, whether I
say what's just or not. For that's the virtue or excellence of a juror,[1] just as
the orator's lies in telling the truth.

The text of *Apology*, translated by C. D. C. Reeve, is reprinted from *The Trials
of Socrates: Six Classic Texts*, edited by C. D. C. Reeve. Copyright © 2002, Hackett
Publishing Co.

[1] A member of an Athenian jury (a *dikastēs*) combined the responsibilities that
are divided between judge and jury in our legal system. Hence *dikastēs* is sometimes
translated as "judge" and sometimes (as in the present translation) as "juror."

The first thing justice demands, then, men of Athens, is that I defend myself from the first false accusations made against me and from my first accusers, and then from the later accusations and the later accusers. You see, many people have been accusing me in front of you for very many years now—and nothing they say is true. And I fear them more than Anytus[2] and the rest, though the latter are dangerous as well. But the earlier ones, gentlemen, are more dangerous. They got hold of most of you from childhood and persuaded you with their accusations against me—accusations no more true than the current ones. They say there's a man called Socrates, a "wise" man, a thinker about things in the heavens, an investigator of all things below the earth, and someone who makes the weaker argument the stronger. Those who've spread this rumor, men of Athens, are my dangerous accusers, since the people who hear them believe that those who investigate such things do not acknowledge the gods either. Moreover, those accusers are numerous and have been accusing me for a long time now. Besides, they also spoke to you at that age when you would most readily believe them, when some of you were children or young boys. Thus they simply won their case by default, as there was no defense. But what's most unreasonable in all this is that I can't discover even their names and tell them to you—unless one of them happens to be a comic playwright. In any case, the ones who used malicious slander to persuade you—as well as those who persuaded others after having been persuaded themselves—all of these are impossible to deal with. One cannot bring any of them here to court or cross-examine them. One must literally fight with shadows to defend oneself and cross-examine with no one to respond.

So you too, then, should allow, as I claimed, that there are two groups of accusers: those who accused me just now and the older ones I've been discussing. Moreover, you should consider it proper for me to defend myself against the latter first, since you've heard them accusing me earlier, and at much greater length, than these recent ones here.

All right. I must defend myself, then, men of Athens, and try to take away in this brief time prejudices you acquired such a long time ago. Certainly, that's the outcome I'd wish for—if it's in any way better for you and for me—and I'd like to succeed in my defense. But I think it's a difficult task, and I am not at all unaware of its nature. Let it turn out, though, in whatever way pleases the god. I have to obey the law and defend myself.

Let's examine, then, from the beginning, what the charge is from which the slander against me arose—the very one on which Meletus relied when he wrote the present indictment of me. Well, then, what exactly did the

---

[2] Anytus was a democratic leader who helped restore democracy to Athens in 403 BCE after the overthrow of the Thirty Tyrants (32c note), under whom he had lost most of his wealth.

slanderers say to slander me? Just as if they were real accusers their affidavit must be read. It's something like this:

> Socrates commits injustice and is a busybody, in that he investigates the things beneath the earth and in the heavens, makes the weaker argument the stronger, and teaches these things to others. 19c

Indeed, you saw these charges expressed yourselves in Aristophanes' comedy.[3] There, some fellow named Socrates swings around claiming he's walking on air and talking a lot of other nonsense on subjects that I know neither a lot nor a little but nothing at all about. Not that I mean to disparage this knowledge, if anyone's wise in such subjects—I don't want to have to defend myself against more of Meletus' lawsuits!—but I, men of Athens, take no part in them. I call on the majority of you as witnesses to 19d this, and I appeal to you to make it perfectly plain to one another—those of you who've heard me conversing (as many of you have). Tell one another, then, whether any of you has ever heard me discussing such subjects, either briefly or at length, and from this you'll realize that the other things commonly said about me are of the same baseless character.

In any case, none of them is true. And if you've heard from anyone that I undertake to educate people and charge fees, that's not true either. Although, it also seems to me to be a fine thing if anyone's able to educate 19e people in the way Gorgias of Leontini does, and Prodicus of Ceos, and Hippias of Elis.[4] For each of them, gentlemen, can enter any city and persuade the young—who may associate with any of their own fellow citizens they want to free of charge—to abandon those associations, and associate 20a with them instead, pay them a fee, and be grateful to them besides.

Since we're on that topic, I heard that there's another wise gentleman here at present, from Paros. For I happened to run into a man who has spent more money on Sophists than everyone else put together—Callias, the son of Hipponicus.[5] So I questioned him, since he has two sons himself.

---

[3] Aristophanes was an Athenian comic dramatist (c. 450–385 BCE). The version of his play *Clouds* referred to here, which is earlier than the revised version we possess, was first staged in 423 BCE.

[4] All three, like Evenus of Paros mentioned below, were Sophists—itinerant professors who charged sometimes substantial fees for popular lectures and specialized instruction in a wide variety of fields, including natural science, rhetoric, grammar, ethics, and politics. Sophists did not constitute a single school or movement, however, and were neither doctrinally nor organizationally united.

[5] Callias was one of the richest men in Greece and a patron of the Sophists. Plato's *Protagoras* is set in his house.

"Callias," I said, "if your two sons had been born colts or calves, we could engage and pay a knowledgeable supervisor—one of those expert horse breeders or farmers—who could turn them into fine and good examples of their proper virtue or excellence. But now, seeing that they're human beings, whom do you have in mind to engage as a supervisor? Who is it that has the knowledge of *this* virtue, the virtue of human beings and of citizens? I assume you've investigated the matter, because you have two sons. Is there such a person," I asked, "or not?"

"Certainly," he replied.

"Who is he?" I said.

"His name's Evenus, Socrates," he replied, "from Paros. He charges five minas."[6]

I thought Evenus blessedly happy if he truly did possess that expertise and taught it for so modest a fee. I, at any rate, would pride myself and give myself airs if I had knowledge of those things. But in fact, men of Athens, I don't know them.

Now perhaps one of you will interject: "But Socrates, what, then, is *your* occupation? What has given rise to these slanders against you? Surely if you weren't in fact occupied with something out of the ordinary, if you weren't doing something different from most people, all this rumor and talk wouldn't have arisen. Tell us, then, what it is, so that we don't judge you hastily." These are fair questions, I think, for the speaker to ask, and I'll try to show you just what it is that has brought me this slanderous reputation. Listen, then. Perhaps, some of you will think I'm joking. But you may be sure that I'll be telling you the whole truth.

You see, men of Athens, I've acquired this reputation because of nothing other than a sort of wisdom. What sort of wisdom, you ask, is that? The very sort, perhaps, that is *human* wisdom. For it may just be that I really do have that sort of wisdom, whereas the people I mentioned just now may, perhaps, be wise because they possess *superhuman* wisdom. I don't know what else to call it, since I myself certainly don't possess that knowledge, and whoever says I do is lying and speaking in order to slander me.

Please don't create an uproar, men of Athens, even if you think I'm somehow making grand claims. You see, I'm not the author of the story I'm about to tell, though I'll refer you to a reliable source. In fact, as a witness to the existence of my wisdom—if indeed it is a sort of wisdom—and to its nature, I'll present the god at Delphi to you.[7]

---

[6] Evenus is described as a poet (*Phaedo* 60c–e) and as an orator (*Phaedrus* 267a). A few fragments of his elegies survive. A drachma was a day's pay for someone engaged in public works; a mina was a hundred silver drachmas.

[7] Apollo, who was god of, among other things, healing, prophecy, purification, care for young citizens, music, and poetry.

You remember Chaerephon, no doubt.[8] He was a friend of mine from youth and also a friend of your party, who shared your recent exile and restoration.[9] You remember, then, what sort of man Chaerephon was, how intense he was in whatever he set out to do. Well, on one occasion in particular he went to Delphi and dared to ask the oracle[10]—as I said, please don't create an uproar, gentlemen—he asked, exactly as I'm telling you, whether anyone was wiser than myself. The Pythia drew forth the response that no one is wiser. His brother here will testify to you about it, since Chaerephon himself is dead.[11]

Please consider my purpose in telling you this, since I'm about to explain to you where the slander against me has come from. You see, when I heard these things, I thought to myself as follows: "What can the god be saying? What does his riddle mean? For I'm only too aware that I've no claim to being wise in anything either great or small. What can he mean, then, by saying that I'm wisest? Surely he can't be lying: that isn't lawful for him."

For a long time I was perplexed about what he meant. Then, very reluctantly, I proceeded to examine it in the following sort of way. I approached one of the people thought to be wise, assuming that in his company, if anywhere, I could refute the pronouncement and say to the oracle, "Here's someone wiser than I, yet you said I was wisest."

Then I examined this person—there's no need for me to mention him by name; he was one of our politicians. And when I examined him and talked with him, men of Athens, my experience was something like this: I thought this man seemed wise to many people, and especially to himself, but wasn't. Then I tried to show him that he thought himself wise, but wasn't. As a result, he came to dislike me, and so did many of the people present. For my part, I thought to myself as I left, "I'm wiser than that person. For it's likely that neither of us knows anything fine and good, but he thinks he knows something he doesn't know, whereas I, since I don't in fact know, don't think that I do either. At any rate, it seems that I'm wiser than he in just this one small way: that what I don't know, I don't think I

21a

21b

21c

21d

---

[8] A long-time companion of Socrates.

[9] Members of the democratic party left Athens when the Thirty Tyrants came to power in 404 BCE. They returned to power when the tyrants were overthrown in 403.

[10] The Delphic oracle was one of the most famous in antiquity. There were two methods of consulting it. One method, involving the sacrifice of sheep and goats, was quite expensive but resulted in a written response. The other—the so-called method of the two beans—was substantially cheaper but resulted only in a response by lot. Since Chaerephon was notoriously poor, it is probable that he consulted the oracle by the latter method (something also suggested by Socrates' characterization of the priestess as *drawing forth* the response at 21a).

[11] The brother is Chaerecrates.

know." Next, I approached another man, one of those thought to be wiser
than the first, and it seemed to me that the same thing occurred, and so I
came to be disliked by that man too, as well as by many others.

After that, then, I kept approaching one person after another. I realized, with distress and alarm, that I was arousing hostility. Nevertheless,
I thought I must attach the greatest importance to what pertained to the
god. So, in seeking what the oracle meant, I had to go to all those with
any reputation for knowledge. And, by the dog, men of Athens—for I'm
obliged to tell the truth before you—I really did experience something
like this: in my investigation in response to the god, I found that, where
wisdom is concerned, those who had the best reputations were practically
the most deficient, whereas men who were thought to be their inferiors
were much better off. Accordingly, I must present all my wanderings to
you as if they were labors of some sort that I undertook in order to prove
the oracle utterly irrefutable.

You see, after the politicians, I approached the poets—tragic,
dithyrambic,[12] and the rest—thinking that in their company I'd catch
myself in the very act of being more ignorant than they. So I examined
the poems with which they seemed to me to have taken the most trouble
and questioned them about what they meant, in order that I might also
learn something from them at the same time.

Well, I'm embarrassed to tell you the truth, gentlemen, but nevertheless it must be told. In a word, almost all the people present could have
discussed these poems better than their authors themselves. And so, in the
case of the poets as well, I soon realized it wasn't wisdom that enabled
them to compose their poems, but some sort of natural inspiration, of just
the sort you find in seers and soothsayers. For these people, too, say many
fine things, but know nothing of what they speak about. The poets also
seemed to me to be in this sort of situation. At the same time, I realized
that, because of their poetry, they thought themselves to be the wisest of
people about the other things as well when they weren't. So I left their
company, too, thinking that I had gotten the better of them in the very
same way as of the politicians.

Finally, I approached the craftsmen. You see, I was conscious of knowing practically nothing myself, but I knew I'd discover that they, at least,
would know many fine things. And I wasn't wrong about this. On the
contrary, they did know things that I didn't know, and in that respect they
were wiser than I. But, men of Athens, the good craftsmen also seemed
to me to have the very same flaw as the poets: because he performed his
own craft well, each of them also thought himself to be wisest about the

---

[12] A dithyramb was a choral song in honor of the god Dionysus.

other things, the most important ones; and this error of theirs seemed
to overshadow their wisdom. So I asked myself on behalf of the oracle   22e
whether I'd prefer to be as I am, not in any way wise with their wisdom
nor ignorant with their ignorance, or to have both qualities as they did.
And the answer I gave to myself, and to the oracle, was that it profited me
more to be just the way I was.

From this examination, men of Athens, much hostility has arisen against
me of a sort that is harshest and most onerous. This has resulted in many   **23a**
slanders, including that reputation I mentioned of being "wise." You see,
the people present on each occasion think that I'm wise about the subjects
on which I examine others. But in fact, gentlemen, it's pretty certainly the
god who is really wise, and by his oracle he meant that human wisdom is
worth little or nothing. And it seems that when he refers to the Socrates
here before you and uses my name, he makes me an example, as if he were   23b
to say, "That one among you is wisest, mortals, who, like Socrates, has
recognized that he's truly worthless where wisdom's concerned."

So even now I continue to investigate these things and to examine,
in response to the god, any person, citizen, or foreigner I believe to be
wise. Whenever he seems not to be so to me, I come to the assistance of
the god and show him that he's not wise. Because of this occupation, I've
had no leisure worth talking about for either the city's affairs or my own
domestic ones; rather, I live in extreme poverty because of my service
to the god.   23c

In addition to these factors, the young people who follow me around
of their own accord, those who have the most leisure, the sons of the
very rich, enjoy listening to people being cross-examined. They often
imitate me themselves and in turn attempt to cross-examine others. Next,
I imagine they find an abundance of people who think they possess some
knowledge, but in fact know little or nothing. The result is that those they
question are angry not at themselves, but at me, and say that Socrates is a
thoroughly pestilential fellow who corrupts the young. Then, when they're   23d
asked what he's doing or teaching, they've nothing to say, as they don't
know. Yet, so as not to appear at a loss, they utter the stock phrases used
against all who philosophize: "things in the sky and beneath the earth,"
and "not acknowledging the gods," and "making the weaker argument the
stronger." For they wouldn't be willing to tell the truth, I imagine: that it
has become manifest they pretend to know, but know nothing. So, seeing
that these people are, I imagine, ambitious, vehement, and numerous, and   23e
have been speaking earnestly and persuasively about me, they've long been
filling your ears with vehement slanders. On the basis of these slanders,
Meletus has brought his charges against me, and Anytus and Lycon along
with him: Meletus is aggrieved on behalf of the poets, Anytus on behalf
of the artisans and politicians, and Lycon on behalf of the orators. So, as I   24a

began by saying, I'd be amazed if I could rid your minds of this slander in the brief time available, when there's so much of it in them.

There, men of Athens, is the truth for you. I've spoken it without concealing or glossing over anything, whether great or small. And yet I pretty much know that I make enemies by doing these very things. And that's further evidence that I'm right—that this is the prejudice against me and these its causes. Whether you investigate these matters now or later, you'll find it to be so.

Enough, then, for my defense before you against the charges brought by my first accusers. Next, I'll try to defend myself against Meletus—who is, he claims, both good and patriotic—and against my later accusers. Once again, then, just as if they were really a different set of accusers, their affidavit must be examined in turn. It goes something like this:

> Socrates is guilty of corrupting the young, and of not acknowl-
> edging the gods the city acknowledges, but new daimonic
> activities instead.

Such, then, is the charge. Let us examine each point in this charge.

Meletus says, then, that I commit injustice by corrupting the young. But I, men of Athens, reply that it's Meletus who is guilty of playing around with serious matters, of lightly bringing people to trial, and of professing to be seriously concerned about things he has never cared about at all—and I'll try to prove this.

Step forward, Meletus, and answer me. You regard it as most important, do you not, that our young people be as good as possible?

I certainly do.

Come, then, and tell these jurors who improves them. Clearly you know, since you care. For having discovered, as you assert, the one who corrupts them—namely, myself—you bring him before these jurors and accuse him. Come, then, speak up, tell the jurors who it is that improves them. Do you see, Meletus, that you remain silent and have nothing to say? Yet don't you think that's shameful and sufficient evidence of exactly what I say, that you care nothing at all? Speak up, my good man. Who improves them?

The laws.

But that's not what I'm asking, my most excellent fellow, but rather which *person,* who knows the laws themselves in the first place, does this?

These gentlemen, Socrates, the jurors.

What are you saying, Meletus? Are they able to educate and improve the young?

Most certainly.

All of them, or some but not others?

All of them.

That's good news, by Hera, and a great abundance of benefactors that you speak of! What, then, about the audience present here? Do they improve the young or not?

Yes, they do so too.

And what about the members of the Council?[13]

Yes, the councilors too.

But, if that's so, Meletus, surely those in the Assembly, the assemblymen, won't corrupt the young, will they? Won't they all improve them too?

Yes, they will too.

But then it seems that all the Athenians except for me make young people fine and good, whereas I alone corrupt them. Is that what you're saying?

Most emphatically, that's what I'm saying.

I find myself, if you're right, in a most unfortunate situation. Now answer me this. Do you think that the same holds of horses? Do people in general improve them, whereas one particular person corrupts them or makes them worse? Or isn't it wholly the opposite: one particular person—or the very few who are horse trainers—is able to improve them, whereas the majority of people, if they have to do with horses and make use of them, make them worse? Isn't that true, Meletus, both of horses and of all other animals? Of course it is, whether you and Anytus say so or not. Indeed, our young people are surely in a very happy situation if only one person corrupts them, whereas all the rest benefit them.

Well then, Meletus, it has been adequately established that you've never given any thought to young people—you've plainly revealed your indifference—and that you care nothing about the issues on which you bring me to trial.

Next, Meletus, tell us, in the name of Zeus, whether it's better to live among good citizens or bad ones. Answer me, sir. Surely, I'm not asking you anything difficult. Don't bad people do something bad to whoever's closest to them at the given moment, whereas good people do something good?

Certainly.

Now is there anyone who wishes to be harmed rather than benefited by those around him? Keep answering, my good fellow. For the law requires you to answer. Is there anyone who wishes to be harmed?

Of course not.

25a

25b

25c

25d

---

[13] The Council consisted of five hundred male citizens over the age of thirty, elected annually by lot, fifty from each of the ten tribes of Athens. The Council met daily (except for some holidays and the like) as a steering committee for the Assembly.

Well, then, when you summon me here for corrupting the young and making them worse, do you mean that I do so intentionally or unintentionally?

Intentionally, I say.

What's that, Meletus? Are you so much wiser at your age than I at mine, that you know bad people do something bad to whoever's closest to them 25e at the given moment, and good people something good? Am I, by contrast, so very ignorant that I don't know even this: that if I do something bad to an associate, I risk getting back something bad from him in return? And is the result, as you claim, that I do so very bad a thing intentionally?

I'm not convinced by you of that, Meletus, and neither, I think, is anyone else. No, either I'm not corrupting the young or, if I am corrupting them, it's unintentionally, so that in either case what you say is false. But 26a if I'm corrupting them unintentionally, the law doesn't require that I be brought to court for such mistakes—that is, unintentional ones—but that I be taken aside for private instruction and admonishment. For it's clear that if I'm instructed, I'll stop doing what I do *un*intentionally. You, however, avoided associating with me and were unwilling to instruct me. Instead, you bring me here, where the law requires you to bring those in need of punishment, not instruction.

Well, men of Athens, what I said before is absolutely clear by this point, namely, that Meletus has never cared about these matters to any extent, great or small. Nevertheless, please tell us now, Meletus, how is it you say 26b I corrupt the young? Or is it absolutely clear, from the indictment you wrote, that it's by teaching them not to acknowledge the gods the city acknowledges, but new daimonic activities instead? Isn't that what you say I corrupt them by teaching?

I most emphatically do say that.

Then, in the name of those very gods we're now discussing, Meletus, speak yet more clearly, both for my sake and for that of these gentlemen. 26c You see, I'm unable to tell what you mean. Is it that I teach people to acknowledge that some gods exist—so that I, then, acknowledge their existence myself and am not an out-and-out atheist and am not guilty of that—yet not, of course, the very ones acknowledged by the city, but different ones? Is that what you're charging me with, that they're different ones? Or are you saying that I myself don't acknowledge any gods at all, and that that's what I teach to others?

That's what I mean, that you don't acknowledge any gods at all.

26d You're a strange fellow, Meletus! What makes you say that? Do I not even acknowledge that the sun and the moon are gods, then, as other men do?

No, by Zeus, gentlemen of the jury, he doesn't, since he says that the sun's a stone and the moon earth.

My dear Meletus, do you think it's Anaxagoras[14] you're accusing? Are you that contemptuous of the jury? Do you think they're so illiterate that they don't know that the books of Anaxagoras of Clazomenae are full of such arguments? And, in particular, do young people learn these views from me, views they can occasionally acquire in the Orchestra[15] for a drachma at most and that they'd ridicule Socrates for pretending were his own—especially as they're so strange? In the name of Zeus, is that really how I seem to you? Do I acknowledge the existence of no god at all?

26e

No indeed, by Zeus, none at all.

You aren't at all convincing, Meletus, not even, it seems to me, to yourself. You see, men of Athens, this fellow seems very arrogant and intemperate to me and to have written this indictment simply out of some sort of arrogance, intemperance, and youthful rashness. Indeed, he seems to have composed a sort of riddle in order to test me: "Will the so-called wise Socrates recognize that I'm playing around and contradicting myself? Or will I fool him along with the other listeners?" You see, he seems to me to be contradicting himself in his indictment, as if he were to say, "Socrates is guilty of not acknowledging gods, but of acknowledging gods." And that's just childish playing around, isn't it?

27a

Please examine with me, gentlemen, why it seems to me that this is what he's saying. And you, Meletus, answer us. But you, gentlemen, please remember what I asked of you at the beginning: don't create an uproar if I make my arguments in my accustomed manner.

27b

Is there anyone, Meletus, who acknowledges that human activities exist but doesn't acknowledge human beings? Make him answer, gentlemen, and don't let him make one protest after another. Is there anyone who doesn't acknowledge horses but does acknowledge equine activities? Or who doesn't acknowledge that musicians exist but does acknowledge musical activities? There's no one, best of men—if you don't want to answer, I must answer for you and for the others here. But at least answer my next question. Is there anyone who acknowledges the existence of daimonic activities but doesn't acknowledge daimons?

27c

No, there isn't.

How good of you to answer, if reluctantly and when compelled to by these gentlemen. Well then, you say that I acknowledge daimonic activities, whether new or familiar, and teach about them. But then, on your account, I do at any rate acknowledge daimonic activities, and to this you've sworn in your indictment against me. However, if I acknowledge daimonic

---

[14] Some of the views of Anaxagoras of Clazomenae (c. 500–428 BCE) are discussed at *Phaedo* 97b–99d.

[15] The Orchestra was part of the marketplace (*agora*) in Athens.

activities, surely it's absolutely necessary that I acknowledge daimons. Isn't that so? Yes, it is—I assume you agree, since you don't answer. But don't 27d we believe that daimons are either gods or, at any rate, children of gods? Yes or no?

Of course.

Then, if indeed I do believe in daimons, as you're saying, and if daimons are gods of some sort, that's precisely what I meant when I said that you're presenting us with a riddle and playing around: you're saying that I don't believe in gods and, on the contrary, that I do believe in gods, since in fact I do at least believe in daimons. But if, on the other hand, daimons are children of gods, some sort of bastard offspring of a nymph, or of whomever else tradition says each one is the child, what man could possibly believe that children of gods exist, but not gods? That would be just 27e as unreasonable as believing in the children of horses and asses—namely, mules—while not believing in the existence of horses and asses.

Well then, Meletus, you must have written these things to test us or because you were at a loss about what genuine injustice to charge me with. There's no conceivable way you could persuade any man with even the slightest intelligence that the same person believes in both daimonic activities and gods, and, on the contrary, that this same person believes neither 28a in daimons, nor in gods, nor in heroes.[16]

In fact, then, men of Athens, it doesn't seem to me to require a long defense to show that I'm not guilty of the charges in Meletus' indictment, but what I've said is sufficient. But what I was also saying earlier, that much hostility has arisen against me and among many people—you may be sure that's true. And it's what will convict me, if I am convicted: not Meletus or Anytus, but the slander and malice of many people. It has certainly convicted many other good men as well, and I imagine it will do so again. 28b There's no danger it will stop with me.

But perhaps someone may say, "Aren't you ashamed, Socrates, to have engaged in the sort of occupation that has now put you at risk of death?" I, however, would be right to reply to him, "You're not thinking straight, sir, if you think that a man who's any use at all should give any opposing weight to the risk of living or dying, instead of looking to this alone whenever he does anything: whether his actions are just or unjust, the deeds of a good 28c or bad man. You see, on your account, all those demigods who died on the plain of Troy were inferior people, especially the son of Thetis, who was so contemptuous of danger when the alternative was something shameful. When he was eager to kill Hector, his mother, since she was a goddess,

---

[16] Heroes are demigods (28c), children of gods and mortals, whose existence therefore entails the existence of gods.

spoke to him, I think, in some such words as these: 'My child, if you avenge the death of your friend Patroclus and slay Hector, you will die yourself immediately,' so the poem goes, 'as your death is fated to follow next after Hector's.' But though he heard that, he was contemptuous of death and danger, for he was far more afraid of living as a bad man and of failing to avenge his friends: 'Let me die immediately, then,' it continues, 'once I've given the wrongdoer his just deserts, so that I do not remain here by the curved ships, a laughingstock and a burden upon the earth.' Do you really suppose he gave a thought to death or danger?"

    You see, men of Athens, this is the truth of the matter: Wherever someone has stationed himself because he thinks it best, or wherever he's been stationed by his commander, there, it seems to me, he should remain, steadfast in danger, taking no account at all of death or of anything else, in comparison to what's shameful. I'd therefore have been acting scandalously, men of Athens, if, when I'd been stationed in Potidea, Amphipolis, or Delium[17] by the leaders you had elected to lead me, I had, like many another, remained where they'd stationed me and run the risk of death. But if, when the god stationed me here, as I became thoroughly convinced he did, to live practicing philosophy, examining myself and others, I had—for fear of death or anything else—abandoned my station.

    That would have been scandalous, and someone might have rightly and justly brought me to court for not acknowledging that gods exist, by disobeying the oracle, fearing death, and thinking I was wise when I wasn't. You see, fearing death, gentlemen, is nothing other than thinking one is wise when one isn't, since it's thinking one knows what one doesn't know. I mean, no one knows whether death may not be the greatest of all goods for people, but they fear it as if they knew for certain that it's the worst thing of all. Yet surely this is the most blameworthy ignorance of thinking one knows what one doesn't know. But I, gentlemen, may perhaps differ from most people by just this much in this matter too. And if I really were to claim to be wiser than anyone in any way, it would be in this: that as I don't have adequate knowledge about things in Hades, so too I don't think that I have knowledge. To act unjustly, on the other hand, to disobey someone better than oneself, whether god or man, that I do know to be bad and shameful. In any case, I'll never fear or avoid things that may for all I know be good more than things I know are bad.

    Suppose, then, you're prepared to let me go now and to disobey Anytus, who said I shouldn't have been brought to court at all, but that since I had been brought to court, you had no alternative but to put me to death

28d

28e

29a

29b

29c

---

[17] Three battles in the Peloponnesian War between Athens and its allies and Sparta and its allies.

because, as he stated before you, if I were acquitted, soon your sons would all be entirely corrupted by following Socrates' teachings. Suppose, confronted with that claim, you were to say to me, "Socrates, we will not obey Anytus this time. Instead, we are prepared to let you go. But on the following condition: that you spend no more time on this investigation

29d and don't practice philosophy, and if you're caught doing so, you'll die." Well, as I just said, if you were to let me go on these terms, I'd reply to you, "I've the utmost respect and affection for you, men of Athens, but I'll obey the god rather than you, and as long as I draw breath and am able, I won't give up practicing philosophy, exhorting you and also showing the way to any of you I ever happen to meet, saying just the sorts of things I'm accustomed to say:

> My excellent man, you're an Athenian, you belong to the greatest city, renowned for its wisdom and strength; are you not
29e   ashamed that you take care to acquire as much wealth as possible—and reputation and honor—but that about wisdom and truth, about how your soul may be in the best possible condition, you take neither care nor thought?

Then, if one of you disagrees and says that he *does* care, I won't let him go away immediately, but I'll question, examine, and test him. And if he doesn't seem to me to possess virtue, though he claims he does, I'll reproach

30a him, saying that he treats the most important things as having the least value, and inferior ones as having more. This I will do for anyone I meet, young or old, alien or fellow citizen—but especially for you, my fellow citizens, since you're closer kin to me. This, you may be sure, is what the god orders me to do. And I believe that no greater good for you has ever come about in the city than my service to the god. You see, I do nothing else except go around trying to persuade you, both young and old alike,

30b not to care about your bodies or your money as intensely as about how your soul may be in the best possible condition. I say,

> It's not from wealth that virtue comes, but from virtue comes money, and all the other things that are good for human beings, both in private and in public life.

Now if by saying this, I'm corrupting the young, *this* is what you'd have to think to be harmful. But if anyone claims I say something other than this, he's talking nonsense."

"It's in that light," I want to say, "men of Athens, that you should obey Anytus or not, and let me go or not—knowing that I wouldn't act in any

30c other way, not even if I were to die many times over."

Don't create an uproar, men of Athens. Instead, please abide by my request not to create an uproar at what I say, but to listen. For I think it will profit you to listen. You see, I'm certainly going to say some further things to you at which you may perhaps exclaim—but by no means do so.

You may be sure that if you put me to death—a man of the sort I said I was just now—you won't harm me more than you harm yourselves. Certainly, Meletus or Anytus couldn't harm me in any way: that's not possible. For I don't think it's lawful for a better man to be harmed by a   30d worse. He may, of course, kill me, or perhaps banish or disenfranchise me. And these *he* believes to be very bad things, and others no doubt agree. But I don't believe this. Rather, I believe that doing what he's doing now— attempting to kill a man unjustly—is far worse.

So, men of Athens, I'm far from pleading in my own defense now, as might be supposed. Instead, I'm pleading in yours, so that you don't commit a great wrong against the god's gift to you by condemning me.   30e If you put me to death, you won't easily find another like me. For, even if it seems ridiculous to say so, I've literally been attached to the city, as if to a large thoroughbred horse that was somewhat sluggish because of its size and needed to be awakened by some sort of gadfly. It's as just such a gadfly, it seems to me, that the god has attached me to the city—one that awakens, cajoles, and reproaches each and every one of you and never stops alighting everywhere on you the whole day. You won't easily find another   31a like that, gentlemen. So if you obey me, you'll spare my life. But perhaps you'll be resentful, like people awakened from a doze, and slap at me. If you obey Anytus, you might easily kill me. Then you might spend the rest of your lives asleep, unless the god, in his compassion for you, were to send you someone else.

That I am indeed the sort of person to be given as a gift to the city by the god, you may recognize from this: it doesn't seem a merely human   31b matter—does it?—for me to have neglected all my own affairs and to have put up with this neglect of my domestic life for so many years now, but always to have minded your business, by visiting each of you in private, like a father or elder brother, to persuade you to care about virtue. Of course, if I were getting anything out of it or if I were being paid for giving this advice, my conduct would be intelligible. But, as it is, you can plainly see for yourselves that my accusers, who so shamelessly accused me of everything else, couldn't bring themselves to be so utterly shameless as to call a witness to say that I ever once accepted or asked for payment. In   31c fact, it's I who can call what I think is a sufficient witness that I'm telling the truth—my poverty.

But perhaps it may seem strange that I, of all people, give this advice by going around and minding other people's business in private, yet do not venture to go before your Assembly and give advice to the city in public. The reason for that, however, is one you've heard me give many times and in many places: A divine and daimonic thing comes to me—the very thing Meletus made mocking allusion to in the indictment he wrote. It's something that began happening to me in childhood: a sort of voice comes, which, whenever it does come, always holds me back from what I'm about to do but never urges me forward. *It* is what opposes my engaging in politics—and to me, at least, its opposition seems entirely right. For you may be sure, men of Athens, that if I'd tried to engage in politics I'd have perished long ago and have benefited neither you nor myself.

Please don't resent me if I tell you the truth. The fact is that no man will be spared by you or by any other multitude of people if he genuinely opposes a lot of unjust and unlawful actions and tries to prevent them from happening in the city. On the contrary, anyone who really fights for what's just, if indeed he's going to survive for even a short time, must act privately not publicly.

I'll present substantial evidence of that—not words, but what you value, deeds. Listen, then, to what happened to me, so you may see that fear of death wouldn't lead me to submit to a single person contrary to what's just, not even if I were to perish at once for not submitting. The things I'll tell you are of a vulgar sort commonly heard in the law courts, but they're true nonetheless.

You see, men of Athens, I never held any other public office in the city, but I've served on the Council. And it happened that my own tribe, Antiochis, was presiding[18] when you wanted to try the ten generals—the ones who failed to rescue the survivors of the naval battle—as a group.[19] That was unlawful, as you all came to recognize at a later time. On that occasion, I was the only presiding member opposed to your doing something illegal, and I voted against you. And though the orators were ready to lay information against me and have me summarily arrested, and you were shouting and urging them on, I thought that I should face danger on the side of law and justice, rather than go along with you for fear of imprisonment or death when your proposals were unjust.

---

[18] A *phulē* is not a tribe in our sense, but an administrative division of the citizen body, most probably of military origin. The presiding committee of the Council (25a note) consisted of the fifty members of one of the ten tribes, selected by lot to serve for one-tenth of the year. It arranged meetings of the Council and Assembly, received envoys and letters to the state, and conducted other routine business.

[19] After the naval battle at Arginusae on the Ionian coast of Asia Minor (406 BCE), ten Athenian generals were indicted for failing to rescue survivors and to pick up the bodies of the dead. Both Council and Assembly voted to try them as a group, which was against Athenian law.

This happened when the city was still under democratic rule. But later, when the oligarchy had come to power, it happened once more. The Thirty[20] summoned me and four others to the Tholus[21] and ordered us to arrest Leon of Salamis[22] and bring him from Salamis to die. They gave many such orders to many other people too, of course, since they wanted to implicate as many as possible in their crimes. On *that* occasion, however, I showed once again not by words but by deeds that I couldn't care less about death—if that isn't putting it too bluntly—but that all I care about is not doing anything unjust or impious. You see, that government, powerful though it was, didn't frighten me into unjust action: when we came out of the Tholus, the other four went to Salamis and arrested Leon, whereas I left and went home. I might have died for that if the government hadn't fallen shortly afterward. 32d

There are many witnesses who will testify before you about these events. 32e

Do you imagine, then, that I'd have survived all these years if I'd been regularly active in public affairs, and had come to the aid of justice like a good man, and regarded that as most important, as one should? Far from it, men of Athens, and neither would any other man. But throughout my entire life, in any public activities I may have engaged in, it was evident I was the sort of person—and in private life I was the same—who never agreed to anything with anyone contrary to justice, whether with others or with those who my slanderers say are my students. In fact, I've never been anyone's teacher at any time. But if anyone, whether young or old, wanted to listen to me while I was talking and performing my own task, I never begrudged that to him. Neither do I engage in conversation only when I receive a fee and not when I don't. Rather, I offer myself for questioning to rich and poor alike, or, if someone prefers, he may listen to me and answer my questions. And if any one of these turned out well, or did not do so, I can't justly be held responsible, since I never at any time promised any of them that they'd learn anything from me or that I'd teach them. And if anyone says that he learned something from me or heard something in private that all the others didn't also hear, you may be sure he isn't telling the truth. 33a 33b

---

[20] When Athens was defeated by Sparta in 404 BCE, its democratic government was replaced by a brutal oligarchy, the so-called Thirty Tyrants, which survived barely eight months. Two members of the Thirty—Critias and Charmides—were relatives of Plato and appear as Socratic interlocutors in the dialogues named after them. Socrates' association with them is often thought to have been one of the things that led to his indictment.

[21] The Tholus was a dome-shaped building. The presiding committee of the Council (32b note) took its meals there.

[22] Leon is otherwise unknown.

Why, then, you may ask, do some people enjoy spending so much time
with me? You've heard the answer, men of Athens. I told you the whole
truth: it's because they enjoy listening to people being examined who think
they're wise but aren't. For it's not unpleasant. In my case, however, it's
something, you may take it from me, I've been ordered to do by the god,
in both oracles and dreams, and in every other way that divine providence
ever ordered any man to do anything at all.

All these things, men of Athens, are both true and easily tested. I mean,
if I really do corrupt the young or have corrupted them in the past, surely
if any of them had recognized when they became older that I'd given them
bad advice at some point in their youth, they'd now have come forward
themselves to accuse me and seek redress. Or else, if they weren't willing to come themselves, some of their family members—fathers, brothers,
or other relatives—if indeed their kinsmen had suffered any harm from
me—would remember it now and seek redress.

In any case, I see many of these people present here: first of all, there's
Crito, my contemporary and fellow demesman, the father of Critobulus
here;[23] then there's Lysanius of Sphettus, father of Aeschines here;[24] next,
there's Epigenes' father, Antiphon of Cephisia here.[25] Then there are
others whose brothers have spent time in this way: Nicostratus, son of
Theozotides,[26] brother of Theodotus—by the way, Theodotus is dead, so
that Nicostratus is at any rate not being held back by him; and Paralius here,
son of Demodocus, whose brother was Theages;[27] and there's Adeimantus,
the son of Ariston, whose brother is Plato here, and Aeantodorus, whose
brother here is Apollodorus.[28] And there are many others I could mention,
some of whom Meletus most certainly ought to have called as witnesses
in the course of his own speech. If he forgot to do so, let him call them
now—I yield time to him. Let him tell us if he has any such witness. No,
it's entirely the opposite, gentlemen. You'll find that they're all prepared to

33c

33d

33e

34a

---

[23] Crito was a well-off farm owner, able and willing to help his friends financially
(38b, *Crito* 44b–c).

[24] Aeschines of Sphettus (fourth century BCE) was a devoted follower of Socrates,
present at his death (*Phaedo* 59b). He taught oratory and wrote speeches for the law
courts. He also wrote Socratic dialogues, only fragments of which are extant.

[25] Epigenes was present at Socrates' death (*Phaedo* 59b) and was a member of his
circle.

[26] Theozotides introduced two important democratic reforms after the fall of the
Thirty Tyrants (32c note).

[27] Otherwise largely unknown.

[28] Apollodorus, an enthusiastic follower of Socrates, given to emotion (*Phaedo*
59a–b, 117c–d), is the narrator in the *Symposium*.

come to my aid, their corruptor, the one who, Meletus and Anytus claim, is doing harm to their families. Of course, the corrupted ones themselves 34b might indeed have reason to come to my aid. But the *uncorrupted* ones, their relatives, who are older men now, what reason could they possibly have to support me, other than the right and just one: that they know perfectly well that Meletus is lying, whereas I am telling the truth?

Well then, gentlemen, those, and perhaps other similar things, are pretty much all I have to say in my defense. But perhaps one of you might be resentful when he recalls his own behavior. Perhaps when he was contesting even a lesser charge than this charge, he positively entreated the jurors 34c with copious tears, bringing forward his children and many other relatives and friends as well, in order to arouse as much pity as possible. And then he finds that I'll do none of these things, not even when I'm facing what might be considered the ultimate danger. Perhaps someone with these thoughts might feel more willful where I'm concerned and, made angry by these very same thoughts, cast his vote in anger. Well, if there's someone like that among you—of course, I don't expect there to be, but *if* there is—I 34d think it appropriate for me to answer him as follows: "I do indeed have relatives, my excellent man. As Homer puts it,[29] I too 'wasn't born from oak or from rock' but from human parents. And so I do have relatives, sons too, men of Athens, three of them, one already a young man while two are still children. Nonetheless, I won't bring any of them forward here and then entreat you to vote for my acquittal."

Why, you may ask, will I do none of these things? Not because I'm willful, men of Athens, or want to dishonor you—whether I'm boldly facing 34e death or not is a separate story. The point has to do with reputation—yours and mine and that of the entire city: it doesn't seem noble to me to do these things, especially at my age and with my reputation—for whether truly or falsely, it's firmly believed in any case that Socrates is superior to the majority of people in some way. Therefore, if those of you who are 35a believed to be superior—in either wisdom or courage or any other virtue whatever—behave like that, it would be shameful.

I've often seen people of this sort when they're on trial: they're thought to be someone, yet they do astonishing things—as if they imagined they'd suffer something terrible if they died and would be immortal if only you didn't kill them. People like that seem to me to bring such shame to the city that any foreigner might well suppose that those among the Athenians who are superior in virtue—the ones they select from among themselves for 35b political office and other positions of honor—are no better than women. I

---

[29] Homer, *Odyssey* xix.163.

say this, men of Athens, because none of us who are in any way whatever thought to be someone should behave like that, nor, if we attempt to do so, should you allow it. On the contrary, you should make it clear you're far more likely to convict someone who makes the city despicable by staging these pathetic scenes than someone who minds his behavior.

35c   Reputation aside, gentlemen, it doesn't seem just to me to entreat the jury—nor to be acquitted by entreating it—but rather to inform it and persuade it. After all, a juror doesn't sit in order to grant justice as a favor, but to decide where justice lies. And he has sworn on oath not that he'll favor whomever he pleases, but that he'll judge according to law. We shouldn't accustom you to breaking your oath, then, nor should you become accustomed to doing so—neither of us would be doing something holy if we did. Hence don't expect me, men of Athens, to act toward you in ways I
35d   consider to be neither noble, nor just, nor pious—most especially, by Zeus, when I'm being prosecuted for *impiety* by Meletus here. You see, if I tried to persuade and to force you by entreaties, after you've sworn an oath, I clearly would be teaching you not to believe in the existence of gods, and my defense would literally convict me of not acknowledging gods. But that's far from being the case: I do acknowledge them, men of Athens, as none of my accusers does. I turn it over to you and to the god to judge me in whatever way will be best for me and for yourselves.

35e
36a   There are many reasons, men of Athens, why I'm not resentful at this outcome—that you voted to convict me—and this outcome wasn't unexpected by me. I'm much more surprised at the number of votes cast on each side: I didn't think that the decision would be by so few votes but by a great many. Yet now, it seems, that if a mere thirty votes had been cast differently, I'd have been acquitted. Or rather, it seems to me that where Meletus is concerned, I've been acquitted even as things stand. And not merely acquitted. On the contrary, one thing at least is clear to everyone: if Anytus had not come forward with Lycon to accuse me, Meletus would
36b   have been fined a thousand drachmas, since he wouldn't have received a fifth of the votes.

     But be that as it may, the man demands the death penalty for me. Well then, what counterpenalty should I now propose to you, men of Athens? Or is it clear that it's whatever I deserve? What then should it be? What do I deserve to suffer or pay just because I didn't mind my own business throughout my life? Because I didn't care about the things most people care about—making money, managing an estate, or being a general, a popular leader, or holding some other political office, or joining the cabals and factions that come to exist in a city—but thought myself too honest,
36c   in truth, to engage in these things and survive? Because I didn't engage in things, if engaging in them was going to benefit neither you nor myself,

but instead went to each of you privately and tried to perform what I claim is the greatest benefaction? That was what I did. I tried to persuade each of you to care first not about any of his possessions, but about himself and how he'll become best and wisest; and not primarily about the city's possessions, but about the city itself; and to care about all other things in the same way.

What, then, do I deserve to suffer for being such a man? Something   36d
good, men of Athens, if I'm indeed to propose a penalty that I truly deserve. Yes, and the sort of good thing, too, that would be appropriate for me. What, then, is appropriate for a poor man who is a public benefactor and needs to have the leisure to exhort you? Nothing could be more appropriate, men of Athens, than for such a man to be given free meals in the Prytaneum—much more so for him, at any rate, than for any one of you who has won a victory at Olympia, whether with a single horse or with a pair or a team of four.[30] You see, he makes you think you're happy, whereas I make you actually happy. Besides, he doesn't need to be sustained in that way, but I do need it. So if, as justice demands, I must propose a penalty I   36e
deserve, that's the penalty I propose: free meals in the Prytaneum.   37a

Now perhaps when I say this, you may think I'm speaking in a quite willful manner—just as when I talked about appeals to pity and supplications. That's not so, men of Athens, rather it's something like this: I'm convinced that I never intentionally do injustice to any man—but I can't get you to share my conviction, because we've talked together a short time. I say this, because if you had a law, as other men in fact do, not to try a capital charge in a single day, but over several, I think you'd be convinced. But as   37b
things stand, it isn't easy to clear myself of huge slanders in a short time.

Since *I'm* convinced that I've done injustice to no one, however, I'm certainly not likely to do myself injustice, to announce that I deserve something bad and to propose a penalty of that sort for myself. Why should I do that? In order not to suffer what Meletus proposes as a penalty for me, when I say that I don't know whether it's a good or a bad thing? As an alternative to that, am I then to choose one of the things I know very well to be bad and propose it? Imprisonment, for example? And why should I live in prison, enslaved to the regularly appointed officers, the Eleven?[31] All   37c
right, a fine with imprisonment until I pay? But in my case the effect would be precisely the one I just now described, since I haven't the means to pay.

Well then, should I propose exile? Perhaps that's what *you*'d propose for me. But I'd certainly have to have an excessive love of life, men of Athens, to be so irrational as to do that. I see that you, my fellow citizens, were unable to tolerate my discourses and discussions but came to find them so   37d

---

[30] See *Euthyphro* 3a note.

[31] Officials appointed by lot to be in charge of prisons and executions.

burdensome and odious that you're now seeking to get rid of them. Is it likely, then, that I'll infer that others will find them easy to bear? Far from it, men of Athens. It would be a fine life for me, indeed, a man of my age, to go into exile and spend his life exchanging one city for another, because he's always being expelled. You see, I well know that wherever I go, the young will come to hear me speaking, just as they do here. And if I drive them away, they will themselves persuade their elders to expel me; whereas

37e if I don't drive them away, their fathers and relatives will expel me because of these same young people.

Now perhaps someone may say, "But by keeping quiet and minding your own business, Socrates, wouldn't it be possible for you to live in exile for us?" This is the very hardest point on which to convince some of you. You see, if I say that to do *that* would be to disobey the god, and that this is why I can't mind my own business, you won't believe me, since you'll

38a suppose I'm being ironical. But again, if I say it's the greatest good for a man to discuss virtue every day, and the other things you've heard me discussing and examining myself and others about, on the grounds that the unexamined life isn't worth living for a human being, you'll believe me even less when I say that. But in fact, things are just as I claim them to be, men of Athens, though it isn't easy to convince you of them. At the same time, I'm not accustomed to thinking that I deserve anything bad.

38b If I had the means, I'd have proposed a fine of as much as I could afford to pay, since that would have done me no harm at all. But as things stand, I don't have them—unless you want me to propose as much as I'm in fact able to pay. Perhaps I could pay you about a mina of silver. So I propose a fine of that amount.

One moment, men of Athens. Plato here, and Crito, Critobulus, and Apollodorus as well, are urging me to propose thirty minas and saying that they themselves will guarantee it.[32] I propose a fine of that amount, therefore, and these men will be sufficient guarantors to you of the silver.

38c For the sake of a little time, men of Athens, you're going to earn from those who wish to denigrate our city both the reputation and the blame for having killed Socrates—that wise man. For those who wish to reproach you will, of course, claim that I'm wise, even if I'm not. In any case, if you'd waited a short time, this would have happened of its own accord. You, of course, see my age, you see that I'm already far along in life and close to death. I'm saying this not to all of you, but to those who voted for the death

38d penalty. And to those same people I also say this: Perhaps you imagine,

---

[32] Thirty minas (3,000 silver drachmas) was almost ten years' salary for someone engaged in public works.

gentlemen, that I was convicted for lack of the sort of arguments I could have used to convince you, if I'd thought I should do or say anything to escape the penalty. Far from it. I *have* been convicted for a lack—not of arguments, however, but of bold-faced shamelessness and for being unwilling to say the sorts of things to you you'd have been most pleased to hear, with me weeping and wailing, and doing and saying many other things I claim are unworthy of me, but that are the very sorts of things you're used to hearing from everyone else. No, I didn't think then that I should do anything servile because of the danger I faced, and so I don't regret now that I defended myself as I did. I'd far rather die after such a defense than live like that. 38e

You see, whether in a trial or in a war, neither I nor anyone else should contrive to escape death at all costs. In battle, too, it often becomes clear that one might escape death by throwing down one's weapons and turning to supplicate one's pursuers. And in each sort of danger there are many other ways one can contrive to escape death, if one is shameless enough to do or say anything. The difficult thing, gentlemen, isn't escaping death; escaping villainy is much more difficult, since it runs faster than death. And now I, slow and old as I am, have been overtaken by the slower runner while my accusers, clever and sharp-witted as they are, have been overtaken by the faster one—vice. And now I take my leave, convicted by you of a capital crime, whereas they stand forever convicted by the truth of wickedness and injustice. And just as I accept my penalty, so must they. Perhaps, things *had* to turn out this way, and I suppose it's good they have. 39a 39b

Next, I want to make a prophecy to those who convicted me. Indeed, I'm now at the point at which men prophesy most—when they're about to die. I say to you men who condemned me to death that as soon as I'm dead vengeance will come upon you, and it will be much harsher, by Zeus, than the vengeance you take in killing me. You did this now in the belief that you'll escape giving an account of your lives. But I say that quite the opposite will happen to you. There will be more people to test you, whom I now restrain, though you didn't notice my doing so. And they'll be all the harsher on you, since they're younger, and you'll resent it all the more. You see, if you imagine that by killing people you'll prevent anyone from reproaching you for not living in the right way, you're not thinking straight. In fact, to escape is neither possible nor noble. On the contrary, what's best and easiest isn't to put down other people, but to prepare oneself to be the best one can. With that prophecy to those of you who voted to convict me, I take my leave. 39c 39d

However, I'd gladly discuss this result with those who voted for my acquittal while the officers of the court are busy and I'm not yet on my way to 39e the place where I must die. Please stay with me, gentlemen, just for that short time. After all, there's nothing to prevent us from having a talk with one another while it's still in our power. To you whom I regard as friends

40a I'm willing to show the meaning of what has just now happened to me. You see, gentlemen of the jury—for in calling *you* "jurors" I no doubt use the term correctly—an amazing thing has happened to me. In previous times, the usual prophecies of my daimonic sign were always very frequent, opposing me even on trivial matters, if I was about do something that wasn't right. Now, however, something has happened to me, as you can see for yourselves, that one might think to be, and that's generally regarded

40b as being, the worst of all bad things. Yet the god's sign didn't oppose me when I left home this morning, or when I came up here to the law court, or anywhere in my speech when I was about to say something, even though in other discussions it has often stopped me in the middle of what I was saying. Now, however, where this affair is concerned, it has opposed me in nothing I either said or did.

What, then, do I suppose is the explanation for that? I'll tell you. You see, it's likely that what has happened to me is a good thing and that those of you who suppose death to be bad make an incorrect supposition. I've

40c strong evidence of this, since there's no way my usual sign would have failed to oppose me, if I weren't about to achieve something good.

But let's bear in mind that the following is also a strong reason to hope that death may be something good. Being dead is one of two things: either the dead are nothing, as it were, and have no awareness whatsoever of anything at all; or else, as we're told, it's some sort of change, a migration of the soul from here to another place. Now, if there's in fact no awareness, but it's

40d like sleep—the kind in which the sleeper has no dream whatsoever—then death would be an amazing advantage. For I imagine that if someone had to pick a night in which he slept so soundly that he didn't even dream and had to compare all the other nights and days of his life with that one, and then, having considered the matter, had to say how many days or nights of his life he had spent better or more pleasantly than that night—I imagine that not just some private individual, but even the great king,[33] would find

40e them easy to count compared to the other days and nights. Well, if death's like that, *I* say it's an advantage, since, in that case, the whole of time would seem no longer than a single night.

On the other hand, if death's a sort of journey from here to another place, and if what we're told is true, and all who've died are indeed there,

---

[33] The king of Persia, whose wealth and power made him a popular exemplar of human success and happiness. Musaeus, usually associated with Orpheus, was also a legendary bard.

what could be a greater good than that, gentlemen of the jury? If on arriving in Hades and leaving behind the people who claim to be jurors **41a** here, one's going to find those who are truly jurors or judges, the very ones who are said to sit in judgment there too—Minos,[34] Rhadamanthys, Aeachus, Triptolemus, and all the other demigods who were just in their own lifetimes—would the journey be a wretched one?

Or again, what would any one of you not give to talk to Orpheus and Musaeus, Hesiod and Homer?[35] I'd be willing to die many times over, if that were true. You see, for myself, at any rate, spending time there would **41b** be amazing: when I met Palamedes or Ajax, the son of Telemon, or anyone else of old who died because of an unjust verdict, I could compare my own experience with theirs—as I suppose it wouldn't be unpleasing to do. And in particular, the most important thing: I could spend time examining and searching people there, just as I do here, to find out who among them is wise, and who thinks he is, but isn't.

What wouldn't one give, gentlemen of the jury, to be able to examine the leader of the great expedition against Troy, or Odysseus, or Sisyphus,[36] **41c** or countless other men and women one could mention? To talk to them there, to associate with them and examine them, wouldn't that be inconceivable happiness? In any case, the people there certainly don't kill one for doing it. For if what we're told is true, the people there are both happier in all other respects than the people here and also deathless for the remainder of time.

But you too, gentlemen of the jury, should be of good hope in the face of death, and bear in mind this single truth: nothing bad can happen to a **41d** good man, whether in life or in death, nor are the gods unconcerned about his troubles. What has happened to me hasn't happened by chance; rather, it's clear to me that to die now and escape my troubles was a better thing for me. It was for this very reason that my sign never opposed me. And so, for my part, I'm not at all angry with those who voted to condemn me or with my accusers. And yet this wasn't what they had in mind when they were condemning and accusing me. No, they thought to harm me—and for that they deserve to be blamed.

This small favor, however, I ask of them. When my sons come of age, **41e** gentlemen, punish them by harassing them in the very same way that I harassed you, if they seem to you to take care of wealth or anything before virtue, if they think they're someone when they're no one. Reproach them, just as I reproached you: tell them that they don't care for the things they

---

[34] Minos was a legendary king of Crete.

[35] Orpheus was a legendary bard and founder of the mystical religion of Orphism.

[36] Sisyphus is a legendary king and founder of Corinth.

42a should and think they're someone when they're worth nothing. If you will do that, I'll have received my own just deserts from you, as will my sons.

But now it's time to leave, I to die and you to live. Which of us goes to the better thing, however, is unclear to everyone except the god.

CRITO

SOCRATES: Why have you come at this hour, Crito? Isn't it still early?　　43a

CRITO: It is indeed.

SOCRATES: About what time?

CRITO: Just before dawn.

SOCRATES: I'm surprised the prison warden was willing to let you in.

CRITO: He knows me by now, Socrates, I come here so often. And besides I've done him a good turn.

SOCRATES: Have you just arrived or have you been here for a while?

CRITO: For quite a while.

SOCRATES: Then why didn't you wake me right away, instead of sitting　43b
there in silence?

CRITO: In the name of Zeus, Socrates, I wouldn't do that! I only wish I weren't so sleepless and distressed myself. I've been amazed all this time to see how peacefully you were sleeping, and I deliberately kept from waking you, so that you could pass the time as pleasantly as possible. In the past—indeed, throughout my entire life—I've often counted you happy in your disposition, but never more so than in this present misfortune. You bear it so easily and calmly.

SOCRATES: Well, Crito, it would be an error for someone of my age to complain when the time has come when he must die.

CRITO: Other people get overtaken by such misfortunes too, Socrates, but　43c
their age doesn't prevent them in the least from complaining about their fate.

SOCRATES: That's right. But tell me, why *have* you come so early?

CRITO: I bring bad news, Socrates. Not bad in your view, it seems to me, but bad and hard in mine and that of all your friends—and hardest of all, I think, for me to bear.

SOCRATES: What news is that? Or has the ship returned from Delos, at whose return I must die?[1]　　43d

---

The text of *Crito,* translated by C. D. C. Reeve, is reprinted from *The Trials of Socrates: Six Classic Texts,* edited by C. D. C. Reeve. Copyright © 2002, Hackett Publishing Co.

[1] Legend had it that Athens was once obliged to send King Minos of Crete an annual tribute of seven young men and seven maidens to be given to the Minotaur—a

CRITO: No, it hasn't returned *yet,* but I think it will arrive today, judging from the reports of people who've come from Sunium,[2] where they left it. It's clear from these reports that it will arrive today. And so tomorrow, Socrates, you must end your life.

SOCRATES: I pray that it may be for the best, Crito. If it pleases the gods, let it be so. All the same, I don't think it will arrive today.

44a CRITO: What evidence have you for that?

SOCRATES: I'll tell you. I must die on the day after the ship arrives.

CRITO: That's what the authorities say, at least.

SOCRATES: Then I don't think it will arrive today, but tomorrow. My evidence for this comes from a dream I had in the night a short while ago. So it looks as though you chose the right time not to wake me.

CRITO: What was your dream?

SOCRATES: I thought a beautiful, graceful woman came to me, robed in
44b white. She called me and said, "Socrates, you will arrive 'in fertile Phthia' on the third day."[3]

CRITO: What a strange dream, Socrates.

SOCRATES: Yet its meaning is quite clear, Crito—at least, it seems so to me.

CRITO: All too clear, apparently. But look here, Socrates, it's still not too late to take my advice and save yourself. You see, if you die, I won't just suffer a single misfortune. On the contrary, not only will I lose a friend the like of whom I'll never find again, but, in addition, many people, who don't know you or me well, will think that I didn't care about you,
44c since I could have saved you if I'd been willing to spend the money. And indeed what reputation could be more shameful than being thought to value money more than friends? For the majority of people won't believe that it was you yourself who refused to leave this place, though we were urging you to do so.

SOCRATES: But my dear Crito, why should we care so much about what the majority think? After all, the most decent ones, who are worthier of consideration, will believe that matters were handled in just the way they were in fact handled.

---

monster, half man and half bull, that he kept in a labyrinth. With the help of a thread given to him by Minos' daughter Ariadne, Theseus, a legendary king of Athens, made his way through the labyrinth, killed the Minotaur, and escaped, thus ending the tribute. Each year, Athens commemorated these events by sending a mission of thanks to the sanctuary of Apollo on the sacred island of Delos. No executions could take place in Athens until the mission returned from its voyage. See *Phaedo* 58a–c.

[2] A headland on the southeast coast of Attica, about thirty miles from Athens.

[3] Homer, *Iliad* ix.363.

CRITO: But you can surely see, Socrates, that one should care about major-   44d
ity opinion too. Your present situation itself shows clearly that the majority
can do not just minor harms but the very worst things to someone who's
been slandered in front of them.

SOCRATES: I only wish, Crito, that the majority *could* do the very worst
things, then they might also be able to do the very best ones—and everything would be fine. But as it is, they can do neither, since they can't make
someone either wise or unwise—the effects *they* produce are really the
result of chance.

CRITO: Well, if you say so. But tell me this, Socrates. You're not worried   44e
about me and your other friends, are you—fearing that if you escaped, the
informers[4] would give us trouble, and that we might be forced to give up
all our property, pay heavy fines, or even suffer some further penalty? If
you're afraid of anything like that, dismiss it from your mind. After all,   45a
we're surely justified in running this risk to save you or an even greater
one if need be. Now take my advice, and don't refuse me.

SOCRATES: Yes, those things do worry me, Crito, among many others.

CRITO: Then don't fear them: the sum of money that certain people I know
will accept in order to save you and get you out of here isn't that large.
Next, don't you see how cheap these informers are and how little money
is needed to deal with them? My own wealth's available to you, and it, I
think, should be enough. Next, even if your concern for me makes you   45b
unwilling to spend my money, there are foreign visitors here who are willing to spend theirs. One of them, Simmias of Thebes, has even brought
enough money for this very purpose; and Cebes, too, and a good many
others are also willing to contribute. So, as I say, don't let these fears make
you hesitate to save yourself. And don't let it trouble you, as you were
saying in court, that if you went into exile you wouldn't know what to
do with yourself. You see, wherever else you may go, there'll be people to   45c
welcome you. If you want to go to Thessaly, I have friends there who'll
make much of you and protect you, so that no one in Thessaly will give
you any trouble.[5]

Besides, Socrates, I think that what you're doing isn't just: throwing
away your life, when you could save it, and hastening the very sort of fate
for yourself that your enemies would hasten—and indeed have hastened—
in their wish to destroy you. What's more I think you're also betraying

---

[4] The *sukophantai* were individuals who prosecuted others in order to get the
reward offered in Athenian law to successful prosecutors, or as a way of blackmailing
someone who would pay to avoid prosecution, or for personal or political gain of
some other sort.

[5] Thessaly is a region in the north of Greece.

those sons of yours by going away and deserting them when you could
45d   bring them up and educate them. So far as you're concerned, they must
take their chances in life; and the chance they'll get, in all likelihood, is just
the one that orphans usually get when they lose their parents. No. Either
one shouldn't have children at all, or one ought to see their upbringing
and education through to the end. But you seem to me to be choosing the
easiest way out, whereas one should choose whatever a good and brave man
would choose—particularly when one claims to have cared about virtue
throughout one's life.

45e   I feel ashamed on your behalf and on behalf of myself and your friends.
I fear that it's going to seem that this whole business of yours has been
handled with a certain cowardice on our part. The case was brought
to court when it needn't have been brought. Then there was the actual
conduct of the trial. And now, to crown it all, this absurd finale to the
affair. It's going to seem that we let the opportunity slip because of some
vice, such as cowardice, on our part, since we didn't save you nor did
46a   you save yourself, although it was quite possible had we been of even the
slightest use.

See to it, then, Socrates, that all this doesn't turn out badly and a shameful thing both for you and for us. Come, deliberate—or rather, at this hour
it's not a matter of deliberating but of having deliberated already—and
only one decision remains. You see, everything must be done this coming
night; and if we delay, it will no longer be possible. For all these reasons,
Socrates, please take my advice and don't refuse me.

46b   SOCRATES: My dear Crito, your enthusiasm's most valuable, provided it's
of the right sort. But if it isn't, the greater it is, the more difficult it will
be to deal with. We must therefore examine whether we should do what
you advise or not. You see, I'm not the sort of person who's just now for
the first time persuaded by nothing within me except the argument that
on rational reflection seems best to me; I've *always* been like that. I can't
now reject the arguments I stated before just because this misfortune has
befallen me. On the contrary, they seem pretty much the same to me, and
46c   I respect and value the same ones as I did before. So if we have no better
ones to offer in the present situation, you can be sure I won't agree with
you—not even if the power of the majority to threaten us, as if we were
children, with the bogeymen of imprisonment, execution, and confiscation
of property were far greater than it is now.

What, then, is the most reasonable way to examine these matters?
Suppose we first take up the argument you stated about people's opinions.
46d   Is it true or not that one should pay attention to some opinions but not
to others? Or was it true before I had to die, whereas it's now clear that it
was stated idly, for the sake of argument, and is really just childish nonsense? For my part, I'm eager to join you, Crito, in a joint examination

of whether this argument will appear any differently to me, now that I'm here, or the same, and of whether we should dismiss it from our minds or be persuaded by it.

It used to be said, I think, by people who thought they were talking sense, that, as I said a moment ago, one should take some people's opinions seriously but not others. By the gods, Crito, don't you think that was true? 46e You see, in all human probability, *you* are not going to die tomorrow, and so the present situation won't distort your judgment. Consider, then, don't 47a you think it's a sound argument that one shouldn't value all the opinions people have, but some and not others, and not those of everyone, but those of some people and not of others? What do you say? Isn't that true?

CRITO: It is.

SOCRATES: And we should value good opinions, but not bad ones?

CRITO: Yes.

SOCRATES: And the good ones are those of wise people and the bad ones those of unwise people?

CRITO: Of course.

SOCRATES: Come then, what of such questions as this? When a man's primarily engaged in physical training, does he pay attention to the praise 47b or blame or opinion of every man or only to those of the one man who's a doctor or a trainer?

CRITO: Only to those of the one man.

SOCRATES: Then he should fear the blame and welcome the praise of that one man, but not those of the majority of people.

CRITO: Clearly.

SOCRATES: So his actions and exercises, his eating and drinking, should be guided by the opinion of the one man, the knowledgeable and understanding supervisor, rather than on that of all the rest?

CRITO: That's right.

SOCRATES: Well, then, if he disobeys that one man and sets no value on his 47c opinion or his praises but values those of the majority of people who have no understanding, won't something bad happen to him?

CRITO: Of course.

SOCRATES: And what is this bad effect? Where does it occur? In what part of the one who disobeys?

CRITO: Clearly, it's in his body, since that's what it destroys.

SOCRATES: That's right. And isn't the same true in other cases, Crito? No need to go through them all, but, in particular, in cases of just and unjust things, shameful and fine ones, good and bad ones—in cases of what we're now deliberating about—is it the opinion of the majority we should follow

47d   and fear? Or is it the opinion of the one man—if there is one who understands these things—we should respect and fear above all others? On the
grounds that, if we don't follow it, we shall seriously damage and maim
that part of us which, as we used to say, is made better by what's just but is
destroyed by what's unjust. Or is there no truth in that?

CRITO: I certainly think there is, Socrates.

SOCRATES: Come then, suppose we destroy the part of us that is made better
by what's healthy but is seriously damaged by what causes disease when we
don't follow the opinion of people who have understanding. Would our
lives be worth living once it has been seriously damaged? And that part,
47e   of course, is the body, isn't it?

CRITO: Yes.

SOCRATES: Then are our lives worth living with a wretched, seriously
damaged body?

CRITO: Certainly not.

SOCRATES: But our lives *are* worth living when the part of us that's maimed
by what's unjust and benefited by what's just is seriously damaged? Or do
we consider it—whichever part of us it is to which justice and injustice
48a   pertain—to be inferior to the body?

CRITO: Certainly not.

SOCRATES: On the contrary, it's more valuable?

CRITO: Far more.

SOCRATES: Then, my very good friend, we should not give so much thought
to what the majority of people will say about us, but think instead of what
the person who understands just and unjust things will say—the one man
and the truth itself. So your first claim—that we should give thought to
the opinion of the majority about what's just, fine, good, and their opposites—isn't right.

"But," someone might say, "the majority can put us to death."

48b   CRITO: That's certainly clear too. It would indeed be said, Socrates.

SOCRATES: That's right. And yet, my dear friend, the argument we've gone
through still seems the same to me, at any rate, as it did before. And now
examine this further one to see whether we think it still stands or not: the
most important thing isn't living, but living well.

CRITO: Yes, it still stands.

SOCRATES: And the argument that living well, living a fine life, and living
justly are the same—does it still stand or not?

CRITO: It still stands.

SOCRATES: Then in the light of these agreements, we should examine
whether or not it would be just for me to try to get out of here when the

Athenians haven't acquitted me. And if it does seem just, we should make 48c
the attempt, and if it doesn't, we should abandon the effort.

As for those other considerations you raise about loss of money and
people's opinions and bringing up children—they, in truth, Crito, are
appropriate considerations for people who readily put one to death and
would as readily bring one back to life again if they could, without thinking; I mean, the majority of people. For us, however, the argument has
made the decision. There's nothing else to be examined besides the very
thing we just mentioned: whether we—both the ones who are rescued and
also the rescuers themselves—will be acting justly if we pay money to those
who would get me out of here and do them favors, or whether we will in 48d
truth be acting unjustly if we do those things. And if it appears that we
will be acting unjustly in doing them, we have no need at all to give any
opposing weight to our having to die—or suffer in some other way—if we
stay here and mind our behavior when the alternative is doing injustice.

CRITO: What you *say* seems true to me, Socrates. But I wish you'd consider
what we're to *do*.

SOCRATES: Let's examine that question together, my dear friend, and if you
can oppose anything I say, oppose it, and I'll be persuaded by you. But if 48e
you can't, be a good fellow and stop telling me the same thing over and
over, that I should leave here against the will of the Athenians. You see,
I think it very important that I act in this matter having persuaded you,
rather than against your will. Consider, then, the starting point of our
inquiry, to see if you find it adequately formulated, and try to answer my
questions as you really think best. 49a

CRITO: I'll certainly try.

SOCRATES: Do we say that one should never do injustice intentionally? Or
may injustice be done in some circumstances but not in others? Is doing
injustice never good or fine, as we have often agreed in the past? Or have
all these former agreements been discarded during these last few days? Can
you and I at our age, Crito, have spent so long in serious discussion with
one another without realizing that we ourselves were no better than a pair
of children? Or is what we used to say true above all else: that whether the 49b
majority of people agree or not, and whether we must suffer still worse
things than at present or ones that are easier to bear, it's true, all the same,
that doing injustice in any circumstances is bad and shameful for the one
who does it? Is that what we say or not?

CRITO: It is what we say.

SOCRATES: So one should never do injustice.

CRITO: Certainly not.

SOCRATES: So one shouldn't do injustice in return for injustice, as the
majority of people think—seeing that one should *never* do injustice.

49c CRITO: Apparently not.

SOCRATES: Well then, should one do wrong or not?

CRITO: Certainly not, Socrates.

SOCRATES: Well, what about when someone does wrong in return for having suffered wrongdoing? Is that just, as the majority of people think, or not just?

CRITO: It's not just at all.

SOCRATES: No, for there's no difference, I take it, between doing wrong and doing injustice?

CRITO: That's right.

SOCRATES: So one must neither do injustice in return nor wrong any man, no matter what one has suffered at his hands. And, Crito, in agreeing to
49d this, watch out that you're not agreeing to anything contrary to what you believe. You see, I know that only a few people do believe or will believe it. And between those who believe it and those who don't, there's no common basis for deliberation, but each necessarily regards the other with contempt when they see their deliberations. You too, then, should consider very carefully whether you share that belief with me and whether the following is the starting point of our deliberations: that it's never right to do injustice, or to do injustice in return, or to retaliate with bad treatment when one has been treated badly. Or do you disagree and not share this starting point?
49e You see, I've believed this for a long time myself and still believe it now. But if you've come to some other opinion, say so. Instruct me. If you stand by the former one, however, then listen to my next point.

CRITO: Yes, I do stand by it and share it with you, so go on.

SOCRATES: Then I'll state the next point—or rather, ask a question: should one do the things one has agreed with someone to do, provided they are just, or should one cheat?

CRITO: One should do them.

SOCRATES: Then consider what follows. If we leave this place without
50a having persuaded the city, are we treating some people badly—and those whom we should least of all treat in that way—or not? Are we standing by agreements that are just or not?

CRITO: I can't answer your question, Socrates, since I don't understand it.

SOCRATES: Well, look at it this way. Suppose we were about to run away from here—or whatever what we'd be doing should be called. And suppose the Laws and the city community came and confronted us, and said,
50b "Tell us, Socrates, what do you intend to do? Do you intend anything else by this act you're attempting than to destroy us Laws, and the city as a whole, to the extent that you can? Or do you think that a city can continue to exist and not be overthrown if the legal judgments rendered in it have

no force, but are deprived of authority and undermined by the actions of private individuals?"

What shall we say in response to that question, Crito, and to others like it? For there's a lot that one might say—particularly, if one were an orator—on behalf of this law we're destroying, the one requiring that legal judgments, once rendered, have authority. Or shall we say to them, "Yes, that's what we intend, for the city treated us unjustly and didn't judge our lawsuit correctly." Is that what we're to say—or what? 50c

CRITO: Yes, by Zeus, that's what we're to say, Socrates.

SOCRATES: Then what if the Laws replied, "Was that also part of the agreement between you and us, Socrates? Or did you agree to stand by whatever judgments the city rendered?" Then, if we were surprised at the words, perhaps they might say, "Don't be surprised at what we're saying, Socrates, but answer us—since you're so accustomed to using question and answer. Come now, what charge have you to bring against the city and ourselves 50d that you should try to destroy us? In the first place, wasn't it we who gave you birth—wasn't it through us that your father married your mother and produced you? Tell us, do you have some complaint about the correctness of those of us Laws concerned with marriage?"

"No, I have no complaint," I'd reply.

"Well then, what about the Laws dealing with the bringing up and educating of children, under which you were educated yourself? Didn't those of us Laws who regulate that area prescribe correctly when we ordered your father to educate you in the arts and physical training?"

"They prescribed correctly," I'd reply. 50e

"Good. Then since you were born, brought up, and educated, can you deny, first, that you're our offspring and slave, both yourself and your ancestors? And if that's so, do you think that what's just is based on an equality between you and us, that whatever we try to do to you it's just for you to do to us in return? As regards you and your father (or you and your master, if you happened to have one), what's just isn't based on equality, and so you don't return whatever treatment you receive—answering back when you're criticized or striking back when you're struck, or doing many 51a other such things. As regards you and your fatherland and its Laws, then, are these things permitted? If we try to destroy you, believing it to be just, will you try to destroy us Laws and your fatherland, to the extent that you can? And will you claim that you're acting justly in doing so—you the man who really cares about virtue? Or are you so wise that it has escaped your notice that your fatherland is more worthy of honor than your mother and father and all your other ancestors; that it is more to be revered and more sacred and is held in greater esteem both among the gods and among those human beings who have any sense; that you must treat your fatherland 51b

with piety, submitting to it and placating it more than you would your own
father when it is angry; that you must either persuade it or else do whatever
it commands; that you must mind your behavior and undergo whatever
treatment it prescribes for you, whether a beating or imprisonment; that
if it leads you to war to be wounded or killed, that's what you must do,
and that's what is just—not to give way or retreat or leave where you were
stationed, but, on the contrary, in war and law courts, and everywhere else,
to do whatever your city or fatherland commands or else persuade it as to
51c   what is really just; and that while it is impious to violate the will of your
mother or father, it is yet less so than to violate that of your fatherland."

   What are we to say to that, Crito? Are the Laws telling the truth or not?

CRITO: Yes, I think they are.

SOCRATES: "Consider, then, Socrates," the Laws might perhaps continue,
"whether we're also telling the truth in saying this: that you aren't treating us justly in what you're now trying to do. You see, we gave you birth,
upbringing, and education, and have provided you, as well as every other
51d   citizen, with a share of all the fine things we could. Nonetheless, if any
Athenian—who has been admitted to adult status and has observed both
how affairs are handled in the city and ourselves, the Laws—is dissatisfied
with us and wishes to leave, we grant him permission to take his property
and go wherever he pleases. Not one of us Laws stands in his way or forbids
it. If any one of you is dissatisfied with us and the city and wishes to go to
a colony or to live as an alien elsewhere, he may go wherever he wishes
and hold on to what's his.

51e   "*But* if any of you stays here, after he has observed the way we judge
lawsuits and the other ways in which we manage the city, then we say
that he has agreed with us by his action to do whatever we command.
And we say that whoever does not obey commits a threefold injustice: he
disobeys us as his parents; he disobeys us as those who brought him up;
and, after having agreed to obey us, he neither obeys nor persuades us, if
we're doing something that isn't right. Yet we offer him a choice and do
52a   not harshly command him to do what he's told. On the contrary, we offer
two alternatives: he must either persuade us or do what we say. And he
does neither. These, then, are the charges, Socrates, to which we say you
too will become liable, if you do what you have in mind—and you won't
be among the least liable of the Athenians, but among the most."

   Then, if I were to say, "Why is that?" perhaps they might justifiably
reproach me by saying that I am among the Athenians who have made that
agreement with them in the strongest terms.

52b   "Socrates," they would say, "we have the strongest evidence that you
were satisfied with us and with the city. After all, you'd never have stayed
at home here so much more consistently than all the rest of the Athenians

if you weren't also much more consistently satisfied. You never left the city for a festival, except once to go to the Isthmus.[6] You never went anywhere else, except for military service. You never went abroad as other people do. You had no desire to acquaint yourself with other cities or other laws. On the contrary, we and our city sufficed for you. So emphatically did you   52c
choose us and agree to live as a citizen under us, that you even produced children here. *That's* how satisfied you were with the city.

"Moreover, even at your very trial, you could have proposed exile as a counterpenalty if you'd wished, and what you're now trying to do against the city's will, you could then have done with its consent. On that occasion, you prided yourself on not feeling resentful that you had to die. You'd choose death before exile—so you said. Now, however, you feel no shame at those words and show no regard for us Laws as you try to destroy us. You're acting exactly the way the most wretched slave would act by trying   52d
to run away, contrary to your commitments and your agreements to live as a citizen under us.

"First, then, answer us on this very point: are we telling the truth when we say that you agreed, by deeds not words, to live as a citizen under us? Or is that untrue?"

What are we to reply to that, Crito? Mustn't we agree?

CRITO: We must, Socrates.

SOCRATES: "Well then," they might say, "surely you're breaking the commitments and agreements you made with us. You weren't coerced or tricked   52e
into agreeing or forced to decide in a hurry. On the contrary, you had seventy years in which you could have left if you weren't satisfied with us or if you thought those agreements unjust. You, however, preferred neither Sparta nor Crete—places you often say have good law and order—nor any   53a
other Greek or foreign city. On the contrary, you went abroad less often than the lame, the blind, or other handicapped people. Hence it's clear that you, more than any other Athenian, have been consistently satisfied with your city and with us Laws—for who would be satisfied by a city but not by its laws? Won't you, then, stand by your agreements now? Yes, you will, if you're persuaded by us, Socrates, and at least you won't make yourself a laughingstock by leaving the city.

"For consider now: if you break those agreements, if you commit any of these wrongs, what good will you do yourself or your friends? You see,   53b
it's pretty clear that your friends will risk being exiled themselves as well as being disenfranchised and having their property confiscated. As for you, if you go to one of the nearest cities, Thebes or Megara—for they

---

[6] The Isthmus is the narrow strip of land connecting the Peloponnese to the rest of Greece, where the Isthmian Games were held.

both have good laws—you will be arriving there, Socrates, as an enemy of their political systems, and those who care about their own cities will look on you with suspicion, regarding you as one who undermines laws. You will also confirm your jurors in their opinion, so that they will think they

53c judged your lawsuit correctly. For anyone who undermines laws might very well be considered a corruptor of young and ignorant people.

"Will you, then, avoid cities with good law and order, and men of the most respectable kind? And if so, will your life be worth living? Or will you associate with these people and be shameless enough to converse with them? And what will you say, Socrates? The very things that you said here, about how virtue and justice are man's most valuable possessions, along with law and lawful conduct. Don't you think Socrates and everything

53d about him will look unseemly? Surely, you must.

"Or will you keep away from those places and go to Crito's friends in Thessaly? After all, there's complete disorder and laxity there, so perhaps they'd enjoy hearing about your absurd escape from prison when you dressed up in disguise, wore a peasant's leather jerkin or some other such escapee's outfit, and altered your appearance. And will no one remark on the fact that you, an old man, with probably only a short time left to live,

53e were so greedy for life that you dared to violate the most important laws? Perhaps not, provided you don't annoy anyone. Otherwise, you'll hear many disparaging things said about you. Will you live by currying favor with every man and acting the slave—and do nothing in Thessaly besides eat, as if you'd gone to live in Thessaly for a good dinner? As for those

54a arguments about justice and the rest of virtue, where, tell us, will they be?

"Is it that you want to live for your children's sake, then, to bring them up and educate them? Really? Will you bring them up and educate them by taking them to Thessaly and making foreigners of them, so they can enjoy that privilege too? If not, will they be better brought up and educated here without you, provided that you're still alive? 'Of course,' you may say, because your friends will take care of them. Then will they take care of them if you go to Thessaly, but not take care of them if you go to Hades? If those who call themselves your friends are worth anything at all, you

54b surely can't believe that.

"No, Socrates, be persuaded by us who reared you. Don't put a higher value on children, on life, or on anything else than on what's just, so that when you reach Hades you may have all this to offer as your defense before the authorities there. For if you do do that, it doesn't seem that it will be better for you *here,* or for any of your friends, or that it will be more just or more pious. And it won't be better for you when you arrive *there* either. As it is, you'll leave here—if you do leave—as one who has been treated

54c unjustly not by us Laws, but by men. But suppose you leave, suppose you return injustice for injustice and bad treatment for bad treatment in that shameful way, breaking your agreements and commitments with us and doing bad things to those whom you should least of all treat in that way—yourself, your friends, your fatherland, and ourselves. Then we'll be angry with you while you're still alive, and our brothers, the Laws of Hades, won't receive you kindly there, knowing that you tried to destroy us to the extent you could. Come, then, don't let Crito persuade you to follow his advice rather than ours." 54d

That, Crito, my dear friend, is what I seem to hear them saying, you may be sure. And, just like those Corybantes who think they are still hearing the flutes, the echo of their arguments reverberates in me and makes me incapable of hearing anything else. No, as far as my present thoughts go, at least, you may be sure that if you argue against them, you will speak in vain. All the same, if you think you can do any more, please tell me.

CRITO: No, Socrates, I've nothing to say.

SOCRATES: Then, let it be, Crito, and let's act in that way, since that's the 54e
way the god is leading us.

MENO

70a   MENO:[1] Can you tell me, Socrates, is virtue something acquired by teaching? Or is it something acquired not by teaching, but by practice? Or is it something acquired neither by practice nor by learning, but something human beings possess by nature or in some other way?

    SOCRATES: In the past, Meno, the inhabitants of Thessaly were well-reputed among the Greeks—admired for their horsemanship and their wealth. But
70b now for their wisdom too, it seems to me—especially the Larissans, your friend Aristippus' fellow citizens.[2] You have Gorgias to thank for that.[3] When he arrived in Larissa, he acquired as lovers for his wisdom the leading Aleuadae—among them your own lover Aristippus—and the other leading Thessalians as well. And he got you into this habit of answering fearlessly and high-mindedly when anyone asks you anything—as is reasonable enough if you have the knowledge. After all, he too makes himself
70c available to any Greek to ask him any question they want, and none of them fail to get an answer. But here in Athens, my friend, we are in the opposite situation. There has been a drought of wisdom, so to speak, and there is a good chance that wisdom has left these parts to go live with
71a you. At any rate, if you wanted to question anyone who lives here in that way, there is no one who wouldn't laugh and say: "Stranger, apparently you think I am somehow divinely blessed, that I know whether virtue is something acquired by teaching or whatever the way is that human beings get it. I am so far from knowing whether it is something acquired by teaching, or not by teaching, that in fact I do not know at all what in the world virtue itself is."

71b   Well, I am also that way myself, Meno. I share the poverty of my fellow citizens in this matter. I reproach myself for not knowing anything whatever about virtue. But if I do not know what it is, how could I know what *sort* of thing it is? Or do you think it is possible for someone, who

---

The text of *Meno,* translated by C. D. C. Reeve, was first published in *Introductory Readings in Ancient Greek and Roman Philosophy,* edited by C. D. C. Reeve and Patrick Lee Miller. Copyright © 2006, Hackett Publishing Co.

[1] A young aristocrat from Pharsalus in Thessaly.

[2] Aristippus was a member of the Aleuadae, the ruling family of Larissa, the major city of Thessaly in northern Greece, not to be confused with the philosopher of the same name.

[3] See *Apology* 19e and note.

does not know at all who Meno is, to know whether Meno is beautiful or rich or in fact of noble birth, or the opposites of these? Do you think that is possible?

MENO: No, I do not. But, Socrates, do you really not know what virtue is? Are we to report *this* about you to the folks back home? 71c

SOCRATES: Not only that, my friend, but also that I have never met anyone else I thought did know.

MENO: What? Didn't you meet Gorgias[4] when he was here?

SOCRATES: I did.

MENO: And you didn't think he knew?

SOCRATES: I haven't a very good memory, Meno, so I cannot tell you at present what I thought of him then. Maybe he does know. Presumably, you know what he said. So remind me what it was. Or if you prefer, speak for yourself. I imagine you think the same as he. 71d

MENO: I do.

SOCRATES: Well in that case, let's leave him out of it, since in fact he is not here. But as for yourself, by the gods, Meno, what do you say virtue is? Tell me, don't be begrudging. The result may be that I spoke a very lucky falsehood when I said that I had never yet met anyone who knew this, if it comes to light that you and Gorgias do know it.

MENO: I will tell you, Socrates; it is not difficult. First, then, if you want 71e to know a man's virtue, that is easy. This is a man's virtue: to take part in the city's affairs capably, and by doing so to benefit his friends and harm his enemies, while taking care that he himself does not suffer anything like that. If you want a woman's virtue, that is not difficult to describe. She must manage the household well, look after its contents, and be obedient to the man. There is a different virtue for a child, one for a male and one for a female, and for an older man, one for a free man, if you want to know that, and one for a slave, if you want to know that. There are very many 72a other virtues, too, so there is no puzzle about telling you what virtue is. You see, for each of the affairs and stages of life, and in relation to each particular function, there is a virtue for each of us—and it is the same way, I think, Socrates, for vice.

SOCRATES: I seem to be enjoying a great stroke of good luck indeed, Meno, if, while inquiring about one virtue, I have turned up something like a swarm of virtues in your possession. But, Meno, keeping to this image of swarms, suppose I asked you about being a bee, what a bee is, and you said 72b that bees are many and multifarious. What would you reply if I asked you: "Do you mean they are many and multifarious and different from one

---

[4] Gorgias came to Athens in 427 BCE and perhaps on other occasions as well.

another in this—in each being bees? Or do they not differ at all in that, but in some other way—for example, in beauty or size or some other such way?" Tell me, how would you answer if questioned like that?

MENO: This is what I'd say: they do not differ at all one from another in being bees.

72c   SOCRATES: So if I went on and said: "Then tell me about that thing itself, Meno—that in which they do not differ, but are all the same. What do you say *it* is?" No doubt you would have an answer to give me.

MENO: I would.

SOCRATES: It is the same with the virtues, too. Even if they are many and multifarious, surely they all have one identical form, because of which they are all virtues. And it is right, I would suppose, for the one who is answering to look to *that* in order to make clear what virtue actually is to
72d   the one who asked. Or don't you understand what I mean?

MENO: I think I understand. But I don't yet grasp what you are asking as firmly as I would like.

SOCRATES: Is it only about virtue that you think this way, Meno—that there is one for a man, another for a woman's, and so on for the others? Or do you think the same about health and size and strength? Do you think health is one for a man, another for a woman? Or is there the same form everywhere, if it really is health, whether for a man or for anything else
72e   whatever?

MENO: I think health, at any rate, is the same, both for a man and for a woman.

SOCRATES: What about size and strength, then? If in fact a woman is strong, will she be strong by virtue of the same form, by the same strength? By "the same strength" I mean this: strength does not differ at all as regards being strength, whether it is in a man or in a woman. Or do you think there is some difference?

MENO: No, I don't.

73a   SOCRATES: Then will virtue differ, as regards being virtue, whether it is in a child or in an old man, in a woman or in a man?

MENO: Well, I somehow think, Socrates, that this is no longer like those other cases.

SOCRATES: What? Weren't you saying that a man's virtue is to manage a city well, and a woman's a household?

MENO: Yes, I was.

SOCRATES: Well then, is it possible to manage a city well or a household or anything else whatever, while not managing it temperately and justly?

MENO: Certainly not.

SOCRATES: And if they really manage it justly and temperately, isn't it by   73b
means of justice and temperance that they will manage it?

MENO: Necessarily.

SOCRATES: So both men and women will need the same things, if they are
really going to be good—justice and temperance.

MENO: Apparently.

SOCRATES: What about a child and an old man? If they were intemperate
and unjust, could they possibly be good?

MENO: Certainly not.

SOCRATES: But if they were temperate and just?

MENO: Yes.

SOCRATES: So all human beings are good in the same way, since they are   73c
good if they possess the same things.

MENO: So it seems.

SOCRATES: But surely if their virtue were not the same, they would not be
good in the same way.

MENO: Certainly not.

SOCRATES: So, since the virtue of them all is the same, try to tell me, try
to recollect, what Gorgias says it is—and you say with him.

MENO: Well, what else than to be able to rule people? If you are really
inquiring about one thing that covers all of them.   73d

SOCRATES: Yes indeed, I am inquiring about that. But is that same virtue
the virtue of a child, Meno, and of a slave—to be able to rule over their
master? Do you think that the one who rules would still be a slave?

MENO: No, I don't think so at all, Socrates.

SOCRATES: No, that wouldn't be reasonable, my very good man. And consider this further point too. Virtue, you say, is "ability to rule." Are we not
to add "justly," not "unjustly"?

MENO: Yes, I think that's right. For justice, Socrates, is virtue.

SOCRATES: Virtue, Meno? Or *a* virtue?   73e

MENO: What do you mean by that?

SOCRATES: The same as with anything else. For example, roundness, if you
like. I would say about roundness that it is *a* shape, not that it is just simply
shape. My reason for speaking like that is that there are other shapes.

MENO: Yes, and you would be speaking rightly, since I also say that it is not
only justice that is virtue, but that there are other virtues too.

SOCRATES: Which ones are? Tell me. I could mention other shapes to   74a
you, if you asked me to. So you do likewise. Mention some other virtues
to me.

MENO: Well, I think courage is a virtue, and temperance and wisdom and high-mindedness, and very many others.

SOCRATES: As before, Meno, the same thing has happened to us. Again, we have found many virtues when we were inquiring about one, though in a different way than in the previous case. But the one that extends through all of them we cannot find.

MENO: No, for I cannot yet grasp, Socrates, what you are inquiring about—
74b one virtue that covers all of them, as in the other cases.

SOCRATES: That isn't surprising. But I am eager, if I can, to move us closer to it. For you understand, surely, that this is just how it is in all of them: if someone were to ask you, as I asked previously, "What is shape, Meno?" and you said that it was roundness, and he then asked, as I did, "Is roundness shape or *a* shape?" you would no doubt reply that it is *a* shape.

MENO: Of course.

74c SOCRATES: The reason being that there are other shapes too?

MENO: Yes.

SOCRATES: And if he went on to ask you what sorts of shapes, you would tell him?

MENO: I would.

SOCRATES: Again, if he asked you in the same way what color is, and you said "white," and he went on to ask, "Is white color or *a* color?" you would say that it is *a* color, because there are other colors too?

MENO: I would.

SOCRATES: And if he asked you to mention some other colors, you would
74d mention others that are no less colors than white is?

MENO: Yes.

SOCRATES: Then, if he pursued the argument as I did, and said, "We keep arriving at many things. Please don't answer me like that. You call these many things by a single name, and say that none of them is not a shape. And you say that even though they are opposites of one another. So tell me just what is this thing that encompasses the round no less than the straight, the
74e one you call shape, so that you say that the round is no more shape than is the straight?" Or don't you say that?

MENO: I do.

SOCRATES: Well then, when you speak like that, do you mean that the round is no more round than straight, or that the straight is no more straight than round?

MENO: Of course not, Socrates.

SOCRATES: Instead, you mean that the round is no more shape than is the straight, or the straight than the round?

MENO: True.

SOCRATES: Well then, what is this thing of which this is the name— "shape"? Try to say. If you said to the questioner who asked you in this way about shape or color, "I don't understand what you want, my man, nor even what you mean," he would probably be amazed and say, "You don't understand that I am inquiring about what in all these cases is the same?" Even in this case, Meno, would you be unable to answer, if someone were to ask you, "What is it that is the same in all these cases—in the case of the round and the straight and the rest—the thing that you call shape?" Try to say. By doing so you will also get practice for your answer about virtue.   **75a**

MENO: No, please, Socrates, you answer.   **75b**

SOCRATES: You want me to indulge you?

MENO: Yes, indeed.

SOCRATES: And then you will be willing to tell me about virtue?

MENO: I will.

SOCRATES: I must give it a try, since it is worth it.

MENO: It certainly is.

SOCRATES: Come on then, let's try to tell you what shape is. See whether you accept that it is this: shape for us is that thing which, alone among the things that are, always goes along with color. Is that answer enough for you, or are you inquiring after some other sort? You see, I would certainly be satisfied if you told me about virtue in just that way.   **75c**

MENO: But that's silly, Socrates.

SOCRATES: How do you mean?

MENO: I mean that shape, if I am not mistaken, is according to your account what always goes along with color. All right. So if someone were to say that he didn't know color, but had the same puzzle about it as with shape, what sort of answer do you think you would have given him?

SOCRATES: I think a true one. And if my questioner were one of those eristical[5] and contentious wise fellows, I would say to him, "I have given my answer. If what I say isn't correct, your function is to demand an account and then refute it." But if people want to engage in discussion with one another as friends, the way you and I are doing now, they must answer more gently, as it were, and in a more dialectical manner.[6] And it is perhaps more dialectical not to answer with the truth alone, but also to do so in terms which the answerer agrees he knows. I too, then, will try   **75d**

---

[5] Someone who aims at scoring points rather than at discovering the truth. See *Republic* 537e–539c.

[6] See *Republic* 454a.

to answer you in that way. So tell me, is there something you call an end?
75e   I mean something like a limit or a boundary—I mean the same thing by
all of them. Perhaps, Prodicus[7] would disagree with us, but *you* surely say
there is such a thing as having limits or ends. That is the sort of thing I
mean—nothing complex.

MENO: Yes I do. I think I understand what you mean, too.

SOCRATES: Well then, is there something you call a surface, and something
76a   else again you call a solid—for example, the ones in geometry?

MENO: Yes, there is.

SOCRATES: Then you can already understand from these what I say shape
is. You see, in the case of every shape, I say that what a solid meets its limit
in is shape.

MENO: And what do you say color is, Socrates?

SOCRATES: You are outrageous, Meno! You cause an old man trouble,
76b   commanding him to answer, while you yourself aren't willing to recollect
and tell us what Gorgias says virtue is.

MENO: You tell me this, Socrates, and I will tell you that.

SOCRATES: A man would know blindfold, Meno, just from the way you
engage in discussion, that you are beautiful and still have lovers![8]

MENO: How so?

SOCRATES: Because you do nothing except give commands when you
speak, the way spoiled boys do, who act like tyrants while their bloom
76c   lasts. At the same time, too, you have probably noticed my weakness for
beautiful boys. So I will indulge you and answer.

MENO: By all means, indulge me!

SOCRATES: Would you like me to give an answer Gorgias-fashion, the way
it would be easiest for you to follow?

MENO: Yes, of course I would.

SOCRATES: Well then, don't you both talk about certain effluences from
things, the way Empedocles[9] does?

MENO: Certainly.

SOCRATES: And pores into which and through which the effluences travel?

MENO: Indeed.

---

[7] See *Apology* 19e and note.

[8] Boys had older male lovers from the arrival of puberty (probably quite late in the ancient world) until their beard became full.

[9] Empedocles of Acragas in Sicily (c. 492–432 BCE), one of the so-called Presocratic philosophers.

SOCRATES: And some of the effluences fit certain pores, whereas others are too small or too large? 76d

MENO: That's right.

SOCRATES: And is there something you call sight?

MENO: There is.

SOCRATES: Well, from this, then, "grasp what I mean," as Pindar says.[10] Color is an effluence from shapes that is commensurate with sight, and so perceptible.

MENO: I think that is an excellent answer, Socrates.

SOCRATES: Probably because it is put in a way you are accustomed to. At the same time, I suppose, you realize that you could use the same things to say what sound is, and smell, and many other things of that sort. 76e

MENO: Of course.

SOCRATES: It is a "deep" answer indeed, Meno, so it pleases you more than the one about shape.

MENO: Yes, it does.

SOCRATES: Yet, I am convinced it is not a better one, son of Alexidemus. On the contrary, the other is better. And I don't think you would disagree, if you did not have to leave, as you mentioned yesterday, before the celebration of the Mysteries, but could stay and be initiated.[11]

MENO: But I would stay, Socrates, if you could tell me many things like that. 77a

SOCRATES: Then I certainly won't be any less than eager to tell you them—both for your sake and for my own. But I fear I won't be able to give you many answers of that sort. Come on, though, you also keep your promise to me, and try to say what virtue as a whole is. Stop making many out of one, as the jokers say each time someone breaks something, but leave virtue whole and sound and say what it is. You got models, at least, from me. 77b

MENO: In that case, Socrates, I think virtue, as the poets say, is "enjoying beautiful things and having power."[12] And so I say this is what virtue is, to desire beautiful things and have the power to get them.

---

[10] Pindar (518–438 BCE), a lyric poet from Boeotia, was most famous for his poems celebrating the victors in the Olympian, Pythian, and other games.

[11] Eleusis—one of the major demes in Athens (see *Euthyphro* 2b note)—was the center of a cult that played a prominent role in Athenian civic religion. Some of its rituals were secret mysteries, known only to initiates. Initiation began in February, so the dramatic date of the conversation is presumably just before that. Plato uses initiation into the Eleusinian Mysteries as a metaphor for initiation into philosophy at *Symposium* 209e–210a.

[12] Source unknown.

SOCRATES: Do you mean that the one who desires beautiful things desires good ones?

MENO: Yes, of course.

SOCRATES: On the assumption that there are some people who desire bad
77c things, and others good ones? Don't you think, my very good man, that everyone desires good things?

MENO: No, I don't.

SOCRATES: But some desire bad ones?

MENO: Yes.

SOCRATES: Thinking the bad ones are good, do you mean? Or actually recognizing they are bad and desiring them all the same?

MENO: Both, I think.

SOCRATES: Really? You think someone recognizes that the bad things are bad but desires them all the same?

MENO: Of course.

SOCRATES: What do you mean by that he desires? That he possesses them for himself?

MENO: That he possesses them for himself. What else?

77d SOCRATES: Thinking that the bad things benefit the one who gets them? Or knowing that the bad things harm the one who possesses them?

MENO: Some thinking that the bad things benefit; others recognizing that they harm.

SOCRATES: Do you also think that those who think that the bad things benefit recognize that the bad things are bad?

MENO: Not at all, I certainly do not think that.

SOCRATES: Then it is clear that *they*—the ones who do not know about
77e them—don't desire bad things; rather, they desire things that they think are good, though in fact they are bad. Hence, those who don't know about these things and think that they are good clearly do desire good things. Don't they?

MENO: It looks as though they do, anyway.

SOCRATES: What about those who desire bad things, thinking, so you claim, that bad things harm the one who gets them? They recognize, surely, that they will be harmed by them?

MENO: They must.

78a SOCRATES: But don't they think that those who are harmed are—to the extent that they are harmed—wretched?

MENO: They must be aware of that too.

SOCRATES: And that the wretched are unhappy?

MENO: Yes, I think so.

SOCRATES: Is there anyone who wants to be wretched and unhappy?

MENO: I don't think so, Socrates.

SOCRATES: Then no one wants bad things, Meno, if indeed he does not want to be like that. For what is being wretched other than wanting bad things and getting them?

MENO: It looks as though you are right, Socrates—no one wants bad things.   78b

SOCRATES: Well, weren't you saying just now that virtue is wanting good things and having power?

MENO: Yes, I did say that.

SOCRATES: Well, the wanting part of this statement holds of everyone, and so in this respect at least no one is better than anyone else.

MENO: Apparently.

SOCRATES: But it is clear then that if indeed someone is better than someone else, it must be as regards power that he is better.

MENO: Certainly.

SOCRATES: So this, it seems, is virtue according to your account: the power to get good things.

MENO: I think, Socrates, that the way you are interpreting me now is   78c
entirely correct.

SOCRATES: Let's also see, then, whether you are speaking the truth, since you may prove to have spoken correctly. You say that the power to get good things is virtue?

MENO: I do.

SOCRATES: And the things you call good are things like wealth and health aren't they?

MENO: Yes, I think getting gold and silver is good and also honors and public offices in the city.

SOCRATES: But you don't think anything else is good besides things of that sort?

MENO: No, just all things of that sort.

SOCRATES: All right. Getting gold and silver is virtue. So says Meno, family   78d
friend of the Great King![13] Do you add "justly and piously" to this "getting," Meno? Or does that make no difference? Even if someone gets these things *unjustly,* do you call it virtue all the same?

MENO: Certainly not, Socrates.

---

[13] Xerxes I, king of Persia (486–465 BCE), led the unsuccessful invasion of Greece in the Persian Wars. He was regarded as the richest and most powerful ruler imaginable. Meno may have had some hereditary connection with the Persian royal house.

SOCRATES: But vice?

MENO: Certainly.

SOCRATES: So it seems that justice, temperance, piety, or some other part
of virtue must be added to this getting. If not, it will not be virtue, even
though it is a getting of good things.

MENO: No, for how could it be virtue without them?

SOCRATES: And *not* getting gold and silver, either for oneself or for someone
else, when it is not just to do so, isn't this also virtue, this not-getting?

MENO: Apparently.

SOCRATES: So getting good things won't be any more virtue than not getting them. Instead, what is done with justice is virtue, while what is done
without anything like it, is vice.

MENO: I think it must be as you claim.

SOCRATES: Now, didn't we say a moment ago that each of these is a part of
virtue—justice, temperance, and everything of that sort?

MENO: Yes.

SOCRATES: Really, Meno? Are you teasing me?

MENO: Why, Socrates?

SOCRATES: Because I begged you just now not to break virtue into pieces
or exchange it for smaller coins. I even gave you models of how you should
answer. But you pay no attention to that, and tell me that virtue is getting
good things with justice. And justice, you say, is part of virtue.

MENO: I do.

SOCRATES: It follows, then, from what you agree to, that doing whatever
one does with a part of virtue is virtue. For you say that justice is a part of
virtue, as well as each of the others.

MENO: So?

SOCRATES: What I mean is this. I begged you to say what virtue as a whole
is. But you, far from saying what it is, claim that every action is virtue if it
is done with a part of virtue—just as if you had said what virtue as a whole
is and I already know it, and would continue to do so even if you broke
it up into pieces. So it seems to me that you need to start again with the
same question, my friend. What is virtue, if every action done with a part
of virtue is virtue? For that is what someone is saying when he says that
every action done with justice is virtue. Don't you think you need to go
back to the same question? Or do you think someone knows what a part
of virtue is, when he does not know what virtue itself is?

MENO: No, I don't think that.

SOCRATES: No. Also if you remember when I was answering you just now
about shape, I think we rejected that sort of answer—one that tries to

answer in terms of things that are still being inquired about and have not yet been agreed to.

MENO: Yes, and we were right to reject it, Socrates.

SOCRATES: Then, my good Meno, when virtue as a whole is still being inquired about, you shouldn't suppose you will make it clear to anyone by couching your answer in terms of its parts, or that you will make anything else clear by speaking the same way. Rather, you should accept that the same question needs to be asked again. What is this virtue about which you 79e say the things you say? Or do you think I am talking nonsense?

MENO: No, I think what you say is right.

SOCRATES: Then answer again from the beginning. What do both you and that friend of yours say virtue is?

MENO: Socrates, I heard before I ever met you that you are never anything but puzzled yourself and that you make others puzzled too. And now, I 80a see for myself that you are using sorcery on me, drugging me, and simply subduing me with spells, so that I am full of puzzles. Indeed, you seem to me—if I may make a little joke—to be altogether very similar, both in appearance and other respects, to the flat, saltwater stingray, since it too always numbs whoever comes near and touches it. And you, I think, have now done something like that to me. You see, my soul and my mouth feel truly numb, and so I do not have an answer for you. Yet on countless occa- 80b sions, I have talked at length about virtue, in front of lots of people—very well, too, or so *I* thought. But now I cannot say at all what sort of thing it is. And so I think your decision not to travel away from here or live abroad was a good one. For if you did things like this as a foreigner in another city, you might well be arrested as a sorcerer.

SOCRATES: You are a tricky customer, Meno! You almost had me fooled!

MENO: How exactly, Socrates?

SOCRATES: I know why you produced that image of me. 80c

MENO: Why?

SOCRATES: To get a counterimage of yourself in return! I know that all beautiful boys enjoy a game of image-making. After all, it profits them. For the images of beautiful boys, I suppose, are also beautiful. But I am not going to give a counterimage of you. As for me, if the stingray is numb itself, and only for that reason numbs others too, I am like it—otherwise not. You see, it is not that *I* am puzzle-free but make others puzzled. On the contrary, I am completely puzzled myself, and that is how I make others puzzled too. And now, as far as virtue is concerned, I do not know what it 80d is. Perhaps, you knew before you came into contact with me, but now you are like someone who does not know. All the same, I want to consider the matter with you and join you in inquiring about what it is.

MENO: And how are you going to inquire about it, Socrates, when you do not at all know what it is? For what sort of thing, from among the ones you do not know, will you take as the object of your inquiry? And even if you do happen to bump right into it, how are you going to know that *it* is the thing you did not know?

80e   SOCRATES: I understand what you want to say, Meno. Do you see how eristical the argument is that you are spinning? According to it, so it seems, it is not possible for a person to inquire about what he knows, or about what he does not know. After all, he wouldn't inquire about what he knows— since he knows it, and there is no need to inquire about something like that—or about what he does not know—since he does not know what he is to inquire about.

81a   MENO: Well, don't you think it is a beautiful argument, Socrates?

SOCRATES: No, I do not.

MENO: Can you tell me why?

SOCRATES: Yes, I can. You see, I have heard men and women who are wise in divine matters. . . .

MENO: Saying what?

SOCRATES: Something true, I think, and beautiful.

MENO: What is it? And who are the ones who say it?

SOCRATES: The ones who say it are those priests and priestesses who have made it their concern to be able to give an account of their practices.[14]
81b   Pindar says it, too, as well as many other poets who are godlike men. And what they say is this. See whether you think they are telling the truth. They say the human soul is immortal. At one time it comes to an end—which is what people call dying—and at another is born again. But it is never destroyed. Because of this, they say, one should live one's life as piously as possible. For from whomever

> Persephone accepts requital for her ancient
> grief, in the ninth year, to the sun above
> she returns their souls again,
81c   > and from these, stately kings,
> men swift in strength, in wisdom unsurpassed,
> arise. And for the rest of time, heroes holy
> by men they shall be called.[15]

---

[14] Their identity is unknown.

[15] Probably a quotation from Pindar. Persephone, daughter of Demeter and Zeus, and wife of Hades, was queen of the underworld. Her grief, in this instance, was probably for her son, Dionysus, who was devoured by the Titans. Zeus blasted them

Since the soul is immortal, then, and has been born many times, and has seen both the things here and the ones in Hades—in fact, all things—there is nothing it has not learned. So it is in no way surprising that it can recollect about virtue and other things, since it knew them before. For, since all nature is akin, and the soul has learned all things, nothing prevents 81d someone who is recollecting one thing—which men call learning it—from discovering all the rest for himself, provided he is courageous and doesn't get tired of inquiry. For the whole of inquiry or learning, in that case, is recollection. So one should not be persuaded by that eristical argument, since it would make us idle. It is pleasant for men who are soft to hear. But the present one makes us energetic and eager to inquire. Trusting in its 81e truth, I am willing to inquire with you about what virtue is.

MENO: Yes, Socrates. But what do you mean we do not learn, that what we call learning is in fact recollection? Can you teach me that this is so?

SOCRATES: I said a moment ago, Meno, that you were a tricky customer! And now you ask if I can teach you, when I say there is no teaching but 82a only recollection, so that I shall be immediately revealed to have contradicted myself!

MENO: By Zeus, Socrates, I didn't ask you with that in mind, but from force of habit! But if you can somehow show me that it is as you say, please show me.

SOCRATES: Well, it is not easy. All the same, I am willing to try for your sake. Call over to me one of the many attendants you have here, whichever one you like, so that I can demonstrate it for you in his case. 82b

MENO: Certainly. [*Addressing a slave boy*] Come over here.

SOCRATES: Is he a Greek? Does he speak Greek, at least?

MENO: Yes, indeed. He is homegrown.

SOCRATES: Pay attention, then, and see whether he seems to you to be recollecting or learning from me.

MENO: Yes, I will.

SOCRATES: [*Turning to the boy*] Tell me, boy, do you know that a square figure looks like this? [*He draws the square ABCD in Figure 1.*]

BOY: I do.

SOCRATES: A square figure, then, is one that has all these four lines equal [*points to AB, BC, CD, and DA*].[16] 82c

---

with a thunderbolt, but human beings sprang from their ashes, and so are involved in their guilt and must make atonement to Persephone.

[16] Strictly speaking, a rhombus is not a square, since a square must have four equal angles as well. The equality of the sides is the pertinent feature for the demonstration.

BOY: Certainly.

SOCRATES: And doesn't it also have these across the middle equal [*points to EF, GH*]?

BOY: Yes.

SOCRATES: Now couldn't there be a larger figure of this sort [*points to ABCD*] or a smaller one [*points to AGIE or one of the other inner squares*]?

BOY: Certainly.

SOCRATES: Then, if this side [*AB*] were two feet, and this one [*BC*] were two feet, how many feet would the whole be? Look at it this way. If it were two feet this way [*AB*], but only one this way [*BF*], wouldn't the figure [*ABFE*] be one times two feet?

BOY: Yes.

Figure 1

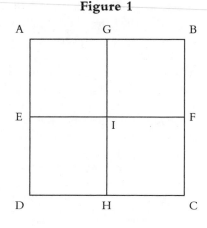

82d SOCRATES: But since it is also two feet in this direction [*BC*], isn't it twice two?

BOY: It is.

SOCRATES: So it is twice two feet?

BOY: Yes.

SOCRATES: How many feet, then, is twice two? Count them and tell me?

BOY: [*Counting the interior squares*] Four, Socrates.

SOCRATES: Now, couldn't there be another figure twice the size of this one [*ABCD*], but similar to it, having all its lines [*AB, BC, CD, DA, GH, EF*] equal just like this one?

BOY: Yes.

SOCRATES: How many feet will it be?

BOY: Eight.

SOCRATES: Come on then, try to tell me how long each side in it will be. In
82e this one [*ABCD*], it is two feet. What is it in the one that is twice the size?

BOY: Clearly then, Socrates, it will be twice the size.

SOCRATES: Do you see, Meno, that I am not teaching him anything, but that all I am doing is asking questions? And at this point he thinks he knows how long a side will result in a figure of eight feet. Do you not agree?

MENO: I do.

SOCRATES: Well, does he know?

MENO: Certainly not.

SOCRATES: But he thinks, at least, that it results from a side twice as long.

MENO: Yes.

SOCRATES: Now watch him recollect in order, which is the way one should recollect. [*Turning back to the boy*] Now you tell me this. You say that a figure twice the size results from a side twice as long? I mean one like this, **83a** not long in this way [*AB*] and short in that [*BF*], but equal in all directions, as this one [*ABCD*] is, but twice its size, or eight feet. See if you still think it will result from a side twice as long.

BOY: Yes, I do.

SOCRATES: Well, isn't this line [*AJ*] twice as long as this [*AB*] if we add a second line of the same length [*BJ*] from here [*B*]? [*He draws the line BJ in Figure 2.*]

BOY: Certainly.

SOCRATES: And it [*AJ*], you say, will result in a figure of eight feet, if there are four like it?

BOY: Yes.

SOCRATES: Then let's draw four equal sides starting from it. [*Socrates draws JK, KL, LD.*] Wouldn't it [*AJKL*] be what you say is eight feet?

Figure 2

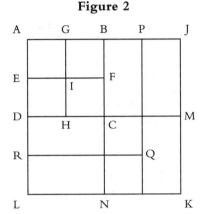

SOCRATES: Then let's draw four equal sides starting from it. [*Socrates draws JK, KL, LD.*] Wouldn't it [*AJKL*] be what you say is eight feet?   **83b**

BOY: Certainly.

SOCRATES: Now, in it there are these four figures [*ABCD, BJMC, CMKN, DCNL*], each of which is equal to this four-foot one [*ABCD*].

BOY: Yes.

SOCRATES: Then, how big is it? Isn't it four times as big?

BOY: Certainly.

SOCRATES: Then is four times the same size as twice?

BOY: No, by Zeus, it isn't!

SOCRATES: Then how many times is it the same as?

BOY: Four times.

SOCRATES: So from a line twice as long, my boy, a figure results that is not twice as big, but four times.   **83c**

BOY: That's true.

SOCRATES: For a figure of four times four feet is sixteen feet. Isn't it?

BOY: Yes.

SOCRATES: So a figure of eight feet results from what line? Didn't this one [*AJ*] result in a figure four times as big?

BOY: It did.

SOCRATES: And this quarter here [*ABCD*] results from this half here [*AB*]?

BOY: Yes.

SOCRATES: All right. But isn't the eight-foot figure double this one [*ABCD*] and half this one [*AJKL*]?

BOY: Yes.

SOCRATES: Will it result from a line longer than this one [*AB*] but shorter than this one here [*AJ*]? Or won't it?

BOY: Yes, I think so.

83d   SOCRATES: Good. You see, what you think is what you should give as your answer. So tell me, isn't this one [*AB*] two feet, and this one [*AJ*] four?

BOY: Yes.

SOCRATES: Then the line from which the eight-foot figure results must be greater than this two-foot one [*AB*], but less than this four-foot one [*AJ*].

BOY: It must.

83e   SOCRATES: Then try to tell me how long you think it is.

BOY: Three feet.

SOCRATES: Well, if indeed it is to be three feet, let's take half of this line [*BJ*] as well [*he marks the point P in Figure 2*] and it [*AP*] will be three feet. For there are two here [*AB*] and one here [*BP*]. And over here [*he marks the point R*], similarly, there are two feet here [*AD*] and one here [*DR*]. And the resulting figure [*he completes the square APQR*] is the one you mention.

BOY: Yes.

SOCRATES: Then if this [*AR*] is three and this [*AP*] is three, isn't the whole figure that results three times three feet?

BOY: Apparently so.

SOCRATES: And three times three is how many feet?

BOY: Nine.

SOCRATES: But the one that was twice the size had to be how many feet?

BOY: Eight.

SOCRATES: So the eight-foot figure does not at all result from the three-foot line either.

BOY: No, indeed.

SOCRATES: But from which one does it result? Try to tell us exactly. If you 84a   don't want to calculate its length, point to which one it results from.

BOY: But, by Zeus, Socrates, I really don't know.

SOCRATES: [*Turning to Meno*] Do you see, Meno, what point he has reached as he proceeds on the path of recollection? At first, he did not know what the side of the eight-foot figure is, just as he does not at all know at this point either. But then he at least thought he knew, answered confidently as if he knew, and didn't think he was puzzled. At this point, however, he now does believe he is puzzled, and as he does not in fact know, he does not think he does either.

84b

MENO: That's true.

SOCRATES: Then isn't he now better off as regards the thing he did not know?

MENO: I agree with that too.

SOCRATES: By making him puzzled, then, and numbing him like a stingray, have we done him any harm?

MENO: No, I don't think so.

SOCRATES: We have certainly done something useful, it seems, as regards finding out how the matter stands. For now he might actually inquire into it with pleasure, since he does not know, whereas before he thought he could easily speak well in front of lots of people and on lots of occasions about the figure that is twice the size, and how it must have a side twice as long.

84c

MENO: So it seems.

SOCRATES: Well, do you think he would have tried to inquire or learn about what he thought he knew, before he fell into puzzlement, came to believe that he did not know, and became anxious to know?

MENO: I don't think so, Socrates.

SOCRATES: So didn't numbing profit him?

MENO: I think so.

SOCRATES: Observe, then, what he will discover starting from this puzzlement, as he inquires with me—but I shall only be asking questions, not teaching. You be on your guard to see whether you discover me teaching or expounding something to him at any point, instead of questioning him about his own beliefs. [*Socrates turns back to the slave boy, erasing everything from Figure 2 except the square ABCD.*] Now you tell me, isn't this our four-foot figure? You understand?

84d

BOY: I do.

SOCRATES: [*Beginning to draw Figure 3*] And we can add this other one here that is equal to it [*draws BJMC*]?

BOY: Yes.

SOCRATES: And this third one that is equal to each of them [*draws MKNC*]?

BOY: Yes.

SOCRATES: Then we could fill in this one in the corner [*draws NLD*]?

BOY: Certainly.

SOCRATES: Then won't these four equal figures result?

BOY: Yes.

84e SOCRATES: Then, this whole resulting one [*AJKL*] is how many times as big as this one [*ABCD*]?

BOY: Four times.

SOCRATES: But we needed one that was twice as big. Don't you remember?

BOY: Certainly.

Figure 3

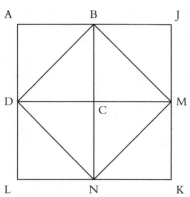

SOCRATES: Now doesn't this line from corner to corner [*he draws BD as an example of the sort of line he means*] cut each of these figures [*the four interior*
85a *squares*] in two?

BOY: Yes.

SOCRATES: Then aren't the four resulting lines [*he draws BM, MN, ND*] equal, the ones enclosing this figure [*BMND*]?

BOY: Yes, they are.

SOCRATES: Now consider. How large is this figure?

BOY: I don't know.

SOCRATES: Has each of these lines cut off the inner half of these four figures? Or not?

BOY: Yes.

SOCRATES: Then how many of this size [*BCD*] are there in this one [*BMND*]?

BOY: Four.

SOCRATES: And how many in this [*ABCD*]?

BOY: Two.

SOCRATES: And what is four to two?

BOY: It is twice it.

SOCRATES: How many feet in this [*BMND*] as a result?

BOY: Eight.

85b SOCRATES: From what line?

BOY: From this one [*BD*].

SOCRATES: From the one that stretches from one corner to the other of the four-foot one?

BOY: Yes.

SOCRATES: Experts call that the diagonal.[17] Hence if "diagonal" is its name, it would be from the diagonal, you say, Meno's slave boy, that the twice-as-big figure results.

BOY: Yes, certainly, Socrates.

SOCRATES: [*Turning to Meno*] What do you think, Meno? Is there any belief he gave as an answer that is not his own?

MENO: No, they are his own. 85c

SOCRATES: And yet he did not know the answer, as we said a short while ago.

MENO: That's right.

SOCRATES: But these beliefs were in him, at least, were they not?

MENO: Yes.

SOCRATES: So the one who does not have knowledge about whatever things he does not know has true beliefs in him about the things he does not know?

MENO: Apparently.

SOCRATES: And now, by contrast, these beliefs have been stirred up in him like a dream. But if someone asks him these same questions many times and in many ways, you know that in the end he will have knowledge of them that is no less exact than anyone else's. 85d

MENO: So it seems.

SOCRATES: Then he will have knowledge without being taught by anyone but only questioned, since *he* will have recovered the knowledge *from inside himself.*

MENO: Yes.

SOCRATES: But recovering knowledge himself from within himself is recollection, is it not?

MENO: Of course.

SOCRATES: So didn't he either get the knowledge he now has at some time or else always have it?

MENO: Yes.

SOCRATES: Well, if he always had it, he would always have known. And if he got it at some time, at least he did not get it in his present life. Or did someone teach him to do geometry? For if so, he will do the same in every part of geometry, and in all other subjects too. Is there anyone, then, who 85e

---

[17] *Diametron:* a word also used for the diameter of a circle, the axis of a sphere, and the hypotenuse of a triangle.

has taught him all that? You certainly ought to know, especially since he was born and brought up in your household.

MENO: No, I know no one has ever taught him.

SOCRATES: But he has these beliefs, does he not?

MENO: Apparently, he must, Socrates.

SOCRATES: Well, if he did not get them in his present life, isn't it clear now

86a that he got or learned them at some other time?

MENO: Apparently.

SOCRATES: At that time, then, when he was not a human being?[18]

MENO: Yes.

SOCRATES: Well, if for whatever time he is a human being, and for whatever time he is not one, there are true beliefs in him, which result in knowledge when awakened by questioning, won't his soul be for all time in a state of learnedness? For it is clear that for all time he either is, or is not, a human being.

MENO: Apparently.

86b SOCRATES: Then if the truth about the things that are is always in our soul, the soul is immortal. So you should confidently try to inquire about and to recollect what you do not happen to know at present—that is, what you do not remember.

MENO: I think you are right, Socrates, but I do not know *how*.

SOCRATES: I think I am too, Meno. And while there are other aspects of the argument on which I would not entirely insist, that we shall be better and more courageous and less idle if we think we should inquire about what we do not know than if we think that it is not possible to find what

86c we do not know and that we shouldn't inquire about it—that is something I would fight for to the death, if I could, both in word and deed.

MENO: Yes, I think you are right about that, at least, Socrates.

SOCRATES: Since we agree, then, that one should inquire about what one does not know, do you want us to try to inquire together about what virtue is?

MENO: I certainly do. Nevertheless, Socrates, what I would most like to consider and hear about is the very thing I asked at the beginning: should

86d we inquire on the assumption that virtue is something present in human beings by teaching, or by nature, or in what way?

SOCRATES: Well, Meno, if I ruled not only myself but you as well, we would not consider whether virtue is acquired by teaching or not before inquiring about what it is. However, since you are not even trying to rule

---

[18] Before his soul was embodied in a human body. See *Republic* 619e–620c.

yourself—in order to remain free, I suppose—but are trying to rule me and succeeding in ruling me, I shall agree. What else am I to do? So it seems we must consider what sort of thing something is when we do not yet know what it is. If you won't do anything else, though, at least relax your rule a little bit for my sake, and agree to investigate *from a hypothesis* whether it is acquired by teaching or whatever. By "from a hypothesis," I mean, the way geometers often conduct their investigations. When someone asks them, for example, whether this figure [*Socrates points to ABCD in Figures 2 and 3*] can be inscribed in this circle [*Figure 4*] as a triangle, one of them might reply, "I don't know yet whether it is the sort that can, but I think I have a hypothesis, so to speak, which is useful in dealing with the question. If this figure [*ABCD*] is such that,

Figure 4

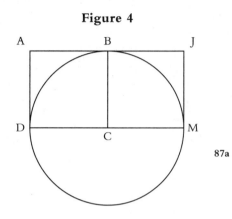

when one applies it to the given line here [*points to AJ*], it falls short by a figure similar to the one applied [*BCMJ*], I think one thing follows, and another if it is impossible for this to happen. By adopting a hypothesis, then, I am willing to tell you whether it is possible or not to inscribe it in the circle."[19] It is the same for us, too, where virtue is concerned. Since we do not know what it is or what sort of thing it is, let's consider by adopting a hypothesis whether it is something acquired by teaching, or not something acquired by teaching. Let's proceed as follows: Among the things belonging to the soul, what sort would virtue have to be if it is to be something not acquired by teaching, or not something acquired by teaching? First, if it is a different sort of thing than knowledge, or the same sort, is it acquired by teaching or not—or as we said just now, acquired by recollection? It makes no difference to us which name is used. Let's say, acquired by teaching. Or isn't this, at least, clear to everyone, that a person is not taught anything except knowledge?

MENO: I think so.

SOCRATES: But *if* virtue is some sort of knowledge, it clearly would be acquired by teaching.

MENO: Of course.

SOCRATES: So we finished with that quickly: if it is the one sort of thing, it is acquired by teaching; if the other, not.

---

[19] The interpretation of Figure 4 is conjectural.

MENO: Certainly.

SOCRATES: Next, it seems, we should consider whether virtue is knowledge or a different sort of thing than knowledge.

87d   MENO: Yes, I think we should consider that next.

SOCRATES: Well then, do we say that it—I mean, virtue—is something good? And does this hypothesis stay put for us, that it is a good thing?

MENO: Certainly.

SOCRATES: Then if there is something that is good, other than and separate from knowledge, perhaps virtue might not be some sort of knowledge. But if nothing is good that is not included in knowledge, we may correctly suspect that it is some sort of knowledge.

MENO: That's right.

SOCRATES: And it is by virtue that we are good.

MENO: Yes.

87e   SOCRATES: And if good, beneficial. For all good things are beneficial. Aren't they?

MENO: Yes.

SOCRATES: Then virtue is a beneficial thing.

MENO: That necessarily follows from the things we have agreed to.

SOCRATES: Then let's consider one by one the sorts of things that benefit us. Health does, we say, and strength and beauty and wealth. These and things like them are the ones we say are beneficial. Aren't they?

MENO: Yes.

88a   SOCRATES: But these same things, we say, sometimes harm. Or do you disagree with that?

MENO: No, I agree.

SOCRATES: Consider, then, what guides each of these when they benefit us, and what when they harm. Doesn't it benefit when there is correct use, and harm when there isn't?

MENO: Certainly.

SOCRATES: In addition, then, let's also consider the ones having to do with the soul. Temperance is one, you say, and justice and courage and ease-in-learning and good memory and high-mindedness and everything of that sort?

MENO: I do.

88b   SOCRATES: Consider, then. Don't the ones among them that seem to you to be not knowledge, but something other than knowledge, sometimes harm and sometimes benefit? Take courage, for example. If courage is not wisdom, but a sort of boldness, then, when a person is bold without understanding, isn't he harmed, when with understanding, benefited?

MENO: Yes.

SOCRATES: Similarly, too, with temperance and ease-in-learning. When things are learned or acquired by training together with understanding, aren't they beneficial, when without understanding, harmful?

MENO: Very much so.

SOCRATES: In a word, then, all of the soul's undertakings and acts of endurance, when guided by wisdom, end in happiness, when by folly, in the opposite.   88c

MENO: It seems so.

SOCRATES: So if virtue is one of the things in the soul and is necessarily beneficial, it must be wisdom, since in fact all the others having to do with the soul, taken by themselves, are neither beneficial nor harmful, but become harmful or beneficial when wisdom or folly is added. According to this   88d
argument, then, since virtue is beneficial it must be some sort of wisdom.

MENO: Yes, I think so.

SOCRATES: In fact, in the case of all the others too—wealth and the rest—that we said just now are sometimes good, sometimes harmful, isn't something similar true? When wisdom guides the rest of the soul, it makes all the other things in the soul beneficial, while foolishness makes them harmful. Similarly, with these things too, when the soul uses and guides them   88e
correctly, doesn't it make them beneficial, when not correctly, harmful?

MENO: Certainly.

SOCRATES: And doesn't the wise one guide correctly, the foolish one incorrectly?

MENO: That's right.

SOCRATES: Then, can't we say the same in the case of all of them? In human beings all the rest depend on the soul. Those of the soul itself depend on wisdom, if they are going to be good things. And so, by this argument, what is beneficial would be wisdom. And we say that virtue is a beneficial   89a
thing?

MENO: Certainly.

SOCRATES: So we say that virtue is wisdom, either the whole thing or some part of it?

MENO: I think what we are saying, Socrates, is quite right.

SOCRATES: If that is so, then, good men would not be good by nature.

MENO: No, I don't think they would.

SOCRATES: Indeed, if they were, the following would also be the case. If good men were good by nature, we would surely have people who

89b recognized those of the young who were good by nature. And when they
had pointed them out to us, we would guard them in our acropolis,[20] seal-
ing them up much more carefully than gold, so that no one could corrupt
them, but that they, when they reached maturity, might be useful to their
cities.

MENO: That seems reasonable enough, Socrates.

SOCRATES: So, since good men are not good by nature, are they so by
89c learning?

MENO: That now seems necessary to me. And clearly, Socrates, on our
hypothesis that virtue is knowledge, it is acquired by teaching.

SOCRATES: Perhaps so, by Zeus! But perhaps we weren't right to agree to
that.

MENO: It certainly seemed right a moment ago.

SOCRATES: Yes, but if any of it is going to be sound, it must seem right not
just a moment ago, but also now and in the future.

89d MENO: Well then, what is it? What is it you are thinking that makes you
uneasy about it and makes you fear that virtue is not knowledge?

SOCRATES: I shall tell you, Meno. That it is acquired by teaching, if indeed
it is knowledge—*that* I do not retract as incorrect. But consider whether
you think it is reasonable to fear that it is not knowledge. Tell me this: if
anything whatever is acquired by teaching—not just virtue—mustn't there
be teachers and learners of it?

MENO: I think so.

89e SOCRATES: Then again won't the opposite hold? If there were neither teachers nor learners of something, wouldn't it be right to conjecture that it is
not acquired by teaching?

MENO: That's right. But don't you think there are teachers of virtue?

SOCRATES: I have often inquired, certainly, to see if there are any teachers of
it, but try as I may, I can't find any. Yet I carried out my inquiry with many
people, especially those I thought most experienced in the matter. And in
fact, Meno, Anytus here has sat down beside us at just the right time. Let's
share our inquiry with him. It would be reasonable for us to share it. For,
90a first, Anytus is the son of a wealthy and wise father, Anthemion,[21] who
has become wealthy not by chance or as a result of a gift—like Ismenias
of Thebes, who recently acquired the wealth of Polycrates[22]—but by his

---

[20] A fortified high place in a city, where public treasures were kept.

[21] On Anytus, see *Apology* 18b note. About Anthemion we know pretty much
only what we are told here.

[22] Polycrates, a leading Athenian democrat, wrote (a lost) *Accusation of Socrates.*
Xenophon's *Socrates' Defense to the Jury* is thought to be a response to it. Ismenias

own wisdom and carefulness. Next, as regards other things too, he seems not to be a haughty, scornful, or offensive citizen, but a moderate and well-behaved man. Finally, he brought up and educated Anytus well, as the majority of Athenians think—at any rate, they choose him for their highest offices.[23] It is right, then, to inquire with such people to see whether there are any teachers of virtue or not, and who they are. So Anytus, please inquire with us, with me and your friend Meno here, into his matter of who the teachers of virtue might be. Consider it this way. If we wanted Meno here to become a good doctor, what teachers would we send him to? Wouldn't we send him to doctors?

ANYTUS: Certainly.

SOCRATES: What if we wanted him to become a good shoemaker? Wouldn't we send him to shoemakers?[24]

ANYTUS: Yes.

SOCRATES: And similarly in all the other cases?

ANYTUS: Certainly.

SOCRATES: Then consider the same cases again and tell me this. We say that we would be right to send him to doctors if we want him to become a doctor. When we say this, are we saying that we would be sensible to send him to those who claim to possess the art rather than those who don't, and who charge a fee for this very thing, and declare themselves to be teachers of anyone who wants to come to them and learn? Isn't it with these considerations in mind that we would be right to send him there?

ANYTUS: Yes.

SOCRATES: And doesn't the same apply to flute-playing and the rest? It would be the height of ignorance, if we wanted to make someone a flute-player, to be unwilling to send him to those who undertake to teach the art, but to trouble other people, when they neither claim to be teachers nor have a single learner in the thing we want the one we send to learn from them. Don't you think that would be the height of irrationality?

ANYTUS: Yes, I do, by Zeus, and of lack of education besides!

SOCRATES: That's right. So now you and I can deliberate together about your guest Meno here. You see, he has been telling me for a long time, Anytus, that he wants the wisdom and virtue by which people manage

90b

90c

90d

90e

91a

---

may have accepted money from Polycrates to help overthrow the Thirty Tyrants and restore the democracy. Ismenias is mentioned at *Republic* 336a in a context that suggests Platonic disapproval.

[23] Anytus was chosen as general in 409 BCE and may have held other offices as well.

[24] Anytus and his father may have been tanners.

their households and cities well, look after their parents, and know how to welcome fellow citizens and foreigners and send them off, in a way worthy of a good man. Consider then, to whom it would be right for us to send him to learn this virtue. Or, is it absolutely clear, according to our discussion just now, that we should send him to those who undertake to be teachers of virtue, declare themselves available to any Greek who wants to learn, and charge a set fee for it?

91b

ANYTUS: And who do you say these people are, Socrates?

SOCRATES: You surely know as well as I do that they are the ones people call Sophists.

91c ANYTUS: In the name of Heracles,[25] be quiet, Socrates! May no one belonging to me, whether family members or friends, citizens or foreigners, be seized by such madness as to go to those people, and be ruined. For they plainly pervert and corrupt those who associate with them.

SOCRATES: What are you saying, Anytus? Do they alone differ so much from others who claim to know how to do some good, that they not only don't benefit what one entrusts to them, like the others, but do the opposite

91d and actually corrupt it? And they openly claim to deserve payment for doing *that*? I don't know, frankly, how I am to believe you. Indeed, I know that one man, Protagoras, earned more money from this sort of wisdom than Phidias—who produced such conspicuously beautiful work—and ten other sculptors combined. Anyway, what you say is incredible. Those who repair old shoes and mend cloaks couldn't escape detection for thirty days

91e if they gave back the cloaks and shoes in worse condition than they got them. On the contrary, if they did that, they would soon starve to death. So how could Protagoras escape detection by the whole of Greece, if, for more than forty years, he corrupted those who associated with him and sent them off worse than when they came? He was almost seventy years old, I think, when he died and had practiced his art for forty years. And in all that time, right up to the present day, his good reputation hasn't diminished. And Protagoras is not the only one. On the contrary, there are many others

92a as well, some earlier than he, some still alive. On your account, are we to say that they led the young astray and ruined them knowingly, or in a way that escaped detection even by themselves? Are we to claim they are as mad as that, those who some say are the wisest people there are?

ANYTUS: They are far from mad, Socrates. The young people who give them money are much more so, and their relatives who allow them do

92b it are even madder than they. But by far the maddest of all are the cities that allow these men in when they arrive and don't expel any citizen or foreigner who attempts to do anything like that.

---

[25] See *Euthyphro* 4a and note.

SOCRATES: Has one of these Sophists wronged you, Anytus? Why are you so hard on them?

ANYTUS: No, by Zeus, I have never associated with any of them or allowed anyone of mine to do so.

SOCRATES: So you have absolutely no experience of these men?

ANYTUS: No, and hope to remain that way.

SOCRATES: You are a strange fellow! How do you know whether there is 92c anything good or bad in this undertaking of theirs, if you have absolutely no experience of it?

ANYTUS: It's easy! I *know* who these people are. Whether I lack or don't lack experience of them has nothing to do with it.

SOCRATES: Perhaps you are a prophet, Anytus! For I wonder how else you could know about them, given the things you yourself say. Really though, we weren't inquiring about who the people are that will make Meno wicked if he goes to them. Let *these* be the Sophists, if you like. But tell us, 92d and do some good for this family friend of yours by telling him, to whom should he go in so large a city in order to become worthy of mention for the virtue I described just now.

ANYTUS: Why don't you tell him yourself?

SOCRATES: But I did say who I thought the teachers of these things are. But you said I was talking nonsense. And perhaps there is something in what you say. But now it is your turn to tell him to which of the Athenians he should go. Name whomever you like. 92e

ANYTUS: Why should he be told one person's name? Without exception, any fine and good Athenian he happens to meet will make him better than the Sophists, provided he is willing to believe them.

SOCRATES: Did these men become fine and good by chance? Without having learned from anyone, are they nevertheless able to teach others what they themselves didn't learn? 93a

ANYTUS: I think they learned from their predecessors, who were fine and good men too. Or don't you think there have been many good men in this city?

SOCRATES: I think, Anytus, both that there are men here who are good in political affairs, and that there have been just as many in the past. But were they also good teachers of their own virtue? You see, that is what our discussion is about, not whether there are good men here or not, or whether there have been in the past, but whether virtue really is acquired by teaching—that is what we have been considering for a long time. But 93b to consider that is to consider this: do good men, whether now or in the past, also know how to pass on to someone else this virtue that makes them good, or is it something a person cannot pass on or receive from someone else? That is what Meno and I have been inquiring about for a long time. On the basis of your own account, consider it this way: Wouldn't you say

93c   that Themistocles[26] was a good man?

ANYTUS: Yes, among the best of them all.

SOCRATES: Then wouldn't you also say that he was a good teacher of his own virtue if anyone was?

ANYTUS: I suppose so—if he *wanted* to be.

SOCRATES: Do you think he wouldn't have wanted others to become fine and good men, not even his own son? Do you think he begrudged it to him and deliberately did not pass on the virtue that made him good himself?

93d   Haven't you heard that Themistocles had his son Cleophantus taught to be a good horseman? Why, he could stay standing upright on horseback, throw the javelin from horseback while standing upright, and do many other amazing things, which Themistocles had had him educated in and made clever at, and which depend on having good teachers. Haven't you heard that from older people?

ANYTUS: I have.

SOCRATES: So no one could claim that his son's *nature* was bad.

93e   ANYTUS: No, they probably couldn't.

SOCRATES: What about this? Have you ever heard anyone young or old say that Themistocles' son Cleophantus was a good and wise man in the way his father was?

ANYTUS: Certainly not.

SOCRATES: So are we to think that he wanted to educate his son in those other things, but not to make him any better than his neighbors when it came to the wisdom he himself possessed—*if*, of course, virtue really is acquired by teaching.

ANYTUS: By Zeus, probably not!

SOCRATES: That is your sort of teacher of virtue for you, then—the one even you agree was among the best in the past. But let's consider another,

94a   Aristides son of Lysimachus.[27] Don't you agree that he was good?

ANYTUS: I certainly do, absolutely.

---

[26] Themistocles (c. 524–459 BCE) was an Athenian statesman and chief architect of the Greek victory in the war against the Persians. He was ostracized by Athens at the end of the 470s and was later condemned to death in his absence, on suspicion of intriguing with the Persians against Greece.

[27] Lysimachus was a prominent fifth-century Athenian statesman, noted for his justice. Like his near contemporary, Themistocles, he was ostracized by Athens in 483–482 BCE on suspicion of being a Persian sympathizer.

SOCRATES: Well, didn't he too do the best job of any Athenian of educating his son Lysimachus in anything that depended on teachers? But do you think he made him a better man than anyone else? You have associated with him, I assume, and see what he is like. Or take Pericles,[28] if you prefer—since he was a man of such high-minded wisdom. You know he brought up two sons, Paralus and Xanthippus?   94b

ANYTUS: I do.

SOCRATES: You also know, then, that he taught them to be horsemen second to none in Athens, and that he had them educated in musical and physical training and all the other things that depend on expertise, so as to be second to none. Didn't he want to make them good men, then? I think he did want to, but that it may be something that can't be acquired by teaching. And lest you think it was only a few utterly useless Athenians who were incapable of this undertaking, consider that Thucydides also brought up two sons, Melesias and Stephanus.[29] He educated them well in   94c
other things, and made them the finest wrestlers in Athens. For he gave one to Xanthias to train, and the other to Eudorus—and they were thought to be the finest wrestlers of their time. Don't you remember?

ANYTUS: Yes, I have heard that.

SOCRATES: Well, isn't it clear that he would never have taught his sons expensive things, but failed to teach them at no expense what would make   94d
them good men—*if* this were acquired by teaching? Was Thucydides a useless man, perhaps, who didn't have many friends among the Athenians and their allies? No, he belonged to a prominent family and had great power in the city and in the rest of Greece. So if it were acquired by teaching, he would have found someone to make his sons good men, whether a fellow countryman or a foreigner, if he himself didn't have the leisure to do it   94e
because he was taking care of the city. But I suspect, Anytus my friend, that virtue is not something acquired by teaching.

ANYTUS: It seems to me, Socrates, that you readily speak ill of people. I would advise you—if you are willing to trust me—to be careful. Perhaps, in other cities too, it is easier to do evil to people than good. It certainly is in this one. But then, I think you know that as well as I.   **95a**

SOCRATES: I think Anytus is angry, Meno, and I am not surprised. You see, in the first place, he thinks I am disparaging these men. Second, he thinks

---

[28] Pericles (c. 495–429 BCE) was the most important democratic leader in Athens, from the 440s until his death. He was involved in the building program of the 440s and 430s that resulted in the Parthenon and much else.

[29] Thucydides (born c. 500 BCE) was the leading conservative opponent of Pericles. He was ostracized c. 443. The great historian of the same name may have been his grandson.

he is one of them. But if he ever comes to know what speaking ill is really like, he will stop being angry. At present, however, he doesn't know. Tell me, though, are there also fine and good men in your country?

MENO: Certainly.

95b   SOCRATES: Then are they willing to offer themselves as teachers to the young men?

MENO: No, by Zeus, they aren't, Socrates! But sometimes you hear them say it is acquired by teaching, sometimes that it isn't.

SOCRATES: Are we to say they are teachers of this thing, then, when they do not even agree about *that*?

MENO: It seems not, Socrates.

SOCRATES: What about these Sophists, then, who alone profess to be so, do you think they are teachers of virtue?

95c   MENO: In fact, that's what I particularly admire about Gorgias, Socrates, that you never hear him promise to teach it. He even ridicules the others when he hears them promise. It is *speaking* he thinks he should make people clever at.

SOCRATES: So you don't think the Sophists are teachers of virtue, either?

MENO: I can't tell, Socrates. Like most people, sometimes I think so, sometimes not.

SOCRATES: Do you know it isn't just you or the other politicians who sometimes think that it is acquired by teaching, sometimes that it isn't? Do

95d   you know even the poet Theognis says the same thing?[30]

MENO: In which verses?

SOCRATES: In his elegiacs where he says—

> Drink and eat with them, and with them
> Sit, be pleasing to those with great power.
> You will learn noble things, you see, from noble men.
> But if with bad ones you mix,

95e   > You will lose even what understanding you already have.

Do you see that in these lines he speaks as if virtue is acquired by teaching?

MENO: Yes, apparently so.

SOCRATES: In others, though, he makes a little change:

> If understanding could be produced and put into a man,

he says roughly that

> Many and great would be the fees earned

---

[30] Theognis was a sixth-century BCE elegiac poet from Megara.

by those able to do it, and that

> Never from a good father would a bad son be born,
> If words of wisdom are trusted. But teaching   **96a**
> Will never make a bad man good.

Do you see that he makes opposite claims about one and the same thing?

MENO: Apparently so.

SOCRATES: Well, can you name any other thing that those who say they are teachers of it are not only not generally agreed to be teachers of it to others, but are not even agreed to know it themselves, but instead to be useless at the very thing they claim to teach? Or that those who are generally agreed **96b** to be fine and good men themselves sometimes say that it is acquired by teaching, sometimes that it isn't? Would you say that those who are that confused about anything are teachers of it in the proper sense?

MENO: No, by Zeus, I cannot.

SOCRATES: Then if neither the Sophists nor the fine and good men themselves are teachers of the thing, is it not clear that no other people are?

MENO: No, I don't think they are.

SOCRATES: But if there are no *teachers,* there are no learners either?   **96c**

MENO: I think that's right.

SOCRATES: But didn't we agree that a thing of which there are neither teachers nor learners is not acquired by teaching?

MENO: We did agree.

SOCRATES: Now, isn't it the case that there are no teachers of virtue to be seen anywhere?

MENO: That's right.

SOCRATES: And if there are no teachers, there are no learners either?

MENO: Apparently so.

SOCRATES: So virtue isn't something acquired by teaching?

MENO: It seems not, if our way of considering it is in fact correct. So I really **96d** wonder, Socrates, whether there aren't ever any good men at all—or else what could be the way those who come to be good do so?

SOCRATES: It looks, Meno, as though you and I are pretty useless men, and Gorgias has not adequately educated you or Prodicus or me. Above all, then, we ought to pay attention to ourselves and search out someone who will make us better *one way or another.* I say this in view of our recent **96e** inquiry, because we ridiculously failed to see that it is not only under the guidance of knowledge that people conduct their affairs correctly and well. And that may be why the knowledge is also escaping us of the way in which men who are good become so.

MENO: What do you mean, Socrates?

97a SOCRATES: I mean this. That good men must be beneficial is something we correctly agreed couldn't be otherwise. Didn't we?

MENO: Yes.

SOCRATES: And that they will be beneficial if they guide us correctly in our affairs is also something we agreed to correctly, I suppose?

MENO: Yes.

SOCRATES: But that it is not possible to guide correctly if one is not wise is something, it looks like, we agreed to *incorrectly*.

MENO: How do you mean?

SOCRATES: I shall tell you. If someone who knew the road to Larissa,[31] or anywhere else you like, were to walk there and guide others, wouldn't he guide them correctly and well?

MENO: Certainly.

97b SOCRATES: But what if someone had a correct belief as to which road it was, though he had never gone on it and had no knowledge of it, wouldn't he also guide them correctly?

MENO: Certainly.

SOCRATES: And as long as he has correct belief, I suppose, about what the other one has knowledge of, he will be no worse a guide than the one who is wise about it, even though he has only true belief, not wisdom.

MENO: No, no worse.

SOCRATES: So true belief is no worse a guide to the correctness of action than wisdom. And that is what we left out just now in considering what **97c** sort of thing virtue was. We said that wisdom alone is a guide to acting correctly, whereas there was, it seems, true belief as well.

MENO: Yes, it seems so.

SOCRATES: So correct belief is no less beneficial than knowledge.

MENO: Except by this much, Socrates—the one with knowledge will always hit the mark, while the one with correct belief will sometimes hit it, sometimes not.

SOCRATES: What do you mean? Won't the one who always has correct opinion always hit it, as long as his belief is correct?

MENO: That does seem necessary to me. So, I wonder, Socrates, if that's **97d** right, why knowledge is much more highly valued than correct belief, and what it is that makes one different from the other.

---

[31] The city of Larissa in Thessaly was close to Meno's hometown, Pharsalus.

SOCRATES: Do you know, then, why you wonder about this, or shall I tell you?

MENO: By all means tell me.

SOCRATES: It is because you haven't paid attention to the statues of Daedalus.[32] But perhaps there aren't any in your country.

MENO: In reference to what do you say that?

SOCRATES: That they, too, if they aren't tied down, run away and flee, but if they are tied down, stay put.

MENO: So what?   97e

SOCRATES: It is not of much value to acquire one of his works that is untied, since, like a runaway slave, it won't stay put. But a tied-down one is worth a lot, since his works are very beautiful. In reference to what do I say that? In reference to true beliefs. For true beliefs—as long as they stay put—are a beautiful thing, too, and everything they bring about is good. They aren't willing to stay put for long, however, but flee from a person's soul. So   **98a** they aren't of much value until someone ties them down by reasoning out the explanation. And that, Meno my friend, is recollection—as we agreed before. When they are tied down, they first become bits of knowledge, then they stay put. That is why knowledge is more valuable than true belief, and it is being tied down that makes knowledge different from true belief.

MENO: Yes, by Zeus, Socrates, it does seem to be something like that!

SOCRATES: And yet I, too, speak as someone who doesn't know, but con-jectures. However, in saying that correct belief is a different thing than   98b knowledge—there, I think, I am not at all conjecturing. On the contrary, if there were anything else that I would say I know—and there are few things I would say it about—at any rate, I would put down this, too, as one of the things I know.

MENO: And you would be right, Socrates.

SOCRATES: Well then, is it not correct to say that when correct belief guides, the outcome of each action is no worse than when knowledge does?

MENO: I think that's right too.

SOCRATES: So correct belief is not worse than knowledge or any less ben-   98c eficial when it comes to actions, nor the man who has correct belief than the one who has knowledge.

MENO: That's true.

SOCRATES: And we agreed that the good man is beneficial.

MENO: Yes.

---

[32] See *Euthyphro* 11b–e and note.

SOCRATES: Then, since it is not only through knowledge that good men—if they exist—are good and beneficial to their cities, but also through correct belief, and since neither of these is something people possess by nature,

98d neither knowledge nor true belief . . . or do you think either of them is possessed by nature?

MENO: No, I do not.

SOCRATES: Then, since neither is possessed by nature, good men will not have goodness by nature, either.

MENO: Certainly not.

SOCRATES: Then, since they do not have it by nature, we next set out to consider whether it is something acquired by teaching.

MENO: Yes.

SOCRATES: And didn't it seem that it would be acquired by teaching, if virtue were wisdom?

MENO: Yes.

SOCRATES: And that if it were acquired by teaching, it would be wisdom?

MENO: Certainly.

98e SOCRATES: And that if there were teachers, it would be acquired by teaching, but if there weren't, it wouldn't be acquired by teaching?

MENO: Yes.

SOCRATES: But we agreed there aren't any teachers of it?

MENO: That's right.

SOCRATES: So we agreed that it is not acquired by teaching and is not wisdom?

MENO: Certainly.

SOCRATES: But we do agree that it *is* good?

MENO: Yes.

SOCRATES: And that what guides correctly is beneficial and good?

MENO: Certainly.

99a SOCRATES: And that what alone guides correctly is two things, true belief and knowledge, and only if he has these does a person guide correctly. For the things that come about correctly by chance do not come about through human guidance, and in those where a man does guide toward the right thing, you find one of these two, true belief or knowledge.

MENO: I think that's right.

SOCRATES: Then, since it is not acquired by teaching, virtue is no longer knowledge, either.

MENO: Apparently not.

SOCRATES: So, of the two good and beneficial things, one has been ruled out, and so it cannot be knowledge that is a guide in political affairs.

MENO: It seems not.

SOCRATES: Then it is not by some sort of wisdom, or by being wise, that men such as Themistocles and his associates, or those whom Anytus here just mentioned, guided their cities. For this very reason, they can't make others like themselves, seeing that they aren't what they are on account of knowledge.

MENO: It seems to be as you say, Socrates.

SOCRATES: Then, if it is not by knowledge, the remaining possibility is that it is by true belief, that it is by using *it* that political men guide their cities correctly, since they are no different as regards wisdom from soothsayers and prophets. For the latter, too, while divinely inspired, say many true things, but have no knowledge whatsoever about the things they say.

MENO: It looks that way.

SOCRATES: Then isn't it right, Meno, to call these men godlike—the ones who without understanding achieve many great successes in the things they do and say?

MENO: Certainly.

SOCRATES: So wouldn't we be right to call the soothsayers and prophets we mentioned just now godlike, as well as all the poets? And to say that the politicians are by no means the least godlike of them, since they are inspired and possessed by the god, when they achieve success in saying many great things, while knowing nothing about the things they say?

MENO: Certainly.

SOCRATES: Women too, I suppose, Meno, call good men godlike; and when the Spartans praise a good man, they say, "He is a godlike man."

MENO: And apparently, Socrates, they are right in doing it. But perhaps Anytus here will be annoyed at you for saying so.

SOCRATES: I am not concerned about that. We shall talk with him again, Meno, some other time. For the present, if we have inquired and spoken correctly throughout this entire discussion, virtue is not acquired by nature or by teaching, but comes to be present by divine dispensation, without understanding, in those in whom it does come to be present—provided, of course, there is not some political man who is able to make someone else a politician. If there were, he could pretty much be said to be among the living what Homer said Tiresias was among the dead. Among those in Hades, he said, "He alone is wise, the others flit around as shadows."[33] In

99b

99c

99d

99e

100a

---

[33] Homer, *Odyssey* x.495.

the same way here, such a man would be like a truly real thing in comparison to shadows as regards virtue.

100b   MENO: I think what you said is absolutely right, Socrates.

SOCRATES: On the basis of this reasoning, then, Meno, it appears to us that it is by divine dispensation that virtue comes to be present in those in whom it comes to be present. But we will know that with certainty when, before inquiring about the way virtue comes to be present in people, we first try to inquire about what virtue itself is by itself. Now, however, it is time for me to go be somewhere. Try to persuade your friend Anytus here, too, of the things you yourself have been persuaded of, so that he will be more gentle. You see, if you do persuade him, you will also profit

100c   the Athenians.[34]

---

[34] A prophetic allusion, presumably, to Anytus' role in having Socrates executed, thereby depriving Athens of his beneficial services.

PHAEDO

ECHECRATES:[1] Were you with Socrates yourself, Phaedo,[2] on the day when   **57a**
he drank the poison in prison, or did someone else tell you about it?

PHAEDO: I was there myself, Echecrates.

ECHECRATES: What are the things he said before he died? And how did he
die? I should be glad to hear this. Hardly anyone from Phlius visits Athens
nowadays, nor has any stranger come from Athens for some time who could
give us a clear account of what happened, except that he drank the poison   **57b**
and died, but nothing more.

PHAEDO: Did you not even hear how the trial went?   **58a**

ECHECRATES: Yes, someone did tell us about that, and we wondered that
he seems to have died a long time after the trial took place. Why was that,
Phaedo?

PHAEDO: That was by chance, Echecrates. The day before the trial, as it
happened, the prow of the ship that the Athenians send to Delos had been
crowned with garlands.

ECHECRATES: What ship is that?

PHAEDO: It is the ship in which, the Athenians say, Theseus once sailed to
Crete, taking with him the two lots of seven victims.[3] He saved them and
was himself saved. The Athenians vowed then to Apollo, so the story goes,   **58b**
that if they were saved they would send a mission to Delos every year. And
from that time to this they send such an annual mission to the god. They
have a law to keep the city pure while it lasts, and no execution may take
place once the mission has begun until the ship has made its journey to
Delos and returned to Athens, and this can sometimes take a long time if   **58c**
the winds delay it. The mission begins when the priest of Apollo crowns
the prow of the ship, and this happened, as I say, the day before Socrates'
trial. That is why Socrates was in prison a long time between his trial and
his execution.

The text of *Phaedo,* translated by G. M. A. Grube, is reprinted with minor adaptations from Plato: *Phaedo,* Second Edition. Copyright © 1980, Hackett Publishing Co.

[1] Echecrates was a native of Phlius, in the northeast Peloponnese, where the conversation takes place. He was a student of the Pythagorean philosophers, Philolaus
and Eurytus of Tarentum.

[2] Phaedo of Elis, in the northwest Peloponnese, was a young follower of Socrates.

[3] See *Crito* 43d note.

ECHECRATES: What about his actual death, Phaedo? What did he say? What did he do? Who of his friends were with him? Or did the authorities not allow them to be present and he died with no friends present?

58d   PHAEDO: By no means. Some were present, in fact, a good many.

ECHECRATES: Please be good enough to tell us all that occurred as fully as possible, unless you have some pressing business.

PHAEDO: I have the time and I will try to tell you the whole story, for nothing gives me more pleasure than to call Socrates to mind, whether talking about him myself, or listening to someone else do so.

ECHECRATES: Your hearers will surely be like you in this, Phaedo. So do try to tell us every detail as exactly as you can.

58e   PHAEDO: I certainly found being there an astonishing experience. Although I was witnessing the death of one who was my friend, I had no feeling of pity, for the man appeared happy in both manner and words as he died nobly and without fear, Echecrates, so that it struck me that even in going down to the underworld he was going with the gods' blessing and that he

59a   would fare well when he got there, if anyone ever does. That is why I had no feeling of pity, such as would seem natural in my sorrow, nor indeed of pleasure, as we engaged in philosophical discussion as we were accustomed to do—for our arguments were of that sort—but I had a strange feeling, an unaccustomed mixture of pleasure and pain at the same time as I reflected that he was just about to die. All of us present were affected in much the same way, sometimes laughing, then weeping; especially one of

59b   us, Apollodorus[4]—you know the man and his ways.

ECHECRATES: Of course I do.

PHAEDO: He was quite overcome; but I was myself disturbed, and so were the others.

ECHECRATES: Who, Phaedo, were those present?

PHAEDO: Among the local people there was Apollodorus, whom I mentioned, Critobulus and his father,[5] also Hermogenes, Epigenes, Aeschines, and Antisthenes. Ctesippus of Paeania was there, Menexenus, and some others. Plato, I believe, was ill.

ECHECRATES: Were there some foreigners present?

---

[4] See *Apology* 34a.

[5] The father of Critobulus is Crito, after whom the dialogue *Crito* is named. Several of the other friends of Socrates mentioned here also appear in other dialogues. For example, Epigenes is mentioned in the *Apology,* as is Aeschines. Simmias and Cebes are mentioned in *Crito* 45b as having come to Athens with enough money to secure Socrates' escape.

PHAEDO: Yes, Simmias from Thebes with Cebes and Phaedondes, and from   59c
Megara, Euclides and Terpsion.[6]

ECHECRATES: What about Aristippus and Cleombrotus? Were they there?

PHAEDO: No. They were said to be in Aegina.[7]

ECHECRATES: Was there anyone else?

PHAEDO: I think these were about all.

ECHECRATES: Well then, what do you say the conversation was about?

PHAEDO: I will try to tell you everything from the beginning. On the
previous days also both the others and I used to visit Socrates. We foregath-   59d
ered at daybreak at the court where the trial took place, for it was close to
the prison, and each day we used to wait around talking until the prison
should open, for it did not open early. When it opened we used to go in
to Socrates and spend most of the day with him. On this day we gathered
rather early, because when we left the prison on the previous evening we   59e
were informed that the ship from Delos had arrived, and so we told each
other to come to the usual place as early as possible. When we arrived the
gatekeeper who used to answer our knock came out and told us to wait and
not go in until he told us to. "The Eleven,"[8] he said, "are freeing Socrates
from his bonds and telling him how his death will take place today." After
a short time he came and told us to go in. We found Socrates recently   60a
released from his chains, and Xanthippe[9]—you know her—sitting by him,
holding their baby. When she saw us, she cried out and said the sort of
thing that women usually say: "Socrates, this is the last time your friends
will talk to you and you to them." Socrates looked at Crito. "Crito," he
said, "let someone take her home." And some of Crito's people led her away
lamenting and beating her breast.

Socrates sat up on the bed, bent his leg, and rubbed it with his hand, and   60b
as he rubbed he said: "What a strange thing that which men call pleasure
seems to be, and how astonishing the relation it has with what is thought
to be its opposite, namely pain! A man cannot have both at the same time.
Yet if he pursues and catches the one, he is almost always bound to catch
the other also, like two creatures with one head. I think that if Aesop had
noted this he would have composed a fable that a god wished to reconcile   60c
their opposition but could not do so, so he joined their two heads together,

---

6 Euclides and Terpsion are both speakers in Plato's *Theaetetus*. Euclides is said
to have founded the Megarian school of philosophy. Terpsion and Cleombrotus are
otherwise unknown.

7 Island in the Saronic Gulf, quite close to Athens.

8 See *Apology* 37c.

9 Socrates' wife.

and therefore when a man has the one, the other follows later. This seems
to be happening to me. My bonds caused pain in my leg, and now pleasure
seems to be following."

Cebes intervened and said: "By Zeus, yes, Socrates, you did well to
remind me. Evenus[10] asked me the day before yesterday, as others had done
before, what induced you to write poetry after you came to prison, you
60d   who had never composed any poetry before, putting the fables of Aesop
into verse and composing the hymn to Apollo. If it is of any concern to
you that I should have an answer to give to Evenus when he repeats his
question, as I know he will, tell me what to say to him."

Tell him the truth, Cebes, he said, that I did not do this with the idea
60e   of rivaling him or his poems, for I knew that would not be easy, but I tried
to find out the meaning of certain dreams and to satisfy my conscience in
case it was this kind of art they were frequently bidding me to practice.
The dreams were something like this: the same dream often came to me
in the past, now in one shape now in another, but saying the same thing:
"Socrates," it said, "practice and cultivate the arts." In the past I imagined
that it was instructing and advising me to do what I was doing, such as
61a   those who encourage runners in a race, that the dream was thus bidding
me do the very thing I was doing, namely, to practice the art of philosophy,
this being the highest kind of art, and I was doing that.

But now, after my trial took place, and the festival of the god was
preventing my execution, I thought that, in case my dream was bidding
me to practice this popular art, I should not disobey it but compose
poetry. I thought it safer not to leave here until I had satisfied my con-
61b   science by writing poems in obedience to the dream. So I first wrote
in honor of the god of the present festival. After that I realized that a
poet, if he is to be a poet, must compose fables, not arguments. Being
no teller of fables myself, I took the stories I knew and had at hand, the
fables of Aesop, and I versified the first ones I came across. Tell this to
Evenus, Cebes, wish him well and bid him farewell, and tell him, if he
is wise, to follow me as soon as possible. I am leaving today, it seems, as
61c   the Athenians so order it.

Said Simmias: "What kind of advice is this you are giving to Evenus,
Socrates? I have met him many times, and from my observation he is not
at all likely to follow it willingly."

How so, said he, is Evenus not a philosopher?

I think so, Simmias said.

Then Evenus will be willing, like every man who partakes worthily of
philosophy. Yet perhaps he will not take his own life, for that, they say,

---

[10] See *Apology* 20b. He is also mentioned at *Phaedrus* 267a.

is not lawful.[11] As he said this, Socrates put his feet on the ground and
remained in this position during the rest of the conversation.   61d

Then Cebes asked: "How do you mean, Socrates, that it is not right to
do oneself violence, and yet that the philosopher will be willing to follow
one who is dying?"

Come now, Cebes, have you and Simmias, who keep company with
Philolaus,[12] not heard about such things?

Nothing definite, Socrates.

Indeed, I too speak about this from hearsay, but I do not mind telling
you what I have heard, for it is perhaps most appropriate for one who is
about to depart yonder to tell and examine tales about what we believe   61e
that journey to be like. What else could one do in the time we have until
sunset?

But whatever is the reason, Socrates, for people to say that it is not right
to kill oneself? As to your question just now, I have heard Philolaus say
this when staying in Thebes and I have also heard it from others, but I have
never heard anyone give a clear account of the matter.

Well, he said, we must do our best, and you may yet hear one. And it   62a
may well astonish you if this subject, alone of all things, is simple, and it is
never, as with everything else, better at certain times and for certain people
to die than to live. And if this is so, you may well find it astonishing that
those for whom it is better to die are wrong to help themselves, and that
they must wait for someone else to benefit them.

And Cebes, lapsing into his own dialect,[13] laughed quietly and said:
"Zeus knows it is."

Indeed, said Socrates, it does seem unreasonable when put like that,   62b
but perhaps there is reason to it. There is the explanation that is put in the
language of the mysteries, that we men are in a kind of prison, and that
one must not free oneself or run away. That seems to me an impressive
doctrine and one not easy to understand fully. However, Cebes, this seems
to me well expressed, that the gods are our guardians and that men are one
of their possessions. Or do you not think so?

I do, said Cebes.

And would you not be angry if one of your possessions killed itself when   62c
you had not given any sign that you wished it to die, and if you had any
punishment you could inflict, you would inflict it?

---

[11] *Themiton:* in accord with divine rather than human law, as at 67b and *Apology*
21b, 30c–d.

[12] Philolaus of Croton (c. 470–390 BCE), his book, only fragments of which
survive, was probably the first by a Pythagorean.

[13] That is, into Boeotian (rather than Attic) Greek.

Certainly, he said.

Perhaps then, put in this way, it is not unreasonable that one should not kill oneself before a god had indicated some necessity to do so, like the necessity now put upon us.

That seems likely, said Cebes. As for what you were saying, that philosophers should be willing and ready to die, that seems strange, Socrates, if what we said just now is reasonable, namely, that a god is our protector and that we are his possessions. It is not logical that the wisest of men should not resent leaving this service in which they are governed by the best of masters, the gods, for a wise man cannot believe that he will look after himself better when he is free. A foolish man might easily think so, that he must escape from his master; he would not reflect that one must not escape from a good master but stay with him as long as possible, because it would be foolish to escape. But the sensible man would want always to remain with one better than himself. So, Socrates, the opposite of what was said before is likely to be true; the wise would resent dying, whereas the foolish would rejoice at it.

I thought that when Socrates heard this he was pleased by Cebes' argumentation. Glancing at us, he said: "Cebes is always on the track of some arguments; he is certainly not willing to be at once convinced by what one says."

Said Simmias: "But actually, Socrates, I think myself that Cebes has a point now. Why should truly wise men want to avoid the service of masters better than themselves, and leave them easily? And I think Cebes is aiming his argument at you, because you are bearing leaving us so lightly, and leaving those good masters, as you say yourself, the gods."

You are both justified in what you say, and I think you mean that I must make a defense against this, as if I were in court.

You certainly must, said Simmias.

Come then, he said, let me try to make my defense to you more convincing than it was to the jury. For, Simmias and Cebes, I should be wrong not to resent dying if I did not believe that I should go first to other wise and good gods, and then to men who have died and are better than men are here. Be assured that, as it is, I expect to join the company of good men. This last I would not altogether insist on, but if I insist on anything at all in these matters, it is that I shall come to gods who are very good masters. That is why I am not so resentful, because I have good hope that some future awaits men after death, as we have been told for years, a much better future for the good than for the wicked.

Well now, Socrates, said Simmias, do you intend to keep this belief to yourself as you leave us, or would you share it with us? I certainly think it would be a blessing for us too, and at the same time it would be your defense if you convince us of what you say.

62d

62e

63a

63b

63c

63d

I will try, he said, but first let us see what it is that Crito here has, I think, been wanting to say for quite a while.

What else, Socrates, said Crito, but what the man who is to give you the poison has been telling me for some time, that I should warn you to talk as little as possible. People get heated when they talk, he says, and one should not be heated when taking the poison, as those who do must sometimes 63e
drink it two or three times.

Socrates replied: "Take no notice of him; only let him be prepared to administer it twice or, if necessary, three times."

I was rather sure you would say that, Crito said, but he has been bothering me for some time.

Let him be, he said. I want to make my argument before you, my judges, as to why I think that a man who has truly spent his life in philosophy is probably right to be of good cheer in the face of death and to be very hopeful that after death he will attain the greatest blessings yonder. I will try 64a
to tell you, Simmias and Cebes, how this may be so. I am afraid that other people do not realize that the one aim of those who practice philosophy in the proper manner is to practice for dying and death. Now if this is true, it would be strange indeed if they were eager for this all their lives and then resent it when what they have wanted and practiced for a long time comes upon them.

Simmias laughed and said: "By Zeus, Socrates, you made me laugh, though I was in no laughing mood just now. I think that the majority, on 64b
hearing this, will think that it describes the philosophers very well, and our people in Thebes would thoroughly agree that philosophers are nearly dead and that the majority of men is well aware that they deserve to be.

And they would be telling the truth, Simmias, except for their being aware. They are not aware of the way true philosophers are nearly dead, nor of the way they deserve to be, nor of the sort of death they deserve. But never mind them, he said, let us talk among ourselves. Do we believe 64c
that there is such a thing as death?

Certainly, said Simmias.

Is it anything else than the separation of the soul from the body? Do we believe that death is this, namely, that the body comes to be separated by itself apart from the soul, and the soul comes to be separated by itself apart from the body? Is death anything else than that?

No, that is what it is, he said.

Consider then, my good sir, whether you share my belief, for this will lead us to a better knowledge of what we are investigating. Do you think 64d
it is the part of a philosopher to be concerned with such so-called pleasures as those of food and drink?

By no means.

What about the pleasures of sex?

Not at all.

What of the other pleasures concerned with the service of the body? Do you think such a man prizes them greatly, the acquisition of distinguished clothes and shoes and the other bodily ornaments? Do you think he values these or despises them, except insofar as one cannot do without them?

I think the true philosopher despises them.

Do you not think, he said, that in general such a man's concern is not with the body but that, as far as he can, he turns away from the body towards the soul?

I do.

So in the first place, such things show clearly that the philosopher more than other men frees the soul from association with the body as much as possible?

Apparently.

A man who finds no pleasure in such things and has no part in them is thought by the majority not to deserve to live and to be close to death; the man, that is, who does not care for the pleasures of the body.

What you say is certainly true.

Then what about the actual acquiring of knowledge? Is the body an obstacle when one associates with it in the search for knowledge? I mean, for example, do men find any truth in sight or hearing, or are not even the poets forever telling us that we do not see or hear anything accurately, and surely if those two physical senses are not clear or precise, our other senses can hardly be accurate, as they are all inferior to these.[14] Do you not think so?

I certainly do, he said.

When then, he asked, does the soul grasp the truth? For whenever it attempts to examine anything with the body, it is clearly deceived by it.

True.

Is it not in reasoning if anywhere that any reality[15] becomes clear to the soul?

Yes.

And indeed the soul reasons best when none of these senses troubles it, neither hearing nor sight, nor pain nor pleasure, but when it is most by itself, taking leave of the body and as far as possible having no contact or association with it in its search for reality.

That is so.

And it is then that the soul of the philosopher most disdains the body, flees from it and seeks to be by itself?

---

14 See *Republic* 507c–508a.

15 That is any of *ta onta*—"any of the things that *are*."

It appears so.

What about the following, Simmias? Do we say that there is such a thing as the Just itself,[16] or not?

We do say so, by Zeus.

And the Beautiful, and the Good?

Of course.

And have you ever seen any of these things with your eyes?

In no way, he said.

Or have you ever grasped them with any of your bodily senses? I am speaking of all things such as Bigness, Health, Strength, and, in a word, the reality[17] of all other things, that which each of them essentially is. Is what is most true in them contemplated through the body, or is this 65e
the position: Whoever of us prepares himself best and most accurately to grasp that thing itself which he is investigating will come closest to the knowledge of it?

Obviously.

Then he will do this most perfectly who approaches the object with thought alone, without associating any sight with his thought, or dragging in any sense perception with his reasoning, but who, using pure thought 66a
alone, tries to track down each reality pure and by itself, freeing himself as far as possible from eyes and ears and, in a word, from the whole body, because the body confuses the soul and does not allow it to acquire truth and wisdom whenever it is associated with it. Will not that man reach reality, Simmias, if anyone does?

What you say, said Simmias, is indeed true.

All these things will necessarily make the true philosophers believe and 66b
say to each other something like this: "There is likely to be something such as a path to guide us out of our confusion, because as long as we have a body and our soul is fused with such an evil we shall never adequately attain what we desire, which we affirm to be the truth. The body keeps us busy in a thousand ways because of its need for nurture. Moreover, if certain diseases befall it, they impede our search for the truth. It fills us with wants, 66c
desires, fears, all sorts of illusions and much nonsense, so that, as it is said, in truth and in fact no thought of any kind ever comes to us from the body. Only the body and its desires cause war, civil discord, and battles, for all wars are due to the desire to acquire wealth,[18] and it is the body and the

---

16 A standard way of referring to the Platonic form of justice.

17 *Ousia:* participle of the verb "to be" (*einai*). An account or definition of the *ousia* (being, substance, essence) of F answers the question "What is F?" by specifying what F really is. See *Euthyphro* 11a–b, *Meno* 72b–e, *Republic* 534b.

18 See *Republic* 373d–e.

66d   care of it, to which we are enslaved, which compel us to acquire wealth, and all this makes us too busy to practice philosophy. Worst of all, if we do get some respite from it and turn to some investigation, everywhere in our investigations the body is present and makes for confusion and fear, so that it prevents us from seeing the truth.

    "It really has been shown to us that, if we are ever to have pure knowledge, we must escape from the body and observe things in themselves with 66e   the soul by itself. It seems likely that we shall, only then, when we are dead, attain that which we desire and of which we claim to be lovers, namely, wisdom, as our argument shows, not while we live; for if it is impossible to attain any pure knowledge with the body, then one of two things is true: either we can never attain knowledge or we can do so after death. Then and 67a   not before, the soul is by itself apart from the body. While we live, we shall be closest to knowledge if we refrain as much as possible from association with the body and do not join with it more than we must, if we are not infected with its nature but purify ourselves from it until the god himself frees us. In this way we shall escape the contamination of the body's folly; we shall be likely to be in the company of people of the same kind, and by our own efforts we shall know all that is pure, which is presumably the 67b   truth, for it is not lawful for the impure to attain the pure."

    Such are the things, Simmias, that all those who love learning in the proper manner must say to one another and believe. Or do you not think so?

    I certainly do, Socrates.

    And if this is true, my friend, said Socrates, there is good hope that on 67c   arriving where I am going, if anywhere, I shall acquire what has been our chief preoccupation in our past life, so that the journey that is now ordered for me is full of good hope, as it is also for any other man who believes that his mind has been prepared and, as it were, purified.

    It certainly is, said Simmias.

    And does purification not turn out to be what we mentioned in our argument some time ago, namely, to separate the soul as far as possible from the body and accustom it to gather itself and collect itself out of every part of the body and to dwell by itself as far as it can both now and in the 67d   future, freed, as it were, from the bonds of the body?

    Certainly, he said.

    And that freedom and separation of the soul from the body is called death?

    That is altogether so.

    It is only those who practice philosophy in the right way, we say, who always most want to free the soul; and this release and separation of the soul from the body is the preoccupation of the philosophers?

    So it appears.

Therefore, as I said at the beginning, it would be ridiculous for a man to train himself in life to live in a state as close to death as possible, and then   67e to resent it when it comes?

Ridiculous, of course.

In fact, Simmias, he said, those who practice philosophy in the right way are in training for dying and they fear death least of all men. Consider it from this point of view: If they are altogether estranged from the body and desire to have their soul by itself, would it not be quite absurd for them to be afraid and resentful when this happens? If they did not gladly set out for a place, where, on arrival, they may hope to attain that for which they had yearned during their lifetime, that is, wisdom, and where they would   68a be rid of the presence of that from which they are estranged?

Many men, at the death of their lovers, wives, or sons, were willing to go to the underworld, driven by the hope of seeing there those for whose company they longed, and being with them. Will then a true lover of wisdom, who has a similar hope and knows that he will never find it to any extent except in Hades, be resentful of dying and not gladly undertake the journey thither? One must surely think so, my friend, if he is a true phi-   68b losopher, for he is firmly convinced that he will not find pure knowledge anywhere except there. And if this is so, then, as I said just now, would it not be highly unreasonable for such a man to fear death?

It certainly would, by Zeus, he said.

Then you have sufficient indication, he said, that any man whom you see resenting death was not a lover of wisdom but a lover of the body, and   68c also a lover of wealth or of honors, either or both.[19]

It is certainly as you say.

And, Simmias, he said, does not what is called courage belong especially to men of this disposition?

Most certainly.

And the quality of temperance which even the majority call by that name, that is, not to get swept off one's feet by one's passions, but to treat them with disdain and orderliness, is this not suited only to those who most of all despise the body and live the life of philosophy?

Necessarily so, he said.   68d

If you are willing to reflect on the courage and temperance of other people, you will find them strange.

In what way, Socrates?

You know that they all consider death a great evil?

Definitely, he said.

---

[19] See *Republic* 436c–442d, 580d–586e.

And the brave among them face death, when they do, for fear of greater evils?

That is so.

Therefore, it is fear and terror that make all men brave, except the philosophers. Yet it is illogical to be brave through fear and cowardice.

68e   It certainly is.

What of the temperate among them? Is their experience not similar? Is it licentiousness of a kind that makes them temperate? We say this is impossible, yet their experience of this simple-minded temperance turns out to be similar: they fear to be deprived of other pleasures which they desire, so they keep away from some pleasures because they are overcome

69a   by others. Now to be mastered by pleasure is what they call licentiousness, but what happens to them is that they master certain pleasures because they are mastered by others. This is like what we mentioned just now, that in some way it is a kind of licentiousness that has made them temperate.

That seems likely.

My good Simmias, I fear this is not the right exchange to attain virtue, to exchange pleasures for pleasures, pains for pains, and fears for fears, the greater for the less like coins, but that the only valid currency for which all these things should be exchanged is wisdom. With this we have real

69b   courage and temperance and justice and, in a word, true virtue, with wisdom, whether pleasures and fears and all such things be present or absent. When these are exchanged for one another in separation from wisdom, such virtue is only an illusory appearance of virtue; it is in fact fit for slaves,

69c   without soundness or truth, whereas, in truth, temperance and courage and justice are a purging away of all such things, and wisdom itself is a kind of cleansing or purification. It is likely that those who established the mystic rites for us were not inferior persons but were speaking in riddles long ago when they said that whoever arrives in the underworld uninitiated and unsanctified will wallow in the mire, whereas he who arrives there purified and initiated will dwell with the gods. There are indeed, as those concerned with the mysteries say, many who carry the thyrsus but

69d   the Bacchants are few.[20] These latter are, in my opinion, no other than those who have practiced philosophy in the right way. I have in my life left nothing undone in order to be counted among these as far as possible, as I have been eager to be in every way. Whether my eagerness was right and we accomplished anything we shall, I think, know for certain in a short time, god willing, on arriving yonder.

This is my defense, Simmias and Cebes, that I am likely to be right to

69e   leave you and my masters here without resentment or complaint, believing

---

[20] That is, the true worshipers of Dionysus, as opposed to those who only carry the external symbols of his worship.

that there, as here, I shall find good masters and good friends. If my defense is more convincing to you than to the Athenian jury, it will be well.

When Socrates finished, Cebes intervened: Socrates, he said, everything else you said is excellent, I think, but men find it very hard to believe   **70a** what you said about the soul. They think that after it has left the body it no longer exists anywhere, but that it is destroyed and dissolved on the day the man dies, as soon as it leaves the body; and that, on leaving it, it is dispersed like breath or smoke, has flown away and gone and is no longer anything anywhere.[21] If indeed it gathered itself together and existed by itself and escaped those evils you were recently enumerating, there would then be much good hope, Socrates, that what you say is true; but to believe   70b this requires a good deal of faith and persuasive argument, to believe that the soul still exists after a man has died and that it still possesses some capability and intelligence.

What you say is true, Cebes, Socrates said, but what shall we do? Do you want to discuss whether this is likely to be true or not?

Personally, said Cebes, I should like to hear your opinion on the subject.

I do not think, said Socrates, that anyone who heard me now, not even a comic poet, could say that I am babbling and discussing things that do   70c not concern me,[22] so we must examine the question thoroughly, if you think we should do so. Let us examine it in some such a manner as this: whether the souls of men who have died exist in the underworld or not. We recall an ancient theory that souls arriving there come from here, and then again that they arrive here and are born here from the dead. If that is true, that the living come back from the dead, then surely our souls must exist there, for they could not come back if they did not exist, and this is   70d a sufficient proof that these things are so if it truly appears that the living never come from any other source than from the dead. If this is not the case we should need another argument.

Quite so, said Cebes.

Do not, he said, confine yourself to humanity if you want to understand this more readily, but take all animals and all plants into account, and, in short, for all things which come to be, let us see whether they come to be in this way, that is, from their opposites if they have such, as the beautiful   70e is the opposite of the ugly and the just of the unjust, and a thousand other things of the kind. Let us examine whether those that have an opposite must necessarily come to be from their opposite and from nowhere else, as, for example, when something comes to be larger it must necessarily become larger from having been smaller before.

---

21 See Homer, *Iliad* xvi.856, xxii.362, xxiii.100–4 (cited at *Republic* 387a).

22 See *Apology* 19b–c; Aristophanes, *Clouds* 1485.

Yes.

Then if something smaller comes to be, it will come from something
71a larger before, which became smaller?

That is so, he said.

And the weaker comes to be from the stronger, and the swifter from
the slower?

Certainly.

Further, if something worse comes to be, does it not come from the
better, and the juster from the more unjust?

Of course.

So we have sufficiently established that all things come to be in this way,
opposites from opposites?

Certainly.

There is a further point, something such as this, about these opposites:
Between each of those pairs of opposites there are two processes: from the
71b one to the other and then again from the other to the first; between the
larger and the smaller there is increase and decrease, and we call the one
increasing and the other decreasing?

Yes, he said.

And so too there is separation and combination, cooling and heating,
and all such things, even if sometimes we do not have a name for the
process, but in fact it must be everywhere that they come to be from one
another, and that there is a process of becoming from each into the other?

Assuredly, he said.

71c Well then, is there an opposite to living, as sleeping is the opposite of
being awake?

Quite so, he said.

What is it?

Being dead, he said.

Therefore, if these are opposites, they come to be from one another, and
there are two processes of generation between the two?

Of course.

I will tell you, said Socrates, one of the two pairs I was just talking
about, the pair itself and the two processes, and you will tell me the other.
I mean, to sleep and to be awake; to be awake comes from sleeping, and to
71d sleep comes from being awake. Of the two processes one is going to sleep,
the other is waking up.

Do you accept that, or not?

Certainly.

You tell me in the same way about life and death. Do you not say that
to be dead is the opposite of being alive? I do. And they come to be from
one another?

Yes.

What comes to be from being alive?

Being dead.

And what comes to be from being dead?

One must agree that it is being alive.

Then, Cebes, living creatures and things come to be from the dead?

So it appears, he said.   71e

Then our souls exist in the underworld. That seems likely.

Then in this case one of the two processes of becoming is clear, for dying is clear enough, is it not?

It certainly is.

What shall we do then?

Shall we not supply the opposite process of becoming? Is nature to be lame in this case? Or must we provide a process of becoming opposite to dying?

We surely must.

And what is that?

Coming to life again.

Therefore, he said, if there is such a thing as coming to life again, it would be a process of coming from the dead to the living?   72a

Quite so.

It is agreed between us then that the living come from the dead in this way no less than the dead from the living, and, if that is so, it seems to be a sufficient proof that the souls of the dead must be somewhere whence they can come back again.

I think, Socrates, he said, that this follows from what we have agreed on.

Consider in this way, Cebes, he said, that, as I think, we were not wrong to agree. If the two processes of becoming did not always balance each other as if they were going round in a circle, but generation proceeded   72b
from one point to its opposite in a straight line and it did not turn back again to the other opposite or take any turning, do you realize that all things would ultimately be in the same state, be affected in the same way, and cease to become?

How do you mean? he said.

It is not hard to understand what I mean. If, for example, there was such a process as going to sleep, but no corresponding process of waking up, you realize that in the end everything would show the story of Endymion[23] to   72c
have no meaning. There would be no point to it because everything would have the same experience as he had and be asleep. And if everything were combined and nothing separated, the saying of Anaxagoras[24] would soon

---

[23] Endymion was granted eternal sleep by Zeus.

[24] Mentioned at *Apology* 26d. Some of his views are discussed later on (97b–99d).

be true, "that all things were mixed together." In the same way, my dear Cebes, if everything that partakes of life were to die and remain in that state and not come to life again, would not everything ultimately have to be dead and nothing alive? Even if the living came from some other source, and all that lived died, how could all things avoid being absorbed in death?

It could not be, Socrates, said Cebes, and I think what you say is altogether true.

I think, Cebes, said he, that this is very definitely the case and that we were not deceived when we agreed on this: Coming to life again in truth exists, the living come to be from the dead, and the souls of the dead exist.

Furthermore, Socrates, Cebes rejoined, such is also the case if that theory is true that you are accustomed to mention frequently, that for us learning is no other than recollection. According to this, we must at some previous time have learned what we now recollect. This is possible only if our soul existed somewhere before it took on this human shape. So according to this theory too, the soul is likely to be something immortal.

Cebes, Simmias interrupted, what are the proofs of this? Remind me, for I do not quite recall them at the moment.

There is one excellent argument, said Cebes, namely that when men are interrogated in the right manner, they always give the right answer of their own accord, and they could not do this if they did not possess the knowledge and the right explanation inside them. Then if one shows them a diagram or something else of that kind, this will show most clearly that such is the case.[25]

If this does not convince you, Simmias, said Socrates, see whether you agree if we examine it in some such way as this, for do you doubt that what we call learning is recollection?

It is not that I doubt, said Simmias, but I want to experience the very thing we are discussing, recollection, and from what Cebes undertook to say, I am now remembering and am pretty nearly convinced. Nevertheless, I should like to hear now the way you were intending to explain it.

This way, he said. We surely agree that if anyone recollects anything, he must have known it before.

Quite so, he said.

Do we not also agree that when knowledge comes to mind in this way, it is recollection? What way do I mean? Like this: When a man sees or hears or in some other way perceives one thing and not only knows that thing but also thinks of another thing of which the knowledge is not the same but different, are we not right to say that he recollects the second thing that comes into his mind?

---

[25] See *Meno* 81e ff.

How do you mean?

Things such as this: To know a man is surely a different knowledge from knowing a lyre.

Of course.

Well, you know what happens to lovers: whenever they see a lyre, a garment, or anything else that their beloved is accustomed to use, they know the lyre, and the image of the boy to whom it belongs comes into their mind. This is recollection, just as someone, on seeing Simmias, often recollects Cebes, and there are thousands of other such occurrences.

Thousands indeed, said Simmias.

Is this kind of thing not recollection of a kind, he said, especially so 73e when one experiences it about things that one had forgotten, because one had not seen them for some time? — Quite so.

Further, he said, can a man seeing the picture of a horse or a lyre recollect a man, or seeing a picture of Simmias recollect Cebes? — Certainly.

Or seeing a picture of Simmias, recollect Simmias himself? — He certainly can.

In all these cases the recollection can be occasioned by things that are similar, but it can also be occasioned by things that are dissimilar? — It can. 74a

When the recollection is caused by similar things, must one not of necessity also experience this: to consider whether the similarity to that which one recollects is deficient in any respect or complete? — One must.

Consider, he said, whether this is the case: We say that there is something that is equal. I do not mean a stick equal to a stick or a stone to a stone, or anything of that kind, but something else beyond all these, the Equal itself. Shall we say that this exists or not?

Indeed we shall, by Zeus, said Simmias, most definitely. 74b

And do we know what this is? — Certainly.

Whence have we acquired the knowledge of it? Is it not from the things we mentioned just now, from seeing sticks or stones or some other things that are equal we come to think of that other which is different from them? Or doesn't it seem to you to be different? Look at it also this way: Do not equal stones and sticks sometimes, while remaining the same, appear to one to be equal and to another to be unequal? — Certainly they do.

But what of the equals themselves? Have they ever appeared unequal to you, or Equality to be Inequality? 74c

Never, Socrates.

These equal things and the Equal itself are therefore not the same?

I do not think they are the same at all, Socrates.

But it is definitely from the equal things, though they are different from that Equal, that you have derived and grasped the knowledge of equality?

Very true, Socrates.

Whether it be like them or unlike them?

Certainly.

It makes no difference. As long as the sight of one thing makes you
74d think of another, whether it be similar or dissimilar, this must of necessity
be recollection?

Quite so.

Well then, he said, do we experience something like this in the case of
equal sticks and the other equal objects we just mentioned? Do they seem
to us to be equal in the same sense as what is Equal itself? Is there some
deficiency in their being such as the Equal, or is there not?

A considerable deficiency, he said.

Whenever someone, on seeing something, realizes that that which he
now sees wants to be like some other reality but falls short and cannot be
74e like that other since it is inferior, do we agree that the one who thinks
this must have prior knowledge of that to which he says it is like, but
deficiently so?

Necessarily.

Well, do we also experience this about the equal objects and the Equal
itself, or do we not?

Very definitely.

We must then possess knowledge of the Equal before that time when
75a we first saw the equal objects and realized that all these objects strive to be
like the Equal but are deficient in this.

That is so.

Then surely we also agree that this conception of ours derives from
seeing or touching or some other sense perception, and cannot come into
our mind in any other way, for all these senses, I say, are the same.

They are the same, Socrates, at any rate in respect to that which our
argument wishes to make plain.

75b Our sense perceptions must surely make us realize that all that we perceive through them is striving to reach that which is Equal but falls short
of it; or how do we express it?

Like that.

Then before we began to see or hear or otherwise perceive, we must
have possessed knowledge of the Equal itself if we were about to refer our
sense perceptions of equal objects to it, and realized that all of them were
eager to be like it, but were inferior.

That follows from what has been said, Socrates.

But we began to see and hear and otherwise perceive right after birth?

Certainly.

75c We must then have acquired the knowledge of the Equal before this.

Yes.

It seems then that we must have possessed it before birth.

It seems so.

Therefore, if we had this knowledge, we knew before birth and immediately after not only the Equal, but the Greater and the Smaller and all such
things, for our present argument is no more about the Equal than about
the Beautiful itself, the Good itself, the Just, the Pious, and, as I say, about   75d
all those things which we mark with the seal of "what it is," both when
we are putting questions and answering them. So we must have acquired
knowledge of them all before we were born.

That is so.

If, having acquired this knowledge in each case, we have not forgotten
it, we remain knowing and have knowledge throughout our life, for to
know is to acquire knowledge, keep it and not lose it. Do we not call the
losing of knowledge forgetting?

Most certainly, Socrates, he said.   75e

But, I think, if we acquired this knowledge before birth, then lost it
at birth, and then later by the use of our senses in connection with those
objects we mentioned, we recovered the knowledge we had before, would
not what we call learning be the recovery of our own knowledge, and we
are right to call this recollection?

Certainly.

It was seen to be possible for someone to see or hear or otherwise per-   **76a**
ceive something, and by this to be put in mind of something else which
he had forgotten and which is related to it by similarity or difference. One
of two things follows, as I say: either we were born with the knowledge
of it, and all of us know it throughout life, or those who later, we say, are
learning, are only recollecting, and learning would be recollection.

That is certainly the case, Socrates.

Which alternative do you choose, Simmias? That we are born with this
knowledge or that we recollect later the things of which we had knowledge   76b
previously?

I have no means of choosing at the moment, Socrates.

Well, can you make this choice? What is your opinion about it? A man
who has knowledge would be able to give an account[26] of what he knows,
or would he not?

He must certainly be able to do so, Socrates, he said.

And do you think everybody can give an account of the things we were
mentioning just now?

I wish they could, said Simmias, but I'm afraid it is much more likely that
by this time tomorrow there will be no one left who can do so adequately.

So you do not think that everybody has knowledge of those things?   76c

---

[26] That is, give the sort of account of a form—or thing that *is*—that amounts to a
correct and defensible definition of what it is or of its essence. See 78d, *Republic* 534b–c.

No indeed.

So they recollect what they once learned?

They must.

When did our souls acquire the knowledge of them? Certainly not since we were born as men.

Indeed no.

Before that then?

Yes.

So then, Simmias, our souls also existed apart from the body before they took on human form, and they had intelligence.

Unless we acquire the knowledge at the moment of birth, Socrates, for that time is still left to us.

76d Quite so, my friend, but at what other time do we lose it? We just now agreed that we are not born with that knowledge. Do we then lose it at the very time we acquire it, or can you mention any other time?

I cannot, Socrates. I did not realize that I was talking nonsense.

So this is our position, Simmias? he said. If those realities we are always talking about exist, the Beautiful and the Good and all that kind of reality, and we refer all the things we perceive to that reality, discovering that it

76e existed before and is ours, and we compare these things with it, then, just as they exist, so our soul must exist before we are born. If these realities do not exist, then this argument is altogether futile. Is this the position, that there is an equal necessity for those realities to exist, and for our souls to exist before we were born? If the former do not exist, neither do the latter?

I do not think, Socrates, said Simmias, that there is any possible doubt that it is equally necessary for both to exist, and it is opportune that our

77a argument comes to the conclusion that our soul exists before we are born, and equally so that reality of which you are now speaking.

Nothing is so evident to me personally as that all such things must certainly exist, the Beautiful, the Good, and all those you mentioned just now. I also think that sufficient proof of this has been given.

Then what about Cebes? said Socrates, for we must persuade Cebes also.

He is sufficiently convinced I think, said Simmias, though he is the most difficult of men to persuade by argument, but I believe him to be fully

77b convinced that our soul existed before we were born. I do not think myself, however, that it has been proved that the soul continues to exist after death; the opinion of the majority which Cebes mentioned still stands, that when a man dies his soul is dispersed and this is the end of its existence. What is to prevent the soul coming to be and being constituted from some other source, existing before it enters a human body and then, having done so and departed from it, itself dying and being destroyed?

77c You are right, Simmias, said Cebes. Half of what needed proof has been proved, namely, that our soul existed before we were born, but further proof is needed that it exists no less after we have died, if the proof is to be complete.

It has been proved even now, Simmias and Cebes, said Socrates, if you are ready to combine this argument with the one we agreed on before, that every living thing must come from the dead. If the soul exists before, it must, as it comes to life and birth, come from nowhere else than death 77d and being dead, so how could it avoid existing after death since it must be born again? What you speak of has then even now been proved. However, I think you and Simmias would like to discuss the argument more fully. You seem to have this childish fear that the wind would really dissolve and scatter the soul, as it leaves the body, especially if one happens to die in a 77e high wind and not in calm weather.

Cebes laughed and said: Assuming that we were afraid, Socrates, try to change our minds, or rather do not assume that we are afraid, but perhaps there is a child in us who has these fears; try to persuade him not to fear death like a bogeyman.

You should, said Socrates, sing a charm over him every day until you have charmed away his fears.

Where shall we find a good charmer for these fears, Socrates, he said, 78a now that you are leaving us?

Greece is a large country, Cebes, he said, and there are good men in it; the tribes of foreigners are also numerous. You should search for such a charmer among them all, sparing neither trouble nor expense, for there is nothing on which you could spend your money to greater advantage. You must also search among yourselves, for you might not easily find people who could do this better than yourselves.

That shall be done, said Cebes, but let us, if it pleases you, go back to the argument where we left it. 78b

Of course it pleases me.

Splendid, he said.

We must then ask ourselves something like this: What kind of thing is likely to be scattered? On behalf of what kind of thing should one fear this, and for what kind of thing should one not fear it? We should then examine to which class the soul belongs, and as a result either fear for the soul or be of good cheer.

What you say is true.

Is not anything that is composite and a compound by nature liable to be 78c split up into its component parts, and only that which is noncomposite, if anything, is not likely to be split up?

I think that is the case, said Cebes.

Are not the things that always remain the same and in the same state most likely not to be composite, whereas those that vary from one time to another and are never the same are composite?

I think that is so.

Let us then return to those same things with which we were dealing
78d   earlier,[27] to that reality of whose existence we are giving an account in our
questions and answers; are they ever the same and in the same state, or do
they vary from one time to another; can the Equal itself, the Beautiful itself,
each thing in itself, the real, ever be affected by any change whatever? Or
does each of them that really is, being uniform by itself, remain the same
and never in any way tolerate any change whatever?

It must remain the same, said Cebes, and in the same state, Socrates.

What of the many beautiful particulars, be they men, horses, clothes,
78e   or other such things, or the many equal particulars, and all those which
bear the same name as those others? Do they remain the same or, in total
contrast to those other realities, one might say, never in any way remain
the same as themselves or in relation to each other?

The latter is the case; they are never in the same state.

79a   These latter you could touch and see and perceive with the other senses,
but those that always remain the same can be grasped only by the reasoning
power of the mind? They are not seen but are invisible?

That is altogether true, he said.

Do you then want us to assume two kinds of existences, the visible and
the invisible?

Let us assume this.

And the invisible always remains the same, whereas the visible never
does?

Let us assume that too.

79b   Now one part of ourselves is the body, another part is the soul?
Quite so.

To which class of existence do we say the body is more alike and akin?
To the visible, as anyone can see.

What about the soul? Is it visible or invisible?
It is not visible to men, Socrates, he said.

Well, we meant visible and invisible to human eyes. Or do you think
we meant to some others?

To human eyes.

Then what do we say about the soul? Is it visible or not visible?
Not visible.

So it is invisible? — Yes.

So the soul is more like the invisible than the body, and the body more
79c   like the visible? — Without any doubt, Socrates.

---

[27] At 74a–77a.

Haven't we also said some time ago that when the soul makes use of the body to investigate something, be it through hearing or seeing or some other sense—for to investigate something through the body is to do it through the senses—it is dragged by the body to the things that are never the same, and the soul itself strays and is confused and dizzy, as if it were drunk, insofar as it is in contact with that kind of thing?

Certainly.

But when the soul investigates by itself it passes into the realm of what   79d
is pure, ever existing, immortal and unchanging, and being akin to this, it always stays with it whenever it is by itself and can do so; it ceases to stray and remains in the same state as it is in touch with things of the same kind, and its experience then is what is called wisdom?

Altogether well said and very true, Socrates, he said.

Judging from what we have said before and what we are saying now, to which of these two kinds do you think that the soul is more alike and   79e
more akin?

I think, Socrates, he said, that on this line of argument any man, even the dullest, would agree that the soul is altogether more like that which always exists in the same state rather than like that which does not.

What of the body?

That is like the other.

Look at it also this way: When the soul and the body are together, nature orders the one to be subject and to be ruled, and the other to rule and be   80a
master. Then again, which do you think is like the divine and which like the mortal? Do you not think that the nature of the divine is to rule and to lead, whereas it is that of the mortal to be ruled and be subject?

I do.

Which does the soul resemble?

Obviously, Socrates, the soul resembles the divine, and the body resembles the mortal.

Consider then, Cebes, whether it follows from all that has been said that the soul is most like the divine, deathless, intelligible,[28] uniform,   80b
indissoluble, always in the same state as itself, whereas the body is most like that which is human, mortal, multiform, unintelligible, soluble, and never consistently the same. Have we anything else to say to show, my dear Cebes, that this is not the case?

We have not.

Well then, that being so, is it not natural for the body to dissolve easily, and for the soul to be altogether indissoluble, or nearly so?

---

[28] *Noēton:* the first occurrence of this word in Plato. What is intelligible is an object of thought, not of sense-perception, and so is contrasted with what is perceptible. See *Republic* 507a–b.

80c   Of course.

You realize, he said, that when a man dies, the visible part, the body, which exists in the visible world, and which we call the corpse, whose natural lot it would be to dissolve, fall apart, and be blown away, does not immediately suffer any of these things but remains for a fair time, in fact, quite a long time if the man dies with his body in a suitable condition and at a favorable season? If the body is emaciated or embalmed, as in Egypt, it remains almost whole for a remarkable length of time, and even if the
80d   body decays, some parts of it, namely bones and sinews and the like, are nevertheless, one might say, deathless. Is that not so? — Yes.

Will the soul, the invisible part which makes its way to a region of the same kind, noble and pure and invisible, to Hades in the true sense, to the good and wise god,[29] whither, god willing, my soul must soon be going—will the soul, being of this kind and nature, be scattered and destroyed on leaving the body, as the majority of men say? Far from it, my
80e   dear Cebes and Simmias, but what happens is much more like this: If it is pure when it leaves the body and drags nothing bodily with it, as it had no willing association with the body in life, but avoided it and gathered itself together by itself and always practiced this, which is no other than
81a   practicing philosophy in the right way, in fact, training to die easily. Or is this not training for death?

It surely is.

A soul in this state makes its way to the invisible, which is like itself, the divine and immortal and wise, and arriving there it can be happy, having rid itself of confusion, ignorance, fear, violent desires, and the other human ills and, as is said of the initiates,[30] truly spend the rest of time with the gods. Shall we say this, Cebes, or something different?

This, by Zeus, said Cebes.

81b   But I think that if the soul is polluted and impure when it leaves the body, having always been associated with it and served it, bewitched by physical desires and pleasures to the point at which nothing seems real[31] to it but the physical, which one can touch and see or eat and drink or make use of for sexual enjoyment, and if that soul is accustomed to hate and fear and avoid that which is dim and invisible to the eyes but intelligible and to be grasped by philosophy—do you think such a soul will escape pure
81c   and by itself?

Impossible, he said.

---

[29] "It is much more likely . . . that Hades derives his name [*Haidēs*] not from what cannot be seen [*aidēs,* which means "invisible"], but from the fact that he knows [*eidenai*] everything fine and beautiful" (*Cratylus* 404b).

[30] Those initiated into a religious cult promising eternal rewards.

[31] *Alēthes:* also "true."

It is no doubt permeated by the physical, which constant intercourse and association with the body, as well as considerable practice, has caused to become ingrained in it?

Quite so.

We must believe, my friend, that this bodily element is heavy, ponderous, earthy, and visible. Through it, such a soul has become heavy and is dragged back to the visible region in fear of the unseen and of Hades. It wanders, as we are told, around graves and monuments, where shadowy   81d
phantoms, images that such souls produce, have been seen, souls that have not been freed and purified but share in the visible, and are therefore seen.

That is likely, Socrates.

It is indeed, Cebes. Moreover, these are not the souls of good but of inferior men, which are forced to wander there, paying the penalty for their   81e
previous bad upbringing. They wander until their longing for that which accompanies them, the physical, again imprisons them in a body, and they are then, as is likely, bound to such characters as they have practiced in their life.

What kind of characters do you say these are, Socrates?

Those, for example, who have carelessly practiced gluttony, violence, and drunkenness are likely to join a company of donkeys or of similar animals. Do you not think so?   **82a**

Very likely.

Those who have esteemed injustice highly, and tyranny and plunder, will join the tribes of wolves and hawks and kites, or where else shall we say that they go?

Certainly to those, said Cebes.

And clearly, the destination of the others will conform to the way in which they have behaved?

Clearly, of course.

The happiest of these, who will also have the best destination, are those who have practiced popular and social virtue, which they call modera-   82b
tion and justice and which was developed by habit and practice, without philosophy or understanding?

How are they the happiest?

Because it is likely that they will again join a social and gentle group, either of bees or wasps or ants, and then again the same kind of human group, and so be temperate men.

That is likely.

No one may lawfully[32] join the company of the gods who has not practiced philosophy and is not completely pure when he departs from life,   82c

---

[32] See 61c note.

but only the lover of learning. It is for this reason, my friends Simmias and Cebes, that those who practice philosophy in the right way keep away from all bodily passions, master them and do not surrender themselves to them; it is not at all for fear of wasting their substance and of poverty, which the majority and the money-lovers fear, nor for fear of dishonor and ill repute, like the ambitious and lovers of honors, that they keep away from them.

That would not be natural for them, Socrates, said Cebes.

82d   By Zeus, no, he said. Those who care for their own soul and do not live for the service of their body dismiss all these things. They do not travel the same road as those, since they are aware that they do not know where they are going. Rather, believing that nothing should be done contrary to philosophy and their deliverance and purification, they turn to this and follow wherever philosophy leads.

How so, Socrates?

I will tell you, he said. The lovers of learning know that when philoso-
82e   phy gets hold of their soul, it is imprisoned in and clinging to the body, and that it is forced to examine other things through it as through a cage and not by itself, and that it wallows in every kind of ignorance. Philosophy sees that the worst feature of this imprisonment is that it is due to desires, so that the prisoner himself is contributing to his own incarceration most
83a   of all. As I say, the lovers of learning know that philosophy gets hold of their soul when it is in that state, then gently encourages it and tries to free it by showing them that investigation through the eyes is full of deceit, as is that through the ears and the other senses. Philosophy then persuades the soul to withdraw from the senses insofar as it is not compelled to use them and bids the soul to gather itself together by itself, to trust only itself
83b   and whatever reality, existing by itself, the soul by itself understands, and not to consider as real[33] whatever it examines by other means, for this is different in different circumstances and is sensible and visible, whereas what the soul itself sees is intelligible and invisible. The soul of the true philosopher thinks that this deliverance must not be opposed and so keeps away from pleasures and desires and pains as far as he can; he reflects that violent pleasure or pain or passion does not cause merely such evils as one might expect, such as one suffers when one has been sick or extravagant
83c   through desire, but the greatest and most extreme evil, though one does not reflect on this.

What is that, Socrates? asked Cebes.

That the soul of every man, when it feels violent pleasure or pain in connection with some object, inevitably believes at the same time that what causes such feelings must be very clear and very true, which it is not. Such objects are mostly visible, are they not?

---

[33] *Alēthes:* see 81b and note.

Certainly.

And doesn't such an experience tie the soul to the body most completely? **83d**

How so?

Because every pleasure or pain provides, as it were, another nail to rivet the soul to the body and to weld them together. It makes the soul corporeal, so that it believes real the very things the body says are so. As it shares the beliefs and pleasures of the body, I think it inevitably comes to share its ways and manner of life and is unable ever to reach Hades in a pure state; it is always full of body when it departs, so that it soon falls back into another **83e** body and grows with it as if it had been sewn into it. Because of this, it can have no part in the company of the divine, the pure and uniform.

What you say is very true, Socrates, said Cebes.

This is why genuine lovers of learning are temperate and brave, or do you think it is for the reasons the majority says they are?

I certainly do not. **84a**

Indeed no. This is how the soul of a philosopher would reason: It would not think that while philosophy must free it, it should while being freed surrender itself to pleasures and pains and imprison itself again, thus laboring in vain like Penelope at her web.[34] The soul of the philosopher achieves a calm from such emotions; it follows reason and ever stays with it contemplating what is real, divine, and not an object of belief. Nurtured by this, it considers that one should live in this manner as long as one is alive and, **84b** after death, arrive at what is akin and of the same kind, and escape from human evils. After such nurture there is no danger, Simmias and Cebes, that one should fear that, on parting from the body, the soul would be scattered and dissipated by the winds and no longer be anything anywhere.

When Socrates finished speaking there was a long silence. He appeared **84c** to be concentrating on what had been said, and so were most of us. But Cebes and Simmias were whispering to each other. Socrates observed them and questioned them. Come, he said, do you think there is something lacking in my argument? There are still many doubtful points and many objections for anyone who wants a thorough discussion of these matters. If you are discussing some other subject, I have nothing to say, but if something is puzzling you[35] about this one, do not hesitate to speak for yourselves and expound it if you think the argument could be improved, **84d** and if you think you will better solve your puzzles with my help, take me along with you in the discussion.

I will tell you the truth, Socrates, said Simmias. Both of us have been in difficulty for some time, and each of us has been urging the other to

---

[34] In Homer's *Odyssey,* Penelope picked apart at night what she had woven during the day.

[35] *Aporeiton:* Socrates' method of examination often results in *aporia* or puzzlement.

question you because we wanted to hear what you would say, but we hesitated to bother you, lest it be displeasing to you in your present misfortune.

When Socrates heard this he laughed quietly and said: "Really, Simmias, 84e it would be hard for me to persuade other people that I do not consider my present fate a misfortune if I cannot persuade even you, and you are afraid that it is more difficult to deal with me than before. You seem to think me inferior to the swans in prophecy.[36] They sing before too, but when 85a they realize that they must die they sing most and most beautifully, as they rejoice that they are about to depart to join the god whose servants they are. But men, because of their own fear of death, tell lies about the swans and say that they lament their death and sing in sorrow. They do not reflect that no bird sings when it is hungry or cold or suffers in any other way, neither the nightingale nor the swallow nor the hoopoe,[37] though they do say that these sing laments when in pain. Nor do the swans, but I believe 85b that as they belong to Apollo, they are prophetic, have knowledge of the future, and sing of the blessings of the underworld, sing and rejoice on that day beyond what they did before. As I believe myself to be a fellow servant with the swans and dedicated to the same god, and have received from my master a gift of prophecy not inferior to theirs, I am no more despondent than they on leaving life. Therefore, you must speak and ask whatever you want as long as the authorities allow it."

Well spoken, said Simmias. I will tell you my difficulty, and then Cebes 85c will say why he does not accept what was said. I believe, as perhaps you do, that precise knowledge on that subject is impossible or extremely difficult in our present life, but that it surely shows a very poor spirit not to examine[38] thoroughly what is said about it, and to desist before one is exhausted by an all-around investigation. One should achieve one of these things: learn the truth about these things or find it for oneself, or, if that is impossible, adopt the best and most irrefutable of men's theories, and, borne 85d upon this, sail through the dangers of life as upon a raft, unless someone should make that journey safer and less risky upon a firmer vessel of some divine doctrine. So even now, since you have said what you did, I will feel no shame at asking questions, and I will not blame myself in the future because I did not say what I think. As I examine what we said, both by myself and with Cebes, it does not seem to be adequate.

---

[36] Swans are traditionally associated with Apollo. See, e.g., Sappho *fr.* 208; Aristophanes, *Birds* 769–73.

[37] Tereus raped Philomela, the sister of his wife Procne. As a result, he was transformed into a hoopoe, Procne into a nightingale, and Philomela into a swallow. Hence these birds, if any, should sing lamentations.

[38] *Elengchein:* i.e., submit to the sort of examination characteristically employed by Socrates, which we call an elenchus.

Said Socrates: "You may well be right, my friend, but tell me how it is 85e inadequate."

In this way, as it seems to me, he said: "One might make the same argument about harmony, lyre and strings, that a harmony is something invisible, without body, beautiful and divine in the attuned lyre, whereas the lyre itself and its strings are physical, bodily, composite, earthy, and 86a akin to what is mortal. Then if someone breaks the lyre, cuts or breaks the strings and then insists, using the same argument as you, that the harmony must still exist and is not destroyed because it would be impossible for the lyre and the strings, which are mortal, still to exist when the strings are broken, and for the harmony, which is akin and of the same nature as the divine and immortal, to be destroyed before that which is mortal; he would 86b say that the harmony itself still must exist and that the wood and the strings must rot before the harmony can suffer. And indeed, Socrates, I think you must have this in mind, that we really do suppose the soul to be something of this kind; as the body is stretched and held together by the hot and the cold, the dry and the moist, and other such things, and our soul is a mixture and harmony of those things when they are mixed with each other rightly 86c and in due measure. If then the soul is a kind of harmony or attunement, clearly, when our body is relaxed or stretched without due measure by diseases and other evils, the soul must immediately be destroyed, even if it be most divine, as are the other harmonies found in music and all the works of artists, and the remains of each body last for a long time until they rot or are burned. Consider what we shall say in answer to one who deems 86d the soul to be a mixture of bodily elements and to be the first to perish in the process we call death."

Socrates looked at us keenly, as was his habit, smiled, and said: "What Simmias says is quite fair. If one of you can better address his puzzles, why did he not answer him, for he seems to have handled the argument competently. However, I think that before we answer him, we should hear Cebes' objection, in order that we may have time to deliberate on an 86e answer. When we have heard him we should either agree with them, if we think them in tune with us or, if not, defend our own argument. Come then, Cebes. What is troubling you?"

I tell you, said Cebes, the argument seems to me to be at the same point 87a as before and open to the same objection. I do not deny that it has been very elegantly and, if it is not offensive to say so, sufficiently proved that our soul existed before it took on this present form, but I do not believe the same applies to its existing somewhere after our death. Not that I agree with Simmias' objection that the soul is not stronger and much more lasting than the body, for I think it is superior in all these respects. "Why then," the argument might say, "are you still unconvinced? Since you see that when the man dies, the weaker part continues to exist, do you not think

87b   that the more lasting part must be preserved during that time?" On this
point consider whether what I say makes sense.

Like Simmias, I too need an image, for I think this argument is much
as if one said at the death of an old weaver that the man had not perished
but was safe and sound somewhere, and offered as proof the fact that the
cloak the old man had woven himself and was wearing was still sound and
had not perished. If one was not convinced, he would be asked whether
87c   a man lasts longer than a cloak which is in use and being worn, and if the
answer was that a man lasts much longer, this would be taken as proof that
the man was definitely safe and sound, since the more temporary thing had
not perished. But, Simmias, I do not think that is so, for consider what I
say. Anybody could see that the man who said this was talking nonsense.
That weaver had woven and worn out many such cloaks. He perished after
87d   many of them, but before the last. That does not mean that a man is inferior
and weaker than a cloak. The image illustrates, I think, the relationship
of the soul to the body, and anyone who says the same thing about them
would appear to me to be talking sense, that the soul lasts a long time
while the body is weaker and more short-lived. He might say that each
soul wears out many bodies, especially if it lives many years. If the body
were in a state of flux and perished while the man was still alive, and the
87e   soul wove afresh the body that is worn out, yet it would be inevitable that
whenever the soul perished it would be wearing the last body it wove and
perish only before this last. Then when the soul perished, the body would
show the weakness of its nature by soon decaying and disappearing. So
we cannot trust this argument and be confident that our soul continues to
88a   exist somewhere after our death. For, if one were to concede, even more
than you do, to a man using that argument, if one were to grant him not
only that the soul exists in the time before we are born, but that there is
no reason why the soul of some should not exist and continue to exist after
our death, and thus frequently be born and die in turn; if one were to grant
him that the soul's nature is so strong that it can survive many bodies, but
if, having granted all this, one does not further agree that the soul is not
damaged by its many births and is not, in the end, altogether destroyed
in one of those deaths, he might say that no one knows which death and
88b   dissolution of the body brings about the destruction of the soul, since not
one of us can be aware of this. And in that case, any man who faces death
with confidence is foolish, unless he can prove that the soul is altogether
immortal. If he cannot, a man about to die must of necessity always fear for
his soul, lest the present separation of the soul from the body bring about
the complete destruction of the soul.

88c   When we heard what they said we were all depressed, as we told each
other afterwards. We had been quite convinced by the previous argument,
and they seemed to confuse us again, and to drive us to doubt not only

what had already been said but also what was going to be said, lest we be worthless as critics or the subject itself admitted of no certainty.

ECHECRATES: By the gods, Phaedo, you have my sympathy, for as I listen to you now I find myself saying to myself: "What argument shall we trust, 88d now that that of Socrates, which was extremely convincing, has fallen into discredit?" The statement that the soul is some kind of harmony has a remarkable hold on me, now and always, and when it was mentioned it reminded me that I had myself previously thought so. And now I am again quite in need, as if from the beginning, of some other argument to convince me that the soul does not die along with the man. Tell me then, by Zeus, how Socrates tackled the argument. Was he obviously distressed, as you say you people were, or was he not, but quietly came to the rescue 88e of his argument, and did he do so satisfactorily or inadequately? Tell us everything as precisely as you can.

PHAEDO: I have certainly often admired Socrates, Echecrates, but never more than on this occasion. That he had a reply was perhaps not strange. **89a** What I wondered at most in him was the pleasant, kind, and admiring way he received the young men's argument, and how sharply he was aware of the effect the discussion had on us, and then how well he healed our distress and, as it were, recalled us from our flight and defeat and turned us around to join him in the examination of their argument.

ECHECRATES: How did he do this?

PHAEDO: I will tell you. I happened to be sitting on his right by the couch 89b on a low stool, so that he was sitting well above me. He stroked my head and pressed the hair on the back of my neck, for he was in the habit of playing with my hair at times. "Tomorrow, Phaedo," he said, "you will probably cut this beautiful hair."

Likely enough, Socrates, I said.

Not if you take my advice, he said.

Why not? said I.

It is today, he said, that I shall cut my hair and you yours, if our argument dies on us, and we cannot revive it. If I were you, and the argument escaped me, I would take an oath, as the Argives did, not to let my hair 89c grow before I fought again and defeated the argument of Simmias and Cebes.

But, I said, they say that not even Heracles could fight two people.

Then call on me as your Iolaus, as long as the daylight lasts.

I shall call on you, but in this case as Iolaus calling on Heracles.

It makes no difference, he said, but first there is a certain experience we must be careful to avoid.

What is that? I asked.

89d   That we should not become misologues, as people become misanthropes. There is no greater evil one can suffer than to hate reasonable discourse. Misology and misanthropy arise in the same way. Misanthropy comes when a man without knowledge or skill has placed great trust in someone and believes him to be altogether truthful, sound, and trustworthy; then, a short time afterwards he finds him to be wicked and unreliable, and then this happens in another case; when one has frequently had that experience,

89e   especially with those whom one believed to be one's closest friends, then, in the end, after many such blows, one comes to hate all men and to believe that no one is sound in any way at all. Have you not seen this happen?

I surely have, I said.

This is a shameful state of affairs, he said, and obviously due to an attempt to have human relations without any skill in human affairs, for such skill would lead one to believe, what is in fact true, that the very good

90a   and the very wicked are both quite rare, and that most men are between those extremes.

How do you mean? said I.

The same as with the very tall and the very short, he said. Do you think anything is rarer than to find an extremely tall man or an extremely short one? Or a dog or anything else whatever? Or again, one extremely swift or extremely slow, ugly or beautiful, white or black? Are you not aware that in all those cases the most extreme at either end are rare and few, but those in between are many and plentiful?

Certainly, I said.

90b   Therefore, he said, if a contest of wickedness were established, there too the winners, you think, would be very few?

That is likely, said I.

Likely indeed, he said, but arguments are not like men in this particular. I was merely following your lead just now. The similarity lies rather in this: It is as when one who lacks skill in arguments puts his trust in an argument as being true, then shortly afterwards believes it to be false—as sometimes it is and sometimes it is not—and so with another argument and then another. You know how those in particular who spend their time

90c   studying contradiction in the end believe themselves to have become very wise and that they alone have understood that there is no soundness or reliability in any object or in any argument, but that all that exists simply fluctuates up and down as if it were in the Euripus[39] and does not remain in the same place for any time at all.

What you say, I said, is certainly true.

---

[39] The Euripus is the strait between the island of Euboea and Boeotia on the Greek mainland; its currents were both violent and variable.

It would be pitiable, Phaedo, he said, when there is a true and reliable argument and one that can be understood, if a man who has dealt with 90d such arguments as appear at one time true, at another time untrue, should not blame himself or his own lack of skill but, because of his distress, in the end gladly shift the blame away from himself to the arguments, and spend the rest of his life hating and reviling reasoned discussion and so be deprived of truth and knowledge of reality.

Yes, by Zeus, I said, that would be pitiable indeed.

This then is the first thing we should guard against, he said. We should not allow into our minds the conviction that argumentation has nothing 90e sound about it; much rather we should believe that it is we who are not yet sound and that we must take courage and be eager to attain soundness, you and the others for the sake of your whole life still to come, and I for the sake of death itself. I am in danger at this moment of not having a philosophical 91a attitude about this, but like those who are quite uneducated, I am eager to get the better of you in argument, for the uneducated, when they engage in argument about anything, give no thought to the truth about the subject of discussion but are only eager that those present will accept the position they have set forth. I differ from them only to this extent: I shall not be eager to get the agreement of those present that what I say is true, except incidentally, but I shall be very eager that I should myself be thoroughly convinced that things are so. For I am thinking—see in how contentious a spirit—that if what I say is true, it is a fine thing to be convinced; if, on 91b the other hand, nothing exists after death, at least for this time before I die I shall distress those present less with lamentations, and my folly will not continue to exist along with me—that would be a bad thing—but will come to an end in a short time. Thus prepared, Simmias and Cebes, he said, I come to deal with your argument. If you will take my advice, you will give but little thought to Socrates but much more to the truth. If you think that what I say is true, agree with me; if not, oppose it with every 91c argument and take care that in my eagerness I do not deceive myself and you and, like a bee, leave my sting in you when I go.

We must proceed, he said, and first remind me of what you said if I do not appear to remember it. Simmias, as I believe, is in doubt and fear that the soul, though it is more divine and beautiful than the body, yet predeceases it, being a kind of harmony. Cebes, I thought, agrees with me that 91d the soul lasts much longer than the body, but that no one knows whether the soul often wears out many bodies and then, on leaving its last body, is now itself destroyed. This then is death, the destruction of the soul, since the body is always being destroyed. Are these the questions, Simmias and Cebes, which we must investigate?

They both agreed that they were.   91e

Do you then, he asked, reject all our previous statements, or some but not others?

Some, they both said, but not others.

What, he said, about the statements we made that learning is recollection and that, if this was so, our soul must of necessity exist elsewhere before
92a   us, before it was imprisoned in the body?

For myself, said Cebes, I was wonderfully convinced by it at the time and I stand by it now also, more than by any other statement.

That, said Simmias, is also my position, and I should be very surprised if I ever changed my opinion about this.

But you must change your opinion, my Theban friend, said Socrates, if you still believe that a harmony is a composite thing, and that the soul is a kind of harmony of the elements of the body in a state of tension, for surely
92b   you will not allow yourself to maintain that a composite harmony existed before those elements from which it had to be composed, or would you?

Never, Socrates, he said.

Do you realize, he said, that this is what you are in fact saying when you state that the soul exists before it takes on the form and body of a man and that it is composed of elements which do not yet exist? A harmony is not like that to which you compare it; the lyre and the strings and the notes,
92c   though still unharmonized, exist; the harmony is composed last of all, and is the first to be destroyed. How will you harmonize this statement with your former one?

In no way, said Simmias.

And surely, he said, a statement about harmony should do so more than any other.

It should, said Simmias.

So your statement is inconsistent? Consider which of your statements you prefer, that learning is recollection or that the soul is a harmony.

I much prefer the former, Socrates. I adopted the latter without proof,
92d   because of a certain probability and plausibility, which is why it appeals to most men. I know that arguments of which the proof is based on probability are pretentious and, if one does not guard against them, they certainly deceive one, in geometry and everything else. The theory of recollection and learning, however, was based on an assumption worthy of acceptance, for our soul was said to exist also before it came into the body, just as the reality does that is of the kind that we qualify by the words "what it is,"
92e   and I convinced myself that I was quite correct to accept it. Therefore, I cannot accept the theory that the soul is a harmony either from myself or anyone else.

93a   What of this, Simmias? Do you think it natural for a harmony, or any other composite, to be in a different state from that of the elements of which it is composed?

Not at all, said Simmias.

Nor, as I think, can it act or be acted upon in a different way than its elements?

He agreed.

One must therefore suppose that a harmony does not direct its components, but is directed by them.

He accepted this.

A harmony is therefore far from making a movement, or uttering a sound, or doing anything else, in a manner contrary to that of its parts.

Far from it indeed, he said.

Does not the nature of each harmony depend on the way it has been harmonized?

I do not understand, he said.

Will it not, if it is more and more fully harmonized, be more and more fully a harmony, and if it is less and less fully harmonized, it will be less 93b and less fully a harmony?

Certainly.

Can this be true about the soul, that one soul is more and more fully a soul than another, or is less and less fully a soul, even to the smallest extent?

Not in any way.

Come now, by Zeus, he said. One soul is said to have intelligence and virtue and to be good, another to have folly and wickedness and to be bad. Are those things truly said?   93c

They certainly are.

What will someone who holds the theory that the soul is a harmony say that those things are which reside in the soul, that is, virtue and wickedness? Are these some other harmony and disharmony? That the good soul is harmonized and, being a harmony, has within itself another harmony, whereas the evil soul is both itself a lack of harmony and has no other within itself?

I don't know what to say, said Simmias, but one who holds that assumption must obviously say something of that kind.

We have previously agreed, he said, that one soul is not more and not 93d less a soul than another, and this means that one harmony is not more and more fully, or less and less fully, a harmony than another.

Is that not so?

Certainly.

Now that which is no more and no less a harmony is not more or less harmonized. Is that so?

It is.

Can that which is neither more nor less harmonized partake more or less of harmony, or does it do so equally?

Equally.

Then if a soul is neither more nor less a soul than another, it has been
93e harmonized to the same extent?

This is so.

If that is so, it would have no greater share of disharmony or of harmony?

It would not.

That being the case, could one soul have more wickedness or virtue than
another, if wickedness is disharmony and virtue harmony?

It could not.

94a But rather, Simmias, according to correct reasoning, no soul, if it is a
harmony, will have any share of wickedness, for harmony is surely altogether this very thing, harmony, and would never share in disharmony.

It certainly would not.

Nor would a soul, being altogether this very thing, a soul, share in
wickedness?

How could it, in view of what has been said?

So it follows from this argument that all the souls of all living creatures
will be equally good, if souls are by nature equally this very thing, souls.

I think so, Socrates.

Does our argument seem right, he said, and does it seem that it should
94b have come to this, if the hypothesis that the soul is a harmony was correct?

Not in any way, he said.

Further, of all the parts of a man, can you mention any other part that
rules him than his soul, especially if it is a wise soul?

I cannot.

Does it do so by following the affections of the body or by opposing
them? I mean, for example, that when the body is hot and thirsty the soul
draws him to the opposite, to not drinking; when the body is hungry, to
not eating, and we see a thousand other examples of the soul opposing the
94c affections of the body. Is that not so?

It certainly is.

On the other hand, we previously agreed that if the soul were a harmony, it would never be out of tune with the stress and relaxation and the
striking of the strings or anything else done to its composing elements, but
that it would follow and never direct them?

We did so agree, of course.

Well, does it now appear to do quite the opposite, ruling over all the
94d elements of which one says it is composed, opposing nearly all of them
throughout life, directing all their ways, inflicting harsh and painful punishment on them, at times in physical culture and medicine, at other times
more gently by threats and exhortations, holding converse with desires and
passions and fears as if it were one thing talking to a different one, as Homer
wrote somewhere in the Odyssey where he says that Odysseus "struck his

breast and rebuked his heart saying, 'Endure, my heart, you have endured
worse than this'"?[40]   94e

Do you think that when he composed this the poet thought that his
soul was a harmony, a thing to be directed by the affections of the body?
Did he not rather regard it as ruling over them and mastering them, itself
a much more divine thing than a harmony?

Yes, by Zeus, I think so, Socrates.

Therefore, my good friend, it is quite wrong for us to say that the soul is
a harmony, and in saying so we would disagree both with the divine poet   95a
Homer and with ourselves.

That is so, he said.

Very well, said Socrates. Harmonia of Thebes seems somehow reasonably propitious to us. How and by what argument, my dear Cebes, can we
propitiate Cadmus?[41]

I think, Cebes said, that you will find a way. You dealt with the argument about harmony in a manner that was quite astonishing to me. When
Simmias was speaking of his difficulties I was very much wondering
whether anyone would be able to deal with his argument, and I was quite   95b
dumbfounded when right away he could not resist your argument's first
onslaught. I should not wonder, therefore, if that of Cadmus suffered the
same fate.

My good sir, said Socrates, do not boast, lest some malign influence
upset the argument we are about to make. However, we leave that to the
care of the god, but let us come to grips with it in the Homeric fashion, to
see if there is anything in what you say. The sum of your problem is this:
You consider that the soul must be proved to be immortal and indestructible before a philosopher on the point of death, who is confident that he   95c
will fare much better in the underworld than if he had led any other kind of
life, can avoid being foolish and simpleminded in this confidence. To prove
that the soul is strong, that it is divine, that it existed before we were born as
men, all this, you say, does not show the soul to be immortal but only long-
lasting. That it existed for a very long time before, that it knew much and
acted much, makes it no more immortal because of that; indeed, its very   95d
entering into a human body was the beginning of its destruction, like a
disease; it would live that life in distress and would in the end be destroyed
in what we call death. You say it makes no difference whether it enters a
body once or many times as far as the fear of each of us is concerned, for

---

[40] *Odyssey* xx.17–18.

[41] Harmonia was in legend the wife of Cadmus, the founder of Thebes. Socrates'
punning joke is simply that, having dealt with Harmonia (harmony), we must now
deal with Cadmus (i.e., Cebes, the other Theban).

95e it is natural for a man who is no fool to be afraid, if he does not know and cannot prove that the soul is immortal. This, I think, is what you maintain, Cebes; I deliberately repeat it often, in order that no point may escape us, and that you may add or subtract something if you wish.

And Cebes said: "There is nothing that I want to add or subtract at the moment. That is what I say."

Socrates paused for a long time, deep in thought. He then said: "This is no unimportant problem that you raise, Cebes, for it requires a thorough

96a investigation of the cause of generation and destruction. I will, if you wish, give you an account of my experience in these matters. Then if something I say seems useful to you, make use of it to persuade us of your position."

I surely do wish that, said Cebes.

Listen then, and I will, Cebes, he said. When I was a young man I was wonderfully keen on that wisdom which they call natural science, for I thought it splendid to know the causes of everything, why it comes to be, why it perishes, and why it exists. I was often changing my mind in the

96b investigation, in the first instance, of questions such as these: Are living creatures nurtured when heat and cold produce a kind of putrefaction, as some say? Do we think with our blood, or air, or fire, or none of these, and does the brain provide our senses of hearing and sight and smell, from which come memory and opinion, and from memory and opinion which has become stable, comes knowledge? Then again, as I investigated how these things perish and what happens to things in the sky and on the earth,

96c finally I became convinced that I have no natural aptitude at all for that kind of investigation, and of this I will give you sufficient proof. This investigation made me quite blind even to those things which I and others thought that I clearly knew before, so that I unlearned what I thought I knew before, about many other things and specifically about how men grew. I thought before that it was obvious to anybody that men grew

96d through eating and drinking, for food adds flesh to flesh and bones to bones, and in the same way appropriate parts were added to all other parts of the body, so that the man grew from an earlier small bulk to a large bulk later, and so a small man became big. That is what I thought then. Do you not think it was reasonable?

I do, said Cebes.

Then further consider this: I thought my opinion was satisfactory, that when a large man stood by a small one he was taller by a head, and so a

96e horse was taller than a horse. Even clearer than this, I thought that ten was more than eight because two had been added, and that a two-cubit length is larger than a cubit because it surpasses it by half its length.

And what do you think now about those things?

That I am far, by Zeus, from believing that I know the cause of any of those things. I will not even allow myself to say that where one is added

to one either the one to which it is added or the one that is added becomes
two, or that the one added and the one to which it is added become two   **97a**
because of the addition of the one to the other. I wonder that, when each
of them is separate from the other, each of them is one, nor are they then
two, but that, when they come near to one another, this is the cause of
their becoming two, the coming together and being placed closer to one
another. Nor can I any longer be persuaded that when one thing is divided,
this division is the cause of its becoming two, for just now the cause of
becoming two was the opposite. At that time it was their coming close   **97b**
together and one was added to the other, but now it is because one is taken
and separated from the other.

I do not any longer persuade myself that I know why a unit or anything
else comes to be, or perishes or exists by the old method of investigation,
and I do not accept it, but I have a confused method of my own. One day
I heard someone reading, as he said, from a book of Anaxagoras,[42] and
saying that it is Mind that directs and is the cause of everything. I was   **97c**
delighted with this cause and it seemed to me good, in a way, that Mind
should be the cause of all. I thought that if this were so, the directing Mind
would direct everything and arrange each thing in the way that was best.
If then one wished to know the cause of each thing, why it comes to be
or perishes or exists, one had to find what was the best way for it to be,
or to be acted upon, or to act. On these premises then it befitted a man   **97d**
to investigate only, about this and other things, what is best. The same
man must inevitably also know what is worse, for that is part of the same
knowledge. As I reflected on this subject I was glad to think that I had
found in Anaxagoras a teacher about the cause of things after my own
heart, and that he would tell me, first, whether the earth is flat or round,
and then would explain why it is so of necessity, saying which is better, and   **97e**
that it was better to be so. If he said it was in the middle of the universe,
he would go on to show that it was better for it to be in the middle, and
if he showed me those things I should be prepared never to desire any   **98a**
other kind of cause. I was ready to find out in the same way about the sun
and the moon and the other heavenly bodies, about their relative speed,
their turnings, and whatever else happened to them, how it is best that
each should act or be acted upon. I never thought that Anaxagoras, who
said that those things were directed by Mind, would bring in any other
cause for them than that it was best for them to be as they are. Once he
had given the best for each as the cause for each and the general cause of   **98b**
all, I thought he would go on to explain the common good for all, and I
would not have exchanged my hopes for a fortune. I eagerly acquired his

---

[42] Anaxagoras of Clazomenae (c. 500–428 BCE). Mentioned at *Apology* 26d.

books and read them as quickly as I could in order to know the best and
the worst as soon as possible.

This wonderful hope was dashed as I went on reading and saw that the
man made no use of Mind, nor gave it any responsibility for the manage-

98c   ment of things, but mentioned as causes air and ether and water and many
other strange things. That seemed to me much like saying that Socrates'
actions are all due to his mind, and then in trying to tell the causes of
everything I do, to say that the reason that I am sitting here is because
my body consists of bones and sinews, because the bones are hard and
are separated by joints, that the sinews are such as to contract and relax,

98d   that they surround the bones along with flesh and skin which hold them
together, then as the bones are hanging in their sockets, the relaxation and
contraction of the sinews enable me to bend my limbs, and that is the cause
of my sitting here with my limbs bent.

Again, he would mention other such causes for my talking to you:
sounds and air and hearing, and a thousand other such things, but he would

98e   neglect to mention the true causes, that, after the Athenians decided it was
better to condemn me, for this reason it seemed best to me to sit here and
more right to remain and to endure whatever penalty they ordered. For,
by the dog, I think these sinews and bones could long ago have been in

99a   Megara or among the Boeotians, taken there by my belief as to the best
course, if I had not thought it more right and honorable to endure whatever
penalty the city ordered rather than escape and run away. To call those
things causes is too absurd. If someone said that without bones and sinews
and all such things, I should not be able to do what I decided, he would
be right, but surely to say that they are the cause of what I do, and not

99b   that I have chosen the best course, even though I act with my mind, is to
speak very lazily and carelessly. Imagine not being able to distinguish the
real cause from that without which the cause would not be able to act as a
cause. It is what the majority appear to do, like people groping in the dark;
they call it a cause, thus giving it a name that does not belong to it. That is
why one man surrounds the earth with a vortex to make the heavens keep
it in place, another makes the air support it like a wide lid. As for their

99c   capacity of being in the best place they could possibly be put, this they
do not look for, nor do they believe it to have any divine force, but they
believe that they will some time discover a stronger and more immortal
Atlas to hold everything together more, and they do not believe that the
truly good and "binding" binds and holds them together. I would gladly
become the disciple of any man who taught the workings of that kind of
cause. However, since I was deprived and could neither discover it myself
nor learn it from another, do you wish me to give you an explanation of

99d   how, as a second best, I busied myself with the search for the cause, Cebes?

I would wish it above all else, he said.

After this, he said, when I had wearied of investigating things, I thought that I must be careful to avoid the experience of those who watch an eclipse of the sun, for some of them ruin their eyes unless they watch its reflection in water or some such material. A similar thought crossed my mind, and I   99e feared that my soul would be altogether blinded if I looked at things with my eyes and tried to grasp them with each of my senses. So I thought I must take refuge in discussions and investigate the truth of things by means of words. However, perhaps this analogy is inadequate, for I certainly do not admit that one who investigates things by means of words is dealing with   **100a** images any more than one who looks at facts. However, I started in this manner: taking as my hypothesis in each case the theory that seemed to me the most compelling, I would consider as true, about cause and everything else, whatever agreed with this, and as untrue whatever did not so agree. But I want to put my meaning more clearly, for I do not think that you understand me now.

No, by Zeus, said Cebes, not very well.

This, he said, is what I mean. It is nothing new, but what I have never   100b stopped talking about, both elsewhere and in the earlier part of our conversation. I am going to try to show you the kind of cause with which I have concerned myself. I turn back to those oft-mentioned things and proceed from them. I assume the existence of a Beautiful, itself by itself, of a Good and a Great and all the rest. If you grant me these and agree that they exist, I hope to show you the cause as a result, and to find the soul to be immortal.

Take it that I grant you this, said Cebes, and hasten to your conclusion.   100c

Consider then, he said, whether you share my opinion as to what follows, for I think that, if there is anything beautiful besides the Beautiful itself, it is beautiful for no other reason than that it shares in that Beautiful, and I say so with everything. Do you agree to this sort of cause? — I do.

I no longer understand or recognize those other sophisticated causes, and if someone tells me that a thing is beautiful because it has a bright color or shape or any such thing, I ignore these other reasons—for all these confuse   100d me—but I simply, naively, and perhaps foolishly cling to this, that nothing else makes it beautiful other than the presence of, or the sharing in, or however you may describe its relationship to that Beautiful we mentioned, for I will not insist on the precise nature of the relationship, but that all beautiful things are beautiful by the Beautiful. That, I think, is the safest answer I can give myself or anyone else. And if I stick to this I think I shall never fall into error. This is the safe answer for me or anyone else to give,   100e namely, that it is through Beauty that beautiful things are made beautiful. Or do you not think so too? — I do.

And that it is through Bigness that big things are big and the bigger are bigger, and that smaller things are made small by Smallness? — Yes.

And you would not accept the statement that one man is taller than another by a head and the shorter man shorter by the same, but you would

101a   bear witness that you mean nothing else than that everything that is bigger is made bigger by nothing else than by Bigness, and that is the cause of its being bigger, and the smaller is made smaller only by Smallness, and this is why it is smaller. I think you would be afraid that some opposite argument would confront you if you said that someone is bigger or smaller by a head, first, because the bigger is bigger and the smaller smaller by the same, then because the bigger is bigger by a head which is small, and this would be

101b   strange, namely, that someone is made bigger by something small. Would you not be afraid of this?

I certainly would, said Cebes, laughing.

Then you would be afraid to say that ten is more numerous than eight by two, and that this is the cause of the excess, and not Numerousness and because of Numerousness, or that two cubits is bigger than one cubit by half and not by Bigness, for this is the same fear. — Certainly.

Then would you not avoid saying that when one is added to one it is the

101c   addition and when it is divided it is the division that is the cause of two? And you would loudly exclaim that you do not know how else each thing can come to be except by sharing in the particular reality in which it shares, and in these cases you do not know of any other cause of becoming two except by sharing in Twoness, and that the things that are to be two must share in this, as that which is to be one must share in Oneness, and you would dismiss these additions and divisions and other such subtleties, and leave them to those wiser than yourself to answer. But you, afraid, as they

101d   say, of your own shadow and your inexperience, would cling to the safety of your own hypothesis and give that answer. If someone then attacked your hypothesis itself, you would ignore him and would not answer until you had examined whether the consequences that follow from it agree with one another or contradict one another. And when you must give an account of your hypothesis itself you will proceed in the same way: you will assume another hypothesis, the one which seems to you best of the higher ones until you come to something acceptable, but you will not jumble the two

101e   as the debaters do by discussing the hypothesis and its consequences at the same time, if you wish to discover any truth. This they do not discuss at all nor give any thought to, but their wisdom enables them to mix everything up and yet to be pleased with themselves, but if you are a philosopher I

102a   think you will do as I say.

What you say is very true, said Simmias and Cebes together.

ECHECRATES: Yes, by Zeus, Phaedo, and they were right; I think he made these things wonderfully clear to anyone of even small intelligence.

PHAEDO: Yes indeed, Echecrates, and all those present thought so too.

ECHECRATES: And so do we who were not present but hear of it now. What was said after that?

PHAEDO: As I recall it, when the above had been accepted, and it was agreed that each of the Forms existed, and that other things acquired their name by having a share in them, he followed this up by asking: If you say these things are so, when you then say that Simmias is taller than Socrates but shorter than Phaedo, do you not mean that there is in Simmias both tallness and shortness? — I do. 102b

But, he said, do you agree that the words of the statement "Simmias is taller than Socrates" do not express the truth of the matter? It is not, surely, the nature of Simmias to be taller than Socrates because he is Simmias but because of the tallness he happens to have? Nor is he taller than Socrates because Socrates is Socrates, but because Socrates has smallness compared with the tallness of the other? — True. 102c

Nor is he shorter than Phaedo because Phaedo is Phaedo, but because Phaedo has tallness compared with the shortness of Simmias? — That is so.

So then Simmias is called both short and tall, being between the two, presenting his shortness to be overcome by the tallness of one, and his tallness to overcome the shortness of the other. He smilingly added, I seem to be going to talk like a book, but it is as I say. The other agreed. 102d

My purpose is that you may agree with me. Now it seems to me that not only Tallness itself is never willing to be tall and short at the same time, but also that the tallness in us will never admit the short or be overcome, but one of two things happens: either it flees and retreats whenever its opposite, the short, approaches, or it is destroyed by its approach. It is not willing to endure and admit shortness and be other than it was, whereas I admit and endure shortness and still remain the same person and am this short man. But Tallness, being tall, cannot venture to be small. In the same way, the short in us is unwilling to become or to be tall ever, nor does any other of the opposites become or be its opposite while still being what it was; either it goes away or is destroyed when that happens. — I altogether agree, said Cebes. 102e

103a

When he heard this, someone of those present—I have no clear memory of who it was—said: "By the gods, did we not agree earlier in our discussion[43] to the very opposite of what is now being said, namely, that the larger came from the smaller and the smaller from the larger, and that this simply was how opposites came to be, from their opposites, but now I think we are saying that this would never happen?"

On hearing this, Socrates inclined his head towards the speaker and said: "You have bravely reminded us, but you do not understand the difference 103b

---

[43] See 70d–71a.

between what is said now and what was said then, which was that an opposite thing came from an opposite thing; now we say that the opposite itself could never become opposite to itself, neither that in us nor that in nature. Then, my friend, we were talking of things that have opposite qualities and naming these after them, but now we say that these opposites themselves, from the presence of which in them things get their name, never can toler-

103c ate the coming to be from one another." At the same time he looked to Cebes and said: "Does anything of what this man says also disturb you?"

Not at the moment, said Cebes, but I do not deny that many things do disturb me.

We are altogether agreed then, he said, that an opposite will never be opposite to itself. — Entirely agreed.

Consider then whether you will agree to this further point. There is something you call hot and something you call cold. — There is.

103d Are they the same as what you call snow and fire? — By Zeus, no.

So the hot is something other than fire, and the cold is something other than snow? — Yes.

You think, I believe, that being snow it will not admit the hot, as we said before, and remain what it was and be both snow and hot, but when the hot approaches it will either retreat before it or be destroyed. — Quite so.

So fire, as the cold approaches, will either go away or be destroyed; it will never venture to admit coldness and remain what it was, fire and

103e cold. — What you say is true.

It is true then about some of these things that not only the Form itself deserves its own name for all time, but there is something else that is not the Form but has its character whenever it exists. Perhaps I can make my meaning clearer: the Odd must always be given this name we now mention. Is that not so? — Certainly.

Is it the only one of existing things to be called odd—this is my ques-

104a tion—or is there something else than the Odd which one must nevertheless also always call odd, as well as by its own name, because it is such by nature as never to be separated from the Odd? I mean, for example, the number three and many others. Consider three: do you not think that it must always be called both by its own name and by that of the Odd, which is not the same as three? That is the nature of three, and of five, and of half of all

104b the numbers; each of them is odd, but it is not the Odd. Then again, two and four and the whole other column of numbers; each of them, while not being the same as the Even, is always even. Do you not agree? — Of course.

Look now. What I want to make clear is this: Not only do those opposites not admit each other, but this is also true of those things which, while not being opposite to each other yet always contain the opposites, and it seems that these do not admit that Form which is opposite to that which is in them; when it approaches them, they either perish or give way. Shall we

not say that three will perish or undergo anything before, while remaining   104c
three, becoming even? — Certainly, said Cebes.

Yet surely two is not the opposite of three? — Indeed it is not.

It is then not only opposite Forms that do not admit each other's approach, but also some other things that do not admit the onset of opposites. — Very true.

Do you then want us, if we can, to define what these are? — I surely do.

Would they be the things that compel whatever they occupy not only   104d
to contain their Form but also always that of some opposite? — How do you mean?

As we were saying just now, you surely know that what the Form of three occupies must be not only three but also odd. — Certainly.

And we say that the opposite Form to the Form that achieves this result could never come to it. — It could not.

Now it is Oddness that has done this? — Yes.

And opposite to this is the Form of the Even? — Yes.

So then the Form of the Even will never come to three? — Never.   104e

Then three has no share in the Even? — Never.

So three is uneven? — Yes.

As for what I said we must define, that is, what kind of things, while not being opposites to something, yet do not admit the opposite, as, for example, the triad, though it is not the opposite of the Even, yet does not admit it because it always brings along the opposite of the Even, and so the dyad in relation to the Odd, fire to the Cold, and very many other things, see whether you would define it thus: Not only does the opposite not admit   **105a**
its opposite, but that which brings along some opposite into that which it occupies; that which brings this along will not admit the opposite to that which it brings along. Refresh your memory; it is no worse for being heard often. Five does not admit the form of the Even, nor will ten, its double, admit the form of the Odd. The double itself is an opposite of something else, yet it will not admit the form of the Odd. Nor do one-and-a-half and   105b
other such fractions admit the form of the Whole, nor will one-third, and so on, if you follow me and agree to this.

I certainly agree, he said, and I follow you.

Tell me again from the beginning, he said, and do not answer in the words of the question, but do as I do. I say that beyond that safe answer, which I spoke of first, I see another safe answer. If you should ask me what, coming into a body, makes it hot, my reply would not be that safe and ignorant one, that it is heat, but our present argument provides a more   105c
sophisticated answer, namely, fire, and if you ask me what, on coming into a body, makes it sick, I will not say sickness but fever. Nor, if asked the presence of what in a number makes it odd, I will not say oddness but

oneness, and so with other things. See if you now sufficiently understand what I want. — Quite sufficiently.

Answer me then, he said, what is it that, present in a body, makes it living? — A soul.

105d   And is that always so? — Of course.

Whatever the soul occupies, it always brings life to it? — It does.

Is there, or is there not, an opposite to life? — There is.

What is it? — Death.

So the soul will never admit the opposite of that which it brings along, as we agree from what has been said?

Most certainly, said Cebes.

Well, and what do we call that which does not admit the form of the even? — The uneven.

What do we call that which will not admit the just and that which will not admit the musical?

105e   The unmusical, and the other the unjust.

Very well, what do we call that which does not admit death?

The deathless, he said. Now the soul does not admit death? — No.

So the soul is deathless? — It is.

Very well, he said. Shall we say that this has been proved, do you think? Quite adequately proved, Socrates.

Well now, Cebes, he said, if the uneven were of necessity indestructible,
106a   surely three would be indestructible? — Of course.

And if the non-hot were of necessity indestructible, then whenever anyone brought heat to snow, the snow would retreat safe and unthawed, for it could not be destroyed, nor again could it stand its ground and admit the heat? — What you say is true.

In the same way, if the non-cold were indestructible, then when some cold attacked the fire, it would neither be quenched nor destroyed, but retreat safely. — Necessarily.

106b   Must then the same not be said of the deathless? If the deathless is also indestructible, it is impossible for the soul to be destroyed when death comes upon it. For it follows from what has been said that it will not admit death or be dead, just as three, we said, will not be even nor will the odd; nor will fire be cold, nor the heat that is in the fire. But, someone might say, what prevents the odd, while not becoming even as has been agreed,
106c   from being destroyed, and the even to come to be instead? We could not maintain against the man who said this that it is not destroyed, for the uneven is not indestructible. If we had agreed that it was indestructible, we could easily have maintained that at the coming of the even, the odd and the three have gone away and the same would hold for fire and the hot and the other things. — Surely.

And so now, if we are agreed that the deathless is indestructible, the soul, besides being deathless, is indestructible. If not, we need another argument.   106d

There is no need for one as far as that goes, for hardly anything could resist destruction if the deathless, which lasts forever, would admit destruction.

All would agree, said Socrates, that the god, and the Form of life itself, and anything that is deathless, are never destroyed. — All men would agree, by Zeus, to that, and the gods, I imagine, even more so.

If the deathless is indestructible, then the soul, if it is deathless, would   106e
also be indestructible? — Necessarily.

Then when death comes to man, the mortal part of him dies, it seems, but his deathless part goes away safe and indestructible, yielding the place to death. — So it appears.

Therefore the soul, Cebes, he said, is most certainly deathless and inde-structible and our souls will really dwell in the underworld. I have nothing   107a
more to say against that, Socrates, said Cebes, nor can I doubt your argu-ments. If Simmias here or someone else has something to say, he should not remain silent, for I do not know to what further occasion other than the present he could put it off if he wants to say or to hear anything on these subjects.

Certainly, said Simmias, I myself have no remaining grounds for doubt after what has been said; nevertheless, in view of the importance of our subject and my low opinion of human weakness, I am bound still to have   107b
some private misgivings about what we have said.

You are not only right to say this, Simmias, Socrates said, but our first hypotheses require clearer examination, even though we find them con-vincing. And if you analyze them adequately, you will, I think, follow the argument as far as a man can, and if the conclusion is clear, you will look no further. — That is true.

It is right to think then, gentlemen, that if the soul is immortal, it   107c
requires our care not only for the time we call our life, but for the sake of all time, and that one is in terrible danger if one does not give it that care. If death were escape from everything, it would be a great boon to the wicked to get rid of the body and of their wickedness together with their soul. But now that the soul appears to be immortal, there is no escape from evil or salvation for it except by becoming as good and wise as possible,   107d
for the soul goes to the underworld possessing nothing but its education and upbringing, which are said to bring the greatest benefit or harm to the dead right at the beginning of the journey yonder.

We are told that when each person dies, the guardian spirit who was allotted to him in life proceeds to lead him to a certain place, whence those who have been gathered together there must, after being judged, proceed to the underworld with the guide who has been appointed to lead them   107e thither from here. Having there undergone what they must and stayed there the appointed time, they are led back here by another guide after long periods of time. The journey is not as Aeschylus' Telephus[44] describes it.

108a He says that only one single path leads to Hades, but I think it is neither one nor simple, for then there would be no need of guides; one could not make any mistake if there were but one path. As it is, it is likely to have many forks and crossroads; and I base this judgment on the sacred rites and customs here.

The well-ordered and wise soul follows the guide and is not without familiarity with its surroundings, but the soul that is passionately attached

108b to the body, as I said before, hovers around it and the visible world for a long time, struggling and suffering much until it is led away by force and with difficulty by its appointed spirit. When the impure soul which has performed some impure deed joins the others after being involved in unjust killings, or committed other crimes which are akin to these and are actions of souls of this kind, everybody shuns it and turns away, unwilling to be its fellow traveler or its guide; such a soul wanders alone completely at a

108c loss until a certain time arrives and it is forcibly led to its proper dwelling place. On the other hand, the soul that has led a pure and temperate life finds fellow travelers and gods to guide it, and each of them dwells in a place suited to it.

There are many strange places upon the earth, and the earth itself is not such as those who are used to discourse upon it believe it to be in nature or size, as someone has convinced me.

108d Simmias said: "What do you mean, Socrates? I have myself heard many things said about the earth, but certainly not the things that convince you. I should be glad to hear them."

Indeed, Simmias, I do not think it requires the skill of Glaucus[45] to tell you what they are, but to prove them true requires more than that skill, and I should perhaps not be able to do so. Also, even if I had the knowledge, my remaining time would not be long enough to tell the tale. However, nothing prevents my telling you what I am convinced is the shape of the

108e earth and what its regions are.

Even that is sufficient, said Simmias.

Well then, he said, the first thing of which I am convinced is that if the earth is a sphere in the middle of the heavens, it has no need of air or

109a any other force to prevent it from falling. The homogeneous nature of the heavens on all sides and the earth's own equipoise are sufficient to hold it, for an object balanced in the middle of something homogeneous will

---

[44] The *Telephus* of Aeschylus is not extant.

[45] A proverbial expression whose origin and specific meaning are obscure.

have no tendency to incline more in any direction than any other but will remain unmoved. This, he said, is the first point of which I am persuaded.

And rightly so, said Simmias.

Further, the earth is very large, and we live around the sea in a small portion of it between Phasis and the pillars of Heracles, like ants or frogs around a swamp; many other peoples live in many such parts of it. Everywhere about the earth there are numerous hollows of many kinds and shapes and sizes into which the water and the mist and the air have gathered. The earth itself is pure and lies in the pure sky where the stars are situated, which the majority of those who discourse on these subjects call the ether. The water and mist and air are the sediment of the ether and they always flow into the hollows of the earth. We, who dwell in the hollows of it, are unaware of this and we think that we live above, on the surface of the earth. It is as if someone who lived deep down in the middle of the ocean thought he was living on its surface. Seeing the sun and the other heavenly bodies through the water, he would think the sea to be the sky; because he is slow and weak, he has never reached the surface of the sea or risen with his head above the water or come out of the sea to our region here, nor seen how much purer and more beautiful it is than his own region, nor has he ever heard of it from anyone who has seen it.

Our experience is the same: Living in a certain hollow of the earth, we believe that we live upon its surface; the air we call the heavens, as if the stars made their way through it; this too is the same: Because of our weakness and slowness we are not able to make our way to the upper limit of the air; if anyone got to this upper limit, if anyone came to it or reached it on wings and his head rose above it, then just as fish on rising from the sea see things in our region, he would see things there and, if his nature could endure to contemplate them, he would know that there is the true heaven, the true light, and the true earth, for the earth here, these stones and the whole region, are spoiled and eaten away, just as things in the sea are by the salt water.

Nothing worth mentioning grows in the sea, nothing, one might say, is fully developed; there are caves and sand and endless slime and mud wherever there is earth—not comparable in any way with the beauties of our region. So those things above are in their turn far superior to the things we know. Indeed, if this is the moment to tell a tale, Simmias, it is worth hearing about the nature of things on the surface of the earth under the heavens.

At any rate, Socrates, said Simmias, we should be glad to hear this story.

Well then, my friend, in the first place it is said that the earth, looked at from above, looks like those spherical balls made up of twelve pieces of leather; it is multicolored, and of these colors those used by our painters give us an indication; up there the whole earth has these colors, but much brighter and purer than these; one part is sea-green and of marvelous beauty, another is golden, another is white, whiter than chalk or snow; the earth is composed also of the other colors, more numerous and beautiful than any we have seen. The very hollows of the earth, full of water and air, gleaming among the variety of other colors, present a color of their own so that the whole is seen as a continuum of variegated colors. On the surface of the earth the plants grow with corresponding beauty, the trees and the flowers and the fruits, and so with the hills and the stones, more beautiful in their smoothness and transparency and color. Our precious stones here are but fragments, our carnelians, jaspers, emeralds, and the rest. All stones there are of that kind, and even more beautiful. The reason is that there they are pure, not eaten away or spoiled by decay and brine, or corroded by the water and air which have flowed into the hollows here and bring ugliness and disease upon earth, stones, the other animals, and plants. The earth itself is adorned with all these things, and also with gold and silver and other metals. These stand out, being numerous and massive and occurring everywhere, so that the earth is a sight for the blessed. There are many other living creatures upon the earth, and also men, some living inland, others at the edge of the air, as we live on the edge of the sea, others again live on islands surrounded by air close to the mainland. In a word, what water and the sea are to us, the air is to them, and the ether is to them what the air is to us. The climate is such that they are without disease, and they live much longer than people do here; their eyesight, hearing, and intelligence and all such are as superior to ours as air is superior to water and ether to air in purity; they have groves and temples dedicated to the gods, in which the gods really dwell, and they communicate with them by speech and prophecy and by the sight of them; they see the sun and moon and stars as they are, and in other ways their happiness is in accord with this.

This then is the nature of the earth as a whole and of its surroundings; around the whole of it there are many regions in the hollows; some are deeper and more open than that in which we live; others are deeper and have a narrower opening than ours, and there are some that have less depth and more width. All these are connected with each other below the surface of the earth in many places by narrow and broader channels, and thus have outlets through which much water flows from one to another as into mixing bowls; huge rivers of both hot and cold water thus flow beneath the earth eternally, much fire and large rivers of fire, and many of wet mud, both more pure and more muddy, such as those flowing in advance of the lava and the stream of lava itself in Sicily. These streams then fill up every and all regions as the flow reaches each, and all these places move up and down with the oscillating movement of the earth. The natural cause of the oscillation is as follows: One of the hollows of the earth, which is also the biggest, pierces through the whole earth; it is that which Homer mentioned when he said: "Far down where is the deepest pit below the earth . . . ,"[46] and which he elsewhere, and many other poets, call Tartarus; into this chasm all the rivers flow together, and again flow out of it, and each river is affected by the nature of the land through which it flows. The reason for their flowing into and out of Tartarus is that this water has no bottom 112b or solid base but it oscillates up and down in waves, and the air and wind about it do the same, for they follow it when it flows to this or that part of the earth. Just as when people breathe, the flow of air goes in and out, so here the air oscillates with the water and creates terrible winds as it goes in and out. Whenever the water retreats to what we call the lower part of 112c the earth, it flows into those parts and fills them up as if the water were pumped in; when it leaves that part for this, it fills these parts again, and the parts filled flow through the channels and through the earth and in each case arrive at the places to which the channels lead and create seas and marshes and rivers and springs. From there the waters flow under the earth again, some flowing around larger and more numerous regions, some 112d around smaller and shallower ones, then flow back into Tartarus, some at a point much lower than where they issued forth, others only a little way, but all of them at a lower point, some of them at the opposite side of the chasm, some on the same side; some flow in a wide circle round the earth once or many times like snakes, then go as far down as possible, then go back into the chasm of Tartarus. From each side it is possible to flow down as far as the center, but not beyond, for this part that faces the river flow 112e from either side is steep.

There are many other large rivers of all kinds, and among these there are four of note; the biggest which flows on the outside (of the earth) in a circle is called Oceanus; opposite it and flowing in the opposite direction is the Acheron; it flows through many other deserted regions and further underground makes its way to the Acherusian lake to which the souls **113a** of the majority come after death and, after remaining there for a certain appointed time, longer for some, shorter for others, they are sent back to birth as living creatures. The third river issues between the first two, and close to its source it falls into a region burning with much fire and makes a lake larger than our sea, boiling with water and mud. From there it goes in a circle, foul and muddy, and winding on its way it comes, among other 113b places, to the edge of the Acherusian lake but does not mingle with its waters; then, coiling many times underground it flows lower down into Tartarus; this is called the Pyriphlegethon, and its lava streams throw off fragments of it in various parts of the earth. Opposite this the fourth river issues forth, which is called Stygion, and it is said to flow first into a terrible 113c

---

[46] *Iliad* viii.14; cf. viii.481.

and wild region, all of it blue-gray in color, and the lake that this river forms by flowing into it is called the Styx. As its waters fall into the lake they acquire dread powers; then diving below and winding round it flows in the opposite direction from the Pyriphlegethon and into the opposite side of the Acherusian lake; its waters do not mingle with any other; it too flows in a circle and into Tartarus opposite the Pyriphlegethon. The name of that fourth river, the poets tell us, is Cocytus.[47]

113d   Such is the nature of these things. When the dead arrive at the place to which each has been led by his guardian spirit, they are first judged as to whether they have led a good and pious life. Those who have lived an average life make their way to the Acheron and embark upon such vessels as there are for them and proceed to the lake. There they dwell and are purified by penalties for any wrongdoing they may have committed; they
113e   are also suitably rewarded for their good deeds as each deserves. Those who are deemed incurable because of the enormity of their crimes, having committed many great sacrileges or wicked and unlawful murders and other such wrongs—their fitting fate is to be hurled into Tartarus never to emerge from it. Those who are deemed to have committed great but curable crimes, such as doing violence to their father or mother in a fit of
114a   temper but who have felt remorse for the rest of their lives, or who have killed someone in a similar manner, these must of necessity be thrown into Tartarus, but a year later the current throws them out, those who are guilty of murder by way of Cocytus, and those who have done violence to their parents by way of the Pyriphlegethon. After they have been carried along to the Acherusian lake, they cry out and shout, some for those they have killed, others for those they have maltreated, and calling them they then pray to them and beg them to allow them to step out into the lake and to
114b   receive them. If they persuade them, they do step out and their punishment comes to an end; if they do not, they are taken back into Tartarus and from there into the rivers, and this does not stop until they have persuaded those they have wronged, for this is the punishment which the judges imposed on them.
114c   Those who are deemed to have lived an extremely pious life are freed and released from the regions of the earth as from a prison; they make their way up to a pure dwelling place and live on the surface of the earth. Those who have purified themselves sufficiently by philosophy live in the future altogether without a body; they make their way to even more beautiful dwelling places which it is hard to describe clearly, nor do we now have the time to do so. Because of the things we have enunciated, Simmias, one must make every effort to share in virtue and wisdom in one's life, for the reward is beautiful and the hope is great.

---

[47] For these features of the underworld, see *Odyssey* x.511 ff., xi.157.

No sensible man would insist that these things are as I have described   114d
them, but I think it is fitting for a man to risk the belief—for the risk is a
noble one—that this, or something like this, is true about our souls and
their dwelling places, since the soul is evidently immortal, and a man
should repeat this to himself as if it were an incantation, which is why I
have been prolonging my tale. That is the reason why a man should be of
good cheer about his own soul, if during life he has ignored the pleasures   114e
of the body and its ornamentation as of no concern to him and doing
him more harm than good, but has seriously concerned himself with the
pleasures of learning, and adorned his soul not with alien but with its own
ornaments, namely, moderation, righteousness, courage, freedom, and   **115a**
truth, and in that state awaits his journey to the underworld.

Now you, Simmias, Cebes, and the rest of you, Socrates continued,
will each take that journey at some other time but my fated day calls me
now, as a tragic character might say, and it is about time for me to have my
bath, for I think it better to have it before I drink the poison and save the
women the trouble of washing the corpse.

When Socrates had said this Crito spoke. Very well, Socrates, what are   115b
your instructions to me and the others about your children or anything
else? What can we do that would please you most? — Nothing new, Crito,
said Socrates, but what I am always saying, that you will please me and
mine and yourselves by taking good care of your own selves in whatever
you do, even if you do not agree with me now, but if you neglect your own
selves, and are unwilling to live following the tracks, as it were, of what we
have said now and on previous occasions, you will achieve nothing even
if you strongly agree with me at this moment.   115c

We shall be eager to follow your advice, said Crito, but how shall we
bury you?

In any way you like, said Socrates, if you can catch me and I do not
escape you. And laughing quietly, looking at us, he said: I do not convince
Crito that I am this Socrates talking to you here and ordering all I say, but
he thinks that I am the thing which he will soon be looking at as a corpse,
and so he asks how he shall bury me. I have been saying for some time and   115d
at some length that after I have drunk the poison I shall no longer be with
you but will leave you to go and enjoy some good fortunes of the blessed,
but it seems that I have said all this to him in vain in an attempt to reas-
sure you and myself too. Give a pledge to Crito on my behalf, he said, the
opposite pledge to that he gave the jury.[48] He pledged that I would stay;
you must pledge that I will not stay after I die, but that I shall go away, so
that Crito will bear it more easily when he sees my body being burned or   115e
buried and will not be angry on my behalf, as if I were suffering terribly,

---

[48] See *Apology* 38b.

and so that he should not say at the funeral that he is laying out, or carrying out, or burying Socrates. For know you well, my dear Crito, that to express oneself badly is not only faulty as far as the language goes, but does some harm to the soul. You must be of good cheer, and say you are burying my **116a** body, and bury it in any way you like and think most customary.

After saying this he got up and went to another room to take his bath, and Crito followed him and he told us to wait for him. So we stayed, talking among ourselves, questioning what had been said, and then again talking of the great misfortune that had befallen us. We all felt as if we had lost a father and would be orphaned for the rest of our lives. When he had **116b** washed, his children were brought to him—two of his sons were small and one was older—and the women of his household came to him. He spoke to them before Crito and gave them what instructions he wanted. Then he sent the women and children away, and he himself joined us. It was now close to sunset, for he had stayed inside for some time. He came and sat down after his bath and conversed for a short while, when the officer **116c** of the Eleven[49] came and stood by him and said: "I shall not reproach you as I do the others, Socrates. They are angry with me and curse me when, obeying the orders of my superiors, I tell them to drink the poison. During the time you have been here I have come to know you in other ways as the noblest, the gentlest, and the best man who has ever come here. So now too I know that you will not make trouble for me; you know who is responsible and you will direct your anger against them. You know what **116d** message I bring. Fare you well, and try to endure what you must as easily as possible." The officer was weeping as he turned away and went out. Socrates looked up at him and said: "Fare you well also; we shall do as you bid us." And turning to us he said: "How pleasant the man is! During the whole time I have been here he has come in and conversed with me from time to time, a most agreeable man. And how genuinely he now weeps for me. Come, Crito, let us obey him. Let someone bring the poison if it is ready; if not, let the man prepare it."

116e But Socrates, said Crito, I think the sun still shines upon the hills and has not yet set. I know that others drink the poison quite a long time after they have received the order, eating and drinking quite a bit, and some of them enjoy intimacy with their loved ones. Do not hurry; there is still some time.

It is natural, Crito, for them to do so, said Socrates, for they think they derive some benefit from doing this, but it is not fitting for me. I do not **117a** expect any benefit from drinking the poison a little later, except to become ridiculous in my own eyes for clinging to life, and be sparing of it when there is none left. So do as I ask and do not refuse me.

---

[49] See *Apology* 37c.

Hearing this, Crito nodded to the slave who was standing near him; the slave went out and after a time came back with the man who was to administer the poison, carrying it made ready in a cup. When Socrates saw him he said: "Well, my good man, you are an expert in this; what must one do?" — "Just drink it and walk around until your legs feel heavy, and then lie down and it will act of itself." And he offered the cup to Socrates, 117b who took it quite cheerfully, Echecrates, without a tremor or any change of feature or color, but looking at the man from under his eyebrows as was his wont, asked: "What do you say about pouring a libation from this drink? It is allowed?" — "We only mix as much as we believe will suffice," said the man.

I understand, Socrates said, but one is allowed, indeed one must, utter a 117c prayer to the gods that the journey from here to yonder may be fortunate. This is my prayer and may it be so.

And while he was saying this, he was holding the cup, and then drained it calmly and easily. Most of us had been able to hold back our tears reasonably well up till then, but when we saw him drinking it and after he drank it, we could hold them back no longer; my own tears came in floods against my will. So I covered my face. I was weeping for myself, not for him—for my misfortune in being deprived of such a comrade. Even before me, Crito 117d was unable to restrain his tears and got up. Apollodorus[50] had not ceased from weeping before, and at this moment his noisy tears and anger made everybody present break down, except Socrates. "What is this," he said, "you strange fellows. It is mainly for this reason that I sent the women away, to avoid such unseemliness, for I am told one should die in good-omened 117e silence. So keep quiet and control yourselves."

His words made us ashamed, and we checked our tears. He walked around, and when he said his legs were heavy he lay on his back as he had been told to do, and the man who had given him the poison touched his body, and after a while tested his feet and legs, pressed hard upon his foot, and asked him if he felt this, and Socrates said no. Then he pressed his calves, and made his way up his body and showed us that it was cold 118a and stiff. He felt it himself and said that when the cold reached his heart he would be gone. As his belly was getting cold Socrates uncovered his head—he had covered it—and said—these were his last words — "Crito, we owe a cock to Asclepius;[51] make this offering to him and do not forget." — "It shall be done," said Crito, "tell us if there is anything else." But there was no answer. Shortly afterwards Socrates made a movement;

---

[50] See *Apology* 34a.

[51] Asclepius is the god of healing. A cock was sacrificed to him by the sick people who slept in his temples, hoping for a cure.

the man uncovered him and his eyes were fixed. Seeing this Crito closed his mouth and his eyes.

Such was the end of our comrade, Echecrates, a man who, we would say, was of all those we have known the best, and also the wisest and the most upright.

Symposium

"The only thing I say I understand," Socrates tells us in the *Symposium*, "is *ta erōtika*" (177d)—"the art or craft of love [*hē erōtikē technē*]," which the god *Erōs* gives to him in the *Phaedrus* (257a). But are we really to believe that the man who affirms when on trial for his life that he knows himself to be wise "in anything either great or small" (*Apology* 21b) knows something as significant as the art of love? No. The claim is a nontrivial play on words facilitated by the fact that the noun *erōs* ("love") and the verb *erōtan* ("to ask questions") seem to be etymologically connected. Socrates knows about the art of love in that—but just insofar as—he knows how to ask questions, how to converse elenctically.

As a man who loves boys in an idiosyncratic, because elenctic, way, Socrates is placed in potential conflict with the norms of a peculiar Athenian social institution, that of *paiderastia*—the socially regulated intercourse between an older Athenian male (*erastēs*) and a teenage boy (*erōmenos, pais*), through which the latter was supposed to learn virtue. This potential, as we know, was realized with tragic consequences when Socrates was found guilty of corrupting the young men of Athens and condemned to death. The effect on Plato is palpable in his works, turning very many of them into defenses—not always uncritical—of Socrates, and of what Socrates represented for the young men he encountered. Plato's account in the *Symposium* of one such relationship—that with the brilliant and beautiful Alcibiades—is an illuminating case in point.

Alcibiades was so in love with Socrates—"it was obvious," the *Symposium* (222c) tells us—that when asked to speak of love, he speaks of his beloved. No general theories of love for him, just the vividly remembered story of the times he spent with a man so extraordinary there has never been anyone like him—a man so powerfully erotic he turned the conventional world of love upside down: "he presents himself as your lover, and, before you know it, you're in love with him yourself!" (222b).

Most of the people who speak in the *Symposium* are representatives of the various kinds of people from whom Athenians (or Athenian men, at any rate) acquired their views about erotic love. We have a tragic poet (Agathon), a comic poet (Aristophanes), a doctor (Eryximachus), an older man (Pausanias), and a younger man (Phaedrus). These are the equivalents of the erotic authorities from whom we learn about love: novelists, journalists, moviemakers (Agathon, Aristophanes), and doctors (Eryximachus).

We lack an exact equivalent for Pausanias and Phaedrus, but the sometimes suggested "older man" or "younger woman" are perhaps rough analogues.

The stories these people tell about love, though independently interesting, seem to be intended to show how inadequate the views of these representatives of conventional erotic wisdom actually are. As theories of love they are, indeed, pretty comic. Nonetheless, most of them contain some grain of what Plato takes to be the truth about love. Phaedrus claims that "Love is the most ancient of the gods, the most honored, and the most powerful in helping men gain virtue and blessedness" (180b), and this, appropriately modified, is endorsed by Socrates and Diotima. Pausanias introduces the distinction between same-sex boy-love and love between the sexes, which is also endorsed by Diotima. Eryximachus broadens the field of love, "it occurs everywhere in the universe" (186a), and connects it specifically to the good—the power of love "is far greater when Love is directed, in temperance and justice, toward the good" (188d). Again, both elements are preserved in Diotima's story. Aristophanes introduces the idea of the incompleteness of the lover, which is endorsed by Socrates in his questioning of Agathon. Finally, Agathon introduces the crucial distinction between what love itself is and what its effects or consequences are, a distinction that is also endorsed by Socrates.

So the acknowledged authorities on erotic love have grasped something of its real nature; they have grasped what Diotima, who is supposed to have taught the truth about love to Socrates, will later refer to as "images" of love, but they have mistaken these images for love itself. Moreover, it is clearly the particular brand of love that each of them favors or suffers from that has caused him to settle not just for any old image of love but for one that matches his brand. Thus, for Agathon and Pausanias the canonical image of true love—the quintessential love story—features the right sort of older man and the right sort of younger one (the latter is more prominent in Phaedrus' version, the former in Pausanias'). For Eryximachus the image of true love is painted in the languages of his own beloved medicine and of all the other crafts and sciences. For Aristophanes it is painted in the language of comedy (albeit a comic language tinged with tragic hues). For Agathon it is painted in the loftier tones of tragedy (tones whose very loftiness make us laugh). In ways that these interlocutors are unaware of, then, but that Plato knows, their love stories are themselves manifestations of their loves and the inversions or perversions expressed and embodied in them—hence the unmistakable aura of parody that surrounds his presentation of their views. These men think their stories are the truth about love but they are really love's delusions. As such, however, they are of course essential parts of that truth. For the power of love to engender delusive images of the beautiful is as much a part of the truth about it as its power to lead to the beautiful itself.

What we all really love, according to Diotima, is the good—that is to say, we want good things to be ours forever. Because we are mortal, the closest we can come to satisfying this desire is to initiate an endless cycle of reproduction in which each new generation has good things. We achieve this, in a famous phrase, by "giving birth in beauty" (206b). What does this mean? Like Pausanias, Diotima recognizes two fundamentally different kinds of love, two fundamentally different varieties of the desire to give birth in beauty. In the case of lovers of opposite sexes, who are "pregnant in body," such giving birth consists in producing children who resemble, and so share in the beauty of their parents (209a). Lovers of the same sex, however, are a different story. What they give birth to is "wisdom and the rest of virtue" (209a). When a man who is pregnant in soul finds a beautiful boy, Diotima says, it "makes him instantly teem with ideas and arguments about virtue" (209b), or "beautiful ideas" (210a). Giving birth to virtue and giving birth to ideas about it or accounts of it are obviously different, but some of the other phrases Diotima uses show us how to mitigate the difference. For what such lovers want is to give birth to accounts of virtue of a particular sort—ones that can be used in "the proper ordering of cities and households" (209a), and so can "make young men better" (210c).

If the lover's accounts are to achieve this goal, however, they mustn't be the product of distorting fantasy, as some feminists think our concept of romantic love itself is. What is intended to insure that they will not is their openness to reality—an openness guaranteed by the fact that in the course of his ascent the lover must study the beauty of ways of life and laws and the beauty of the sciences (210c). What he gains from these studies are the conceptual resources needed to see the world, including the human world, aright—to gain knowledge of it. This is not the project we undertake when we reflect on our own love stories in hopes of understanding them (often a project provoked by an unhappy ending). It is instead the project of philosophy, as Plato conceives of it. That is why it culminates in the birth of "many gloriously beautiful ideas and theories, in unstinting love of wisdom" (210d). Yet the grander project intersects with ours in an interesting way. The terms or concepts we use to tell our love stories must themselves be coherent if the stories we use them to tell are themselves to be coherently livable.

In Plato's view, this means that they must be the concepts the true lover uses once he has seen the beautiful itself—the concepts whose correlates are forms. If they are not, they will be incoherent and the lover who employs them will find himself embroiled in a love story he cannot fully understand, a love story whose incoherence the elenchus, or psychoanalysis, or just plain critical scrutiny will reveal. It is this incoherence, indeed, encountered at lower stages in the ascent, that leads the correct lover, under pressure from his rational desire for truth and consistency, and the pain of inconsistency, to climb to the next stage. We can see Diotima, then, not only as revealing the other more abstract loves that a true lover of boys must have, but also as exploring the conditions concepts must meet if they are to figure in genuinely coherent love stories.

SYMPOSIUM

APOLLODORUS:[1] In fact, your question does not find me unprepared. Just   **172a**
the other day, as it happens, I was walking to the city from my home in
Phaleron[2] when a man I know, who was making his way behind me, saw
me and called from a distance:

"The gentleman from Phaleron!" he yelled, trying to be funny. "Hey,
Apollodorus, wait!"

So I stopped and waited.

"Apollodorus, I've been looking for you!" he said. "You know there
once was a gathering at Agathon's[3] when Socrates, Alcibiades, and their   **172b**
friends had dinner together; I wanted to ask you about the speeches they
made on Love. What were they? I heard a version from a man who had it
from Phoenix,[4] Philip's son, but it was badly garbled, and he said you were
the one to ask. So please, will you tell me all about it? After all, Socrates is
your friend—who has a better right than you to report his conversation?
But before you begin," he added, "tell me this: were you there yourself?"

"Your friend must have really garbled his story," I replied, "if you think   **172c**
this affair was so recent that I could have been there."

"I did think that," he said.

"Glaucon,[5] how could you? You know very well Agathon hasn't lived
in Athens for many years, while it's been less than three that I've been
Socrates' companion and made it my job to know exactly what he says and
does each day. Before that, I simply drifted aimlessly. Of course, I used   **173a**
to think that what I was doing was important, but in fact I was the most
worthless man on earth—as bad as you are this very moment: I used to
think philosophy was the last thing a man should do."

"Stop joking, Apollodorus," he replied. "Just tell me when the party
took place."

The text of *Symposium*, translated by Alexander Nehamas and Paul Woodruff, is
reprinted with minor adaptations from Plato, *Symposium*. Copyright © 1989, Hackett
Publishing Co.

[1] See *Apology* 34a.

[2] A port town in Attica, southwest of Athens.

[3] Agathon was a Greek tragedian.

[4] Otherwise unknown.

[5] Possibly the father of Charmides (mentioned at 222b), but most likely Plato's
brother and Socrates' interlocutor in the *Republic*.

"When we were still children, when Agathon won the prize with his first tragedy. It was the day after he and his troupe held their victory celebration."

"So it really was a long time ago," he said. "Then who told you about it? Was it Socrates himself?"

173b   "Oh, for god's sake, of course not!" I replied. "It was the very same man who told Phoenix, a fellow called Aristodemus, from Cydatheneum,[6] a real runt of a man, who always went barefoot. He went to the party because, I think, he was obsessed with Socrates—one of the worst cases at that time. Naturally, I checked part of his story with Socrates, and Socrates agreed with his account."

"Please tell me, then," he said. "You speak and I'll listen, as we walk to the city. This is the perfect opportunity."

So this is what we talked about on our way; and that's why, as I said

173c before, I'm not unprepared. Well, if I'm to tell *you* about it too—I'll be glad to. After all, my greatest pleasure comes from philosophical conversation, even if I'm only a listener, whether or not I think it will be to my advantage. All other talk, especially the talk of rich businessmen like you, bores me to tears, and I'm sorry for you and your friends because you think your affairs are important when really they're totally trivial. Perhaps, in

173d your turn, you think I'm a failure, and, believe me, I think that what you think is true. But as for all of you, I don't just *think* you are failures—I know it for a fact.

FRIEND: You'll never change, Apollodorus! Always nagging, even at yourself! I do believe you think everybody—yourself first of all—is totally worthless, except, of course, Socrates. I don't know exactly how you came to be called "the maniac," but you certainly talk like one, always furious with everyone, including yourself—but not with Socrates!

173e APOLLODORUS: Of course, my dear friend, it's perfectly obvious why I have these views about us all: it's simply because I'm a maniac, and I'm raving!

FRIEND: It's not worth arguing about this now, Apollodorus. Please do as I asked: tell me the speeches.

APOLLODORUS: All right. . . . Well, the speeches went something like this— but I'd better tell you the whole story from the very beginning, as

174a Aristodemus told it to me.

He said, then, that one day he ran into Socrates, who had just bathed and put on his fancy sandals—both very unusual events. So he asked him where he was going, and why he was looking so good.

---

[6] Aristodemus is also mentioned as a companion of Socrates in Xenophon, *Memorabilia* i.4, but is otherwise largely unknown. Cydatheneum was a deme (administrative unit) within the walled city of Athens.

Socrates replied, "I'm going to Agathon's for dinner. I managed to avoid yesterday's victory party—I really don't like crowds—but I promised to be there today. So, naturally, I took great pains with my appearance: I'm going to the house of a good-looking man; I had to look my best. But let me ask you this," he added, "I know you haven't been invited to the dinner; how would you like to come anyway?"   174b

And Aristodemus answered, "I'll do whatever you say."

"Come with me, then," Socrates said, "and we shall prove the proverb wrong; the truth is, 'Good men go uninvited to Goodman's feast.'[7] Even Homer himself, when you think about it, did not much like this proverb; he not only disregarded it, he violated it. Agamemnon,[8] of course, is one of his great warriors, while he describes Menelaus as a 'limp spearman.'   174c And yet, when Agamemnon offers a sacrifice and gives a feast, Homer has the weak Menelaus arrive uninvited at his superior's table."[9]

Aristodemus replied to this, "Socrates, I am afraid Homer's description is bound to fit me better than yours. Mine is a case of an obvious inferior arriving uninvited at the table of a man of letters. I think you'd better figure out a good excuse for bringing me along, because, you know, I won't admit I've come without an invitation. I'll say I'm your guest."   174d

"Let's go," he said. "We'll think about what to say 'as we proceed the two of us along the way.'"[10]

With these words, they set out. But as they were walking, Socrates began to think about something, lost himself in thought, and kept lagging behind. Whenever Aristodemus stopped to wait for him, Socrates would urge him to go on ahead. When he arrived at Agathon's he found the gate   174e wide open, and that, Aristodemus said, caused him to find himself in a very embarrassing situation: a household slave saw him the moment he arrived and took him immediately to the dining room, where the guests were already lying down on their couches, and dinner was about to be served.

As soon as Agathon saw him, he called:

"Welcome, Aristodemus! What perfect timing! You're just in time for dinner! I hope you're not here for any other reason—if you are, forget it. I looked all over for you yesterday, so I could invite you, but I couldn't

---

[7] Agathon's name could be translated as "Goodman." The proverb is, "Good men go uninvited to an inferior man's feast."

[8] King of Mycenae. He led the Greek forces in the Trojan War. Menelaus, husband of Helen (whose abduction by Paris caused that war), was Agamemnon's brother.

[9] Menelaus calls on Agamemnon at *Iliad* ii.408. Menelaus is called a limp spearman at xvii.587.

[10] An allusion to *Iliad* x.224, "When two go together, one has an idea before the other."

find you anywhere. But where is Socrates? How come you didn't bring him along?"

So I turned around (Aristodemus said), and Socrates was nowhere to be seen. And I said that it was actually Socrates who had brought *me* along as his guest.

"I'm delighted he did," Agathon replied. "But where is he?"

175a   "He was directly behind me, but I have no idea where he is now."

"Go look for Socrates," Agathon ordered a slave, "and bring him in. Aristodemus," he added, "you can share Eryximachus'[11] couch."

A slave brought water, and Aristodemus washed himself before he lay down. Then another slave entered and said: "Socrates is here, but he's gone off to the neighbor's porch. He's standing there and won't come in even though I called him several times."

"How strange," Agathon replied. "Go back and bring him in. Don't leave him there."

But Aristodemus stopped him. "No, no," he said. "Leave him alone. It's
175b   one of his habits: every now and then he just goes off like that and stands motionless, wherever he happens to be. I'm sure he'll come in very soon, so don't disturb him; let him be."

"Well, all right, if you really think so," Agathon said, and turned to the slaves: "Go ahead and serve the rest of us. What you serve is completely up to you; pretend nobody's supervising you—as if I ever did! Imagine that we are all your own guests, myself included. Give us good reason to
175c   praise your service."

So they went ahead and started eating, but there was still no sign of Socrates. Agathon wanted to send for him many times, but Aristodemus wouldn't let him. And, in fact, Socrates came in shortly afterward, as he always did—they were hardly halfway through their meal. Agathon, who, as it happened, was all alone on the farthest couch, immediately called: "Socrates, come lie down next to me. Who knows, if I touch you, I may
175d   catch a bit of the wisdom that came to you under my neighbor's porch. It's clear *you've* seen the light. If you hadn't, you'd still be standing there."

Socrates sat down next to him and said, "How wonderful it would be, dear Agathon, if the foolish were filled with wisdom simply by touching the wise. If only wisdom were like water, which always flows from a full cup into an empty one when we connect them with a piece of yarn—well, then I would consider it the greatest prize to have the chance to lie down
175e   next to you. I would soon be overflowing with your wonderful wisdom. My own wisdom is of no account—a shadow in a dream—while yours is

---

[11] Eryximachus of Athens, like his father Acumenus before him, was a doctor and friend of Phaedrus (*Phaedrus* 268a).

bright and radiant and has a splendid future. Why, young as you are, you're so brilliant I could call more than thirty thousand Greeks as witnesses."[12]

"Now you've gone *too* far, Socrates," Agathon replied. "Well, eat your dinner. Dionysus will soon enough be the judge of our claims to wisdom!"[13]

Socrates took his seat after that and had his meal, according to Aristodemus. When dinner was over, they poured a libation to the god, sang a hymn, and—in short—followed the whole ritual. Then they turned their attention to drinking. At that point Pausanias[14] addressed the group: **176a**

"Well, gentlemen, how can we arrange to drink less tonight? To be honest, I still have a terrible hangover from yesterday, and I could really use a break. I daresay most of you could, too, since you were also part of the celebration. So let's try not to overdo it." **176b**

Aristophanes[15] replied: "Good idea, Pausanias. We've got to make a plan for going easy on the drink tonight. I was over my head last night myself, like the others."

After that, up spoke Eryximachus, son of Acumenus: "Well said, both of you. But I still have one question: How do *you* feel, Agathon? Are you strong enough for serious drinking?"

"Absolutely not," replied Agathon. "I've no strength left for anything."

"What a lucky stroke for us," Eryximachus said, "for me, for Aristodemus, **176c** for Phaedrus,[16] and the rest—that you large-capacity drinkers are already exhausted. Imagine how weak drinkers like ourselves feel after last night! Of course I don't include Socrates in my claims: he can drink or not, and will be satisfied whatever we do. But since none of us seems particularly eager to overindulge, perhaps it would not be amiss for me to provide you with some accurate information as to the nature of intoxication. If I have learned anything from medicine, it is the following point: inebriation is **176d** harmful to everyone. Personally, therefore, I always refrain from heavy drinking; and I advise others against it—especially people who are suffering the effects of a prévious night's excesses."

"Well," Phaedrus interrupted him, "I always follow your advice, especially when you speak as a doctor. In this case, if the others know what's good for them, they too will do just as you say."

---

[12] The theater of Dionysus, where Agathon's plays were staged, actually held between ten thousand and twenty thousand.

[13] Dionysus was the god of wine and drunkenness.

[14] Pausianias of Cerameis (a deme slightly northwest of Athens).

[15] See *Apology* 19c note.

[16] Socrates' interlocutor in the eponymous *Phaedrus*. He was exiled, as was Alcibiades, accused of profaning the Eleusinian Mysteries.

176e   At that point they all agreed not to get drunk that evening; they decided to drink only as much as pleased them.

"It's settled, then," said Eryximachus. "We are resolved to force no one to drink more than he wants. I would like now to make a further motion: let us dispense with the flute-girl who just made her entrance; let her play for herself or, if she prefers, for the women in the house. Let us instead spend our evening in conversation. If you are so minded, I would like to propose a subject."

177a   They all said they were quite willing, and urged him to make his proposal. So Eryximachus said:

"Let me begin by citing Euripides' *Melanippe:* 'Not mine the tale.' What I am about to tell belongs to Phaedrus here, who is deeply indignant on this issue, and often complains to me about it:

"'Eryximachus,' he says, 'isn't it an awful thing! Our poets have composed hymns in honor of just about any god you can think of; but has a single one of them given one moment's thought to the god of love,

177b   ancient and powerful as he is? As for our fancy intellectuals, they have written volumes praising Heracles and other heroes (as did the distinguished Prodicus).[17] Well, perhaps *that's* not surprising, but I've actually read a book by an accomplished author who saw fit to extol the usefulness of salt! How

177c   *could* people pay attention to such trifles and never, not even once, write a proper hymn to Love? How could anyone ignore so great a god?'

"Now, Phaedrus, in my judgment, is quite right. I would like, therefore, to take up a contribution, as it were, on his behalf, and gratify his wish. Besides, I think this a splendid time for all of us here to honor the god. If

177d   you agree, we can spend the whole evening in discussion, because I propose that each of us give as good a speech in praise of Love as he is capable of giving, in proper order from left to right. And let us begin with Phaedrus, who is at the head of the table and is, in addition, the father of our subject."

"No one will vote against that, Eryximachus," said Socrates. "How could *I* vote 'No,' when the only thing I say I understand is the art of love? Could Agathon and Pausanias? Could Aristophanes, who thinks of

177e   nothing but Dionysus and Aphrodite?[18] No one I can see here now could vote against your proposal.

"And though it's not quite fair to those of us who have to speak last, if the first speeches turn out to be good enough and to exhaust our subject, I promise we won't complain. So let Phaedrus begin, with the blessing of Fortune; let's hear his praise of Love."

They all agreed with Socrates, and pressed Phaedrus to start. Of course,

178a   Aristodemus couldn't remember exactly what everyone said, and I myself

---

[17] See *Apology* 19e and note.

[18] Goddess of love.

don't remember everything he told me. But I'll tell you what he remembered best, and what I consider the most important points.

As I say, he said Phaedrus spoke first, beginning more or less like this:

Love is a great god, wonderful in many ways to gods and men, and most marvelous of all is the way he came into being. We honor him as one of the most ancient gods, and the proof of his great age is this: the parents of 178b Love have no place in poetry or legend. According to Hesiod, the first to be born was Chaos,

> . . . but then came
> Earth, broad-chested, a seat for all, forever safe,
> And Love.[19]

And Acusilaus agrees with Hesiod: after Chaos came Earth and Love, these two.[20] And Parmenides tells of this beginning:

> The very first god [she] designed was Love.[21]

All sides agree, then, that Love is one of the most ancient gods. As such, 178c he gives to us the greatest goods. I cannot say what greater good there is for a young boy than a gentle lover, or for a lover than a boy to love. There is a certain guidance each person needs for his whole life, if he is to live well; and nothing imparts this guidance—not high kinship, not public honor, not wealth—nothing imparts this guidance as well as Love. What guidance do I mean? I mean a sense of shame at acting shamefully, and a 178d sense of pride in acting well. Without these, nothing fine or great can be accomplished, in public or in private.

What I say is this: if a man in love is found doing something shameful, or accepting shameful treatment because he is a coward and makes no defense, then nothing would give him more pain than being seen by the boy he loves—not even being seen by his father or his comrades. We see the same 178e thing also in the boy he loves, that he is especially ashamed before his lover when he is caught in something shameful. If only there were a way to start a city or an army made up of lovers and the boys they love! Theirs would be the best possible system of society, for they would hold back from all that is shameful, and seek honor in each other's eyes. Even a few of them, in **179a** battle side by side, would conquer all the world, I'd say. For a man in love would never allow his loved one, of all people, to see him leaving ranks or dropping weapons. He'd rather die a thousand deaths! And as for leaving

---

[19] *Theogony* 116–20, 118 omitted.

[20] Acusilaus was an early-fifth–century writer of genealogies.

[21] Parmenides of Elea (fifth-century philosopher), B13.

the boy behind, or not coming to his aid in danger—why, no one is so base that true Love could not inspire him with courage, and make him as brave as if he'd been born a hero. When Homer says a god 'breathes might' into some of the heroes, this is really Love's gift to every lover.[22]

179b

Besides, no one will die for you but a lover, and a lover will do this even if she's a woman. Alcestis is proof to everyone in Greece that what I say is true.[23] Only she was willing to die in place of her husband, although his father and mother were still alive. Because of her love, she went so far beyond his parents in family feeling that she made them look like outsiders, as if they belonged to their son in name only. And when she did this her deed struck everyone, even the gods, as nobly done. The gods were so delighted, in fact, that they gave her the prize they reserve for a handful chosen from the throngs of noble heroes—they sent her soul back from the dead. As you can see, the eager courage of love wins highest honors from the gods.

179c

179d

Orpheus, however, they sent unsatisfied from Hades, after showing him only an image of the woman he came for. They did not give him the woman herself, because they thought he was soft (he was, after all, a cithara-player) and did not dare to die like Alcestis for Love's sake, but contrived to enter living into Hades. So they punished him for that, and made him die at the hands of women.[24]

179e

The honor they gave to Achilles,[25] the son of Thetis, is another matter. They sent him to the Isles of the Blest because he dared to stand by his lover Patroclus and avenge him, even after he had learned from his mother that he would die if he killed Hector, but that if he chose otherwise he'd go home and end his life as an old man. Instead he chose to die for Patroclus, and more than that, he did it for a man whose life was already over. The gods were highly delighted at this, of course, and gave him special honor, because he made so much of his lover. Aeschylus talks nonsense when he claims Achilles was the lover;[26] he was more beautiful than Patroclus, more beautiful than all the heroes, and still beardless. Besides he was much younger, as Homer says.

180a

---

[22] Cf. *Iliad* x.482, xv.262; *Odyssey* ix.381.

[23] Alcestis was the self-sacrificing wife of Admetus, to whom Apollo gave a chance to live if anyone would go to Hades in his place.

[24] Orpheus was a musician of legendary powers, who charmed his way into the underworld in search of his dead wife, Eurydice.

[25] Champion of the Greeks in the Trojan War. Patroclus was his friend.

[26] In his play, *The Myrmidons*. In Homer there is no hint of sexual attachment between Achilles and Patroclus.

In truth, the gods honor virtue most highly when it belongs to Love. They are more impressed and delighted, however, and are more generous 180b with a loved one who cherishes his lover, than with a lover who cherishes the boy he loves. A lover is more godlike than his boy, you see, since he is inspired by a god. That's why they gave a higher honor to Achilles than to Alcestis, and sent him to the Isles of the Blest.

Therefore I say Love is the most ancient of the gods, the most honored, and the most powerful in helping men gain virtue and blessedness, whether they are alive or have passed away.

That was more or less what Phaedrus said according to Aristodemus. 180c There followed several other speeches which he couldn't remember very well. So he skipped them and went directly to the speech of Pausanias.

Phaedrus (Pausanias began), I'm not quite sure our subject has been well defined. Our charge has been simple—to speak in praise of Love. This would have been fine if Love himself were simple, too, but as a matter of fact, there are two kinds of Love. In view of this, it might be better to begin by making clear which kind of Love we are to praise. Let me therefore 180d try to put our discussion back on the right track and explain which kind of Love ought to be praised. Then I shall give him the praise he deserves, as the god he is.

It is a well-known fact that Love and Aphrodite are inseparable. If, therefore, Aphrodite were a single goddess, there could also be a single Love; but, since there are actually two goddesses of that name, there also are two kinds of Love. I don't expect you'll disagree with me about the two goddesses, will you? One is an older deity, the motherless daughter of Uranus, the god of heaven: she is known as Urania, or Heavenly Aphrodite. The other goddess is younger, the daughter of Zeus and Dione: her name is Pandemos, or Common Aphrodite. It follows, therefore, that there is 180e a Common as well as a Heavenly Love, depending on which goddess is Love's partner. And although, of course, all the gods must be praised, we must still make an effort to keep these two gods apart.

The reason for this applies in the same way to every type of action: considered in itself, no action is either good or bad, honorable or shameful. Take, for example, our own case. We had a choice between drinking, singing, or having a conversation. Now, in itself none of these is better than 181a any other: how it comes out depends entirely on how it is performed. If it is done honorably and properly, it turns out to be honorable; if it is done improperly, it is disgraceful. And my point is that exactly this principle applies to being in love: Love is not in himself noble and worthy of praise; that depends on whether the sentiments he produces in us are themselves noble.

181b   Now the Common Aphrodite's Love is himself truly common. As such, he strikes wherever he gets a chance. This, of course, is the love felt by the vulgar, who are attached to women no less than to boys, to the body more than to the soul, and to the least intelligent partners, since all they care about is completing the sexual act. Whether they do it honorably or not is of no concern. That is why they do whatever comes their way, sometimes good, sometimes bad; and which one it is, is incidental to their purpose. For the Love who moves them belongs to a much younger goddess, who,

181c   through her parentage, partakes of the nature both of the female and the male.

Contrast this with the Love of Heavenly Aphrodite. This goddess, whose descent is purely male (hence this love is for boys), is considerably older and therefore free from the lewdness of youth. That's why those who are inspired by her Love are attracted to the male: they find pleasure in what is by nature stronger and more intelligent. But, even within the group that is

181d   attracted to handsome boys, some are not moved purely by this Heavenly Love; those who are do not fall in love with little boys; they prefer older ones whose cheeks are showing the first traces of a beard—a sign that they have begun to form minds of their own. I am convinced that a man who falls in love with a young man of this age is generally prepared to share everything with the one he loves—he is eager, in fact, to spend the rest of his own life with him. He certainly does not aim to deceive him—to take advantage of him while he is still young and inexperienced and then, after exposing him to ridicule, to move quickly on to someone else.

As a matter of fact, there should be a law forbidding affairs with young

181e   boys. If nothing else, all this time and effort would not be wasted on such an uncertain pursuit—and what is more uncertain than whether a particular boy will eventually make something of himself, physically or mentally? Good men, of course, are willing to make a law like this for themselves, but those other lovers, the vulgar ones, need external restraint. For just this reason we have placed every possible legal obstacle to their seducing our own

182a   wives and daughters. These vulgar lovers are the people who have given love such a bad reputation that some have gone so far as to claim that taking *any* man as a lover is in itself disgraceful. Would anyone make this claim if he weren't thinking of how hasty vulgar lovers are, and therefore how unfair to their loved ones? For nothing done properly and in accordance with our customs would ever have provoked such righteous disapproval.

I should point out, however, that, although the customs regarding Love in most cities are simple and easy to understand, here in Athens (and in Sparta[27] as well) they are remarkably complex. In places where the people

---

[27] Major city of the Peloponnese. Athens' rival in the fifth and fourth centuries.

are inarticulate, like Elis or Boeotia,[28] tradition straightforwardly approves 182b
taking a lover in every case. No one there, young or old, would ever
consider it shameful. The reason, I suspect, is that, being poor speakers,
they want to save themselves the trouble of having to offer reasons and
arguments in support of their suits.

By contrast, in places like Ionia[29] and almost every other part of the
Persian empire, taking a lover is always considered disgraceful. The Persian
empire is absolute; that is why it condemns love as well as philosophy and
sport. It is no good for rulers if the people they rule cherish ambitions for
themselves or form strong bonds of friendship with one another. That 182c
these are precisely the effects of philosophy, sport, and especially of Love
is a lesson the tyrants of Athens learned directly from their own experience: Didn't their reign come to a dismal end because of the bonds uniting
Harmodius and Aristogiton in love and affection?[30]

So you can see that plain condemnation of Love reveals lust for power
in the rulers and cowardice in the ruled, while indiscriminate approval 182d
testifies to general dullness and stupidity.

Our own customs, which, as I have already said, are much more difficult
to understand, are also far superior. Recall, for example, that we consider
it more honorable to declare your love rather than to keep it a secret, especially if you are in love with a youth of good family and accomplishment,
even if he isn't all that beautiful. Recall also that a lover is encouraged in
every possible way; this means that what he does is not considered shameful. On the contrary, conquest is deemed noble, and failure shameful. And 182e
as for *attempts* at conquest, our custom is to praise lovers for totally extraordinary acts—so extraordinary, in fact, that if they performed them for any
other purpose whatever, they would reap the most profound contempt. 183a
Suppose, for example, that in order to secure money, or a public post, or
any other practical benefit from another person, a man were willing to do
what lovers do for the ones they love. Imagine that in pressing his suit he
went to his knees in public view and begged in the most humiliating way,
that he swore all sorts of vows, that he spent the night at the other man's
doorstep, that he were anxious to provide services even a slave would have
refused—well, you can be sure that everyone, his enemies no less than his

---

[28] Elis was a city in the northwest Peloponnese; Boeotia, an area in northern
Greece.

[29] Area on the central northwest coast of Asia Minor where many great settlements
were located.

[30] Harmodius and Aristogiton attempted to overthrow the tyrant Hippias in 514
BCE. Although their attempt failed, the tyranny fell three years later, and the lovers
were celebrated as tyrannicides.

183b friends, would stand in his way. His enemies would jeer at his fawning servility, while his friends, ashamed on his behalf, would try everything to bring him back to his senses. But let a lover act in any of these ways, and everyone will immediately say what a charming man he is! No blame attaches to his behavior: custom treats it as noble through and through. And what is even more remarkable is that, at least according to popular wisdom, the gods will forgive a lover even for breaking his vows—a lover's vow, our people say, is no vow at all. The freedom given to the lover by 183c both gods and men according to our custom is immense.

In view of all this, you might well conclude that in our city we consider the lover's desire and the willingness to satisfy it as the noblest things in the world. When, on the other hand, you recall that fathers hire attendants for their sons as soon as they're old enough to be attractive, and that an attendant's main task is to prevent any contact between his charge and his suitors; when you recall how mercilessly a boy's own friends tease him if they catch him at it, and how strongly their elders approve and even 183d encourage such mocking—when you take all this into account, you're bound to come to the conclusion that we Athenians consider such behavior the most shameful thing in the world.

In my opinion, however, the fact of the matter is this. As I said earlier, love is, like everything else, complex: considered simply in itself, it is neither honorable nor a disgrace—its character depends entirely on the behavior it gives rise to. To give oneself to a vile man in a vile way is truly disgraceful behavior; by contrast, it is perfectly honorable to give oneself honorably to the right man. Now you may want to know who counts as vile in this context. I'll tell you: it is the common, vulgar lover, who 183e loves the body rather than the soul, the man whose love is bound to be inconstant, since what he loves is itself mutable and unstable. The moment the body is no longer in bloom, "he flies off and away,"[31] his promises and vows in tatters behind him. How different from this is a man who loves the right sort of character, and who remains its lover for life, attached as he is to something that is permanent.

We can now see the point of our customs: they are designed to separate 184a the wheat from the chaff, the proper love from the vile. That's why we do everything we can to make it as easy as possible for lovers to press their suits and as difficult as possible for young men to comply; it is like a competition, a kind of test to determine to which sort each belongs. This explains two further facts: First, why we consider it shameful to yield too quickly: the passage of time in itself provides a good test in these matters. Second, why we also consider it shameful for a man to be seduced by money or political

---

[31] *Iliad* ii.71.

power, either because he cringes at ill-treatment and will not endure it or   184b
because, once he has tasted the benefits of wealth and power, he will not
rise above them. None of these benefits is stable or permanent, apart from
the fact that no genuine affection can possibly be based upon them.

Our customs, then, provide for only one honorable way of taking a man
as a lover. In addition to recognizing that the lover's total and willing subju-
gation to his beloved's wishes is neither servile nor reprehensible, we allow   184c
that there is one—and only one—further reason for willingly subjecting
oneself to another which is equally above reproach: that is subjection for
the sake of virtue. If someone decides to put himself at another's disposal
because he thinks that this will make him better in wisdom or in any
other part of virtue, we approve of his voluntary subjection: we consider
it neither shameful nor servile. Both these principles—that is, both the
principle governing the proper attitude toward the lover of young men and
the principle governing the love of wisdom and of virtue in general—must   184d
be combined if a young man is to accept a lover in an honorable way.
When an older lover and a young man come together and each obeys the
principle appropriate to him—when the lover realizes that he is justified
in doing anything for a loved one who grants him favors, and when the
young man understands that he is justified in performing any service for
a lover who can make him wise and virtuous—and when the lover is able   184e
to help the young man become wiser and better, and the young man is
eager to be taught and improved by his lover—then, and only then, when
these two principles coincide absolutely, is it ever honorable for a young
man to accept a lover.

Only in this case, we should notice, is it never shameful to be deceived;
in every other case it is shameful, both for the deceiver and the person he
deceives. Suppose, for example, that someone thinks his lover is rich and   **185a**
accepts him for his money; his action won't be any less shameful if it turns
out that he was deceived and his lover was a poor man after all. For the
young man has already shown himself to be the sort of person who will do
anything for money—and that is far from honorable. By the same token,
suppose that someone takes a lover in the mistaken belief that this lover is a
good man and likely to make him better himself, while in reality the man
is horrible, totally lacking in virtue; even so, it is noble for him to have   185b
been deceived. For he too has demonstrated something about himself: that
he is the sort of person who will do anything for the sake of virtue—and
what could be more honorable than that? It follows, therefore, that giving
in to your lover for virtue's sake is honorable, whatever the outcome. And
this, of course, is the Heavenly Love of the heavenly goddess. Love's value
to the city as a whole and to the citizens is immeasurable, for he compels
the lover and his loved one alike to make virtue their central concern. All
other forms of love belong to the vulgar goddess.   185c

Phaedrus, I'm afraid this hasty improvisation will have to do as my contribution on the subject of Love.

When Pausanias finally came to a pause (I've learned this sort of fine figure from our clever rhetoricians), it was Aristophanes' turn, according to Aristodemus. But he had such a bad case of the hiccups—he'd probably stuffed himself again, though, of course, it could have been anything—that making a speech was totally out of the question. So he turned to the doctor, 185d Eryximachus, who was next in line, and said to him:

"Eryximachus, it's up to you—as well it should be. Cure me or take my turn."

"As a matter of fact," Eryximachus replied, "I shall do both. I shall take your turn—you can speak in my place as soon as you feel better—and I shall also cure you. While I am giving my speech, you should hold your breath for as long as you possibly can. This may well eliminate your hic-185e cups. If it fails, the best remedy is a thorough gargle. And if even this has no effect, then tickle your nose with a feather. A sneeze or two will cure even the most persistent case."

"The sooner you start speaking, the better," Aristophanes said. "I'll follow your instructions to the letter."

This, then, was the speech of Eryximachus:

Pausanias introduced a crucial consideration in his speech, though in my opinion he did not develop it sufficiently. Let me therefore try to carry 186a his argument to its logical conclusion. His distinction between the two species of Love seems to me very useful indeed. But if I have learned a single lesson from my own field, the science of medicine, it is that Love does not occur only in the human soul; it is not simply the attraction we feel toward human beauty: it is a significantly broader phenomenon. It certainly occurs within the animal kingdom, and even in the world of plants. In fact, it occurs everywhere in the universe. Love is a deity of the 186b greatest importance: he directs everything that occurs, not only in the human domain, but also in that of the gods.

Let me begin with some remarks concerning medicine—I hope you will forgive my giving pride of place to my own profession. The point is that our very bodies manifest the two species of Love. Consider for a moment the marked difference, the radical dissimilarity, between healthy and diseased constitutions and the fact that dissimilar subjects desire and love objects that are themselves dissimilar. Therefore, the love manifested in health is fundamentally distinct from the love manifested in disease. And now recall that, as Pausanias claimed, it is as honorable to yield to a good

man as it is shameful to consort with the debauched. Well, my point is   186c
that the case of the human body is strictly parallel. Everything sound and
healthy in the body must be encouraged and gratified; that is precisely the
object of medicine. Conversely, whatever is unhealthy and unsound must
be frustrated and rebuffed: that's what it is to be an expert in medicine.

In short, medicine is simply the science of the effects of Love on reple-
tion and depletion of the body, and the hallmark of the accomplished   186d
physician is his ability to distinguish the Love that is noble from the Love
that is ugly and disgraceful. A good practitioner knows how to affect the
body and how to transform its desires; he can implant the proper species
of Love when it is absent and eliminate the other sort whenever it occurs.
The physician's task is to effect a reconciliation and establish mutual love
between the most basic bodily elements. Which are those elements? They
are, of course, those that are most opposed to one another, as hot is to cold,
bitter to sweet, wet to dry, cases like those. In fact, our ancestor Asclepius[32]   186e
first established medicine as a profession when he learned how to produce
concord and love between such opposites—that is what those poet fellows
say, and—this time—I concur with them.

Medicine, therefore, is guided everywhere by the god of Love, and so   **187a**
are physical education and farming as well. Further, a moment's reflection
suffices to show that the case of poetry and music, too, is precisely the same.
Indeed, this may have been just what Heraclitus had in mind, though his
mode of expression certainly leaves much to be desired. The one, he says,
"being at variance with itself is in agreement with itself "like the attunement of a bow or a lyre."[33] Naturally, it is patently absurd to claim that
an attunement or a harmony is in itself discordant or that its elements are
still in discord with one another. Heraclitus probably meant that an expert
musician creates a harmony by resolving the prior discord between high
and low notes. For surely there can be no harmony so long as high and   187b
low are still discordant; harmony, after all, is consonance, and consonance
is a species of agreement. Discordant elements, as long as they are still in
discord, cannot come to an agreement, and they therefore cannot produce
a harmony. Rhythm, for example, is produced only when fast and slow,
though earlier discordant, are brought into agreement with each other.   187c
Music, like medicine, creates agreement by producing concord and love
between these various opposites. Music is therefore simply the science of
the effects of Love on rhythm and harmony.

---

[32] A mythical figure regarded as the first doctor.

[33] Heraclitus of Ephesus, a philosopher of the early fifth century, was known for
his enigmatic sayings.

These effects are easily discernible if you consider the constitution of rhythm and harmony in themselves; Love does not occur in both his forms in this domain. But the moment you consider, in their turn, the effects of rhythm and harmony on their audience—either through composition, which creates new verses and melodies, or through musical education, which teaches the correct performance of existing compositions—complications arise directly, and they require the treatment of a good practitioner. Ultimately, the identical argument applies once again: the love felt by good people or by those whom such love might improve in this regard must be encouraged and protected. This is the honorable, heavenly species of Love, produced by the melodies of Urania, the Heavenly Muse. The other, produced by Polyhymnia, the muse of many songs, is common and vulgar.[34] Extreme caution is indicated here: we must be careful to enjoy his pleasures without slipping into debauchery—this case, I might add, is strictly parallel to a serious issue in my own field, namely, the problem of regulating the appetite so as to be able to enjoy a fine meal without unhealthy aftereffects.

In music, therefore, as well as in medicine and in all the other domains, in matters divine as well as in human affairs, we must attend with the greatest possible care to these two species of Love, which are, indeed, to be found everywhere. Even the seasons of the year exhibit their influence. When the elements to which I have already referred—hot and cold, wet and dry—are animated by the proper species of Love, they are in harmony with one another: their mixture is temperate, and so is the climate. Harvests are plentiful; men and all other living things are in good health; no harm can come to them. But when the sort of Love that is crude and impulsive controls the seasons, he brings death and destruction. He spreads the plague and many other diseases among plants and animals; he causes frost and hail and blights. All these are the effects of the immodest and disordered species of Love on the movements of the stars and the seasons of the year, that is, on the objects studied by the science called astronomy.

Consider further the rites of sacrifice and the whole area with which the art of divination is concerned; that is, the interaction between men and gods. Here, too, Love is the central concern: our object is to try to maintain the proper kind of Love and to attempt to cure the kind that is diseased. For what is the origin of all impiety? Our refusal to gratify the orderly kind of Love, and our deference to the other sort, when we should have been guided by the former sort of Love in every action in connection with our parents, living or dead, and with the gods. The task of divination is to keep watch over these two species of Love and to doctor them

187d

187e

188a

188b

188c

---

[34] Urania and Polyhymnia appear as Muses in Hesiod, *Theogony* 75–79. Eryximachus has made them correspond to Pausanias' Urania and Pandemos.

as necessary. Divination, therefore, is the practice that produces loving affection between gods and men; it is simply the science of the effects of Love on justice and piety.

189d

Such is the power of Love—so varied and great that in all cases it might be called absolute. Yet even so it is far greater when Love is directed, in temperance and justice, toward the good, whether in heaven or on earth: happiness and good fortune, the bonds of human society, concord with the gods above—all these are among his gifts.

Perhaps I, too, have omitted a great deal in this discourse on Love. If so, I assure you, it was quite inadvertent. And if in fact I have overlooked certain points, it is now your task, Aristophanes, to complete the argument—unless, of course, you are planning on a different approach. In any case, proceed; your hiccups seem cured.

188e

Then Aristophanes took over (so Aristodemus said): "The hiccups have stopped all right—but not before I applied the Sneeze Treatment to them. Makes me wonder whether the 'orderly sort of Love' in the body calls for the sounds and itchings that constitute a sneeze, because the hiccups stopped immediately when I applied the Sneeze Treatment."

189a

"You're good, Aristophanes," Eryximachus answered. "But watch what you're doing. You are making jokes before your speech, and you're forcing me to prepare for you to say something funny, and to put up my guard against you, when otherwise you might speak at peace."

189b

Then Aristophanes laughed. "Good point, Eryximachus. So let me 'unsay what I have said.' But don't put up your guard. I'm not worried about saying something funny in my coming oration. That would be pure profit, and it comes with the territory of my Muse. What I'm worried about is that I might say something ridiculous."

"Aristophanes, do you really think you can take a shot at me, and then escape? Use your head! Remember, as you speak, that you will be called upon to give an account. Though perhaps, if I decide to, I'll let you off."

189c

"Eryximachus," Aristophanes said, "indeed I do have in mind a different approach to speaking than the one the two of you used, you and Pausanias. You see, I think people have entirely missed the power of Love, because, if they had grasped it, they'd have built the greatest temples and altars to him and made the greatest sacrifices. But as it is, none of this is done for him, though it should be, more than anything else! For he loves the human race more than any other god, he stands by us in our troubles, and he cures those ills we humans are most happy to have mended. I shall, therefore, try to explain his power to you; and you, please pass my teaching on to everyone else."

189d

First you must learn what Human Nature was in the beginning and what has happened to it since, because long ago our nature was not what it is now, but very different. There were three kinds of human beings, that's my first point—not two as there are now, male and female. In addi-

189e   tion to these, there was a third, a combination of those two; its name survives, though the kind itself has vanished. At that time, you see, the word "androgynous" really meant something: a form made up of male and female elements, though now there's nothing but the word, and that's used as an insult. My second point is that the shape of each human being was completely round, with back and sides in a circle; they had four hands each,

190a   as many legs as hands, and two faces, exactly alike, on a rounded neck. Between the two faces, which were on opposite sides, was one head with four ears. There were two sets of sexual organs, and everything else was the way you'd imagine it from what I've told you. They walked upright, as we do now, whatever direction they wanted. And whenever they set out to run fast, they thrust out all their eight limbs, the ones they had then, and spun rapidly, the way gymnasts do cartwheels, by bringing their legs around straight.

Now here is why there were three kinds, and why they were as I

190b   described them: The male kind was originally an offspring of the sun, the female of the earth, and the one that combined both genders was an off-spring of the moon, because the moon shares in both. They were spherical, and so was their motion, because they were like their parents in the sky.

In strength and power, therefore, they were terrible, and they had great ambitions. They made an attempt on the gods, and Homer's story about Ephialtes and Otus was originally about them: how they tried to make an

190c   ascent to heaven so as to attack the gods.[35] Then Zeus and the other gods met in council to discuss what to do, and they were sore perplexed. They couldn't wipe out the human race with thunderbolts and kill them all off, as they had the giants, because that would wipe out the worship they receive, along with the sacrifices we humans give them. On the other hand, they couldn't let them run riot. At last, after great effort, Zeus had an idea.

"I think I have a plan," he said, "that would allow human beings to exist and stop their misbehaving: they will give up being wicked when they lose

190d   their strength. So I shall now cut each of them in two. At one stroke they will lose their strength and also become more profitable to us, owing to the increase in their number. They shall walk upright on two legs. But if I find they still run riot and do not keep the peace," he said, "I will cut them in two again, and they'll have to make their way on one leg, hopping."

---

[35] *Iliad* v.385, *Odyssey* xi.305 ff. Ephialtes and Otus were giants.

So saying, he cut those human beings in two, the way people cut   190e
sorb-apples before they dry them or the way they cut eggs with hairs. As
he cut each one, he commanded Apollo to turn its face and half its neck
toward the wound, so that each person would see that he'd been cut and
keep better order. Then Zeus commanded Apollo to heal the rest of the
wound, and Apollo did turn the face around, and he drew skin from all
sides over what is now called the stomach, and there he made one mouth,
as in a pouch with a drawstring, and fastened it at the center of the stomach.
This is now called the navel. Then he smoothed out the other wrinkles, of   **191a**
which there were many, and he shaped the breasts, using some such tool as
shoemakers have for smoothing wrinkles out of leather on the form. But
he left a few wrinkles around the stomach and the navel, to be a reminder
of what happened long ago.

Now, since their natural form had been cut in two, each one longed for
its own other half, and so they would throw their arms about each other,
weaving themselves together, wanting to grow together. In that condition
they would die from hunger and general idleness, because they would
not do anything apart from each other. Whenever one of the halves died   191b
and one was left, the one that was left still sought another and wove itself
together with that. Sometimes the half he met came from a woman, as
we'd call her now, sometimes it came from a man; either way, they kept
on dying.

Then, however, Zeus took pity on them, and came up with another
plan: he moved their genitals around to the front! Before then, you see,
they used to have their genitals outside, like their faces, and they cast seed
and made children, not in one another, but in the ground, like cicadas. So   191c
Zeus brought about this relocation of genitals, and in doing so he invented
interior reproduction, *by* the man *in* the woman. The purpose of this was
so that, when a man embraced a woman, he would cast his seed and they
would have children; but when male embraced male, they would at least
have the satisfaction of intercourse, after which they could stop embracing,
return to their jobs, and look after their other needs in life. This, then, is
the source of our desire to love each other. Love is born into every human   191d
being; it calls back the halves of our original nature together; it tries to
make one out of two and heal the wound of human nature.

Each of us, then, is a "matching half" of a human whole, because each
was sliced like a flatfish, two out of one, and each of us is always seeking
the half that matches him. That's why a man who is split from the double
sort (which used to be called "androgynous") runs after women. Many
lecherous men have come from this class, and so do the lecherous women
who run after men. Women who are split from a woman, however, pay no   191e
attention at all to men; they are oriented more toward women, and lesbians
come from this class. People who are split from a male are male-oriented.

192a While they are boys, because they are chips off the male block, they love men and enjoy lying with men and being embraced by men; those are the best of boys and lads, because they are the most manly in their nature. Of course, some say such boys are shameless, but they're lying. It's not because they have no shame that such boys do this, you see, but because they are bold and brave and masculine, and they tend to cherish what is like themselves. Do you want me to prove it? Look, these are the only kind of boys who grow up to be politicians. When they're grown men, they are lovers of

192b young men, and they naturally pay no attention to marriage or to making babies, except insofar as they are required by local custom. They, however, are quite satisfied to live their lives with one another unmarried. In every way, then, this sort of man grows up as a lover of young men and a lover of Love, always rejoicing in his own kind.

And so, when a person meets the half that is his very own, whatever his orientation, whether it's to young men or not, then something wonderful

192c happens: the two are struck from their senses by love, by a sense of belonging to one another, and by desire, and they don't want to be separated from one another, not even for a moment.

These are the people who finish out their lives together and still cannot say what it is they want from one another. No one would think it is the intimacy of sex—that mere sex is the reason each lover takes so great and deep a joy in being with the other. It's obvious that the soul of every lover

192d longs for something else; his soul cannot say what it is, but like an oracle it has a sense of what it wants, and like an oracle it hides behind a riddle. Suppose two lovers are lying together and Hephaestus[36] stands over them with his mending tools, asking, "What is it you human beings really want from each other?" And suppose they're perplexed, and he asks them again: "Is this your heart's desire, then—for the two of you to become parts of the same whole, as near as can be, and never to separate, day or night? Because if that's your desire, I'd like to weld you together and join you

192e into something that is naturally whole, so that the two of you are made into one. Then the two of you would share one life, as long as you lived, because you would be one being, and by the same token, when you died, you would be one and not two in Hades, having died a single death. Look at your love, and see if this is what you desire: wouldn't this be all the good fortune you could want?"

Surely you can see that no one who received such an offer would turn it down; no one would find anything else that he wanted. Instead, everyone would think he'd found out at last what he had always wanted: to come together and melt together with the one he loves, so that one person

---

[36] Armorer to the gods. Cf. *Odyssey* viii.266 ff.

emerged from two. Why should this be so? It's because, as I said, we used
to be complete wholes in our original nature, and now "Love" is the name
for our pursuit of wholeness, for our desire to be complete.   193a

Long ago we were united, as I said; but now the god has divided us as
punishment for the wrong we did him, just as the Spartans divided the
Arcadians.[37] So there's a danger that if we don't keep order before the gods,
we'll be split in two again, and then we'll be walking around in the condition of people carved on gravestones in bas-relief, sawn apart between the
nostrils, like half dice. We should encourage all men, therefore, to treat
the gods with all due reverence, so that we may escape this fate and find
wholeness instead. And we will, if Love is our guide and our commander.   193b
Let no one work against him. Whoever opposes Love is hateful to the gods,
but if we become friends of the god and cease to quarrel with him, then
we shall find the young men that are meant for us and win their love, as
very few men do nowadays.

Now don't get ideas, Eryximachus, and turn this speech into a comedy.
Don't think I'm pointing this at Pausanias and Agathon. Probably, they
both do belong to the group that are entirely masculine in nature. But I   193c
am speaking about everyone, men and women alike, and I say there's just
one way for the human race to flourish: we must bring love to its perfect
conclusion, and each of us must win the favors of his very own young
man, so that he can recover his original nature. If that is the ideal, then,
of course, the nearest approach to it is best in present circumstances, and
that is to win the favor of young men who are naturally sympathetic to us.

If we are to give due praise to the god who can give us this blessing,
then, we must praise Love. Love does the best that can be done for the time   193d
being: he draws us toward what belongs to us. But for the future, Love
promises the greatest hope of all: if we treat the gods with due reverence,
he will restore to us our original nature, and by healing us, he will make
us blessed and happy.

"That," he said, "is my speech about Love, Eryximachus. It is rather different from yours. As I begged you earlier, don't make a comedy of it. I'd
prefer to hear what all the others will say—or, rather, what each of them
will say, since Agathon and Socrates are the only ones left."   193e

"I found your speech delightful," said Eryximachus, "so I'll do as you
say. Really, we've had such a rich feast of speeches on Love, that if I couldn't

---

[37] Arcadia included the city of Mantinea, which opposed Sparta, and was rewarded
for this by having its population divided and dispersed in 385 BCE. Aristophanes
seems to be referring anachronistically to those events. Such anachronisms are not
uncommon in Plato.

vouch for the fact that Socrates and Agathon are masters of the art of love, I'd be afraid that they'd have nothing left to say. But as it is, I have no fears on this score."

194a   Then Socrates said, "That's because *you* did beautifully in the contest, Eryximachus. But if you ever get in my position, or rather the position I'll be in after Agathon's spoken so well, then you'll really be afraid. You'll be at your wit's end, as I am now."

"You're trying to bewitch me, Socrates," said Agathon, "by making me think the audience expects great things of my speech, so I'll get flustered."

194b   "Agathon!" said Socrates, "How forgetful do you think I am? I saw how brave and dignified you were when you walked right up to the theater platform along with the actors and looked straight out at that enormous audience. You were about to put your own writing on display, and you weren't the least bit panicked. After seeing that, how could I expect you to be flustered by us, when we are so few?"

"Why, Socrates," said Agathon. "You must think I have nothing but theater audiences on my mind! So you suppose I don't realize that, if you're intelligent, you find a few sensible men much more frightening than a senseless crowd?"

194c   "No," he said, "It wouldn't be very handsome of me to think you crude in any way, Agathon. I'm sure that if you ever run into people you consider wise, you'll pay more attention to them than to ordinary people. But you can't suppose we're in that class; we were at the theater too, you know, part of the ordinary crowd. Still, if you did run into any wise men, other than yourself, you'd certainly be ashamed at the thought of doing anything ugly in front of them. Is that what you mean?"

"That's true," he said.

"On the other hand, you wouldn't be ashamed to do something ugly in front of ordinary people. Is that it?"

194d   At that point Phaedrus interrupted: "Agathon, my friend, if you answer Socrates, he'll no longer care whether we get anywhere with what we're doing here, so long as he has a partner for discussion. Especially if he's handsome. Now, like you, I enjoy listening to Socrates in discussion, but it is my duty to see to the praising of Love and to exact a speech from every one of this group. When each of you two has made his offering to the god, then you can have your discussion."

194e   "You're doing a beautiful job, Phaedrus," said Agathon. "There's nothing to keep me from giving my speech. Socrates will have many opportunities for discussion later."

I wish first to speak of how I ought to speak, and only then to speak. In my opinion, you see, all those who have spoken before me did not so much celebrate the god as congratulate human beings on the good things that come to them from the god. But who it is who gave these gifts, what he is like—no one has spoken about that. Now, only one method is correct **195a** for every praise, no matter whose: you must explain what qualities in the subject of your speech enable him to give the benefits for which we praise him. So now, in the case of Love, it is right for us to praise him first for what he is and afterward for his gifts.

I maintain, then, that while all the gods are happy, Love—if I may say so without giving offense—is the happiest of them all, for he is the most beautiful and the best. His great beauty lies in this: First, Phaedrus, he is the youngest of the gods. He proves my point himself by fleeing old age in 195b headlong flight, fast-moving though it is (that's obvious—it comes after us faster than it should). Love was born to hate old age and will come nowhere near it. Love always lives with young people and is one of them: the old story holds good that like is always drawn to like. And though on many other points I agree with Phaedrus, I do not agree with this: that Love is more ancient than Cronus and Iapetus.[38] No, I say that he is the youngest of the gods and stays young forever. 195c

Those old stories Hesiod and Parmenides tell about the gods—those things happened under Necessity, not Love, if what they say is true. For not one of all those violent deeds would have been done—no castrations, no imprisonments—if Love had been present among them. There would have been peace and brotherhood instead, as there has been now as long as Love has been king of the gods.

So he is young. And besides being young, he is delicate. It takes a poet as good as Homer to show how delicate the god is. For Homer says that 195d Mischief is a god and that she is delicate—well, that her feet are delicate, anyway! He says:

> . . . hers are delicate feet: not on the ground
> Does she draw nigh; she walks instead upon the heads of men.[39]

A lovely proof, I think, to show how delicate she is: she doesn't walk on 195e anything hard; she walks only on what is soft. We shall use the same proof about Love, then, to show that he is delicate. For he walks not on earth, not even on people's skulls, which are not really soft at all, but in the softest of all the things that are, there he walks, there he has his home. For he makes his home in the characters, in the souls, of gods and men—and not even in every soul that comes along: when he encounters a soul with a harsh character, he turns away; but when he finds a soft and gentle character, he

---

[38] Cronus was the father of Zeus, who castrated, deposed, and imprisoned him. Iapetus was Cronus' brother.

[39] *Iliad* xix.92–93. "Mischief" translates *Atē*.

settles down in it. Always, then, he is touching with his feet and with the whole of himself what is softest in the softest places. He must therefore be most delicate.

196a He is youngest, then, and most delicate; in addition he has a fluid, supple shape. For if he were hard, he would not be able to enfold a soul completely or escape notice when he first entered it or withdrew. Besides, his graceful good looks prove that he is balanced and fluid in his nature. Everyone knows that Love has extraordinary good looks, and between ugliness and Love there is unceasing war.

And the exquisite coloring of his skin! The way the god consorts with 196b flowers shows that. For he never settles in anything, be it a body or a soul, that cannot flower or has lost its bloom. His place is wherever it is flowery and fragrant; there he settles, there he stays.

Enough for now about the beauty of the god, though much remains still to be said. After this, we should speak of Love's moral character.[40] The main point is that Love is neither the cause nor the victim of any injustice; he does no wrong to gods or men, nor they to him. If anything 196c has an effect on him, it is never by violence, for violence never touches Love. And the effects he has on others are not forced, for every service we give to love we give willingly. And whatever one person agrees on with another, when both are willing, that is right and just; so say "the laws that are kings of society."[41]

And besides justice, he has the biggest share of temperance. For temperance, by common agreement, is power over pleasures and passions, and no pleasure is more powerful than Love! But if they are weaker, they are under the power of Love, and *he* has the power; and because he has power over pleasures and passions, Love is exceptionally temperate.

196d And as for manly bravery, "Not even Ares can stand up to" Love![42] For Ares has no hold on Love, but Love does on Ares—love of Aphrodite, so runs the tale.[43] But he who has hold is more powerful than he who is held; and so, because Love has power over the bravest of the others, he is bravest of them all.

Now I have spoken about the god's justice, temperance, and bravery; his wisdom remains.[44] I must try not to leave out anything that can be

---

[40] "Moral character": *aretē*, i.e., virtue.

[41] A proverbial expression.

[42] From Sophocles: "Even Ares cannot withstand Necessity." Ares is the god of war.

[43] See *Odyssey* viii.266–366. Aphrodite's husband Hephaestus made a snare that caught Ares in bed with Aphrodite.

[44] "Wisdom" translates *sophia* in the first instance; afterward in this passage it is "skill" or "art."

said on this. In the first place—to honor *our* profession as Eryximachus did his—the god is so skilled a poet that he can make others into poets: once   196e
Love touches him, *anyone* becomes a poet,

> . . . howe'er uncultured he had been before.[45]

This, we may fittingly observe, testifies that Love is a good poet, good, in sum, at every kind of artistic production. For you can't give to another what you don't have yourself, and you can't teach what you don't know.

And as to the production of animals—who will deny that they are all   **197a**
born and begotten through Love's skill?

And as for artisans and professionals—don't we know that whoever has this god for a teacher ends up in the light of fame, while a man untouched by Love ends in obscurity? Apollo, for one, invented archery, medicine, and prophecy when desire and love showed the way. Even he, therefore, would be a pupil of Love, and so would the Muses in music, Hephaestus in bronze   197b
work, Athena in weaving, and Zeus in "the governance of gods and men."

That too is how the gods' quarrels were settled, once Love came to be among them—love of beauty, obviously, because love is not drawn to ugliness. Before that, as I said in the beginning, and as the poets say, many dreadful things happened among the gods, because Necessity was king. But once this god was born, all goods came to gods and men alike through love of beauty.

This is how I think of Love, Phaedrus: first, he is himself the most   197c
beautiful and the best; after that, if anyone else is at all like that, Love is responsible. I am suddenly struck by a need to say something in poetic meter,[46] that it is he who—

> Gives peace to men and stillness to the sea,
> Lays winds to rest, and careworn men to sleep.

Love fills us with togetherness and drains all of our divisiveness away.   197d
Love calls gatherings like these together. In feasts, in dances, and in ceremonies, he gives the lead. Love moves us to mildness, removes from us wildness. He is giver of kindness, never of meanness. Gracious, kindly—let wise men see and gods admire! Treasure to lovers, envy to others, father of elegance, luxury, delicacy, grace, yearning, desire. Love cares well for good men, cares not for bad ones. In pain, in fear, in desire, or speech, Love is our best guide and guard; he is our comrade and our savior. Ornament of   197e
all gods and men, most beautiful leader and the best! Every man should

---

[45] Euripides, *Stheneboea*.

[46] After these two lines of poetry, Agathon continues with an extremely poetical prose peroration.

follow Love, sing beautifully his hymns, and join with him in the song he sings that charms the mind of god or man.

This, Phaedrus, is the speech I have to offer. Let it be dedicated to the god, part of it in fun, part of it moderately serious, as best I could manage.

198a   When Agathon finished, Aristodemus said, everyone there burst into applause, so becoming to himself and to the god did they think the young man's speech.

Then Socrates glanced at Eryximachus and said, "Now do you think I was foolish to feel the fear I felt before? Didn't I speak like a prophet a while ago when I said that Agathon would give an amazing speech and I would be tongue-tied?"

"You were prophetic about one thing, I think," said Eryximachus, "that Agathon would speak well. But you, tongue-tied? No, I don't believe that."

198b   "Bless you," said Socrates. "How am I not going to be tongue-tied, I or anyone else, after a speech delivered with such beauty and variety? The other parts may not have been so wonderful, but that at the end! Who would not be struck dumb on hearing the beauty of the words and phrases? Anyway, I was worried that I'd not be able to say anything that came close to them in beauty, and so I would almost have run away and escaped, if there had been a place to go. And, you see, the speech reminded

198c   me of Gorgias, so that I actually experienced what Homer describes: I was afraid that Agathon would end by sending the Gorgian head,[47] awesome at speaking in a speech, against my speech, and this would turn me to stone by striking me dumb. Then I realized how ridiculous I'd been to agree

198d   to join with you in praising Love and to say that I was a master of the art of love, when I knew nothing whatever of this business, of how anything whatever ought to be praised. In my foolishness, I thought you should tell the truth about whatever you praise, that this should be your basis, and that from this a speaker should select the most beautiful truths and arrange them most suitably. I was quite vain, thinking that I would talk well and that I knew the truth about praising anything whatever. But now it appears that this is not what it is to praise anything whatever; rather, it is to apply

198e   to the object the grandest and the most beautiful qualities, whether he actually has them or not. And if they are false, that is no objection; for the proposal, apparently, was that everyone here make the rest of us think he is praising Love—and not that he actually praise him. I think that is why you stir up every word and apply it to Love; your description of him and his

---

[47] "Gorgian head" is a pun on "Gorgon's head." In his peroration Agathon had spoken in the style of Gorgias (see *Apology* 19d–e), and this style was considered to be irresistibly powerful. The sight of a Gorgon's head would turn a man to stone.

gifts is designed to make him look better and more beautiful than anything else—to ignorant listeners, plainly, for of course he wouldn't look that way **199a** to those who knew. And your praise did seem beautiful and respectful. But I didn't even know the method for giving praise; and it was in ignorance that I agreed to take part in this. So "the tongue" promised, and "the mind" did not.[48] Goodbye to that! I'm not giving another eulogy using that method, not at all—I wouldn't be able to do it!—but, if you wish, I'd like to tell the truth my way. I want to avoid any comparison with your speeches, so as not to give you a reason to laugh at me. So look, Phaedrus, 199b would a speech like this satisfy your requirement? You will hear the truth about Love, and the words and phrasing will take care of themselves."

Then Aristodemus said that Phaedrus and the others urged him to speak in the way he thought was required, whatever it was.

"Well then, Phaedrus," said Socrates, "allow me to ask Agathon a few little questions, so that, once I have his agreement, I may speak on that basis."

"You have my permission," said Phaedrus. "Ask away." 199c

After that, said Aristodemus, Socrates began: "Indeed, Agathon, my friend, I thought you led the way beautifully into your speech when you said that one should first show the qualities of Love himself, and only then those of his deeds. I must admire that beginning. Come, then, since you have beautifully and magnificently expounded his qualities in other ways, tell me this, too, about Love. Is Love such as to be a love of something or of nothing? I'm not asking if he is born *of* some mother or father, (for 199d the question whether Love is love of mother or of father would really be ridiculous), but it's as if I'm asking this about a father—whether a father is the father *of* something or not. You'd tell me, of course, if you wanted to give me a good answer, that it's *of* a son or a daughter that a father is the father. Wouldn't you?"

"Certainly," said Agathon.

"Then does the same go for the mother?"

He agreed to that also.

"Well, then," said Socrates, "answer a little more fully, and you will 199e understand better what I want. If I should ask, 'What about this: a brother, just insofar as he *is* a brother, is he the brother of something or not?'"

He said that he was.

"And he's of a brother or a sister, isn't he?"

He agreed.

"Now try to tell me about love," he said. "Is Love the love of nothing or of something?"

---

[48] The allusion is to Euripides, *Hippolytus* 612.

"Of something, surely!"

200a "Then keep this object of love in mind, and remember what it is. But tell me this much: does Love desire that of which it is the love, or not?"

"Certainly," he said.

"At the time he desires and loves something, does he actually have what he desires and loves at that time, or doesn't he?"

"He doesn't. At least, that wouldn't be likely," he said.

"Instead of what's *likely*," said Socrates, "ask yourself whether it's *necessary* that this be so: a thing that desires something of which it is in need; **200b** otherwise, if it were not in need, it would not desire it. I can't tell you, Agathon, how strongly it strikes me that this is necessary. But how about you?"

"I think so too."

"Good. Now then, would someone who is tall, want to be tall? Or someone who is strong want to be strong?"

"Impossible, on the basis of what we've agreed."

"Presumably because no one is in need of those things he already has."

"True."

"But maybe a strong man could want to be strong," said Socrates, "or a fast one fast, or a healthy one healthy: in cases like these, you might think people really do want to be things they already are and do want to **200c** have qualities they already have—I bring them up so they won't deceive us. But in these cases, Agathon, if you stop to think about them, you will see that these people are what they are at the present time, whether they want to be or not, by a logical necessity. And who, may I ask, would ever bother to desire what's necessary in any event? But when someone says 'I am healthy, but that's just what I want to be,' or 'I am rich, but that's just what I want to be,' or 'I desire the very things that I have,' let us say to him: 'You already have riches and health and strength in your **200d** possession, my man, what you want is to possess these things in time to come, since in the present, whether you want to or not, you have them. Whenever you say, *I desire what I already have,* ask yourself whether you don't mean this: *I want the things I have now to be mine in the future as well.*' Wouldn't he agree?"

According to Aristodemus, Agathon said that he would.

So Socrates said, "Then this is what it is to love something which is not at hand, which the lover does not have: it is to desire the preservation of what he now has in time to come, so that he will have it then."

200e "Quite so," he said.

"So such a man or anyone else who has a desire desires what is not at hand and not present, what he does not have, and what he is not, and that of which he is in need; for such are the objects of desire and love."

"Certainly," he said.

"Come, then," said Socrates. "Let us review the points on which we've agreed. Aren't they, first, that Love is the love of something, and, second, that he loves things of which he has a present need?"

"Yes," he said.   201a

"Now, remember, in addition to these points, what you said in your speech about what it is that Love loves. If you like, I'll remind you. I think you said something like this: that the gods' quarrels were settled by love of beautiful things, for there is no love of ugly ones. Didn't you say something like that?"

"I did," said Agathon.

"And that's a suitable thing to say, my friend," said Socrates. "But if this is so, wouldn't Love have to be a desire for beauty, and never for ugliness?"

He agreed.

"And we also agreed that he loves just what he needs and does not have."   201b

"Yes," he said.

"So Love needs beauty, then, and does not have it."

"Necessarily," he said.

"So! If something needs beauty and has got no beauty at all, would you still say that it is beautiful?"

"Certainly not."

"Then do you still agree that Love is beautiful, if those things are so?"

Then Agathon said, "It turns out, Socrates, I didn't know what I was talking about in that speech."

"It was a beautiful speech, anyway, Agathon," said Socrates. "Now take   201c
it a little further. Don't you think that good things are always beautiful as well?"

"I do."

"Then if Love needs beautiful things, and if all good things are beautiful, he will need good things too."

"As for me, Socrates," he said, "I am unable to contradict you. Let it be as you say."

"Then it's the truth, my beloved Agathon, that you are unable to contradict," he said. "It is not hard at all to contradict Socrates."

Now I'll let you go. I shall try to go through for you the speech about   201d
Love I once heard from a woman of Mantinea, Diotima—a woman who was wise about many things besides this: once she even put off the plague for ten years by telling the Athenians what sacrifices to make. She is the one who taught me the art of love, and I shall go through her speech as best I can on my own, using what Agathon and I have agreed to as a basis.

Following your lead, Agathon, one should first describe who Love is and what he is like, and afterward describe his works—I think it will be easiest   201e
for me to proceed the way Diotima did and tell you how she questioned me.

You see, I had told her almost the same things Agathon told me just now: that Love is a great god and that he belongs to beautiful things.[49] And she used the very same arguments against me that I used against Agathon; she showed how, according to my very own speech, Love is neither beautiful nor good.

So I said, "What do you mean, Diotima? Is Love ugly, then, and bad?"

But she said, "Watch your tongue! Do you really think that, if a thing is not beautiful, it has to be ugly?"

202a   "I certainly do."

"And if a thing's not wise, it's ignorant? Or haven't you found out yet that there's something in between wisdom and ignorance?"

"What's that?"

"It's judging things correctly without being able to give a reason. Surely you see that this is not the same as knowing—for how could knowledge be unreasoning? And it's not ignorance either—for how could what hits the truth be ignorance? Correct judgment, of course, has this character: it is *in between* understanding and ignorance."

"True," said I, "as you say."

202b   "Then don't force whatever is not beautiful to be ugly, or whatever is not good to be bad. It's the same with Love: when you agree he is neither good nor beautiful, you need not think he is ugly and bad; he could be something in between," she said.

"Yet everyone agrees he's a great god," I said.

"Only those who don't know?" she said. "Is that how you mean 'everyone'? Or do you include those who do know?"

"Oh, everyone together."

And she laughed. "Socrates, how could those who say that he's not a
202c   god at all agree that he's a great god?"

"Who says that?" I asked.

"You, for one," she said, "and I for another."

"How can you say this!" I exclaimed.

"That's easy," said she. "Tell me, wouldn't you say that all gods are beautiful and happy? Surely you'd never say a god is not beautiful or happy?"

"Zeus! Not I," I said.

"Well, by calling anyone 'happy,' don't you mean they possess good and beautiful things?"

"Certainly."

---

[49] The Greek is ambiguous between "Love loves beautiful things" and "Love is one of the beautiful things." Agathon had asserted the former (197b, 201a), and this will be a premise in Diotima's argument, but Agathon asserted the latter as well (195a), and this is what Diotima proceeds to refute.

"What about Love? You agreed he needs good and beautiful things, and   202d
that's why he desires them—because he needs them."

"I certainly did."

"Then how could he be a god if he has no share in good and beautiful
things?"

"There's no way he could, apparently."

"Now do you see? You don't believe Love is a god either!"

"Then, what could Love be?" I asked. "A mortal?"

"Certainly not."

"Then, what is he?"

"He's like what we mentioned before," she said. "He is in between
mortal and immortal."

"What do you mean, Diotima?"

"He's a great spirit, Socrates. Everything spiritual, you see, is in between   202e
god and mortal."

"What is their function?" I asked.

"They are messengers who shuttle back and forth between the two,
conveying prayer and sacrifice from men to gods, while to men they bring
commands from the gods and gifts in return for sacrifices. Being in the
middle of the two, they round out the whole and bind fast the all to all.
Through them all divination passes, through them the art of priests in
sacrifice and ritual, in enchantment, prophecy, and sorcery. Gods do not   **203a**
mix with men; they mingle and converse with us through spirits instead,
whether we are awake or asleep. He who is wise in any of these ways is a
man of the spirit, but he who is wise in any other way, in a profession or
any manual work, is merely a mechanic. These spirits are many and various,
then, and one of them is Love."

"Who are his father and mother?" I asked.

"That's rather a long story," she said. "I'll tell it to you, all the same."   203b

"When Aphrodite was born, the gods held a celebration. Poros, the son
of Metis, was there among them.[50] When they had feasted, Penia came
begging, as poverty does when there's a party, and stayed by the gates.
Now Poros got drunk on nectar (there was no wine yet, you see) and,
feeling drowsy, went into the garden of Zeus, where he fell asleep. Then
Penia schemed up a plan to relieve her lack of resources: she would get a
child from Poros. So she lay beside him and got pregnant with Love. That   203c
is why Love was born to follow Aphrodite and serve her: because he was
conceived on the day of her birth. And that's why he is also by nature a
lover of beauty, because Aphrodite herself is especially beautiful.

---

[50] *Poros* means "way" or "resource." *Aporia* ("puzzle") means not having a way
to proceed. Poros' mother's name, *Mētis,* means "cunning." *Penia* means "poverty."

"As the son of Poros and Penia, his lot in life is set to be like theirs. In the first place, he is always poor, and he's far from being delicate and beautiful (as ordinary people think he is); instead, he is tough and shriveled 203d and shoeless and homeless, always lying on the dirt without a bed, sleeping at people's doorsteps and in roadsides under the sky, having his mother's nature, always living with Need. But on his father's side he is a schemer after the beautiful and the good; he is brave, impetuous, and intense, an awesome hunter, always weaving snares, resourceful in his pursuit of intelligence, a lover of wisdom through all his life, a genius with enchantments, potions, and clever pleadings.

203e "He is by nature neither immortal nor mortal. But now he springs to life when he gets his way; now he dies—all in the very same day. Because he is his father's son, however, he keeps coming back to life, but then anything he finds his way to always slips away, and for this reason Love is never completely without resources, nor is he ever rich.

"He is in between wisdom and ignorance as well. In fact, you see, none 204a of the gods loves wisdom or wants to become wise—for they are wise— and no one else who is wise already loves wisdom; on the other hand, no one who is ignorant will love wisdom either or want to become wise. For what's especially difficult about being ignorant is that you are content with yourself, even though you're neither beautiful and good nor intelligent. If you don't think you need anything, of course you won't want what you don't think you need."

"In that case, Diotima, who *are* the people who love wisdom, if they are neither wise nor ignorant?"

204b "That's obvious," she said. "A child could tell you. Those who love wisdom fall in between those two extremes. And Love is one of them, because he is in love with what is beautiful, and wisdom is extremely beautiful. It follows that Love *must* be a lover of wisdom and, as such, is in between being wise and being ignorant. This, too, comes to him from his parentage, from a father who is wise and resourceful and a mother who is not wise and lacks resource.

"My dear Socrates, that, then, is the nature of the Spirit called Love. 204c Considering what you thought about Love, it's no surprise that you were led into thinking of Love as you did. On the basis of what you say, I conclude that you thought Love was *being loved,* rather than *being a lover.* I think that's why Love struck you as beautiful in every way: because it is what is really beautiful and graceful that deserves to be loved, and this is perfect and highly blessed; but being a lover takes a different form, which I have just described."

So I said, "All right then, my friend. What you say about Love is beautiful, but if you're right, what use is Love to human beings?"

"I'll try to teach you that, Socrates, after I finish this. So far I've been   204d
explaining the character and the parentage of Love. Now, according to you,
he is love for beautiful things. But suppose someone asks us, 'Socrates and
Diotima, what is the point of loving beautiful things?'"

"It's clearer this way: 'The lover of beautiful things has a desire; what
does he desire?'"

"That they become his own," I said.

"But that answer calls for still another question, that is, 'What will this
man have, when the beautiful things he wants have become his own?'"

I said there was no way I could give a ready answer to that question.

Then she said, "Suppose someone changes the question, putting 'good'   204e
in place of 'beautiful,' and asks you this: 'Tell me, Socrates, a lover of good
things has a desire; what does he desire?'"

"That they become his own," I said.

"And what will he have, when the good things he wants have become
his own?"

"This time it's easier to come up with the answer," I said. "He'll have
happiness."

"That's what makes happy people happy, isn't it—possessing good things.   **205a**
There's no need to ask further, 'What's the point of wanting happiness?'
The answer you gave seems to be final."

"True," I said.

"Now this desire for happiness, this kind of love—do you think it is
common to all human beings and that everyone wants to have good things
forever and ever? What would you say?"

"Just that," I said. "It is common to all."

"Then, Socrates, why don't we say that everyone is in love," she asked,
"since everyone always loves the same things? Instead, we say some people   205b
are in love and others not; why is that?"

"I wonder about that myself," I said.

"It's nothing to wonder about," she said. "It's because we divide out a
special kind of love, and we refer to it by the word that means the whole—
'love'; and for the other kinds of love we use other words."

"What do you mean?" I asked.

"Well, you know, for example, that 'poetry' has a very wide range, when
it is used to mean 'creativity.'[51] After all, everything that is responsible
for creating something out of nothing is a kind of poetry; and so all the
creations of every craft and profession are themselves a kind of poetry, and   205c
everyone who practices a craft is a poet."

---

[51] "Poetry" translates *poiēsis,* lit. "making," which can be used for any kind of production or creation. However, the word *poiētēs,* lit. "maker," was used mainly for poets.

"True."

"Nevertheless," she said, "as you also know, these craftsmen are not called poets. We have other words for them, and out of the whole of poetry we have marked off one part, the part the Muses give us with melody and rhythm, and we refer to this by the word that means the whole. For this alone is called 'poetry,' and those who practice this part of poetry are called poets."

"True."

205d "That's also how it is with love. The main point is this: every desire for good things or for happiness is 'the supreme and treacherous love' in everyone. But those who pursue this along any of its many other ways—through making money, or through the love of sports, or through philosophy—we don't say that *these* people are in love, and we don't call them lovers. It's only when people are devoted exclusively to one special kind of love that we use these words that really belong to the whole of it: 'love' and 'in love' and 'lovers.'"

"I am beginning to see your point," I said.

"Now there is a certain story," she said, "according to which lovers are those people who seek their other halves. But according to my story, 205e a lover does not seek the half or the whole, unless, my friend, it turns out to be good as well. I say this because people are even willing to cut off their own arms and legs if they think they are diseased. I don't think an individual takes joy in what belongs to him personally unless by 'belonging to me' he means 'good' and by 'belonging to another' he means 'bad.' That's because what everyone loves is really nothing other than the good. 206a Do you disagree?"

"Zeus! Not I," I said.

"Now, then," she said. "Can we simply say that people love the good?"

"Yes," I said.

"But shouldn't we add that, in loving it, they want the good to be theirs?"

"We should."

"And not only that," she said. "They want the good to be theirs forever, don't they?"

"We should add that too."

"In a word, then, love is wanting to possess the good forever."

"That's very true," I said.

206b "This, then, is the object of love," she said. "In view of that, how do people pursue it if they are truly in love? What is the real purpose of love? Can you say?"

"If I could, Diotima," I said, "I wouldn't be your student, filled with admiration for your wisdom, and trying to learn these very things."

"Well, I'll tell you," she said. "It is giving birth in beauty, whether in body or in soul."

"It would take divination to figure out what you mean. I can't."

"Well, I'll tell you more clearly," she said. "All of us are pregnant,   206c
Socrates, both in body and in soul, and, as soon as we come to a certain
age, we naturally desire to give birth. Now no one can possibly give birth
in anything ugly; only in something beautiful. That's because when a man
and a woman come together in order to give birth, this is a godly affair.
Pregnancy, reproduction—this is an immortal thing for a mortal animal to
do, and it cannot occur in anything that is out of harmony, but ugliness is
out of harmony with all that is godly. Beauty, however, is in harmony with   206d
the divine. Therefore the goddess who presides at childbirth—she's called
Moira or Eilithuia—is really Beauty.[52] That's why, whenever pregnant
animals or persons draw near to beauty, they become gentle and joyfully
disposed and give birth and reproduce; but near ugliness they frown and
draw back in pain; they turn away and shrink back and do not reproduce,
and because they hold on to what they carry inside them, the labor is painful. This is the source of the great excitement about beauty that comes to
anyone who is pregnant and already teeming with life: beauty releases them
from their great pain. You see, Socrates," she said, "what Love wants is not   206e
beauty, as you think it is."

"Well, what is it, then?"

"Reproduction and birth in beauty."

"Maybe," I said.

"Certainly," she said. "Now, why reproduction? It's because reproduction goes on forever; it is what mortals have in place of immortality. A lover
must desire immortality along with the good, if what we agreed earlier   **207a**
was right, that Love wants to possess the good forever. It follows from our
argument that Love must desire immortality."

All this she taught me, on those occasions when she spoke on the art
of love. And once she asked, "What do you think causes love and desire,
Socrates? Don't you see what an awful state a wild animal is in when it
wants to reproduce? Footed and winged animals alike, all are plagued by
the disease of Love. First they are sick for intercourse with each other, then   207b
for nurturing their young—for their sake the weakest animals stand ready
to do battle against the strongest and even to die for them, and they may be
racked with famine in order to feed their young. They would do anything
for their sake. Human beings, you'd think, would do this because they
understand the reason for it; but what causes wild animals to be in such a
state of love? Can you say?"   207c

And I said again that I didn't know.

---

[52] Moira is known mainly as a Fate, but she was also identified with the birth
goddess Eilithuia.

So she said, "How do you think you'll ever master the art of love, if you don't know that?"

"But that's why I came to you, Diotima, as I just said. I knew I needed a teacher. So tell me what causes this, and everything else that belongs to the art of love."

"If you really believe that Love by its nature aims at what we have often agreed it does, then don't be surprised at the answer," she said. "For among 207d   animals the principle is the same as with us, and mortal nature seeks so far as possible to live forever and be immortal. And this is possible in one way only: by reproduction, because it always leaves behind a new young one in place of the old. Even while each living thing is said to be alive and to be the same—as a person is said to be the same from childhood till he turns into an old man—even then he never consists of the same things, though he is called the same, but he is always being renewed and in other respects passing away, in his hair and flesh and bones and blood and his entire body. 207e   And it's not just in his body, but in his soul, too, for none of his manners, customs, opinions, desires, pleasures, pains, or fears ever remains the same, but some are coming to be in him while others are passing away. And what is still far stranger than that is that not only does one branch of knowledge come to be in us while another passes away and that we are never the same even in respect of our knowledge, but that each single piece of knowledge 208a   has the same fate. For what we call *studying* exists because knowledge is leaving us, because forgetting is the departure of knowledge, while studying puts back a fresh memory in place of what went away, thereby preserving a piece of knowledge, so that it seems to be the same. And in that way everything mortal is preserved, not, like the divine, by always being the same in every way, but because what is departing and aging leaves behind 208b   something new, something such as it had been. By this device, Socrates," she said, "what is mortal shares in immortality, whether it is a body or anything else, while the immortal has another way. So don't be surprised if everything naturally values its own offspring, because it is for the sake of immortality that everything shows this zeal, which is Love."

Yet when I heard her speech I was amazed, and spoke: "Well," said I, "Most wise Diotima, is this really the way it is?"

208c   And in the manner of a perfect sophist she said, "Be sure of it, Socrates. Look, if you will, at how human beings seek honor. You'd be amazed at their irrationality, if you didn't have in mind what I spoke about and if you hadn't pondered the awful state of love they're in, wanting to become famous and 'to lay up glory immortal forever,' and how they're ready to brave any danger for the sake of this, much more than they are for their children; and they are prepared to spend money, suffer through all sorts 208d   of ordeals, and even die for the sake of glory. Do you really think that Alcestis would have died for Admetus," she asked, "or that Achilles would have died after Patroclus, or that your Codrus would have died so as to preserve the throne for his sons,[53] if they hadn't expected the memory of their virtue—which we still hold in honor—to be immortal? Far from it," she said. "I believe that anyone will do anything for the sake of immortal virtue and the glorious fame that follows; and the better the people, the more they will do, for they are all in love with immortality.

208e

"Now, some people are pregnant in body, and for this reason turn more to women and pursue love in that way, providing themselves through childbirth with immortality and remembrance and happiness, as they think, for all time to come; while others are pregnant in soul—because there surely *are* those who are even more pregnant in their souls than in their bodies, and these are pregnant with what is fitting for a soul to bear and bring to birth. And what is fitting? Wisdom and the rest of virtue, which all poets beget, as well as all the craftsmen who are said to be creative. But by far the greatest and most beautiful part of wisdom deals with the proper ordering of cities and households, and that is called temperance and justice. When someone has been pregnant with these in his soul from early youth, while he is still a virgin, and, having arrived at the proper age, desires to beget and give birth, he too will certainly go about seeking the beauty in which he would beget; for he will never beget in anything ugly. Since he is pregnant, then, he is much more drawn to bodies that are beautiful than to those that are ugly; and if he also has the luck to find a soul that is beautiful and noble and well-formed, he is even more drawn to this combination; such a man makes him instantly teem with ideas and arguments about virtue—the qualities a virtuous man should have and the customary activities in which he should engage; and so he tries to educate him. In my view, you see, when he makes contact with someone beautiful and keeps company with him, he conceives and gives birth to what he has been carrying inside him for ages. And whether they are together or apart, he remembers that beauty. And in common with him he nurtures the newborn; such people, therefore, have much more to share than do the parents of human children, and have a firmer bond of friendship, because the children in whom they have a share are more beautiful and more immortal. Everyone would rather have such children than human ones, and would look up to Homer, Hesiod, and the other good poets with envy and admiration for the offspring they have left behind—offspring, which, because they are immortal themselves, provide their parents with immortal glory and remembrance. For example," she said, "those are the

209a

209b

209c

209d

---

[53] Codrus was the legendary last king of Athens. He gave his life to satisfy a prophecy that promised victory to Athens if their king was killed by the invading Dorians.

sort of children Lycurgus[54] left behind in Sparta as the saviors of Sparta and virtually all of Greece. Among you the honor goes to Solon[55] for his creation of your laws. Other men in other places everywhere, Greek or barbarian, have brought a host of beautiful deeds into the light and begotten every kind of virtue. Already many shrines have sprung up to honor them for their immortal children, which hasn't happened yet to anyone for human offspring.

"Even you, Socrates, could probably come to be initiated into these rites of love. But as for the purpose of these rites when they are done correctly—that is the final and highest mystery, and I don't know if you are capable of it. I myself will tell you," she said, "and I won't stint any effort. And you must try to follow if you can.

"A lover who goes about this matter correctly must begin in his youth to devote himself to beautiful bodies. First, if the leader leads aright, he should love one body and beget beautiful ideas there; then he should realize that the beauty of any one body is brother to the beauty of any other and that if he is to pursue beauty of form he'd be very foolish not to think that the beauty of all bodies is one and the same. When he grasps this, he must become a lover of all beautiful bodies, and he must think that this wild gaping after just one body is a small thing and despise it.

"After this he must think that the beauty of people's souls is more valuable than the beauty of their bodies, so that if someone is decent in his soul, even though he is scarcely blooming in his body, our lover must be content to love and care for him and to seek to give birth to such ideas as will make young men better. The result is that our lover will be forced to gaze at the beauty of activities and laws and to see that all this is akin to itself, with the result that he will think that the beauty of bodies is a thing of no importance. After customs he must move on to various kinds of knowledge. The result is that he will see the beauty of knowledge and be looking mainly not at beauty in a single example—as a servant would who favored the beauty of a little boy or a man or a single custom (being a slave, of course, he's low and small-minded)—but the lover is turned to the great sea of beauty, and, gazing upon this, he gives birth to many gloriously beautiful ideas and theories, in unstinting love of wisdom,[56] until, having grown and been strengthened there, he catches sight of such knowledge, and it is the knowledge of such beauty. . . .

---

[54] Lycurgus was supposed to have been the founder of the oligarchic laws and stern customs of Sparta.

[55] Solon (c. 640–560 BCE) was an Athenian statesman and poet and founder of the Athenian constitution.

[56] I.e., philosophy.

"Try to pay attention to me," she said, "as best you can. You see, the   210e
man who has been thus far guided in matters of Love, who has beheld
beautiful things in the right order and correctly, is coming now to the goal
of Loving: all of a sudden he will catch sight of something wonderfully
beautiful in its nature; that, Socrates, is the reason for all his earlier labors:

"First, it always *is* and neither comes to be nor passes away, neither   **211a**
waxes nor wanes. Second, it is not beautiful this way and ugly that way,
nor beautiful at one time and ugly at another, nor beautiful in relation to
one thing and ugly in relation to another; nor is it beautiful here but ugly
there, as it would be if it were beautiful for some people and ugly for others. Nor will the beautiful appear to him in the guise of a face or hands
or anything else that belongs to the body. It will not appear to him as one
idea or one kind of knowledge. It is not anywhere in another thing, as in
an animal, or in earth, or in heaven, or in anything else, but itself by itself
with itself, it is always one in form; and all the other beautiful things share   211b
in that, in such a way that when those others come to be or pass away, this
does not become the least bit smaller or greater nor suffer any change. So
when someone rises by these stages, through loving boys correctly, and
begins to see this beauty, he has almost grasped his goal. This is what it is to
go aright, or be led by another, into the mystery of Love: one goes always   211c
upward for the sake of this Beauty, starting out from beautiful things and
using them like rising stairs: from one body to two and from two to all
beautiful bodies, then from beautiful bodies to beautiful customs, and from
customs to learning beautiful things, and from these lessons he arrives in
the end at this lesson, which is learning of this very Beauty, so that in the
end he comes to know just what it is to be beautiful.

"And there in life, Socrates, my friend," said the woman from Mantinea,   211d
"there if anywhere should a person live his life, beholding that Beauty.
If you once see that, it won't occur to you to measure beauty by gold or
clothing or beautiful boys and youths—who, if you see them now, strike
you out of your senses, and make you, you and many others, eager to be
with the boys you love and look at them forever, if there were any way to
do that, forgetting food and drink, everything but looking at them and
being with them. But how would it be, in our view," she said, "if someone
got to see the Beautiful itself, absolute, pure, unmixed, not polluted by   211e
human flesh or colors or any other great nonsense of mortality, but if he
could see the divine Beauty itself in its one form? Do you think it would be
a poor life for a human being to look there and to behold it by that which   **212a**
he ought, and to be with it? Or haven't you remembered," she said, "that
in that life alone, when he looks at Beauty in the only way that Beauty can
be seen—only then will it become possible for him to give birth not to
images of virtue (because he's in touch with no images), but to true virtue
(because he is in touch with the true Beauty). The love of the gods belongs

to anyone who has given birth to true virtue and nourished it, and if any human being could become immortal, it would be he."

212b   This, Phaedrus and the rest of you, was what Diotima told me. I was persuaded. And once persuaded, I try to persuade others too that human nature can find no better workmate for acquiring this than Love. That's why I say that every man must honor Love, why I honor the rites of Love myself and practice them with special diligence, and why I commend them to others. Now and always I praise the power and courage of Love so far 212c   as I am able. Consider this speech, then, Phaedrus, if you wish, a speech in praise of Love. Or if not, call it whatever and however you please to call it.

Socrates' speech finished to loud applause. Meanwhile, Aristophanes was trying to make himself heard over their cheers in order to make a response to something Socrates had said about his own speech. Then, all of a sudden, there was even more noise. A large drunken party had arrived at the courtyard door and they were rattling it loudly, accompanied by the shrieks of some flute-girl they had brought along. Agathon at that point called to his slaves:

212d   "Go see who it is. If it's people we know, invite them in. If not, tell them the party's over, and we're about to turn in."

A moment later they heard Alcibiades[57] shouting in the courtyard, very drunk and very loud. He wanted to know where Agathon was, he demanded to see Agathon at once. Actually, he was half-carried into the house by the flute-girl and by some other companions of his, but, at the 212e   door, he managed to stand by himself, crowned with a beautiful wreath of violets and ivy and ribbons in his hair.

"Good evening, gentlemen. I'm plastered," he announced. "May I join your party? Or should I crown Agathon with this wreath—which is all I came to do, anyway—and make myself scarce? I really couldn't make it yesterday," he continued, "but nothing could stop me tonight! See, I'm wearing the garland myself. I want this crown to come directly from my head to the head that belongs, I don't mind saying, to the cleverest and

---

[57] Alcibiades (452–404 BCE) was a controversial Athenian statesman. He was thirty-six in 416 (the dramatic date of Agathon's party). In 415, during the Peloponnesian War with Sparta, he was appointed joint leader of a daring, perhaps foolhardy, military expedition against Sicily—an expedition he advocated and encouraged before the Athenian Assembly. He was recalled on religious charges, alleged to have mutilated statues of the god Hermes and parodied the secret initiation rites of the Eleusinian Mysteries. Rather than face these charges, he helped the Spartans against the Athenians. In 407, he rejoined the Athenians. Agents of Persia, with whom the Spartans had allied themselves, assassinated him in 404.

best looking man in town. Ah, you laugh; you think I'm drunk! Fine, go
ahead—I know I'm right anyway. Well, what do you say? May I join you   213a
on these terms? Will you have a drink with me or not?"

Naturally they all made a big fuss. They implored him to join them,
they begged him to take a seat, and Agathon called him to his side. So
Alcibiades, again with the help of his friends, approached Agathon. At the
same time, he kept trying to take his ribbons off so that he could crown
Agathon with them, but all he succeeded in doing was to push them further
down his head until they finally slipped over his eyes. What with the ivy
and all, he didn't see Socrates, who had made room for him on the couch as
soon as he saw him. So Alcibiades sat down between Socrates and Agathon   213b
and, as soon as he did so, he put his arms around Agathon, kissed him, and
placed the ribbons on his head.

Agathon asked his slaves to take Alcibiades' sandals off. "We can all three
fit on my couch," he said.

"What a good idea!" Alcibiades replied. "But wait a moment! Who's
the third?"

As he said this, he turned around, and it was only then that he saw
Socrates. No sooner had he seen him than he leaped up and cried:

"Good lord, what's going on here? It's Socrates! You've trapped me
again! You always do this to me—all of a sudden you'll turn up out of   213c
nowhere where I least expect you! Well, what do you want now? Why
did you choose this particular couch? Why aren't you with Aristophanes
or anyone else we could tease you about? But no, you figured out a way to
find a place next to the most handsome man in the room!"

"I beg you, Agathon," Socrates said, "protect me from this man! You
can't imagine what it's like to be in love with him: from the very first
moment he realized how I felt about him, he hasn't allowed me to say two
words to anybody else—what am I saying, I can't so much as look at an   213d
attractive man but he flies into a fit of jealous rage. He yells; he threatens;
he can hardly keep from slapping me around! Please, try to keep him under
control. Could you perhaps make him forgive me? And if you can't, if he
gets violent, will you defend me? The fierceness of his passion terrifies me!"

"I shall never forgive you!" Alcibiades cried. "I promise you, you'll
pay for this! But for the moment," he said, turning to Agathon, "give me   213e
some of these ribbons. I'd better make a wreath for him as well—look at
that magnificent head! Otherwise, I know, he'll make a scene. He'll be
grumbling that, though I crowned you for your first victory, I didn't honor
him even though he has never lost an argument in his life."

So Alcibiades took the ribbons, arranged them on Socrates' head, and
lay back on the couch. Immediately, however, he started up again:

"Friends, you look sober to me; we can't have that! Let's have a drink!
Remember our agreement? We need a master of ceremonies; who should

it be? . . . Well, at least till you are all too drunk to care, I elect . . . myself!
Who else? Agathon, I want the largest cup around. . . . No! Wait! You!
Bring me that cooling jar over there!"

He'd seen the cooling jar, and he realized it could hold more than two
214a quarts of wine. He had the slaves fill it to the brim, drained it, and ordered
them to fill it up again for Socrates.

"Not that the trick will have any effect on *him*," he told the group.
"Socrates will drink whatever you put in front of him, but no one yet has
seen him drunk."

The slave filled the jar and, while Socrates was drinking, Eryximachus
said to Alcibiades:

214b "This is certainly most improper. We cannot simply pour the wine
down our throats in silence: we must have some conversation, or at least a
song. What we are doing now is hardly civilized."

What Alcibiades said to him was this:

"O Eryximachus, best possible son to the best possible, the most temperate father: Hi!"

"Greetings to you, too," Eryximachus replied. "Now what do you suggest we do?"

"Whatever you say. Ours to obey you, 'For a medical mind is worth a
million others.'[58] Please prescribe what you think fit."

"Listen to me," Eryximachus said. "Earlier this evening we decided
214c to use this occasion to offer a series of encomia of Love. We all took
our turn—in good order, from left to right—and gave our speeches, each
according to his ability. You are the only one not to have spoken yet,
though, if I may say so, you have certainly drunk your share. It's only
proper, therefore, that you take your turn now. After you have spoken,
you can decide on a topic for Socrates on your right; he can then do the
same for the man to his right, and we can go around the table once again."

"Well said, O Eryximachus," Alcibiades replied. "But do you really
think it's fair to put my drunken ramblings next to your sober orations?
And anyway, my dear fellow, I hope you didn't believe a single word
214d Socrates said: the truth is just the opposite! He's the one who will most
surely beat me up if I dare praise anyone else in his presence—even a god!"

"Hold your tongue!" Socrates said.

"By god, don't you dare deny it!" Alcibiades shouted. "I would never—
never—praise anyone else with you around."

"Well, why not just do that, if you want?" Eryximachus suggested.
"Why don't you offer an encomium to Socrates?"

---

[58] *Iliad* xi.514.

"What do you mean?" asked Alcibiades. "Do you really think so,   214e
Eryximachus? Should I unleash myself upon him? Should I give him his
punishment in front of all of you?"

"Now, wait a minute," Socrates said. "What do you have in mind? Are
you going to praise me only in order to mock me? Is that it?"

"I'll only tell the truth—please, let me!"

"I would certainly like to hear the truth from you. By all means, go
ahead," Socrates replied.

"Nothing can stop me now," said Alcibiades. "But here's what you can
do: if I say anything that's not true, you can just interrupt, if you want, and
correct me; at worst, there'll be mistakes in my speech, not lies. But you
can't hold it against me if I don't get everything in the right order—I'll say   215a
things as they come to mind. It is no easy task for one in my condition to
give a smooth and orderly account of your bizarreness!"

I'll try to praise Socrates, my friends, but I'll have to use an image. And
though he may think I'm trying to make fun of him, I assure you my image
is no joke: it aims at the truth. Look at him! Isn't he just like a statue of
Silenus? You know the kind of statue I mean; you'll find them in any shop   215b
in town. It's a Silenus sitting, his flute[59] or his pipes in his hands, and it's
hollow. It's split right down the middle, and inside it's full of tiny statues of
the gods. Now look at him again! Isn't he also just like the satyr Marsyas?[60]

Nobody, not even you, Socrates, can deny that you *look* like them. But
the resemblance goes beyond appearance, as you're about to hear.

You are impudent, contemptuous, and vile! No? If you won't admit it,
I'll bring witnesses. And you're quite a flute-player, aren't you? In fact,
you're much more marvelous than Marsyas, who needed instruments to cast   215c
his spells on people. And so does anyone who plays his tunes today—for
even the tunes Olympus[61] played are Marsyas' work, since Olympus learned
everything from him. Whether they are played by the greatest flautist or
the meanest flute-girl, his melodies have in themselves the power to possess
and so reveal those people who are ready for the god and his mysteries.

---

[59] This is the conventional translation of the word, but the *aulos* was in fact a reed
instrument and not a flute. It was held by the ancients to be the instrument that most
strongly arouses the emotions.

[60] Satyrs had the sexual appetites and manners of wild beasts and were usually
portrayed with large erections. Sometimes they had horses' tails or ears, sometimes
the traits of goats. Marsyas, in myth, was a satyr who dared to compete in music with
Apollo and was skinned alive for his impudence.

[61] Olympus was a legendary musician who was said to be loved by Marsyas and to
have made music that drove its listeners out of their senses.

That's because his melodies are themselves divine. The only difference between you and Marsyas is that you need no instruments; you do exactly what he does, but with words alone. You know, people hardly ever take a speaker seriously, even if he's the greatest orator; but let anyone—man, woman, or child—listen to you or even to a poor account of what you say—and we are all transported, completely possessed.

If I were to describe for you what an extraordinary effect his words have always had on me (I can feel it this moment even as I'm speaking), you might actually suspect that I'm drunk! Still, I swear to you, the moment he starts to speak, I am beside myself: my heart starts leaping in my chest, the tears come streaming down my face, even the frenzied Corybantes[62] seem sane compared to me—and, let me tell you, I am not alone. I have heard Pericles[63] and many other great orators, and I have admired their speeches. But nothing like this ever happened to me: they never upset me so deeply that my very own soul started protesting that my life—*my* life!—was no better than the most miserable slave's. And yet that is exactly how this Marsyas here at my side makes me feel all the time: he makes it seem that my life isn't worth living! You can't say that isn't true, Socrates. I know very well that you could make me feel that way this very moment if I gave you half a chance. He always traps me, you see, and he makes me admit that my political career is a waste of time, while all that matters is just what I most neglect: my personal shortcomings, which cry out for the closest attention. So I refuse to listen to him; I stop my ears and tear myself away from him, for, like the Sirens,[64] he could make me stay by his side till I die.

Socrates is the only man in the world who has made me feel shame—ah, you didn't think I had it in me, did you? Yes, he makes me feel ashamed: I know perfectly well that I can't prove he's wrong when he tells me what I should do; yet, the moment I leave his side, I go back to my old ways: I cave in to my desire to please the crowd. My whole life has become one constant effort to escape from him and keep away, but when I see him, I feel deeply ashamed, because I'm doing nothing about my way of life, though I have already agreed with him that I should. Sometimes, believe me, I think I would be happier if he were dead. And yet I know that if he dies I'll be even more miserable. I can't live with him, and I can't live without him! What *can* I do about him?

---

[62] The Corybantes were legendary worshipers of Cybele, who brought about their own derangement through music and dance.

[63] Pericles (c. 495–429 BCE) was an Athenian statesman, orator, and democratic leader. Alcibiades was his ward.

[64] The Sirens were mythical women whose singing led sailors to their deaths. See Homer, *Odyssey* xii.

That's the effect of this satyr's music—on me and many others. But that's the least of it. He's like these creatures in all sorts of other ways; his powers are really extraordinary. Let me tell you about them, because, you can be sure of it, none of you really understands him. But, now I've started, I'm going to show you what he really is.   216d

To begin with, he's crazy about beautiful boys; he constantly follows them around in a perpetual daze. Also, he likes to say he's ignorant and knows nothing. Isn't this just like Silenus? Of course it is! And all this is just on the surface, like the outsides of those statues of Silenus. I wonder, my fellow drinkers, if you have any idea what a sober and temperate man he proves to be once you have looked inside. Believe me, it couldn't matter less to him whether a boy is beautiful. You can't imagine how little he cares whether a person is beautiful, or rich, or famous in any other   216e way that most people admire. He considers all these possessions beneath contempt, and that's exactly how he considers all of us as well. In public, I tell you, his whole life is one big game—a game of irony. I don't know if any of you have seen him when he's really serious. But I once caught him when he was open like Silenus' statues, and I had a glimpse of the figures he keeps hidden within: they were so godlike—so bright and beautiful, so utterly amazing—that I no longer had a choice—I just had to do whatever   **217a** he told me.

What I thought at the time was that what he really wanted was *me,* and that seemed to me the luckiest coincidence: all I had to do was to let him have his way with me, and he would teach me everything he knew— believe me, I had a lot of confidence in my looks. Naturally, up to that time we'd never been alone together; one of my attendants had always been present. But with this in mind, I sent the attendant away, and met Socrates alone. (You see, in this company I must tell the whole truth: so pay attention. And, Socrates, if I say anything untrue, I want you to correct me.)   217b

So there I was, my friends, alone with him at last. My idea, naturally, was that he'd take advantage of the opportunity to tell me whatever it is that lovers say when they find themselves alone; I relished the moment. But no such luck! Nothing of the sort occurred. Socrates had his usual sort of conversation with me, and at the end of the day he went off.

My next idea was to invite him to the gymnasium with me. We took   217c exercise together, and I was sure that this would lead to something. He took exercise and wrestled with me many times when no one else was present. What can I tell you? I got nowhere. When I realized that my ploy had failed, I decided on a frontal attack. I refused to retreat from a battle I myself had begun, and I needed to know just where matters stood. So what I did was to invite him to dinner, as if *I* were his lover and he my young prey! To tell the truth, it took him quite a while to accept my invitation, but one day he finally arrived. That first time he left right after dinner: 217d

I was too shy to try to stop him. But on my next attempt, I started some discussion just as we were finishing our meal and kept him talking late into the night. When he said he should be going, I used the lateness of the hour as an excuse and managed to persuade him to spend the night at my house. He had had his meal on the couch next to mine, so he just made himself comfortable and lay down on it. No one else was there.

217e

Now you must admit that my story so far has been perfectly decent; I could have told it in any company. But you'd never have heard me tell the rest of it, as you're about to do, if it weren't that, as the saying goes, 'there's truth in wine when the slaves have left'—and when they're present, too. Also, would it be fair to Socrates for me to praise him and yet to fail to reveal one of his proudest accomplishments? And, furthermore, you know what people say about snakebite—that you'll only talk about it with your fellow victims: only they will understand the pain and forgive you for all

218a the things it made you do. Well, something much more painful than a snake has bitten me in my most sensitive part—I mean my heart, or my soul, or whatever you want to call it, which has been struck and bitten by philosophy, whose grip on young and eager souls is much more vicious than a viper's and makes them do the most amazing things. Now, all you

218b people here, Phaedrus, Agathon, Eryximachus, Pausanias, Aristodemus, Aristophanes—I need not mention Socrates himself—and all the rest, have all shared in the madness, the Bacchic frenzy of philosophy. And that's why you will hear the rest of my story; you will understand and forgive both what I did then and what I say now. As for the house slaves and for anyone else who is not an initiate, my story's not for you: block your ears!

To get back to the story. The lights were out; the slaves had left; the

218c time was right, I thought, to come to the point and tell him freely what I had in mind. So I shook him and whispered:

"Socrates, are you asleep?"

"No, no, not at all," he replied.

"You know what I've been thinking?"

"Well, no, not really."

"I think," I said, "you're the only worthy lover I have ever had—and yet, look how shy you are with me! Well, here's how I look at it. It would be really stupid not to give you anything you want: you can have me, my

218d belongings, anything my friends might have. Nothing is more important to me than becoming the best man I can be, and no one can help me more than you to reach that aim. With a man like you, in fact, I'd be much more ashamed of what wise people would say if I did *not* take you as my lover, than I would of what all the others, in their foolishness, would say if I did."

He heard me out, and then he said in that absolutely inimitable ironic manner of his:

"Dear Alcibiades, if you are right in what you say about me, you are already more accomplished than you think. If I really have in me the power to make you a better man, then you can see in me a beauty that   218e
is really beyond description and makes your own remarkable good looks pale in comparison. But, then, is this a fair exchange that you propose? You seem to me to want more than your proper share: you offer me the merest appearance of beauty, and in return you want the thing itself, 'gold in exchange for bronze.'[65]   **219a**

"Still, my dear boy, you should think twice, because you could be wrong, and I may be of no use to you. The mind's sight becomes sharp only when the body's eyes go past their prime—and you are still a good long time away from that."

When I heard this I replied:

"I really have nothing more to say. I've told you exactly what I think. Now it's your turn to consider what you think best for you and me."

"You're right about that," he answered. "In the future, let's consider   219b
things together. We'll always do what seems the best to the two of us."

His words made me think that my own had finally hit their mark, that he was smitten by my arrows. I didn't give him a chance to say another word. I stood up immediately and placed my mantle over the light cloak which, though it was the middle of winter, was his only clothing. I slipped underneath the cloak and put my arms around this man—this utterly unnatural, this truly extraordinary man—and spent the whole night next   219c
to him. Socrates, you can't deny a word of it. But in spite of all my efforts, this hopelessly arrogant, this unbelievably insolent man—he turned me down! He spurned my beauty, of which I was so proud, members of the jury—for this is really what you are: you're here to sit in judgment of Socrates' amazing arrogance and pride. Be sure of it, I swear to you by all the gods and goddesses together, my night with Socrates went no further than if I had spent it with my own father or older brother!   219d

How do you think I felt after that? Of course, I was deeply humiliated, but also I couldn't help admiring his natural character, his temperance, his fortitude—here was a man whose strength and wisdom went beyond my wildest dreams! How could I bring myself to hate him? I couldn't bear to lose his friendship. But how could I possibly win him over? I knew very well that money meant much less to him than enemy weapons ever meant to   219e
Ajax,[66] and the only trap by means of which I had thought I might capture

---

[65] *Iliad* vi.232–36 tells the famous story of the exchange by Glaucus of golden armor for bronze.

[66] Ajax, a hero of the Greek army at Troy, carried an enormous shield and so was virtually invulnerable to enemy weapons.

him had already proved a dismal failure. I had no idea what to do, no purpose in life; ah, no one else has ever known the real meaning of slavery!

All this had already occurred when Athens invaded Potidaea,[67] where we served together and shared the same mess. Now, first, he took the hardships of the campaign much better than I ever did—much better, in fact, than anyone in the whole army. When we were cut off from our supplies, as often happens in the field, no one else stood up to hunger as well as he did. And yet he was the one man who could really enjoy a feast; and though he didn't much want to drink, when he had to, he could drink the best of us under the table. Still, and most amazingly, no one ever saw him drunk (as we'll straightaway put to the test).

Add to this his amazing resistance to the cold—and, let me tell you, the winter there is something awful. Once, I remember, it was frightfully cold; no one so much as stuck his nose outside. If we absolutely had to leave our tent, we wrapped ourselves in anything we could lay our hands on and tied extra pieces of felt or sheepskin over our boots. Well, Socrates went out in that weather wearing nothing but this same old light cloak, and even in bare feet he made better progress on the ice than the other soldiers did in their boots. You should have seen the looks they gave him; they thought he was only doing it to spite them!

So much for that! But you should hear what else he did during that same campaign,

The exploit our strong-hearted hero dared to do.[68]

One day, at dawn, he started thinking about some problem or other; he just stood outside, trying to figure it out. He couldn't resolve it, but he wouldn't give up. He simply stood there, glued to the same spot. By midday, many soldiers had seen him, and, quite mystified, they told everyone that Socrates had been standing there all day, thinking about something. He was still there when evening came, and after dinner some Ionians moved their bedding outside, where it was cooler and more comfortable (all this took place in the summer), but mainly in order to watch if Socrates was going to stay out there all night. And so he did; he stood on the very same spot until dawn! He only left next morning, when the sun came out, and he made his prayers to the new day.

And if you would like to know what he was like in battle—this is a tribute he really deserves. You know that I was decorated for bravery during that campaign: well, during that very battle, Socrates single-handedly

---

[67] Potidaea, a city in Thrace allied to Athens, was induced by Corinth to revolt in 432 BCE. The city was besieged by the Athenians and eventually defeated in a bloody local war, 432–430 BCE.

[68] *Odyssey* iv.242, 271.

saved my life! He absolutely did! He just refused to leave me behind when   220e
I was wounded, and he rescued not only me but my armor as well. For my
part, Socrates, I told them right then that the decoration really belonged
to you, and you can blame me neither for doing so then nor for saying so
now. But the generals, who seemed much more concerned with my social
position, insisted on giving the decoration to me, and, I must say, you were
more eager than the generals themselves for me to have it.

You should also have seen him at our horrible retreat from Delium.[69]
I was there with the cavalry, while Socrates was a foot soldier. The army   221a
had already dispersed in all directions, and Socrates was retreating together
with Laches. I happened to see them just by chance, and the moment I did
I started shouting encouragements to them, telling them I was never going
to leave their side, and so on. That day I had a better opportunity to watch
Socrates than I ever had at Potidaea, for, being on horseback, I wasn't in
very great danger. Well, it was easy to see that he was remarkably more
collected than Laches.[70] But when I looked again I couldn't get your words,   221b
Aristophanes, out of my mind: in the midst of battle he was making his
way exactly as he does around town,

> . . . with swagg'ring gait and roving eye.[71]

He was observing everything quite calmly, looking out for friendly
troops and keeping an eye on the enemy. Even from a great distance it was
obvious that this was a very brave man, who would put up a terrific fight
if anyone approached him. This is what saved both of them. For, as a rule,
you try to put as much distance as you can between yourself and such men
in battle; you go after the others, those who run away helter-skelter.   221c

You could say many other marvelous things in praise of Socrates.
Perhaps he shares some of his specific accomplishments with others. But,
as a whole, he is unique; he is like no one else in the past and no one in the
present—this is by far the most amazing thing about him. For we might
be able to form an idea of what Achilles was like by comparing him to
Brasidas or some other great warrior, or we might compare Pericles with
Nestor or Antenor or one of the other great orators.[72] There is a parallel for   221d

---

[69] At Delium, a town on the coast just north of Attica, a major Athenian expeditionary force was routed by a Boeotian army in 424 BCE.

[70] Well-known Athenian general who died at the battle of Mantinea (418 BCE). He appears in the eponymous *Laches,* which discusses courage.

[71] Cf. Aristophanes, *Clouds* 362.

[72] Brasidas, among the most effective Spartan generals during the Peloponnesian War, was mortally wounded while defeating the Athenians at Amphipolis in 422 BCE (Thucydides iv.102–16). Antenor (for the Trojans) and Nestor (for the Greeks) were the legendary wise men of the Trojan War.

everyone—everyone else, that is. But this man here is so bizarre, his ways and his ideas are so unusual, that, search as you might, you'll never find anyone else, alive or dead, who's even remotely like him. The best you can do is not to compare him to anything human, but to liken him, as I do, to Silenus and the satyrs, and the same goes for his ideas and arguments.

Come to think of it, I should have mentioned this much earlier: even his ideas and arguments are just like those hollow statues of Silenus. If you were to listen to his arguments, at first they'd strike you as totally ridiculous; they're clothed in words as coarse as the hides worn by the most vulgar satyrs. He's always going on about pack asses, or blacksmiths, or cobblers, or tanners; he's always making the same tired old points in the same tired old words. If you are foolish, or simply unfamiliar with him, you'd find it impossible not to laugh at his arguments. But if you see them when they open up like the statues, if you go behind their surface, you'll realize that no other arguments make any sense. They're truly worthy of a god, bursting with figures of virtue inside. They're of great—no, of the greatest—importance for anyone who wants to become a truly good man.

Well, gentlemen, this is my praise of Socrates, though I haven't spared him my reproach, either; I told you how horribly he treated me—and not only me but also Charmides, Euthydemus,[73] and many others. He has deceived us all: he presents himself as your lover, and, before you know it, you're in love with him yourself! I warn you, Agathon, don't let him fool you! Remember our torments; be on your guard: don't wait, like the fool in the proverb, to learn your lesson from your own misfortune.[74]

Alcibiades' frankness provoked a lot of laughter, especially since it was obvious that he was still in love with Socrates, who immediately said to him:

"You're perfectly sober after all, Alcibiades. Otherwise you could never have concealed your motive so gracefully: how casually you let it drop, almost like an afterthought, at the very end of your speech! As if the real point of all this has not been simply to make trouble between Agathon and me! You think that I should be in love with you and no one else, while you, and no one else, should be in love with Agathon—well, we were *not*

---

[73] Charmides was Plato's uncle, a member of Socrates' circle, and a supporter of the oligarchic Thirty Tyrants, who briefly controlled Athens in 404 BCE. He was killed in 303 fighting the counterrevolutionary democrats. Euthydemus (not to be confused with the sophist of the same name) is unknown outside the various Platonic dialogues (including the *Republic*) in which he is mentioned.

[74] Cf. *Iliad* xvii.32.

deceived; we've seen through your little satyr play. Agathon, my friend, don't let him get away with it: let no one come between us!"

Agathon said to Socrates:

"I'm beginning to think you're right; isn't it proof of that that he literally came between us here on the couch? Why would he do this if he weren't set on separating us? But he won't get away with it; I'm coming right over to lie down next to you." 222e

"Wonderful," Socrates said. "Come here, on my other side."

"My god!" cried Alcibiades. "How I suffer in his hands! He kicks me when I'm down; he never lets me go. Come, don't be selfish, Socrates; at least, let's compromise: let Agathon lie down between us."

"Why, that's impossible," Socrates said. "You have already delivered your praise of me, and now it's my turn to praise whoever's on my right. But if Agathon were next to you, he'd have to praise me all over again instead of having me speak in his honor, as I very much want to do in any case. Don't be jealous; let me praise the boy." 223a

"Oh, marvelous," Agathon cried. "Alcibiades, nothing can make me stay next to you now. I'm moving no matter what. I simply *must* hear what Socrates has to say about me."

"There we go again," said Alcibiades. "It's the same old story: when Socrates is around, nobody else can get close to a good-looking man. Look how smoothly and plausibly he found a reason for Agathon to lie down next to him!" 223b

And then, all of a sudden, while Agathon was changing places, a large drunken group, finding the gates open because someone was just leaving, walked into the room and joined the party. There was noise everywhere, and everyone was made to start drinking again in no particular order.

At that point, Aristodemus said, Eryximachus, Phaedrus, and some others among the original guests made their excuses and left. He himself fell asleep and slept for a long time (it was winter, and the nights were quite long). He woke up just as dawn was about to break; the roosters were crowing already. He saw that the others had either left or were asleep on their couches and that only Agathon, Aristophanes, and Socrates were still awake, drinking out of a large cup which they were passing around from left to right. Socrates was talking to them. Aristodemus couldn't remember exactly what they were saying—he'd missed the first part of their discussion, and he was half-asleep anyway—but the main point was that Socrates was trying to prove to them that authors should be able to write both comedy and tragedy: the skillful tragic dramatist should also be a comic poet. He was about to clinch his argument, though, to tell the truth, sleepy as they were, they were hardly able to follow his reasoning. In fact, Aristophanes fell asleep in the middle of the discussion, and very soon thereafter, as day was breaking, Agathon also drifted off. 223c 223d

But after getting them off to sleep, Socrates got up and left, and Aristodemus followed him, as always. He said that Socrates went directly to the Lyceum, washed up, spent the rest of the day just as he always did, and only then, as evening was falling, went home to rest.

Phaedrus

In the *Phaedrus* (chiefly in Socrates' second speech in praise of love) we find a more detailed account of the psychology and art of love than in the *Symposium*. The soul, whether divine or human, Socrates claims, is like "the natural union of a team of winged horses and their charioteer" (*Phaedrus* 246a). Whereas in a divine soul all three elements are "good and come from good stock," in a human soul the white horse (familiar from *Republic*, Book iv, as the honor-loving spirited element) is "beautiful and good and from stock of the same sort," while the black one (the *Republic's* appetitive element) is "the opposite and has the opposite sort of bloodline," so that "chariot-driving in our case is inevitably a painfully difficult business" (246b). When spirit together with the charioteer (who is the analogue of the *Republic's* rational element, there too identified with what is truly human rather than bestial in us; *Republic* 588b–589a) "leads us by reasoning toward what is best," we possess temperance (*Phaedrus* 237e). But when "desire takes command in us and drags us without reasoning toward pleasure, then its command is known as 'outrageousness'" (238a). Of this excess, gluttony is one species, but erotic love another (238b–c). This is the bad kind of love—Pandemotic in the *Symposium*—that Lysias rightly disparages in the speech Phaedrus admires and reads to Socrates (230e–234c).

In Socrates' view, however, there is also another kind of love, namely, a madness "which someone shows when he sees the beauty we have down here and is reminded of true beauty; then he takes wing and flutters in his eagerness to rise up, but is unable to do so; and he gazes aloft, like a bird, paying no attention to what is down below—and that is what brings on him the charge that he has gone mad" (249d). This madman is the philosopher of the *Symposium,* who when he falls in love with a boy is led by his love to ascend by stages to the Platonic form of the beautiful. What makes his madness a divine gift, however, is that the ascent is now revealed as involving recollection of a prior prenatal ascent taken in the company of a god.

Followers of Zeus (the king of the gods), for example, choose someone to love whose soul resembles their patron god. So they seek someone who "has a talent for philosophy and the guidance of others, and once they have found him and are in love with him they do everything to develop that talent" (252e). Nonetheless, the falling itself involves a huge psychological upheaval. The black horse of appetite immediately urges toward sexual intercourse. The white horse—"controlled, then as always, by its sense of shame" (254a)—holds itself and the chariot of the soul back. Eventually, however, the black horse forces both the charioteer and the white horse to "go up to the boy and suggest to him the pleasures of sex." Again they balk, "angry in their belief that they are being made to do things that are dreadfully wrong." But finally, "when they see no end to their trouble, they are led forward, reluctantly agreeing to do as they have been told." As they come close to the beloved, however, to initiate intercourse, the flashing face of the beloved reminds the charioteer of the beautiful itself, so that his memory "again where it stands on the sacred pedestal next to Self-control." He becomes frightened and "falls over backwards awestruck, and at the same time has to pull the reins back so fiercely that both horses are set on their haunches, one falling back voluntarily with no resistance, but the other insolent and quite unwilling." Eventually, "the bad horse has suffered this same thing time after time, it stops being so insolent; now it is humble enough to follow the charioteer's warnings" (254e). If this control of appetite by reason and spirit continues—even when the boy has accepted his lover and embraces, kisses, and lies down with him—and draws them to "follow the assigned regimen of philosophy," they are blessedly happy here on earth, and, if they live such a life for three successive incarnations, they regrow their wings and rejoin the entourage of their god (255e–256b).

When followers of Ares (the god of war) fall in love, on the other hand, they "adopt a lower way of living, with ambition in place of philosophy" (256b). When they are drinking together, for example, or are careless in some other way, the "undisciplined horses will catch their souls off guard," and since the man's recollection of beauty is dimmer and is not rekindled by philosophical conversation, they end up having sex together—something "ordinary people would take to be the happiest choice of all." Nonetheless, they don't have sex very often, because "they have not approved of what they are doing by their whole minds." So while the degree of their love and happiness is less than the philosophical pair and, on their death, "they are wingless," still they have an impulse, coming from love, to try to gain them. Hence they aren't punished in the next life, but helped on the way to future happiness together.

The love that is divine madness is a good thing, therefore, especially when, accompanied by "philosophical discussions" (257b), it leads to the beautiful itself and the other forms, which are what we truly love and crave. The question is what makes a discussion philosophical? What makes it of the sort to be included in the true art of love that the philosopher who loves the beautiful itself practices? The answer now proposed is that it must be a *technē* or craft, and so must have the defining characteristics of one. As applied to love itself, for example, it must begin with a definition of love, and reach its conclusions by ordering its discussion in relation to it

(263d–e). And this definition, in turn, must be established by what Socrates refers to as collection and division (266b).

Collection is a process of "seeing together things that are scattered about everywhere and collecting them into one kind" (265d). It is a process that we, unlike other animals, are able to engage in it, because our souls include a rational element that has prior acquaintance with forms: "a soul that never [prenatally] saw the truth cannot take a human shape, since a human being must understand speech in terms of general forms, proceeding to bring many perceptions together into a reasoned unity" (249b–c).

Once a form has been reached in this way, division begins. This is a matter of cutting "up each kind according to its species along its natural joints" (265e). As an example, Socrates cites the case of love itself:

> just as each single body has parts that naturally come in pairs of the same name (one of them being called the right-hand and the other the left-hand one), so the speeches, having considered unsoundness of mind to be by nature one single kind within us, proceeded to cut it up—the first speech [Socrates' reorganized version of Lysias' attack on love] cut its left-hand part, and continued to cut until it discovered among these parts a sort of love that can be called "left-handed," which it correctly denounced; the second speech [Socrates' own defense of love], in turn, led us to the right-hand part of madness; discovered a love that shares its name with the other but is actually divine; set it out before us, and praised it as the cause of our greatest goods. (265e–266b)

Thus, while each speech tells only half the story, the two together show how correct division should proceed. The goal, however, isn't just truth or correctness, but explanatory adequacy. Thus, if the form in question "we must investigate its power: What things does it have what natural power of acting upon? By what things does it have what natural disposition to be acted upon?" If it is complex, we should count its subforms, and consider the same things about them as about the simple ones (270d). That Socrates—the archetypal searcher for explanatory definitions (*Euthyphro* 6d–e)—should pronounce himself "a lover of these divisions and collections" is no surprise, therefore (266b).

Philosophy aims at true definitions and true stories based on those definitions. It also aims at persuasion, since the philosophical lover wants to persuade his boy to follow him on the path to the forms. Philosophy and rhetoric must thus go together, which means that rhetoric, too, must be developed as a *techne*. It must, first, distinguish and give definitions of the various kinds of souls and kinds of speeches, revealing their respective capacities and susceptibilities, and, second, "coordinate each kind of soul with the kind of speech appropriate to it, . . . [explaining] why one kind of soul is necessarily convinced by one kind of speech while another necessarily remains unconvinced" (271b). Mastery of such a science, however, requires one further thing: "the orator must learn all this well, then put his theory into practice and develop the ability to discern each kind clearly as it occurs in the actions of real life" (271d–e). It isn't enough, in other words, to know what kinds of speeches affect what kinds of soul; the philosophical rhetorician must also know that this man in front of him is of such and such a kind, and be able to talk in such a way that will prove convincing to him.

PHAEDRUS

SOCRATES: Phaedrus,[1] my friend! Where have you been? And where are   227a
you going?

PHAEDRUS: I was with Lysias, the son of Cephalus,[2] Socrates, and I am
going for a walk outside the city walls because I was with him for a long
time, sitting there the whole morning. You see, I'm keeping in mind the
advice of our mutual friend Acumenus,[3] who says it's more refreshing to
walk along country roads than city streets.   227b

SOCRATES: He is quite right, too, my friend. So Lysias, I take it, is in the
city?

PHAEDRUS: Yes, at the house of Epicrates,[4] which used to belong to
Morychus,[5] near the temple of the Olympian Zeus.

SOCRATES: What were you doing there? Oh, I know: Lysias must have been
entertaining you with a feast of eloquence.

PHAEDRUS: You'll hear about it, if you are free to come along and listen.

SOCRATES: What? Don't you think I would consider it "more important
than the most pressing engagement," as Pindar says, to hear how you and
Lysias spent your time?[6]

PHAEDRUS: Lead the way, then.   227c

SOCRATES: If only you will tell me.

PHAEDRUS: In fact, Socrates, you're just the right person to hear the speech
that occupied us, since, in a roundabout way, it was about love. It is aimed

---

The text of *Phaedrus*, translated by Alexander Nehamas and Paul Woodruff, is
reprinted with minor adaptations from Plato, *Phaedrus*. Copyright © 1995, Hackett
Publishing Co.

[1] See *Symposium* 176c note.

[2] Lysias of Thurii and Athens (459–c. 380 BCE), a well-known orator and writer of
legal speeches. His brother, Polemarchus, and father, Cephalus, appear in the *Republic*.

[3] A relative of the doctor Eryximachus, who speaks in the *Symposium*, and a doctor
himself.

[4] Epicrates of Cephisia (born in the 440s and active through 390 BCE), rhetorician and politician.

[5] Mentioned several times by Aristophanes (see *Symposium* 176b note) for his luxurious way of life.

[6] Pindar of Cynoscephalae (518–438 BCE) was a lyric poet from Boeotia, most
famous for his poems celebrating the victors in the Olympic and other games. Plato
is adapting his *Isthmian* i.2.

at seducing a beautiful boy, but the speaker is not in love with him—this is actually what is so clever and elegant about it: Lysias argues that it is better to give your favors to someone who does not love you than to someone who does.

SOCRATES: What a wonderful man! I wish he would write that you should give your favors to a poor rather than to a rich man, to an older rather than to a younger one—that is, to someone like me and most other people:

227d then his speeches would be really sophisticated, and they'd contribute to the public good besides! In any case, I am so eager to hear it that I would follow you even if you were walking all the way to Megara, as Herodicus[7] recommends, to touch the wall and come back again.

PHAEDRUS: What on earth do you mean, Socrates? Do you think that a

228a mere dilettante like me could recite from memory in a manner worthy of him a speech that Lysias, the best of our writers, took such time and trouble to compose? Far from it—though actually I would rather be able to do that than come into a large fortune!

SOCRATES: Oh, Phaedrus, if I don't know my Phaedrus I must be forgetting who I am myself—and neither is the case. I know very well that he did not hear Lysias' speech only once: he asked him to repeat it over and over again,

228b and Lysias was eager to oblige. But not even that was enough for him. In the end, he took the book himself and pored over the parts he liked best. He sat reading all morning long, and when he got tired, he went for a walk, having learned—I am quite sure—the whole speech by heart, unless it was extraordinarily long. So he started for the country, where he could practice reciting it. And running into a man who is sick with passion for hearing speeches, seeing him—just seeing him—he was filled with delight: he had found a partner for his frenzied dance, and he urged him to lead the way.

228c But when that lover of speeches asked him to recite it, he played coy and pretended that he did not want to. In the end, of course, he was going to recite it even if he had to force an unwilling audience to listen. So, please, Phaedrus, beg him to do it right now. He'll do it soon enough anyway.

PHAEDRUS: Well, I'd better try to recite it as best I can: you'll obviously not leave me in peace until I do so one way or another.

SOCRATES: You are absolutely right.

228d PHAEDRUS: That's what I'll do, then. But, Socrates, it really is true that I did not memorize the speech word for word; instead, I will give a careful summary of its general sense, listing all the ways he said the lover differs from the non-lover, in the proper order.

---

[7] A medical expert. Socrates criticizes him at *Republic* 406a–b.

SOCRATES: Only if you first show me what you are holding in your left hand under your cloak, my friend. I strongly suspect you have the speech itself. And if I'm right, you can be sure that, though I love you dearly, I'll never, as long as Lysias himself is present, allow you to practice your own speechmaking on me. Come on, then, show me.   228e

PHAEDRUS: Enough, enough. You've dashed my hopes of using you as my training partner, Socrates. All right, where do you want to sit while we read?

SOCRATES: Let's leave the path here and walk along the Ilisus; then we can sit quietly wherever we find the right spot.   229a

PHAEDRUS: How lucky, then, that I am barefoot today—you, of course, are always so. The easiest thing to do is to walk right in the stream; this way, we'll also get our feet wet, which is very pleasant, especially at this hour and season.

SOCRATES: Lead the way, then, and find us a place to sit.

PHAEDRUS: Do you see that very tall plane tree?[8]

SOCRATES: Of course.

PHAEDRUS: It's shady, with a light breeze; we can sit or, if we prefer, lie down on the grass there.   229b

SOCRATES: Lead on, then.

PHAEDRUS: Tell me, Socrates, isn't it from somewhere near this stretch of the Ilisus that people say Boreas carried Oreithuia away?[9]

SOCRATES: So they say.

PHAEDRUS: Couldn't this be the very spot? The stream is lovely, pure and clear: just right for girls to be playing nearby.

SOCRATES: No, it is two or three hundred yards farther downstream, where one crosses to get to the district of Agra.[10] I think there is even an altar to Boreas there.   229c

PHAEDRUS: I hadn't noticed it. But tell me, Socrates, in the name of Zeus, do you really believe that that legend is true?

SOCRATES: Actually, it would not be out of place for me to reject it, as our intellectuals do. I could then tell a clever story: I could claim that a gust of the North Wind blew her over the rocks where she was playing with

---

[8] *Platanos:* a European sycamore or buttonwood tree. Perhaps a pun on "Plato" (*Platōn*).

[9] According to the legend, Oreithuia, daughter of the Athenian king Erechtheus, was abducted by Boreas (personification of the north wind) while she was playing along the banks of the Ilisis with her friend Pharmaceia.

[10] One of the demes of classical Athens.

Pharmaceia; and once she was killed that way people said she had been
229d   carried off by Boreas—or was it, perhaps, from the Areopagus?[11] The story
is also told that she was carried away from there instead. Now, Phaedrus,
such explanations are amusing enough, but they are a job for a man I cannot
envy at all. He'd have to be far too ingenious and work too hard—mainly
because after that he will have to go on and give a rational account of the
form of the Hippocentaurs, and then of the Chimera; and a whole flood
of Gorgons and Pegasuses and other monsters, in large numbers and absurd
229e   forms, will overwhelm him.[12] Anyone who does not believe in them, who
wants to explain them away and make them plausible by means of some
sort of rough ingenuity, will need a great deal of time.

But I have no time for such things; and the reason, my friend, is this. I
am still unable, as the Delphic inscription orders, to know myself;[13] and it
really seems to me ridiculous to look into other things before I have under-
230a   stood that. This is why I do not concern myself with them. I accept what is
generally believed, and, as I was just saying, I look not into them but into
my own self: Am I a beast more complicated and savage than Typhon,[14] or
am I a tamer, simpler animal with a share in a divine and gentle nature?
But look, my friend—while we were talking, haven't we reached the tree
you were taking us to?

230b   PHAEDRUS: That's the one.

SOCRATES: By Hera,[15] it really is a beautiful resting place. The plane tree is
tall and very broad; the chaste-tree,[16] high as it is, is wonderfully shady, and
since it is in full bloom, the whole place is filled with its fragrance. From
under the plane tree the loveliest spring runs with very cool water—our
feet can testify to that. The place appears to be dedicated to Achelous
and some of the Nymphs, if we can judge from the statues and votive
230c   offerings.[17] Feel the freshness of the air; how pretty and pleasant it is; how

---

[11] "The Hill of Ares" (god of war), located northwest of the Acropolis in Athens;
it was the seat of a civic council, also called the Areopagus.

[12] A Hippocentaur was half man, half horse; the Chimera had a lion's head, a
goat's body, and a serpent's tail; a Gorgon was a woman with snakes for hair; Pegasus
was a winged horse.

[13] *Gnōthi sauton* ("know yourself"): inscribed in the temple of Apollo at Delphi.

[14] A fabulous, multiform beast with a hundred heads resembling many different
animal species. See *Republic* 588c ff.

[15] Wife of Zeus, queen of the Greek pantheon, guardian of marriage.

[16] *Agnos:* a tall tree rather like a willow. It is associated with chastity because *hagnos*
means "chaste."

[17] Achelous was a river god. Nymphs were benevolent, female deities particularly
associated with streams, woods, and mountains.

it echoes with the summery, sweet song of the cicadas' chorus! The most exquisite thing of all, of course, is the grassy slope: it rises so gently that you can rest your head perfectly when you lie down on it. You've really been the most marvelous guide, my dear Phaedrus.

PHAEDRUS: And you, my remarkable friend, appear to be totally out of place. Really, just as you say, you seem to need a guide, not to be one of the locals. Not only do you never travel abroad—as far as I can tell, you never even set foot beyond the city walls. 230d

SOCRATES: Forgive me, my friend. I am devoted to learning; landscapes and trees have nothing to teach me—only the people in the city can do that. But you, I think, have found a potion to charm me into leaving. For just as people lead hungry animals forward by shaking branches of fruit before them, you can lead me all over Attica or anywhere else you like simply by waving in front of me the leaves of a book containing a speech. But now, 230e having gotten as far as this place this time around, I intend to lie down; so choose whatever position you think will be most comfortable for you, and read on.

PHAEDRUS: Listen, then:[18]

"You understand my situation: I've told you how good it would be for us, in my opinion, if this worked out. In any case, I don't think I should lose the chance to get what I am asking for, merely because I don't happen to be in love with you. 231a

"A man in love will wish he had not done you any favors once his desire dies down, but the time will never come for a man who's not in love to change his mind. That is because the favors he does for you are not forced but voluntary; and he does the best that he possibly can for you, just as he would for his own business.

"Besides, a lover keeps his eye on the balance sheet—where his interests have suffered from love, and where he has done well; and when he adds up all the trouble he has taken, he thinks he's long since given the boy he 231b loved a fair return. A non-lover, on the other hand, can't complain about love's making him neglect his own business; he can't keep a tab on the trouble he's been through, or blame you for the quarrels he's had with his relatives. Take away all those headaches and there's nothing left for him to do but put his heart into whatever he thinks will give pleasure.

"Besides, suppose a lover does deserve to be honored because, as they say, he is the best friend his loved one will ever have, and he stands ready 231c to please his boy with all those words and deeds that are so annoying to everyone else. It's easy to see (if he is telling the truth) that the next time he falls in love he will care more for his new love than for the old one,

---

[18] It is unclear whether this is a genuine speech by Lysias or a Platonic parody.

and it's clear he'll treat the old one shabbily whenever that will please the new one.

"And anyway, what sense does it make to throw away something like that on a person who has fallen into such a miserable condition that those 231d who have suffered it don't even try to defend themselves against it? A lover will admit that he's more sick than sound in the head. He's well aware that he is not thinking straight; but he'll say he can't get himself under control. So when he does start thinking straight, why would he stand by decisions he had made when he was sick?

"Another point: if you were to choose the best of those who are in love with you, you'd have a pretty small group to pick from; but you'll have a large group if you don't care whether he loves you or not and just pick the one who suits you best; and in that larger pool you'll have a much better 231e hope of finding someone who deserves your friendship.

"Now suppose you're afraid of conventional standards and the stigma that will come to you if people find out about this. Well, it stands to 232a reason that a lover—thinking that everyone else will admire him for his success as much as he admires himself—will fly into words and proudly declare to all and sundry that his labors were not in vain. Someone who does not love you, on the other hand, can control himself and will choose to do what is best, rather than seek the glory that comes from popular reputation.

"Besides, it's inevitable that a lover will be found out: many people will see that he devotes his life to following the boy he loves. The result is that 232b whenever people see you talking with him they'll think you are spending time together just before or just after giving way to desire. But they won't even begin to find fault with people for spending time together if they are not lovers; they know one has to talk to someone, either out of friendship or to obtain some other pleasure.

"Another point: have you been alarmed by the thought that it is hard for friendships to last? Or that when people break up, it's ordinarily just as 232c awful for one side as it is for the other, but when you've given up what is most important to you already, then your loss is greater than his? If so, it would make more sense for you to be afraid of lovers. For a lover is easily annoyed, and whatever happens, he'll think it was designed to hurt him. That is why a lover prevents the boy he loves from spending time with other people. He's afraid that wealthy men will outshine him with their money, while men of education will turn out to have the advantage of greater intelligence. And he watches like a hawk everyone who may have 232d any other advantage over him! Once he's persuaded you to turn those people away, he'll have you completely isolated from friends; and if you show more sense than he does in looking after your own interests, you'll come to quarrel with him.

"But if a man really does not love you, if it is only because of his excellence that he got what he asked for, then he won't be jealous of the people who spend time with you. Quite the contrary! He'll hate anyone who does not want to be with you; he'll think they look down on him while those who spend time with you do him good; so you should expect friendship, rather than enmity, to result from this affair.   232e

"Another point: lovers generally start to desire your body before they know your character or have any experience of your other traits, with the result that even they can't tell whether they'll still want to be friends with you after their desire has passed. Non-lovers, on the other hand, are friends with you even before they achieve their goal, and you've no reason   233a
to expect that benefits received will ever detract from their friendship for you. No, those things will stand as reminders of more to come.

"Another point: you can expect to become a better person if you are won over by me, rather than by a lover. A lover will praise what you say and what you do far beyond what is best, partly because he is afraid of being disliked, and partly because desire has impaired his judgment. Here is how   233b
love draws conclusions: When a lover suffers a reverse that would cause no pain to anyone else, love makes him think he's accursed! And when he has a stroke of luck that's not worth a moment's pleasure, love compels him to sing its praises. The result is, you should feel sorry for lovers, not admire them.

"If my argument wins you over, I will, first of all, give you my time with no thought of immediate pleasure; I will plan instead for the benefits that are to come, since I am master of myself and have not been over-   233c
whelmed by love. Small problems will not make me very hostile, and big ones will make me only gradually, and only a little, angry. I will forgive you for unintentional errors and do my best to keep you from going wrong intentionally. All this, you see, is the proof of a friendship that will last a long time.

"Have you been thinking that there can be no strong friendship in the absence of erotic love? Then you ought to remember that we would not care so much about our children if that were so, nor about our fathers and   233d
mothers. And we wouldn't have had any trustworthy friends, since those relationships did not come from such a desire but from doing quite different things.

"Besides, if it were true that we ought to give the biggest favor to those who need it most, then we should all be helping out the very poorest people, not the best ones, because people we've saved from the worst troubles will give us the most thanks. For instance, the right people to invite to a dinner party would be beggars and people who need to sate their   233e
hunger, because they're the ones who'll be fond of us, follow us, knock on our doors, take the most pleasure with the deepest gratitude, and pray for

234a our success. No, it's proper, I suppose, to grant your favors to those who are best able to return them, not to those in the direst need—that is, not to those who merely desire the thing, but to those who really deserve it—not to people who will take pleasure in the bloom of your youth, but to those who will share their goods with you when you are older; not to people who achieve their goal and then boast about it in public, but to those who will keep a modest silence with everyone; not to people whose devotion is short-lived, but to those who will be steady friends their whole lives; not to the people who look for an excuse to quarrel as soon as their desire has passed, but to those who will prove their worth when the bloom of your

234b youth has faded. Now, remember what I said and keep this in mind: friends often criticize a lover for bad behavior; but no one close to a non-lover ever thinks that desire has led him into bad judgment about his interests.

"And now I suppose you'll ask me whether I'm urging you to give your favors to everyone who is not in love with you. No. As I see it, a lover

234c would not ask you to give in to all your lovers either. You would not, in that case, earn as much gratitude from each recipient, and you would not be able to keep one affair secret from the others in the same way. But this sort of thing is not supposed to cause any harm, and really should work to the benefit of both sides.

"Well, I think this speech is long enough. If you are still longing for more, if you think I have passed over something, just ask."

How does the speech strike you, Socrates? Don't you think it's simply superb, especially in its choice of words?

234d SOCRATES: It's a miracle, my friend; I'm in ecstasy. And it's all your doing, Phaedrus: I was looking at you while you were reading and it seemed to me the speech had made you radiant with delight; and since I believe you understand these matters better than I do, I followed your lead, and following you I shared your Bacchic frenzy.

PHAEDRUS: Come, Socrates, do you think you should joke about this?

SOCRATES: Do you really think I am joking, that I am not serious?

234e PHAEDRUS: You are not at all serious, Socrates. But now tell me the truth, in the name of Zeus, god of friendship: Do you think that any other Greek could say anything more impressive or more complete on this same subject?

SOCRATES: What? Must we praise the speech even on the ground that its author has said what the situation demanded, and not instead simply on the ground that he has spoken in a clear and concise manner, with a precise turn of phrase? If we must, I will have to go along for your sake, since—

235a surely because I am so ignorant—that passed me by. I paid attention only to the speech's style. As to the other part, I wouldn't even think that Lysias himself could be satisfied with it. For it seemed to me, Phaedrus—unless, of course, you disagree—that he said the same things two or even three times, as if he really didn't have much to say about the subject, almost as if he just weren't very interested in it. In fact, he seemed to me to be showing off, trying to demonstrate that he could say the same thing in two different ways, and say it just as well both times.

PHAEDRUS: You are absolutely wrong, Socrates. That is in fact the best   235b
thing about the speech: He has omitted nothing worth mentioning about the subject, so that no one will ever be able to add anything of value to complete what he has already said himself.

SOCRATES: You go too far: I can't agree with you about that. If, as a favor to you, I accept your view, I will stand refuted by all the wise men and women of old who have spoken or written about this subject.

PHAEDRUS: Who are these people? And where have you heard anything   235c
better than this?

SOCRATES: I can't tell you offhand, but I'm sure I've heard better somewhere; perhaps it was the lovely Sappho or the wise Anacreon or even some writer of prose.[19] So, what's my evidence? The fact, my dear friend, that my breast is full and I feel I can make a different speech, even better than Lysias'. Now I am well aware that none of these ideas can have come from me—I know my own ignorance. The only other possibility, I think, is that I was filled, like an empty jar, by the words of other people streaming in   235d
through my ears, though I'm so stupid that I've even forgotten where and from whom I heard them.

PHAEDRUS: But, my dear friend, you couldn't have said a better thing! Don't bother telling me when and from whom you've heard this, even if I ask you—instead, do exactly what you said: You've just promised to make another speech making more points, and better ones, without repeating a word from my book. And I promise you that, like the Nine Archons, I shall set up in return a life-sized, golden statue at Delphi, not only of myself, but also of you.[20]   235e

SOCRATES: You're a real friend, Phaedrus, good as gold, to think I'm claiming that Lysias failed in absolutely every respect and that I can make a speech that is different on every point from his. I am sure that that couldn't happen even to the worst possible author. In our own case, for example, do you think that anyone could argue that one should favor the non-lover rather than the lover without praising the former for keeping his wits about

---

[19] Sappho was a lyric poet, born on the island of Lesbos in the second half of the seventh century BCE and known for her poetry about love. Anacreon, also a lyric poet, flourished in Teos in the middle of the sixth century BCE.

[20] The archons were Athenian magistrates chosen by lot. On taking office, they swore an oath to set up a golden statue at the temple of Apollo at Delphi if they violated the laws.

236a him or condemning the latter for losing his—points that are essential to make—and still have something left to say? I believe we must allow these points, and concede them to the speaker. In their case, we cannot praise their novelty but only their skillful arrangement; but we can praise both the arrangement and the novelty of the nonessential points that are harder to think up.

PHAEDRUS: I agree with you; I think that's reasonable. This, then, is what I shall do. I will allow you to presuppose that the lover is less sane than **236b** the non-lover—and if you are able to add anything of value to complete what we already have in hand, you will stand in hammered gold beside the offering of the Cypselids in Olympia.[21]

SOCRATES: Oh, Phaedrus, I was only criticizing your beloved in order to tease you—did you take me seriously? Do you think I'd really try to match the product of his wisdom with a fancier speech?

PHAEDRUS: Well, as far as that goes, my friend, you've fallen into your own **236c** trap. You have no choice but to give your speech as best you can: otherwise you will force us into trading vulgar jibes the way they do in comedy. Don't make me say what you said: "Socrates, if I don't know my Socrates, I must be forgetting who I am myself," or "He wanted to speak, but he was being coy." Get it into your head that we shall not leave here until you recite what you claimed to have "in your breast." We are alone, in a deserted place, and **236d** I am younger and stronger. From all this, "take my meaning"[22] and don't make me force you to speak when you can do so willingly.

SOCRATES: But, my dear Phaedrus, I'll be ridiculous—a mere dilettante, improvising on the same topics as a seasoned professional!

PHAEDRUS: Do you understand the situation? Stop playing hard to get! I know what I can say to make you give your speech.

SOCRATES: Then please don't say it!

PHAEDRUS: Oh, yes, I will. And what I say will be an oath. I swear to **236e** you—by which god, I wonder? How about this very plane tree?—I swear in all truth that, if you don't make your speech right next to this tree here, I shall never, never again recite another speech for you—I shall never utter another word about speeches to you!

SOCRATES: My oh my, what a horrible man you are! You've really found the way to force a lover of speeches to do just as you say!

PHAEDRUS: So why are you still twisting and turning like that?

---

[21] The Cypselids were rulers of Corinth during a period of great prosperity in the seventh century BCE.

[22] Plato attributes this phrase to Pindar at *Meno* 76d.

SOCRATES: I'll stop—now that you've taken this oath. How could I possibly give up such treats?

PHAEDRUS: Speak, then.   237a

SOCRATES: Do you know what I'll do?

PHAEDRUS: What?

SOCRATES: I'll cover my head while I'm speaking. In that way, as I'm going through the speech as fast as I can, I won't get embarrassed by having to look at you and lose the thread of my argument.

PHAEDRUS: Just give your speech! You can do anything else you like.

SOCRATES: Come to me, O you clear-voiced Muses, whether you are called so because of the quality of your song or from the musical people of Liguria,[23] "come, take up my burden"[24] in telling the tale that this fine fellow forces upon me so that his companion may now seem to him even more clever than he did before: 237b

There once was a boy, a youth rather, and he was very beautiful, and had very many lovers. One of them was wily and had persuaded him that he was not in love, though he loved the lad no less than the others. And once in pressing his suit to him, he tried to persuade him that he ought to give his favors to a man who did not love him rather than to one who did. And this is what he said:

"If you wish to reach a good decision on any topic, my boy, there is only one way to begin: You must know what the decision is about, or else   237c
you are bound to miss your target altogether. Ordinary people cannot see that they do not know the true nature of a particular subject, so they proceed as if they did; and because they do not work out an agreement at the start of the inquiry, they wind up as you would expect—in conflict with themselves and each other. Now you and I had better not let this happen to us, since we criticize it in others. Because you and I are about to discuss whether a boy should make friends with a man who loves him rather than with one who does not, we should agree on defining what love is and what effects it has. Then we can look back and refer to that as we try to   237d
find out whether to expect benefit or harm from love. Now, as everyone plainly knows, love is some kind of desire; but we also know that even men who are not in love have a desire for what is beautiful. So how shall we distinguish between a man who is in love and one who is not? We must realize that each of us is ruled by two principles which we follow wherever they lead: one is our inborn desire for pleasures, the other is our acquired judgment that pursues what is best. Sometimes these two are in agreement;

---

[23] Liguria is what is now known as the French Riviera.

[24] Apparently a quotation from an unknown source.

237e   but there are times when they quarrel inside us, and then sometimes one
        of them gains control, sometimes the other. Now when judgment is in
        control and leads us by reasoning toward what is best, that sort of self-
        control is called "temperance"; but when desire takes command in us and
238a   drags us without reasoning toward pleasure, then its command is known as
        "outrageousness [*hubris*]." Now outrageousness has as many names as the
        forms it can take, and these are quite diverse. Whichever form stands out
        in a particular case gives its name to the person who has it—and that is not
        a pretty name to be called, not worth earning at all. If it is desire for food
        that overpowers a person's reasoning about what is best and suppresses his
238b   other desires, it is called gluttony and it gives him the name of a glutton,
        while if it is desire for drink that plays the tyrant and leads the man in that
        direction, we all know what name we'll call him then! And now it should
        be clear how to describe someone appropriately in the other cases: call the
        man by that name—sister to these others—that derives from the sister of
        these desires that controls him at the time. As for the desire that has led us
        to say all this, it should be obvious already, but I suppose things said are
        always better understood than things unsaid: The unreasoning desire that
        overpowers a person's considered impulse to do right and is driven to take
238c   pleasure in beauty, its force reinforced by its kindred desires for beauty in
        human bodies—this desire, all-conquering in its forceful drive, takes its
        name from the word for force [*rhōmē*] and is called love [*erōs*]."
            There, Phaedrus my friend, don't you think, as I do, that I'm in the grip
        of something divine?

        PHAEDRUS: This is certainly an unusual flow of words for you, Socrates.

        SOCRATES: Then be quiet and listen. There's something really divine about
238d   this place, so don't be surprised if I'm quite taken by the Nymphs' madness
        as I go on with the speech. I'm on the edge of speaking in dithyrambs[25]
        as it is.

        PHAEDRUS: Very true!

        SOCRATES: Yes, and you're the cause of it. But hear me out; the attack may
        yet be prevented. That, however, is up to the god; what we must do is face
        the boy again in the speech:
            "All right then, my brave friend, now we have a definition for the
        subject of our decision; now we have said what it really is; so let us keep
238e   that in view as we complete our discussion. What benefit or harm is likely
        to come from the lover or the non-lover to the boy who gives him favors?
        It is surely necessary that a man who is ruled by desire and is a slave to
        pleasure will turn his boy into whatever is most pleasing to himself. Now
        a sick man takes pleasure in anything that does not resist him, but sees

        ───────────────

        [25] See *Symposium* 175e note on Dionysus.

anyone who is equal or superior to him as an enemy. That is why a lover
will not willingly put up with a boyfriend who is his equal or superior, but   **239a**
is always working to make the boy he loves weaker and inferior to himself.
Now, the ignorant man is inferior to the wise one, the coward to the brave,
the ineffective speaker to the trained orator, the slow-witted to the quick.
By necessity, a lover will be delighted to find all these mental defects and
more, whether acquired or innate in his boy; and if he does not, he will
have to supply them or else lose the pleasure of the moment. The necessary
consequence is that he will be jealous and keep the boy away from the good   239b
company of anyone who would make a better man of him; and that will
cause him a great deal of harm, especially if he keeps him away from what
would most improve his mind—and that is, in fact, divine philosophy, from
which it is necessary for a lover to keep his boy a great distance away, out
of fear the boy will eventually come to look down on him. He will have
to invent other ways, too, of keeping the boy in total ignorance and so
in total dependence on himself. That way the boy will give his lover the
most pleasure, though the harm to himself will be severe. So it will not
be of any use to your intellectual development to have as your mentor and   239c
companion a man who is in love.

"Now let's turn to your physical development. If a man is bound by
necessity to chase pleasure at the expense of the good, what sort of shape
will he want you to be in? How will he train you, if he is in charge? You
will see that what he wants is someone who is soft, not muscular, and not
trained in full sunlight but in dappled shade—someone who has never
worked out like a man, never touched hard, sweaty exercise. Instead, he
goes for a boy who has known only a soft unmanly style of life, who makes
himself pretty with cosmetics because he has no natural color at all. There   239d
is no point in going on with this description: it is perfectly obvious what
other sorts of behavior follow from this. We can take up our next topic
after drawing all this to a head: the sort of body a lover wants in his boy
is one that will give confidence to the enemy in a war or other great crisis
while causing alarm to friends and even to his lovers. Enough of that; the
point is obvious.

"Our next topic is the benefit or harm to your possessions that will come   239e
from a lover's care and company. Everyone knows the answer, especially
a lover: His first wish will be for a boy who has lost his dearest, kindliest
and godliest possessions—his mother and father and other close relatives.
He would be happy to see the boy deprived of them, since he would expect
them either to block him from the sweet pleasure of the boy's company or   **240a**
to criticize him severely for taking it. What is more, a lover would think
any money or other wealth the boy owns would only make him harder
to snare and, once snared, harder to handle. It follows by absolute necessity that wealth in a boyfriend will cause his lover to envy him, while his

poverty will be a delight. Furthermore, he will wish for the boy to stay wifeless, childless, and homeless for as long as possible, since that's how long he desires to go on plucking his sweet fruit.

240b   "There are other troubles in life, of course, but some divinity has mixed most of them with a dash of immediate pleasure. A flatterer, for example, may be an awful beast and a dreadful nuisance, but nature makes flattery rather pleasant by mixing in a little culture with its words. So it is with a mistress—for all the harm we accuse her of causing—and with many other creatures of that character, and their callings: at least they are delightful company for a day. But besides being harmful to his boyfriend, a lover is

240c simply disgusting to spend the day with. 'Youth delights youth,' as the old proverb runs—because, I suppose, friendship grows from similarity, as boys of the same age go after the same pleasures. But you can even have too much of people your own age. Besides, as they say, it is miserable for anyone to be forced into anything by necessity—and this (to say nothing of the age difference) is most true for a boy with his lover. The older man clings to the younger day and night, never willing to leave him, driven by

240d necessity and goaded on by the sting that gives him pleasure every time he sees, hears, touches, or perceives his boy in any way at all, so that he follows him around like a servant, with pleasure.

   "As for the boy, however, what comfort or pleasure will the lover give to him during all the time they spend together? Won't it be disgusting in the extreme to see the face of that older man who's lost his looks? And everything that goes with that face—why, it is a misery even to hear them

240e mentioned, let alone actually handle them, as you would constantly be forced to do! To be watched and guarded suspiciously all the time, with everyone! To hear praise of yourself that is out of place and excessive! And then to be falsely accused—which is unbearable when the man is sober and not only unbearable but positively shameful when he is drunk and lays into you with a pack of wild barefaced insults!

   "While he is still in love he is harmful and disgusting, but after his love fades he breaks his trust with you for the future, in spite of all the promises he has made with all those oaths and entreaties which just barely kept

241a you in a relationship that was troublesome at the time, in hope of future benefits. So, then, by the time he should pay up, he has made a change and installed a new ruling government in himself: right-minded reason in place of the madness of love. The boy does not even realize that his lover is a different man. He insists on his reward for past favors and reminds him of what they had done and said before—as if he were still talking to the same man! The lover, however, is so ashamed that he does not dare tell the boy how much he has changed or that there is no way, now that

241b he is in his right mind and under control again, that he can stand by the promises he had sworn to uphold when he was under that old mindless

regime. He is afraid that if he acted as he had before he would turn out the same and revert to his old self. So now he is a refugee, fleeing from those old promises on which he must default by necessity; he, the former lover, has to switch roles and flee, since the coin has fallen the other way,[26] while the boy must chase after him, angry and cursing. All along he has been completely unaware that he should never have given his favors to a man who was in love—and who therefore had by necessity lost his mind. He should much rather have done it for a man who was not in love and had his wits about him. Otherwise it follows necessarily that he'd be giving   241c
himself to a man who is deceitful, irritable, jealous, disgusting, harmful to his property, harmful to his physical fitness, and absolutely devastating to the cultivation of his soul, which truly is, and will always be, the most valuable thing to gods and men.

"These are the points you should bear in mind, my boy. You should know that the friendship of a lover arises without any good will at all. No, like food, its purpose is to sate hunger. 'Do wolves love lambs? That's how lovers befriend a boy!'"[27]   241d

That's it, Phaedrus. You won't hear another word from me, and you'll have to accept this as the end of the speech.

PHAEDRUS: But I thought you were right in the middle—I thought you were about to speak at the same length about the non-lover, to list his good points and argue that it's better to give one's favors to him. So why are you stopping now, Socrates?

SOCRATES: Didn't you notice, my friend, that even though I am criticizing   241e
the lover, I have passed beyond lyric into epic poetry?[28] What do you suppose will happen to me if I begin to praise his opposite? Don't you realize that the Nymphs to whom you so cleverly exposed me will take complete possession of me? So I say instead, in a word, that every shortcoming for which we blamed the lover has its contrary advantage, and the non-lover possesses it. Why make a long speech of it? That's enough about them both. This way my story will meet the end it deserves, and I will cross the river   242a
and leave before you make me do something even worse.

PHAEDRUS: Not yet, Socrates, not until this heat is over. Don't you see that it is almost exactly noon, "straight-up" as they say? Let's wait and discuss the speeches, and go as soon as it turns cooler.

---

[26] In a game like tag, Plato's contemporaries tossed a shell, which could land bright side or dark side up, to decide who should chase whom.

[27] Perhaps an allusion to Homer, *Iliad* xxii.262–63.

[28] Epic poetry glorified its hero; lyric poets, such as Sappho and Anacreon, complained about the effects of love.

SOCRATES: You're really superhuman when it comes to speeches, Phaedrus; you're truly amazing. I'm sure you've brought into being more of the speeches that have been given during your lifetime than anyone else, whether you composed them yourself or in one way or another forced others to make them; with the single exception of Simmias the Theban, you are far ahead of the rest.[29] Even as we speak, I think, you're managing to cause me to produce yet another one.

PHAEDRUS: Oh, how wonderful! But what do you mean? What speech?

SOCRATES: My friend, just as I was about to cross the river, the familiar divine sign came to me which, whenever it occurs, holds me back from something I am about to do. I thought I heard a voice coming from this very spot, forbidding me to leave until I made atonement for some offense against the gods. In effect, you see, I am a seer, and though I am not particularly good at it, still—like people who are just barely able to read and write—I am good enough for my own purposes. I recognize my offense clearly now. In fact, the soul too, my friend, is itself a sort of seer; that's why, almost from the beginning of my speech, I was disturbed by a very uneasy feeling, as Ibycus puts it, that "for offending the gods I am honored by men."[30] But now I understand exactly what my offense has been.

PHAEDRUS: Tell me, what is it?

SOCRATES: Phaedrus, that speech you carried with you here—it was horrible, as horrible as the speech you made me give.

PHAEDRUS: How could that be?

SOCRATES: It was foolish, and close to being impious. What could be more horrible than that?

PHAEDRUS: Nothing—if, of course, what you say is right.

SOCRATES: Well, then? Don't you believe that Love is the son of Aphrodite?[31] Isn't he one of the gods?

PHAEDRUS: This is certainly what people say.

SOCRATES: Well, Lysias certainly doesn't and neither does your speech, which you charmed me through your potion into delivering myself. But if Love is a god or something divine—which he is—he can't be bad in any way; and yet our speeches just now spoke of him as if he were. That is their offense against Love. And they've compounded it with their utter foolishness in parading their dangerous falsehoods and preening themselves over perhaps deceiving a few silly people and coming to be admired by them.

---

[29] Simmias is one of Socrates' two questioners in the *Phaedo*.

[30] Sixth-century lyric poet from Regium in southern Italy.

[31] See *Symposium* 177e note.

And so, my friend, I must purify myself. Now for those whose offense lies in telling false stories about matters divine, there is an ancient rite of purification—Homer did not know it, but Stesichorus did. When he lost his sight for speaking ill of Helen, he did not, like Homer, remain in the dark about the reason why. On the contrary, true follower of the Muses that he was, he understood it and immediately composed these lines:

> There's no truth to that story:
> You never sailed that lovely ship,
> You never reached the tower of Troy.[32]   243b

And as soon as he completed the poem we call the Palinode, he immediately regained his sight. Now I will prove to be wiser than Homer and Stesichorus to this small extent: I will try to offer my Palinode to Love before I am punished for speaking ill of him—with my head bare, no longer covered in shame.

PHAEDRUS: No words could be sweeter to my ears, Socrates.

SOCRATES: You see, my dear Phaedrus, you understand how shameless the   243c
speeches were, my own as well as the one in your book. Suppose a noble and gentle man, who was (or had once been) in love with a boy of similar character, were to hear us say that lovers start serious quarrels for trivial reasons and that, jealous of their beloved, they do him harm—don't you think that man would think we had been brought up among the most vulgar of sailors, totally ignorant of love among the freeborn? Wouldn't he most certainly refuse to acknowledge the flaws we attributed to Love?   243d

PHAEDRUS: Most probably, Socrates.

SOCRATES: Well, that man makes me feel ashamed, and as I'm also afraid of Love himself, I want to wash out the bitterness of what we've heard with a more tasteful speech. And my advice to Lysias, too, is to write as soon as possible a speech urging one to give similar favors to a lover rather than to a non-lover.

PHAEDRUS: You can be sure he will. For once you have spoken in praise of the lover, I will most definitely make Lysias write a speech on the same topic.   243e

SOCRATES: I do believe you will, so long as you are who you are.

PHAEDRUS: Speak on, then, in full confidence.

SOCRATES: Where, then, is the boy to whom I was speaking? Let him hear this speech, too. Otherwise he may be too quick to give his favors to the non-lover.

---

[32] Stesichorus was a lyric and dithyrambic poet of the early sixth century BCE. In his famous Palinode, or "taking-it-back" poem, he explained away the evidence for Helen's (willing) abduction by Paris—the alleged precipitating cause of the Trojan War.

PHAEDRUS: He is here, always right by your side, whenever you want him.

SOCRATES: You'll have to understand, beautiful boy, that the previous speech was by Phaedrus, Pythocles' son, from Myrrhinus, while the one I am about to deliver is by Stesichorus, Euphemus' son, from Himera.[33] And here is how the speech should go:

"'There's no truth to that story'—that when a lover is available you should give your favors to a man who doesn't love you instead, because he is in control of himself while the lover has lost his head. That would have been fine to say if madness were bad, pure and simple; but in fact the best things we have come from madness, when it is given as a gift of the god.

"The prophetess of Delphi and the priestesses at Dodona[34] are out of their minds when they perform that fine work of theirs for all of Greece, either for an individual person or for a whole city, but they accomplish little or nothing when they are in control of themselves. We will not mention the Sibyl[35] or the others who foretell many things by means of god-inspired prophetic trances and give sound guidance to many people—that would take too much time for a point that's obvious to everyone. But here's some evidence worth adding to our case: The people who designed our language in the old days never thought of madness as something to be ashamed of or worthy of blame; otherwise they would not have used the word 'manic' for the finest experts of all—the ones who tell the future—thereby weaving insanity into prophecy. They thought it was wonderful when it came as a gift of the god, and that's why they gave its name to prophecy; but nowadays people don't know the fine points, so they stick in a 't' and call it 'mantic.' Similarly, the clear-headed study of the future, which uses birds and other signs, was originally called *oionoïstic,* since it uses reasoning to bring intelligence (*nous*) and learning (*historia*) into human thought; but now modern speakers call it *oiōnistic,* putting on airs with their long 'ō'. To the extent, then, that prophecy, *mantic,* is more perfect and more admirable than sign-based prediction, *oiōnistic,* in both name and achievement, madness (*mania*) from a god is finer than self-control of human origin, according to the testimony of the ancient language givers.

"Next, madness can provide relief from the greatest plagues of trouble that beset certain families because of their guilt for ancient crimes: it turns up among those who need a way out; it gives prophecies and takes refuge

---

[33] Etymologically: "Stesichorus, son of Good Speaker, from the Land of Desire." Myrrhinus was one of the demes of ancient Athens.

[34] The priestesses at the temple of Apollo at Delphi and of Zeus at Dodona in Epirus were thought to deliver their oracular utterance while in a divinely inspired trance.

[35] Originally the name of a single prophetess, then a generic term.

in prayers to the gods and in worship, discovering mystic rites and purifica-   244e
tions that bring the man it touches[36] through to safety for this and all time
to come. So it is that the right sort of madness finds relief from present
hardships for a man it has possessed.

"Third comes the kind of madness that is possession by the Muses,   **245a**
which takes a tender virgin soul and awakens it to a Bacchic frenzy of
songs and poetry that glorifies the achievements of the past and teaches
them to future generations. If anyone comes to the gates of poetry and
expects to become an adequate poet by acquiring expert knowledge of the
subject without the Muses' madness, he will fail, and his self-controlled
verses will be eclipsed by the poetry of men who have been driven out
of their minds.

"There you have some of the fine achievements—and I could tell you   245b
even more—that are due to god-sent madness. We must not have any fear
on this particular point, then, and we must not let anyone disturb us or
frighten us with the claim that you should prefer a friend who is in control
of himself to one who is disturbed. Besides proving that point, if he is to
win his case, our opponent must show that love is not sent by the gods as a
benefit to a lover and his boy. And we, for our part, must prove the oppo-   245c
site, that this sort of madness is given us by the gods to ensure our greatest
good fortune. It will be a proof that convinces the wise if not the clever.

"Now we must first understand the truth about the nature of the soul,
divine or human, by examining what it does and what is done to it. Here
begins the proof:

"Every soul is immortal. That is because whatever is always in motion is
immortal, while what moves, and is moved by, something else stops living
when it stops moving. So it is only what moves itself that never desists from
motion, since it does not leave off being itself. In fact, this self-mover is
also the source[37] and spring of motion in everything else that moves; and
a source has no beginning. That is because anything that has a beginning   245d
comes from some source, but there is no source for this, since a source that
got its start from something else would no longer be the source. And since
it cannot have a beginning, then necessarily it cannot be destroyed. That
is because if a source were destroyed it could never get started again from
anything else and nothing else could get started from it—that is, if everything gets started from a source. This then is why a self-mover is a source of
motion. And *that* is incapable of being destroyed or starting up; otherwise
all heaven and everything that has been started up would collapse, come to   245e
a stop, and never have cause to start moving again. But since we have found

---

[36] That is, a person who is mad.

[37] *Archē:* often translated as the technical expression "first principle."

that a self-mover is immortal, we should have no qualms about declaring that this is the very essence and principle of a soul, for every bodily object that is moved from outside has no soul, while a body whose motion comes from within, from itself, does have a soul, that being the nature of a soul; and if this is so—that whatever moves itself is essentially a soul—then it

246a follows necessarily that soul should have neither birth nor death.

"That, then, is enough about the soul's immortality. Now here is what we must say about its structure. To describe what the soul actually is would require a very long account, altogether a task for a god in every way; but to say what it is like is humanly possible and takes less time. So let us do the second in our speech. Let us then liken the soul to the natural union of a team of winged horses and their charioteer. The gods have horses and charioteers that are themselves all good and come from good stock besides,

246b while everyone else has a mixture. To begin with, our driver is in charge of a pair of horses; second, one of his horses is beautiful and good and from stock of the same sort, while the other is the opposite and has the opposite sort of bloodline. This means that chariot-driving in our case is inevitably a painfully difficult business.

"And now I should try to tell you why living things are said to include both mortal and immortal beings. All soul looks after all that lacks a soul, and patrols all of heaven, taking different shapes at different times. So long

246c as its wings are in perfect condition it flies high, and the entire universe is its dominion; but a soul that sheds its wings wanders until it lights on something solid, where it settles and takes on an earthly body, which then, owing to the power of this soul, seems to move itself. The whole combination of soul and body is called a living thing, or animal, and has the designation 'mortal' as well. Such a combination cannot be immortal, not on any reasonable account. In fact it is pure fiction, based neither on observation nor on adequate reasoning, that a god is an immortal living

246d thing which has a body and a soul, and that these are bound together by nature for all time—but of course we must let this be as it may please the gods, and speak accordingly.

"Let us turn to what causes the shedding of the wings, what makes them fall away from a soul. It is something of this sort: By their nature wings have the power to lift up heavy things and raise them aloft where the gods all dwell, and so, more than anything that pertains to the body, they are

246e akin to the divine, which has beauty, wisdom, goodness, and everything of that sort. These nourish the soul's wings, which grow best in their presence; but foulness and ugliness make the wings shrink and disappear.

"Now Zeus, the great commander in heaven, drives his winged chariot first in the procession, looking after everything and putting all things in order. Following him is an army of gods and spirits arranged in eleven sections.[38] Hestia[39] is the only one who remains at the home of the gods; all **247a** the rest of the twelve are lined up in formation, each god in command of the unit to which he is assigned. Inside heaven are many wonderful places from which to look and many aisles which the blessed gods take up and back, each seeing to his own work, while anyone who is able and wishes to do so follows along, since jealousy has no place in the gods' chorus. When they go to feast at the banquet they have a steep climb to the high tier at the rim of heaven; on this slope the gods' chariots move easily, since they **247b** are balanced and well under control, but the other chariots barely make it. The heaviness of the bad horse drags its charioteer toward the earth and weighs him down if he has failed to train it well, and this causes the most extreme toil and struggle that a soul will face. But when the souls we call immortals reach the top, they move outward and take their stand on the high ridge of heaven, where its circular motion carries them around as they **247c** stand while they gaze upon what is outside heaven.

"The place beyond heaven—none of our earthly poets has ever sung or ever will sing its praises enough! Still, this is the way it is—risky as it may be, you see, I must attempt to speak the truth, especially since the truth is my subject. What is in this place is without color and without shape and without solidity, a being that really is what it is, the subject of all true knowledge, visible only to intelligence, the soul's steersman. Now a god's **247d** mind is nourished by intelligence and pure knowledge, as is the mind of any soul that is concerned to take in what is appropriate to it, and so it is delighted at last to be seeing what is real and watching what is true, feeding on all this and feeling wonderful, until the circular motion brings it around to where it started. On the way around it has a view of Justice as it is; it has a view of Self-control; it has a view of Knowledge—not the knowledge that is close to change, that becomes different as it knows the different things which we consider real down here. No, it is the knowledge of what really **247e** is what it is. And when the soul has seen all the things that are as they are and feasted on them, it sinks back inside heaven and goes home. On its arrival, the charioteer stables the horses by the manger, throws in ambrosia, and gives them nectar to drink besides.

"Now that is the life of the gods. As for the other souls, one that fol- **248a** lows a god most closely, making itself most like that god, raises the head of its charioteer up to the place outside and is carried around in the circular motion with the others. Although distracted by the horses, this soul does

---

[38] The twelve principal gods were central to civic religion in classical Greece; an altar to them, placed in the marketplace in Athens, was considered the center of the city for the purposes of measurement.

[39] Goddess of hearth and home.

have a view of Reality, just barely. Another soul rises at one time and falls at another, and because its horses pull it violently in different directions, it sees some real things and misses others. The remaining souls are all eagerly straining to keep up, but are unable to rise; they are carried around below the surface, trampling and striking one another as each tries to get ahead of 248b   the others. The result is terribly noisy, very sweaty, and disorderly. Many souls are crippled by the incompetence of the drivers, and many wings break much of their plumage. After so much trouble, they all leave without having seen reality, uninitiated, and when they have gone they will depend on what they think is nourishment—their own opinions.

    "The reason there is so much eagerness to see the plain where truth stands is that this pasture has the grass that is the right food for the best 248c   part of the soul, and it is the nature of the wings that lift up the soul to be nourished by it. Besides, the law of Destiny is this: If any soul becomes a companion to a god and catches sight of any true thing, it will be unharmed until the next circuit; and if it is able to do this every time, it will always be safe. If, on the other hand, it does not see anything true because it could not keep up, and by some accident takes on a burden of forgetfulness and wrongdoing, then it is weighed down, sheds its wings and falls to earth. 248d   At that point, according to the law, the soul is not born into a wild animal in its first incarnation; but a soul that has seen the most will be planted in the seed of a man who will become a lover of wisdom or of beauty, or who will be cultivated in the arts and prone to erotic love. The second sort of soul will be put into someone who will be a lawful king or warlike commander; the third, a statesman, a manager of a household, or a financier; the fourth will be a trainer who loves exercise or a doctor who cures the body; the fifth will lead the life of a prophet or priest of the mysteries. To 248e   the sixth the life of a poet or some other representational artist is properly assigned; to the seventh the life of a manual laborer or farmer; to the eighth the career of a sophist or demagogue; and to the ninth a tyrant.

    "Of all these, any who have led their lives with justice will change to a better fate, and any who have led theirs with injustice, to a worse one. In fact, no soul returns to the place from which it came for ten thousand years, 249a   since its wings will not grow before then, except for the soul of a man who practices philosophy without guile or who loves boys philosophically. If, after the third cycle of one thousand years, the last-mentioned souls have chosen such a life three times in a row, they grow their wings back, and they depart in the three-thousandth year. As for the rest, once their first life is over, they come to judgment; and, once judged, some are condemned to go to places of punishment beneath the earth and pay the full penalty for their injustice, while the others are lifted up by justice to a place in heaven where they live in the manner the life they led in human form has earned 249b   them. In the thousandth year both groups arrive at a choice and allotment of second lives, and each soul chooses the life it wants. From there, a human soul can enter a wild animal, and a soul that was once human can move from an animal to a human being again. But a soul that never saw the truth cannot take a human shape, since a human being must understand speech in terms of general forms, proceeding to bring many perceptions together into a reasoned unity. That process is the recollection of the things our soul saw when it was traveling with god, when it disregarded the things we now call real and lifted up its head to what is truly real instead.

249c

"For just this reason it is fair that only a philosopher's mind grows wings, since its memory always keeps it as close as possible to those realities by being close to which the gods are divine. A man who uses reminders of these things correctly is always at the highest, most perfect level of initiation, and he is the only one who is perfect as perfect can be. He stands outside human concerns and draws close to the divine; ordinary people think he is disturbed and rebuke him for this, unaware that he is possessed by god. Now this takes me to the whole point of my discussion of the fourth kind of madness—that which someone shows when he sees the beauty we have down here and is reminded of true beauty; then he takes wing and flutters in his eagerness to rise up, but is unable to do so; and he gazes aloft, like a bird, paying no attention to what is down below—and that is what brings on him the charge that he has gone mad. This is the best and noblest of all the forms that possession by god can take for anyone who has it or is connected to it, and when someone who loves beautiful boys is touched by this madness he is called a lover. As I said, nature requires that the soul of every human being has seen reality; otherwise, no soul could have entered this sort of living thing. But not every soul is easily reminded of the reality there by what it finds here—not souls that got only a brief glance at the reality there, not souls who had such bad luck when they fell down here that they were twisted by bad company into lives of injustice so that they forgot the sacred objects they had seen before. Only a few remain whose memory is good enough; and they are startled when they see an image of what they saw up there. Then they are beside themselves, and their experience is beyond their comprehension because they cannot fully grasp what it is that they are seeing.

249d

249e

250a

250b

"Justice and self-control do not shine out through their images down here, and neither do the other objects of the soul's admiration; the senses are so murky that only a few people are able to make out, with difficulty, the original of the likenesses they encounter here. But beauty was radiant to see at that time when the souls, along with the glorious chorus (we [philosophers] were with Zeus, while others followed other gods), saw that blessed and spectacular vision and were ushered into the mystery that we may rightly call the most blessed of all. And we who celebrated it were wholly perfect and free of all the troubles that awaited us in time to come,

250c

and we gazed in rapture at sacred revealed objects that were perfect, and simple, and unshakeable and blissful. That was the ultimate vision, and we saw it in pure light because we were pure ourselves, not buried in this thing we are carrying around now, which we call a body, locked in it like an oyster in its shell.

"Well, all that was for love of a memory that made me stretch out my speech in longing for the past. Now beauty, as I said, was radiant among the other objects; and now that we have come down here we grasp it spar-kling through the clearest of our senses. Vision, of course, is the sharpest of our bodily senses, although it does not see wisdom. It would awaken a terribly powerful love if an image of wisdom came through our sight as clearly as beauty does, and the same goes for the other objects of inspired love. But now beauty alone has this privilege, to be the most clearly visible and the most loved. Of course a man who was initiated long ago or who has become defiled is not to be moved abruptly from here to a vision of Beauty itself when he sees what we call beauty here; so instead of gazing at the latter reverently, he surrenders to pleasure and sets out in the man-ner of a four-footed beast, eager to make babies; and, wallowing in vice, he goes after unnatural pleasure too, without a trace of fear or shame. A recent initiate, however, one who has seen much in heaven—when he sees a godlike face or bodily form that has captured Beauty well, first he shudders and a fear comes over him like those he felt at the earlier time; then he gazes at him with the reverence due a god, and if he weren't afraid people would think him completely mad, he'd even sacrifice to his boy as if he were the image of a god. Once he has looked at him, his chill gives way to sweating and a high fever, because the stream of beauty that pours into him through his eyes warms him up and waters the growth of his wings. Meanwhile, the heat warms him and melts the places where the wings once grew, places that were long ago closed off with hard scabs to keep the sprouts from coming back; but as nourishment flows in, the feather shafts swell and rush to grow from their roots beneath every part of the soul (long ago, you see, the entire soul had wings). Now the whole soul seethes and throbs in this condition. Like a child whose teeth are just starting to grow in, and its gums are all aching and itching—that is exactly how the soul feels when it begins to grow wings. It swells up and aches and tingles as it grows them. But when it looks upon the beauty of the boy and takes in the stream of particles flowing into it from his beauty (that is why this is called "desire"),[40] when it is watered and warmed by this, then all its pain subsides and is replaced by joy. When, however, it is separated from the boy and runs dry, then the openings of the passages in which the

---

[40] *Himeros:* from *merē* ("particles"), *ienai* ("go"), and *rhein* ("flow").

feathers grow are dried shut and keep the wings from sprouting. Then the stump of each feather is blocked in its desire and it throbs like a pulsing artery while the feather pricks at its passageway, with the result that the whole soul is stung all around, and the pain simply drives it wild—but then, when it remembers the boy in his beauty, it recovers its joy. From the outlandish mix of these two feelings—pain and joy—comes anguish and helpless raving: in its madness the lover's soul cannot sleep at night or stay 251e put by day; it rushes, yearning, wherever it expects to see the person who has that beauty. When it does see him, it opens the sluice-gates of desire and sets free the parts that were blocked up before. And now that the pain and the goading have stopped, it can catch its breath and once more suck in, for the moment, this sweetest of all pleasures. This it is not at all willing 252a to give up, and no one is more important to it than the beautiful boy. It forgets mother and brothers and friends entirely and doesn't care at all if it loses its wealth through neglect. And as for proper and decorous behavior, in which it used to take pride, the soul despises the whole business. Why, it is even willing to sleep like a slave, anywhere, as near to the object of its longing as it is allowed to get! That is because in addition to its reverence for one who has such beauty, the soul has discovered that the boy is the only doctor for all that terrible pain. 252b

"This is the experience we humans call love, you beautiful boy (I mean the one to whom I am making this speech).⁴¹ You are so young that what the gods call it is likely to strike you as funny. Some of the successors of Homer, I believe, report two lines from the less well-known poems, of which the second is quite indecent and does not scan very well. They praise love this way:

> Yes, mortals call him powerful winged "Love";
> But because of his need to thrust out the wings,
> the gods call him "Shove."⁴²

You may believe this or not as you like. But, seriously, the cause of love 252c is as I have said, and this is how lovers really feel.

"If the man who is taken by love used to be an attendant on Zeus, he will be able to bear the burden of this feathered force with dignity. But if it is one of Ares' troops who has fallen prisoner of love—if that is the god with whom he took the circuit—then if he has the slightest suspicion that the boy he loves has done him wrong, he turns murderous, and he is ready to make a sacrifice of himself as well as the boy.

---

⁴¹ The boy being courted by the non-lover in the fictional example.

⁴² The lines are probably Plato's invention, as the language is not consistently Homeric. The pun is on *erōs* and *pterōs* ("the winged one").

252d   "So it is with each of the gods: everyone spends his life honoring the god in whose chorus he danced, and emulates that god in every way he can, so long as he remains undefiled and in his first life down here. And that is how he behaves with everyone at every turn, not just with those he loves. Everyone chooses his love after his own fashion from among those who are beautiful, and then treats the boy like his very own god, building him up and adorning him as an image to honor and worship. Those who

252e   followed Zeus, for example, choose someone to love who is a Zeus himself in the nobility of his soul. So they make sure he has a talent for philosophy and the guidance of others, and once they have found him and are in love with him they do everything to develop that talent. If any lovers have not yet embarked on this practice, then they start to learn, using any source they can and also making progress on their own. They are well equipped

253a   to track down their god's true nature with their own resources because of their driving need to gaze at the god, and as they are in touch with the god by memory they are inspired by him and adopt his customs and practices, so far as a human being can share a god's life. For all of this they know they have the boy to thank, and so they love him all the more; and if they draw their inspiration from Zeus, then, like the Bacchants,[43] they pour it into the soul of the one they love in order to help him take on as much of their own

253b   god's qualities as possible. Hera's followers look for a kingly character, and once they have found him they do all the same things for him. And so it is for followers of Apollo or any other god: They take their god's path and seek for their own a boy whose nature is like the god's; and when they have got him they emulate the god, convincing the boy they love and training him to follow their god's pattern and way of life, so far as is possible in each case. They show no envy, no mean-spirited lack of generosity, toward the boy, but make every possible effort to draw him into being totally like

253c   themselves and the god to whom they are devoted. This, then, is any true lover's heart's desire: if he follows that desire in the manner I described, this friend who has been driven mad by love will secure a consummation for the one he has befriended that is as beautiful and blissful as I said—if, of course, he captures him. Here, then, is how the captive is caught:

          "Remember how we divided each soul in three at the beginning of our story—two parts in the form of horses and the third in that of a chari-

253d   oteer? Let us continue with that. One of the horses, we said, is good, the other not; but we did not go into the details of the goodness of the good horse or the badness of the bad. Let us do that now. The horse that is on the right, or nobler, side is upright in frame and well jointed, with a high neck and a regal nose; his coat is white, his eyes are black, and he is a lover

---

[43] Worshipers of Dionysus, not Zeus.

of honor with temperance and self-control; companion to true glory, he
needs no whip, and is guided by verbal commands alone. The other horse
is a crooked great jumble of limbs with a short bull-neck, a pug nose, black   253e
skin, and bloodshot white eyes; companion to wild boasts and indecency,
he is shaggy around the ears—deaf as a post—and just barely yields to
horsewhip and goad combined. Now when the charioteer looks love in
the eye, his entire soul is suffused with a sense of warmth and starts to fill
with tingles and the goading of desire. As for the horses, the one who is
obedient to the charioteer is still controlled, then as always, by its sense   254a
of shame, and so prevents itself from jumping on the boy. The other one,
however, no longer responds to the whip or the goad of the charioteer; it
leaps violently forward and does everything to aggravate its yokemate and
its charioteer, trying to make them go up to the boy and suggest to him the
pleasures of sex. At first the other two resist, angry in their belief that they
are being made to do things that are dreadfully wrong. At last, however,   254b
when they see no end to their trouble, they are led forward, reluctantly
agreeing to do as they have been told. So they are close to him now, and
they are struck by the boy's face as if by a bolt of lightning. When the
charioteer sees that face, his memory is carried back to the real nature of
Beauty, and he sees it again where it stands on the sacred pedestal next to
Self-control. At the sight he is frightened, falls over backwards awestruck,   254c
and at the same time has to pull the reins back so fiercely that both horses
are set on their haunches, one falling back voluntarily with no resistance,
but the other insolent and quite unwilling. They pull back a little further;
and while one horse drenches the whole soul with sweat out of shame and
awe, the other—once it has recovered from the pain caused by the bit and
its fall—bursts into a torrent of insults as soon as it has caught its breath,
accusing its charioteer and yokemate of all sorts of cowardice and unmanli-
ness for abandoning their position and their agreement. Now once more it   254d
tries to make its unwilling partners advance, and gives in grudgingly only
when they beg it to wait till later. Then, when the promised time arrives,
and they are pretending to have forgotten, it reminds them; it struggles, it
neighs, it pulls them forward and forces them to approach the boy again
with the same proposition; and as soon as they are near, it drops its head,
straightens its tail, bites the bit, and pulls without any shame at all. The
charioteer is now struck with the same feelings as before, only worse, and   254e
he's falling back as he would from a starting gate; and he violently yanks
the bit back out of the teeth of the insolent horse, only harder this time, so
that he bloodies its foul-speaking tongue and jaws, sets its legs and haunches
firmly on the ground, and 'gives it over to pain.'[44] When the bad horse has

---

[44] Cf. *Iliad* v.397 and *Odyssey* xvii.567.

suffered this same thing time after time, it stops being so insolent; now it is humble enough to follow the charioteer's warnings, and when it sees the beautiful boy it dies of fright, with the result that now at last the lover's soul follows its boy in reverence and awe.

255a "And because he is served with all the attentions due a god by a lover who is not pretending otherwise but is truly in the throes of love, and because he is by nature disposed to be a friend of the man who is serving him (even if he has already been set against love by school friends or others who say that it is shameful to associate with a lover, and initially rejects the lover in consequence), as time goes forward he is brought by his ripening age and a sense of what must be to a point where he lets the man spend

255b time with him. It is a decree of fate, you see, that bad is never friends with bad, while good cannot fail to be friends with good. Now that he allows his lover to talk and spend time with him, and the man's good will is close at hand, the boy is amazed by it as he realizes that all the friendship he has from his other friends and relatives put together is nothing compared to that of this friend who is inspired by a god.

"After the lover has spent some time doing this, staying near the boy (and even touching him during sports and on other occasions), then the

255c spring that feeds the stream Zeus named 'Desire' when he was in love with Ganymede begins to flow mightily in the lover and is partly absorbed by him, and when he is filled it overflows and runs away outside him. Think how a breeze or an echo bounces back from a smooth solid object to its source; that is how the stream of beauty goes back to the beautiful boy and sets him aflutter. It enters through his eyes, which are its natural route

255d to the soul; there it waters the passages for the wings, starts the wings growing, and fills the soul of the loved one with love in return. Then the boy is in love, but has no idea what he loves. He does not understand, and cannot explain, what has happened to him. It is as if he had caught an eye disease from someone else, but could not identify the cause; he does not realize that he is seeing himself in the lover as in a mirror. So when the lover is near, the boy's pain is relieved just as the lover's is, and when they are apart he yearns as much as he is yearned for, because he has a mirror

255e image of love in him—'backlove'—though he neither speaks nor thinks of it as love, but as friendship. Still, his desire is nearly the same as the lover's, though weaker: he wants to see, touch, kiss, and lie down with him; and of course, as you might expect, he acts on these desires soon after they occur.

"When they are in bed, the lover's undisciplined horse has a word to say to the charioteer—that after all its sufferings it is entitled to a little

256a fun. Meanwhile, the boy's bad horse has nothing to say, but swelling with desire, confused, it hugs the lover and kisses him in delight at his great good will. And whenever they are lying together it is completely unable, for its own part, to deny the lover any favor he might beg to have. Its yokemate,

however, along with its charioteer, resists such requests with modesty and reason. Now if the victory goes to the better elements in both their minds, which lead them to follow the assigned regimen of philosophy, their life here below is one of bliss and shared understanding. They are modest and   256b
fully in control of themselves now that they have enslaved the part that brought trouble into the soul and set free the part that gave it virtue. After death, when they have grown wings and become weightless, they have won the first of three rounds in these, the true Olympic Contests. There is no greater good than this that either human self-control or divine madness can offer a man. If, on the other hand, they adopt a lower way of living, with ambition in place of philosophy, then pretty soon when they are careless   256c
because they have been drinking or for some other reason, the pair's undisciplined horses will catch their souls off guard and together bring them to commit that act which ordinary people would take to be the happiest choice of all; and when they have consummated it once, they go on doing this for the rest of their lives, but sparingly, since they have not approved of what they are doing with their whole minds. So these two also live in mutual friendship (though weaker than that of the philosophical pair), both while they are in love and after they have passed beyond it, because they   256d
realize they have exchanged such firm vows that it would be forbidden for them ever to break them and become enemies. In death they are wingless when they leave the body, but their wings are bursting to sprout, so the prize they have won from the madness of love is considerable, because those who have begun the sacred journey in lower heaven may not by law be sent into darkness for the journey under the earth; their lives are bright and happy as they travel together, and thanks to their love they will grow   256e
wings together when the time comes.

"These are the rewards you will have from a lover's friendship, my boy, and they are as great as divine gifts should be. A non-lover's companionship, on the other hand, is diluted by human self-control; all it pays are cheap, human dividends, and though the slavish attitude it engenders in a friend's soul is widely praised as virtue, it tosses the soul around for nine thousand years on the earth and leads it, mindless, beneath it.   **257a**

"So now, dear Love, this is the best and most beautiful Palinode[45] we could offer as payment for our debt, especially in view of the rather poetical choice of words Phaedrus made me use. Forgive us our earlier speeches in return for this one; be kind and gracious toward my expertise at love, which is your own gift to me: do not, out of anger, take it away or disable it; and grant that I may be held in higher esteem than ever by those who are beautiful. If Phaedrus and I said anything that shocked you in   257b

---

[45] See 243b note.

our earlier speech, blame it on Lysias, who was its father, and put a stop
to his making speeches of this sort; convert him to philosophy like his
brother Polemarchus[46] so that his lover here may no longer play both sides
as he does now, but simply devote his life to Love through philosophical
discussions."

PHAEDRUS: I join you in your prayer, Socrates. If this is really best for us,
257c   may it come to pass. As to your speech, I admired it from the moment you
began: You managed it much better than your first one. I'm afraid that
Lysias' effort to match it is bound to fall flat, if of course he even dares to
try to offer a speech of his own. In fact, my marvelous friend, a politician
I know was only recently taking Lysias to task for just that reason: All
through his invective, he kept calling him a "speech writer." So perhaps
his pride will keep him from writing this speech for us.

SOCRATES: Ah, what a foolish thing to say, young man. How wrong you
257d   are about your friend: he can't be intimidated so easily! But perhaps you
thought the man who was taking him to task meant what he said as a
reproach?

PHAEDRUS: He certainly seemed to, Socrates. In any case, you are surely
aware yourself that the most powerful and renowned politicians are
ashamed to compose speeches or leave any writings behind; they are afraid
that in later times they may come to be known as "sophists."

SOCRATES: Phaedrus, you don't understand the expression "Pleasant
257e   Bend"—it originally referred to the long bend of the Nile.[47] And, besides
the bend, you also don't understand that the most ambitious politicians love
speechwriting and long for their writings to survive. In fact, when they
write one of their speeches, they are so pleased when people praise it that
they add at the beginning a list of its admirers everywhere.

PHAEDRUS: What do you mean? I don't understand.

258a   SOCRATES: Don't you know that the first thing politicians put in their
writings is the names of their admirers?

PHAEDRUS: How so?

SOCRATES: "Resolved," the author often begins, "by the Council" or "by
the People" or by both, and "So-and-so said"[48]—meaning himself, the
writer, with great solemnity and self-importance. Only then does he go
on with what he has to say, showing off his wisdom to his admirers, often

---

[46] See 227a note.

[47] *Glukus agkōn:* apparently, a familiar example of something that means the opposite of what it says—though called "pleasant," it was really a long, nasty bend.

[48] This is the standard form for decisions, including legislation, made by the
Athenian Assembly, but not that for political speeches.

composing a very long document. Do you think there's any difference between that and a written speech?

PHAEDRUS: No, I don't.   258b

SOCRATES: Well, then, if it remains on the books, he is delighted and leaves the stage a poet. But if it is struck down, if he fails as a speech writer and isn't considered worthy of having his work written down, he goes into deep mourning, and his friends along with him.

PHAEDRUS: He certainly does.

SOCRATES: Clearly, then, they don't feel contempt for speechwriting; on the contrary, they are in awe of it.

PHAEDRUS: Quite so.

SOCRATES: There's this too. What of an orator or a king who acquires enough power to match Lycurgus, Solon, or Darius[49] as a lawgiver and   258c
acquires immortal fame as a speech writer in his city? Doesn't he think that he is equal to the gods while he is still alive? And don't those who live in later times believe just the same about him when they behold his writings?

PHAEDRUS: Very much so.

SOCRATES: Do you really believe then that any one of these people, whoever he is and however much he hates Lysias, would reproach him for being a writer?

PHAEDRUS: It certainly isn't likely in view of what you said, for he would probably be reproaching his own ambition as well.

SOCRATES: This, then, is quite clear: Writing speeches is not in itself a   258d
shameful thing.

PHAEDRUS: How could it be?

SOCRATES: It's not speaking or writing well that's shameful; what's really shameful is to engage in either of them shamefully or badly.

PHAEDRUS: That is clear.

SOCRATES: So what distinguishes good from bad writing? Do we need to ask this question of Lysias or anyone else who ever did or will write any-thing—whether a public or a private document, poetic verse or plain prose?

PHAEDRUS: You ask if we need to? Why else should one live, I say, if not   258e
for pleasures of this sort? Certainly not for those you cannot feel unless you are first in pain, like most of the pleasures of the body, and which for this reason we call the pleasures of slaves.

SOCRATES: It seems we clearly have the time. Besides, I think that the cicadas, who are singing and carrying on conversations with one another in

---

[49] On Lycurgus and Solon, see *Symposium* 209d notes. Darius (died 486 BCE) was king of Persia.

259a   the heat of the day above our heads, are also watching us. And if they saw
the two of us avoiding conversation at midday like most people, diverted
by their song and, sluggish of mind, nodding off, they would have every
right to laugh at us, convinced that a pair of slaves had come to their resting place to sleep like sheep gathering around the spring in the afternoon.
But if they see us in conversation, steadfastly navigating around them as if
they were the Sirens,[50] they will be very pleased and immediately give us

259b   the gift from the gods they are able to give to mortals.

PHAEDRUS: What is this gift? I don't think I have heard of it.

SOCRATES: Everyone who loves the Muses[51] should have heard of this. The
story goes that the cicadas used to be human beings who lived before the
birth of the Muses. When the Muses were born and song was created for
the first time, some of the people of that time were so overwhelmed with

259c   the pleasure of singing that they forgot to eat or drink; so they died without
even realizing it. It is from them that the race of the cicadas came into
being; and, as a gift from the Muses, they have no need of nourishment
once they are born. Instead, they immediately burst into song, without
food or drink, until it is time for them to die. After they die, they go to
the Muses and tell each one of them which mortals have honored her. To
Terpsichore they report those who have honored her by their devotion to

259d   the dance and thus make them dearer to her. To Erato, they report those
who honored her by dedicating themselves to the affairs of love, and so
too with the other Muses, according to the activity that honors each. And
to Calliope, the oldest among them, and Urania, the next after her, who
preside over the heavens and all discourse, human and divine, and sing
with the sweetest voice, they report those who honor their special kind of
music by leading a philosophical life.

There are many reasons, then, why we should talk and not waste our
afternoon in sleep.

PHAEDRUS: By all means, let's talk.

259e   SOCRATES: Well, then, we ought to examine the topic we proposed just
now: When is a speech well written and delivered, and when is it not?

PHAEDRUS: Plainly.

SOCRATES: Won't someone who is to speak well and nobly have to have in
mind the truth about the subject he is going to discuss?

PHAEDRUS: What I have actually heard about this, Socrates, my friend, is

260a   that it is not for the intending orator to learn what is really just, but only

---

[50] See *Symposium* 216a note.

[51] Although they were usually referred to collectively in this period, each of the
Muses was assigned as a sort of patron saint to one of the arts—Terpsichore to dance,
Erato to lyric poetry, Urania to astronomy, Calliope (eventually) to epic poetry.

what will seem just to the crowd who will act as judges. Nor again what is really good or noble, but only what will seem so. For that is what persuasion proceeds from, not truth.

SOCRATES: Anything that wise men say, Phaedrus, "is not lightly to be cast aside";[52] we must consider whether it might be right. And what you just said, in particular, must not be dismissed.

PHAEDRUS: You're right.

SOCRATES: Let's look at it this way, then.

PHAEDRUS: How?

SOCRATES: Suppose I were trying to convince you that you should fight   260b your enemies on horseback, and neither one of us knew what a horse is, but I happened to know this much about you, that Phaedrus believes a horse is the tame animal with the longest ears—

PHAEDRUS: But that would be ridiculous, Socrates.

SOCRATES: Not quite yet, actually. But if I were seriously trying to convince you, having composed a speech in praise of the donkey in which I called it a horse and claimed that having such an animal is of immense value both at home and in military service, that it is good for fighting and for carrying your baggage and that it is useful for much else besides—   260c

PHAEDRUS: Well, that would be totally ridiculous.

SOCRATES: Well, which is better? To be ridiculous and a friend? Or clever and an enemy?

PHAEDRUS: The former.

SOCRATES: And so, when a rhetorician who does not know good from bad addresses a city which knows no better and attempts to sway it, not praising a miserable donkey as if it were a horse, but bad as if it were good, and, having studied what the people believe, persuades them to do something bad instead of good—with that as its seed, what sort of crop do you think rhetoric can harvest?   260d

PHAEDRUS: A crop of really poor quality.

SOCRATES: But could it be, my friend, that we have mocked the art of speaking more rudely than it deserves? For it might perhaps reply, "What bizarre nonsense! Look, I am not forcing anyone to learn how to make speeches without knowing the truth; on the contrary, my advice, for what it is worth, is to take me up only after mastering the truth. But I do make this boast: even someone who knows the truth couldn't produce conviction on the basis of a systematic art without me."

PHAEDRUS: Well, is that a fair reply?   260e

---

[52] Homer, *Iliad* ii.361.

SOCRATES: Yes, it is—if, that is, the arguments now advancing upon rhetoric testify that it is an art. For it seems to me as if I hear certain arguments approaching and protesting that that is a lie and that rhetoric is not an art but an artless practice. As the Spartan said, there is no genuine art of speaking without a grasp of truth, and there never will be.

261a PHAEDRUS: We need to hear these arguments, Socrates. Come, produce them, and examine them: What is their point? How do they make it?

SOCRATES: Come to us, then, noble creatures; convince Phaedrus, him of the beautiful offspring,[53] that unless he pursues philosophy properly he will never be able to make a proper speech on any subject either. And let Phaedrus be the one to answer.

PHAEDRUS: Let them put their questions.

SOCRATES: Well, then, isn't the rhetorical art, taken as a whole, a way of directing the soul by means of speech, not only in the lawcourts and on other public occasions but also in private? Isn't it one and the same art

261b whether its subject is great or small, and no more to be held in esteem—if it is followed correctly—when its questions are serious than when they are trivial? Or what have you heard about all this?

PHAEDRUS: Well, certainly not what *you* have! Artful speaking and writing is found mainly in the lawcourts; also perhaps in the Assembly. That's all I've heard.

SOCRATES: Well, have you only heard of the rhetorical treatises of Nestor and Odysseus—those they wrote in their spare time in Troy? Haven't you also heard of the works of Palamedes?[54]

261c PHAEDRUS: No, by Zeus, I haven't even heard of Nestor's—unless by Nestor you mean Gorgias,[55] and by Odysseus, Thrasymachus[56] or Theodorus.[57]

SOCRATES: Perhaps. But let's leave these people aside. Answer this question yourself: What do adversaries do in the lawcourts? Don't they speak on opposite sides? What else can we call what they do?

PHAEDRUS: That's it, exactly.

SOCRATES: About what is just and what is unjust?

PHAEDRUS: Yes.

---

[53] Phaedrus' offspring are philosophical speeches or discussions.

[54] Nestor and Odysseus were Homeric heroes known for their speaking ability (*Iliad* i.249, iii.223). Palamedes, who does not figure in Homer, was proverbial for his cunning.

[55] See *Symposium* 198c note.

[56] See *Republic* 328b note.

[57] Theodorus of Byzantium is otherwise largely unknown.

SOCRATES: And won't whoever does this artfully make the same thing appear to the same people sometimes just and sometimes, when he prefers, unjust? 261d

PHAEDRUS: Of course.

SOCRATES: And when he addresses the Assembly, he will make the city approve a policy at one time as a good one, and reject it—the very same policy—as just the opposite at another.

PHAEDRUS: Right.

SOCRATES: Now, don't we know that the Eleatic Palamedes is such an artful speaker that his listeners will perceive the same things to be both similar and dissimilar, both one and many, both at rest and also in motion?[58]

PHAEDRUS: Most certainly.

SOCRATES: We can therefore find the practice of speaking on opposite sides not only in the lawcourts and in the Assembly. Rather, it seems that one 261e
single art—if, of course, it is an art in the first place—governs all speaking. By means of it one can make out as similar anything that can be so assimilated, to everything to which it can be made similar, and expose anyone who tries to hide the fact that that is what he is doing.

PHAEDRUS: What do you mean by that?

SOCRATES: I think it will become clear if we look at it this way. Where is deception most likely to occur—regarding things that differ much or things that differ little from one another?

PHAEDRUS: Regarding those that differ little. **262a**

SOCRATES: At any rate, you are more likely to escape detection, as you shift from one thing to its opposite, if you proceed in small steps rather than in large ones.

PHAEDRUS: Without a doubt.

SOCRATES: Therefore, if you are to deceive someone else and to avoid deception yourself, you must know precisely the respects in which things are similar and dissimilar to one another.

PHAEDRUS: Yes, you must.

SOCRATES: And is it really possible for someone who doesn't know what each thing truly is to detect a similarity—whether large or small—between something he doesn't know and anything else?

PHAEDRUS: That is impossible. 262b

SOCRATES: Clearly, therefore, the state of being deceived and holding beliefs contrary to what is the case comes upon people by reason of certain similarities.

---

[58] The Eleatic Palamedes is Zeno of Elea, the author of the famous paradoxes about motion.

PHAEDRUS: That is how it happens.

SOCRATES: Could someone, then, who doesn't know what each thing is ever have the art to lead others little by little through similarities away from what is the case on each occasion to its opposite? Or could he escape this being done to himself?

PHAEDRUS: Never.

262c SOCRATES: Therefore, my friend, the art of a speaker who doesn't know the truth and chases opinions instead is likely to be a ridiculous thing—not an art at all!

PHAEDRUS: So it seems.

SOCRATES: So, shall we look for instances of what we called the artful and the artless in the speech of Lysias you carried here and in our own speeches?

PHAEDRUS: That's the best thing to do—because, as it is, we are talking quite abstractly, without enough examples.

SOCRATES: In fact, by some chance the two speeches do, as it seems, contain
262d an example of the way in which someone who knows the truth can toy with his audience and mislead them. For my part, Phaedrus, I hold the local gods responsible for this—also, perhaps, the messengers of the Muses who are singing over our heads may have inspired me with this gift: certainly I don't possess any art of speaking.

PHAEDRUS: Fine, fine. But explain what you mean.

SOCRATES: Come, then—read me the beginning of Lysias' speech.

262e PHAEDRUS: "You understand my situation: I've told you how good it would be for us, in my opinion, if we could work this out. In any case, I don't think I should lose the chance to get what I am asking for, merely because I don't happen to be in love with you. A man in love will wish he had not done you any favors—"

SOCRATES: Stop. Our task is to say how he fails and writes artlessly. Right?

263a PHAEDRUS: Yes.

SOCRATES: Now isn't this much absolutely clear: We are in accord with one another about some of the things we discourse about and in discord about others?

PHAEDRUS: I think I understand what you are saying; but, please, can you make it a little clearer?

SOCRATES: When someone utters the word "iron" or "silver," don't we all think of the same thing?

PHAEDRUS: Certainly.

SOCRATES: But what happens when we say "just" or "good"? Doesn't each one of us go in a different direction? Don't we differ with one another and even with ourselves?

PHAEDRUS: We certainly do.

SOCRATES: Therefore, we agree about the former and disagree about the   263b
latter.

PHAEDRUS: Right.

SOCRATES: Now in which of these two cases are we more easily deceived?
And when does rhetoric have greater power?

PHAEDRUS: Clearly, when we wander in different directions.

SOCRATES: It follows that whoever wants to acquire the art of rhetoric must
first make a systematic division and grasp the particular character of each
of these two kinds of thing, both the kind where most people wander in
different directions and the kind where they do not.

PHAEDRUS: What a splendid thing, Socrates, he will have understood if   263c
he grasps *that*!

SOCRATES: Second, I think, he must not be mistaken about his subject;
he must have a sharp eye for the class to which whatever he is about to
discuss belongs.

PHAEDRUS: Of course.

SOCRATES: Well, now, what shall we say about love? Does it belong to the
class where people differ or to that where they don't?

PHAEDRUS: Oh, surely the class where they differ. Otherwise, do you think
you could have spoken of it as you did a few minutes ago, first saying that
it is harmful both to lover and beloved and then immediately afterward
that it is the greatest good?

SOCRATES: Very well put. But now tell me this—I can't remember at all   263d
because I was completely possessed by the gods: Did I define love at the
beginning of my speech?

PHAEDRUS: Oh, absolutely, by Zeus, you most certainly did.

SOCRATES: Alas, how much more artful with speeches the Nymphs, daughters of Achelous,[59] and Pan, son of Hermes,[60] are, according to what you
say, than Lysias, son of Cephalus! Or am I wrong? Did Lysias too, at the
start of his love-speech, compel us to assume that love is the single thing
that he himself wanted it to be? Did he then complete his speech by arrang-   263e
ing everything in relation to that? Will you read its opening once again?

PHAEDRUS: If you like. But what you are looking for is not there.

SOCRATES: Read it, so that I can hear it in his own words.

---

[59] See 230b note.

[60] Pan was a god, half man and half goat, associated with the pastoral world, and
with the nymphs. Hermes, the son of Zeus and the nymph Maia, is, above all, the
messenger god, who carries out the orders of Zeus.

PHAEDRUS: "You understand my situation: I've told you how good it would be for us, in my opinion, if we could work this out. In any case, I don't think I should lose the chance to get what I am asking for, merely because

264a I don't happen to be in love with you. A man in love will wish he had not done you any favors, once his desire dies down—"

SOCRATES: He certainly seems a long way from doing what we wanted. He doesn't even start from the beginning but from the end, making his speech swim upstream on its back. His first words are what a lover would say to his boy as he was concluding his speech. Am I wrong, Phaedrus, dear heart?

264b PHAEDRUS: Well, Socrates, that was the end for which he gave the speech!

SOCRATES: And what about the rest? Don't the parts of the speech appear to have been thrown together at random? Is it evident that the second point had to be made second for some compelling reason? Is that so for any of the parts? I at least—of course I know nothing about such matters—thought the author said just whatever came to mind next, though not without a certain noble willfulness. But you, do you know any principle of speech-composition compelling him to place these things one after another in this order?

PHAEDRUS: It's very generous of you to think that I can understand his

264c reasons so clearly.

SOCRATES: But surely you will admit at least this much: Every speech must be put together like a living creature, with a body of its own; it must be neither without head nor without legs; and it must have a middle and extremities that are fitting both to one another and to the whole work.

PHAEDRUS: How could it be otherwise?

SOCRATES: But look at your friend's speech: Is it like that or is it otherwise? Actually, you'll find that it's just like the epigram people say is inscribed on the tomb of Midas the Phrygian.[61]

264d PHAEDRUS: What epigram is that? And what's the matter with it?

SOCRATES: It goes like this:

> A maid of bronze am I, on Midas' tomb I lie
> As long as water flows, and trees grow tall
> Shielding the grave where many come to cry
> That Midas rests here I say to one and all.

264e I'm sure you notice that it makes no difference at all which of its verses comes first, and which last.

PHAEDRUS: You are making fun of our speech, Socrates.

---

[61] Legendary eighth-century BCE king of Phrygia, famous for his golden touch.

SOCRATES: Well, then, if that upsets you, let's leave that speech aside—even though I think it has plenty of very useful examples, provided one tries to emulate them as little as possible—and turn to the others. I think it is important for students of speechmaking to pay attention to one of their features.

PHAEDRUS: What do you mean?   265a

SOCRATES: They were in a way opposite to one another. One claimed that one should give one's favors to the lover; the other, to the non-lover.

PHAEDRUS: Most manfully, too.

SOCRATES: I thought you were going to say "madly," which would have been the truth, and is also just what I was looking for: We did say, didn't we, that love is a kind of madness?

PHAEDRUS: Yes.   265b

SOCRATES: And that there are two kinds of madness, one produced by human illness, the other by a divinely inspired release from normally accepted behavior?

PHAEDRUS: Certainly.

SOCRATES: We also distinguished four parts within the divine kind and connected them to four gods. Having attributed the inspiration of the prophet to Apollo, of the mystic to Dionysus, of the poet to the Muses, and the fourth part of madness to Aphrodite and to Love, we said that the madness of love is the best. We used a certain sort of image to describe love's passion; perhaps it had a measure of truth in it, though it may also have led us astray. And having whipped up a not altogether implausible speech, we sang playfully, but also appropriately and respectfully, a story-   265c like hymn to my master and yours, Phaedrus—to Love, who watches over beautiful boys.

PHAEDRUS: And I listened to it with the greatest pleasure.

SOCRATES: Let's take up this point about it right away: How was the speech able to proceed from censure to praise?

PHAEDRUS: What exactly do you mean by that?

SOCRATES: Well, everything else in it really does appear to me to have been spoken in play. But part of it was given with Fortune's guidance, and there were in it two kinds of things the nature of which it would be quite wonderful to grasp by means of a systematic art.   265d

PHAEDRUS: Which things?

SOCRATES: The first consists in seeing together things that are scattered about everywhere and collecting them into one kind, so that by defining each thing we can make clear the subject of any instruction we wish to give. Just so with our discussion of love: Whether its definition was or was not correct, at least it allowed the speech to proceed clearly and consistently with itself.

PHAEDRUS: And what is the other thing you are talking about, Socrates?

265e   SOCRATES: This, in turn, is to be able to cut up each kind according to its species along its natural joints, and to try not to splinter any part, as a bad butcher might do. In just this way, our two speeches placed all mental derangements into one common kind. Then, just as each single body has

266a   parts that naturally come in pairs of the same name (one of them being called the right-hand and the other the left-hand one), so the speeches, having considered unsoundness of mind to be by nature one single kind within us, proceeded to cut it up—the first speech cut its left-hand part, and continued to cut until it discovered among these parts a sort of love that can be called "left-handed," which it correctly denounced; the second speech, in turn, led us to the right-hand part of madness; discovered a love that shares its name with the other but is actually divine; set it out before

266b   us, and praised it as the cause of our greatest goods.

PHAEDRUS: You are absolutely right.

SOCRATES: Well, Phaedrus, I am myself a lover of these divisions and collections, so that I may be able to think and to speak; and if I believe that someone else is capable of discerning a single thing that is also by nature capable of encompassing many, I follow "straight behind, in his tracks, as if he were a god."[62] God knows whether this is the right name for those who can do this correctly or not, but so far I have always called them "dialecti-

266c   cians." But tell me what I must call them now that we have learned all this from Lysias and you. Or is it just that art of speaking that Thrasymachus and the rest of them use, which has made them masters of speechmaking and capable of producing others like them—anyhow those who are willing to bring them gifts and to treat them as if they were kings?

PHAEDRUS: They may behave like kings, but they certainly lack the knowledge you're talking about. No, it seems to me that you are right in calling the sort of thing you mentioned dialectic; but, it seems to me, rhetoric still eludes us.

266d   SOCRATES: What are you saying? Could there be anything valuable which is independent of the methods I mentioned and is still grasped by art? If there is, you and I must certainly honor it, and we must say what part of rhetoric it is that has been left out.

PHAEDRUS: Well, there's quite a lot, Socrates: everything, at any rate, written up in the books on the art of speaking.

---

[62] Adapted from Homer, *Odyssey* ii.406.

SOCRATES: You were quite right to remind me. First, I believe, there is the Preamble with which a speech must begin. This is what you mean, isn't it—the fine points of the art?

PHAEDRUS: Yes.   266e

SOCRATES: Second come the Statement of Facts and the Evidence of Witnesses concerning it; third, Indirect Evidence; fourth, Claims to Plausibility. And I believe at least that excellent Byzantine word-wizard adds Confirmation and Supplementary Confirmation.

PHAEDRUS: You mean the worthy Theodorus?[63]

SOCRATES: Quite. And he also adds Refutation and Supplementary   **267a**
Refutation, to be used both in prosecution and in defense. Nor must we forget the most excellent Evenus of Paros,[64] who was the first to discover Covert Implication and Indirect Praise and who—some say—has even arranged Indirect Censures in verse as an aid to memory: a wise man indeed! And Tisias[65] and Gorgias? How can we leave them out when it is they who realized that what is likely must be held in higher honor than what is true; they who, by the power of their language, make small things appear great and great things small; they who express modern ideas in ancient garb, and ancient ones in modern dress; they who have discovered   267b
how to argue both concisely and at infinite length about any subject? Actually, when I told Prodicus[66] this last, he laughed and said that only he had discovered the art of proper speeches: What we need are speeches that are neither long nor short but of the right length.

PHAEDRUS: Brilliantly done, Prodicus!

SOCRATES: And what about Hippias[67] How can we omit him? I am sure our friend from Elis would cast his vote with Prodicus.

PHAEDRUS: Certainly.

SOCRATES: And what shall we say of the whole gallery of terms Polus[68] set up—speaking with Reduplication, Speaking in Maxims, Speaking in   267c
Images—and of the terms Licymnius[69] gave him as a present to help him explain Good Diction?

---

[63] See 261c note.

[64] See *Apology* 20b note.

[65] A fifth-century BCE teacher of rhetoric from Syracuse.

[66] A fifth-century BCE teacher of rhetoric from Ceos, with an interest in fine distinctions of meaning and the correctness of names.

[67] A contemporary of Socrates from Elis, who claimed expertise in astronomy, physics, grammar, poetry, and other subjects.

[68] A pupil of Gorgias.

[69] A dithyrambic poet and teacher of rhetoric from Chios.

PHAEDRUS: But didn't Protagoras[70] actually use similar terms?

SOCRATES: Yes, Correct Diction, my boy, and other wonderful things. As to the art of making speeches bewailing the evils of poverty and old age, the prize, in my judgment, goes to the mighty Chalcedonian.[71] He it is also who knows best how to inflame a crowd and, once they are inflamed, how to hush them again with his words' magic spell, as he says himself. And let's not forget that he is as good at producing slander as he is at refuting it, whatever its source may be.

As to the way of ending a speech, everyone seems to be in agreement, though some call it Recapitulation and others by some other name.

PHAEDRUS: You mean, summarizing everything at the end and reminding the audience of what they've heard?

SOCRATES: That's what I mean. And if you have anything else to add about the art of speaking—

PHAEDRUS: Only minor points, not worth making.

SOCRATES: Well, let's leave minor points aside. Let's hold what we do have closer to the light so that we can see precisely the power of the art these things produce.

PHAEDRUS: A very great power, Socrates, especially in front of a crowd.

SOCRATES: Quite right. But now, my friend, look closely: Do you think, as I do, that its fabric is a little threadbare?

PHAEDRUS: Can you show me?

SOCRATES: All right, tell me this. Suppose someone came to your friend Eryximachus or his father Acumenus[72] and said: "I know treatments to raise or lower (whichever I prefer) the temperature of people's bodies; if I decide to, I can make them vomit or make their bowels move, and all sorts of things. On the basis of this knowledge, I claim to be a physician; and I claim to be able to make others physicians as well by imparting it to them." What do you think they would say when they heard that?

PHAEDRUS: What could they say? They would ask him if he also knew to whom he should apply such treatments, when, and to what extent.

SOCRATES: What if he replied, "I have no idea. My claim is that whoever learns from me will manage to do what you ask on his own"?

PHAEDRUS: I think they'd say the man's mad if he thinks he's a doctor just because he read a book or happened to come across a few potions; he knows nothing of the art.

---

[70] A famous, early sophist (c. 490–420 BCE) from Abdera.

[71] I.e., Thrasymachus.

[72] See *Symposium* 175a note.

SOCRATES: And suppose someone approached Sophocles and Euripides and claimed to know how to compose the longest passages on trivial topics and the briefest ones on topics of great importance, that he could make them pitiful if he wanted, or again, by contrast, terrifying and menacing, and so on. Suppose further that he believed that by teaching this he was imparting the knowledge of composing tragedies—   268d

PHAEDRUS: Oh, I am sure they too would laugh at anyone who thought a tragedy was anything other than the proper arrangement of these things: They have to fit with one another and with the whole work.

SOCRATES: But I am sure they wouldn't reproach him rudely. They would react more like a musician confronted by a man who thought he had mastered harmony because he was able to produce the highest and lowest notes on his strings. The musician would not say fiercely, "You stupid man, you   268e
are out of your mind!" As befits his calling, he would speak more gently: "My friend, though that too is necessary for understanding harmony, someone who has gotten as far as you have may still know absolutely nothing about the subject. What you know is what it's necessary to learn before you study harmony, but not harmony itself."

PHAEDRUS: That's certainly right.

SOCRATES: So Sophocles would also tell the man who was showing off to   **269a**
them that he knew the preliminaries of tragedy, but not the art of tragedy itself. And Acumenus would say his man knew the preliminaries of medicine, but not medicine itself.

PHAEDRUS: Absolutely.

SOCRATES: And what if the "honey-tongued Adrastus"[73] (or perhaps Pericles)[74] were to hear of all the marvelous techniques we just discussed— Speaking Concisely and Speaking in Images and all the rest we listed and proposed to examine under the light? Would he be angry or rude, as you   269b
and I were, with those who write of those techniques and teach them as if they are rhetoric itself, and say something coarse to them? Wouldn't he—being wiser than we are—reproach us as well and say, "Phaedrus and Socrates, you should not be angry with these people—you should be sorry for them. The reason they cannot define rhetoric is that they are ignorant of dialectic. It is their ignorance that makes them think they have discovered what rhetoric is when they have mastered only what it is necessary to learn   269c
as preliminaries. So they teach these preliminaries and imagine their pupils

---

[73] Described in the *Iliad* as a former king of Sicyon (ii.572), leader of the first Argive expedition against Thebes. His name became a byword for eloquence. The quotation is from the early Spartan poet Tyrtaeus, *fr.* ix.8.

[74] See *Symposium* 215e note.

have received a full course in rhetoric, thinking the task of using each of them persuasively and putting them together into a whole speech is a minor matter, to be worked out by the pupils from their own resources"?

PHAEDRUS: Really, Socrates, the art these men present as rhetoric in their courses and handbooks is no more than what you say. In my judgment, at least, your point is well taken. But how, from what source, could one 269d   acquire the art of the true rhetorician, the really persuasive speaker?

SOCRATES: Well, Phaedrus, becoming good enough to be an accomplished competitor is probably—perhaps necessarily—like everything else. If you have a natural ability for rhetoric, you will become a famous rhetorician, provided you supplement your ability with knowledge and practice. To the extent that you lack any one of them, to that extent you will be less than perfect. But, insofar as there is an art of rhetoric, I don't believe the right method for acquiring it is to be found in the direction Lysias and Thrasymachus have followed.

PHAEDRUS: Where can we find it then?

269e   SOCRATES: My dear friend, maybe we can see now why Pericles was in all likelihood the greatest rhetorician of all.

PHAEDRUS: How is that?

SOCRATES: All the great arts require endless talk and ethereal speculation 270a   about nature: This seems to be what gives them their lofty point of view and universal applicability. That's just what Pericles mastered—besides having natural ability. He came across Anaxagoras, who was just that sort of man, got his full dose of ethereal speculation, and understood the nature of mind and mindlessness—just the subject on which Anaxagoras had the most to say.[75] From this, I think, he drew for the art of rhetoric what was useful to it.

PHAEDRUS: What do you mean by that?

270b   SOCRATES: Well, isn't the method of medicine in a way the same as the method of rhetoric?

PHAEDRUS: How so?

SOCRATES: In both cases we need to determine the nature of something—of the body in medicine, of the soul in rhetoric. Otherwise, all we'll have will be an empirical and artless practice. We won't be able to supply, on the basis of an art, a body with the medicines and diet that will make it healthy and strong, or a soul with the reasons and customary rules for conduct that will impart to it the convictions and virtues we want.

PHAEDRUS: That is most likely, Socrates.

---

[75] See *Phaedo* 97b–99d.

SOCRATES: Do you think, then, that it is possible to reach a serious under-   270c
standing of the nature of the soul without understanding the nature of the
world as a whole?

PHAEDRUS: Well, if we're to listen to Hippocrates, Asclepius' descendant,[76]
we won't even understand the body if we don't follow that method.

SOCRATES: He speaks well, my friend. Still, Hippocrates aside, we must
consider whether argument supports that view.

PHAEDRUS: I agree.

SOCRATES: Consider, then, what both Hippocrates and true argument say
about nature. Isn't this the way to think systematically about the nature
of anything? First, we must consider whether the object regarding which   270d
we intend to become experts and capable of transmitting our expertise is
simple or complex. Then, if it is simple, we must investigate its power:
What things does it have what natural power of acting upon? By what
things does it have what natural disposition to be acted upon? If, on the
other hand, it takes many forms, we must enumerate them all and, as we
did in the simple case, investigate how each is naturally able to act upon
what and how it has a natural disposition to be acted upon by what.

PHAEDRUS: It seems so, Socrates.

SOCRATES: Proceeding by any other method would be like walking with
the blind. Conversely, whoever studies anything on the basis of an art must   270e
never be compared to the blind or the deaf. On the contrary, it is clear that
someone who teaches another to make speeches as an art will demonstrate
precisely the essential nature of that to which speeches are to be applied.
And that, surely, is the soul.

PHAEDRUS: Of course.

SOCRATES: This is therefore the object toward which the speaker's whole   **271a**
effort is directed, since it is in the soul that he attempts to produce conviction. Isn't that so?

PHAEDRUS: Yes.

SOCRATES: Clearly, therefore, Thrasymachus and anyone else who teaches
the art of rhetoric seriously will, first, describe the soul with absolute
precision and enable us to understand what it is: whether it is one and
homogeneous by nature or takes many forms, like the shape of bodies,
since, as we said, that's what it is to demonstrate the nature of something.

PHAEDRUS: Absolutely.

SOCRATES: Second, he will explain how, in virtue of its nature, it acts and
is acted upon by certain things.

---

[76] Hippocrates, a contemporary of Socrates, was a famous doctor. Asclepius is the
god of healing.

PHAEDRUS: Of course.

271b SOCRATES: Third, he will classify the kinds of speech and of soul there are, as well as the various ways in which they are affected, and explain what causes each. He will then coordinate each kind of soul with the kind of speech appropriate to it. And he will give instructions concerning the reasons why one kind of soul is necessarily convinced by one kind of speech while another necessarily remains unconvinced.

PHAEDRUS: This, I think, would certainly be the best way.

SOCRATES: In fact, my friend, no speech will ever be a product of art, whether it is a model or one actually given, if it is delivered or written in

271c any other way—on this or on any other subject. But those who now write *Arts of Rhetoric*—we were just discussing them[77]—are cunning people: they hide the fact that they know very well everything about the soul. Well, then, until they begin to speak and write in this way, we mustn't allow ourselves to be convinced that they write on the basis of the art.

PHAEDRUS: What way is that?

SOCRATES: It's very difficult to speak the actual words, but as to how one should write in order to be as artful as possible—that I am willing to tell you.

PHAEDRUS: Please do.

SOCRATES: Since the nature of speech is in fact to direct the soul, whoever

271d intends to be a rhetorician must know how many kinds of soul there are. Their number is so-and-so many; each is of such-and-such a sort; hence some people have such-and-such a character and others have such-and-such. Those distinctions established, there are, in turn, so-and-so many kinds of speech, each of such-and-such a sort. People of such-and-such a character are easy to persuade by speeches of such-and-such a sort in connection with such-and-such an issue for this particular reason, while people of such-and-such another sort are difficult to persuade for those particular reasons.

The orator must learn all this well, then put his theory into practice and

271e develop the ability to discern each kind clearly as it occurs in the actions of real life. Otherwise he won't be any better off than he was when he was still listening to those discussions in school. He will now not only be able to say what kind of person is convinced by what kind of speech; on meeting someone he will be able to discern what he is like and make clear

272a to himself that the person actually standing in front of him is of just this particular sort of character he had learned about in school—to that he must now apply speeches of such-and-such a kind in this particular way in order

---

[77] See 266c ff.

to secure conviction about such-and-such an issue. When he has learned all this—when, in addition, he has grasped the right occasions for speaking and for holding back; and when he has also understood when the time is right for Speaking Concisely or Appealing to Pity or Exaggeration or for any other of the kinds of speech he has learned and when it is not—then, and only then, will he have finally mastered the art well and completely. But if his speaking, his teaching, or his writing lacks any one of these elements and he still claims to be speaking with art, you'll be better off if you don't believe him.

272b

"Well, Socrates and Phaedrus," the author of this discourse might say, "do you agree? Could we accept an art of speaking presented in any other terms?"

PHAEDRUS: That would be impossible, Socrates. Still, it's evidently rather a major undertaking.

SOCRATES: You're right. And that's why we must turn all our arguments every which way and try to find some easier and shorter route to the art: we don't want to follow a long rough path for no good reason when we can choose a short smooth one instead.

272c

Now, try to remember if you've heard anything helpful from Lysias or anybody else. Speak up.

PHAEDRUS: It's not for lack of trying, but nothing comes to mind right now.

SOCRATES: Well, then, shall I tell you something I've heard people say who care about this topic?

PHAEDRUS: Of course.

SOCRATES: We do claim, after all, Phaedrus, that it is fair to give the wolf's side of the story as well.

PHAEDRUS: That's just what you should do.

272d

SOCRATES: Well, these people say that there is no need to be so solemn about all this and stretch it out to such lengths. For the fact is, as we said ourselves at the beginning of this discussion, that one who intends to be an able rhetorician has no need to know the truth about the things that are just or good or yet about the people who are such either by nature or upbringing. No one in a lawcourt, you see, cares at all about the truth of such matters. They only care about what is convincing. This is called "the likely," and that is what a man who intends to speak according to art should concentrate on. Sometimes, in fact, whether you are prosecuting or defending a case, you must not even say what actually happened, if it was not likely to have happened—you must say something that is likely instead. Whatever you say, you should pursue what is likely and leave the truth aside: the whole art consists in cleaving to that throughout your speech.

272e

273a

PHAEDRUS: That's an excellent presentation of what people say who profess to be expert in speeches, Socrates. I recall that we raised this issue briefly earlier on, but it seems to be their single most important point.

SOCRATES: No doubt you've churned through Tisias' book[78] quite carefully. Then let Tisias tell us this also: By "the likely" does he mean anything but what is accepted by the crowd?

273b

PHAEDRUS: What else?

SOCRATES: And it's likely it was when he discovered this clever and artful technique that Tisias wrote that if a weak but spunky man is taken to court because he beat up a strong but cowardly one and stole his cloak or something else, neither one should tell the truth. The coward must say that the spunky man didn't beat him up all by himself, while the latter must rebut this by saying that only the two of them were there, and fall back on that well-worn plea, "How could a man like me attack a man like him?" The strong man, naturally, will not admit his cowardice, but will try to invent some other lie, and may thus give his opponent the chance to refute him. And in other cases, speaking as the art dictates will take similar forms. Isn't that so, Phaedrus?

273c

PHAEDRUS: Of course.

SOCRATES: Phew! Tisias—or whoever else it was and whatever name he pleases to use for himself—seems to have discovered an art which he has disguised very well! But now, my friend, shall we or shall we not say to him—

273d

PHAEDRUS: What?

SOCRATES: This: "Tisias, some time ago, before you came into the picture, we were saying that people get the idea of what is likely through its similarity to the truth. And we just explained that in every case the person who knows the truth knows best how to determine similarities. So, if you have something new to say about the art of speaking, we shall listen. But if you don't, we shall remain convinced by the explanations we gave just before: No one will ever possess the art of speaking, to the extent that any human being can, unless he acquires the ability to enumerate the sorts of characters to be found in any audience, to divide everything according to its kinds, and to grasp each single thing firmly by means of one form. And no one can acquire these abilities without great effort—a laborious effort a sensible man will make not in order to speak and act among human beings, but so as to be able to speak and act in a way that pleases the gods as much as possible. Wiser people than ourselves, Tisias, say that a reasonable man must put his mind to being pleasant not to his fellow slaves (though this

273e

---

[78] See 267a note.

may happen as a side effect) but to his masters, who are wholly good. So,   274a
if the way round is long, don't be astonished: we must make this detour for
the sake of things that are very important, not for what you have in mind.
Still, as our argument asserts, if that is what you want, you'll get it best as
a result of pursuing our own goal.

PHAEDRUS: What you've said is wonderful, Socrates—if only it could be
done!

SOCRATES: Yet surely whatever one must go through on the way to an
honorable goal is itself honorable.   274b

PHAEDRUS: Certainly.

SOCRATES: Well, then, that's enough about artfulness and artlessness in
connection with speaking.

PHAEDRUS: Quite.

SOCRATES: What's left, then, is aptness and ineptness in connection with
writing: What feature makes writing good, and what inept? Right?

PHAEDRUS: Yes.

SOCRATES: Well, do you know how best to please god when you either use
words or discuss them in general?

PHAEDRUS: Not at all. Do you?

SOCRATES: I can tell you what I've heard the ancients said, though they   274c
alone know the truth. However, if we could discover that ourselves, would
we still care about the speculations of other people?

PHAEDRUS: That's a silly question. Still, tell me what you say you've heard.

SOCRATES: Well, this is what I've heard. Among the ancient gods of
Naucratis[79] in Egypt there was one to whom the bird called the ibis is
sacred. The name of that divinity was Theuth,[80] and it was he who first
discovered number and calculation, geometry and astronomy, as well as   274d
the games of checkers and dice, and, above all else, writing.

Now the king of all Egypt at that time was Thamus, who lived in
the great city in the upper region that the Greeks call Egyptian Thebes;
Thamus is what they call Ammon.[81] Theuth came to exhibit his arts to him
and urged him to disseminate them to all the Egyptians. Thamus asked
him about the usefulness of each art, and while Theuth was explaining it,
Thamus praised him for whatever he thought was right in his explanations   274e
and criticized him for whatever he thought was wrong.

---

[79] A Greek trading colony.

[80] Theuth (or Thoth) was the Egyptian god of writing, measuring, and calculation,
represented on early monuments as an ibis.

[81] Ammon, king of the Egyptian gods, is identified by the Egyptians with the sun
god Ra, and by the Greeks (who call him Thamus) with Zeus.

The story goes that Thamus said much to Theuth, both for and against each art, which it would take too long to repeat. But when they came to writing, Theuth said: "O King, here is something that, once learned, will make the Egyptians wiser and will improve their memory; I have discovered a potion for memory and for wisdom." Thamus, however, replied: "O most expert Theuth, one man can give birth to the elements of an art, but only another can judge how they can benefit or harm those who will use them. And now, since you are the father of writing, your affection for it has made you describe its effects as the opposite of what they really are. In fact, it will introduce forgetfulness into the soul of those who learn it: they will not practice using their memory because they will put their trust in writing, which is external and depends on signs that belong to others, instead of trying to remember from the inside, completely on their own. You have not discovered a potion for remembering, but for reminding; you provide your students with the appearance of wisdom, not with its reality. Your invention will enable them to hear many things without being properly taught, and they will imagine that they have come to know much while for the most part they will know nothing. And they will be difficult to get along with, since they will merely appear to be wise instead of really being so."

PHAEDRUS: Socrates, you're very good at making up stories from Egypt or wherever else you want!

SOCRATES: But, my friend, the priests of the temple of Zeus at Dodona say that the first prophecies were the words of an oak. Everyone who lived at that time, not being as wise as you young ones are today, found it rewarding enough in their simplicity to listen to an oak or even a stone, so long as it was telling the truth, while it seems to make a difference to you, Phaedrus, who is speaking and where he comes from. Why, though, don't you just consider whether what he says is right or wrong?

PHAEDRUS: I deserved that, Socrates. And I agree that the Theban king was correct about writing.

SOCRATES: Well, then, those who think they can leave written instructions for an art, as well as those who accept them, thinking that writing can yield results that are clear or certain, must be quite naive and truly ignorant of Ammon's prophetic judgment: otherwise, how could they possibly think that words that have been written down can do more than remind those who already know what the writing is about?

PHAEDRUS: Quite right.

SOCRATES: You know, Phaedrus, writing shares a strange feature with painting. The offspring of painting stand there as if they are alive, but if anyone asks them anything, they remain most solemnly silent. The same is true of written words. You'd think they were speaking as if they had some understanding, but if you question anything that has been said because you want to learn more, it continues to signify just that very same thing forever. When it has once been written down, every discourse roams about everywhere, reaching indiscriminately those with understanding no less than those who have no business with it, and it doesn't know to whom it should speak and to whom it should not. And when it is faulted and attacked unfairly, it always needs its father's support; alone, it can neither defend itself nor come to its own support.

PHAEDRUS: You are absolutely right about that, too.

SOCRATES: Now tell me, can we discern another kind of discourse, a legitimate brother of this one? Can we say how it comes about, and how it is by nature better and more capable?

PHAEDRUS: Which one is that? How do you think it comes about?

SOCRATES: It is a discourse that is written down, with knowledge, in the soul of the listener; it can defend itself, and it knows for whom it should speak and for whom it should remain silent.

PHAEDRUS: You mean the living, breathing discourse of the man who knows, of which the written one can be fairly called an image.

SOCRATES: Absolutely right. And tell me this. Would a sensible farmer, who cared about his seeds and wanted them to yield fruit, plant them in all seriousness in the gardens of Adonis in the middle of the summer and enjoy watching them bear fruit within seven days?[82] Or would he do this as an amusement and in honor of the holiday, if he did it at all? Wouldn't he use his knowledge of farming to plant the seeds he cared for when it was appropriate and be content if they bore fruit seven months later?

PHAEDRUS: That's how he would handle those he was serious about, Socrates, quite differently from the others, as you say.

SOCRATES: Now what about the man who knows what is just, noble, and good? Shall we say that he is less sensible with his seeds than the farmer is with his?

PHAEDRUS: Certainly not.

SOCRATES: Therefore, he won't be serious about writing them in ink, sowing them, through a pen, with words that are as incapable of speaking in their own defense as they are of teaching the truth adequately.

PHAEDRUS: That wouldn't be likely.

275e

276a

276b

276c

---

[82] Adonis spent eight months of the year with Aphrodite, goddess of sexual love, and the four winter months with Persephone, goddess of the underworld. Gardens of Adonis were pots or windowboxes used for forcing seeds during the Athenian midsummer festival of Adonis. The seeds quickly germinated in the hot sun, but the young plants withered there just as quickly.

276d SOCRATES: Certainly not. When he writes, it's likely he will sow gardens of letters for the sake of amusing himself, storing up reminders for himself "when he reaches forgetful old age"[83] and for everyone who wants to follow in his footsteps, and will enjoy seeing them sweetly blooming. And when others turn to different amusements, watering themselves with drinking parties and everything else that goes along with them, he will rather spend his time amusing himself with the things I have just described.

276e PHAEDRUS: Socrates, you are contrasting a vulgar amusement with the very noblest—with the amusement of a man who can while away his time telling stories of justice and the other matters you mentioned.

SOCRATES: That's just how it is, Phaedrus. But it is much nobler to be serious about these matters, and use the art of dialectic. The dialectician chooses a proper soul and plants and sows within it discourse accompanied by knowledge—discourse capable of helping itself as well as the man
277a who planted it, which is not barren but produces a seed from which more discourse grows in the character of others. Such discourse makes the seed forever immortal and renders the man who has it as happy as any human being can be.

PHAEDRUS: What you describe is really much nobler still.

SOCRATES: And now that we have agreed about this, Phaedrus, we are finally able to decide the issue.

PHAEDRUS: What issue is that?

SOCRATES: The issue which brought us to this point in the first place: We wanted to examine the attack made on Lysias on account of his writing
277b speeches, and to ask which speeches are written artfully and which not. Now, I think that we have answered that question clearly enough.

PHAEDRUS: So it seemed; but remind me again how we did it.

SOCRATES: First, you must know the truth concerning everything you are speaking or writing about; you must learn how to define each thing in itself; and, having defined it, you must know how to divide it into kinds until you reach something indivisible. Second, you must understand the
277c nature of the soul, along the same lines; you must determine which kind of speech is appropriate to each kind of soul, prepare and arrange your speech accordingly, and offer a complex and elaborate speech to a complex soul and a simple speech to a simple one. Then, and only then, will you be able to use speech artfully, to the extent that its nature allows it to be used that way, either in order to teach or in order to persuade. This is the whole point of the argument we have been making.

PHAEDRUS: Absolutely. That is exactly how it seemed to us.

---

[83] Apparent quotation. Source unknown.

SOCRATES: Now how about whether it's noble or shameful to give or write   277d
a speech—when it could be fairly said to be grounds for reproach, and when
not? Didn't what we said just a little while ago make it clear—

PHAEDRUS: What was that?

SOCRATES: That if Lysias or anybody else ever did or ever does write—
privately or for the public, in the course of proposing some law—a political document which he believes to embody clear knowledge of lasting
importance, then this writer deserves reproach, whether anyone says so or
not. For to be unaware of the difference between a dream-image and the
reality of what is just and unjust, good and bad, must truly be grounds for   277e
reproach even if the crowd praises it with one voice.

PHAEDRUS: It certainly must be.

SOCRATES: On the other hand, take a man who thinks that a written discourse on any subject can only be a great amusement, that no discourse
worth serious attention has ever been written in verse or prose, and that
those that are recited in public without questioning and explanation, in the
manner of the rhapsodes, are given only in order to produce conviction. He
believes that at their very best these can only serve as reminders to those
who already know. And he also thinks that only what is said for the sake   **278a**
of understanding and learning, what is truly written in the soul concerning what is just, noble, and good can be clear, perfect, and worth serious
attention: Such discourses should be called his own legitimate children,
first the discourse he may have discovered already within himself and then
its sons and brothers who may have grown naturally in other souls insofar   **278b**
as these are worthy; to the rest, he turns his back. Such a man, Phaedrus,
would be just what you and I both would pray to become.

PHAEDRUS: I wish and pray for things to be just as you say.

SOCRATES: Well, then: our playful amusement regarding discourse is complete. Now you go and tell Lysias that we came to the spring which is
sacred to the Nymphs and heard words charging us to deliver a message to
Lysias and anyone else who composes speeches, as well as to Homer and   **278c**
anyone else who has composed poetry either spoken or sung, and third, to
Solon and anyone else who writes political documents that he calls laws: If
any one of you has composed these things with a knowledge of the truth,
if you can defend your writing when you are challenged, and if you can
yourself make the argument that your writing is of little worth, then you
must be called by a name derived not from these writings but rather from
those things that you are seriously pursuing.   **278d**

PHAEDRUS: What name, then, would you give such a man?

SOCRATES: To call him wise, Phaedrus, seems to me too much, and proper
only for a god. To call him wisdom's lover—a philosopher—or something
similar would fit him better and be more seemly.

PHAEDRUS: That would be quite appropriate.

SOCRATES: On the other hand, if a man has nothing more valuable than what he has composed or written, spending long hours twisting it around, pasting parts together and taking them apart—wouldn't you be right to call him a poet or a speech writer or an author of laws?

PHAEDRUS: Of course.

SOCRATES: Tell that, then, to your friend.

PHAEDRUS: And what about you? What shall you do? We must surely not forget your own friend.

SOCRATES: Whom do you mean?

PHAEDRUS: The beautiful Isocrates.[84] What are you going to tell him, Socrates? What shall we say he is?

SOCRATES: Isocrates is still young, Phaedrus. But I want to tell you what I foresee for him.

PHAEDRUS: What is that?

SOCRATES: It seems to me that by his nature he can outdo anything that Lysias has accomplished in his speeches; and he also has a nobler character. So I wouldn't be at all surprised if, as he gets older and continues writing speeches of the sort he is composing now, he makes everyone who has ever attempted to compose a speech seem like a child in comparison. Even more so if such work no longer satisfies him and a higher, divine impulse leads him to more important things. For nature, my friend, has placed the love of wisdom in his mind.

That is the message I will carry to my beloved, Isocrates, from the gods of this place; and you have your own message for your Lysias.

PHAEDRUS: So it shall be. But let's be off, since the heat has died down a bit.

SOCRATES: Shouldn't we offer a prayer to the gods here before we leave?

PHAEDRUS: Of course.

SOCRATES: O dear Pan[85] and all the other gods of this place, grant that I may be beautiful inside. Let all my external possessions be in friendly harmony with what is within. May I consider the wise man rich. As for gold, let me have as much as a temperate man could bear and carry with him.

Do we need anything else, Phaedrus? I believe my prayer is enough for me.

PHAEDRUS: Make it a prayer for me as well. Friends have everything in common.

SOCRATES: Let's be off.

---

[84] An Athenian teacher and orator (436–338 BCE) whose school was more famous in its day than Plato's Academy.

[85] See 263d note.

Republic

The *Republic* is specifically about the virtue of justice and about whether it pays better dividends in terms of happiness than does injustice. It begins, therefore, with a characteristically Socratic search for the definition of justice (331b–c). Polemarchus provides the first candidate: justice is giving to each what he is owed (331e). Socrates proceeds to examine this definition by testing its consistency with other beliefs Polemarchus holds and is unwilling to abandon. When it proves to be inconsistent with them, it is accepted as having been refuted (335e). Socrates must be presupposing, therefore, that some of Polemarchus' sincerely held ethical beliefs are true, since inconsistency with false beliefs is no guarantee of falsehood. The problem is that there seems to be little reason to accept this presupposition.

Socrates' next interlocutor, Thrasymachus, explains why. He argues that those who are stronger in any society—the rulers—control education and socialization through legislation and enforcement. But Thrasymachus believes that the rulers, like everyone else, are self-interested. Hence they make laws and adopt conventions—including linguistic conventions—that are in their own best interests, not those of their weaker subjects. It is these conventions that largely determine a subject's conception of justice and the other virtues. By being trained to follow or obey them, therefore, a subject is unwittingly adopting an ideology—a code of values and behavior—that serves his ruler's, rather than his own, interests. Consequently, Thrasymachus defines justice, not as what socialized subjects, like Socrates and Polemarchus, think it is (something genuinely noble and valuable that promotes their own happiness), but as what it really is in all cities: *the interest of the stronger.*

As he did with Polemarchus, Socrates uses the elenchus to try to refute Thrasymachus. But his attempts are not found wholly adequate, either by Thrasymachus himself or by the other interlocutors (350d–e, 357a–b, 358b–c). And we can see why: by arguing that ethical beliefs are an ideologically contaminated social product, Thrasymachus has undercut the elenchus altogether. Socrates may tie *Thrasymachus* in knots, but his *theory* is invulnerable to elenctic refutation (as Thrasymachus points out at 349a). For elenctic refutation appeals to ideologically contaminated ideas in order to counter his theory, but his theory maintains that these have no validity.

That is why Plato has Socrates abandon the elenchus in subsequent books and attempt to answer Thrasymachus (whose views are taken over by Glaucon and Adeimantus) by developing a positive defense of justice of his own.

At the center of Socrates' defense of justice stand the philosopher–kings—who unite political power and authority with philosophical knowledge of the transcendent, unchanging form of the good (the good itself)—and the ideal city they come to rule, Kallipolis (beautiful or noble city in Greek). Because this knowledge is based, as Socrates argues, in mathematics and science, it is unmediated by conventionally controlled concepts of good and bad, just and unjust. Hence it is free from the distorting influence of power or ideology, and so immune to the challenge Thrasymachus poses to the elenchus.

What the philosopher–kings do is construct a political system—including a system of socialization and education—that will distribute the benefits of their specialized knowledge of the good among the citizens at large. The system they construct relies on Plato's theory of the soul or mind, the seat of consciousness, emotion, desire, and decision making. According to this theory, there are three fundamentally different kinds of desires: *appetitive* ones for food, drink, sex, and the money with which to acquire them; *spirited* ones for honor, victory, and good reputation; and *rational* ones for knowledge and truth (437b ff., 580d ff.). Each type of desire "rules" in the soul of a different type of person, determining his values. People most value what they most desire, and so those ruled by one type of desire have very different conceptions of what is valuable or good or of what would make them happy than someone ruled by another type of desire. Just which type of desire rules an individual's soul depends on the relative strengths of his desires and on the kind of education and socialization he receives. The fundamental goal of ethical or political education isn't to provide knowledge, therefore, but to socialize desires, so as to turn people around (to the degree possible) from the pursuit of what they *falsely* believe to be happiness to the pursuit of *true* happiness (518b–519d).

The famous Allegory of the Cave illustrates the effects of such education (514a). Uneducated people, tethered by their unsocialized appetites, see only images of models of the good (shadows cast by puppets on the walls of the cave). They are not virtuous to any degree, since they act simply on their whims. When their appetites are shaped through physical training and that mix of reading and writing, dance and song that the Greeks call *mousikē* (musical training), they are released from these bonds and are ruled by their socialized appetites. They have at least that level of virtue required to act prudently and postpone gratification. Plato refers to them as *money-lovers,* because they pursue money as the best means of reliably satisfying their appetitive desires in the long term (580d–581a). They see models of the good (the puppets that cast the shadows), for stable satisfaction of appetitive desires *is* a sort of good.

Further education, this time in mathematical science, leaves people eligible for it ruled by their spirited desires. They are *honor-lovers,* who seek success in difficult endeavors and the honor and approval it brings. They have the true beliefs about virtue required for such success, and hence that greater level of virtue Plato calls civic virtue (430c).

Finally, further education in dialectic (a sort of philosophical training that is a descendant of the Socratic elenchus) and practical city management results in people who are bound only by their rational desires. They are free from illusion and see not mere images of the good but the good itself. They are *wisdom-lovers* or philosophers, who have knowledge rather than mere true belief about virtue, and so are fully virtuous.

Not everyone, however, is able to benefit from these various types of education: there are some at each stage whose desires are too strong for education to break. That is why there are producers, guardians, and philosopher–kings in the ideal city. That is why, too, these groups can cooperate with one another in a just system, where the money-loving producers trade their products for the protection provided by the honor-loving guardians and the knowledge provided by the wisdom-loving kings, rather than competing with them for the very same goods (462e–463b). Nonetheless, everyone in this ideal system is enabled to travel as far toward the sun (the good) as education can take him given the innate strength of his desires. Thus everyone comes as close to being fully virtuous, and so to pursuing and achieving genuine happiness, as he can. It is this that makes Plato's city both an ethical and a prudential ideal, both maximally just and maximally happy. And because it is both, it constitutes a response to the Thrasymachean challenge raised anew by Glaucon and Adeimantus in Book ii of the *Republic.* For if maximal justice and maximal happiness go together, then it pays in terms of happiness to be just rather than unjust.

Note on the translation: The *Republic* is largely in reported speech. Socrates is relating a conversation he had in the past. Here, for ease of reading, his report is cast as an explicit dialogue in direct speech with identified speakers.

REPUBLIC

BOOK I

327a

327b

327c

SOCRATES' NARRATION BEGINS: *I went down to the Piraeus yesterday with Glaucon, the son of Ariston, to say a prayer to the goddess, and also because I wanted to see how they would manage the festival, since they were holding it for the first time. I thought the procession of the local residents was beautiful, but the show put on by the Thracians was no less so, in my view. After we had said our prayer and watched the procession, we started back toward town. Then Polemarchus, the son of Cephalus, saw us from a distance as we were hurrying homeward, and told his slave boy to run and ask us to wait for him. The boy caught hold of my cloak from behind.*

SLAVE: Polemarchus wants you to wait.

I turned around and asked where he was.

SLAVE: He is coming up behind you; please wait for him.

GLAUCON: All right, we will.

Shortly after that, Polemarchus caught up with us. Adeimantus, Glaucon's brother, was with him, and so were Niceratus, the son of Nicias, and some others, all of whom were apparently on their way from the procession.

POLEMARCHUS: It looks to me, Socrates, as if you two are hurrying to get away to town.

SOCRATES: That isn't a bad guess.

POLEMARCHUS: But do you see how many we are?

SOCRATES: Certainly.

POLEMARCHUS: Well, then, either you must prove yourselves stronger than all these people or you will have to stay here.

SOCRATES: Isn't there another alternative still: that we persuade you that you should let us go?

POLEMARCHUS: But could you persuade us, if we won't listen?

GLAUCON: There is no way we could.

POLEMARCHUS: Well, we won't listen; you had better make up your mind to that.

ADEIMANTUS: You mean to say you don't know that there is to be a torch   **328a**
race on horseback for the goddess tonight?

SOCRATES: On horseback? That is something new. Are they going to race
on horseback and hand the torches on in relays, or what?

POLEMARCHUS: In relays. And, besides, there will be an all-night celebration that will be worth seeing. We will get up after dinner and go to see
the festivities. We will meet lots of young men there and have a discussion.
So stay and do as we ask.   **328b**

GLAUCON: It looks as if we will have to stay.

SOCRATES: If you think so, we must.

*So, we went to Polemarchus' house, and there we found Lysias[1] and
Euthydemus, the brothers of Polemarchus, and what is more, Thrasymachus
of Chalcedon[2] was there too, and Charmantides of Paeania, and Clitophon,
the son of Aristonymus. Polemarchus' father, Cephalus, was also inside, and
I thought he looked quite old. You see, I hadn't seen him for some time. He*   **328c**
*was sitting on a sort of chair with cushions and had a wreath on his head, as
he had been offering a sacrifice in the courtyard. We sat down beside him, since
some chairs were arranged in a circle there. As soon as he saw me, Cephalus
greeted me:*

Socrates, you don't often come down to the Piraeus to see us. Yet you
should. If it were still easy for me to make the trip to town, you wouldn't   **328d**
have to come here. On the contrary, we would come to you. But as it is,
you ought to come here more often. I want you to know, you see, that in
my case at least, as the other pleasures—the bodily ones—wither away, my
appetites for discussions and their pleasures grow stronger. So please do as I
ask: have your conversation with these young men, and stay here with us,
as you would with your close friends and relatives.

SOCRATES: I certainly will, Cephalus. In fact, I enjoy engaging in discussion with the very old. I think we should learn from them—since they   **328e**
are like people who have traveled a road that we too will probably have to
follow—what the road is like, whether rough and difficult or smooth and
easy. And I would be particularly glad to find out from you what you think
about it, since you have reached the point in life the poets call old age's
threshold. Is it a difficult time of life? What have you to report about it?

CEPHALUS: By Zeus, Socrates, I will tell you exactly what I think. You see,   **329a**
a number of us who are more or less the same age often get together, so as

---

[1] See *Phaedrus*.

[2] Thrasymachus of Chalcedon (fl. c. 430–400 BCE) was a Sophist and rhetorician
of note.

to preserve the old saying.[3] When they meet, the majority of our members lament, longing for the lost pleasures of their youth and reminiscing about sex, drinking parties, feasts, and the other things that go along with them. They get irritated, as if they had been deprived of very great things, and had lived well then but are not living now. Some others, too, even moan about the abuse heaped on old people by their relatives, and for *that* reason recite a litany of all the evils old age has caused them. But I don't think they blame the real cause, Socrates. After all, if that were the cause, I too would have had the same experiences, at least as far as old age is concerned, and so would everyone else of my age. But as it is, I have met others in the past who don't feel that way—in particular, the poet Sophocles. I was once present when he was asked by someone, "How are you as far as sex goes, Sophocles? Can you still make love to a woman?" "Quiet, man," he replied, "I am very glad to have escaped from all that, like a slave who has escaped from a deranged and savage master." I thought at the time what he said was sensible, and I still do. You see, old age brings peace and freedom from all such things. When the appetites cease to stress and importune us, everything Sophocles said comes to pass, and we escape from many insane masters. But in these matters, and in those concerning one's relatives, the real cause isn't old age, Socrates, but the way people live. If they are orderly and contented, old age, too, is only moderately onerous; if they aren't, both old age, Socrates, *and* youth are hard to bear.

I admired him for saying that, and I wanted him to tell me more, so I urged him on.

I imagine when you say that, Cephalus, the masses do not accept it. On the contrary, they think you bear old age more easily, not because of the way you live, but because you are wealthy. For the wealthy, they say, have many consolations.

CEPHALUS: That's true, they are not convinced. And there is something in their objection, though not as much as they think. Themistocles' retort is relevant here. When someone from Seriphus insulted him by saying his high reputation was due to his city, not to himself, he replied that, had he been a Seriphian, he would not be famous; but nor would the other, had he been an Athenian. The same account applies to those who are not rich and find old age hard to bear: a good person would not easily bear old age if it were coupled with poverty, but one who wasn't good would not be contented even if he were wealthy.

SOCRATES: Did you inherit most of your wealth, Cephalus, or did you make it yourself?

---

[3] "God ever draws together like to like."

CEPHALUS: What did I make for myself, Socrates, you ask. As a money- 330b
maker I am in between my grandfather and my father. You see, my grandfather and namesake inherited about the same amount of wealth as I possess
and multiplied it many times. However, my father, Lysanias, diminished
that amount to even less than I have now. As for me, I am satisfied to leave
my sons here no less, but a little more, than I inherited.

SOCRATES: The reason I asked is that you do not seem particularly to love
money. And those who have not made it themselves are usually like that. 330c
But those who have made it themselves love it twice as much as anyone
else. For just as poets love their poems and fathers their children, so those
who have made money take their money seriously both as something they
have made themselves and—just as other people do—because it is useful.
This makes them difficult even to be with, since they are unwilling to
praise anything except money.

CEPHALUS: That's true.

SOCRATES: Indeed, it is. But tell me something else. What do you think 330d
is the greatest good you have enjoyed as a result of being very wealthy?

CEPHALUS: What I have to say probably would not persuade the masses.
But you are well aware, Socrates, that when someone thinks his end is
near, he becomes frightened and concerned about things he did not fear
before. It is then that the stories told about Hades, that a person who has
been unjust here must pay the penalty there—stories he used to make fun
of—twist his soul this way and that for fear they are true. And whether 330e
because of the weakness of old age, or because he is now closer to what
happens in Hades and has a clearer view of it, or whatever it is, he is filled
with foreboding and fear, and begins to calculate and consider whether he
has been unjust to anyone. If he finds many injustices in his life, he often
even awakes from sleep in terror, as children do, and lives in anticipation of
evils to come. But someone who knows he has not been unjust has sweet **331a**
good hope as his constant companion—a nurse to his old age, as Pindar
says. For he puts it charmingly, Socrates, when he says that when someone
lives a just and pious life,

> Sweet hope is in his heart
> Nurse and companion to his age
> Hope, captain of the ever-twisting
> Mind of mortal men.

How amazingly well he puts that. It is in this connection I would say the
possession of wealth is most valuable, not for every man, but for a good
and orderly one. Not cheating someone even unintentionally, not lying 331b
to him, not owing a sacrifice to some god or money to a person, and as a
result departing for that other place in fear—the possession of wealth makes

no small contribution to this. It has many other uses, too, but putting one thing against the other, Socrates, I would say that for a man with any sense, that is how wealth is most useful.

331c SOCRATES: A fine sentiment, Cephalus. But speaking of that thing itself, justice, are we to say it is simply speaking the truth and paying whatever debts one has incurred? Or is it sometimes just to do these things, sometimes unjust? I mean this sort of thing, for example: everyone would surely agree that if a man borrows weapons from a sane friend, and if he goes mad and asks for them back, the friend should not return them, and would not be just if he did. Nor should anyone be willing to tell the whole truth to someone in such a state.

331d CEPHALUS: That's true.

SOCRATES: Then the following is not the definition of justice: to speak the truth and repay what one has borrowed. Polemarchus interrupted: It certainly is, Socrates, if indeed we are to trust Simonides at all.

CEPHALUS: Well, then, I will hand over the discussion to you, since it is time for me to look after the sacrifices.

POLEMARCHUS: Am I, Polemarchus, not heir of all your possessions?

Cephalus replied with a laugh:

Certainly.

And off he went to the sacrifice.

SOCRATES: Then tell us, heir to the discussion, just what Simonides said
331e about justice that you think is correct.

POLEMARCHUS: He said it is just to give to each what is owed to him. And a fine saying it is, in my view.

SOCRATES: Well, now, it is not easy to disagree with Simonides, since he is a wise and godlike man. But what exactly does he mean? Perhaps you know, Polemarchus, but I do not understand. Clearly, he does not mean what we said a moment ago—namely, giving back to someone whatever he has lent to you, even if he is out of his mind when he asks
332a for it. And yet what he has lent to you is surely something that is owed to him, isn't it?

POLEMARCHUS: Yes.

SOCRATES: But when he is out of his mind, it is, under no circumstances, to be given to him?

POLEMARCHUS: True.

SOCRATES: Then it seems Simonides must have meant something else when he says that to return what is owed is just.

POLEMARCHUS: Something else indeed, by Zeus! He meant friends owe something good to their friends, never something bad.

SOCRATES: I understand. You mean someone does not give a lender what
he is owed by giving him gold, when the giving and taking would be   332b
harmful, and both he and the lender are friends. Isn't that what you say
Simonides meant?

POLEMARCHUS: It certainly is.

SOCRATES: Now what about this? Should one also give to one's enemies
whatever is owed to them?

POLEMARCHUS: Yes, by all means. What is *in fact* owed to them. And what
an enemy owes an enemy, in my view, is also precisely what is appropriate—something bad.

SOCRATES: It seems, then, Simonides was speaking in riddles—just like a
poet!—when he said what justice is. For what he meant, it seems, is that   332c
it is just to give to each *what is appropriate to him,* and this is what he called
giving him *what he is owed.*

POLEMARCHUS: What else did you think he meant?

SOCRATES: Then what, in the name of Zeus, do you think he would answer
if someone asked him: "Simonides, what owed or appropriate things does
the craft we call medicine give, and to which things?"

POLEMARCHUS: Clearly, he would say it gives drugs, food, and drink to
bodies.

SOCRATES: And what owed or appropriate things does the craft we call
cooking give, and to which things?

POLEMARCHUS: It gives pleasant flavors to food.   332d

SOCRATES: Good. Now what does the craft we would call justice give, and
to whom or what does it give it?

POLEMARCHUS: If we are to follow the previous answers, Socrates, it gives
benefit to friends and harm to enemies.

SOCRATES: Does Simonides mean, then, that treating friends well and
enemies badly is justice?

POLEMARCHUS: I believe so.

SOCRATES: And who is most capable of treating sick friends well and enemies badly in matters of disease and health?

POLEMARCHUS: A doctor.

SOCRATES: And who can do so best in a storm at sea?   332e

POLEMARCHUS: A ship's captain.

SOCRATES: What about the just person? In what actions and what work is
he most capable of benefiting friends and harming enemies?

POLEMARCHUS: In wars and alliances, I imagine.

SOCRATES: All right. Now when people are not sick, Polemarchus, a doctor
is useless to them.

POLEMARCHUS: True.

SOCRATES: And so is a ship's captain to those who are not sailing?

POLEMARCHUS: Yes.

SOCRATES: So to people who are not at war, a just man is useless?

POLEMARCHUS: No, I don't think that at all.

SOCRATES: So justice is also useful in peacetime?

333a　POLEMARCHUS: Yes, it is useful.

SOCRATES: And so is farming, isn't it?

POLEMARCHUS: Yes.

SOCRATES: For providing produce?

POLEMARCHUS: Yes.

SOCRATES: And shoemaking as well, of course?

POLEMARCHUS: Yes.

SOCRATES: For the acquisition of shoes, I suppose you would say?

POLEMARCHUS: Of course.

SOCRATES: Tell me, then, what is justice useful for using or acquiring in peacetime?

POLEMARCHUS: Contracts, Socrates.

SOCRATES: And by contracts you mean partnerships, or what?

POLEMARCHUS: Partnerships, of course.

333b　SOCRATES: So is it a just man who is a good and useful partner in a game of checkers, or an expert checkers player?

POLEMARCHUS: An expert checkers player.

SOCRATES: And in laying bricks and stones, is a just person a better and more useful partner than a builder?

POLEMARCHUS: Not at all.

SOCRATES: Well, in what kind of partnership, then, is a just person a better partner than a builder or a lyre player, in the way a lyre player is better than a just person at hitting the right notes?

POLEMARCHUS: In money matters, I think.

SOCRATES: Except, I presume, Polemarchus, in using money. You see,
333c　whenever one needs to buy or sell a horse jointly, I think a horse breeder is a more useful partner. Isn't he?

POLEMARCHUS: Apparently.

SOCRATES: And when it is a boat, a boat builder or a ship's captain?

POLEMARCHUS: It would seem so.

SOCRATES: In what joint use of silver or gold, then, is a just person a more useful partner than anyone else?

POLEMARCHUS: When yours must be deposited for safekeeping, Socrates.

SOCRATES: You mean whenever there is no need to use it, but only to keep it?

POLEMARCHUS: Of course.

SOCRATES: So when money is not being used, that is when justice is useful for it?   333d

POLEMARCHUS: It looks that way.

SOCRATES: And when one needs to keep a pruning knife safe, justice is useful both in partnerships and for the individual. When you need to use it, however, it is the craft of vine pruning that is useful?

POLEMARCHUS: Apparently.

SOCRATES: And would you also say that when one needs to keep a shield and a lyre safe and not use them, justice is a useful thing, but when you need to use them it is the soldier's craft or the musician's that is useful?

POLEMARCHUS: I would have to.

SOCRATES: And so in all other cases, too, justice is useless when they are in use, but useful when they are not?

POLEMARCHUS: It looks that way.

SOCRATES: Then justice cannot be something excellent, can it, my friend,   333e
if it is only useful for useless things. But let's consider the following point. Isn't the person who is cleverest at landing a blow, whether in boxing or any other kind of fight, also cleverest at guarding against it?

POLEMARCHUS: Of course.

SOCRATES: And the one who is clever at guarding against disease is also cleverest at producing it unnoticed?

POLEMARCHUS: That is my view, at any rate.

SOCRATES: And the one who is a good guardian of an army is the very one   **334a**
who can steal the enemy's plans and dispositions?

POLEMARCHUS: Of course.

SOCRATES: So whenever someone is a clever guardian of something, he is also clever at stealing it.

POLEMARCHUS: It seems so.

SOCRATES: So if a just person is clever at guarding money, he must also be clever at stealing it.

POLEMARCHUS: So the argument suggests, at least.

SOCRATES: It seems, then, that a just person has turned out to be a kind of thief. You probably got that idea from Homer. For he loves Autolycus, the maternal grandfather of Odysseus, whom he describes as better than   334b everyone at stealing and swearing false oaths.[4] According to you, Homer, and Simonides, then, justice seems to be some sort of craft of stealing—one that benefits friends and harms enemies. Isn't that what you meant?

POLEMARCHUS: No, by Zeus, it isn't. But I do not know anymore what I meant. I still believe this, however, that benefiting one's friends and harming one's enemies is justice.

334c
SOCRATES: Speaking of friends, do you mean those a person believes to be good and useful, or those who actually are good and useful, even if he does not believe they are, and similarly with enemies?

POLEMARCHUS: Probably, one loves those one considers good and useful and hates those one considers bad.

SOCRATES: But don't people make mistakes about this, so that lots of those who seem to them to be good and useful aren't, and vice versa?

POLEMARCHUS: They do.

SOCRATES: So, for them, good people are enemies and bad ones friends?

POLEMARCHUS: Of course.

SOCRATES: All the same, it is then just for them to benefit bad people and harm good ones?

POLEMARCHUS: Apparently.

334d
SOCRATES: Yet good people are just and are not the sort to do injustice.

POLEMARCHUS: True.

SOCRATES: According to your account, then, it is just to do bad things to those who do no injustice.

POLEMARCHUS: Not at all, Socrates. It is *my account* that seems to be bad.

SOCRATES: It is just, then, is it, to harm unjust people and benefit just ones?

POLEMARCHUS: That seems better than the other view.

SOCRATES: Then it follows, Polemarchus, that it is just for many people—
334e
the ones who are mistaken in their judgment—to harm their friends, since they are bad for them, and benefit their enemies, since they are good. And so we will find ourselves claiming the very opposite of what we said Simonides meant.

POLEMARCHUS: Yes, that certainly follows. But let's change our definition. For it looks as though we did not define friends and enemies correctly.

SOCRATES: How did we define them, Polemarchus?

POLEMARCHUS: We said that a friend is someone who is believed to be good.

SOCRATES: And how are we to change that now?

---

[4] *Odyssey* xix.392–98.

POLEMARCHUS: Someone who is both believed to be good and is good is a friend; someone who is believed to be good, but is not, is believed to be a friend but is not. And the same goes for enemies.   **335a**

SOCRATES: According to that account, then, a good person will be a friend and a bad one an enemy.

POLEMARCHUS: Yes.

SOCRATES: So you want us to add something to what we said before about the just man. Then we said that it is just to treat friends well and enemies badly. Now you want us to add to this: to treat a friend well, *provided he is good,* and to harm an enemy, *provided he is bad?*

POLEMARCHUS: Yes, that seems well put to me.   335b

SOCRATES: Should a just man really harm anyone whatsoever?

POLEMARCHUS: Of course. He should harm those who are both bad and enemies.

SOCRATES: When horses are harmed, do they become better or worse?

POLEMARCHUS: Worse.

SOCRATES: With respect to the virtue that makes dogs good, or to the one that makes horses good?

POLEMARCHUS: With respect to the one that makes horses good.

SOCRATES: And when dogs are harmed, they become worse with respect to the virtue that makes dogs, not horses, good?

POLEMARCHUS: Necessarily.

SOCRATES: And what about human beings, comrade; shouldn't we say that, when they are harmed, they become worse with respect to human virtue?   335c

POLEMARCHUS: Of course.

SOCRATES: But isn't justice human virtue?

POLEMARCHUS: Yes, that's necessarily so, too.

SOCRATES: Then, my dear Polemarchus, people who have been harmed are bound to become more unjust.

POLEMARCHUS: So it seems.

SOCRATES: Now, can musicians use music to make people unmusical?

POLEMARCHUS: No, they can't.

SOCRATES: Or can horsemen use horsemanship to make people unhorsemanlike?

POLEMARCHUS: No.

SOCRATES: Well, then, can just people use justice to make people unjust? In a word, can good people use their virtue or goodness to make people bad?   335d

POLEMARCHUS: No, they can't.

SOCRATES: For it isn't the function of heat to cool things down, I imagine, but that of its opposite.

POLEMARCHUS: Yes.

SOCRATES: Nor the function of dryness to make things wet, but that of its opposite.

POLEMARCHUS: Of course.

SOCRATES: So the function of a good person isn't to harm, but that of his opposite.

POLEMARCHUS: Apparently.

SOCRATES: And a just person is a good person?

POLEMARCHUS: Of course.

SOCRATES: So it isn't the function of a just person to harm a friend or anyone else, Polemarchus, but that of his opposite, an unjust person.

335e   POLEMARCHUS: I think you are absolutely right, Socrates.

SOCRATES: So if someone tells us it is just to give to each what he is owed, and understands by this that a just man should harm his enemies and benefit his friends, the one who says it is not wise. I mean, what he says is not true. For it has become clear to us that it is never just to harm anyone.

POLEMARCHUS: I agree.

SOCRATES: You and I will fight as partners, then, against anyone who tells us that Simonides, Bias, Pittacus, or any of our other wise and blessedly happy men said this.

POLEMARCHUS: I, for my part, am willing to be your partner in the battle.

336a   SOCRATES: Do you know whose saying I think it is, that it is just to benefit friends and harm enemies?

POLEMARCHUS: Whose?

SOCRATES: I think it is a saying of Periander, or Perdiccas, or Xerxes, or Ismenias of Thebes, or some other wealthy man who thought he had great power.

POLEMARCHUS: That's absolutely true.

SOCRATES: All right. Since it has become apparent, then, that neither justice nor the just consists in benefiting friends and harming enemies, what else should one say it is?

336b   *Now, while we were speaking, Thrasymachus had tried many times to take over the discussion but was restrained by those sitting near him, who wanted to hear our argument to the end. When we paused after what I had just said, however, he could not keep quiet any longer: crouched up like a wild beast about to spring, he hurled himself at us as if to tear us to pieces. Polemarchus and I were frightened and flustered as he roared into our midst:*

What nonsense you two have been talking all this time, Socrates! Why do   336c
you act like naïve people, giving way to one another? If you really want to
know what justice is, don't just ask questions and then indulge your love
of honor by refuting the answers. You know very well it is easier to ask
questions than to answer them. Give an answer yourself and tell us what *you*
say the just is. And don't tell me it is the right, the beneficial, the profitable,   336d
the gainful, or the advantageous, but tell me clearly and exactly what you
mean. For I won't accept such nonsense from you.

His words startled me and, looking at him, I was afraid. And I think if I had
not seen him before he looked at me, I would have been dumbstruck.[5] *But as*
it was, I happened to look at him just as he began to be exasperated by our
argument, so I was able to answer; and trembling a little, I said: 336e

Do not be too hard on us, Thrasymachus. If Polemarchus and I made an
error in our investigation of the accounts, you may be sure we did so involuntarily. If we were searching for gold, we would never voluntarily give
way to each other, if by doing so we would destroy our chance of finding
it. So do not think that in searching for justice, a thing more honorable
than a large quantity of gold, we would foolishly give way to one another
or be less than completely serious about finding it. You surely must not
think that, my friend, but rather—as I do—that we are incapable of finding
it. Hence it is surely far more appropriate for us to be pitied by you clever
people than to be given rough treatment.

When he heard that, he gave a loud sarcastic laugh: **337a**

By Heracles! That is Socrates' usual irony for you! I knew this would happen. I even told these others earlier that you would be unwilling to answer,
that you would be ironic and do anything rather than give an answer, if
someone questioned *you*.

SOCRATES: That is because you are a wise fellow, Thrasymachus. You knew
very well if you ask someone how much twelve is, and in putting the question you warn him, "Don't tell me, man, that twelve is twice six, or three   337b
times four, or six times two, or four times three; for I won't accept such
nonsense from you"—it was obvious to you, I imagine, that no one could
respond to a person who inquired in that way. But suppose he said to you:
"What do you mean, Thrasymachus; am I not to give any of the answers
you mention, not even if twelve happens to be one of those things? You
are amazing. Do you want me to say something other than the truth? Or
do you mean something else?" What answer would you give him?   337c

THRASYMACHUS: Well, so you think the two cases are alike?

---

[5] It was a Greek superstition that anyone seen by a wolf before he saw it was struck
dumb.

SOCRATES: Why shouldn't I? But even if they are not alike, yet seem so to the person you asked, do you think he is any less likely to give the answer that seems right to him, whether we forbid him to do so or not?

THRASYMACHUS: Is that what you are going to do, give one of the forbidden answers?

SOCRATES: I would not be surprised—provided it is the one that seems right to me after I have investigated the matter.

THRASYMACHUS: What if I show you another answer about justice, one
337d   that is different from all these and better than any of them? What penalty would you deserve then?

SOCRATES: The very one that is appropriate for someone who does not know—what else? And what is appropriate is to learn from the one who does know. That, therefore, is what I deserve to suffer.

THRASYMACHUS: What a pleasant fellow you are! But in addition to learning, you must pay money.

SOCRATES: I will if I ever have any.

GLAUCON: He has it already. If it is a matter of money, speak, Thrasymachus. We will all contribute for Socrates.

337e   THRASYMACHUS: Oh yes, sure, so that Socrates can carry on as usual: he gives no answer himself, and if someone else does, he takes up his account and refutes it.

SOCRATES: How can someone give an answer, my excellent man, when, first of all, he does not know and does not claim to know, and then, even if he does have some opinion about the matter, is forbidden by no ordinary man to express any of the things he thinks? No, it is much more appropri-
338a   ate for you to answer, since you say you do know and can tell us. Don't be obstinate. Give your answer as a favor to me and do not begrudge your teaching to Glaucon and the others.

While I was saying this, Glaucon and the others begged him to do as I asked. Thrasymachus clearly wanted to speak in order to win a good reputation, since he thought he had a very good answer. But he pretended to want to win a victory at my expense by having me do the answering. However, he agreed in the end, and then said:

338b   That is Socrates' wisdom for you: he himself isn't willing to teach but goes around learning from others and isn't even grateful to them.

SOCRATES: When you say I learn from others, you are right, Thrasymachus; but when you say I do not give thanks, you are wrong. I give as much as I can. But I can give only praise, since I have no money. And just how enthusiastically I give it, when someone seems to me to speak well, you will know as soon as you have answered, since I think you will speak well.

THRASYMACHUS: Listen, then. I say justice is nothing other than what is advantageous for the stronger. Well, why don't you praise me? No, you are unwilling.

338c

SOCRATES: First, I must understand what you mean. For, as things stand, I do not. What is advantageous for the stronger, you say, is just. What on earth do you mean, Thrasymachus? Surely you do not mean something like this: Polydamas, the pancratist,[6] is stronger than we are. Beef is advantageous for his body. So, this food is also both advantageous and just for us who are weaker than he?

338d

THRASYMACHUS: You disgust me, Socrates. You interpret my account in the way that does it the most evil.

SOCRATES: That's not it at all, my very good man; I only want you to make your meaning clearer.

THRASYMACHUS: Don't you know, then, that some cities are ruled by a tyranny, some by a democracy, and some by an aristocracy?

SOCRATES: Of course I do.

THRASYMACHUS: And that what is stronger in each city is the ruling element?

SOCRATES: Certainly.

THRASYMACHUS: And each type of rule makes laws that are advantageous for itself: democracy makes democratic ones, tyranny tyrannical ones, and so on with the others. And by so legislating, each declares that what is just for its subjects is what is advantageous for itself—the ruler—and it punishes anyone who deviates from this as lawless and unjust. That, Socrates, is what I say justice is, the same in all cities: what is advantageous for the established rule. Since the established rule is surely stronger, anyone who does the rational calculation correctly will conclude that the just is the same everywhere—what is advantageous for the stronger.

338e

339a

SOCRATES: Now I see what you mean. Whether it is true or not, I will try to find out. But you yourself have answered that what is just is what is advantageous, Thrasymachus, whereas you forbade me to answer that. True, you have added *for the stronger* to it.

339b

THRASYMACHUS: And I suppose you think that is an insignificant addition.

SOCRATES: It isn't clear yet whether it is significant. What *is* clear is that we must investigate whether or not it is true. I agree that what is just is something advantageous. But you add *for the stronger*. I do not know about that. We will have to look into it.

---

[6] *Pancration* was a mixture of boxing and wrestling combined with kicking and strangling.

THRASYMACHUS: Go ahead and look.

SOCRATES: That is just what I am going to do. Tell me, then, you also claim, don't you, that it is just to obey the rulers?

THRASYMACHUS: I do.

339c SOCRATES: And are the rulers in each city infallible, or are they liable to error?

THRASYMACHUS: No doubt, they are liable to error.

SOCRATES: So, when they attempt to make laws, they make some correctly, others incorrectly?

THRASYMACHUS: I suppose so.

SOCRATES: And a law is correct if it prescribes what is advantageous for the rulers themselves, and incorrect if it prescribes what is disadvantageous for them? Is that what you mean?

THRASYMACHUS: It is.

SOCRATES: And whatever laws the rulers make must be obeyed by their subjects, and that is what is just?

THRASYMACHUS: Of course.

339d SOCRATES: According to your account, then, it isn't only just to do what is advantageous for the stronger, but also the opposite: what is not advantageous.

THRASYMACHUS: What is that you are saying?

SOCRATES: The same as you, I think. But let's examine it more closely. Haven't we agreed that the rulers are sometimes in error as to what is best for themselves when they give orders to their subjects, and yet that it is just for their subjects to do whatever their rulers order? Wasn't that agreed?

THRASYMACHUS: I suppose so.

339e SOCRATES: You will also have to suppose, then, that you have agreed that it is just to do what is disadvantageous for the rulers and those who are stronger, whenever they unintentionally order what is bad for themselves. But you say, too, that it is just for the others to obey the orders the rulers gave. You are very wise, Thrasymachus, but doesn't it necessarily follow that it is just to do the opposite of what you said, since the weaker are then ordered to do what is disadvantageous for the stronger?

340a POLEMARCHUS: By Zeus, Socrates, that's absolutely clear.

And Clitophon interrupted:

Of course it is, if you are to be his witness, at any rate.

POLEMARCHUS: Who needs a witness? Thrasymachus himself agrees that the rulers sometimes issue orders that are bad for them, and that it is just for the others to obey them.

CLITOPHON: That, Polemarchus, is because Thrasymachus maintained that it is just to obey the orders of the rulers.

POLEMARCHUS: Yes, Clitophon, and he also maintained that what is advantageous for the stronger is just. And having maintained both principles, he went on to agree that the stronger sometimes order the weaker, who are subject to them, to do things that are disadvantageous for the stronger themselves. From these agreements it follows that what is advantageous for the stronger is no more just than what is not advantageous. 340b

CLITOPHON: But what he meant by what is advantageous for the stronger is what the stronger *believes* to be advantageous for him. That is what he maintained the weaker must do, and that is what he maintained is what is just.

POLEMARCHUS: But it is not what he said.

SOCRATES: It makes no difference, Polemarchus. If Thrasymachus wants to put it that way now, let's accept it. But tell me, Thrasymachus, is that what you intended to say, that what is just is what the stronger believes to be advantageous for him, whether it is in fact advantageous for him or not? Is that what we are to say you mean? 340c

THRASYMACHUS: Not at all. Do you think I would call someone who is in error stronger at the very moment he errs?

SOCRATES: I did think you meant that, when you agreed that the rulers are not infallible but sometimes make errors. 340d

THRASYMACHUS: That is because you are a quibbler in arguments, Socrates. I mean, when someone makes an error in the treatment of patients, do you call him a doctor in virtue of the fact that he made that very error? Or, when someone makes an error in calculating, do you call him an accountant in virtue of the fact that he made that very error in calculation? I think we express ourselves in words that, taken literally, do say that a doctor is in error, or an accountant, or a grammarian. But each of these, to the extent that he is what we call him, never makes errors, so that, according to the precise account (and you are a stickler for precise accounts), no craftsman ever makes errors. It is when his knowledge fails him that he makes an error, and, in virtue of the fact that he made that error, he is no craftsman. No craftsman, wise man, or ruler makes an error at the moment when he is ruling, even though everyone will say that a physician or a ruler makes errors. It is in this loose way that you must also take the answer I gave just now. But the most precise answer is this: a ruler, to the extent that he is a ruler, never makes errors and unerringly decrees what is best for himself, and that is what his subject must do. Thus, as I said from the first, it is just to do what is advantageous for the stronger. 340e

341a

SOCRATES: Well, Thrasymachus, so you think I quibble, do you?

THRASYMACHUS: Yes, I do.

SOCRATES: And you think that I asked the questions I did in a premeditated attempt to do you evil in the argument?

THRASYMACHUS: I am certain of it. But it won't do you any good. You will never be able to do me evil by covert means, and without them, you will never be able to overpower me by argument.

341b

SOCRATES: Bless you, Thrasymachus; I would not so much as try! But to prevent this sort of confusion from happening to us again, would you define whether you mean the ruler and stronger in the ordinary sense or in what you were just now calling the precise sense, when you say that it is just for the weaker to do what is advantageous for him, since he is the stronger?

THRASYMACHUS: I mean the ruler in the most precise sense. Now do *that* evil, if you can, and practice your quibbling on it—I ask no favors. But you will find there is nothing you can do.

341c

SOCRATES: Do you think that I am crazy enough to try to shave a lion[7] and quibble with Thrasymachus?

THRASYMACHUS: Well, you certainly tried just now, although you were a good-for-nothing at it, too!

SOCRATES: That's enough of that! Tell me: is a doctor—in the precise sense, the one you mentioned before—a moneymaker or someone who treats the sick? Tell me about the one who is really a doctor.

THRASYMACHUS: Someone who treats the sick.

SOCRATES: What about a ship's captain? Is the true captain a ruler of sailors, or a sailor?

341d

THRASYMACHUS: A ruler of sailors.

SOCRATES: In other words, we should not take any account of the fact that he sails in a ship, and he should not be called a sailor for that reason. For it is not because he is sailing that he is called a ship's captain, but because of the craft he practices and his rule over sailors?

THRASYMACHUS: True.

SOCRATES: And is there something that is advantageous for each of these?

THRASYMACHUS: Certainly.

SOCRATES: And isn't it also the case that the natural aim of the craft is to consider and provide what is advantageous for each?

THRASYMACHUS: Yes, that is its aim.

SOCRATES: And is anything advantageous for each of the crafts themselves besides being as complete as possible?

---

[7] Proverbial characterization of an almost impossible task.

THRASYMACHUS: How do you mean?   341e

SOCRATES: It is like this: suppose you asked me whether it is satisfactory for a body to be a body, or whether it needs something else. I would answer, "Of course it needs something. In fact, that is why the craft of medicine has been discovered—because a body is deficient and it is not satisfactory for it to be like that. To provide what is advantageous, that is what the craft was developed for." Do you think I am speaking correctly in saying this, or not?

THRASYMACHUS: Correctly.   342a

SOCRATES: What about medicine itself? Is it deficient? Does a craft need some further virtue, as the eyes are in need of sight and the ears of hearing, so that another craft is needed to consider and provide what is advantageous for them? Does a craft have some similar deficiency itself, so that each craft needs another to consider what is advantageous for it? And does the craft that does the considering need still another, and so on without end? Or does each consider by itself what is advantageous for it? Does it need neither   342b itself nor another craft to consider what—in light of its own deficiency—is advantageous for it? Indeed, is there no deficiency or error in any craft? And is it inappropriate for any craft to consider what is advantageous for anything besides that with which it deals? And since it is itself correct, is it without fault or impurity so long as it is wholly and precisely the craft it is? Consider this with that precision of language you mentioned. Is it so or not?

THRASYMACHUS: It appears to be so.

SOCRATES: Doesn't it follow that medicine does not consider what is advantageous for medicine, but for the body?   342c

THRASYMACHUS: Yes.

SOCRATES: And horse breeding does not consider what is advantageous for horse breeding, but for horses? Indeed, no other craft considers what is advantageous for itself—since it has no further needs—but what is advantageous for that with which it deals?

THRASYMACHUS: Apparently so.

SOCRATES: Now surely, Thrasymachus, the various crafts rule over and are stronger than that with which they deal?

He gave in at this point as well, very reluctantly.

SOCRATES: So no kind of knowledge considers or enjoins what is advantageous for itself, but what is advantageous for the weaker, which is subject   342d to it.

He finally agreed to this too, although he tried to fight it. When he had agreed, however, I said:

Surely then, no doctor, to the extent that he is a doctor, considers or enjoins what is advantageous for himself, but what is advantageous for his patient?

For we agreed that a doctor, in the precise sense, is a ruler of bodies, not a moneymaker. Isn't that what we agreed?

THRASYMACHUS: Yes.

SOCRATES: So a ship's captain, in the precise sense, is a ruler of sailors, not a sailor?

THRASYMACHUS: That is what we agreed.

SOCRATES: Doesn't it follow that a ship's captain and ruler won't consider and enjoin what is advantageous for a captain, but what is advantageous for a sailor and his subject?

He reluctantly agreed.

SOCRATES: So then, Thrasymachus, no one in any position of rule, to the extent that he is a ruler, considers or enjoins what is advantageous for himself, but what is advantageous for his subject—that on which he practices his craft. It is to his subject and what is advantageous and proper for it that he looks, and everything he says and does, he says and does for it.

When we reached this point in the argument and it was clear to all that his account of justice had turned into its opposite, instead of answering, Thrasymachus said:

Tell me, Socrates, do you still have a wet nurse?

SOCRATES: What is that? Shouldn't you be giving answers rather than asking such things?

THRASYMACHUS: Because she is letting you run around sniveling and doesn't wipe your nose when you need it, since it is her fault that you do not know the difference between sheep and shepherds.

SOCRATES: What exactly is it I do not know?

THRASYMACHUS: You think that shepherds and cowherds consider what is good for their sheep and cattle, and fatten them and take care of them with some aim in mind other than what is good for their master and themselves. Moreover, you believe that rulers in cities—true rulers, that is—think about their subjects in a different way than one does about sheep, and that what they consider night and day is something other than what is advantageous for themselves. You are so far from understanding justice and what is just, and injustice and what is unjust, that you do not realize that justice is really the good of another, what is advantageous for the stronger and the ruler, and harmful to the one who obeys and serves. Injustice is the opposite, it rules those simpleminded—for that is what they really are—just people, and the ones it rules do what is advantageous for the other who is stronger; and they make the one they serve happy, but they do not make themselves the least bit happy.

You must consider it as follows, Socrates, or you will be the most naïve of all: a just man must always get less than does an unjust one. First, in their contracts with one another, when a just man is partner to an unjust, you will never find, when the partnership ends, that the just one gets more than the unjust, but less. Second, in matters relating to the city, when taxes are to be paid, a just man pays more on an equal amount of property, an unjust one less; but when the city is giving out refunds, a just man gets nothing while an unjust one makes a large profit. Finally, when each of them holds political office, a just person—even if he is not penalized in other ways—finds that his private affairs deteriorate more because he has to neglect them, that he gains no advantage from the public purse because of his justice, and that he is hated by his relatives and acquaintances because he is unwilling to do them an unjust favor. The opposite is true of an unjust man in every respect. I mean, of course, the person I described before: the man of great power who does better.[8] He is the one you should consider if you want to figure out how much more advantageous it is for the individual to be unjust than just. You will understand this most easily if you turn your thoughts to injustice of the most complete sort, the sort that makes those who do injustice happiest, and those who suffer it—those who are unwilling to do injustice—most wretched. The sort I mean is tyranny, because it uses both covert means and force to appropriate the property of others—whether it is sacred or secular, public or private—not little by little, but all at once. If someone commits a part of this sort of injustice and gets caught, he is punished and greatly reproached—temple robbers,[9] kidnappers, housebreakers, robbers, and thieves are what these partly unjust people are called when they commit those harms. When someone appropriates the possessions of the citizens, on the other hand, and then kidnaps and enslaves the possessors as well, instead of these shameful names he is called happy and blessed: not only by the citizens themselves, but even by all who learn that he has committed the whole of injustice. For it is not the fear of doing injustice, but of suffering it, that elicits the reproaches of those who revile injustice.

So you see, Socrates, injustice, if it is on a large enough scale, is stronger, freer, and more masterful than justice. And, as I said from the beginning, justice is what is advantageous for the stronger, while injustice is profitable and advantageous for oneself.

343e

344a

344b

344c

---

[8] Do better (*pleonektein*): an important notion in the *Republic,* connected to *pleonexia,* wanting to get and have more and more. *Pleonexia* is the chief cause of injustice (359c), since it leads one to try to get what belongs to other people, what isn't *one's own.* This concept is contrasted with *doing or having one's own,* which is, or is the cause of, justice (434a, 441e).

[9] The temples served as public treasuries, so a temple robber is the equivalent of a present-day bank robber.

344d   *Having, like a bath attendant, emptied this great flood of words into our ears*
         all at once, Thrasymachus was thinking of leaving. But those present wouldn't
         let him. They made him stay and give an account of what he had said. And
         I myself was particularly insistent:

You are marvelous, Thrasymachus; after hurling such a speech at us, you
surely cannot be thinking of leaving before you have adequately instructed
us—or learned yourself—whether you are right or not. Or do you think
344e   it is a trivial matter you are trying to determine, and not rather a way of
life—the one that would make living life that way most profitable for each
of us?

THRASYMACHUS: Do you mean that I do not think it is a serious matter?

SOCRATES: Either that, or you care nothing for us and so are not worried
about whether we will live better or worse lives because of our ignorance of
what you claim to know. No, be a good fellow and show some willingness
345a   to teach us—you won't do badly for yourself if you help a group as large
as ours. For my own part, I will tell you that I am not persuaded. I do not
believe that injustice is more profitable than justice, not even if you should
give it full scope to do what it wants. Suppose, my good fellow, that there
is an unjust person, and suppose he *does* have the power to do injustice,
whether by covert means or open warfare; nonetheless, he does not per-
345b   suade me that injustice is more profitable than justice. Perhaps someone
here besides myself feels the same as I do. So, blessed though you are, you
are going to have to fully persuade us that we are wrong to value justice
more highly than injustice in deliberating.

THRASYMACHUS: And how am I to persuade you? If you are not persuaded
by what I said just now, what more can I do? Am I to take my argument
and pour it into your very soul?

SOCRATES: No, by Zeus, do not do that! But first, stick to what you have
said, or, if you change your position, do it openly and do not try to deceive
345c   us. You see, Thrasymachus, having defined the true doctor—to continue
examining the things you said before—you did not consider it necessary
to maintain the same level of exactness when you later turned to the true
shepherd. You do not think a shepherd—to the extent that he is a shepherd—fattens sheep with the aim of doing what is best for them. But you
think that, like a guest about to be entertained at a feast, his aim is to eat
well or to make a future sale—as if he were a moneymaker rather than a
345d   shepherd. But of course, the only concern of the craft of shepherding is to
provide what is best for that with which it deals, since it itself is adequately
provided with all it needs to be at its best, as we know, when it does not
fall short in any way of being the craft of shepherding. That is why I, at

any rate, thought it necessary for us to agree before[10] that every kind of rule—to the extent that it is a kind of rule—does not seek anything other than what is best for the thing it rules and cares for, and this is true both in political and in private rule. But do you think that those who rule cit-   345e
ies—the ones who are truly rulers—rule willingly?

THRASYMACHUS: I do not think it, by Zeus, I know it.

SOCRATES: But, Thrasymachus, don't you realize that in other kinds of rule there is no willing ruler? On the contrary, they demand wages on the assumption that their ruling will benefit not themselves, but their subjects. For tell me, don't we say that each craft differs from every other in the   **346a**
power it has? Blessed though you are, please don't answer contrary to your belief, so that we can come to some definite conclusion.

THRASYMACHUS: Yes, that is what differentiates them.

SOCRATES: And doesn't each craft provide us with a particular benefit, different from the others? For example, medicine provides us with health, captaincy with safety at sea, and so on with the others?

THRASYMACHUS: Certainly.

SOCRATES: And doesn't wage-earning provide us with wages, since that is what it is capable of doing? Or would you call medicine the same craft as   346b
captaincy? Indeed, if you want to define matters precisely, as you proposed, even if someone who is a ship's captain becomes healthy because what is advantageous for him is sailing on the sea, you would not for that reason call what he does medicine, would you?

THRASYMACHUS: Of course not.

SOCRATES: Nor would you call wage-earning medicine, even if someone becomes healthy while earning wages?

THRASYMACHUS: Of course not.

SOCRATES: Nor would you call medicine wage-earning, even if someone earns pay while healing?

THRASYMACHUS: No.   346c

SOCRATES: We are agreed then, aren't we, that each craft brings its own special benefit?

THRASYMACHUS: Yes, we are.

SOCRATES: So whatever benefit all craftsmen jointly receive must clearly derive from their joint practice of some additional craft that is the same for each of them.

THRASYMACHUS: It seems so.

---

[10] 341e–342e above.

SOCRATES: And we say that the additional craft in question, which benefits the craftsmen by earning them wages, is the craft of wage-earning?

He reluctantly agreed.

346d SOCRATES: Then this very benefit, receiving wages, is not provided to each of them by his own craft. On the contrary, if we are to examine the matter precisely, medicine provides health and wage-earning provides a wage; house-building provides a house, and wage-earning, which accompanies it, provides a wage; and so on with the other crafts. Each of them does its own work and benefits that with which it deals. So, wages aside, is there any benefit that craftsmen get from their craft?

THRASYMACHUS: Apparently not.

346e SOCRATES: But he still provides a benefit, even when he works for nothing?

THRASYMACHUS: Yes, I think he does.

SOCRATES: Then, it is clear now, Thrasymachus, that no type of craft or rule provides what is beneficial for itself; but, as we have been saying for some time, it provides and enjoins what is beneficial for its subject, and aims at what is advantageous for *it*—the weaker, not the stronger. That is why I said just now, my dear Thrasymachus, that no one chooses to rule voluntarily and take other people's troubles in hand and straighten them out, but each asks for wages. You see, anyone who is going to practice his

347a type of craft well never does or enjoins what is best for himself—at least not when he is acting as his craft prescribes—but what is best for his subject. It is because of this, it seems, that wages must be provided to a person if he is going to be willing to rule, whether they are in the form of money or honor or a penalty if he refuses.

GLAUCON: What do you mean, Socrates? I am familiar with the first two kinds of wages, but I do not understand what penalty you mean, or how you can call it a wage.

SOCRATES: Then you do not understand the sort of wages for which the

347b best people rule, when they are willing to rule. Don't you know that those who love honor and those who love money are despised, and rightly so?

GLAUCON: I do.

SOCRATES: Well, then, that is why good people won't be willing to rule for the sake of money or honor. You see, if they are paid wages openly for ruling, they will be called hirelings, and if they take them covertly as the fruits of their rule, they will be called thieves. On the other hand, they won't rule for the sake of honor either, since they are not ambitious honor-lovers. So, if they are going to be willing to rule, some compulsion

347c or punishment must be brought to bear on them—that is probably why wanting to rule when one does not have to is thought to be shameful. Now, the greatest punishment for being unwilling to rule is being ruled by someone worse than oneself. And I think it is fear of that that makes good people rule when they do rule. They approach ruling, not as though they were going to do something good or as though they were going to enjoy themselves in it, but as something compulsory, since it cannot be entrusted to anyone better than—or even as good as—themselves. In a city 347d of good men, if it came into being, the citizens would fight in order *not to rule,* just as they now do in order to rule. There it would be quite clear that anyone who is really and truly a ruler does not naturally seek what is advantageous for himself, but what is so for his subject. As a result, anyone with any sense would prefer to be benefited by another than to go to the trouble of benefiting him. So I cannot at all agree with Thrasymachus that justice is what is advantageous for the stronger. But we will look further 347e into that another time. What Thrasymachus is now saying—that the life of an unjust person is better than that of a just one—seems to be of far greater importance. Which life would you choose, Glaucon? And which of our views do you think is closer to the truth?

GLAUCON: I think the life of a just person is more profitable.

SOCRATES: Did you hear all the good things Thrasymachus attributed a 348a moment ago to the unjust man?

GLAUCON: I did, but I am not persuaded.

SOCRATES: Then do you want us to persuade him, if we can find a way, that what he says is not true?

GLAUCON: Of course I do.

SOCRATES: Well, if we oppose him with a speech parallel to his speech enumerating in turn the many good things that come from being just, and he replies, and then we do, we will have to count and measure the good 348b things mentioned on each side, and we will need a jury to decide the case. But if, on the other hand, we investigate the question, as we have been doing, by seeking agreement with each other, we ourselves can be both jury and advocates at once.

GLAUCON: Certainly.

SOCRATES: Then which approach do you prefer?

GLAUCON: The second.

SOCRATES: Come on then, Thrasymachus, answer us from the beginning. You say, don't you, that complete injustice is more profitable than complete justice?

THRASYMACHUS: I certainly have said that. And I have told you why. 348c

SOCRATES: Well, then, what do you say about this? Do you call one of the two a virtue and the other a vice?

THRASYMACHUS: Of course.

SOCRATES: That is to say, you call justice a virtue and injustice a vice?

THRASYMACHUS: Is that likely, sweetest one, when I say that injustice is profitable and justice is not?

SOCRATES: Then what exactly do you say?

THRASYMACHUS: The opposite.

SOCRATES: That justice is a vice?

THRASYMACHUS: No, just very noble naiveté.[11]

348d SOCRATES: So you call injustice deviousness?

THRASYMACHUS: No, I call it being prudent.

SOCRATES: Do you also consider unjust people to be wise and good, Thrasymachus?

THRASYMACHUS: Yes, if they commit complete injustice and can bring cities and whole nations under their power. Perhaps, you thought I meant pickpockets? Not that such crimes aren't also profitable, if they are not found out. But they are not worth discussing by comparison to what I described.

348e SOCRATES: Yes, I am not unaware of what you mean. But this did surprise me: that you include injustice with virtue and wisdom, and justice with their opposites.

THRASYMACHUS: Nevertheless, that is where I put them.

SOCRATES: That is now a harder problem, comrade, and it is not easy to know what to say in response. If you had declared that injustice is more profitable, but agreed that it is a vice or shameful, as some others do, we could be discussing the matter on the basis of conventional norms. But now, obviously, you will say that injustice is fine and strong and apply to

349a it all the attributes we used to apply to justice, since you dare to include it with virtue and wisdom.

THRASYMACHUS: You have guessed my views exactly.

SOCRATES: All the same, we must not shrink from pursuing the argument and looking into this, just as long as I take you to be saying what you really think. You see, I believe that you really are not joking now, Thrasymachus, but saying what you believe to be the truth.

THRASYMACHUS: What difference does it make to you, whether I believe it or not? Isn't it *my account* you are supposed to be refuting?

349b SOCRATES: It makes no difference. But here is a further question I would like you to try to answer: do you think that a just person wants to do better than another just person?

---

[11] *Euētheia, kakoētheia:* Thrasymachus uses *euētheia* in the bad sense, to mean stupidity. Socrates takes him to mean it in the good sense of being straightforward, and so contrasts it with *kakoētheia*—deviousness. See 400e.

THRASYMACHUS: Not at all. Otherwise, he would not be the civilized and naïve person he actually is.

SOCRATES: What about than the just action?

THRASYMACHUS: No, not than that, either.

SOCRATES: And does he claim that he deserves to do better than an unjust person and believe that it is just for him to do so, or doesn't he believe that?

THRASYMACHUS: He would want to do better than him, and he would claim to deserve to do so, but he would not be able.

SOCRATES: That is not what I am asking, but whether a just person wants, and claims to deserve, to do better than an unjust person, but not than a just one? 349c

THRASYMACHUS: He does.

SOCRATES: What about an unjust person? Does he claim that he deserves to do better than a just person or a just action?

THRASYMACHUS: Of course he does; he thinks he deserves to do better than everyone.

SOCRATES: Then will an unjust person also do better than an *unjust* person or an *unjust* action, and will he strive to get the most he can for himself from everyone?

THRASYMACHUS: He will.

SOCRATES: Then let's put it this way: a just person does not do better than someone like himself, but someone unlike himself, whereas an unjust person does better than those who are like *and* those who are unlike him. 349d

THRASYMACHUS: Very well put.

SOCRATES: Now, an unjust person is wise and good, and a just one is neither?

THRASYMACHUS: That is well put, too.

SOCRATES: So isn't an unjust person also *like* a wise and good person, while the just person is not?

THRASYMACHUS: Of course. How could he fail to be like people who have such qualities, when he has them himself? But the unjust person is not like them.

SOCRATES: Fine. Then each of them has the qualities of the people he is like?

THRASYMACHUS: What else could he have?

SOCRATES: All right, Thrasymachus. Do you call one person musical and another non-musical? 349e

THRASYMACHUS: I do.

SOCRATES: Which of them is wise in music and which is not?

THRASYMACHUS: The musical one is wise, presumably, and the other not wise.

SOCRATES: And in the things in which he is wise, he is good; and in the things in which he is not wise, he is bad?

THRASYMACHUS: Yes.

SOCRATES: Isn't the same true of a doctor?

THRASYMACHUS: It is.

SOCRATES: Do you think, then, Thrasymachus, that a man who is a musician, when he is tuning his lyre and tightening and loosening the strings, wants to do better than another musician, and does he claim that that is what he deserves?

THRASYMACHUS: I do not.

SOCRATES: But he does want to do better than a non-musician?

THRASYMACHUS: Necessarily.

350a SOCRATES: What about a doctor? When he is prescribing food and drink, does he want to do better than another doctor or than medical practice?

THRASYMACHUS: Certainly not.

SOCRATES: But he does want to do better than a non-doctor?

THRASYMACHUS: Yes.

SOCRATES: In any branch of knowledge or ignorance, do you think that a knowledgeable person would intentionally try to take more for himself than another knowledgeable person, or to do or say more, and not rather exactly what the one like himself would do in the same situation?

THRASYMACHUS: No, I imagine it must be as you say.

SOCRATES: And what about an ignorant person? Doesn't he want to do **350b** better than both a knowledgeable person and an ignorant one?

THRASYMACHUS: I suppose so.

SOCRATES: A knowledgeable person is wise?

THRASYMACHUS: I agree.

SOCRATES: And a wise one is good?

THRASYMACHUS: I agree.

SOCRATES: So, a good and wise person does not want to do better than someone like himself, but someone both unlike and opposite to him.

THRASYMACHUS: So it seems.

SOCRATES: But a bad and ignorant person wants to do better than both his like and his opposite.

THRASYMACHUS: Apparently.

SOCRATES: Well, Thrasymachus, we found that an unjust person tries to do better than those like him and those unlike him. Didn't you say that?

THRASYMACHUS: I did.

SOCRATES: And that a just person won't do better than those like him, but   350c
those unlike him?

THRASYMACHUS: Yes.

SOCRATES: Then a just person is like a wise and good person, and an unjust
person is like an ignorant and bad one.

THRASYMACHUS: It looks that way.

SOCRATES: Moreover, we agreed that each has the qualities of the one he
resembles.

THRASYMACHUS: Yes, we did.

SOCRATES: A just person has turned out to be good and wise, then, and an
unjust one ignorant and bad.

Thrasymachus agreed to all this, not easily as I am telling it, but reluctantly,   350d
with toil, trouble, and—since it was summer—a quantity of sweat that was
amazing to behold. And then I saw something I had never seen before—
Thrasymachus blushing. But in any case, after we had agreed that justice is
virtue and wisdom and that injustice is vice and ignorance, I said:

All right, let's take that as established. But we also said that injustice is a
strong thing, or don't you remember that, Thrasymachus?

THRASYMACHUS: I remember. But I am not satisfied with what you are
now saying. I could make a speech about it, but if I did, I know that you
would say I was engaging in demagoguery. So, either allow me to say as
much as I want to say or, if you want to keep on asking questions, go ahead   350e
and ask them, and I shall say to you—as one does to old women telling
stories—"All right," and nod or shake my head.

SOCRATES: No, don't do that; not contrary to your own belief.

THRASYMACHUS: Then I will answer to please you, since you won't let me
make a speech. What else do you want?

SOCRATES: Nothing, by Zeus. But if that is what you are going to do, do
it, and I will ask the questions.

THRASYMACHUS: Ask them, then.

SOCRATES: All right, I will ask precisely what I asked before, so that we
may proceed in an orderly fashion with our argument about what sort of
thing justice is, as opposed to injustice. For it was claimed, I believe, that   **351a**
injustice is stronger and more powerful than justice. But now, if justice
is indeed wisdom and virtue, it will be easy to show, I suppose, that it is
stronger than injustice, since injustice is ignorance—no one could now be
ignorant of that. However, I, at any rate, do not want to consider the matter
in such simple terms, Thrasymachus, but to look into it in some such way
as this: would you say that a city may be unjust and try to enslave other   351b

cities unjustly, and succeed at enslaving them, and hold them in subjection which it enslaved in the past?

THRASYMACHUS: Of course. And that is what the best city will especially do, the one that is most completely unjust.

SOCRATES: I understand that that is your argument, but the point I want to examine is this: will the city that becomes stronger than another achieve this power without justice, or will it need the help of justice?

351c THRASYMACHUS: If what you said a moment ago stands, and justice is wisdom, it will need the help of justice; but if things are as I stated, it will need the help of injustice.

SOCRATES: I am impressed, Thrasymachus, that you are not merely nodding or shaking your head, but giving these fine answers.

THRASYMACHUS: That is because I am trying to please you.

SOCRATES: You are doing well at it, too. So please me some more by answering this question: do you think that a city, an army, a band of robbers or thieves, or any other group with a common unjust purpose would be able to achieve it if its members were unjust to each other?

THRASYMACHUS: Of course not.

351d SOCRATES: What if they were not unjust to one another? Would they achieve more?

THRASYMACHUS: Certainly.

SOCRATES: Because, Thrasymachus, injustice causes factions, hatreds, and quarrels among them, while justice brings friendship and a sense of common purpose. Isn't that so?

THRASYMACHUS: I will say it is, in order not to disagree with you.

SOCRATES: You are still doing well on that front, which is very good of you. So tell me this: if the function of injustice is to produce hatred wherever it occurs, then whenever it arises, whether among free men or slaves, won't it make them hate one another, form factions, and be unable to achieve 351e any common purpose?

THRASYMACHUS: Of course.

SOCRATES: What if it arises between two people? Won't they be at odds, hate each other, and be enemies both to one another and to just people?

THRASYMACHUS: They will.

SOCRATES: Well, then, my amazing fellow, if injustice arises within a single individual, will it lose its power or will it retain it undiminished?

THRASYMACHUS: Let's say that it retains it undiminished.

SOCRATES: Apparently, then, its power is such that whenever it comes to exist in something—whether in a city, a family, an army, or anything else whatsoever—it makes that thing, first of all, incapable of acting in concert

with itself, because of the faction and difference it creates; and, second of $\quad$ 352a
all, an enemy to itself, and to what is in every way its opposite: namely,
justice. Isn't that so?

THRASYMACHUS: Of course.

SOCRATES: And in a single individual, too, I presume, it will produce the
very same effects that it is in its nature to produce. First, it will make him
incapable of acting because of inner faction and not being of one mind with
himself; second, it will make him his own enemy as well as the enemy of
just people. Isn't that right?

THRASYMACHUS: Yes.

SOCRATES: But, my dear fellow, aren't the gods also just?

THRASYMACHUS: Let's say they are. $\quad$ 352b

SOCRATES: Then an unjust person will also be an enemy of the gods,
Thrasymachus, while a just person will be their friend?

THRASYMACHUS: Feast yourself confidently on the argument! Don't worry,
I won't oppose you, so as not to arouse the enmity of our friends here.

SOCRATES: Come on, then, complete the banquet for me by continuing
to answer as you have been doing now. We have shown that just people
are wiser and better and more capable of acting, while unjust ones are not
even able to act together. For whenever we speak of men who are unjust $\quad$ 352c
acting together to effectively achieve a common goal, what we say is not
altogether true. They would never have been able to keep their hands off
each other if they were completely unjust. But clearly there must have been
some sort of justice in them that at least prevented them from doing injustice among themselves at the same time as they were doing it to others. And
it was this that enabled them to achieve what they did. When they started
doing unjust things, they were only halfway corrupted by their injustice.
For those who are wholly bad and completely unjust are also completely
incapable of acting. All this I now see to be the truth, and not what you first $\quad$ 352d
maintained. However, we must now examine the question, as we proposed
to do before,[12] of whether just people also live better and are happier than
unjust ones. I think it is clear even now from what we have said that this
is so, but we must consider it further. After all, the argument concerns no
ordinary topic, but the way we ought to live.

THRASYMACHUS: Go ahead and consider.

SOCRATES: I will. Tell me, do you think there is such a thing as the function of a horse? $\quad$ 352e

THRASYMACHUS: I do.

---

[12] 347e.

SOCRATES: And would you take the function of a horse or of anything else to be that which one can do only with it, or best with it?

THRASYMACHUS: I don't understand.

SOCRATES: Let me put it this way: is it possible for you to see with anything except eyes?

THRASYMACHUS: Certainly not.

SOCRATES: Or for you to hear with anything except ears?

THRASYMACHUS: No.

SOCRATES: Would it be right, then, for us to say that these things are their functions?

THRASYMACHUS: Of course.

353a SOCRATES: Again, couldn't you use a dagger, a carving knife, or lots of other things in pruning a vine?

THRASYMACHUS: Certainly.

SOCRATES: But nothing would do a better job than a pruning knife designed for the purpose?

THRASYMACHUS: That's true.

SOCRATES: Shall we take pruning to be its function, then?

THRASYMACHUS: Yes.

SOCRATES: Now I think you will understand better what I was asking earlier when I asked whether the function of each thing is what it alone can do or what it can do better than anything else.

353b THRASYMACHUS: I do understand, and I think that that is the function of anything.

SOCRATES: All right. Does there seem to you also to be a virtue for each thing to which some function is assigned? Let's go over the same ground again. We say that eyes have some function?

THRASYMACHUS: They do.

SOCRATES: So eyes also have a virtue?

THRASYMACHUS: They do.

SOCRATES: And ears have a function?

THRASYMACHUS: Yes.

SOCRATES: So they also have a virtue?

THRASYMACHUS: They have a virtue too.

SOCRATES: What about everything else? Doesn't the same hold?

THRASYMACHUS: It does.

353c SOCRATES: Well, then. Could eyes perform their function well if they lacked their proper virtue but had the vice instead?

THRASYMACHUS: How could they? For don't you mean if they had blindness instead of sight?

SOCRATES: Whatever their virtue is. You see, I am not now asking about that, but about whether it is by means of their own proper virtue that their function performs the things it performs well, and by means of vice badly?

THRASYMACHUS: What you say is true.

SOCRATES: So, if ears are deprived of their own virtue, they too perform their function badly?

THRASYMACHUS: Of course.

SOCRATES: And the same argument applies to everything else?   353d

THRASYMACHUS: So it seems to me, at least.

SOCRATES: Come on, then, and let's next consider this: does the soul have some function that you could not perform with anything else—for example, taking care of things, ruling, deliberating, and all other such things? Is there anything else besides a soul to which you could rightly assign these and say that they are special to it?

THRASYMACHUS: No, there is nothing else.

SOCRATES: Then what about living? Don't we say that it is a function of a soul?

THRASYMACHUS: Absolutely.

SOCRATES: And don't we also say that a soul has a virtue?

THRASYMACHUS: We do.

SOCRATES: Will a soul ever perform its functions well, then, Thrasymachus,   353e
if it is deprived of its own proper virtue, or is that impossible?

THRASYMACHUS: It is impossible.

SOCRATES: It is necessary, then, that a bad soul rules and takes care of things badly, and that a good soul does all these things well?

THRASYMACHUS: It is necessary.

SOCRATES: Now, didn't we agree that justice is a soul's virtue and injustice its vice?

THRASYMACHUS: Yes, we did agree.

SOCRATES: So a just soul and a just man will live well and an unjust one badly.

THRASYMACHUS: Apparently so, according to your argument.

SOCRATES: And surely anyone who lives well is blessed and happy, and   354a
anyone who does not is the opposite.

THRASYMACHUS: Of course.

SOCRATES: Therefore, a just person is happy and an unjust one wretched.

THRASYMACHUS: Let's say so.

SOCRATES: But surely it is profitable, not to be wretched, but to be happy.

THRASYMACHUS: Of course.

SOCRATES: So then, blessed Thrasymachus, injustice is never more profitable than justice.

THRASYMACHUS: Let that be your banquet, Socrates, at the feast of Bendis.

SOCRATES: Given by you, Thrasymachus, after you became gentle with me and ceased to be difficult. Yet I have not had a good banquet. But that is my fault, not yours. I seem to have behaved like those gluttons who snatch at every dish that passes and taste it before having properly savored the preceding one. Before finding the first thing we inquired about—namely, what justice is—I let that go, and turned to investigate whether it is a kind of vice and ignorance or a kind of wisdom and virtue. Then an argument came up about injustice being more profitable than justice, and I could not refrain from abandoning the previous one and following up on it. Hence the result of the discussion, so far as I am concerned, is that I know nothing. For when I do not know what justice is, I will hardly know whether it is a kind of virtue or not, or whether a person who has it is happy or unhappy.

BOOK II

SOCRATES' NARRATION CONTINUES: *When I had said this, I thought I had done with the discussion. But it all turned out to be only a prelude, as it were. You see, Glaucon, who is always very courageous in everything, refused on this occasion, too, to accept Thrasymachus' capitulation. Instead, he said:*

Do you want to *seem* to have persuaded us, Socrates, that it is better in every way to be just rather than unjust, or do you want to *really* persuade us of this?

SOCRATES: I want to really persuade you, if I can.

GLAUCON: Well, then, you certainly are not doing what you want. Tell me, do you think there is a sort of good we would choose to have, not because we desire its consequences, but because we would welcome it for its own sake—enjoying, for example, and all the harmless pleasures from which nothing results afterward beyond enjoying having them?

SOCRATES: Certainly, I think there is such a thing.

GLAUCON: And is there a sort of good we love for its own sake, and also for the sake of its consequences—knowing, for example, and seeing, and being healthy? For we welcome such things, I imagine, on both counts.

SOCRATES: Yes.

GLAUCON: And do you also recognize a third kind of good, which includes physical training, medical treatment when sick, and both medicine itself

and other ways of making money? We would say that these are burdensome but beneficial to us, and we would not choose to have them for their
own sake, but for the sake of the wages and other things that are their   357d
consequences.

SOCRATES: Yes, certainly, there is also this third kind. But what of it?

GLAUCON: In which of them do you place justice?

SOCRATES: I myself put it in the finest one—the one that anyone who is   358a
going to be blessed with happiness must love both because of itself and
because of its consequences.

GLAUCON: That is not what the masses think. On the contrary, they think
it is of the burdensome kind: the one that must be practiced for the sake of
the wages and the popularity that come from a good reputation, but that
is to be avoided just because of itself.

SOCRATES: I know that is the general view. Thrasymachus has been faulting
justice and praising injustice on these grounds for some time. But it seems
that I am a slow learner.

GLAUCON: Come on, then, listen to what I have to say as well, and see   358b
whether you still have that problem. You see, I think Thrasymachus gave
up before he had to, as if he were a snake you had charmed. Yet, to my
way of thinking, there was still no demonstration on either side. For I want
to hear what justice and injustice are, and what power each has when it is
just by itself in the soul. I want to leave out of account the wages and the
consequences of each of them.

So, if you agree, I will renew the argument of Thrasymachus. First,
I will state what sort of thing people consider justice to be, and what its   358c
origins are. Second, I will argue that all who practice it do so unwillingly,
as something compulsory, not as something good. Third, I will argue that
they have good reason to act as they do. For the life of the unjust person
is, they say, much better than that of the just one.

It isn't, Socrates, that I believe any of that myself. I am perplexed, indeed,
and my ears are deafened listening to Thrasymachus and countless others.
But I have yet to hear anyone defend justice in the way I want, as being   358d
better than injustice. I want to hear it praised just by itself, and I think that
I am most likely to learn this from you. That is why I am going to speak at
length in praise of the unjust life: by doing so, I will be showing you the
way I want to hear you denouncing injustice and praising justice. But see
whether you want me to do what I am saying or not.

SOCRATES: I want it most of all. Indeed, what subject could a person with
any sense enjoy talking and hearing about more often?   358e

GLAUCON: Excellent sentiments. Now, listen to what I said I was going to
discuss first—what justice is like and what its origins are. People say, you

see, that to do injustice is naturally good and to suffer injustice bad. But the
badness of suffering it far exceeds the goodness of doing it. Hence, those
who have done and suffered injustice and who have tasted both—the ones
who lack the power to do it and avoid suffering it—decide that it is profit-
359a able to come to an agreement with each other neither to do injustice nor
to suffer it. As a result, they begin to make laws and covenants; and what
the law commands, they call lawful and just. That, they say, is the origin
and very being[1] of justice. It is in between the best and the worst. The
best is to do injustice without paying the penalty; the worst is to suffer it
without being able to take revenge. Justice is in the middle between these
359b two extremes. People love it, not because it is a good thing, but because
they are too weak to do injustice with impunity. Someone who has the
power to do it, however—someone who is truly a man—would not make
an agreement with anyone, neither to do injustice nor to suffer it. For
him, that would be insanity. That is the nature of justice, according to the
argument, Socrates, and those are its natural origins.

We can see most clearly that those who practice it do so unwillingly,
because they lack the power to do injustice, if we imagine the following
359c thought-experiment. Suppose we grant to the just and the unjust person
the freedom to do whatever they like. We can then follow both of them
and see where their appetites would lead. And we will catch the just person
red-handed, traveling the same road as the unjust one. The reason for this
is the desire to do better. This is what every nature naturally pursues as
good. But by law and force, it is made to deviate from this path and honor
equality.

They would especially have the freedom I am talking about if they had
359d the power that the ancestor of Gyges of Lydia is said to have possessed. The
story goes that he was a shepherd in the service of the ruler of Lydia. There
was a violent thunderstorm, and an earthquake broke open the ground
and created a chasm at the place where he was tending his sheep. Seeing
this, he was filled with amazement and went down into it. And there, in
addition to many other amazing things of which we are told stories, he
saw a hollow, bronze horse. There were windowlike openings in it and,
peeping in, he saw a corpse, which seemed to be of more than human size,
359e wearing nothing but a gold ring on its finger. He took off the ring and
came out of the chasm. He wore the ring at the usual monthly meeting of
shepherds that reported to the king on the state of the flocks. And as he
was sitting among the others, he happened to turn the setting of the ring
toward himself, toward the inside of his hand. When he did this, he became

---

[1] *Ousia* ("being" or "substance") is an abstract noun derived from the verb *einai*
("to be"). The being of justice is what justice really or essentially is.

invisible to those sitting near him, and they went on talking as if he had   360a
gone. He was amazed at this and, fingering the ring, he turned the setting
outward again and became visible. So, he experimented with the ring
to test whether it indeed had this power—and it did. If he turned the
setting inward, he became invisible; if he turned it outward, he became
visible again. As soon as he realized this, he arranged to become one of the
messengers sent to report to the king. On arriving there, he seduced the   360b
king's wife, attacked the king with her help, killed him, and in this way
took over the kingdom.

Let's suppose, then, that there were two such rings, one worn by the
just person, the other by the unjust. Now no one, it seems, would be so
incorruptible that he would stay on the path of justice, or bring himself to
keep away from other people's possessions and not touch them, when he
could take whatever he wanted from the marketplace with impunity, go
into people's houses and have sex with anyone he wished, kill or release   360c
from prison anyone he wished, and do all the other things that would
make him like a god among humans. And in so behaving, he would do no
differently than the unjust person, but both would pursue the same course.

This, some would say, is strong evidence that no one is just willingly,
but only when compelled. No one believes justice to be a good thing when
it is kept private, since whenever either person thinks he can do injustice
with impunity, he does it. Indeed, all men believe that injustice is far more
profitable to themselves than is justice. And what they believe is true, so   360d
the exponent of this argument will say. For someone who did not want to
do injustice, given this sort of opportunity, and who did not touch other
people's property, would be thought most wretched and most foolish by
everyone aware of the situation. Though, of course, they would praise him
in public, deceiving each other for fear of suffering injustice. So much for
my second topic.

As for decision itself about the life of the two we are discussing, if we
contrast the extremes of justice and injustice, we shall be able to make the   360e
decision correctly; but if we don't, we won't. What, then, is the contrast
I have in mind? It is this: we will subtract nothing from the injustice of
the unjust person, and nothing from the justice of the just one. On the
contrary, we will take each to be perfect in his own pursuit. First, then,
let the unjust person act like clever craftsmen. An eminent ship's captain
or doctor, for example, knows the difference between what his craft can
and cannot do. He attempts the first but lets the second go by. And if   361a
he happens to slip, he can put things right. In the same way, if he is to
be completely unjust, let the unjust person correctly attempt unjust acts
and remain undetected. The one who is caught should be thought inept.
For the extreme of injustice is to be believed to be just without actually being so. And our completely unjust person must be given complete

injustice—nothing must be subtracted from it. We must allow that, while doing the greatest injustice, he has nonetheless provided himself with the

361b   greatest reputation for justice. If he does happen to slip up, he must be able to put it right, either through his ability to speak persuasively if any of his unjust activities are discovered, or to use force if force is needed, because he is courageous and strong and has provided himself with wealth and friends.

Having hypothesized such a person, let's now put the just man next to him in our argument—someone who is simple and noble and who, as Aeschylus says, does not want to be believed to be good, but to be so.[2] We

361c   must take away his reputation. For a reputation for justice would bring him honor and rewards, so that it would not be clear whether he is being just for the sake of justice, or for the sake of those honors and rewards. We must strip him of everything except justice, and make his situation the opposite of the unjust person's. Though he does no injustice, he must have the greatest reputation for it, so that he may be tested with regard to justice by seeing whether or not he can withstand a bad reputation and its consequences. Let him stay like that, unchanged, until he is dead—just, but

361d   all his life believed to be unjust. In this way, both will reach the extremes, the one of justice and the other of injustice, and we will be able to judge which of them is happier.

SOCRATES: Whew! My dear Glaucon, how vigorously you have scoured each of the men in our competition, just as you would a pair of statues for an art competition.

GLAUCON: I am doing the best I can. Since the two are as I have described, in any case, it should not be difficult to complete the account of the sort of life that awaits each of them, but it must be done. And if what I say sounds

361e   crude, Socrates, remember that it is not *I* who speak, but those who praise injustice at the expense of justice. They will say that the just person in such circumstances will be whipped, stretched on a rack, chained, blinded with a

362a   red-hot iron, and, at the end, when he has suffered every sort of bad thing, he will be impaled, and will realize then that one should not want to be just, but to be believed to be just. Indeed, Aeschylus' words are far more correctly applied to the unjust man. For people will say that it is really the unjust person who does not want to be believed to be unjust, but actually to be so, because he bases his practice on the truth about things and does not allow reputation to regulate his life. He is the one who "harvests a deep

362b   furrow in his mind, where wise counsels propagate." First, he rules his city because of his reputation for justice. Next, he marries into any family he

---

[2] In Aeschylus, *Seven against Thebes* 592–94, it is said of Amphiaraus, "he did not wish to be believed to be the best but to be it." The passage continues with the words Glaucon quotes below at 362a–b.

wishes, gives his children in marriage to anyone he wishes, has contracts and partnerships with anyone he wants, and, besides benefiting himself in all these ways, he profits because he is not disgusted by doing injustice. In any contest, public or private, he is the winner and does better than his enemies. And by doing better than them, he becomes wealthy, benefits his friends, and harms his enemies. He makes adequate sacrifices to the gods and sets up magnificent offerings to them, and takes much better care of the gods—and, indeed, of the human beings he favors—than the just person. So he may reasonably expect that the gods, in turn, will love him more than the just person. That is why they say, Socrates, that gods and humans provide a better life for the unjust person than for the just one.

362c

When Glaucon had said this, I had it in mind to respond, but his brother Adeimantus intervened:

362d

You surely do not think that the argument has been adequately stated?

SOCRATES: Why shouldn't I?

ADEIMANTUS: The most important point has not been mentioned.

SOCRATES: Well, then, as the saying goes, a man's brother must stand by him.[3] So if Glaucon has omitted something, you must help him. Though, for my part at any rate, what he has already said is quite enough to throw me to the canvas and make me incapable of coming to the aid of justice.

362e

ADEIMANTUS: Nonsense. But listen to what more I have to say, as well. You see, in order to clarify what Glaucon has in mind, we should also fully explore the arguments that are opposed to the ones he gave—those that praise justice and disparage injustice. As you know, when fathers speak to their sons to give them advice, they say that one must be just, as do all those who have others in their charge. But they do not praise justice itself, only the good reputation it brings: the inducement they offer is that if we are reputed to be just, then, as a result of our reputation, we will get political offices, good marriages, and all the things that Glaucon recently said that the just man would get as a result of having a good reputation. But these people have even more to say about the consequences of reputation. For by throwing in being well thought of by the gods, they have plenty of good things to talk about—all the ones the gods are said to give to those who are pious. For example, the noble Hesiod and Homer say such things. For Hesiod says that the gods make the oak trees "bear acorns at the top, bees in the middle, and fleecy sheep heavy laden with wool" for those who are just, and tells of many other good things akin to these.[4] And Homer says pretty much the same:

363a

363b

---

[3] See Homer, *Odyssey* xvi.97–98.

[4] Hesiod, *Works and Days* 332–33.

When a good king, in his piety,
363c   Upholds justice, the black earth bears
Wheat and barley for him, and his trees are heavy with fruit,
His sheep bear lambs unfailingly and the sea yields up its fish.[5]

Musaeus and his son claim that the gods give just people even more exciting goods than these. In their account, they lead the just to Hades, seat them on couches, provide them with a symposium of pious people, crown them
363d   with wreaths, and make them spend all their time drinking—as if they thought eternal drunkenness was the finest wage of virtue. Others stretch even further the wages that virtue receives from the gods. For they say that someone who is pious and keeps his promises leaves his children's children and a whole race behind him. In these and other similar ways, they praise justice. But the impious and unjust they bury in mud in Hades, and they compel them to carry water in a sieve. They bring them into bad repute
363e   while they are still alive. And all those penalties that Glaucon gave to just people who are thought to be unjust, they give to the unjust ones. But they have nothing else to say.

That, then, is the praise and blame given to each. But in addition, Socrates, there is another kind of argument about justice and injustice for you to consider—one that is used both by private individuals and by poets.
364a   With one voice they all chant the hymn that justice and temperance are fine things, but difficult and onerous, while intemperance and injustice are sweet and easy to acquire and are only shameful by repute and convention. They also say that unjust deeds are, for the most part, more profitable than just ones; and whereas they are perfectly willing to bestow public and private honors on bad people—provided they have wealth and other types of power—and to declare them to be happy, they dishonor and disregard
364b   those who happen to be in any way weak or poor, even though they admit that they are better than the others.

But most amazing of all are the accounts they give of the gods and virtue, and how it is that the gods, too, assign misfortune and a bad life to many good people, and the opposite fate to their opposites. Begging priests and prophets go to the doors of rich people and persuade them that, through sacrifices and charms, they have acquired a god-given power: if the rich person or any of his ancestors has committed an injustice, they can
364c   fix it with pleasant rituals. And if he wishes to injure an enemy, he will be able to harm a just one or an unjust one alike at little cost, since by means of spells and enchantments they can persuade the gods to do their bidding.

And the poets are brought forward as witnesses to all these accounts. Some harp on the ease of vice, on the grounds that

---

[5] Homer, *Odyssey* xix.109.

Vice in abundance is easy to get,
The road is smooth and begins beside you,   364d
But the gods have put sweat between us and virtue

and a road that is long, rough, and steep.[6] Others quote Homer to bear
witness that the gods can be influenced by humans, since he too said:

Even the gods themselves can be swayed by prayer.
And with sacrifices and soothing promises,
Incense and libation-drinking, human beings turn them from their
    purpose,   364e
When someone has transgressed and sinned.[7]

And they present a noisy throng of books by Musaeus and Orpheus—who
are the offspring, they claim, of Selene and the Muses—on which they base
their rituals. And they persuade not only private individuals, but whole
cities, that there are in fact absolutions and purifications for unjust deeds.
For the living, these consist of ritual sacrifices and pleasant games. But there
are also special rites for the dead. These initiations, as they call them, free   365a
people from evils hereafter, while terrible things await those who have not
performed the rituals.

With so many things of this sort, my dear Socrates, being said about
virtue and vice, and about how human beings and gods honor them, what
effect do we suppose they have on the souls of young people? I mean those
who are naturally gifted and able to flit, so to speak, from one of these sayings to another and gather from them an impression of what sort of people
they should be, and of how best to travel the road of life. He would surely   365b
ask himself Pindar's question: "Is it by justice or by crooked tricks that I
will scale the higher wall," and so live out my life surrounded by secure
defenses? And he will answer: "As for what people say, they say that there
is no advantage in my being just if I am not also thought just, whereas the
troubles and penalties of being just are apparent; but the unjust person,
who has secured for himself a reputation for justice, lives the life of a god.
Since, then, 'opinion forcibly overcomes truth,' and 'controls happiness,'
as the wise men say, I must surely turn entirely to it.[8] I should create an   365c
illusionist painting of virtue around me to deceive those who come near,
but keep behind it the wise Archilochus' greedy and cunning fox."

"But surely," someone will object, "it is not easy for evil to remain
always hidden." We will reply that nothing great is easy. And, in any case,
if we are to be happy, we must go where the tracks of the arguments lead.   365d

---

[6] *Works and Days* 287–89, with minor alterations.

[7] *Iliad* ix.497–501, with minor alterations.

[8] The quotation is attributed to Simonides, who is cited by Polemarchus in Book i.

To remain undiscovered we will form secret societies and political clubs.
And there are teachers of persuasion to make us clever in dealing with
assemblies and law courts. Therefore, partly by persuasion, partly by force,
we will contrive to do better than other people, without paying the penalty.

"But surely we cannot hide from the gods or overpower them by force!"
Well, if the gods do not exist, or do not concern themselves with human
affairs, why should we worry at all about hiding from them? On the other
hand, if they do exist, and do care about us, we know nothing about them

365e   except what we have learned from the laws and from the poets who give
their genealogies. But these are the very people who tell us that the gods
can be persuaded and influenced by sacrifices, gentle prayers, and offerings. Hence, we should believe them on both matters, or on neither. If we
believe them, we should be unjust and offer sacrifices from the fruits of our

366a   injustice. For if we are just, our only gain is not to be punished by the gods,
but we will lose the profits of our injustice. But if we are unjust, we will
get those profits, and afterward we will entreat the gods and, persuading
them, escape with our crimes and transgressions unpunished.

"But in Hades, won't we pay the penalty for crimes committed here,
either ourselves or through our children's children?" "My friend," the
young man will say as he does his rational calculation, "mystery rites and
the gods of absolution have great power. The greatest cities tell us this, as do

366b   those children of the gods who have become the gods' poets and prophets
and reveal it to be so."

On the basis of what further argument, then, should we choose justice
over the greatest injustice? For if we possess such injustice with a false
façade, we will do as we have a mind to among gods and humans, both
while we are living and when we are dead, as both the masses and the emi-

366c   nent claim. So given all that has been said, Socrates, what device could get
someone with any power—whether of mind, wealth, body, or family—to
be willing to honor justice, and not laugh aloud when he hears it praised?

Indeed, if anyone can show that what we have said is false, and has
adequate knowledge that justice is best, what he feels for unjust people
won't be anger, but a large measure of forgiveness. After all, he knows
that apart from someone of godlike character who is disgusted by doing
injustice, or someone who has gained knowledge and avoids injustice for

366d   that reason, no one is just willingly. Through cowardice or old age or some
other weakness, people do indeed object to injustice. But it is obvious that
they do so only because they lack the power to do injustice. For the first
of them to gain that power is the first to do as much injustice as he can.

And all this has no other cause than the one that led to the whole of
Glaucon's and my argument with you, Socrates. "Socrates, you amazing

366e   man," we said, "of all of you who claim to praise justice, beginning from
the earliest heroes of old whose accounts survive up to the men of the

present day, not one has ever blamed injustice or praised justice except by mentioning the reputations, honors, and rewards that are their consequences. No one has ever adequately described what each does itself, through its own power, by its presence in the soul of the person who possesses it, even if it remains hidden from gods and humans. No one, whether in poetry or in private discussions, has adequately argued that injustice is the greatest evil a soul can have in it, and justice the greatest good. If all of **367a** you had spoken in this way and had tried to persuade us from our earliest youth, we would not now be guarding against one another's injustice, but each would be his own best guardian, afraid that by doing injustice he would be living on intimate terms with the worst thing possible."

That, Socrates, and probably other things in addition, are what Thrasymachus (or possibly someone else) might say in discussing justice and injustice—crudely inverting their power, in my view. But I—for I **367b** have no reason to hide anything from you—want to hear the opposite from you, and that is why I am speaking with all the force I can muster. So do not merely demonstrate to us by argument that justice is stronger than injustice, but tell us what each one itself does, because of itself, to someone who possesses it, that makes the one bad and the other good. Follow Glaucon's advice and do not take reputations into account.[9] For if you do not deprive justice and injustice of their true reputations and attach false ones to them, we will say that it is not justice you are praising, but its reputation; nor injustice you are condemning, but its reputation; and that you are encouraging us to be unjust but keep it secret. In that case, we will **367c** say that you agree with Thrasymachus that justice is the good of another, the advantage of the stronger, while injustice is one's own advantage and profit, though not the advantage of the weaker.

You agree that justice is one of the greatest goods, the ones that are worth having for the sake of their consequences, but much more so for their own sake—such as seeing, hearing, knowing, being healthy, of course, and all the others that are genuine goods by nature and not simply by repute. **367d** This is what I want you to praise about justice. How does it—because of its very self—benefit its possessor, and how does injustice harm him? Leave wages and reputations for others to praise.

I can put up with other people praising justice and blaming injustice in that way—extolling the reputations and wages of the one and denigrating those of the other. But I won't put up with that from you (unless you insist on it). For you have spent your whole life investigating this and nothing else. So do not merely demonstrate to us by argument that justice is stron- **367e** ger than injustice, but show what effect each one itself has, because of itself,

---

[9] At 361b–c.

on the person who has it—the one for good, the other for bad—whether it remains hidden from gods and human beings or not.

Now, I had always admired the natural characters of Glaucon and Adeimantus, but I was especially pleased when I heard what they had to say on this occasion, and I replied:

368a   Sons of that man,[10] Glaucon's lover was not wrong to begin the elegy he wrote, when you distinguished yourselves at the battle of Megara, by addressing you as "Sons of Ariston, godlike family of a famous man." That, my dear friends, was well said, in my view. For something altogether godlike must have affected you if you are not convinced that injustice is better than justice and yet can speak like that on its behalf. And I do believe that you really are unconvinced by your own words. I infer this

368b   from your general character, since if I had only your arguments to go on, I would not trust you. The more I trust you, however, the more I am at a loss as to what to do. I do not see how I can be of help. Indeed, I believe I am incapable of it. And here is my evidence: I thought that what I said to Thrasymachus showed that justice is better than injustice, but you won't accept that from me as a proof. On the other hand, I do not see how I can refuse my help. For I fear that it may even be impious to have breath in

368c   one's body and the ability to speak, and yet stand idly by and not defend justice when it is being prosecuted. The best thing, then, is to give justice any assistance I can.

Glaucon and the others begged me not to abandon the argument but to help in every way to track down what justice and injustice each is, and the truth about their respective benefits. So I told them what I had in mind:

The investigation we are undertaking is not an easy one, in my view, but requires keen eyesight. So, since we are not clever people, I think we

368d   should adopt the method of investigation that we would use if, lacking keen eyesight, we were told to identify small letters from a distance, and then noticed that the same letters existed elsewhere in a larger size and on a larger surface. We would consider it a godsend, I think, to be allowed to identify the larger ones first, and then to examine the smaller ones to see whether they are really the same.

ADEIMANTUS: Of course we would. But how is this case similar to our

368e   investigation of justice in your view?

SOCRATES: I will tell you. We say, don't we, that there is a justice that belongs to a single man, and also one that belongs to a whole city?

---

[10] Sometimes taken to be a facetious, indexical reference to Thrasymachus, whose heirs (sons) in the argument Glaucon and Adeimantus self-confessedly are. It is more likely, however, that it is an honorific expression equivalent in meaning to "that well-known man."

ADEIMANTUS: Certainly.

SOCRATES: And a city is larger than a single man?

ADEIMANTUS: Yes, it is larger.

SOCRATES: Perhaps, then, there will be more justice in the larger thing, and it will be easier to discern. So, if you are willing, let's first find out what sort of thing justice is in cities, and afterward look for it in the individual, **369a** to see if the larger entity is similar in form to the smaller one.

ADEIMANTUS: I think that is a fine idea.

SOCRATES: If, in our discussion, we could look at a city coming to be, wouldn't we also see its justice coming to be, and its injustice as well?

ADEIMANTUS: We probably would.

SOCRATES: And once that process is completed, could we expect to find what we are looking for more easily?   369b

ADEIMANTUS: Yes, much more easily.

SOCRATES: Do you think we should try to carry it out then? It is no small task, in my view. So, think it over.

ADEIMANTUS: It has been thought over. Don't do anything besides try.

SOCRATES: Well, then, a city comes to exist, I believe, because none of us is individually self-sufficient, but each has many needs he cannot satisfy. Or do you think that a city is founded on some other principle?

ADEIMANTUS: No, none.

SOCRATES: Then because we have many needs, and because one of us calls on another out of one need, and on a third out of a different need, we   369c gather many into a single settlement as partners and helpers. And we call such a shared settlement a city. Isn't that so?

ADEIMANTUS: Yes, indeed.

SOCRATES: And if they share things with one another—if they give something to one another, or take something from one another—don't they do so because each believes that this is better for himself?

ADEIMANTUS: Of course.

SOCRATES: Come on, then, let's, in our discussion, create a city from the beginning. But its real creator, it seems, will be our need.

ADEIMANTUS: Certainly.

SOCRATES: Now, the first and greatest of our needs is to provide food in   369d order to sustain existence and life.

ADEIMANTUS: Yes, absolutely.

SOCRATES: The second is for shelter, and the third is for clothes and things of that sort.

ADEIMANTUS: That's right.

SOCRATES: Tell me, then, how will a city be able to provide all this? Won't one person have to be a farmer, another a builder, and another a weaver? And shouldn't we add a shoemaker to them, or someone else to take care of our bodily needs?

ADEIMANTUS: Of course.

SOCRATES: A city with the barest necessities, then, would consist of four or five men?

369e

ADEIMANTUS: Apparently.

SOCRATES: Well, then, should each of them contribute his own work for the common use of all? I mean, should a farmer, although he is only one person, provide food for four people, and spend quadruple the time and labor to provide food to be shared by them all? Or should he not be concerned about everyone else? Should he produce one quarter the food in one quarter the time for himself alone? Should he spend the other three quarters providing a house, a cloak, and shoes? Should he save himself the bother of sharing with other people and mind his own business on his own?

370a

ADEIMANTUS: The first alternative, Socrates, is perhaps easier.

SOCRATES: There is nothing strange in that, by Zeus. You see, it occurred to me while you were speaking that, in the first place, we are not all born alike. On the contrary, each of us differs somewhat in nature from the others, one being suited to one job, another to another. Or don't you think so?

370b

ADEIMANTUS: I do.

SOCRATES: Well, then, would one person do better work if he practiced many crafts or if he practiced one?

ADEIMANTUS: If he practiced one.

SOCRATES: And it is also clear, I take it, that if one misses the opportune moment in any job, the work is spoiled.

ADEIMANTUS: It is clear.

SOCRATES: That, I take it, is because the thing that has to be done won't wait until the doer has the leisure to do it. No, instead the doer must, of necessity, pay close attention to what has to be done and not leave it for his idle moments.

370c

ADEIMANTUS: Yes, he must.

SOCRATES: The result, then, is that more plentiful and better-quality goods are more easily produced, if each person does one thing for which he is naturally suited and does it at the opportune moment, because his time is freed from all the others.

ADEIMANTUS: Absolutely.

SOCRATES: Then, Adeimantus, we are going to need more than four citizens to provide the things we have mentioned. For a farmer won't make

his own plow, it seems, if it is going to be a good one, nor his hoe, nor any
of his other farm implements. Nor will a carpenter—and he, too, needs   370d
lots of tools. And the same is true of a weaver and a shoemaker, isn't it?

ADEIMANTUS: It is.

SOCRATES: So carpenters, metalworkers, and many other craftsmen of that
sort will share our little city and make it bigger.

ADEIMANTUS: Yes, indeed.

SOCRATES: Yet it still would not be a great settlement, even if we added
cowherds, shepherds, and other herdsmen, so that the farmers would have
cows to do their plowing, the builders oxen to share with the farmers in   370e
hauling their materials, and the weavers and shoemakers hides and fleeces
to use.

ADEIMANTUS: It would not be a small city either, if it had to hold all that.

SOCRATES: Moreover, it is almost impossible, at any rate, to establish the
city itself in the sort of place where it will need no imports.

ADEIMANTUS: Yes, that is impossible.

SOCRATES: Then we will need still other people who will import whatever
is needed from another city.

ADEIMANTUS: We will.

SOCRATES: And if our servant goes empty-handed to another city, without
any of the things needed by those from whom he is trying to get what his
own people need, he will come away empty-handed, won't he?   **371a**

ADEIMANTUS: I should think so.

SOCRATES: Our citizens, then, must produce not only enough for themselves at home, but also goods of the right quality and quantity to satisfy
the needs of others.

ADEIMANTUS: Yes, they must.

SOCRATES: So we will need more farmers and other craftsmen in our city.

ADEIMANTUS: Yes.

SOCRATES: And also other servants, I imagine, who are to take care of
imports and exports. These are merchants, aren't they?

ADEIMANTUS: Yes.

SOCRATES: We will need merchants too, then.

ADEIMANTUS: Of course.

SOCRATES: And if the trade is carried on by sea, we will need a great many   371b
others who have expert knowledge of the business of the sea.

ADEIMANTUS: A great many, indeed.

SOCRATES: Again, within the city itself, how will people share with one
another the things they each produce? It was in order to *share,* after all, that
we associated with one another and founded a city.

ADEIMANTUS: Clearly, they must do it by buying and selling.

SOCRATES: Then we will need a marketplace and a currency for such exchange.

ADEIMANTUS: Yes, indeed.

SOCRATES: So if a farmer or any other craftsman brings some of his products

371c to the marketplace, and he does not arrive at the same time as those who want to exchange things with him, is he to sit idly in the marketplace, neglecting his own craft?

ADEIMANTUS: Not at all. On the contrary, there will be people who notice this situation and provide the requisite service—in well-organized cities, they are generally those whose bodies are weakest and who are not fit to do any other sort of work. Their job is to wait there in the marketplace

371d and exchange money for the goods of those who have something to sell, and then to exchange goods for the money of those who want to buy them.

SOCRATES: This need, then, causes retailers to be present in our city. Those who wait in the marketplace, and provide this service of buying and selling, are called retailers, aren't they, whereas those who travel between cities are merchants?

ADEIMANTUS: Yes, that's right.

SOCRATES: There are also other servants, I think, whose minds would not

371e altogether qualify them for membership in our community, but whose bodies are strong enough for hard labor. So they sell the use of their strength for a price called a wage, and that is why they are called wage-earners. Isn't that so?

ADEIMANTUS: Yes.

SOCRATES: So the wage-earners too, it seems, serve to complete our city?

ADEIMANTUS: I think so.

SOCRATES: Well, then, Adeimantus, has our city now grown to completeness?

ADEIMANTUS: Maybe it has.

SOCRATES: Then where are justice and injustice to be found in it? With which of the people we considered did they come in?

372a ADEIMANTUS: I have no idea, Socrates, unless it is somewhere in some need that these people have of one another.

SOCRATES: Perhaps what you say is right. We must look into it and not back off. First, then, let's see what sort of life people will lead who have been provided for in this way. They will make food, wine, clothes, and shoes, won't they? And they will build themselves houses. In the summer, they will mostly work naked and barefoot, but in the winter they will

372b wear adequate clothing and shoes. For nourishment, they will provide

themselves with barley meal and wheat flour, which they will knead and bake into noble cakes and loaves and serve up on a reed or on clean leaves. They will recline on couches strewn with yew and myrtles and feast with their children, drink their wine, and, crowned with wreaths, hymn the gods. They will enjoy having sex with one another, but they will produce no more children than their resources allow, lest they fall into either pov- 372c
erty or war.

At this point Glaucon interrupted and said:

It seems that you make your people feast without any relishes.[11]

SOCRATES: True enough, I was forgetting that they will also have relishes— salt, of course, and olives and cheese, and they will boil roots and vegetables the way they boil them in the country. We will give them desserts too, I imagine, consisting of figs, chickpeas, and beans. And they will roast myrtles and acorns before the fire and drink in moderation. And so they 372d
will live in peace and good health, it seems, and when they die at a ripe old age, they will pass on a similar sort of life to their children.

GLAUCON: If you were founding a city of pigs, Socrates, isn't that just what you would provide to fatten *them?*

SOCRATES: What, then, would you have me do, Glaucon?

GLAUCON: Just what is conventional. If they are not to suffer hardship, they should recline on proper couches, I suppose, dine at tables, and have the relishes and desserts that people have nowadays. 372e

SOCRATES: All right, I understand. It isn't merely the origins of a city that we are considering, it seems, but those of a city that is *luxurious,* too. And that may not be a bad idea. For by examining such a city, we might perhaps see how justice and injustice grow up in cities. Yet the true city, in my view, is the one we have described: the healthy one, as it were. But if you also want to look at a feverish city, so be it. There is nothing to stop us. You see, the things I mentioned earlier, and the way of life I described, won't satisfy 373a
some people, it seems; but couches, tables, and other furniture will have to be added to it, and relishes, of course, and incense, perfumes, prostitutes, pastries—and the multifariousness of each of them. In particular, we can- not just provide them with the necessities[12] we mentioned at first, such as houses, clothes, and shoes; no, instead we will have to get painting and embroidery going, and procure gold and ivory and all sorts of everything of that sort. Isn't that so?

GLAUCON: Yes.

---

[11] Anything eaten with such staples as barley and wheat breads.
[12] See 558d–559d.

373b   SOCRATES: Then we will have to enlarge our city again: the healthy one is
       no longer adequate. On the contrary, we must now increase it in size and
       population and fill it with a multitude of things that go beyond what is
       necessary for a city—hunters, for example, and all those imitators. Many of
       the latter work with shapes and colors; many with music—poets and their
       assistants, rhapsodes,[13] actors, choral dancers, theatrical producers. And
       there will have to be craftsmen of multifarious devices, including, among
373c   other things, those needed for the adornment of women. In particular,
       then, we will need more servants—don't you think—such as tutors, wet
       nurses, nannies, beauticians, barbers, and relish cooks and meat cooks, too?
       Moreover, we will also need people to farm pigs. This animal did not exist
       in our earlier city, since there was no need for it, but we will need it in
       this one. And we will also need large numbers of other meat-producing
       animals, won't we, if someone is going to eat them?

       GLAUCON: We certainly will.

       SOCRATES: And if we live like that, won't we have a far greater need for
373d   doctors than we did before?

       GLAUCON: Yes, far greater.

       SOCRATES: And the land, I take it, that used to be adequate to feed the
       population we had then will now be small and inadequate. Or don't you
       agree?

       GLAUCON: I do.

       SOCRATES: Won't we have to seize some of our neighbors' land, then, if
       we are to have enough for pasture and plowing? And won't our neighbors
       want to seize part of ours in turn, if they too have abandoned themselves
       to the endless acquisition of money and overstepped the limit of their
373e   necessary desires?

       GLAUCON: Yes, that is quite inevitable, Socrates.

       SOCRATES: And the next step will be war, Glaucon, don't you agree?

       GLAUCON: I do.

       SOCRATES: Now, let's not say yet whether the effects of war are good or bad,
       but only that we have now found the origin of war: it comes from those
       same factors, the occurrence of which is the source of the greatest evils for
       cities and the individuals in them.

       GLAUCON: Indeed, it does.

       SOCRATES: The city must be further enlarged, then, my dear Glaucon, and
       not just a little, but by the size of a whole army. It will do battle with the
374a   invaders in defense of the city's wealth, and of all the other things we just
       described.

---

[13] People who memorized epic poems and gave dramatic recitations of them.

GLAUCON: Why so? Aren't the inhabitants themselves adequate for that purpose?

SOCRATES: No, not, at any rate, if the agreement that you and the rest of us made when we were founding the city was a good one. I think we agreed, if you remember, that it is impossible for a single person to practice many crafts well.

GLAUCON: True, we did say that.

SOCRATES: Well, then, don't you think that warfare is a craft? 374b

GLAUCON: It is, indeed.

SOCRATES: So, should we be more concerned about the craft of shoemaking than the craft of warfare?

GLAUCON: Not at all.

SOCRATES: Well, now, we prevented a shoemaker from trying to be a farmer, weaver, or builder at the same time, instead of just a shoemaker, in order to ensure that the shoemaker's job was done well. Similarly, we also assigned just the one job for which he had a natural aptitude to each of the other people, and said that he was to work at it his whole life, free from 374c having to do any of the other jobs, so as not to miss the opportune moments for performing it well. But isn't it of the greatest importance that warfare be carried out well? Or is fighting a war so easy that a farmer, a shoemaker, or any other artisan can be a soldier at the same time, even though no one can become so much as a good checkers player or dice player if he considers it only as a sideline and does not practice it from childhood? Can someone just pick up a shield, or any other weapon or instrument of war and imme- 374d diately become a competent fighter in an infantry battle or whatever other sort of battle it may be, even though no other tool makes someone who picks it up a craftsman or an athlete, or is even of any service to him unless he has acquired knowledge of it and has had sufficient practice?

GLAUCON: If tools could do that, they would be valuable indeed.

SOCRATES: Then to the degree that the guardians' job is of greatest impor- 374e tance, it requires the most freedom from other things, as well as the greatest craft and practice.

GLAUCON: I should think so.

SOCRATES: And doesn't it also require a person whose nature is suited to that very practice?

GLAUCON: Certainly.

SOCRATES: Then our task, it seems, is to select, if we can, which natures, which sorts of natures, suit people to guard the city.

GLAUCON: Yes, that is our task.

SOCRATES: By Zeus, it is no trivial task that we have taken on, then. All the same, we must not shrink from it, but do the best we can.

375a GLAUCON: No, we must not.

SOCRATES: Do you think that there is any difference, when it comes to the job of guarding, between the nature of a noble hound and that of a well-bred youth?

GLAUCON: What do you mean?

SOCRATES: I mean that both of them have to be sharp-eyed, quick to catch what they see, and strong, too, in case they have to fight what they capture.

GLAUCON: Yes, they need all these things.

SOCRATES: And they must be courageous, surely, if indeed they are to fight well.

GLAUCON: Of course.

SOCRATES: Now, will a horse, a dog, or any other animal be courageous if
375b it is not spirited? Or haven't you noticed just how invincible and unbeatable spirit is, so that its presence makes the whole soul fearless and unconquerable in any situation?

GLAUCON: I have noticed that.

SOCRATES: Then it is clear what physical qualities the guardians should have.

GLAUCON: Yes.

SOCRATES: And as far as their souls are concerned, they must, at any rate, be spirited.

GLAUCON: That too.

SOCRATES: But with natures like that, Glaucon, how will they avoid behaving like savages to one another and to the other citizens?

GLAUCON: By Zeus, it won't be easy for them.

375c SOCRATES: But surely they must be gentle to their own people and harsh to their enemies. Otherwise, they will not wait around for others to destroy them, but will do it themselves first.

GLAUCON: That's true.

SOCRATES: What are we to do, then? Where are we to find a character that is both gentle and high-spirited at the same time? For, of course, a gentle nature is the opposite of the spirited kind.

GLAUCON: Apparently.

SOCRATES: But surely if someone lacks either of these qualities, he cannot be a good guardian. Yet the combination of them seems to be impossible.
375d And so it follows, then, that a good guardian is impossible.

GLAUCON: I am afraid so.

I could not see a way out, and on reexamining what had gone before, I said:

We deserve to be stuck, my dear Glaucon. For we have lost track of the analogy we put forward.

GLAUCON: How do you mean?

SOCRATES: We have overlooked the fact that there *are* natures of the sort we thought impossible, ones that include these opposite qualities.

GLAUCON: Where?

SOCRATES: You can see the combination in other animals, too, but especially in the one to which we compared the guardian. For you know, of course, that noble hounds naturally have a character of that sort. They 375e are as gentle as can be to those they are familiar with and know, but the opposite to those they do not know.

GLAUCON: Yes, I do know that.

SOCRATES: So the combination we want is possible, after all, and what we are seeking in a good guardian is not contrary to nature.

GLAUCON: No, I suppose not.

SOCRATES: Now, don't you think that our future guardian, besides being spirited, must also be, by nature, philosophical?

GLAUCON: How do you mean? I don't understand.   **376a**

SOCRATES: It too is something you see in dogs, and it should make us wonder at the merit of the beast.

GLAUCON: In what way?

SOCRATES: In that when a dog sees someone it does not know, it gets angry even before anything bad happens to it. But when it knows someone, it welcomes him, even if it has never received anything good from him. Have you never wondered at that?

GLAUCON: I have never paid it any mind until now. But it is clear that a dog does do that sort of thing.

SOCRATES: Well, that seems to be a naturally refined quality, and one that 376b is truly philosophical.

GLAUCON: In what way?

SOCRATES: In that it judges anything it sees to be either a friend or an enemy on no other basis than that it knows the one and does not know the other. And how could it be anything besides a lover of learning if it defines what is its own and what is alien to it in terms of knowledge and ignorance?

GLAUCON: It surely could not be anything but.

SOCRATES: But surely the love of learning and philosophy are the same, aren't they?

GLAUCON: Yes, they are the same.

SOCRATES: Then can't we confidently assume that the same holds for a
376c human being too—that if he is going to be gentle to his own and those
he knows, he must be, by nature, a lover of learning and a philosopher?

GLAUCON: We can.

SOCRATES: Philosophy, then, and spirit, speed, and strength as well, must
all be combined in the nature of anyone who is going to be a really fine
and good guardian of our city.

GLAUCON: Absolutely.

SOCRATES: Then that is what he would have to be like at the outset. But
how are we to bring these people up and educate them? Will inquiring
into that topic bring us any closer to the goal of our inquiry, which is to
376d discover the origins of justice and injustice in a city? We want our account
to be adequate, but we do not want it to be any longer than necessary.

And Glaucon's brother replied:

I for one certainly expect that this inquiry will help us.

SOCRATES: By Zeus, in that case, my dear Adeimantus, we must not abandon it, even if it turns out to be a somewhat lengthy affair.

ADEIMANTUS: No, we must not.

SOCRATES: Come on, then, and like people in a fable telling stories at their
leisure, let's in our discussion educate these men.

ADEIMANTUS: Yes, let's.

376e SOCRATES: What, then, will the education be? Or is it difficult to find
a better one than the one that has been discovered over a long period of
time—physical training for bodies and musical training for the soul?[14]

ADEIMANTUS: Yes, it is.

SOCRATES: Now, won't we start musical training before physical training?

ADEIMANTUS: Of course.

SOCRATES: And you include stories under musical training, don't you?

ADEIMANTUS: I do.

SOCRATES: But aren't there two kinds of stories, one true and the other
false?

ADEIMANTUS: Yes.

377a SOCRATES: And education must make use of both, but first of the false ones?

ADEIMANTUS: I do not understand what you mean.

SOCRATES: Don't you understand that we first begin by telling stories to
children? And surely they are false on the whole, though they have some
truth in them. And we use stories on children before physical training.

---

[14] Musical training included poetry and stories, as well as music proper.

ADEIMANTUS: That's true.

SOCRATES: That, then, is what I meant by saying that musical training should be taken up before physical training.

ADEIMANTUS: And you were right.

SOCRATES: Now, you know, don't you, that the beginning of any job is of greatest importance, especially when we are dealing with anything young 377b and tender? For that is when it is especially malleable and best takes on whatever pattern one wishes to impress on it.

ADEIMANTUS: Precisely so.

SOCRATES: Shall we carelessly allow our children to hear any old stories made up by just anyone, then, and to take beliefs into their souls that are, for the most part, the opposite of the ones we think they should hold when they are grown up?

ADEIMANTUS: We certainly won't allow that at all.

SOCRATES: So our first task, it seems, is to supervise the storytellers: if they 377c make up a good story, we must accept it; if not, we must reject it. We will persuade nurses and mothers to tell the acceptable ones to their children, and to spend far more time shaping their souls with these stories than they do shaping their bodies by handling them. Many of the stories they tell now, however, must be thrown out.

ADEIMANTUS: Which sorts?

SOCRATES: In the more significant stories, we will see the less significant ones as well. For surely the more significant ones and the less significant ones both follow the same pattern and have the same effects. Don't you think so?

ADEIMANTUS: Indeed, I do. But I do not understand at all what more 377d significant ones you mean.

SOCRATES: The ones Homer, Hesiod, and other poets tell us. After all, they surely composed false stories, which they told and are still telling to people.

ADEIMANTUS: Which stories do you mean? And what is the fault you find in them?

SOCRATES: The first and greatest fault that one ought to find, especially if the falsehood has no good features.

ADEIMANTUS: Yes, but what *is* it?

SOCRATES: Using a story to create a bad image of what the gods and heroes 377e are like, just as a painter might paint a picture that is not at all like the things he is trying to paint.

ADEIMANTUS: Yes, you are right to find fault with that. But what cases in particular, what sorts of cases, do you mean?

SOCRATES: First, the greatest falsehood about the greatest things has no good features—I mean Hesiod telling us about how Uranus behaved, how **378a** Cronus punished him for it, and how he was in turn punished by his own son.[15] But even if these stories were true, they should be passed over in silence, I would think, and not told so casually to the foolish and the young. And if, for some reason, they must be told, only a very few people should hear them—people who are pledged to secrecy and have had to sacrifice not just a pig, but something so great and scarce that the number of people who hear them is kept as small as possible.

ADEIMANTUS: Yes, those stories are certainly troubling.

378b **SOCRATES:** And they should not be told in our city, Adeimantus. No young person should hear it said that if he were to commit the worst crimes, he would be doing nothing amazing, or that if he were to inflict every sort of punishment on an unjust father, he would only be doing the same as the first and greatest of the gods.

ADEIMANTUS: No, by Zeus, I do not think myself that these stories are fit to be told.

SOCRATES: Indeed, we must not allow *any* stories about gods warring, fighting, or plotting against one another if we want the guardians of our city to think that it is shameful to be easily provoked into mutual hatred. After **378c** all, those stories are not true either. Still less should battles between gods and giants, or the many other multifarious hostilities of gods and heroes toward their families and friends, occur in the stories the guardians hear or in the embroidered pictures they see. On the contrary, if we are somehow going to persuade our people that no citizen has ever hated another, and that it is impious to do so, then *those* are the things their male and female **378d** elders should tell them from childhood on. And the poets they listen to as they grow older should be compelled to tell them the same sort of thing. Stories about Hera being chained by her son, on the other hand, or about Hephaestus being hurled from the heavens by his father when he tried to save his mother from a beating, or about the battle of the gods in Homer, should not be admitted into our city, either as allegories or non-allegories. For the young cannot distinguish what is allegorical from what is not. And the beliefs they absorb at that age are difficult to erase and tend to become **378e** unalterable. For these reasons, then, we should probably take the utmost

---

[15] Uranus prevented his wife, Gaia, from giving birth to his children by blocking them up inside her. Gaia gave a sickle to one of these children, Cronus, which he used to castrate his father when Uranus next had intercourse with her. Cronus ate the children he had by his wife, Rhea, until, by deceiving him with a stone, she was able to save Zeus from suffering this fate. Zeus then overthrew his father.

care to ensure that the first stories they hear about virtue are the best ones for them to hear.

ADEIMANTUS: Yes, that makes sense. But if, at this point too, someone were once again to ask us what stories these are, how should we reply?

SOCRATES: You and I are not poets at present, Adeimantus, but we are founding a city. And it is appropriate for the founders to know the patterns on which the poets must base their stories, and from which they must not deviate. But they should not themselves make up any poems.

379a

ADEIMANTUS: That's right. But what precisely are the patterns that stories about the gods must follow?

SOCRATES: Something like this: whether in epic, lyric, or tragedy, a god must always be represented as he is.

ADEIMANTUS: Yes, he must.

SOCRATES: Now, gods,[16] of course, are really good, aren't they, and must be described as such?

379b

ADEIMANTUS: Certainly.

SOCRATES: And surely nothing good is harmful, is it?

ADEIMANTUS: I suppose not.

SOCRATES: Well, can what is not harmful do any harm?

ADEIMANTUS: No, never.

SOCRATES: And can what does no harm do anything bad?

ADEIMANTUS: No, it can't do that either.

SOCRATES: But what does nothing bad could not be the cause of anything bad, could it?

ADEIMANTUS: No, it could not.

SOCRATES: What about what is good? Is it beneficial?

ADEIMANTUS: Yes.

SOCRATES: So, it is the cause of doing well?

ADEIMANTUS: Yes.

SOCRATES: What is good is not the cause of all things, then. Instead, it is the cause of things that are good, while of bad ones it is not the cause.

ADEIMANTUS: Exactly.

379c

SOCRATES: So, since gods are good, they are not—as the masses claim—the cause of everything. Instead, they are a cause of only a few things that happen to human beings, while of most they are not the cause. For good things are fewer than bad ones in our lives. Of the good things, they

---

[16] *Ho theos:* literally, "the god." But the definite article is almost certainly functioning as a universal quantifier, as in "The swallow is a migratory bird."

alone are the cause, but we must find some other cause for the bad ones, not the gods.

ADEIMANTUS: That's absolutely true in my view.

379d SOCRATES: Then we won't accept from Homer—or from anyone else—the foolish mistake he makes about the gods when he says: "There are two urns at the threshold of Zeus, one filled with good fates, the other with bad ones," and the person to whom Zeus gives a mixture of these "sometimes meets with a bad fate, sometimes with a good one." But the one who receives his fate entirely from the second urn, "evil famine drives over the 379e divine earth." Nor will we tolerate the saying that "Zeus is the dispenser of both good and bad to mortals." As for the breaking of the oaths and the truce by Pandarus, if anyone tells us that it was brought about by Athena and Zeus, or that Themis and Zeus were responsible for strife and conten- 380a tion among the gods, we won't praise him. Nor will we allow the young to hear the words of Aeschylus: "A god makes mortals guilty, when he wants to destroy a house utterly."[17] And if anyone composes a poem, such as the one those lines are from, about the sufferings of Niobe, or about the house of Pelops, or the tale of Troy, or anything else of that sort, he should be required to say that these things are not the works of a god. Or, if they are the works of a god, then the poet must look for roughly the sort of account of them we are now seeking: he must say that the actions of the gods are 380b good and just, and that the people they punish are benefited by them. We won't allow him to say that those who are punished are made wretched, and that it was a god who made them so; but we will allow him to say that bad people are wretched because they are in need of punishment, and that in paying the penalty they are benefited by that god. But as for saying that a god, who is himself good, is the cause of evils, we will fight that in every way. We won't allow anyone to say it in his own city, if it is to be 380c well governed, or anyone to hear it either—whether young or old, whether with meter or without meter. For these stories are impious, disadvantageous to us, and not in concord with one another.

ADEIMANTUS: I like your law, and I will vote with you for it.

SOCRATES: This, then, will be one of the laws or patterns relating to gods that speakers and poets will have to follow: that gods are not the cause of all things, but only of good ones.

ADEIMANTUS: And an entirely satisfactory one it is.

380d SOCRATES: Now, what about this second law? Do you think that gods are sorcerers who deliberately take different forms at different times, sometimes

---

[17] The first three quotations are from *Iliad* xxiv.527–32. The sources for the fourth, and for the quotation from Aeschylus, are unknown. The story of Athena urging Pandarus to break the truce is told at *Iliad* iv.73–126.

by changing on their own and altering their own form into a large number of shapes, sometimes by deceiving us into thinking they have done so? Or are they simple beings, and least of all likely to abandon their own form?

ADEIMANTUS: I can't say offhand.

SOCRATES: Well, if something abandons its own form, mustn't it either cause the change itself or be changed by something else?   380e

ADEIMANTUS: It must.

SOCRATES: Now, the best things are least liable to alteration or change, aren't they? For example, a body is altered by food, drink, and labors, and all plants by sun, winds, and other similar affections—but the healthiest and strongest is least altered, isn't that so?   381a

ADEIMANTUS: Of course.

SOCRATES: And wouldn't a soul that is most courageous and most knowledgeable be least disturbed or altered by any outside influence?

ADEIMANTUS: Yes.

SOCRATES: And the same account surely also applies even to manufactured items, such as implements, houses, and clothes: those that are good and well made are least altered by time or any other influences.

ADEIMANTUS: That's right.

SOCRATES: So whatever is in good condition—whether due to nature or craft or both—is least subject to change by something else.   381b

ADEIMANTUS: It seems so.

SOCRATES: But gods, of course, as well as the things belonging to them, are best in every way.

ADEIMANTUS: They certainly are.

SOCRATES: So, on this view, gods would be least likely to have many forms.

ADEIMANTUS: Least likely, indeed.

SOCRATES: Then would they change or alter themselves?

ADEIMANTUS: Clearly so, if indeed they are altered at all.

SOCRATES: Do they change themselves into something better and more beautiful, or into something worse and uglier, than themselves?

ADEIMANTUS: It would have to be into something worse, if indeed they are altered at all. For surely we won't say that gods are deficient in either   381c
beauty or virtue.

SOCRATES: You are absolutely right. And do you think, Adeimantus, that anyone, whether god or human, would deliberately make himself worse in any way?

ADEIMANTUS: No, that is impossible.

SOCRATES: It is also impossible, then, for a god to want to alter himself. On the contrary, since each god is, it seems, as beautiful and as good as possible, he must always unqualifiedly retain his own form.

ADEIMANTUS: In my view, at least, that is absolutely necessary.

381d SOCRATES: None of our poets, then, my very good man, is to say that "The gods, like strangers from foreign lands, assume many disguises when they visit our cities."[18] Nor must they tell lies about Proteus and Thetis, or present Hera, in their tragedies or other poems, disguised as a priestess collecting alms for "the life-giving sons of the Argive river Inachus,"[19] or

381e tell us any of the many other such lies. Nor should mothers, influenced by these stories, which terrify children, tell bad tales about gods who go wandering around at night in the guises of many strange and multifarious beings, lest they blaspheme the gods and, at the same time, make their children too cowardly.

ADEIMANTUS: Indeed, they should not.

SOCRATES: But, though the gods themselves are the sorts of things that cannot change, do they make us think that they appear in multifarious guises, deceiving us and using sorcery on us?

ADEIMANTUS: Perhaps they do.

SOCRATES: What? Would a god be willing to lie by presenting in word or
382a deed what is only an illusion?

ADEIMANTUS: I don't know.

SOCRATES: Don't you know that all gods and humans hate a true lie, if one may call it that?

ADEIMANTUS: What do you mean?

SOCRATES: I mean that no one intentionally wants to lie about the most important things to what is most important in himself. On the contrary, he fears to hold a lie there more than anything.

ADEIMANTUS: I still don't understand.

SOCRATES: That is because you think I am saying something deep. I simply
382b mean that to lie and to have lied to the soul about the things that are,[20] and to be ignorant, and to have and hold a lie there, is what everyone would least of all accept; indeed, they especially hate it there.

ADEIMANTUS: They certainly do.

---

[18] *Odyssey* xvii.485–86.

[19] Inachus was the father of Io, who was persecuted by Hera because Zeus was in love with her. The source for the part of the story Plato quotes is unknown.

[20] Because of the ambiguity of the verb *einai* ("to be"), a thing that is could be: (1) a thing that exists (existential "is"); (2) a thing that is beautiful (say) (predicative "is"); (3) a thing that is true or something that is (veridical "is").

SOCRATES: But surely, as I was saying just now, it would be most correct to say that it is truly speaking a lie—the ignorance in the soul of the one to whom the lie was told. For a lie in words is a sort of imitation of this affection in the soul, an image of it that comes into being after it, and not   382c
an altogether pure lie. Isn't that so?

ADEIMANTUS: Yes, it is.

SOCRATES: A real lie, then, is hated not only by the gods, but also by human beings.

ADEIMANTUS: I think it is.

SOCRATES: What about a lie in words? Aren't there times when it is useful, and so does not merit hatred? What about when we are dealing with enemies, or with so-called friends who, because of insanity or ignorance, are attempting to do something bad? Isn't it a useful drug for preventing them? And consider the case of those stories we were talking about just now—those we tell because we do not know the truth about those ancient   382d
events: by making the lies that they contain as much like the truth as possible, don't we make them useful?

ADEIMANTUS: We most certainly do.

SOCRATES: In which of these ways, then, could a lie be useful to a god? Would he lie by making likenesses of the truth about ancient events because of his ignorance of them?

ADEIMANTUS: It would be ridiculous to think that.

SOCRATES: Then there is nothing of the lying poet in a god?

ADEIMANTUS: Not in my view.

SOCRATES: Would he lie, then, through fear of his enemies?

ADEIMANTUS: Hardly.   382e

SOCRATES: Because of the foolishness or insanity of his family or friends, then?

ADEIMANTUS: No one who is foolish or mad is a friend of the gods.

SOCRATES: So a god has no reason to lie?

ADEIMANTUS: None.

SOCRATES: So both what is daimonic[21] and what is divine are entirely free of lies.

ADEIMANTUS: Absolutely.

SOCRATES: A god, then, is altogether simple, true in both word and deed. He does not change himself or deceive others by means of images, by words, or by sending signs, whether they are awake or dreaming.

---

[21] See *Apology* 27c–d.

ADEIMANTUS: That is my view—at any rate, now that I have heard what
383a you have to say.

SOCRATES: You agree, then, that this is the second pattern people must
follow when speaking or composing poems about the gods: the gods are
not sorcerers who change themselves, nor do they mislead us by telling
lies in word or deed.

ADEIMANTUS: I agree.

SOCRATES: Even though we praise many things in Homer, then, we won't
approve of Zeus' sending the dream to Agamemnon, nor of Aeschylus
383b when he makes Thetis say that Apollo sang, in prophecy at her wedding:

> About the good luck my children would have,
> Free of disease throughout their long lives,
> And of all the blessings the friendship of the gods would bring me.
> I hoped that Phoebus' divine mouth would be free of lies,
> Endowed as it is with the craft of prophecy.
> But the very god who sang, the one at the feast,
> The one who said all that, he himself it is
> Who killed my son.[22]

383c Whenever anyone says such things about a god, we will be angry with
him, refuse him a chorus,[23] and not allow teachers to use what he says for
the education of the young—not if our guardians are going to be as god-
fearing and godlike as human beings can be.

ADEIMANTUS: I agree completely about these patterns, and I would use
them as laws.

BOOK III

SOCRATES' NARRATION CONTINUES:

386a SOCRATES: Where the gods are concerned, then, it seems that those are
the sorts of stories the future guardians should and should not hear from
childhood on, if they are to honor the gods and their parents, and not treat
lightly their friendship with one another.

ADEIMANTUS: I am sure we are right about that.

---

[22] At *Iliad* ii.1–34, Zeus sends a dream to Agamemnon to promise success if he
attacks Troy immediately. The promise is false. The source for the quotation from
Aeschylus is unknown.

[23] I.e., deny him the funding necessary to hire a chorus of actors and produce his
play.

SOCRATES: What about if they are to be courageous? Shouldn't they be told stories that will make them least likely to fear death? Or do you think that anyone ever becomes courageous if he has that fear in his heart?   386b

ADEIMANTUS: No, by Zeus, I do not.

SOCRATES: What about if someone believes that Hades exists and is full of terrible things? Can anyone with that fear be unafraid of death and prefer it to defeat in battle and slavery?

ADEIMANTUS: Not at all.

SOCRATES: Then we must also supervise those who try to tell such stories, it seems, and ask them not to disparage the life in Hades in this undiscriminating way, but to speak well of it, since what they now tell us is neither true nor beneficial to future warriors.   386c

ADEIMANTUS: Yes, we must.

SOCRATES: We will start with the following lines, then, and expunge everything like them: "I would rather labor on earth in another man's service, a man who is landless, with little to live on, than be king over all the dead";[1] and this: "He feared that his home should be revealed to mortals and immortals as dreadful, dank, and hated even by the gods;"[2]   386d and: "Alas, there survives in the Halls of Hades a soul, a mere phantasm, with its wits completely gone";[3] and this: "He alone can think others to be flitting shadows";[4] and: "The soul, leaving his limbs, made its way to Hades, lamenting its fate, leaving manhood and youth behind";[5] and this: **387a** "His soul went below the earth like smoke, screeching as it went";[6] and:

> As when bats in an awful cave
> Fly around screeching if one of them falls
> From the cluster on the ceiling, all clinging to one another,
> so their souls went screeching.[7]

---

[1] *Odyssey* xi.489–91. Odysseus is being addressed by Achilles in Hades.

[2] *Iliad* xx.64–65. Hades is afraid that the earth will split open and reveal what his home is like.

[3] *Iliad* xxiii.103–4. Achilles speaks these lines as the soul of the dead Patroclus leaves for Hades.

[4] *Odyssey* x.493–95. Circe speaking to Odysseus about the prophet Tiresias.

[5] *Iliad* xvi.856–57. The words refer to Patroclus, who has just been mortally wounded by Hector.

[6] *Iliad* xxiii.100. The soul referred to is that of Patroclus.

[7] *Odyssey* xiv.6–9. The souls are those of Penelope's suitors, whom Odysseus has killed.

387b We will beg Homer and the rest of the poets not to be angry if we delete these and all similar passages—not because they are not poetic and pleasing to the masses when they hear them, but because the more poetic they are, the more they should be kept away from the ears of children and men who are to be free and to fear slavery more than death.

ADEIMANTUS: Absolutely.

387c SOCRATES: Then, in addition, we must also get rid of the terrible and frightening names that occur in such passages: Cocytus, Styx,[8] "those below," "the sapless ones," and all the other names of the same pattern that supposedly make everyone who hears them shudder. Perhaps they are useful for other purposes, but our fear is that all that shuddering will make our guardians more emotional and soft than they ought to be.

ADEIMANTUS: And our fear is justified.

SOCRATES: Should we remove them, then?

ADEIMANTUS: Yes.

SOCRATES: And follow the opposite pattern in speech and poetry?

ADEIMANTUS: Clearly.

387d SOCRATES: Shall we also remove the lamentations and pitiful speeches of famous men?

ADEIMANTUS: If what we did before was necessary, so is that.

SOCRATES: Consider, though, whether we will be right to remove them or not. What we claim is that a good man won't think that death is a terrible thing for another good one to suffer—even if the latter happens to be his friend.

ADEIMANTUS: Yes, we do claim that.

SOCRATES: So, he won't mourn for him as if he had suffered a terrible fate.

ADEIMANTUS: Certainly not.

SOCRATES: But we also claim this: a good person is most self-sufficient
387e when it comes to living well, and is distinguished from other people by having the least need of anyone or anything else.

ADEIMANTUS: True.

SOCRATES: So it is less terrible for him than for anyone else to be deprived of a son, brother, possessions, or the like.

ADEIMANTUS: Yes, much less.

SOCRATES: So, he will lament it the least and bear it the most calmly when some such misfortune overtakes him.

ADEIMANTUS: Of course.

---

[8] "Cocytus" means river of wailing or lamenting; "Styx," river of hatred.

SOCRATES: We would be right, then, to remove the lamentations of famous men. We would leave them to women (provided they are not excellent women) and cowardly men, so that those we say we are training to guard   388a
our land will feel disgust at doing such things.

ADEIMANTUS: That's right.

SOCRATES: In addition, then, we will have to ask Homer and the other poets not to represent Achilles, who was the son of a goddess, as:

> Lying now on his side, now on his back, now again
> On his belly; then standing up to wander distracted
> This way and that on the shore of the unharvested sea;[9]

or to make him pick up ashes with both hands and pour them over his head,   388b
weeping and lamenting to the extent and in the manner Homer describes;[10] or to represent Priam, a close descendant of the gods, as "begging and rolling around in dung, as he calls upon each of his men by name."[11] And yet more insistently than that, we will ask them at least not to make the gods lament and say: "Woe is me, unfortunate that I am, wretched mother of a great son."[12] But, if they do make the gods do such things, at least they   388c
must not dare to represent *the greatest of the gods* in so unlikely a fashion as to make him say: "Alas, with my own eyes I see a man who is most dear to me being chased around the city, and my heart laments";[13] or "Woe is me, that Sarpedon, who is most dear to me, should be fated to be killed by Patroclus, the son of Menoetius."[14] You see, my dear Adeimantus, if   388d
our young people listen seriously to these stories without ridiculing them as not worth hearing, none of them is going to consider such things to be unworthy of a mere human being like himself, or rebuke himself if it occurred to him to do or say any of them. On the contrary, without shame or perseverance, he would chant many dirges and laments at the slightest sufferings.

ADEIMANTUS: That's absolutely true.

SOCRATES: But that must not happen, as our argument has shown—and we   388e
must remain persuaded by it until someone shows us a better one.

ADEIMANTUS: No, it must not.

---

[9] *Iliad* xxiv.3–12.

[10] *Iliad* xviii.23–24.

[11] *Iliad* xxii.414–15.

[12] *Iliad* xviii.54. Thetis, the mother of Achilles, is mourning his fate among the Nereids.

[13] *Iliad* xxii.168–69. Zeus is watching Hector being pursued by Achilles.

[14] *Iliad* xvi.433–34.

SOCRATES: Moreover, they must not be lovers of laughter either. For whenever anyone gives in to violent laughter, a violent reaction pretty much always follows.

ADEIMANTUS: I agree.

SOCRATES: So, if someone represents worthwhile people as overcome by laughter, we must not accept it, and we will accept it even less if they
389a   represent the gods in that way.

ADEIMANTUS: Much less.

SOCRATES: Then we must not accept the following sorts of sayings about the gods from Homer: "And unquenchable laughter arose among the blessed gods as they saw Hephaestus limping through the hall."[15] According to your argument, they must be rejected.

ADEIMANTUS: Yes, if you want to attribute it to me, but they must be
389b   rejected in any case.

SOCRATES: Moreover, we have to be concerned about truth as well. For if what we said just now is correct and a lie is really useless to the gods, but useful to human beings as a form of drug, it is clear that it must be assigned to doctors, whereas private individuals must have nothing to do with it.

ADEIMANTUS: It is clear.

SOCRATES: It is appropriate for the rulers, then, if anyone, to lie because of enemies or citizens for the good of the city. But no one else may have anything to do with it. On the contrary, we will say that for a private individual to lie to such rulers is as bad a mistake as for a sick person not to tell
389c   his doctor or an athlete his trainer the truth about his physical condition, or for someone not to tell the captain the things that are true about the ship and the sailors, or about how he himself or one of his fellow sailors is faring—indeed, it is a worse mistake.

ADEIMANTUS: That's absolutely true.

389d   SOCRATES: So, if anyone else is caught telling lies in the city—"any of the craftsmen, whether a prophet, a doctor who heals the sick, or a carpenter who works in wood"[16]—he will be punished for introducing a practice that is as subversive and destructive of a city as of a ship.

ADEIMANTUS: Indeed it is, at any rate, if what people do is influenced by what he says.

SOCRATES: What about temperance? Won't our young people also need that?

ADEIMANTUS: Of course.

---

[15] *Iliad* i.599–600.

[16] *Odyssey* xvii.384.

SOCRATES: And don't the greatest parts of temperance—at any rate for the
majority of people—consist in obedience to the rulers and ruling over the   389e
pleasures of drink, sex, and food for themselves?

ADEIMANTUS: That is my view, anyway.

SOCRATES: So we will claim, I imagine, that it is fine to say the sort of
thing that Diomedes says in Homer: "Sit down in silence, my friend, and
be persuaded by my story";[17] and what follows it: "The Achaeans went in
silently, breathing valor, afraid of their commanders";[18] and anything else
of that sort.

ADEIMANTUS: Yes, it is fine.

SOCRATES: But what about things like, "You drunkard, with the eyes of
a dog and the heart of a deer," and what follows it?[19] Are they, then, fine
things to say? And what about all the other headstrong things that private   **390a**
individuals say to their rulers in works of prose or poetry?

ADEIMANTUS: No, they are not fine.

SOCRATES: That, I imagine, is because they are not suitable for inculcating temperance in the young people who hear them. But it would not be
surprising if they were found pleasant in some other context. What do
you think?

ADEIMANTUS: The same as you.

SOCRATES: What about making the wisest man say that the best thing of
all, as it seems to him, is when "the tables are well laden with bread and
meat, and the wine-bearer draws wine from the mixing bowl, brings it,
and pours it in the cups"?[20] Do you think that hearing things like that is   390b
suitable for inculcating self-mastery in young people? Or that "death by
starvation is the most pitiful fate"?[21] Or about how Zeus stayed awake alone
deliberating, when all the other gods and mortals were asleep, and then easily forgot all his plans because of his sexual appetite, and was so overcome   390c
by the sight of Hera that he did not even want to go to their bedroom, but
to possess her there on the ground, saying that his appetite for her was even
greater than it was when they first made love to one another "without their

---

[17] *Iliad* iv.412. Agamemnon has unfairly rebuked Diomedes for cowardice.
Diomedes' squire protests, but Diomedes quiets him with these words. By obeying,
the squire exhibits the kind of moderation that most people can come to possess.

[18] A mix of *Iliad* iii.8 and iv.431.

[19] *Iliad* i.225. Achilles is insulting his commander, Agamemnon.

[20] *Odyssey* ix.8–10.

[21] *Odyssey* xii.342. Eurylochus urges the men to slay the cattle of Helios in
Odysseus' absence.

parents' knowledge"?[22] Or what about the chaining together of Ares and Aphrodite by Hephaestus[23] for similar reasons?

ADEIMANTUS: No, by Zeus, that does not seem suitable to me.

390d SOCRATES: On the other hand, if there are any words or deeds of famous men that express perseverance in the face of everything, surely they must be seen and heard. For example, "He struck his chest and spoke to his heart: 'Bear up, my heart, you have suffered more shameful things than this.'"[24]

ADEIMANTUS: Absolutely.

SOCRATES: And we must not, of course, allow our men to be bribable with gifts or to be money-lovers.

390e ADEIMANTUS: Certainly not.

SOCRATES: Then they must not sing: "Gifts persuade gods, and gifts persuade revered kings."[25] Nor must we praise Phoenix, the tutor of Achilles, for being moderate, when he advises Achilles to take the gifts and defend the Achaeans, but not to lay aside his anger without gifts.[26] Nor should we agree that Achilles himself was such a money-lover as to accept the gifts of Agamemnon, or to release a corpse when he got paid for it, but otherwise

391a to refuse.[27]

ADEIMANTUS: No, it certainly is not right to praise such things.

SOCRATES: It is only out of respect for Homer, indeed, that I hesitate to say that it is positively impious to accuse Achilles of such things, or to believe them when others say them. Or to believe that he said to Apollo: "You have injured me, Farshooter, most deadly of the gods; And I would punish you,

391b if only I had the power."[28] Or that he disobeyed the river—a god—and was ready to fight it.[29] Or that he consecrated hair to the dead Patroclus, which he had already consecrated to the other river, Sphercheius:"To the hero, Patroclus, I give my hair to take with him."[30] We must not believe that he did that. Nor is it true that he dragged the dead Hector around the tomb of Patroclus[31] or massacred the captives on his pyre.[32] So we will deny these

---

[22] *Iliad* xiv.294–341.

[23] *Odyssey* viii.266 ff.

[24] *Odyssey* xx.17–18. The speaker is Odysseus.

[25] The source of the passage is unknown.

[26] *Iliad* ix.602–3.

[27] *Iliad* xix.278 ff., xxiv.594.

[28] *Iliad* xxii.15, 20.

[29] *Iliad* xxi.232 ff.

[30] *Iliad* xxiii.151–52.

[31] *Iliad* xiv.14–18.

[32] *Iliad* xxiii.175.

things. Nor will we allow our people to believe that Achilles—the son of a goddess and of Peleus (who was himself the most temperate of men and the grandson of Zeus), and the pupil of the most wise Cheiron—was so full of inner disorder as to have two opposite diseases within him: illiberality accompanied by the love of money on the one hand, and arrogance toward gods and humans on the other. 391c

ADEIMANTUS: That's right.

SOCRATES: Moreover, we will neither believe nor allow it to be said that Theseus, the son of Poseidon, and Peirithous, the son of Zeus, ever attempted those terrible rapes,[33] nor that any other child of a god and hero dared to do any of the terrible and impious deeds that are now falsely attributed to them. We will compel the poets either to deny that they did such things, or else to deny that they were children of the gods. But they must not say both or attempt to persuade our young people that the gods produce evils, nor that heroes are no better than humans. After all, as we were saying earlier, these things are neither pious nor true. For we demonstrated, I take it, that it is impossible for the gods to produce evils. 391d 391e

ADEIMANTUS: We certainly did.

SOCRATES: And they are also positively harmful to those who hear them. You see, everyone will be ready to excuse himself when he is bad, if he has been persuaded that similar things are done and were done by "close descendants of the gods, near kin of Zeus, whose ancestral altar is in the ether on Ida's peak," and "in whom the blood of daimons has not weakened."[34] That is why we must put a stop to such stories; if we do not, they will produce in our young people a very casual attitude to evil. 392a

ADEIMANTUS: Exactly.

SOCRATES: What kind of stories are still left, then, about which we must determine whether or not they may be told? I mean, we have discussed how gods, heroes, daimons, and things in Hades should be portrayed.

ADEIMANTUS: We have.

SOCRATES: Then wouldn't stories about human beings be left?

ADEIMANTUS: Obviously so.

SOCRATES: But it is not possible, my friend, to discuss them here.

ADEIMANTUS: Why not?

SOCRATES: Because what we are going to say, I imagine, is that poets and prose writers get the greatest things concerning human beings wrong. They say that many unjust people are happy and many just ones wretched, 392b

---

[33] According to some legends, Theseus and Peirithous abducted Helen and tried to abduct Persephone from Hades.

[34] Thought to be from Aeschylus' lost play *Niobe*.

that doing injustice is profitable if it escapes detection, and that justice is another's good but one's own loss. We will forbid them to say such things, I imagine, and order them to sing and tell the opposite. Don't you think so?

ADEIMANTUS: No, I *know* so.

SOCRATES: Well, then, if you agree that what I said is correct, won't I say to you that you have conceded the point we were investigating all along?

392c   ADEIMANTUS: And your claim would be correct.

SOCRATES: Then we won't come to an agreement about what stories should be told about human beings until we have discovered what sort of thing justice is, and how, given its nature, it profits the one who has it, whether he is believed to be just or not.

ADEIMANTUS: That's absolutely right.

SOCRATES: Our discussion of the content of stories is complete, then. Our next task, I take it, is to investigate their style. And then we will have completely investigated both what they should say and how they should say it.

ADEIMANTUS: I don't understand what you mean.

SOCRATES: Well, we must see that you do. Maybe this will help you to grasp
392d   it better: isn't everything said by poets and storytellers a narration of past, present, or future events?

ADEIMANTUS: Of course.

SOCRATES: And don't they proceed by narration alone, narration through imitation, or both?

ADEIMANTUS: I need a still clearer understanding of that, too.

SOCRATES: What a ridiculously unclear teacher I seem to be! So, I will do what incompetent speakers do: I won't try to deal with the subject as a
392e   whole. Instead, I will take up a particular example and use that to explain what I mean. Tell me, do you know the beginning of the *Iliad* where the poet tells us that Chryses begged Agamemnon to release his daughter, that Agamemnon got angry, and that Chryses, having failed to get what he
393a   wanted, prayed to his god[35] to punish the Achaeans?

ADEIMANTUS: I do.

SOCRATES: You know, then, that up to the lines, "He begged all the Achaeans, but especially the commanders of the army, the two sons of Atreus,"[36] the poet himself is speaking and is not trying to make us think that the speaker is anyone but himself. After that, however, he speaks as if he himself were Chryses, and tries as hard as he can to make us think that
393b   the speaker is not Homer, but the priest himself, who is an old man. And

---

[35] Apollo.

[36] *Iliad* i.15 ff.

all the rest of his narration of the events in Ilium and Ithaca, and all of the *Odyssey,* are written in pretty much the same way.

ADEIMANTUS: Yes, they are.

SOCRATES: Now, each of the speeches, as well as the material between them, is narration, isn't it?

ADEIMANTUS: Of course.

SOCRATES: But when he makes a speech as if he were someone else, won't we say that he makes his own style as much like that of the person he tells us is about to speak? 393c

ADEIMANTUS: We certainly will.

SOCRATES: Now, to make oneself like someone else in voice or appearance is to imitate the person one makes oneself like, isn't it?

ADEIMANTUS: Of course.

SOCRATES: Then in a passage of that sort, it seems, he, and the rest of poets as well, produce their narration through imitation.

ADEIMANTUS: Yes, indeed.

SOCRATES: But if the poet never disguised himself, his entire poem would be narration without imitation. To prevent you from saying that you still do not understand, I will tell you what that would be like. If Homer said that 393d Chryses came with a ransom for his daughter to supplicate the Achaeans, especially the kings, and if after that Homer had gone on speaking, not as if he had become Chryses, but still as Homer, you know that it would not be imitation but narration pure and simple. It would have gone something like this—I will speak without meter since I am not a poet: the priest came and prayed that the gods would grant it to the Achaeans to capture Troy and have a safe return home, and he entreated them to accept the ransom 393e and free his daughter, out of reverence for the god. When he had said this, the others approved of it and consented. But Agamemnon was angry and ordered him to leave and never return, or else his priestly wand and the wreaths of the god would not protect him. He said that the priest's daughter would grow old in Argos by his side sooner than be freed. He ordered Chryses to leave and not make him angry if he wanted to get home safely. **394a** When the old man heard this, he was frightened and went off in silence. And once he had left the camp, he prayed at length to Apollo, invoking the cult names of the god, reminding him of his past gifts, and asking to be repaid for any that had found favor with him, whether they were temples he had built or victims he had sacrificed. He prayed that, in return for these things, the arrows of the god would make the Achaeans pay for his tears. That, comrade, is how we get pure narration without any imitation. 394b

ADEIMANTUS: I understand.

SOCRATES: Also understand, then, that the opposite occurs when one omits the words between the speeches and leaves the speeches on their own.

ADEIMANTUS: I understand that, too; it is what happens in tragedies, for example.

SOCRATES: You have got it absolutely right. And now I think I can make clear to you what I could not before. One sort of poetry and storytelling employs only imitation—tragedy, as you said, and comedy. Another sort, which you find primarily in dithyrambs,[37] employs only narration by the poet himself. A third sort, which uses both, is what we find in epic poetry and many other places. Do you follow me?

ADEIMANTUS: Yes, now I understand what you meant.

SOCRATES: And before that, as you remember, we said that we had already dealt with *content*, but that we had yet to investigate *style*.

ADEIMANTUS: Yes, I remember.

SOCRATES: What I meant, then, was just this: we need to come to an agreement about whether to allow our poets to narrate as imitators, or as imitators of some things, but not others—and what sorts of things these are; or not to allow them to imitate at all.

ADEIMANTUS: I imagine that you are considering whether we will admit tragedy and comedy into our city or not.

SOCRATES: Perhaps so, but it may be an even wider question than that. I really do not know yet. But wherever the wind of argument blows us, so to speak, that is where we must go.

ADEIMANTUS: Yes, well put.

SOCRATES: What I want you to consider, then, Adeimantus, is whether our guardians should be imitators or not. Or does the answer follow from what we have said already—namely, that whereas each individual can practice one pursuit well, he cannot practice many well, and if he tried to do this and dabbled in many things, he would surely fail to achieve distinction in all of them?

ADEIMANTUS: Of course. Why wouldn't it?

SOCRATES: Then doesn't the same principle also apply to imitation—namely, that a single individual cannot imitate many things as well as he can imitate one?

ADEIMANTUS: No, he cannot.

SOCRATES: Then he will hardly be able to practice any pursuit worth talking about while at the same time imitating lots of things and being an imitator. For, as you know, even when two sorts of imitation are thought

---

[37] Choral song to the god Dionysus.

to be closely akin, the same people are not able to practice both of them well simultaneously. The writing of tragedy and comedy is an example. Didn't you just call both of these imitations?

ADEIMANTUS: I did, and you are quite right; the same people cannot do both.

SOCRATES: Nor can they be both rhapsodes and actors simultaneously.

ADEIMANTUS: True.

SOCRATES: Indeed, the same men cannot be used as both tragic and comic actors. And all these are imitations, aren't they?   395b

ADEIMANTUS: They are.

SOCRATES: And human nature, Adeimantus, seems to me to be minted in even smaller coins than this, so that an individual can neither imitate many things well nor perform well the actions themselves of which those imitations are likenesses.

ADEIMANTUS: That's absolutely true.

SOCRATES: So, if we are to preserve our first argument, that our guardians must be kept away from all other crafts so as to be the most exact craftsmen of the city's freedom, and practice nothing at all except what contributes to   395c
this, then they must neither do nor imitate anything else. But if they imitate anything, they must imitate right from childhood what is appropriate for them—that is to say, people who are courageous, temperate, pious, free, and everything of that sort. On the other hand, they must not be clever at doing or imitating illiberal or shameful actions, so that they won't acquire a taste for the real thing from imitating it. Or haven't you noticed that imitations, if they are practiced much past youth, get established in the   395d
habits and nature of body, tones of voice, and mind?

ADEIMANTUS: I have indeed.

SOCRATES: Since those we claim to care about are *men,* then, and men who must become good, we won't allow them to imitate a *woman,* young or old, as she abuses her husband, quarrels with the gods, brags because she thinks herself happy, or suffers misfortune and is possessed by sorrows and lamen-   395e
tations—and still less a woman who is ill, passionately in love, or in labor.

ADEIMANTUS: Absolutely not.

SOCRATES: Nor must they imitate either male or female slaves doing servile actions.

ADEIMANTUS: No, they must not.

SOCRATES: Nor cowardly, bad men, it seems, or those whose actions are the opposite of what we described just now—men who libel and ridicule each other, and use shameful language when drunk or even when sober, or who wrong themselves and others by word or deed in the other ways that are   396a typical of such people. And they must not get into the habit, I take it, of acting or talking like madmen. They must *know,* of course, about mad and evil men and women, but they must not do or imitate anything they do.

ADEIMANTUS: That's absolutely true.

SOCRATES: What about metalworkers or other craftsmen, or those who row in triremes, or their coxswains, or the like—should they imitate them?

ADEIMANTUS: No, they should not, since they are not allowed even to pay any mind to those pursuits.

SOCRATES: And what about neighing horses, bellowing bulls, roaring rivers, the crashing sea, thunder, or the like—will they imitate them?

ADEIMANTUS: No, they have already been forbidden to be mad or to imitate madmen.

SOCRATES: So you are saying, if I understand you, that there is one kind of style and narration that a really good and fine person would use whenever he had to say something, and another kind, unlike that one, which his opposite by nature and education would always favor, and in which he would narrate his story.

ADEIMANTUS: What kinds are they?

SOCRATES: In my view, when a moderate man comes upon the words or actions of a good man in the course of a narration, he will be willing to report them as if he were that man himself, and he won't be ashamed of that sort of imitation. He will be most willing to imitate the good man when he is acting in a faultless and intelligent manner, but less willing and more reluctant to do so when he is upset by disease, passion, drunkenness, or some other misfortune. When he comes upon a character who is beneath him, however, he will be unwilling to make himself resemble this inferior character in any serious way—except perhaps for a brief period in which he is doing something good. On the contrary, he will be ashamed to do something like that, both because he is unpracticed in the imitation of such people, and also because to shape and mold himself on an inferior pattern disgusts him. In his mind he despises that, except when it is for the sake of amusement.

ADEIMANTUS: Probably so.

SOCRATES: Won't he use the sorts of narration, then, that we described in dealing with the Homeric epics a moment ago? And though his style of speaking will involve both imitation and the other sort of narration, won't imitation play a small part even in a long story? Or am I talking nonsense?

ADEIMANTUS: Not at all. That must indeed be the pattern followed by that sort of speaker.

SOCRATES: As for the other sort of speaker, the more inferior he is, the more willing he will be to narrate anything and to consider nothing beneath

396b

396c

396d

396e

397a

him. Hence he will undertake to imitate, before a large audience and in a serious way, all the things we just mentioned: thunder and the sounds of winds, hail, axles, and pulleys; trumpets, flutes, pipes, and all the other instruments; and even the cries of dogs, sheep, and birds. And his style will consist entirely of imitation in voice and gesture, won't it, with possibly a small bit of plain narration thrown in? 397b

ADEIMANTUS: Yes, that must be so, too.

SOCRATES: Well, then, that is what I meant when I said that there are two kinds of style.

ADEIMANTUS: And you were right; there are.

SOCRATES: Now, one of them involves little variation.[38] Hence if an appropriate harmony and rhythm are provided for this style, won't anyone who speaks in it correctly come close to speaking in a single harmony and, what is more, in a rhythm of pretty much the same sort, since the variations involved in it are slight?

ADEIMANTUS: Yes, that's precisely what he will do. 397c

SOCRATES: What about the other kind of style? Won't it need the opposite: namely, every harmony and every rhythm, if it, too, is going to be spoken in properly, since it is multifarious in the forms of its variations?

ADEIMANTUS: Yes, that's very much what it is like.

SOCRATES: Now, doesn't every poet and speaker adopt a style that fits one or the other of these patterns, or a mixture of both?

ADEIMANTUS: Necessarily.

SOCRATES: What are we to do, then? Shall we admit all of these into our city, or one of the pure sorts, or the mixed one? 397d

ADEIMANTUS: If my view prevails, we will admit only the pure imitator of the good person.

SOCRATES: And yet, Adeimantus, the mixed style *is* pleasing. And the one that is most pleasing to children, their tutors, and the vast majority of people is the opposite of the one you chose.

ADEIMANTUS: Yes, it is the most pleasing.

SOCRATES: But perhaps you would say that it does not harmonize with our constitution, because there is no twofold or manifold man among us, since 397e each does only one job.

ADEIMANTUS: Indeed, it does not harmonize with it.

SOCRATES: And isn't that the reason that it is only in a city like ours that we will find a shoemaker who is a shoemaker, not a ship's captain who also

---

[38] *Metabolē:* variation in general, but also a technical term in music for the transition from one harmony to another.

makes shoes; and a farmer who is a farmer, not a juror who also farms; and a soldier who is a soldier, not a moneymaker who also soldiers, and so on?

ADEIMANTUS: True, it is.

398a SOCRATES: Suppose, then, that a man whose wisdom enabled him to become multifarious and imitate everything were to arrive in person in our city and want to give a performance of his poems. It seems that we would bow down before him as someone holy, amazing, and pleasing. But we would tell him that there is no man like him in our city, and that it is not in accord with divine law for there to be one. Then we would anoint his head with perfumes, crown him with a woolen wreath,[39] and send him away to another city. But, for our own benefit, we would employ a more austere and less pleasant poet and storyteller ourselves—one who would **398b** imitate the speech of a good person and make his stories fit the patterns we laid down at the beginning, when we undertook to educate our soldiers.

ADEIMANTUS: Yes, that is certainly what we would do, if it were up to us.

SOCRATES: And now, my friend, it looks to me as though we have completed our discussion of the branch of musical training that deals with speech and stories. After all, we have discussed both what is to be said and how it is to be said.

ADEIMANTUS: Yes, it seems that way to me, too.

SOCRATES: Wouldn't what is left for us to discuss next, then, be lyric odes **398c** and songs?

ADEIMANTUS: Clearly.

SOCRATES: And couldn't anyone discover by now what to say about what they must be like, if indeed it is going to be concordant with what has already been said?

And Glaucon laughed and said:

I am afraid, Socrates, that "anyone" does not include me. You see, it is not sufficiently clear to me at the moment what we are to say, though I have my suspicions.

398d SOCRATES: Nonetheless, you are sufficiently clear about this: first, that a song consists of three elements—speech, harmony, and rhythm.

GLAUCON: Yes, I do know that, at least.

SOCRATES: Now, as far as speech is concerned, at any rate, it is no different, is it, from speech that is not part of a song, in that it must still be spoken in conformity to the patterns we established just now?

GLAUCON: True.

SOCRATES: Further, the harmony and rhythm must fit the speech.

---

[39] As was traditionally done to statues of the gods.

GLAUCON: Of course.

SOCRATES: But we said that there is no longer a need for dirges and lamentations in words.[40]

GLAUCON: No, there is not.

SOCRATES: What are the lamenting harmonies, then? You tell me; you are musical.

GLAUCON: The mixo-Lydian, the syntono-Lydian, and some others of that sort.

SOCRATES: Shouldn't we exclude them, then? After all, they are even useless for helping women to be as good as they should be, let alone men.

GLAUCON: We certainly should.

SOCRATES: Now, surely drunkenness is also entirely inappropriate for our guardians, and softness and idleness as well.

GLAUCON: Of course.

SOCRATES: What, then, are the soft harmonies, and the ones suitable for drinking parties?

GLAUCON: There are some Ionian ones that are called "relaxed," and also some Lydian ones.

SOCRATES: Could you use any of them, my friend, on men who are warriors?

GLAUCON: No, never. So it looks as though you have got the Dorian and Phrygian left.

SOCRATES: I do not know the harmonies, so just leave me that harmony that would appropriately imitate the vocal sounds and tones[41] of a courageous person engaged in battle or in other work that he is forced to do, and who—even when he fails and faces wounds or death or some other misfortune—always grapples with what chances to occur, in a disciplined and resolute way. And also leave me another harmony for when he is engaged in peaceful enterprises, or in those he is not forced to do but does willingly; or for when he is trying to persuade someone of something, or entreating a god though prayer, or a human being through instruction and advice; or for when he is doing the opposite—patiently listening to someone else, who is entreating or instructing him, or trying to change his mind through persuasion. Leave me the harmony that will imitate him, when he does not behave arrogantly when these things turn out as he intends;

398e

399a

399b

---

[40] 387d–388e.

[41] *Phthongos, prosōdia: phthongos* is a human voice, an animal cry, or more generally a sound of some sort; *prosōdia* is the tone or accent of a syllable, or a song accompanied by music.

399c but, on the contrary, is temperate and moderate in all these enterprises, and satisfied with their outcomes. Leave me these two harmonies, then—the forced and the willing—that will best imitate the voices of temperate and courageous men in good fortune and in bad.

GLAUCON: You are asking to be left with the very ones I just mentioned.

SOCRATES: Well, then, we will have no need for multi-stringed or poly-harmonic instruments to accompany our odes and songs.

GLAUCON: No, it seems to me we won't.

399d SOCRATES: Then we won't maintain craftsmen who make triangular lutes, harps, and all other such multi-stringed and polyharmonic instruments.

GLAUCON: Apparently not.

SOCRATES: What about flute-makers and flute players? Will you allow them into the city? Or isn't the flute the most multi-stringed of all?[42] And aren't polyharmonic instruments all imitations of it?

GLAUCON: Clearly, they are.

SOCRATES: You have the lyre and the cithara left, then, as useful in our city; and in the countryside, by contrast, there would be a sort of pipe for the herdsman to play.

GLAUCON: That is what our argument suggests, anyway.

399e SOCRATES: Well we are certainly not doing anything new, my friend, in preferring Apollo and his instruments to Marsyas and his.[43]

GLAUCON: No, by Zeus, I suppose we aren't.

SOCRATES: And, by the dog,[44] we have certainly been unwittingly repurifying the city we described as luxurious a while ago.

GLAUCON: That just shows how temperate we are.

SOCRATES: Then let's complete the purification. Now, the next topic after harmonies is the discussion of rhythms. We should not chase after complexity or multifariousness in the basic elements.[45] On the contrary, we should 400a try to discover the rhythms of a life that is ordered and courageous, and then adapt the metrical foot and the melody to the speech characteristic of

---

[42] The flute is characterized as multistringed because of the number of different notes it is capable of producing.

[43] After Athena had invented the flute, she discarded it because playing it distorted her features. It was picked up by the satyr Marsyas, who was foolish enough to challenge Apollo (inventor of the lyre) to a musical contest. He was defeated, and Apollo flayed him alive. Satyrs were bestial in their behavior and desires—especially their sexual desires.

[44] Probably the dog-headed Egyptian god Anubis.

[45] Rhythm is poetic meter, and the elements are the metrical feet.

it, not the speech to them. What rhythms these would be is for you to say, just as you did in the case of the harmonies.

GLAUCON: No, by Zeus, I cannot tell you that. However, I can tell you from observation that there are three kinds of metrical feet[46] out of which the others are constructed, just as there are four, in the case of voices, from which come all the harmonies.[47] But I cannot tell you which sort imitates which sort of life.

SOCRATES: Well, then, we will also have to consult with Damon, on this point, and ask him which metrical feet suit illiberality, arrogance, madness, and the other vices, and which their opposites. I think I have heard him using the unclear terms "warlike," "complex," "fingerlike," and "heroic" to describe one foot, which he arranged, I do not know how, to be equal up and down in the interchange of long and short.[48] And I think he called one foot an iamb and another a trochee, and assigned long and short quantities to them. In the case of some of these, I think he approved or disapproved of the tempo of the foot as much as of the rhythm itself, or of some combination of the two—I cannot tell you which. But, as I said, we will leave these things to Damon, since to decide them would take a long discussion. Or do you think we should try it?

GLAUCON: No, by Zeus, I do not.

SOCRATES: But you are able to decide this, at least, aren't you: that grace goes along with good rhythm and lack of grace with bad rhythm?

GLAUCON: Of course.

SOCRATES: Furthermore, good rhythm goes along with fine speaking and is similar to it, while bad rhythm goes along with the opposite sort, and the same goes for harmony and disharmony; since, as we said just now, rhythm and harmony must conform to speech, and not vice versa.

GLAUCON: Yes, they certainly must conform to speech.

SOCRATES: And what about the style of speaking and what is said? Don't they go along with the character of the speaker's soul?

GLAUCON: Of course.

400b

400c

400d

---

[46] Probably those in which the foot is divided in the ratio of: (1) 2:2—e.g., the dactyl ($\_\smile\smile$) or the spondee ($\_ \_$); (2) 3:2—e.g., the paeon ($\smile\smile\smile\_$); (3) 1:2 or 2:1—e.g., the iamb ($\smile\_$) or the trochee ($\_\smile$).

[47] The precise reference is unclear.

[48] The foot being described is probably the dactyl ($\_\smile\smile$): it is warlike and heroic, because Greek heroic poetry was written in dactylic hexameter; complex, because it consists of a long syllable and two short ones; equal up and down in the interchange of long and short, because a long syllable is equal in length to two short ones; and fingerlike, because the first joint on a finger is roughly equal in length to the other two.

SOCRATES: And don't all the rest go along with the style of speaking?

GLAUCON: Yes.

400e SOCRATES: Fine speech, then, as well as harmony, grace, and rhythm, go along with naiveté. I do not mean the foolishness for which naiveté is a euphemism, but the quality a mind has when it is equipped with a truly good and fine character.

GLAUCON: Absolutely.

SOCRATES: And mustn't our young people try to achieve these on every occasion, if they are going to do the job that is really theirs?

GLAUCON: Yes, they must indeed.

401a SOCRATES: Now, surely painting and all the crafts similar to it are full of them, as are embroidery, architecture, and likewise the manufacture of implements generally; and so, furthermore, is the nature of bodies and that of the other things that grow. For in all these there is grace or the lack of it. And lack of grace, bad rhythm, and disharmony are akin to bad speech and bad character, while their opposites are akin to and imitate their opposite—a character that is temperate and good.

GLAUCON: Absolutely.

401b SOCRATES: Is it only poets we have to supervise, then, compelling them either to embody the image of a good character in their poems or else not to practice their craft among us? Or mustn't we also supervise all the other craftsmen, and forbid them to represent a character that is bad, intemperate, illiberal, and graceless, in their images of living beings, in their buildings, or in any of the other products of their craft? And mustn't the one who finds this impossible be prevented from practicing in our city, so that our guardians will not be brought up on images of evil as in a meadow of bad 401c grass, where they crop and graze every day from all that surrounds them until, little by little, they unwittingly accumulate a great evil in their souls? Instead, mustn't we look for craftsmen who are naturally capable of pursuing what is fine and graceful in their work, so that our young people will live in a healthy place and be benefited on all sides as the influence exerted by those fine works affects their eyes and ears like a healthy breeze from wholesome regions, and imperceptibly guides them from earliest 401d childhood into being similar to, friendly toward, and concordant with the beauty of reason?

GLAUCON: Yes, that would be by far the best education for them.

SOCRATES: Then aren't these the reasons, Glaucon, that musical training is most important? First, because rhythm and harmony permeate the innermost element of the soul, affect it more powerfully than anything else, and bring it grace, such education makes one graceful if one is properly 401e trained, and the opposite if one is not. Second, because anyone who has

been properly trained will quickly notice if something has been omitted from a thing, or if that thing has not been well crafted or well grown. And so, since he feels disgust correctly, he will praise fine things, be pleased by them, take them into his soul, and, through being nourished by them, become fine and good. What is ugly or shameful, on the other hand, he   402a
will correctly condemn and hate while he is still young, before he is able to grasp the reason. And, because he has been so trained, he will welcome the reason when it comes and recognize it easily because of its kinship with himself.

GLAUCON: Yes, it seems to me that these are the goals of musical training.

SOCRATES: It is like learning to read, then. We became adequately proficient only when the few letters that there are did not escape us in any of the different words in which they are scattered about; and when we did not disregard them, either in a small word or a great one, as if they were not worth noticing; but tried hard to distinguish them wherever they   402b
occur, knowing that we would not be competent readers until we knew our letters.

GLAUCON: True.

SOCRATES: And isn't it also true that if there are images of letters reflected in water or mirrors, we won't know them until we know the letters themselves, for both abilities are parts of the same craft and discipline?

GLAUCON: Absolutely.

SOCRATES: Then, by the gods, aren't I right in saying that neither we nor the guardians we claim to be educating will be musically trained until we know the different forms of temperance, courage, generosity, high-   402c
mindedness, and all their kindred, and their opposites, too, which are carried around all over the place; and see them in the things in which they are, both themselves and their images; and do not disregard them, either in small things or in great, but accept that the knowledge of both belongs to the same craft and discipline?

GLAUCON: Yes, that necessarily follows.

SOCRATES: Then, if the fine habits in someone's soul and those in his physi-   402d
cal form agree and are in concord with one another, so that both share the same pattern, wouldn't that be the most beautiful sight for anyone capable of seeing it?

GLAUCON: By far.

SOCRATES: And surely the most beautiful is also the most loveable, isn't it?

GLAUCON: Of course.

SOCRATES: A really musical person, then, would passionately love people who are most like that. But a disharmonious person, he would not passionately love.

GLAUCON: No, he would not—at least, not if the defect were in the soul. If it were only in the body, however, he would put up with it and still be willing to embrace the boy who had it.

402e SOCRATES: I understand that you love or have loved such a boy yourself, and I agree with you. But tell me this: does excessive pleasure share anything in common with temperance?

GLAUCON: How can it? It surely drives one no less mad than pain does.

SOCRATES: What about with any other virtue?

403a GLAUCON: Never.

SOCRATES: Then, what about with arrogance and intemperance?

GLAUCON: Yes, with them most of all.

SOCRATES: Can you think of any pleasure that is greater or keener than sexual pleasure?

GLAUCON: No, I cannot—or of a more insane one either.

SOCRATES: But isn't the right sort of passion a naturally moderate and musically educated passion for order and beauty?

GLAUCON: Yes.

SOCRATES: Then nothing insane and nothing akin to dissoluteness can be involved in the right love?

GLAUCON: No, they cannot.

403b SOCRATES: Then sexual pleasure must not be involved, must it, and the lover and the boy who passionately love and are loved in the right way must have no share in it?

GLAUCON: No, by Zeus, Socrates, it must not be involved.

SOCRATES: It seems, then, that you will lay it down as a law in the city we are founding that a lover—if he can persuade his boyfriend to let him—may kiss him, be with him, and touch him, as a father would a son, for the sake of beautiful things. But in all other respects, his association with the one he cares about must never seem to go any further than this. Otherwise, he
403c will be reproached as untrained in music, and as lacking in appreciation for beautiful things.

GLAUCON: That's right.

SOCRATES: Do you agree, then, that our account of musical training has come to an end? At any rate, it ought to end where it has ended; for surely training in the musical crafts ought to end in a passion for beauty.

GLAUCON: I agree.

SOCRATES: Now, after musical training, our young people must be given physical training.

GLAUCON: Of course.

SOCRATES: And in this, too, they must have a careful training, which starts in childhood and continues throughout life. It would, I believe, be some- 403d thing like this—but you should consider what you think, too. You see, I, for my part, do not believe that a healthy body, by means of its own virtue, makes the soul good. On the contrary, I believe that the opposite is true: a good soul, by means of its own virtue, makes the body as good as possible. What do you think?

GLAUCON: I think so, too.

SOCRATES: Then if we give adequate care to the mind, entrust it with the detailed supervision of the body, and content ourselves with indicating the general patterns to be followed rather than going on at great length, wouldn't we be proceeding in the right way? 403e

GLAUCON: Yes, indeed.

SOCRATES: Now, we said that our prospective guardians must avoid drunkenness. For surely a guardian is the last person who should get so drunk that he does not know where on earth he is.

GLAUCON: Yes, it would be ridiculous for a *guardian* to need a guardian himself!

SOCRATES: What about food? These men are athletes in the greatest contest, aren't they?

GLAUCON: Yes.

SOCRATES: Then would the regimen of ordinary, trained athletes be suitable for them? **404a**

GLAUCON: Maybe.

SOCRATES: But it seems to be a soporific sort of regimen and unreliable as regards health. Or haven't you noticed that these athletes sleep their lives away, and that if they deviate even a little from their orderly regimen, they become seriously and violently ill?

GLAUCON: I have noticed that.

SOCRATES: Then we need a more refined sort of training for our warrior-athletes, since they must be like sleepless hounds, as it were, who have the keenest possible sight and hearing, and whose health is not so precarious that it cannot sustain the frequent changes of water and diet generally, and 404b the heat waves and winter storms typical of war.

GLAUCON: I agree.

SOCRATES: Wouldn't the best physical training, then, be akin to the simple musical training we described a moment ago?

GLAUCON: How do you mean?

SOCRATES: I mean a simple and good physical training, and one that is especially adapted to the conditions of war.

GLAUCON: In what way?

SOCRATES: You could learn *that* even from Homer. For you know that when
404c his heroes are at war, he does not portray them banqueting on fish[49]—even
though they are by the sea in the Hellespont—or boiled meat, but roasted
meat only, which is the sort most easily available to soldiers. For it is pretty
much always easier to use an open fire than to carry pots and pans around
everywhere.

GLAUCON: Quite right.

SOCRATES: Nor, I believe, does Homer mention rich sauces anywhere. In
fact, isn't everyone else who is in training also aware that if he is planning
to stay in good physical condition, he must avoid such things altogether?

GLAUCON: Yes, and they are certainly right to be aware of it and to avoid
them.

SOCRATES: If you think they are right to do that, my dear Glaucon, you
404d apparently do not approve of Syracusan cuisine or complex Sicilian relishes.

GLAUCON: I suppose not.

SOCRATES: Then you also object to men having a Corinthian girlfriend, [50]
if they are planning to be in good physical condition.

GLAUCON: Absolutely.

SOCRATES: And also to their enjoying the reputed delights of Attic pastries?

GLAUCON: I would have to.

SOCRATES: And the reason for that, I take it, is that we would be right to
compare this sort of diet, and this lifestyle, to the polyharmonic songs and
404e lyric odes that make use of every sort of rhythm.

GLAUCON: Of course.

SOCRATES: There complexity engendered intemperance, didn't it, and here
it engenders illness; whereas simplicity in musical training engenders temperance in the soul, and in physical training health in the body?

GLAUCON: That's absolutely true.

405a SOCRATES: And as intemperance and disease breed in a city, aren't many
law courts and surgeries opened? And don't the legal and medical profes-
sions give themselves airs when even free men in large numbers take them
very seriously?

GLAUCON: How could it be otherwise?

---

[49] Fish was a luxury item in Plato's Athens.

[50] Corinthian prostitutes enjoyed an international reputation in the Classical
period.

SOCRATES: Could you find better evidence that a city's education is in a bad and shameful state than when eminent doctors and lawyers are needed, not only by inferior people and handicraftsmen, but by those who claim to have been brought up in the manner of free men? Indeed, don't you think it is shameful and strong evidence of lack of education to be compelled to make use of a justice imposed by others, as if they were one's masters and judges, because one lacks such qualities oneself? 405b

GLAUCON: That is the most shameful thing of all.

SOCRATES: Do you really think so? Isn't it even more shameful not just to spend a good part of one's life in court defending oneself and prosecuting someone else, but to be so vulgar that one is persuaded to take pride in this and regard oneself as amazingly clever at doing injustice, and as so accomplished at every trick and turn that one can wiggle through any loophole, and avoid punishment—and to do all that for the sake of little worthless things, and because one is ignorant of how much better and finer it is to arrange one's own life so that one won't need to find a judge who is asleep? 405c

GLAUCON: Yes, that is even more shameful.

SOCRATES: What about needing the craft of medicine for something besides wounds or some seasonal illnesses? What about needing it because idleness and the regimen we described has filled one full of gasses and phlegm, like a stagnant swamp, so that sophisticated Asclepiad doctors are compelled to come up with names like "flatulence" and "catarrh" to describe one's diseases? Don't you think that is shameful? 405d

GLAUCON: Yes, it is; and those truly are strange new names for diseases.

SOCRATES: And of a sort that I do not imagine even existed in the time of Asclepius himself. My evidence for this is that his sons at Troy did not criticize the woman who treated the wounded Eurypylus with Pramneian wine that had lots of barley meal and grated cheese sprinkled on it, even though such treatment is now thought to cause inflammation. Moreover, they did not criticize Patroclus, who prescribed the treatment.[51] 405e **406a**

GLAUCON: Yet, surely it *was* a strange drink for someone in that condition.

SOCRATES: Not if you recall that the sort of modern medicine that coddles the disease was not used by the Asclepiads before the time of Herodicus. Herodicus was a physical trainer who became ill and, through a combination of physical training and medicine, tormented first and foremost himself, and then lots of other people as well. 406b

GLAUCON: How did he do that?

---

[51] At *Iliad* xi.580 ff. Eurypylus is wounded, but not treated in this way (see xi.828–36).

However, Machaon, the son of Asclepius, does receive this treatment at xi.624–50.

SOCRATES: By making his death a lengthy process. You see, although he was always tending his illness, he was not able to cure it, since it was terminal. And so he spent his life under medical treatment, with no free time for anything else whatsoever. He suffered torments if he departed even a little from his accustomed regimen; but, thanks to his wisdom, he struggled against death and reached old age.

GLAUCON: A fine reward for his craft that was!

406c SOCRATES: And appropriate for someone who did not know that it was not because of ignorance or inexperience of this kind of medicine that Asclepius failed to teach it to his sons, but because he knew that everyone in a well-regulated city has his own work to do, and that no one has the time to be ill and under treatment all his life. We see how ridiculous this would be in the case of craftsmen, but we do not see it in the case of those who are supposedly happy—the rich.

GLAUCON: What do you mean?

406d SOCRATES: When a carpenter is ill, he expects to get a drug from his doctor that will make him throw up what is making him sick or evacuate it through his bowels; or to get rid of his disease through surgery or cautery. If anyone prescribes a lengthy regimen for him and tells him that he should rest with his head bandaged and so on, he quickly replies that he has no time to be ill, and that it is not profitable for him to live like that, always minding his illness and neglecting the work at hand. After that, he says 406e goodbye to his doctor, resumes his usual regimen, lives doing his own job, and recovers his health; alternatively, if his body cannot withstand the illness, he dies and escapes his troubles.

GLAUCON: That does seem to be the correct way for someone like that to use the craft of medicine.

407a SOCRATES: Isn't that because he had a job to do, and that if he could not do it, it would not profit him to go on living?

GLAUCON: Clearly.

SOCRATES: But a rich person, it is said, has no job assigned to him of the sort that would make his life not worth living if he had to keep away from it.

GLAUCON: So it is said, at least.

SOCRATES: What, have you not heard the saying of Phocylides that once one has the means of life, one must practice virtue?[52]

GLAUCON: And even earlier, in my view.

SOCRATES: Let's not quarrel with him about that. But let's try to find out for ourselves whether this virtue is something a rich person must practice, and

---

[52] Phocylides of Miletus was a mid-sixth–century elegiac and hexameter poet best known for his epigrams.

if his life is not worth living if he does not practice it; or whether nursing an illness, while an obstacle to putting your mind to carpentry and other crafts, is no obstacle whatever to taking Phocylides' advice.   407b

GLAUCON: But, by Zeus, it is: excessive care of the body that goes beyond simple physical training is more of an obstacle than pretty much anything. For it's a nuisance in household management, in military service, and even in sedentary political office.

SOCRATES: And the greatest of all, surely, is that it makes any sort of learning, thought, or private meditation difficult, by forever causing imaginary   407c headaches or dizziness and accusing philosophy of causing them. Hence, wherever this sort of virtue is practiced and submitted to philosophical scrutiny, excessive care of the body hinders it. For it is constantly making you imagine that you are ill and never lets you stop agonizing about your body.

GLAUCON: Yes, probably so.

SOCRATES: Then won't we say that Asclepius knew this, too, and that he invented the craft of medicine for people whose bodies are healthy in nature and habit, but have some specific disease in them? That is the type of person and condition for which he invented it. He rid them of their disease   407d by means of drugs or surgery, and then prescribed their normal regimen, so that affairs of politics would not be harmed. However, he did not attempt to prescribe regimens for those whose bodies were riddled with disease, so that by drawing off a little here and pouring in a little there, he could make their life a prolonged misery and enable them to produce offspring in all probability like themselves. He did not think that he should treat someone who could not live a normal life, since such a person would profit   407e neither himself nor his city.

GLAUCON: Asclepius was a true man of politics, in your view.

SOCRATES: Clearly so. And it was because he was like that, don't you see, that his sons, too, turned out to be good men in the war at Troy, and prac-   **408a** ticed the craft of medicine as I say they did. Don't you remember that they "sucked out the blood and applied gentle drugs" to the wound Pandarus inflicted on Menelaus? But they no more prescribed what he should eat or drink after that than they did for Eurypylus?[53] That was because they assumed that their drugs were sufficient to cure men who were healthy and living an orderly life before being wounded, even if they happened to drink wine mixed with barley and cheese right afterward. But they thought that   408b the lives of naturally sick and intemperate people were profitable neither to themselves nor to anyone else, that the craft of medicine shouldn't be

---

[53] *Iliad* iv.218–19. In the extant text, Machaon is acting alone.

practiced on them, and that they should not be given treatment, not even if they were richer than Midas.

GLAUCON: The sons of Asclepius were indeed very sophisticated, in your view.

SOCRATES: It is the right view to hold of them. And yet it is on just this point that Pindar and the tragedians are not persuaded by us. They say that Asclepius, even though he was the son of Apollo, was bribed with gold to heal a rich man who was already dying, and that that is why he was struck by lightning. But, in view of what we said before, we won't accept both claims from them. On the contrary, we will say that if Asclepius was the son of a god, he was not a money-grubber; and that if he was a money-grubber, he was not the son of a god.

GLAUCON: That's absolutely right. But what do you say about the following, Socrates? Won't we need to have good doctors in our city? And the best, I take it, will be those who have treated the greatest number of healthy and diseased people. In the same way, the best judges will be those who have associated with people with multifarious natures.

SOCRATES: I certainly agree that we need good ones. But do you know which ones I regard as such?

GLAUCON: I will, if you will tell me.

SOCRATES: Well, I will try. However, you ask about things that are not alike in the same question.

GLAUCON: What do you mean?

SOCRATES: Doctors, it is true, would become cleverest if, in addition to learning the craft of medicine, they associated with the greatest possible number of the most diseased bodies right from childhood, had themselves experienced every illness, and were not, by nature, very healthy. After all, they do not treat a body with a body. If they did, we would not allow their bodies to be or become bad. But it is with a soul that a body is treated, and it is not possible for a soul to treat anything well if it is or has become bad itself.

GLAUCON: That's right.

SOCRATES: But a *judge,* my friend, does rule a soul with a soul. And it is not possible for a soul to be nurtured among bad souls from childhood, to have associated with them, and to have itself indulged in every sort of injustice, so as to be able to draw exact inferences from itself about the injustices of others, as in the case of diseases of the body. On the contrary, it itself the craft of medicine, they associated with must have no experience of, and be uncontaminated by, bad characters while it is young, if as a fine and good soul itself, it is going to make judgments about what is just in a healthy way. That is precisely the reason, indeed, that good people are thought to be naïve when they are young and easily deceived by unjust ones: they do not have models within themselves of the behavior of bad ones. 409b

GLAUCON: Yes, indeed, that is precisely what happens to them.

SOCRATES: That is why a good judge must not be young, but old—a late learner of what sort of thing injustice is, who has become aware of it, not as something at home in his own soul, but as an alien thing present in other people's souls. He must have trained himself over many years to discern how naturally bad it is by using his theoretical knowledge, not his own intimate experience of it.

GLAUCON: At any rate, it would seem that *the noblest* judge would be like 409c that.

SOCRATES: And so is the *good* one you asked about, since the one who has a good soul is good. The clever and suspicious person, on the other hand, who has committed many injustices himself and thinks of himself to be unscrupulous and wise, appears clever when he associates with those like himself, because he is on his guard and looks to the models within himself. But when he meets with good people who are older, he is seen to be stupid, distrustful at the wrong time, and ignorant of what a healthy character is, since he has no model of this within himself. But because he meets bad 409d people more often than good ones, he seems more wise than foolish, both to himself and to them as well.

GLAUCON: That's absolutely true.

SOCRATES: Then we must not look for a good judge among people like that, but among the sort we described earlier. For while a bad person could never come to know either vice or virtue, a naturally virtuous person, when educated, will in time acquire knowledge of both virtue and vice. And it is someone like that, and not a bad person, who becomes a wise judge in my view. 409e

GLAUCON: And I share your view.

SOCRATES: Then won't you establish by law in your city both the craft of medicine we mentioned and this craft of judging along with it? And these crafts will care for such of your citizens as have naturally good bodies and souls; but those whose bodies are not like that they will allow to die, while 410a those whose souls are naturally and incurably bad they will themselves put to death.

GLAUCON: Yes, we have seen that that is best both for those who receive such treatment and for the city.

SOCRATES: And so it is clear that *your* young people will be wary of coming to need a judge, since they employ that simple sort of musical training, which we said engenders temperance.

GLAUCON: Of course.

SOCRATES: And won't a person who is musically trained hunt for a type of
410b physical training by following these same tracks, and catch it, if he chooses?
And won't the result be that he will have no need of the craft of medicine,
except when absolutely necessary?

GLAUCON: That's my view, at any rate.

SOCRATES: And he will undertake even the regimens and exertions of
physical training with an eye less to strength than to arousing the spirited
part of his nature, unlike all other athletes who use diets and exertions only
to gain muscle power.

GLAUCON: That's absolutely right.

SOCRATES: Then, doesn't it follow, Glaucon, that those who established
musical training and physical training did not establish them with the aim
410c that some people attribute to them: namely, to treat the body with the
former and the soul with the latter?

GLAUCON: What was it then?

SOCRATES: It looks as though they established both chiefly for the sake of
the soul.

GLAUCON: How so?

SOCRATES: Have you never noticed the mind-set of those who have a life-
long association with physical training but stay away from musical training?
Or, again, that of those who do the opposite?

GLAUCON: What do you mean?

410d SOCRATES: Savagery and toughness, in the one case; softness and over-
cultivation, in the other.

GLAUCON: I have certainly noticed that people who devote themselves
exclusively to physical training turn out to be more savage than they
should, while those who devote themselves to musical training turn out
to be softer than is good for them.

SOCRATES: And surely the savageness derives from the spirited element
of their nature, which, if rightly nurtured, becomes courageous, but, if
overstrained, is likely to become hard and harsh.

GLAUCON: So it seems.

SOCRATES: What about the cultivation? Wouldn't it derive from the philo-
410e sophic element of their nature, which, if relaxed too much, becomes softer
than it should, but, if well nurtured, is cultivated and orderly?

GLAUCON: That's right.

SOCRATES: Now, we said that our guardians must have both these natures.

GLAUCON: Yes, they must.

SOCRATES: And mustn't the two be harmonized with one another?

GLAUCON: Of course.

SOCRATES: And isn't the soul of the person thus harmonized temperate and
courageous?   **411a**

GLAUCON: Certainly.

SOCRATES: And that of the inharmonious person, cowardly and savage?

GLAUCON: Exactly.

SOCRATES: So when someone gives himself over to musical training and
lets the flute pour into his soul through his ears, as through a funnel, those
sweet, soft, and plaintive harmonies we mentioned; and when he spends
his whole life humming, entranced by song, the first result is that whatever
spirit he had, he softens the way he would iron and makes useful, rather
than useless and brittle. But when he keeps at it unrelentingly and charms   411b
his spirit, the next result is that he melts it and dissolves it completely until
he has cut out, so to speak, the very sinews of his soul and makes himself
"a feeble warrior."[54]

GLAUCON: Yes, indeed.

SOCRATES: And if he has a spiritless nature to begin with, this happens
quickly. But if he has a spirited one, his spirit becomes weak and unstable,
quickly inflamed by trivial things and quickly extinguished. As a result,
people like that become irascible and bad-tempered, instead of spirited,   411c
and filled with peevishness.

GLAUCON: Absolutely.

SOCRATES: On the other hand, what about someone who works hard at
physical training, eats very well, and never touches musical training or
philosophy? At first, because his body is in good strong condition, isn't he
full of pride and spirit, and more courageous than he was before?

GLAUCON: He certainly is.

SOCRATES: But what happens if he does nothing but this and never enters
into partnership with a Muse? Even if there was some love of learning in
his soul, because it never tastes any sort of instruction or investigation, and   411d
never participates in any discussion or in any of the rest of musical training, doesn't it become weak, deaf, and blind, because it never receives any
stimulation or nourishment, and its senses are never purified?

GLAUCON: Yes, it does.

SOCRATES: Then a person like that, I take it, becomes an unmusical hater
of argument[55] who no longer uses argument to persuade people, but force
and savagery, behaves like a wild beast, and lives in awkward ignorance   411e
without rhythm or grace.

---

[54] *Iliad* xvii.588.

[55] *Misologos:* the opposite of a philosopher, who is a *philologos,* a lover of argument.
See *Phaedo* 89d–91b.

GLAUCON: That's exactly how it is.

SOCRATES: So I, for one, would claim that it is to deal with *these* two things, so it seems, that a god has given two crafts to human beings—musical training and physical training—to deal with the philosophical and spirited elements, and not, except as a byproduct, with the soul and the body; but with these two, so that they might be harmonized with one another by being stretched and relaxed to the appropriate degree.

412a

GLAUCON: Yes, it seems so.

SOCRATES: Then it is the person who makes the best blend of musical and physical training, and applies them in the most perfect proportion to his soul, that we would be most correct to describe as completely trained in music and as most in harmony—far more so than the one who merely attunes his strings to one another.

GLAUCON: Probably so, Socrates.

SOCRATES: Then won't we also need this sort of person in our city, Glaucon, as a permanent overseer, if indeed its constitution is to be preserved?

412b

GLAUCON: Yes, we will need him most of all.

SOCRATES: Those, then, would be the patterns of their education and upbringing. For why should we enumerate their dances, hunts, chases with hounds, athletic contests, and horse races? After all, it is pretty much clear that they should be consistent with these patterns, and so there should no longer be any difficulty in discovering them.

GLAUCON: No, presumably there should not.

SOCRATES: All right. Now, what is the next question we have to settle? Isn't it which of these same people will rule and which be ruled?

412c

GLAUCON: Of course.

SOCRATES: Well, isn't it clear that the older ones must rule, whereas the younger ones must be ruled?

GLAUCON: Yes, it is clear.

SOCRATES: And that the rulers must be the best among them?

GLAUCON: Yes, that's clear, too.

SOCRATES: And aren't the best farmers the ones who are best at farming?

GLAUCON: Yes.

SOCRATES: In the present case, then, since the rulers must be the best of the guardians, mustn't they be the ones who are best at guarding the city?

GLAUCON: Yes.

SOCRATES: Then mustn't they be knowledgeable and capable in this matter, and, in addition, mustn't they care for the city?

412d

GLAUCON: Yes, they must.

SOCRATES: But a person would care most for what he loved.

GLAUCON: Necessarily.

SOCRATES: And he would love something most if he thought that the same things were advantageous both for it and for himself, and if he thought that when it did well, he would do well, too; and that if it didn't, the opposite would happen.

GLAUCON: That's right.

SOCRATES: Then we must choose from among our guardians the sort of men who seem on the basis of our observation to be most inclined, throughout their entire lives, to do what they believe to be advantageous for the city, and most unwilling to do the opposite.   412e

GLAUCON: Yes, they would be suitable for the job.

SOCRATES: I think, then, that we will have to observe them at every stage of their lives to make sure that they are good guardians of this conviction, and that neither compulsion nor sorcery will cause them to discard or forget their belief that they must do what is best for the city.

GLAUCON: What do you mean by discarding?

SOCRATES: I will tell you. It seems to me that the departure of a belief from someone's mind is either voluntary or involuntary—voluntary when he learns that the belief is false; involuntary in the case of all true beliefs.   413a

GLAUCON: I understand the voluntary sort, but I still need instruction about the involuntary.

SOCRATES: What? Don't you know that people are involuntarily deprived of good things, but voluntarily deprived of bad ones? And isn't being deceived about the truth a bad thing, whereas possessing the truth is a good one? Or don't you think that to believe things that are is to possess the truth?

GLAUCON: No, you are right. And I do think that people are involuntarily deprived of true beliefs.

SOCRATES: Then isn't it through theft, sorcery, and compulsion that this happens?   413b

GLAUCON: Now I do not understand again.

SOCRATES: I suppose I am making myself as clear as a tragic poet! By those who have their beliefs stolen from them, I mean those who are over-persuaded, or those who forget; because argument, in the one case, and time, in the other, takes away their beliefs without their noticing. You understand now, don't you?

GLAUCON: Yes.

SOCRATES: Well then, by those who are compelled, I mean those who are made to change their beliefs by some suffering or pain.

GLAUCON: I understand that, too, and you are right.

413c   SOCRATES: And the victims of sorcery, I think you would agree, are those who change their beliefs because they are charmed by pleasure or terrified by some fear.

GLAUCON: It seems to me that all deception is a form of sorcery.

SOCRATES: Well then, as I was just saying, we must discover which of them are best at safeguarding within themselves the conviction that they must always do what they believe to be best for the city. We must watch them right from childhood, and set them tasks in which a person would be most likely to forget such a conviction or be deceived out of it. And we must select the ones who remember and are difficult to deceive, and reject the

413d   others. Do you agree?

GLAUCON: Yes.

SOCRATES: And we must also subject them to labors, pains, and contests, and watch for the same things there.

GLAUCON: That's right.

SOCRATES: Then we must also set up a third kind of competition for sorcery. Like those who lead colts into noise and tumult to see if they are afraid, we must subject our young people to fears and then plunge them once again into pleasures, so as to test them much more thoroughly than

413e   people test gold in a fire. And if any of them seems to be immune to sorcery, preserves his composure throughout, is a good guardian of himself and of the musical training he has received, and proves himself to be rhythmical and harmonious in all these trials—he is the sort of person who would be most useful, both to himself and to the city. And anyone who is tested as a child, youth, and adult, and always emerges as being without impurities, should be established as a ruler of the city as well as a

414a   guardian, and should be honored in life and receive the most prized tombs and memorials after his death. But those who do not should be rejected. That is the sort of way, Glaucon, that I think rulers and guardians should be selected and established. Though I have provided only a pattern, not the precise details.

GLAUCON: I also think much the same.

SOCRATES: Then wouldn't it really be most correct to call these people

414b   complete guardians—the ones who guard against external enemies and internal friends, so that the former will lack the power, and the latter the desire, to do any evil; but to call the young people to whom we were referring as guardians just now, *auxiliaries* and supporters of the guardians' decrees?

GLAUCON: Yes, I think it would.

SOCRATES: How, then, could we devise one of those useful lies we were talking about a while ago,[56] a single noble lie that would, preferably, persuade even the rulers themselves; but, failing that, the rest of the city? 414c

GLAUCON: What sort of lie?

SOCRATES: Nothing new, but a sort of Phoenician story[57] about something that happened in lots of places prior to this—at least, that is what the poets say and have persuaded people to believe. It has not happened in our day, and I do not know if it could happen. It would take a lot of persuasion to get people to believe it.

GLAUCON: You seem hesitant to tell the story.

SOCRATES: You will realize that I have every reason to hesitate, when I do tell it.

GLAUCON: Out with it. Do not be afraid.

SOCRATES: All right, I will—though I do not know where I will get the audacity or the words to tell it. I will first be trying to persuade the rulers 414d and the soldiers, and then the rest of the city, that the upbringing and the education we gave them were like dreams; that they only imagined they were undergoing all the things that were happening to them, while in fact they themselves were at that time down inside the earth being formed and nurtured, and that their weapons and the rest of their equipment were also manufactured there. When they were entirely completed, the earth, their mother, sent them up, so that now, just as if the land in which they live 414e were their mother and nurse, they must deliberate on its behalf, defend it if anyone attacks it, and regard the other citizens as their earthborn brothers.

GLAUCON: It is not for nothing that you were ashamed to tell your lie earlier.

SOCRATES: No, it was only to be expected. But all the same, you should listen to the rest of the story. "Although all of you in the city are broth- 415a ers," we will say to them in telling our story, "when the god was forming you, he mixed gold into those of you who are capable of ruling, which is why they are the most honorable; silver into the auxiliaries; and iron and bronze into the farmers and other craftsmen. For the most part, you will produce children like yourselves; but, because you are all related, a silver child will occasionally be born to a golden parent, a golden child to a silver 415b parent, and so on. Therefore, the first and greatest command from the god to the rulers is that there is nothing they must guard better or watch more

---

[56] 382a–d.

[57] Apparently a reference, first, to the legend of the Phoenician hero, Cadmus, who sowed the earth with dragon's teeth from which giants grew; and, second, to the *Odyssey,* and the tales Odysseus tells to the Phaeacians.

carefully than the mixture of metals in the souls of their offspring. If an offspring of theirs is born with a mixture of iron or bronze, they must not pity him in any way, but assign him an honor appropriate to his nature and drive him out to join the craftsmen or the farmers. On the other hand, if an offspring of the latter is found to have a mixture of gold or silver, they will honor him and take him up to join the guardians or the auxiliaries. For there is an oracle that the city will be ruined if it ever has an iron or a bronze guardian." So, have you a device that will make them believe this story?

GLAUCON: No, none that would make this group believe it themselves. But I do have one for their sons, for later generations, and for all other people who come after them.

SOCRATES: Well, even that would have a good effect, by making them care more for the city and for each other. For I think I understand what you mean—namely, that all this will go where *tradition* leads. What *we* can do, however, when we have armed our earthborn people, is lead them forth with their rulers at their head. They must go and look for the best place in the city for a military encampment, a site from which they can most easily control anyone in the city who is unwilling to obey the laws, or repel any outside enemy who, like a wolf, attacks the fold. And when they have established their camp and sacrificed to the appropriate gods, they must make their sleeping quarters, mustn't they?

GLAUCON: Yes.

SOCRATES: And mustn't these provide adequate shelter against the storms of winter and the heat of summer?

GLAUCON: Yes, of course. After all, I assume you are talking about their living quarters.

SOCRATES: Yes, but ones for *soldiers,* not moneymakers.

GLAUCON: What difference do you think there is between the two, again?

SOCRATES: I will try to tell you. You see, it is surely the most terrible and most shameful thing in the world for shepherds to rear dogs as auxiliaries to help them with their flocks in such a way that those dogs themselves—because of intemperance, hunger, or some other bad condition—try to do evil to the sheep, acting not like sheepdogs but like wolves.

GLAUCON: Of course, that is terrible.

SOCRATES: So, mustn't we use every safeguard to prevent our auxiliaries from treating the citizens like that—because they are stronger—and becoming savage masters rather than gentle allies?

GLAUCON: Yes, we must.

SOCRATES: And wouldn't they have been provided with the greatest safeguard possible if they have been really well educated?

GLAUCON: But surely they have been.

SOCRATES: That is not something that deserves to be asserted so confidently, my dear Glaucon. But what does deserve it is what we were saying just now, that they must have the right education, whatever it is, if they are going to have what will do most to make them gentle to one another and the ones they are guarding. 416c

GLAUCON: That's right.

SOCRATES: But anyone with any sense will tell us that, besides this education, they must be provided with living quarters and other property of the sort that will neither prevent them from being the best guardians nor encourage them to do evil to the other citizens. 416d

GLAUCON: And he would be right.

SOCRATES: Consider, then, whether or not they should live and be housed in some such way as this, if they are going to be the sort of men we described. First, none of them should possess any private property that is not wholly necessary. Second, none should have living quarters or storerooms that are not open for all to enter at will. Such provisions as are required by temperate and courageous men, who are warrior-athletes, they should receive from the other citizens as wages for their guardianship, the amount being 416e fixed so that there is neither a shortfall nor a surplus at the end of the year. They should have common messes to go to, and should live together like soldiers in a camp. We will tell them that they have gold and silver of a divine sort in their souls as a permanent gift from the gods, and have no need of human gold in addition. And we will add that it is impious for them to defile this divine possession by possessing an admixture of mortal gold, because many impious deeds have been done for the sake of the currency 417a of the masses, whereas their sort is pure. No, they alone among the city's population are forbidden by divine law to handle or even touch gold and silver. They must not be under the same roof as these metals, wear them as jewelry, or drink from gold or silver goblets. And by behaving in that way, they would save both themselves and the city. But if they acquire private land, houses, and money themselves, they will be household managers and farmers instead of guardians—hostile masters of the other citizens, instead of their allies. They will spend their whole lives hating and being 417b hated, plotting and being plotted against, much more afraid of internal than of external enemies—already rushing, in fact, to the brink of their own destruction and that of the rest of the city as well. For all these reasons, let's declare that *that* is how the guardians must be provided with housing and the rest, and establish it as a law. Or don't you agree?

GLAUCON: Of course I do.

BOOK IV

SOCRATES' NARRATION CONTINUES: *Adeimantus interrupted:*

419a How will you defend yourself, Socrates, *he said,* if someone objects that you are not making these men very happy and, furthermore, that it is their own fault that they are not? I mean, the city really belongs to them, yet they derive no good from the city. Others own land, build fine, big houses, acquire furnishings to go along with them, make their own private sacrifices to the gods, entertain guests, and also, of course, possess what you were talking about just now: gold and silver and all the things that those who are going to be blessedly happy are thought to require. Instead of that, he might say, they seem simply to be paid wage-earning auxiliaries 420a established in the city as a garrison, and nothing else.

SOCRATES: Yes, and what is more, they do it just for upkeep and get no wages in addition to their upkeep, as other men do. So, they won't even be able to take a personal trip out of town if they want to, or give presents to their girlfriends, or spend money in whatever other ways they might wish, as people do who are considered happy. You have omitted these and a host of other similar facts from your list of charges.

ADEIMANTUS: Well, let them too be added to the charges.

420b SOCRATES: How will we defend ourselves? Is that what you are asking?

ADEIMANTUS: Yes.

SOCRATES: I think we will discover what to say if we follow the same path as before. You see, our reply will be this: it would not be at all surprising if these people were happiest just as they are. However, in establishing our city, we are not looking to make any one group in it outstandingly happy, but to make the whole city so as far as possible. For we thought that we would be most likely to find justice in such a city, and injustice, by contrast, in the one that is governed worst. And we thought that by observing both cities, we would be able to decide the question we have been inquiring 420c into for so long. At the moment, then, we take ourselves to be forming a happy city—not separating off a few happy people and putting them in it, but making the city as a whole happy. (We will look at the opposite city soon.)[1] Suppose, then, that we were painting a statue[2] and someone came up to us and started to criticize us, saying that we had not applied the most beautiful colors to the most beautiful parts of the statue; because the eyes, which are the most beautiful part, had been painted black rather than purple. We would think it reasonable to offer the following defense:

---

[1] This discussion begins at 445c, but is interrupted and does not resume again until Book viii.

[2] Ancient Greek statues were painted and gilded.

"My amazing fellow, you must not expect us to paint the eyes so beauti-   420d
fully that they no longer look like eyes at all, nor the other parts either.
On the contrary, you must look to see whether, by dealing with each part
appropriately, we are making the whole thing beautiful. Similarly, in the
present case, you must not compel us to give our guardians the sort of happiness that would make them something other than guardians. You see, we
know how to clothe the farmers in purple robes, festoon them with gold   420e
jewelry, and tell them to work the land whenever they please. We know
we could have our potters recline on couches from right to left in front of
the fire,[3] drinking and feasting with their wheel beside them for whenever
they have a desire to make pots. And we can make all the others happy in
the same way, so that the whole city is happy. But please do not urge us to
do this. For if we are persuaded by you, a farmer won't be a farmer, nor a   421a
potter a potter, nor will any of the others from which a city is constituted
remain true to type. But for most of the others, it matters less: cobblers
who become inferior and corrupt, and claim to be what they are not, do
nothing terrible to the city. But if the guardians of our laws and city are
not really what they seem to be, you may be sure that they will destroy the
city utterly and, on the other hand, that they alone have the opportunity
to govern it well and make it happy."

Now, if we are making genuine guardians, the sort least likely to do
the city evil, and if our critic is making pseudo-farmers—feasters happy   421b
at a festival, so to speak, not in a city—he is not talking about a city, but
about something else. What we have to consider, then, is whether our aim
in establishing the guardians is the greatest possible happiness for them,
or whether—since our aim is to see this happiness develop for the whole
city—we should compel and persuade the auxiliaries and guardians to
ensure that they, and all the others as well, are the best possible craftsmen
at their own work; and then, with the whole city developing and being   421c
governed well, leave it to nature to provide each group with its share of
happiness.

ADEIMANTUS: Yes, I think what you say is right.

SOCRATES: Well, then, will you also think me reasonable if I say something
closely related?

ADEIMANTUS: What exactly?

SOCRATES: Take the rest of the craftsmen again, and consider whether these
things corrupt them to such an extent that they actually become bad.

ADEIMANTUS: What things?   421d

---

[3] At formal drinking parties (*sumposia*), the toastmaster sat at the head of the table.
The others sat in order of their importance, from his right counterclockwise around
the table to his left.

SOCRATES: Wealth and poverty.

ADEIMANTUS: What do you mean?

SOCRATES: This: do you think that a potter who has become wealthy will still be willing to devote himself to his craft?

ADEIMANTUS: Not at all.

SOCRATES: Won't he become idler and more careless than he was?

ADEIMANTUS: Much more.

SOCRATES: Then won't he become a worse potter?

ADEIMANTUS: Yes, much worse.

SOCRATES: And surely if poverty prevents him from providing himself with tools, or any of the other things he needs for his craft, he will make poorer products himself and worse craftsmen of his sons or anyone else he teaches.

421e

ADEIMANTUS: Of course.

SOCRATES: So poverty and wealth make the products and the practitioners of the crafts worse.

ADEIMANTUS: Apparently.

SOCRATES: It seems, then, that we have found other things that our guardians must prevent in every way from slipping into the city undetected.

ADEIMANTUS: What things?

422a

SOCRATES: Wealth and poverty. For the former makes for luxury, idleness, and revolution; and the latter for illiberality, bad work, and revolution as well.

ADEIMANTUS: That's right. But consider this, Socrates: how will our city be able to fight a war if it has acquired no wealth—especially if it is compelled to fight a great and wealthy city?

SOCRATES: Obviously, it will be harder to fight one such city, but easier to fight two.

422b

ADEIMANTUS: How do you mean?

SOCRATES: First of all, if our city has to fight a city of the sort you mention, won't it be a case of warrior-athletes fighting rich men?

ADEIMANTUS: Yes, it will.

SOCRATES: Well, then, Adeimantus, don't you think that a single boxer who has had the best possible training could easily fight two non-boxers who are rich and fat?

ADEIMANTUS: Maybe not at the same time.

SOCRATES: Not even if he could start to run away and then turn and hit the one who caught up with him first, and could do this often, out in the stifling heat of the sun? Couldn't a man like that overcome even more than two such enemies?

422c

ADEIMANTUS: It certainly would not be surprising if he could.

SOCRATES: Well, don't you think that rich people have more knowledge and experience of boxing than of how to fight a war?

ADEIMANTUS: I do.

SOCRATES: In all likelihood, then, our athletes will easily be able to fight two or three times their number.

ADEIMANTUS: I will have to grant you that, since I think what you say is right.   422d

SOCRATES: Well, then, what if they sent an envoy to another city with the following true message: "We use no gold or silver. It is against divine law for us to do so, but not for you. So join us in this war and you can have the property of our enemy." Do you think that anyone who heard this message would choose to fight hard, lean hounds, rather than to join the hounds in fighting fat and tender sheep?

ADEIMANTUS: No, I do not. But if the wealth of all other cities were amassed by a single one, don't you think that would endanger your non-wealthy city?

SOCRATES: You are happily innocent if you think that any city besides the one we are constructing deserves to be called a city.   422e

ADEIMANTUS: What should we call them, then?

SOCRATES: We will have to find a "greater" title for the others because each of them is a great many cities, but not *a* city, as they say in the game.[4] They contain two, at any rate, which are at war with one another: the city of the poor and that of the rich. And within each of these, there are a great   423a many more. So if you treat them as one city, you will be making a big mistake. But if you treat them as many and offer one the money, power, and the very inhabitants of another, you will always find many allies and few enemies. And as long as your own city is temperately governed in the way we just arranged, it will be the greatest one—not in reputation; I do not mean that; but the greatest in fact—even if it has only a thousand soldiers to defend it. For you won't easily find one city so great among either Greeks or barbarians, though you will find many that are reputed   423b to be many times greater. Or do you disagree?

ADEIMANTUS: No, by Zeus, I do not.

SOCRATES: This, then, would also provide our rulers with the best limit for determining the proper size of the city, and how much land they should mark off for a city that size, letting the rest go.

---

[4] The reference is obscure; it may be to a saying or proverb, or to a game like checkers.

ADEIMANTUS: What limit is that?

SOCRATES: I think it is this: as long as it is willing to remain one city, it may continue to grow, but not beyond that point.

423c ADEIMANTUS: And it is a good one.

SOCRATES: Then we will also give our guardians this further order, that they are to guard in every possible way against the city's being either small in size or great in reputation, rather than adequate in size and one in number.

ADEIMANTUS: No doubt, *that* will be a trivial instruction for them to follow!

SOCRATES: Here is another that is even more trivial. We mentioned it earlier as well.[5] We said that if an offspring of the guardians is inferior, he must be sent off to join the other citizens, and that if the others have an excellent

423d offspring, he must join the guardians. This was meant to make clear that every other citizen, too, must be assigned to what naturally suits him, with one person assigned to one job so that, practicing his own pursuit, each of them will become not many but one, and the entire city thereby naturally grow to be one, not many.

ADEIMANTUS: Oh, yes, that is a more minor one!

SOCRATES: Really, my good Adeimantus, the orders we are giving them are neither as numerous nor as difficult as one would think. Indeed, they

423e are all insignificant provided, as the saying goes, they safeguard the one great thing—or rather not great but adequate.

ADEIMANTUS: What's that?

SOCRATES: Their education and upbringing. For if a good education makes them moderate men, they will easily discover all this for themselves—and everything else that we are now omitting, such as the possession of women,

424a marriages, and the procreation of children, and how all these must be governed as far as possible by the old proverb that friends share everything in common.

ADEIMANTUS: Yes, that would be best.

SOCRATES: And surely once our constitution is well started, it will, as it were, go on growing cyclically. For good education and upbringing, if they are kept up, produce good natures; and sound natures, which in turn receive such an education, grow up even better than their predecessors in every respect—but particularly with respect to their offspring, as in the case of all the other animals.

424b ADEIMANTUS: Yes, probably so.

---

[5] 415a–c.

SOCRATES: To put it briefly, then, what the overseers of our city must cling to, not allow to become corrupted without their noticing it, and guard against everything, is this: there must be no innovation in musical or physical training that goes against the established order. On the contrary, they must guard against that as much as they can. And they should dread to hear anyone say that "people think most of the song that floats newest from the singer's lips,"[6] in case someone happens to suppose that the poet means not new *songs,* but a new *way of singing,* and praises that. We should not praise such a claim, however, or take it to be what the poet meant. You see, a change to a new kind of musical training is something to beware of as wholly dangerous. For one can never change the ways of training people in music without affecting the greatest political laws. That is what Damon says, and I am convinced he is right. 424c

ADEIMANTUS: You can also count me among those who are convinced.

SOCRATES: It seems, then, that it is in musical training that the guardhouse of our guardians must surely be built. 424d

ADEIMANTUS: At any rate, this sort of lawlessness easily inserts itself undetected.

SOCRATES: Yes, because it is supposed to be only part of a game that, as such, can do no harm.

ADEIMANTUS: And it does not do any—except, of course, that when it has established itself there, it slowly and silently flows over into people's habits and practices. From these it travels forth with greater vigor into private contracts, and then from private contracts it advances with the utmost insolence into the laws and constitution, Socrates, until in the end it overthrows everything public and private. 424e

SOCRATES: Well, is that so?

ADEIMANTUS: I think it is.

SOCRATES: Then, as we were saying at the beginning, our children must take part in games that are more law-abiding right from the start, since, if their games become lawless and the children follow suit, isn't it impossible for them to grow up into excellent and law-abiding men? 425a

ADEIMANTUS: Of course.

SOCRATES: So whenever children play in a good way right from the start and absorb lawfulness from musical training, there is the opposite result: lawfulness follows them in everything and fosters their growth, correcting anything in the city that may have been neglected before.

ADEIMANTUS: That's true.

---

[6] *Odyssey* i.351–52. Our text of Homer is slightly different.

SOCRATES: And so such people rediscover the seemingly insignificant conventional norms their predecessors had destroyed.

ADEIMANTUS: Which sort?

425b SOCRATES: Those dealing with things like this: the silence appropriate for younger people in the presence of their elders; the giving up of seats for them and standing up in their presence; the care of parents; hairstyles; clothing; shoes; the general appearance of the body; and everything else of that sort. Don't you agree?

ADEIMANTUS: I do.

SOCRATES: To legislate about such things is naïve, in my view, since verbal or written decrees will never make them come about or last.

ADEIMANTUS: How could they?

425c SOCRATES: At any rate, Adeimantus, it looks as though the start of someone's education determines what follows. Or doesn't like always encourage like?

ADEIMANTUS: It does.

SOCRATES: And the final outcome of education, I imagine we would say, is a single, complete, and fresh product that is either good or the opposite.

ADEIMANTUS: Of course.

SOCRATES: That is why I, for my part, would not try to legislate about such things.

ADEIMANTUS: And with good reason.

SOCRATES: Then, by the gods, what about all that marketplace business, the contracts people make with one another in the marketplace, for example, 425d and contracts with handicraftsmen, and slanders, injuries, indictments, establishing juries, paying or collecting whatever dues are necessary in marketplace and harbors, and, in a word, the entire regulation of marketplace, city, harbor, or what have you—dare we legislate about any of these?

ADEIMANTUS: No, it would not be appropriate to dictate to men who are fine and good. For they will easily find out for themselves whatever needs 425e to be legislated about such things.

SOCRATES: Yes, my friend, provided that a god grants that the laws we have already described are preserved intact.

ADEIMANTUS: If not, they will spend their lives continually enacting and amending such laws in the hope of finding what is best.

SOCRATES: You mean they will live like those sick people who, because they are intemperate, are not willing to abandon their bad way of life.

ADEIMANTUS: That's right.

426a SOCRATES: Such people really do lead a charming life! Their medical treatment achieves nothing, except to make their illnesses worse and more complex, and they are always hoping that someone will recommend some new drug that will make them healthy.

ADEIMANTUS: Yes, that's exactly what happens to invalids of this sort.

SOCRATES: And isn't it another charming feature of theirs that they think their worst enemy of all is the one who tells them the truth—that until they give up drunkenness, overeating, sexual indulgence, and idleness, then no drug, cautery, or surgery, no charms, amulets, or anything else of that sort will do them any good? 426b

ADEIMANTUS: It is not charming at all. Being harsh to someone who tells the truth is not charming.

SOCRATES: You do not approve of such men, apparently.

ADEIMANTUS: No, by Zeus, I do not.

SOCRATES: Then nor will you approve of an entire city that behaves in the way we were just describing. Or don't you think that such invalids behave in the very same way as cities where the following occurs? Because they are badly governed politically, the citizens are warned not to change the city's whole political system, and the one who does is threatened with the 426c death penalty. But the one who serves these cities most pleasantly, while they remain politically governed in that way; who indulges them, flatters them, anticipates their wishes, and is clever at fulfilling them; isn't he, on that account, honored by them as a good man who is wise in the greatest matters?

ADEIMANTUS: Yes, I think their behavior is the same and I do not approve of it at all.

SOCRATES: What about those who are willing and eager to provide treatment for such cities? Don't you approve of their courage and also their 426d lighthearted irresponsibility?

ADEIMANTUS: I do indeed—except for those who are actually deluded and suppose themselves to be true men of politics because they are praised by the masses.

SOCRATES: What do you mean? Have you no sympathy for these men? Or do you think it is possible for a man who does not know how to measure anything not to believe that he is four cubits tall[7] when many others, who are similarly ignorant, tell him that he is? 426e

ADEIMANTUS: No, I do not think that.

SOCRATES: Then do not be too hard on them. You see, such people are surely the most charming of all. They pass and amend the sorts of laws we have just been describing, and are always expecting that they will find

---

[7] Roughly seven feet. A cubit is between seventeen and twenty-two inches long.

a way to put a stop to cheating on contracts, and the other evildoings I mentioned just now, not realizing that they are really just cutting off a Hydra's head.[8]

427a ADEIMANTUS: Yet that is all they are really doing.

SOCRATES: I would have thought, then, that a true lawgiver should not bother with laws or constitutions of this kind, whether in a politically badly governed or in a politically well-governed city—in the one because it is useless and accomplishes nothing; in the other because some of them are discoverable by anyone, while the others follow automatically from the practices already described.

427b ADEIMANTUS: What remains for us to legislate, then?

SOCRATES: For us, nothing; but for the Delphic Apollo, there remain the greatest, finest, and first of legislations.

ADEIMANTUS: What are they about?

SOCRATES: The establishing of temples and sacrifices, and other forms of service to gods, daimons, and heroes; the burial of the dead, and the services that ensure the favor of those who have gone to the other world. For we, of course, have no knowledge of these things and so, when we are **427c** founding a city, we won't take anyone else's advice, if we have any sense, or employ any interpreter except our ancestral one. And in fact, this god—as he delivers his interpretations from his seat at the navel of the earth[9]—is the ancestral guide on these matters for the whole human race.

ADEIMANTUS: Well put. That is what we must do.

SOCRATES: So then, son of Ariston, your city would now seem to be **427d** founded. As the next step, look inside it, having got hold of an adequate light somewhere. Look yourself and invite your brother and Polemarchus and the rest of us to help you, to see where justice and injustice might be in it, how they differ from one another, and which of the two must be possessed by the person who is going to be happy, whether that fact is hidden from all gods and humans or not.

And Glaucon said:

That's nonsense! You promised you would look for them yourself, because **427e** you said it was impious for you not to defend justice in every way you could.[10]

---

[8] The Hydra was a mythical monster. When one of its heads was cut off, two or three new heads grew in its place. Heracles (or Hercules) had to slay the Hydra as one of his labors.

[9] The oracle of the god is Apollo. His seat is Delphi. A stone there marked the supposed center of the earth.

[10] 368b–c.

SOCRATES: You are right to remind me, and I must do what I promised. But you will have to help.

GLAUCON: We will.

SOCRATES: I expect, then, to find justice in the following way. I think our city, if indeed it has been correctly founded, is completely good.

GLAUCON: Yes, it must be.

SOCRATES: Clearly, then, it is wise, courageous, temperate, and just.

GLAUCON: Clearly.

SOCRATES: Then if we find any of these in it, what remains will be what we have not found?   428a

GLAUCON: Of course.

SOCRATES: Therefore, as in the case of any other four things, if we were looking for one of them in something and recognized it first, that would be enough to satisfy us. But if we recognized the other three first, that itself would enable us to recognize what we were looking for, since clearly it could not be anything other than the one that remains.

GLAUCON: That's right.

SOCRATES: So, since there also happen to be four things we are interested in, mustn't we look for them in the same way?

GLAUCON: Clearly.

SOCRATES: Now, the first thing I think I can see clearly in the city is wis-   428b
dom. And there seems to be something odd about it.

GLAUCON: What?

SOCRATES: I think that the city we described is really wise. And that is because it is prudent,[11] isn't it?

GLAUCON: Yes.

SOCRATES: And surely it is clear that this very thing, prudence, is some sort of knowledge. I mean, it certainly is not through *ignorance* that people do the prudent thing, but through knowledge.

GLAUCON: Clearly.

SOCRATES: But there are, of course, many multifarious sorts of knowledge in the city.

GLAUCON: Certainly.

SOCRATES: So, is it because of the knowledge possessed by the carpenters that the city deserves to be described as wise and prudent?

GLAUCON: Not at all. It is called skilled in carpentry because of that.   428c

---

[11] *Euboulos:* in Greek cities, the *boulē* was the council that had day-to-day responsibility for public affairs.

SOCRATES: So a city shouldn't be called wise because it has the knowledge that deliberates about how wooden things can be best.

GLAUCON: Certainly not.

SOCRATES: What about this, then? What about the knowledge of things made of bronze, or anything else of that sort?

GLAUCON: Not anything of that sort either.

SOCRATES: And not the knowledge of how to produce crops from the soil. On the contrary, it is skilled in farming because of that.

GLAUCON: That's my view.

SOCRATES: Then is there some knowledge in the city we have just founded, which some of its citizens have, that does not deliberate about some particular thing in the city, but about the city as a whole, and about how its internal relations and its relations with other cities will be the best possible.

GLAUCON: There is indeed.

SOCRATES: What is it and who has it?

GLAUCON: It is the craft of guardianship. And the ones who possess it are those rulers we just now[12] called complete guardians.

SOCRATES: Because it has this knowledge, then, how do you describe the city?

GLAUCON: As prudent and really wise.

SOCRATES: Now, do you think that there will be more metalworkers in the city, or more of these true guardians?

GLAUCON: There will be far more metalworkers.

SOCRATES: Of all those who are called by a certain name because they have some sort of knowledge, wouldn't the true guardians be the fewest in number?

GLAUCON: By far.

SOCRATES: So, it is because of the smallest group or part of itself, and the knowledge that is in it—the part that governs and rules—that a city founded according to nature would be wise as a whole. And this class— which seems to be, by nature, the smallest—is the one that inherently possesses a share of the knowledge that alone among all the other sorts of knowledge should be called wisdom.

GLAUCON: That's absolutely true.

SOCRATES: So we have found—though I do not know how—this one of the four and its place in the city, too.

GLAUCON: It seems to me, at least, that it has been well and truly found.

428d

428e

429a

---

12 414b.

SOCRATES: But surely courage and the part of the city it is in, and because of which the city is described as courageous, is not very difficult to spot.

GLAUCON: How so?

SOCRATES: Who would describe a city as cowardly or courageous by look- 429b ing at anything other than that part which defends it and wages war on its behalf?

GLAUCON: No one would look at anything else.

SOCRATES: Because, I take it, whether the others are courageous or cowardly doesn't make it one or the other.

GLAUCON: No, it doesn't.

SOCRATES: So courage, too, belongs to a city because of a part of itself— because it has in that part the power to preserve through everything its belief that the things, and the sorts of things, that should inspire terror are the very things, and sorts of things, that the lawgiver declared to be such 429c in the course of educating it. Or don't you call that courage?

GLAUCON: I do not completely understand what you said. Would you mind repeating it?

SOCRATES: I mean that courage is a sort of preservation.

GLAUCON: What sort of preservation?

SOCRATES: The preservation of the belief, inculcated by the law through education, about what things, and what sorts of things, inspire terror. And by its preservation "through everything," I mean preserving it though pains, pleasures, appetites, and fears and not abandoning it. I will compare 429d it to something I think it resembles, if you like.

GLAUCON: I would like that.

SOCRATES: You know, then, that when dyers want to dye wool purple, they first select from wools of many different colors the ones that are naturally white. Then they give them an elaborate preparatory treatment, so that they will accept the color as well as possible. And only at that point do they dip them in the purple dye. When something is dyed in this way, it holds the dye fast, and no amount of washing, whether with or without 429e detergent, can remove the color. But you also know what happens when things are not dyed in this way, when one dyes wools of other colors, or even these white ones, without preparatory treatment.

GLAUCON: I know they look washed out and ridiculous.

SOCRATES: You should take it, then, that we too were trying as hard as we could to do something similar when we selected our soldiers and educated them in musical and physical training. It was contrived, you should sup- 430a pose, for no purpose other than to ensure that—persuaded by us—they would absorb the laws in the best possible way, just like wool does a dye;

that as a result, their beliefs about what things should inspire terror, and about everything else, would hold fast because they had the proper nature and rearing; so fast that the dye could not be washed out even by those detergents that are so terribly effective at scouring—pleasure, which is 430b much more terribly effective at this than any chalestrian[13] or alkali, and pain and fear and appetite, which are worse than any detergent. This power, then, to preserve through everything the correct and law-inculcated belief about what should inspire terror and what should not is what I, at any rate, call courage. And I will assume it is this, unless you object.

GLAUCON: No, I have no objection. For I presume that the sort of correct belief about these same matters that you find in animals and slaves, which is not the result of education and has nothing at all to do with law, is called something other than courage.

430c SOCRATES: You are absolutely right.

GLAUCON: Well, then, I accept your account of courage.

SOCRATES: Yes, do accept it, at any rate, as my account of *political* courage, and you will be right to accept it. If you like, we will discuss that more fully some other time. You see, at the moment, our inquiry is not about courage but about justice. And for the purpose of that inquiry, I think that what we have said is sufficient.

GLAUCON: You are right.

SOCRATES: Two things, then, remain for us to find in the city: temperance 430d and—the goal of our entire inquiry—justice.

GLAUCON: Yes, indeed.

SOCRATES: How could we find justice, then, so we won't have to bother with temperance any further?

GLAUCON: Well I, for my part, do not know of any, nor would I want justice to appear first if that means that we are not going to investigate temperance any further. So if you want to please me, look for it before the other.

SOCRATES: Of course I want to. It would be wrong not to.

GLAUCON: Go ahead and look, then.

430e SOCRATES: I will. And seen from here, it is more like a sort of concord and harmony than the previous ones.

GLAUCON: How so?

SOCRATES: Temperance is surely a sort of order, the mastery of certain sorts of pleasures and appetites. People indicate as much when they use the term

---

[13] Carbonate of soda from Chalestra, a town and lake in Macedonia.

"self-mastery"—though I do not know in what way. This and other similar things are like tracks that temperance has left. Isn't that so?

GLAUCON: Absolutely.

SOCRATES: Isn't the term "self-mastery" ridiculous, though? For, of course, the one who is master of himself is also the one who is weaker, and the one who is weaker is also the one who masters. After all, the same person is referred to in all these descriptions. **431a**

GLAUCON: Of course.

SOCRATES: It seems to me, however, that what this term is trying to indicate is that within the same person's soul, there is a better thing and a worse one. Whenever the naturally better one masters the worse, this is called being master of oneself. At any rate, it is praised. But whenever, as a result of bad upbringing or associating with bad people, the smaller and better one is mastered by the inferior majority, this is blamed as a disgraceful thing and **431b** is called being weaker than oneself, or being intemperate.

GLAUCON: Yes, that seems plausible.

SOCRATES: Now, then, take a look at our new city and you will find one of these conditions present in it. For you will say that it is rightly described as master of itself, if indeed anything in which the better rules the worse is to be described as temperate and master of itself.

GLAUCON: I am looking, and what you say is true.

SOCRATES: Furthermore, pleasures, pains, and appetites that are numerous and multifarious are things one would especially find in children, women, **431c** household slaves, and in the so-called free members of the masses—that is, the inferior people.

GLAUCON: Yes.

SOCRATES: But the pleasures, pains, and appetites that are simple and moderate, the ones that are led by rational calculation with the aid of understanding and correct belief, you would find in those few people who are born with the best natures and receive the best education.

GLAUCON: That's true.

SOCRATES: Don't you see, then, that this too is present in your city, and that the appetites of the masses—the inferior people—are mastered there by the wisdom and appetites of the few—the best people? **431d**

GLAUCON: I do.

SOCRATES: So, if any city is said to be master of its pleasures and appetites and of itself, it is this one.

GLAUCON: Absolutely.

SOCRATES: So isn't it also temperate because of all this?

GLAUCON: Yes, indeed.

SOCRATES: And moreover, if there is any city in which rulers and subjects share the same belief about who should rule, it is this one. Or don't you agree?

GLAUCON: Yes, I certainly do.

SOCRATES: And in which of them do you say temperance is located when they are in this condition? In the rulers or the subjects?

GLAUCON: In both, I suppose.

SOCRATES: Do you see, then, that the hunch we had just now—that temperance is like a sort of harmony—was quite plausible?

GLAUCON: Why is that?

SOCRATES: Because its operation is unlike that of courage and wisdom, each of which resides in one part and makes the city either courageous or wise. Temperance does not work like that, but has literally been stretched throughout the whole, making the weakest, the strongest, and those in between all sing the same song in unison—whether in wisdom, if you like, or in physical strength, if you prefer; or, for that matter, in numbers, wealth, or anything else. Hence we would be absolutely right to say that this unanimity is temperance—this concord between the naturally worse and the naturally better, about which of the two should rule both in the city and in each individual.

GLAUCON: I agree completely.

SOCRATES: All right. We have now spotted three kinds of virtue in our city. What kind remains, then, that would give the city yet another share of virtue? For it is clear that what remains is justice.

GLAUCON: It is clear.

SOCRATES: So then, Glaucon, we must now station ourselves like hunters surrounding a wood and concentrate our minds, so that justice does not escape us and vanish into obscurity. For it is clear that it is around here somewhere. Keep your eyes peeled and do your best to catch sight of it, and if you happen to see it before I do, show it to me.

GLAUCON: I wish I could help. But it is rather the case that if you use me as a follower who can see only what you point out to him, you will be using me in a more reasonable way.

SOCRATES: Pray for success, then, and follow me.

GLAUCON: I will. You have only to lead.

SOCRATES: And it truly seems to be an impenetrable place and full of shadows. It is dark, at any rate, and difficult to search through. But all the same, we must go on.

GLAUCON: Yes, we must.

And then I caught sight of something and shouted:

SOCRATES: Ah ha! Glaucon, it looks as though there is a track here, and I do not think our quarry will altogether escape us.

GLAUCON: That's good news.

SOCRATES: Oh dear, what a stupid condition in which to find ourselves!

GLAUCON: How so?

SOCRATES: It seems, blessed though you are, that the thing has been rolling around at our feet from the very beginning, and yet, like ridiculous fools, we could not see it. For just as people who are holding something in their hands sometimes search for the very thing they are holding, we did not look in the right direction but gazed off into the distance, and perhaps that is the very reason we did not notice it.   432e

GLAUCON: What do you mean?

SOCRATES: This: I think we have been talking and hearing about it all this time without understanding ourselves, or realizing that we were, in a way, talking about it.

GLAUCON: That was a long prelude! Now I want to hear what you mean!

SOCRATES: Listen, then, and see whether there is anything in what I say. You see, what we laid down at the beginning when we were founding our   **433a** city, about what should be done throughout it—that, I think, or some form of that, is justice. And surely what we laid down and often repeated, if you remember, is that each person must practice one of the pursuits in the city, the one for which he is naturally best suited.

GLAUCON: Yes, we did say that.

SOCRATES: Moreover, we have heard many people say, and have often said ourselves, that justice is doing one's own work and not meddling with what is not one's own.   433b

GLAUCON: Yes, we have.

SOCRATES: This, then, my friend, provided it is taken in a certain way, would seem to be justice—this doing one's own work. And do you know what I take as evidence of that?

GLAUCON: No, tell me.

SOCRATES: After our consideration of temperance, courage, and wisdom, I think that what remains in the city is the power that makes it possible for all of these to arise in it, and that preserves them when they have arisen for as long as it remains there itself. And we did say that justice would be what remained when we had found the other three.[14]   433c

GLAUCON: Yes, that must be so.

---

[14] 428a.

SOCRATES: Yet, surely, if we had to decide which of these will most contribute to making our city good by being present in it, it would be difficult to decide. Is it the agreement in belief between the rulers and the subjects? The preservation among the soldiers of the law-inculcated belief about what should inspire terror and what should not? The wisdom and guardianship of the rulers? Or is what most contributes to making

433d it good the fact that every child, woman, slave, free person, craftsman, ruler, and subject each does his own work and does not meddle with what is not?

GLAUCON: Of course it's a difficult decision.

SOCRATES: It seems, then, that this power—which consists in everyone's doing his own work—rivals wisdom, temperance, and courage in its contribution to the city's virtue.

GLAUCON: It certainly does.

SOCRATES: And wouldn't you say that justice is certainly what rivals them

433e in contributing to the city's virtue?

GLAUCON: Absolutely.

SOCRATES: Look at it this way, too, if you want to be convinced. Won't you assign to the rulers the job of judging lawsuits in the city?

GLAUCON: Of course.

SOCRATES: And will they have any aim in judging other than this: that no citizen should have what is another's or be deprived of what is his own?

GLAUCON: No, they will have none but that.

SOCRATES: Because that is just?

GLAUCON: Yes.

SOCRATES: So from that point of view, too, having and doing of one's own,

434a of what belongs to one, would be agreed to be justice.

GLAUCON: That's right.

SOCRATES: Now, see whether you agree with me about this: if a carpenter attempts to do the work of a shoemaker, or a shoemaker that of a carpenter, or they exchange their tools or honors with one another, or if the same person tries to do both jobs, and all other such exchanges are made, do you think that does any great harm to the city?

GLAUCON: Not really.

SOCRATES: But I imagine that when someone who is, by nature, a craftsman or some other sort of moneymaker is puffed up by wealth, or by having

434b a majority of votes, or by his own strength, or by some other such thing, and attempts to enter the class of soldiers; or when one of the soldiers who is unworthy to do so tries to enter that of judge and guardian, and these exchange their tools and honors; or when the same person tries to do all these things at once, then I imagine you will agree that these exchanges and this meddling destroy the city.

GLAUCON: Absolutely.

SOCRATES: So, meddling and exchange among these three classes is the greatest harm that can happen to the city and would rightly be called the worst evil one could do to it.   434c

GLAUCON: Exactly.

SOCRATES: And wouldn't you say that the worst evil one could do to one's own city is injustice?

GLAUCON: Of course.

SOCRATES: That, then, is what injustice is. But let's put it in reverse: the opposite of this—when the moneymaking, auxiliary, and guardian class each do their own work in the city—is justice, isn't it, and makes the city just?

GLAUCON: That's exactly what I think too.

SOCRATES: Let's not state it as fixedly established just yet. But if this kind of thing is agreed by us to be justice in the case of individual human beings as well, then we can assent to it. For what else will there be for us to say? But if it is not, we will have to look for something else. For the moment, however, let's complete the inquiry in which we supposed that if we first tried to observe justice in some larger thing that possessed it, that would make it easier to see what it is like in an individual human being. We agreed that this larger thing is a city, and so we founded the best city we could, knowing well that justice would of course be present in one that was good. So, let's apply what has come to light for us there to an individual, and if it is confirmed, all will be well. But if something different is found in the case of the individual, we will go back to the city and test it there. And perhaps by examining them side by side and rubbing them together like fire-sticks, we can make justice blaze forth and, once it has come to light, confirm it in our own case.   434d

434e

435a

GLAUCON: Well, the road you describe is the right one, and we should follow it.

SOCRATES: Well, then, if you call a larger thing and a smaller thing by the same name, are they unalike in the respect in which they are called the same, or alike?

GLAUCON: Alike.

SOCRATES: So a just man won't differ at all from a just city with respect to the form of justice but will be like it.   435b

GLAUCON: Yes, he will be like it.

SOCRATES: But now, the city, at any rate, was thought to be just because each of the three natural classes within it did its own job; and to be temperate, courageous, and wise, in addition, because of certain other conditions or states of these same classes.

GLAUCON: That's true.

SOCRATES: Then, my friend, we would expect an individual to have these same kinds of things in his soul, and to be correctly called by the same 435c   names as the city because the same conditions are present in them both.

GLAUCON: Inevitably.

SOCRATES: Well, you amazing fellow, here is another trivial investigation we have stumbled into: does the soul have these three kinds of things in it or not?

GLAUCON: It does not look at all trivial to me. Perhaps, Socrates, there is some truth in the old saying that everything beautiful is difficult.

SOCRATES: Apparently so. In fact, you should be well aware, Glaucon, that 435d   it is my belief we will never ever grasp this matter precisely by methods of inquiry of the sort we are now using in our discussions. However, there is in fact another longer and more time-consuming road that does lead there. But perhaps we can manage to come up to the standard of our previous statements and inquiries.

GLAUCON: Shouldn't we be content with that? It would be enough for me, at least for now.

SOCRATES: Well, then, it will be quite satisfactory for me, too.

GLAUCON: Then do not weary, but go on with the inquiry.

SOCRATES: Well, isn't it absolutely necessary for us to agree to this much: 435e   that the very same kinds of things and conditions exist in each one of us as exist in the city? After all, where else would they come from? You see, it would be ridiculous for anyone to think that spiritedness did not come to be in cities from the private individuals who are reputed to have this quality, such as the Thracians, Scythians, and others who live to the north of us; or that the same is not true of the love of learning, which is mostly 436a   associated with our part of the world; or of the love of money, which is said to be found not least among the Phoenicians and Egyptians.

GLAUCON: It certainly would.

SOCRATES: We may take that as being so, then, and it was not at all difficult to discover.

GLAUCON: No, it certainly was not.

SOCRATES: But this, now, *is* difficult. Do we do each of them with the same thing or, since there are three, do we do one with one and another with another: that is to say, do we learn with one, feel anger with another, and 436b   with yet a third have an appetite for the pleasures of food, sex, and those closely akin to them? Or do we do each of them with the whole of our soul, once we feel the impulse? *That* is what is difficult to determine in a way that is up to the standards of our argument.

GLAUCON: I think so, too.

SOCRATES: Well, then, let's try in this way to determine whether they are the same as one another or different.

GLAUCON: What way?

SOCRATES: It is clear that the same thing cannot do or undergo opposite things; not, at any rate, in the same respect, in relation to the same thing, at the same time. So, if we ever find that happening here, we will know that we are not dealing with one and the same thing, but with many.   436c

GLAUCON: All right.

SOCRATES: Consider, then, what I am about to say.

GLAUCON: Say it.

SOCRATES: Is it possible for the same thing, at the same time, and in the same respect, to be standing still and moving?

GLAUCON: Not at all.

SOCRATES: Let's come to a more precise agreement, in order to avoid disputes later on. You see, if anyone said of a person who is standing still but moving his hands and head, that the same thing is moving and standing still, we would not consider, I imagine, that he should say that; but rather that in one respect the person is standing still, while in another he is moving. Isn't that so?   436d

GLAUCON: It is.

SOCRATES: Then, if the one who said this became still more charming and made the sophisticated point that spinning tops, at any rate, stand still as a whole at the same time as they are also in motion, when, with the peg fixed in the same place, they revolve, or that the same holds of anything else that moves in a circle on the same spot—we would not agree, on the grounds that in such situations it is not in the same respects that these objects are both moving and standing still. On the contrary, we would say that these objects have both a straight axis and a circumference in them, and that with respect to the straight axis they stand still—since they do not wobble   436e to either side—whereas with respect to the circumference they move in a circle. But if their straight axis wobbles to the left or right or front or back at the same time as they are spinning, we will say that they are not standing still in any way.

GLAUCON: And we would be right.

SOCRATES: No such objection will disturb us, then, or make us any more likely to believe that the same thing can—at the same time, in the same respect, and in relation to the same thing—undergo, be, or do opposite things.   437a

GLAUCON: They won't have that effect on me at least.

SOCRATES: All the same, in order to avoid going through all these objections one by one and taking a long time to prove them all untrue, let's hypothesize that what we have said is correct and carry on—with the understanding that if it should ever be shown to be incorrect, all the consequences we have drawn from it will be lost.

GLAUCON: Yes, that's what we should do.

437b SOCRATES: Now, wouldn't you consider assent and dissent, wanting to have something and rejecting it, taking something and pushing it away, as all being pairs of mutual opposites—whether of opposite doings or of opposite undergoings does not matter?

GLAUCON: Yes, they are pairs of opposites.

SOCRATES: What about thirst, hunger, and the appetites as a whole, and also wishing and willing? Would you include all of them somewhere among the kinds of things we just mentioned? For example, wouldn't you say that the 437c soul of someone who has an appetite wants the thing for which it has an appetite, and draws toward itself what it wishes to have; and, in addition, that insofar as his soul wishes something to be given to it, it nods assent to itself as if in answer to a question, and strives toward its attainment?

GLAUCON: I would.

SOCRATES: What about not-willing, not-wishing, and not-having an appetite? Wouldn't we include them among the very opposites, cases in which the soul pushes and drives things away from itself?

GLAUCON: Of course.

437d SOCRATES: Since that is so, won't we say that there is a kind consisting of appetites, and that the most conspicuous examples of them are what we call hunger and thirst?

GLAUCON: We will.

SOCRATES: Isn't the one for food, the other for drink?

GLAUCON: Yes.

SOCRATES: Now, insofar as it is thirst, is it an appetite in the soul for more than what we say it is for? I mean, is thirst a thirst for hot drink or cold, or much drink or little, or—in a word—for drink of a certain sort? Or isn't it rather that if heat is present in addition to thirst, it causes the appetite 437e to be for something cold as well, whereas the addition of cold makes it an appetite for something hot? And if there is much thirst, because of the presence of muchness, won't it cause the desire to be for much drink, and where little for little? But thirst itself will never be for anything other than the very thing that it is in its nature to be an appetite for: namely, drink itself; and, similarly, hunger is for food.

GLAUCON: That's the way it is. By itself, at any rate, each appetite is for its natural object only, while an appetite for an object of this or that sort depends on additions.

SOCRATES: No one should catch us unprepared, then, or disturb us by claiming that no one has an appetite for drink but rather for good drink, nor for food but rather for good food, since everyone's appetite is for good things. And so, if thirst is an appetite, it will be an appetite for good drink or good whatever, and similarly for the other appetites.   **438a**

GLAUCON: Yes, there might seem to be something in that objection.

SOCRATES: But surely, whenever things are related to something, those that are of a particular sort are related to a particular sort of thing, as it seems to me, whereas those that are just themselves are related only to a thing   **438b** that is just itself.

GLAUCON: I do not understand.

SOCRATES: Don't you understand that the greater is such as to be greater than something?

GLAUCON: Of course.

SOCRATES: Than the less?

GLAUCON: Yes.

SOCRATES: And the much greater than the much less. Isn't that so?

GLAUCON: Yes.

SOCRATES: And the once greater than the once less? And the going-to-be greater than the going-to-be less?

GLAUCON: Certainly.

SOCRATES: And doesn't the same hold of the more in relation to the fewer, the double to the half, and everything of that sort; and also of heavier to   **438c** lighter and faster to slower; and, in addition, of hot to cold, and all other similar things?

GLAUCON: Yes, indeed.

SOCRATES: What about the various kinds of knowledge? Aren't they the same way? Knowledge itself is of what can be learned itself (or of whatever we should take the object of knowledge to be), whereas a particular knowledge of a particular sort is of a particular thing of a particular sort. I mean something like this: when knowledge of building houses was developed, it differed from the other kinds of knowledge, and so was called knowledge   **438d** of building. Isn't that so?

GLAUCON: Of course.

SOCRATES: And wasn't that because it was a different sort of knowledge from all the others?

GLAUCON: Yes.

SOCRATES: And wasn't it because it was of a particular sort of thing that it itself became a particular sort of knowledge? And isn't this true of all the crafts and sciences?

GLAUCON: It is.

SOCRATES: Well, then, you should think of that as what I wanted to get across before—if you understand it now—when I said that whenever things are related to something, those that are just themselves are related to things that are just themselves, whereas those of a particular sort are related to 438e things of a particular sort. And I do not at all mean that the sorts in question have to be the same for them both—that the knowledge of health and disease is healthy and diseased, or that that of good and bad things is good and bad. On the contrary, I mean that when knowledge occurred that was not just knowledge of the thing itself that knowledge is of, but of something of a particular sort, which in this case was health and disease, the result was that it itself became a particular sort of knowledge; and this caused it to be no longer called simply knowledge but, with the addition of the particular sort, medical knowledge.

GLAUCON: I understand and I think you are right.

SOCRATES: Returning to thirst, then, wouldn't you include it among the 439a things that are related to something just by being what they are? Surely thirst is related to . . .

GLAUCON: I would. It is related to drink.

SOCRATES: So a particular sort of thirst is for a particular sort of drink. Thirst itself, however, is not for much or little, good or bad, or, in a word, for drink of a particular sort; rather, thirst itself is, by nature, just for drink itself. Right?

GLAUCON: Absolutely.

SOCRATES: Hence the soul of the thirsty person, insofar as it is simply thirsty, does not want anything else except to drink, and this is what it 439b longs for and is impelled to do.

GLAUCON: Clearly.

SOCRATES: Then if anything in it draws it back when it is thirsty, wouldn't it be something different from what thirsts and, like a beast, drives it to drink? For surely, we say, the same thing, in the same respect of itself, in relation to the same thing, and at the same time, cannot do opposite things.

GLAUCON: No, it cannot.

SOCRATES: In the same way, I imagine, it is not right to say of the archer that his hands at the same time push the bow away and draw it toward him. On the contrary, we should say that one hand pushes it away, while 439c the other draws it toward him.

GLAUCON: Absolutely.

SOCRATES: Now, we would say, wouldn't we, that some people are thirsty sometimes, yet unwilling to drink?

GLAUCON: Many people often are.

SOCRATES: What, then, should one say about them? Isn't it that there is an element in their soul urging them to drink, and also one stopping them—something different that masters the one doing the urging?

GLAUCON: I certainly think so.

SOCRATES: Doesn't the element doing the stopping in such cases arise—when it does arise—from rational calculation, while the things that drive and drag are present because of feelings and diseases? 439d

GLAUCON: Apparently so.

SOCRATES: It would not be unreasonable for us to claim, then, that there are two elements, different from one another; and to call the element in the soul with which it calculates, the rationally calculating element; and the one with which it feels passion, hungers, thirsts, and is stirred by other appetites, the irrational and appetitive element, friend to certain ways of being filled and certain pleasures.

GLAUCON: No, it would not. Indeed, it would be a very natural thing for us to do.

SOCRATES: Let's assume, then, that we have distinguished these two kinds 439e of elements in the soul. Now, is the spirited element—the one with which we feel anger—a third kind of thing, or is it the same in nature as one of these others?

GLAUCON: As the appetitive element, perhaps.

SOCRATES: But I once heard a story and I believe it. Leontius, the son of Aglaeon, was going up from the Piraeus along the outside of the North Wall when he saw some corpses with the public executioner nearby. He had an appetitive desire to look at them, but at the same time he was disgusted and turned himself away. For a while he struggled and put his hand over 440a his eyes, but finally, mastered by his appetite, he opened his eyes wide and rushed toward the corpses, saying: "Look for yourselves, you evil wretches; take your fill of the beautiful sight."[15]

GLAUCON: I have also heard that story myself.

SOCRATES: Yet, surely, the story suggests that anger sometimes makes war against the appetites as one thing against another.

---

[15] A fragment of the comedy *Kapēlides* by Theopompus (410–370 BCE) tells us that a certain Leotrophides (emended to Leontius because of Plato's reference here) was known for his love of boys as pale as corpses. So Leontius' desire is probably sexual in origin, and for that reason appetitive. The North and South Walls enclosed an area connecting Athens to Piraeus.

GLAUCON: Yes, it does suggest that.

SOCRATES: And don't we often notice on other occasions that when appetite
440b forces someone contrary to his rational calculation, he reproaches himself
and feels anger at the thing in him that is doing the forcing; and just as if
there were two warring factions, such a person's spirit becomes the ally of
his reason? But spirit partnering the appetites to do what reason has decided
should not be done—I do not imagine you would say that you had ever
seen that, either in yourself or in anyone else.

GLAUCON: No, by Zeus, I would not.

SOCRATES: And what about when a person thinks he is doing some injus-
440c tice? Isn't it true that the nobler he is, the less capable he is of feeling angry
if he suffers hunger, cold, or the like at the hands of someone whom he
believes to be inflicting this on him justly; and won't his spirit, as I say,
refuse to be aroused?

GLAUCON: It is true.

SOCRATES: But what about when a person believes he is being unjustly
treated? Doesn't his spirit boil then, and grow harsh and fight as an ally
of what he holds to be just? And even if it suffers hunger, cold, and every
imposition of that sort, doesn't it stand firm and win out over them, not
440d ceasing its noble efforts until it achieves its purpose, or dies, or, like a dog
being called to heel by a shepherd, is called back by the reason alongside
it and becomes gentle?

GLAUCON: Your simile is perfect. And, in fact, we did put the auxiliaries
in our city to be like obedient sheepdogs for the city's shepherdlike rulers.

SOCRATES: You have understood what I was trying to say very well. But
have you also noticed something else about it?

GLAUCON: What?

440e SOCRATES: That it is the opposite of what we recently thought about the
kind of thing spirit is. You see, then we thought of it as something appetitive.[16] But now, far from saying that, we say that in the faction that
takes place in the soul, it is far more likely to take arms on the side of the
rationally calculating element.

GLAUCON: Absolutely.

SOCRATES: Is it also different from this, then, or is it some kind of rationally
calculating element, so that there are not three kinds of things in the soul,
but two—the rationally calculating element and the appetitive one? Or
rather, just as there were three classes in the city that held it together—the
441a moneymaking, the auxiliary, and the deliberative—is there also this third
element in the soul, the spirited kind, which is the natural auxiliary of

---

[16] 439e.

the rationally calculating element, if it has not been corrupted by bad upbringing?

GLAUCON: There must be a third.

SOCRATES: Yes, provided, at any rate, that it can be shown to be as distinct from the rationally calculating element as it was shown to be from the appetitive one.

GLAUCON: But it is not difficult to show that. After all, one can see it even in small children: they are full of spirit right from birth, but as for rational calculation, some of them seem to me never to possess it, while the masses do so quite late.   441b

SOCRATES: Yes, by Zeus, you put that really well. Besides, one can see in animals that what you say is true. But, in addition to that, our earlier quotation from Homer also bears it out: "He struck his chest and spoke to his heart."[17] You see, in it Homer clearly presents what has calculated about better and worse, rebuking what is irrationally angry as though it were something different.   441c

GLAUCON: That's exactly right.

SOCRATES: Well, we have had a difficult swim through all that, and we are pretty much agreed that the same classes as are in the city are in the soul of each individual, and an equal number of them too.

GLAUCON: That's true.

SOCRATES: Then doesn't it already necessarily follow that the private individual is wise in the same way and because of the same element as is the city?

GLAUCON: Of course.

SOCRATES: And that the city is courageous in the same way and because of the same element as is the private individual? And that in everything else   441d
that pertains to virtue, both are alike?

GLAUCON: Necessarily.

SOCRATES: And so, Glaucon, I take it we will also say that a man is just in exactly the same way as is a city.

GLAUCON: That too follows with absolute necessity.

SOCRATES: But we surely have not forgotten that the city was just because each of the three classes in it does its own work.

GLAUCON: I do not think we have.

SOCRATES: We should also bear in mind, then, that in the case of each one of us as well, the one in whom each of the elements does its own job will be just and do his own job.   441e

---

[17] *Odyssey* xx.17. See 390d.

GLAUCON: Certainly.

SOCRATES: Then isn't it appropriate for the rationally calculating element to rule, since it is really wise and exercises foresight on behalf of the whole soul; and for the spirited kind to obey it and be its ally?

GLAUCON: Of course.

SOCRATES: Now, as we were saying, isn't it a mixture of musical and physical training that makes these elements concordant, tightening and nurturing the first with fine words and learning, while relaxing, soothing, and making gentle the second by means of harmony and rhythm?

GLAUCON: Yes, exactly.

SOCRATES: And these two elements, having been trained in this way and having truly learned their own jobs and been educated, will be put in charge of the appetitive element—the largest one in each person's soul and, by nature, the most insatiable for money. They will watch over it to see that it does not get so filled with the so-called pleasures of the body that it becomes big and strong, and no longer does its own job but attempts to enslave and rule over the classes it is not fitted to rule, thereby overturning the whole life of anyone in whom it occurs.

GLAUCON: Yes, indeed.

SOCRATES: And wouldn't these two elements also do the finest job of guarding the whole soul and body against external enemies—the one by deliberating, the other by fighting, following the ruler, and using its courage to carry out the things on which the former had decided?

GLAUCON: Yes, they would.

SOCRATES: I imagine, then, that we call each individual courageous because of the latter part—that is, when the element of his that is spirited in kind preserves through pains and pleasures the pronouncements of reason about what should inspire terror and what should not.

GLAUCON: That's right.

SOCRATES: But we call him wise, surely, because of the small part that rules in him, makes those pronouncements, and has within it the knowledge of what is advantageous—both for each part and for the whole, the community composed of all three.

GLAUCON: Yes, indeed.

SOCRATES: What about temperance? Isn't he temperate because of the friendly and concordant relations between these same things: namely, when both the ruler and its two subjects share the belief that the rationally calculating element should rule, and do not engage in faction against it?

GLAUCON: Temperance in a city and in a private individual is certainly nothing other than that.

SOCRATES: But surely, now, a person will be just because of what we have so often described and in the way we have so often described.

GLAUCON: Necessarily.

SOCRATES: Well, then, has our justice become in any way blurred? Does it look like anything other than the very thing we found in the city?

GLAUCON: It doesn't seem so to me, at least.

SOCRATES: We could make perfectly sure, if there is still anything in our souls that disputes this, by applying everyday tests to it.   442e

GLAUCON: Which ones?

SOCRATES: For example, if we had to come to an agreement about whether a man similar in nature and training to this city of ours would embezzle gold or silver he had accepted for deposit, who do you think would consider him more likely to do so than men of a different sort?   **443a**

GLAUCON: No one.

SOCRATES: And would he have anything to do with temple robberies, thefts, or betrayals of friends in private life or of cities in public life?

GLAUCON: No, nothing.

SOCRATES: And he would be in no way untrustworthy when it came to promises or other agreements.

GLAUCON: How could he be?

SOCRATES: And surely adultery, disrespect for parents, and neglect of the gods would be more characteristic of any other sort of person than of this one.

GLAUCON: Of any other sort, indeed.

SOCRATES: And isn't the reason for all this the fact that each element within   443b
him does its own job where ruling and being ruled are concerned?

GLAUCON: Yes, that and nothing else.

SOCRATES: Are you still looking for justice to be something besides this power that produces men and cities of the sort we have described?

GLAUCON: No, by Zeus, I am not.

SOCRATES: The dream we had has been completely fulfilled, then—I mean the suspicion we expressed that right from the beginning, when we were founding the city, we had, with the help of some god, chanced to hit upon   443c
the origin and pattern of justice.[18]

GLAUCON: Absolutely.

SOCRATES: So, Glaucon, it really was—which is why it was so helpful—a sort of image of justice, this principle that it is right for someone who is,

---

[18] 432d–433b.

by nature, a shoemaker to practice shoemaking and nothing else, for a carpenter to practice carpentry, and the same for all the others.

GLAUCON: Apparently so.

SOCRATES: And in truth, justice is, it seems, something of this sort. Yet it is not concerned with someone's doing his own job on the outside. On the contrary, it is concerned with what is inside; with himself, really, and the
443d things that are his own. It means that he does not allow the elements in him each to do the job of some other, or the three sorts of elements in his soul to meddle with one another. Instead, he regulates well what is really his own, rules himself, puts himself in order, becomes his own friend, and harmonizes the three elements together, just as if they were literally the three defining notes of an octave—lowest, highest, and middle—as well as any others that may be in between. He binds together all of these and,
443e from having been many, becomes entirely one, temperate and harmonious. Then and only then should he turn to action, whether it is to do something concerning the acquisition of wealth or concerning the care of his body, or even something political, or concerning private contracts. In all these areas, he considers and calls just and fine the action that preserves this inner harmony and helps achieve it, and wisdom the knowledge that oversees such action; and he considers and calls unjust any action that destroys this
444a harmony, and ignorance the *belief* that oversees it.

GLAUCON: That's absolutely true, Socrates.

SOCRATES: Well, then, if we claim to have found the just man, the just city, and what justice really is in them, we won't, I imagine, be thought to be telling a complete lie.

GLAUCON: No, by Zeus, we certainly won't.

SOCRATES: Shall we claim it, then?

GLAUCON: Yes, let's.

SOCRATES: So be it, then. I take it we must look for injustice next.

GLAUCON: Clearly.

444b SOCRATES: Mustn't it, in turn, be a kind of faction among those three— their meddling and interfering with one another's jobs; the rebellion of a part of the soul against the whole in order to rule in it inappropriately, since its nature suits it to be a slave of the ruling class. We will say something like that, I imagine, and that their disorder and wandering is injustice, licentiousness, cowardice, ignorance, and, in a word, the whole of vice.

444c GLAUCON: That is precisely what they are.

SOCRATES: Doing unjust actions, then, and being unjust; and, the opposite, doing just ones—they all surely become clear at once, don't they, provided that both injustice and justice are also clear?

GLAUCON: What do you mean?

SOCRATES: That they do not differ in any way from healthy actions and unhealthy ones, that what the latter are in the body, they are in the soul.

GLAUCON: In what respect?

SOCRATES: Surely, healthy actions engender health, unhealthy ones disease.

GLAUCON: Yes.

SOCRATES: Well, doesn't doing just actions also engender justice, unjust ones injustice?   444d

GLAUCON: Necessarily.

SOCRATES: But to produce health is to put the elements that are in the body in their natural relations of mastering and being mastered by one another; while to produce disease is to establish a relation of ruling and being ruled by one another that is contrary to nature.

GLAUCON: That's right.

SOCRATES: Doesn't it follow, then, that to produce justice is to establish the elements in the soul in a natural relation of mastering and being mastered by one another, while to produce injustice is to establish a relation of ruling and being ruled by one another that is contrary to nature?

GLAUCON: Absolutely.

SOCRATES: Virtue, then, so it seems, is a sort of health, a fine and good state of the soul; whereas vice seems to be a shameful disease and weakness.   444e

GLAUCON: That's right.

SOCRATES: And don't fine practices lead to the possession of virtue, shameful ones to vice?

GLAUCON: Necessarily.

SOCRATES: So it now remains, it seems, for us to consider whether it is more   **445a** profitable to do just actions, engage in fine practices, and be just, whether one is known to be so or not; or to do injustice and be unjust, provided that one does not have to pay the penalty and become a better person as a result of being punished.

GLAUCON: But, Socrates, that question seems to me, at least, to have become ridiculous, now that the two have been shown to be as we described. Life does not seem worth living when the body's natural constitution is ruined, not even if one has food and drink of every sort, all the money in the world, and every political office imaginable. So how—even if one   445b could do whatever one wished, except what would liberate one from vice and injustice and make one acquire justice and virtue—could it be worth living when the natural constitution of the very thing by which we live is ruined and in turmoil?

SOCRATES: Yes, it is ridiculous. All the same, since in fact we have reached a point from which we can see with the utmost clarity, as it were, that these things are so, we must not give up.

GLAUCON: That's absolutely the last thing we should do.

445c   SOCRATES: Come up here, then, so that you can see how many kinds of vice there are—the ones, at any rate, that are worth seeing.

GLAUCON: I am following. Just tell me.

SOCRATES: Well, from the vantage point, so to speak, that we have reached in our argument, it seems to me that there is one kind of virtue and an unlimited number of kinds of vice, four of which are worth mentioning.

GLAUCON: What do you mean?

SOCRATES: It seems likely that there are as many types of soul as there are types of political constitution of a specific kind.

445d   GLAUCON: How many is that?

SOCRATES: Five types of constitution, and five of soul.

GLAUCON: Tell me what they are.

SOCRATES: I will tell you that one type would be the constitution we have been describing. However, there are two ways of referring to it: if one outstanding man emerges among the rulers, it is called a kingship; if more than one, it is called an aristocracy.

GLAUCON: That's true.

SOCRATES: Well, then, that is one of the kinds I had in mind. You see, whether many arise or just one, they won't change any of the laws of the city that are worth mentioning, since they will have been brought up and
445e   educated in the way we described.

GLAUCON: No, they probably won't.

BOOK V

449a   SOCRATES' NARRATION CONTINUES:

SOCRATES: That, then, is the sort of city and constitution—and the sort of man—I call good and correct. And if indeed this one is correct, all the others are bad and mistaken, both as city governments and as ways of organizing the souls of private individuals. The deficient ones fall into four kinds.

GLAUCON: What are they?

I was going to describe them in the order in which I thought they developed out
449b   *of one another.[1] But Polemarchus, who was sitting not far from Adeimantus, extended his hand, gripped the latter's cloak by the shoulder from above, drew Adeimantus toward him, and, leaning forward himself, said some things in his ear. We overheard nothing of what he said, other than this:*

---

[1] See Book viii.

Shall we let it go, then, or what?

ADEIMANTUS: (*Now speaking aloud.*) Certainly not.

SOCRATES: What is it exactly you won't let go?

ADEIMANTUS: You!

SOCRATES: Why exactly?   449c

ADEIMANTUS: We think you are being lazy, that you are robbing us of a whole important section of the argument in order to avoid having to explain it. You thought we would not notice when you said—as though it were something inconsequential—that, as regards women and children, anyone could see that it will be a case of friends sharing everything in common.

SOCRATES: But isn't that correct, Adeimantus?

ADEIMANTUS: Yes, it is. But it is just like all the rest we have discussed; its correctness requires an explanation of how the sharing will be arranged, since there are many ways to bring it about. So, do not omit to tell us about the particular one you have in mind. We have all been waiting for a long   449d
time in the expectation that you would surely discuss how procreation will be handled, how the children that are born will be reared, and the whole subject of what you mean by sharing women and children. You see, we think that this makes a considerable difference—indeed, all the difference—to whether a constitution is correct or incorrect. So now that you are beginning to describe another constitution without having analyzed this matter adequately, we are resolved, as you overheard, not to let you go until you explain all this just as you did the rest.   450a

GLAUCON: Include me, too, as having a share in this vote.

And Thrasymachus said:

In fact, you can take it as the resolution of *all* of us, Socrates.

SOCRATES: What a thing to do, attacking me like that. You have started up a huge discussion about the constitution—it will be like starting from the beginning. I was delighted to think I had already completed its description by this time and was satisfied to have what I had said earlier be accepted as is. You do not realize what a swarm of arguments you are now stirring up   450b
by making this demand. It was because I could see it that I left the topic aside, to avoid all the trouble it would cause us.

THRASYMACHUS: What of it? Don't you think these people have come here now to listen to arguments, not to smelt ore?[2]

SOCRATES: Yes—within moderation, at least.

---

[2] A proverbial expression applied to those who neglect the task at hand for an uncertain profit. Thrasymachus is reminding Socrates of his own words at 336e.

GLAUCON: But surely it is within moderation, Socrates, for people with any sense to listen to such arguments their whole life long. So never mind about *us*. Don't *you* get tired of explaining your views on what we asked about: namely, what the sharing of children and women will amount to for our guardians, and how the children will be brought up while they are still small. After all, the time between birth and the beginning of formal education seems to be the most troublesome period of all. So, try to tell us in what way it should be handled.

SOCRATES: It is not easy to explain, my happy fellow. It raises even more doubts than the topics we have discussed so far. One might, in fact, doubt whether what we proposed is possible, and, even if one granted that it is entirely so, one might still have doubts about whether it would be for the best. That, then, is why I was somewhat hesitant to bring it up: I was afraid, my dear comrade, that our argument might seem to be no more than wishful thinking.

GLAUCON: Do not hesitate at all. You see, your audience won't be inconsiderate, or incredulous, or hostile.

SOCRATES: My very good fellow, are you saying that because you want to encourage me?

GLAUCON: I am.

SOCRATES: Well, you are having precisely the opposite effect. If I were confident that I was speaking with knowledge, your encouragement would be all very well. When one is among knowledgeable and beloved friends, and one is speaking what one knows to be the truth about the greatest and most beloved things, one can feel both secure and confident. But to produce arguments when one is uncertain and searching, as I am doing, is a frightening thing and makes one feel insecure. I am not afraid of being ridiculed—that would be childish, indeed—but I am afraid that if I fail to secure the truth, just where it is most important to do so, I will not only fall myself but drag my friends down as well. So I bow to Adrasteia, Glaucon, for what I am about to say. You see, I suspect that involuntary homicide is a lesser crime than misleading people about beautiful, good, and just norms. That is a risk it would be better to run among enemies than among friends. So you have well and truly encouraged me.

Glaucon laughed and said:

Well, Socrates, if we suffer from any false note you strike in the argument, we will release you, as we would in a homicide case, as guiltless and no deceiver of us. So you may speak with confidence.

SOCRATES: Well, it is true; the one who is acquitted in that situation is guiltless, so the law says. And if it is true there, it is probably true here, too.

GLAUCON: On these grounds, then, tell us.

SOCRATES: I will have to go back again, then, and say now what perhaps
I should have said then in the proper place. But maybe it is all right, after   451c
having completed a male drama, to perform a female one next—especially
when you demand it in this way. For people born and educated as we have
described, then, there is, I believe, no correct way to acquire and employ
children and women other than to follow the path on which we first set
them. Surely, in our argument, we tried to establish the men as guard-dogs
of their flock.

GLAUCON: Yes.

SOCRATES: Then let's proceed by giving corresponding rules for birth and
rearing, and see whether they suit us or not.   451d

GLAUCON: How?

SOCRATES: As follows. Do we think that the females of our guard-dogs
should join in guarding precisely what the males guard, hunt with them,
and share everything with them? Or do we think that they should stay
indoors and look after the house,[3] on the grounds that they are incapable
of doing this because they must bear and rear the puppies, while the males
should work and have the entire care of the flock?

GLAUCON: They should share everything—except that we employ the
females as we would weaker animals, and the males as we would stronger
ones.

SOCRATES: Is it possible, then, to employ an animal for the same tasks as   451e
another if you do not give it the same upbringing and education?

GLAUCON: No, it is not.

SOCRATES: Then if we employ women for the same tasks as men, they must
also be taught the same things.

GLAUCON: Yes.   452a

SOCRATES: Now, we gave the latter musical and physical training.

GLAUCON: Yes.

SOCRATES: So, we must also give these two crafts, as well as military training, to the women, and employ them in the same way.

GLAUCON: That seems reasonable, given what you say.

SOCRATES: But perhaps many of the things we are now saying, because
they are contrary to custom, would seem ridiculous if they were put into
practice.

GLAUCON: Indeed, they would.

---

   [3] Respectable, well-to-do women lived secluded lives in most Greek states: they
were confined to the household (see 579b) and to domestic work and were largely
excluded from the public spheres of culture, politics, and warfare.

SOCRATES: What do you see as the most ridiculous aspect of them? Isn't it obvious that it is the idea of the women exercising stripped in the palestras alongside the men?[4] And not just the young women, but the older ones too—like the old men we see in gymnasiums who, even though their bodies are wrinkled and not pleasant to look at, still love physical training.

452b

GLAUCON: Yes, by Zeus, that *would* look really ridiculous, at least under present conditions.

SOCRATES: Yet, since we have started to discuss the matter, we must not be afraid of the various jokes that the wits will make both about this sort of change in musical and physical training and—even more so—about the change in the bearing of arms and the mounting of cavalry horses.

452c

GLAUCON: You are right.

SOCRATES: But since we have started, we must move on to the rougher part of the law, and ask these wits *not* to do their own job, but to be serious. And we will remind them that it is not long since the *Greeks* thought it shameful and ridiculous (as many barbarians still do) for *men* to be seen stripped, and that when first the Cretans and then the Lacedaemonians began the gymnasiums, the wits of the time had the opportunity to make a comedy of it all. Or don't you think so?

452d

GLAUCON: I certainly do.

SOCRATES: But when it became clear, I take it, to those who employed these practices, that it was better to strip than to cover up all such parts, the laughter in the eyes faded away because of what the arguments had proved to be best. And this showed that it is a fool who finds anything ridiculous except what is bad, or tries to raise a laugh at the sight of anything except what is stupid or bad, or—putting it the other way around—who takes seriously any standard of what is beautiful other than what is good.

452e

GLAUCON: Absolutely.

SOCRATES: Well, then, shouldn't we first agree about whether our proposals are viable or not? And mustn't we give anyone who wishes to do so— whether it is someone who loves a joke or someone serious—the opportunity to dispute whether the female human does have the natural ability to share in *all* the tasks of the male sex, or in none at all, or in some but not others; and, in particular, whether this holds in the case of warfare? By making the best beginning in this way, wouldn't one also be likely to reach the best conclusion?

453a

GLAUCON: Of course.

---

[4] A palestra was a wrestling school and training ground.

SOCRATES: So, would you like us to dispute with one another on their behalf, so that their side of the argument won't be attacked without defenders?

GLAUCON: Why not?

SOCRATES: Then let's say this on their behalf: "Socrates and Glaucon, you   453b
do not need *other people* to dispute you. After all, you yourselves, when you were beginning to found your city, agreed that each one had to do the one job for which he was naturally suited."

GLAUCON: We did agree to that, I think. Of course we did.

SOCRATES: "Can it be, then, that a woman is not by nature very different from a man?"

GLAUCON: Of course she is different.

SOCRATES: "Then isn't it also appropriate to assign a different job to each of them, the one for which they are naturally suited?"

GLAUCON: Certainly.

SOCRATES: "How is it, then, that you are not making a mistake now and   453c
contradicting yourselves, when you say that men and women must do the same jobs, seeing that they have natures that are most distinct?" Do you have any defense, you amazing fellow, against that attack?

GLAUCON: It is not easy to think of one on the spur of the moment. On the contrary, I shall ask—indeed, I am asking—you to explain the argument on our side as well, whatever it is.

SOCRATES: That, Glaucon, and many other problems of the same sort, which I foresaw long ago, was what I was afraid of when I hesitated to tackle the law concerning the possession and upbringing of women and   453d
children.

GLAUCON: No, by Zeus, it certainly does not seem to be a simple matter.

SOCRATES: No, it is not. But the fact is that whether one falls into a small diving pool or into the middle of the greatest sea, one has to swim all the same.

GLAUCON: Of course.

SOCRATES: Then we must swim, too, and try to save ourselves from the sea of argument, hoping for a dolphin to pick us up, or for some other unlikely rescue.[5]

GLAUCON: It seems so.

SOCRATES: Come on, then, let's see if we can find a way out. We have   453e
agreed, of course, that different natures must have different pursuits, and that the natures of a woman and a man are different. But we now say that

---

[5] The story of Arion's rescue by the dolphin is told in Herodotus, *Histories* 1.23–24.

those different natures must have the same pursuits. Isn't that the charge against us?

GLAUCON: Yes, exactly.

454a   SOCRATES: What a noble power, Glaucon, the craft of disputation possesses!

GLAUCON: Why is that?

SOCRATES: Because many people seem to me to fall into it even against their wills, and think they are engaging not in eristic,[6] but in discussion. This happens because they are unable to examine what has been said by dividing it up into kinds. Instead, it is on the purely verbal level that they look for the contradiction in what has been said, and employ eristic, not dialectical discussion, on one another.

GLAUCON: Yes, that certainly does happen to many people. But surely it is not pertinent to us at the moment, is it?

454b   SOCRATES: It most certainly is. At any rate, we are in danger of unconsciously dealing in disputation.

GLAUCON: How?

SOCRATES: We are trying to establish the principle that different natures should not be assigned the same pursuits in a bold and eristic manner, *on the verbal level*. But we did not at all investigate what kind of natural difference or sameness we had in mind, or in what regard the distinction was pertinent, when we assigned different pursuits to different natures and the same ones to the same.

GLAUCON: No, we did not investigate that.

SOCRATES: And because we did not, it is open to us, apparently, to ask
454c   ourselves whether the natures of bald and long-haired men are the same or opposite. And, once we agree that they are opposite, it is open to us to forbid the long-haired ones to be shoemakers, if that is what the bald ones are to be, or *vice versa*.

GLAUCON: But that would be ridiculous.

SOCRATES: And is it ridiculous for any other reason than that we did not have in mind *every* kind of difference and sameness in nature, but were keeping our eyes only on the kind of difference and sameness that was
454d   pertinent to the pursuits themselves? We meant, for example, that a male and female whose souls are suited for medicine have the same nature. Or don't you think so?

GLAUCON: I do.

SOCRATES: But a male doctor and a male carpenter have different ones?

GLAUCON: Of course, completely different.

---

[6] See *Meno* 75d.

SOCRATES: In the case of both the male and the female sex, then, if one of them is shown to be different from the other with regard to a particular craft or pursuit, we will say that is the one who should be assigned to it. But if it is apparent that they differ in this respect alone, that the female bears the offspring while the male mounts the female, we will say it has not yet been demonstrated that a woman is different from a man with regard to 454e what we are talking about, and we will continue to believe our guardians and their women should have the same pursuits.

GLAUCON: And rightly so.

SOCRATES: Next, won't we urge our opponent to tell us the precise craft or pursuit, relevant to the organization of the city, for which a woman's 455a nature and a man's are not the same but different?

GLAUCON: That would be a fair question, at least.

SOCRATES: Perhaps, then, this other person might say, just as you did a moment ago,[7] that it is not easy to give an adequate answer on the spur of the moment, but that after reflection it would not be at all difficult.

GLAUCON: Yes, he might say that.

SOCRATES: Do you want us to ask the one who disputes things in this way, then, to follow us to see whether we can somehow show him that there is no pursuit relevant to the management of the city that is peculiar to 455b women?

GLAUCON: Of course.

SOCRATES: Come on, then, we will say to him, give us an answer: "Is this what you meant by one person being naturally well suited for something and another naturally unsuited: that the one learns it easily, the other with difficulty; that the one, after a little instruction, can discover a lot for himself in the subject being studied, whereas the other, even if he gets a lot of instruction and attention, does not even retain what he was taught; that the bodily capacities of the one adequately serve his mind, while those of the other obstruct his? Are there any other factors than these, by which 455c you distinguish a person who is naturally well suited for each pursuit from one who is not?"

GLAUCON: No one will be able to mention any others.

SOCRATES: Do you know of anything practiced by human beings, then, at which the male sex is not superior to the female in all those ways? Or must we make a long story of it by discussing weaving and the preparation of baked and boiled food—the very pursuits in which the female sex is thought to excel, and in which its defeat would expose it to the greatest ridicule of all?   455d

---

[7] 453c.

GLAUCON: It is true that the one sex shows greater mastery than the other in pretty much every area. Yet there are many women who are better than many men at many things. But on the whole, it is as you say.

SOCRATES: Then, my friend, there is no pursuit relevant to the management of the city that belongs to a woman because she is a woman, or to a man because he is a man; but the various natural capacities are distributed in a similar way between both creatures, and women can share by nature in every pursuit, and men in every one, though for the purposes of all of 455e them women are weaker than men.

GLAUCON: Of course.

SOCRATES: So shall we assign all of them to men and none to women?

GLAUCON: How could we?

SOCRATES: We could not. For we will say, I imagine, that one woman is suited for medicine, another not, and that one is naturally musical, another not.

GLAUCON: Of course.

SOCRATES: Won't one be suited for physical training or war, then, while 456a another is unwarlike and not a lover of physical training?

GLAUCON: I suppose so.

SOCRATES: And one a philosopher (lover of wisdom), another a "misosopher" (hater of wisdom)? And one spirited, another spiritless?

GLAUCON: That too.

SOCRATES: So there is also a woman who is suited to be a guardian, and one who is not. Or wasn't that the sort of nature we selected for our male guardians, too?

GLAUCON: It certainly was.

SOCRATES: A woman and a man can have the same nature, then, relevant to guarding the city—except to the extent that she is weaker and he is stronger.

GLAUCON: Apparently so.

SOCRATES: Women of that sort, then, must be selected to live and guard 456b with men of the same sort, since they are competent to do so and are akin to the men by nature.

GLAUCON: Of course.

SOCRATES: And mustn't we assign the same pursuits to the same natures?

GLAUCON: Yes, the same ones.

SOCRATES: We have come around, then, to what we said before, and we are agreed that it is not against nature to assign musical and physical training to the female guardians.

GLAUCON: Absolutely.

SOCRATES: So, we are not legislating impossibilities or mere fantasies, at any 456c rate, since the law we were proposing is in accord with nature. Rather, it is the contrary laws that we have now that turn out to be more contrary to nature, it seems.

GLAUCON: It does seem that way.

SOCRATES: Now, wasn't our inquiry about whether our proposals were both viable and best?

GLAUCON: Yes, it was.

SOCRATES: And that they are in fact viable has been agreed, hasn't it?

GLAUCON: Yes.

SOCRATES: So, we must next come to an agreement about whether they are for the best?

GLAUCON: Clearly.

SOCRATES: Now, as regards producing a woman who is equipped for guardianship, we won't have one sort of education that will produce our guardian men, will we, and another our women—especially not when it will have the same nature to work on in both cases? 456d

GLAUCON: No, we won't.

SOCRATES: What is your belief about this, then?

GLAUCON: What?

SOCRATES: The notion that one man is better or worse than another—or do you think they are all alike?

GLAUCON: Not at all.

SOCRATES: In the city we are founding, who do you think will turn out to be better men: our guardians, who get the education we have described, or the shoemakers, who are educated in shoemaking?

GLAUCON: What a ridiculous question!

SOCRATES: I realize that. Aren't the guardians the best of the citizens?

GLAUCON: By far.

SOCRATES: And what about the female guardians? Won't they be the best 456e of the women?

GLAUCON: Yes, they are by far the best, too.

SOCRATES: Is there anything better for a city than that the best possible men and women should come to exist in it?

GLAUCON: No, there is not.

SOCRATES: And that is what musical and physical training, employed as we have described, will achieve? 457a

GLAUCON: Of course.

SOCRATES: Then the law we were proposing was not only possible, but also best for a city?

GLAUCON: Yes.

SOCRATES: Then the female guardians must strip, clothing themselves in virtue instead of cloaks. They must share in warfare, and whatever else guarding the city involves, and do nothing else. But within these areas, the women must be assigned lighter tasks than the men, because of the weakness of their sex. And the man who laughs at the sight of women stripped 457b for physical training, when their stripping is for the best, is "plucking the unripe fruit of laughter's wisdom,"[8] and knows nothing, it seems, about what he is laughing at or what he is doing. For it is, and always will be, the finest saying that what is beneficial is beautiful; what is harmful ugly.

GLAUCON: Absolutely.

SOCRATES: May we claim, then, that we are avoiding one wave, as it were, in our discussion of the law about women, so that we are not altogether swept away when we declare that our male and female guardians must share 457c all their pursuits, and that our argument is somehow self-consistent when it states that this is both viable and beneficial?

GLAUCON: It is certainly no small wave that you are avoiding.

SOCRATES: You won't think it is so great when you see the next.

GLAUCON: I won't see it unless you tell me about it.

SOCRATES: The law that is consistent with that one, and with the others that preceded it, is this, I take it.

GLAUCON: What?

SOCRATES: That all these women should be shared among all the men, that 457d no individual woman and man should live together, and that the children, too, should be shared, with no parent knowing its own offspring, and no child its parent.

GLAUCON: That wave *is* far greater and more dubitable than the other, both as regards its viability and its benefit.

SOCRATES: As far as its benefit is concerned, at least, I do not think anyone would argue that the sharing of women and children is not the greatest good, if indeed it is viable. But I imagine there would be a lot of dispute about whether or not it is viable.

457e GLAUCON: No, *both* could very well be disputed.

SOCRATES: You mean I will have to face a coalition of arguments. I thought I had at least escaped one of them—namely, whether you thought the

---

[8] Plato is adapting a phrase of Pindar.

proposal was beneficial—and that I would just be left with the argument about whether it is viable or not.

GLAUCON: Well, you did not escape unnoticed. So you will have to give an argument for both.

SOCRATES: I must pay the penalty. But do me this favor: let me take a holi- **458a** day and act like those lazy people who make a banquet for themselves of their own thoughts when they are walking alone. People like that, as you know, do not bother to find out how any of their appetites might actually be fulfilled, so as to avoid the trouble of deliberating about what is possible and what is not. They assume that what they want is available, and then proceed to arrange all the rest, taking pleasure in going through everything they will do when they get it—thus making their already lazy souls even lazier. Well, I, too, am succumbing to this weakness at the moment and **458b** want to postpone consideration of the viability of our proposals until later. I will assume now that they are viable, if you will permit me to do so, and examine how the rulers will arrange them when they come to pass. And I will try to show that, if they were put into practice, they would be the most beneficial arrangements of all, both for the city and for its guardians. These are the things I will try to examine with you first, leaving the others for later—if indeed you will permit this.

GLAUCON: You have my permission; so proceed with the examination.

SOCRATES: Well, then, I imagine that if indeed our rulers, and likewise their auxiliaries, are worthy of their names, the latter will be prepared to **458c** carry out orders, and the former to give orders, obeying our laws in some cases and imitating them in the others that we leave to their discretion.

GLAUCON: Probably so.

SOCRATES: Now, you are their lawgiver, and in just the way you selected these men, you will select as the women to hand over to them those who have natures as similar to theirs as possible. And because they have shared dwellings and meals, and none of them has any private property of that sort, they will live together; and through mixing together in the gymnasia **458d** and in the rest of their daily life, they will be driven by inborn compulsion, I take it, to have sex with one another. Or don't you think I am talking about necessities here?

GLAUCON: Not *geometric* necessities, certainly, but *erotic* ones; and they prob- ably have a sharper capacity to persuade and attract most people.

SOCRATES: They do, indeed. But the next point, Glaucon, is that for them to have unregulated sexual intercourse with one another, or to do anything else of that sort, would not be a pious thing in a city of happy people, and **458e** the rulers won't allow it.

GLAUCON: No, it would not be just.

SOCRATES: It is clear, then, that we will next have to make marriages as sacred as possible. And sacred marriages will be those that are most beneficial.

GLAUCON: Absolutely.

SOCRATES: How, then, will the most beneficial ones come about? Tell me this, Glaucon. I see you have hunting dogs and quite a flock of noble birds at home.[9] Have you, by Zeus, noticed anything in particular about their "marriages" and breeding?

GLAUCON: Like what?

SOCRATES: In the first place, though they are all noble animals, aren't there some that are, or turn out to be, the very best?

GLAUCON: There are.

SOCRATES: Do you breed from them all to the same extent, then, or do you try hard to breed as far as possible from the best ones?

GLAUCON: From the best ones.

SOCRATES: And do you breed from the youngest, the oldest, or as far as possible from those in their prime?

GLAUCON: From those in their prime.

SOCRATES: And if they were not bred in this way, do you think that your race of birds and dogs would get much worse?

GLAUCON: I do.

SOCRATES: And what do you think about horses and other animals? Is the situation any different with them?

GLAUCON: It would be strange if it were.

SOCRATES: Good heavens, my dear comrade! Then our need for eminent rulers is quite desperate, if indeed the same also holds for the human race.

GLAUCON: Well, it does hold of them. But so what?

SOCRATES: It follows that our rulers will then have to employ a great many drugs. You know that when people do not need drugs for their bodies, and they are prepared to follow a regimen, we regard even an inferior doctor as adequate. But when drugs are needed, we know that a much bolder doctor is required.

GLAUCON: That's true. But what is your point?

SOCRATES: This: it looks as though our rulers will have to employ a great many lies and deceptions for the benefit of those they rule. And you remember, I suppose, we said all such things were useful as a kind of drug.[10]

GLAUCON: And we were correct.

459a, 459b, 459c, 459d *(marginal line references)*

---

[9] Both hunting dogs and aviaries were common in rich Greek households.

[10] 382c–d.

SOCRATES: Well, in the case of marriages and procreation, its correctness is particularly evident.

GLAUCON: How so?

SOCRATES: It follows from our previous agreement that the best men should mate with the best women in as many cases as possible, while the opposite should hold of the worst men and women; and that the offspring of the former should be reared, but not that of the latter, if our flock is going to be an eminent one. And all this must occur without anyone knowing   459e
except the rulers—if, again, our herd of guardians is to remain as free from faction as possible.

GLAUCON: That's absolutely right.

SOCRATES: So then, we will have to establish by law certain festivals and sacrifices at which we will bring together brides and bridegrooms, and our poets must compose suitable hymns for the marriages that take place. We will leave the number of marriages for the rulers to decide. That will   **460a**
enable them to keep the number of males as constant as possible, taking into account war, disease, and everything of that sort; so that the city will, as far as possible, become neither too great nor too small.

GLAUCON: That's right.

SOCRATES: I imagine that some sophisticated lotteries will have to be created, then, so that an inferior person of that sort will blame chance rather than the rulers at each mating time.

GLAUCON: Yes, indeed.

SOCRATES: And presumably, the young men who are good at war or at other things must—among other prizes and awards—be given a greater   460b
opportunity to have sex with the women, in order that a pretext may also be created at the same time for having as many children as possible fathered by such men.

GLAUCON: That's right.

SOCRATES: And then, as offspring are born, won't they be taken by the officials appointed for this purpose, whether these are men or women or both—for surely our offices are also open to both women and men.

GLAUCON: Yes.

SOCRATES: And I suppose they will take the offspring of good parents to the rearing pen and hand them over to special nurses who live in a separate   460c
part of the city. But those of inferior parents, or any deformed offspring of the others, they will hide in a secret and unknown place, as is fitting.[11]

GLAUCON: Yes, if indeed the race of guardians is going to remain pure.

---

[11] Infanticide by exposure was commonly used in ancient Greece as a method of family planning.

SOCRATES: And won't these nurses also take care of the children's feed-ing by bringing the mothers to the rearing pen when their breasts are full, while devising every device to ensure that no mother will recognize her offspring? And won't they provide other women as wet nurses if the mothers themselves have insufficient milk—taking care, however, that the mothers breast-feed the children for only a moderate period of time, and assigning sleepless nights and similar burdens to the nurses and wet nurses?

GLAUCON: You are making childbearing a soft job for the guardians' women.

SOCRATES: Yes, properly so. But let's take up the next thing we proposed. We said, as you know, that offspring should be bred from parents who are in their prime.

GLAUCON: True.

SOCRATES: Do you agree that a woman's prime lasts, on average, for a period of twenty years and a man's for thirty?

GLAUCON: Which years are those?

SOCRATES: A woman should bear children for the city from the age of twenty to that of forty; whereas a man should beget them for the city from the time that he passes his peak as a runner until he reaches fifty-five.

GLAUCON: At any rate, that is the physical and mental prime for both.

SOCRATES: Then if any male who is younger or older than that engages in reproduction for the community, we will say that his offense is neither pious nor just. For the child he fathers for the city, if it escapes discovery, will be begotten and born without the benefit of sacrifices, or of the prayers that priestesses, priests, and the entire city will offer at every marriage festival, asking that from good and beneficial parents ever better and more beneficial offspring should be produced. On the contrary, it will be born in darkness through a terrible act of lack of self-control.

GLAUCON: That's right.

SOCRATES: The same law will apply if a man who is still of breeding age has sex with a woman in her prime when the rulers have not mated them. We will say that he is imposing an illegitimate, unauthorized, and unholy child on the city.

GLAUCON: That's absolutely right.

SOCRATES: But when women and men have passed breeding age, I imagine we will leave them free to have sex with whomever they wish—except that a man may not have sex with his daughter, mother, daughters' daughters, or mother's female ancestors, or a woman with her son and his descendants or her father and his ancestors. And we will permit all that only after telling them to be very careful not to let even a single fetus see the light of day, if one should happen to be conceived; but if one does force its way out,

they must dispose of it on the understanding that no nurture is available
for such a child.

GLAUCON: All that sounds reasonable. But how will they recognize one
another's fathers, daughters, and the others you mentioned?

SOCRATES: They won't. Instead, from the day a man becomes a bride-   461d
groom, he will call all offspring born in the tenth month afterward (and
in the seventh, of course) his sons, if they are male, and his daughters, if
they are female; and they will call him father. Similarly, he will call their
children his grandchildren, and they, in turn, will call the group to which
he belongs grandfathers and grandmothers. And those who were born at
the same time as their mothers and fathers were breeding, they will call
their brothers and sisters. Thus, as we were saying just now, they will avoid
sexual relations with each other. However, the law *will* allow brothers and   461e
sisters to have sex with one another, if the lottery works out that way and
the Pythia[12] approves.

GLAUCON: You are absolutely right.

SOCRATES: That, then, Glaucon, or something like it, is how the sharing
of women and children by the guardians of your city will be handled.
The next point we need to have confirmed by argument, then, is that this
arrangement is both consistent with the rest of the constitution and by far
the best. Isn't that so?

GLAUCON: Yes, by Zeus, it is.   **462a**

SOCRATES: As a beginning step toward reaching agreement, shouldn't we
ask ourselves what we think is the greatest good for the organization of the
city—the one at which the legislator should aim in making its laws—and
what the greatest evil? And then examine whether what we have just
described is in harmony with the tracks of the good we have found, and
in disharmony with those of the bad?

GLAUCON: Absolutely.

SOCRATES: Now, do we know of any greater evil for a city than what tears
it apart and makes it many instead of one? Or any greater good than what   462b
binds it together and makes it one?

GLAUCON: No, we do not.

SOCRATES: Well, doesn't sharing pleasure and pain bind it together—when,
as far as possible, all the citizens feel more or less the same joy or pain at
the same gains or losses?

GLAUCON: Absolutely.

---

[12] See *Apology* 21a.

SOCRATES: On the other hand, doesn't the privatization of these things dissolve the city—when some are overwhelmed with distress and others overjoyed by the same things happening to the city or some of its inhabitants?

462c GLAUCON: Of course.

SOCRATES: And isn't that what happens when people do not apply such phrases as "mine" and "not mine" in unison in the city? And similarly with "someone else's"?

GLAUCON: Precisely.

SOCRATES: Then isn't the city that is best governed the one in which the vast majority of people apply "mine" and "not mine" to the same things on the basis of the same principle?

GLAUCON: Certainly.

SOCRATES: And isn't it the city whose condition is most like that of a single person? I mean, when one of us somehow hurts his finger, you know the entire partnership—the one that binds body and soul together into a single system under the ruling part within it—is aware of this, and all of it as a

462d whole feels the pain in unison with the part that suffers. That is why we say that this person has a pain in his finger. And the same principle applies, doesn't it, to any other part of a person, whether it is suffering pain or relieved by pleasure?

GLAUCON: Yes, the same one. And, to answer your question, the city that manages to come closest to this condition *is* the best-governed one.

SOCRATES: I imagine, then, that whenever one of its citizens has an experience, whether good or bad, such a city will most certainly say that the

462e experience is its own, and all of it together will share his pleasure or pain.

GLAUCON: That must be so, since it is well governed.

SOCRATES: It is time for us to return to our own city, then, to look there for the features we have agreed on and to see whether it, or rather some other city, possesses them to the greatest degree.

GLAUCON: Yes, it is.

SOCRATES: Well, now, what about those other cities? Presumably there are

463a rulers and people in them as well as in ours?

GLAUCON: There are.

SOCRATES: And won't all of them call one another "citizens"?

GLAUCON: Of course.

SOCRATES: But besides "citizens," what do the people in those other cities call the rulers?

GLAUCON: In most, they call them "masters," but in democracies they are called just that—"rulers."

SOCRATES: What about the people in our city? Besides "citizens," what do they call the rulers?

GLAUCON: "Preservers" and "auxiliaries."

SOCRATES: And what do *they* call the people?   463b

GLAUCON: "Paymasters" and "providers."

SOCRATES: What do the rulers in other cities call the people?

GLAUCON: "Slaves."

SOCRATES: And what do the rulers call each other?

GLAUCON: "Co-rulers."

SOCRATES: And ours?

GLAUCON: "Co-guardians."

SOCRATES: Now, can you tell me whether a ruler in other cities could address one of his co-rulers as his kinsman and another as an outsider?

GLAUCON: Many do, at any rate.

SOCRATES: And doesn't he regard and speak of his kinsman as belonging to him, while he regards the outsider as not doing so?

GLAUCON: Yes.

SOCRATES: What about your guardians? Could any of them regard or   463c
address a co-guardian as an outsider?

GLAUCON: Certainly not. He will regard everyone he meets as a brother or a sister, a father or a mother, a son or a daughter, or some ancestor or descendant of these.

SOCRATES: Very well put. But tell me this, too: will your laws require them simply to use these terms of kinship, or must they also do all the things that go along with the names? In the case of fathers, for example, must   463d
they show them the customary respect, solicitude, and obedience owed to parents? Will they fare worse at the hands of gods or men, as people whose actions are neither pious nor just, if they do otherwise? Will these be the sayings that are chanted by all the citizens, and that sound in their ears right from their earliest childhood? Or will they hear something else about their fathers—or the ones they are told to regard as their fathers—or about their other relatives?   463e

GLAUCON: They will hear those. It would be ridiculous if they only mouthed the terms of kinship, without the actions.

SOCRATES: So, in this city more than in any other, when someone is doing well or badly, they will utter in concord the words we mentioned a moment ago, and say "*my* such-and-such is doing well" or "*my* so-and-so is doing badly."

GLAUCON: That's absolutely true.

464a SOCRATES: Well, didn't we say that this conviction and way of talking are accompanied by the having of pleasures and pains in common?

GLAUCON: Yes, and we were right to do so.

SOCRATES: Then won't our citizens share to the fullest, and call "mine," the very same thing? And because they share it, won't they experience to the fullest the sharing of pleasures and pains?

GLAUCON: Of course.

SOCRATES: And—in the context of the rest of the political system—isn't the sharing of women and children by the guardians responsible for it?

GLAUCON: Yes, it is by far the most important cause.

SOCRATES: But we further agreed that this sharing is the greatest good for a city, when we compared a well-governed city to the way a human body relates to pain and pleasure in one of its parts.

GLAUCON: And we were right to agree.

464b SOCRATES: Then we have shown that the cause of the greatest good for our city is the sharing of women and children by the auxiliaries.

GLAUCON: Yes, we certainly have.

SOCRATES: And what is more, it is consistent with what we said before. For we said, as you know, that if these people are going to be real guardians, they should not have private houses, land, or any other possession, **464c** but should receive their upkeep from the other citizens as a wage for their guardianship, and should all eat communally.

GLAUCON: That's right.

SOCRATES: So, as I say, doesn't what was said earlier, as well as what is being said now, make them into even better guardians and prevent them from tearing the city apart by applying the term "mine" not to the same thing, but to different ones—with one person dragging into his own house whatever he, apart from the others, can get his hands on, and another **464d** into a different house to a different wife and children, who create private pleasures and pains at things that are private? Instead of that, don't our guardians share a single conviction about what is their own, aim at the same goal, and, as far as possible, feel pleasure and pain in unison?

GLAUCON: Absolutely.

SOCRATES: What about lawsuits and accusations? Won't they pretty much disappear from among them because they have no private possessions except their own bodies and share all the rest? As a result, won't they be free from faction—at any rate, from the sort of faction that the possession **464e** of property, children, and families causes among people?

GLAUCON: Yes, they will inevitably be entirely free of it.

SOCRATES: Moreover, neither lawsuits for violence nor for assault should justifiably occur among them. For we will declare, surely, that for people to defend themselves against others of the same age is a fine and just thing, since it will compel them to stay in good physical shape.

GLAUCON: That's right.

SOCRATES: This law is also correct for another reason: if a spirited person 465a
vents his anger in this way, he will be less likely to move on to more serious sorts of faction.

GLAUCON: He certainly will.

SOCRATES: As for an older person, he will be authorized to rule and punish all the younger ones.

GLAUCON: Clearly.

SOCRATES: And, unless the rulers command it, it is unlikely that a younger person will ever employ any sort of violence against an older one, or strike him. And I do not imagine he will fail to show him respect in other ways either, since two guardians—fear and shame—are sufficient to prevent it. 465b
Shame will prevent him from laying a hand on his parents, as will the fear that the others would come to his victim's aid—some because they are his sons, some because they are his brothers, and some because they are his fathers.

GLAUCON: Yes, that is what would happen.

SOCRATES: Then won't the laws induce men to live at peace with one another in all respects?

GLAUCON: Very much so.

SOCRATES: And if there is no faction among the guardians, there is no terrible danger that the rest of the city will form factions, either against them or among themselves.

GLAUCON: No, there is not.

SOCRATES: As for the pettiest of the evils the guardians would escape, they 465c
are so unseemly, I hesitate even to mention them: the flatteries of the rich by the poor; the perplexities and sufferings involved in bringing up children; the need to make the money necessary to feed the household—the borrowings, the defaults, and all the things people are compelled to do to provide an income to hand over to their wives and slaves to spend on housekeeping. The various troubles men endure in these areas, my dear 465d
Glaucon, are obvious, quite demeaning, and not worth discussing.

GLAUCON: They are obvious even to the blind.

SOCRATES: They will escape from all these things, then, and live a more blessedly happy life than the most blessedly happy one—that of the victors in the Olympian games.

GLAUCON: How so?

SOCRATES: Surely, these victors are considered happy on account of only a small part of what the guardians possess, since the latter victory is even finer, and their upkeep from public funds more complete.[13] After all, the victory they gain is the salvation of the whole city, and the crown of victory they and their children receive is their upkeep and all the necessities of life. They receive privileges from their own city during their lifetime and a worthy burial after their death.

465e

GLAUCON: Yes, those are very fine rewards.

SOCRATES: Now, do you remember that earlier in our discussion we were rebuked by an argument—I forget whose—to the effect that we had not made our guardians happy, that though it was possible for them to have everything that belongs to the citizens, they actually had nothing? We said, didn't we, that if this happened to come up at some point, we would look into it then, but that our concern at the time was to make our guardians *guardians,* and to make the *city* the happiest possible, rather than looking to any one group within it and molding it for happiness?

466a

GLAUCON: I remember.

SOCRATES: Well, then, if indeed the life of our auxiliaries has been shown to be much finer and better than that of Olympian victors, is there any need to compare it with the lives of shoemakers or any other craftsmen, or with that of the farmers?

466b

GLAUCON: I do not think there is.

SOCRATES: Nevertheless, it is surely right to repeat here what I also said on that earlier occasion: if a guardian tries to become happy in such a way that he is no longer a guardian at all, and is not satisfied with a life that is moderate, stable, and (we claim) best, but is seized by a foolish, adolescent belief about happiness, which incites him to use his power to take everything in the city for himself—he will come to realize the true wisdom of Hesiod's saying that, in a sense, "the half is worth more than the whole."[14]

466c

GLAUCON: If he takes my advice, he will keep to the former life.

SOCRATES: Do you agree, then, that the women should share with the men, in the way we described, in the areas of education, children, and guarding the other citizens; that whether they remain in the city or go out to war, they must guard together and hunt together, as hounds do, and share everything to the extent possible; and that by behaving in this way, they will be doing what is best, not something contrary to the natural

466d

---

[13] See *Apology* 36d.

[14] *Works and Days* 40.

relationship of female to male, and the one they are most naturally fitted to share in with one another?

GLAUCON: I do agree.

SOCRATES: Then doesn't it remain for us to determine whether it is also possible among human beings, as it is among other animals, for this sort of sharing to come about, and if so, how?

GLAUCON: You took the words out of my mouth.

SOCRATES: As far as war is concerned, I think it is clear how they will wage it.   466e

GLAUCON: How?

SOCRATES: They will go to war together. What is more, they will take the children with them to the war, when they are sturdy enough, so that, like the children of other craftsmen, they can see what they will have to do in their own craft when they are grown up. But in addition to observing, they should help and assist in every aspect of war, and take care of their   467a
mothers and fathers. For haven't you noticed in the other crafts how the children of potters, for example, assist and watch for a long time before actually putting their hands to the clay?

GLAUCON: I have, indeed.

SOCRATES: Well, should these people take more care than the guardians in training their children by appropriate experience and observation?

GLAUCON: Of course not. That would be completely ridiculous.

SOCRATES: Besides, every animal will fight better in the presence of its young.   467b

GLAUCON: That's right. But there is a risk, Socrates, and not a small one either, that in the event of a disaster of the sort that is likely to happen in a war, they will lose their children's lives as well as their own, making it impossible for the rest of the city to recover.

SOCRATES: That's true. But, in the first place, do you think they should arrange for the avoidance of all risk?

GLAUCON: Not at all.

SOCRATES: Well, then, if they must face some risk, shouldn't it be one in which they will be improved by success?

GLAUCON: Clearly.

SOCRATES: But you think, do you, that it makes little difference—and so is not worth the risk—whether or not men who are going to be warriors   467c
watch warfare when they are still boys?

GLAUCON: No, it does make a difference to what you are talking about.

SOCRATES: Starting from the assumption, then, that we are to make the children observers of war, we must further devise some way of keeping them safe. Then everything will be fine, won't it?

GLAUCON: Yes.

SOCRATES: Well, in the first place, their fathers won't be ignorant, will they, but rather as knowledgeable as people can be, about which military campaigns are dangerous and which are not?

GLAUCON: Presumably so.

467d SOCRATES: So, they will take the children on the latter, but be wary of taking them on the former.

GLAUCON: That's right.

SOCRATES: And they will not put the worst people in charge of them, I presume, but those whose experience and age qualifies them to be leaders and tutors.

GLAUCON: Yes, that would be proper.

SOCRATES: But we will say that the unexpected happens to many people and on many occasions.

GLAUCON: Yes, indeed.

SOCRATES: So, with that in mind, my friend, we must provide the young children with wings at the outset, so that, if the need arises, they can fly away and escape.

GLAUCON: What do you mean?

467e SOCRATES: We must mount them on horses when they are still very young, and when they have been taught to ride, they must be taken to view the fighting, not on spirited or aggressive horses, but on the fastest and most manageable ones. In this way, they will get the best view of their own future job, and will be able to make the safest escape, if the need arises, by following their older leaders.

468a GLAUCON: I think you are right.

SOCRATES: What about warfare itself? How should your soldiers behave toward one another and the enemy? Are my views correct or not?

GLAUCON: Tell me what they are.

SOCRATES: If one of them leaves his post, throws away his shield, or does anything else of that sort out of cowardice, shouldn't he be demoted to craftsman or farmer?

GLAUCON: Certainly.

468b SOCRATES: And if anyone is captured alive by the enemy, shouldn't he be presented to his captors as a catch to use however they wish?

GLAUCON: Absolutely.

SOCRATES: But if someone distinguishes himself and earns high honors, do you or don't you think that in the first place, while still on campaign, he should be crowned in turn by each of the adolescents and children who are with the army?

GLAUCON: I do.

SOCRATES: What about shaking him by the right hand?

GLAUCON: That too.

SOCRATES: But I do not imagine you would go so far as this.

GLAUCON: As what?

SOCRATES: That he should kiss, and be kissed by, each of them.

GLAUCON: By all means. And I would add to the law that while they are still on campaign, no one he wants to kiss shall be allowed to refuse, so   468c
that if anyone passionately loves another, whether male or female, he will try harder to win the prize for bravery.

SOCRATES: Excellent! For we have already mentioned that more opportunities for marriage will be available for a good man, and that men like him will be selected more often than others for such things, so that as many children as possible may be produced from them.

GLAUCON: Yes, we did mention that.

SOCRATES: Moreover, according to Homer too, it is just to honor in such ways those young people who are good. For Homer says that when   468d
Ajax distinguished himself in battle, he "was rewarded with the whole backbone,"[15] since he considered that to be an appropriate honor for a courageous young man because it honored him and built up his strength at the same time.

GLAUCON: That's absolutely right.

SOCRATES: Then we will follow Homer in this matter, at any rate. I mean that at sacrifices and all other such occasions, we too will honor good men—insofar as they have exhibited their goodness—not only with hymns and all the other things we mentioned, but also with "seats of honor, cuts   468e
of meats, and well-filled cups of wine,"[16] so that while honoring our good men and women, we may train them at the same time.

GLAUCON: That's an excellent idea.

SOCRATES: All right. And if any of those who died while on campaign has had a particularly distinguished death, won't we, in the first place, declare that he belongs to the golden race?

GLAUCON: Absolutely.

---

15 *Iliad* vii.321.

16 *Iliad* viii.162.

SOCRATES: And won't we believe with Hesiod that, whenever any of that
469a race die, they become "unsullied daimons living upon the earth, noble
beings, protectors against evil, guardians of articulate mortals?"[17]

GLAUCON: We will certainly believe that.

SOCRATES: Won't we ask the god, then, to tell us how and with what
distinction these daimons, these godlike people, should be buried, and
perform their burial in whatever way he prescribes?

GLAUCON: Of course.

SOCRATES: And for the remainder of time, won't we regard their graves as
those of daimons, and take care of them and worship at them? And won't
469b we follow these same rites whenever anyone who has been judged outstandingly good throughout his life dies of old age, or in some other way?

GLAUCON: It would be just to do so, at any rate.

SOCRATES: Now, what about enemies? How will our soldiers behave toward
them?

GLAUCON: In what respect?

SOCRATES: First, as regards enslavement, do you think it is just for Greek
cities to enslave other Greeks, or should they try as hard as possible not
even to allow other cities to do so, and make a habit of sparing the Greek
469c race as a precaution against being enslaved by barbarians?

GLAUCON: Sparing them is by far the best course.

SOCRATES: So, they should not possess any Greek slaves themselves, and
should advise the other Greeks to do the same?

GLAUCON: By all means. In that way, at any rate, they would be more likely
to turn against the barbarians and keep their hands off one another.

SOCRATES: What about despoiling the dead? Is it a good thing to strip the
dead of anything besides their armor after a victory? Doesn't it give cowards
469d a pretext for not facing the enemy, since when they are greedily bending
over corpses, they will be performing an important duty? And haven't
many armies been lost because of such plundering?

GLAUCON: Yes, indeed.

SOCRATES: Don't you think it is illiberal and money-loving to strip a corpse?
And isn't it small-minded and womanish to regard a dead body as your
enemy, when the enemy himself has flitted away leaving behind only the
instrument with which he fought? Do you think that people who do this
469e are any different from dogs who get angry with the stones thrown at them
but leave the person throwing them alone?

GLAUCON: No different at all.

---

[17] *Works and Days* 122.

SOCRATES: So they should not strip corpses, should they, or refuse the enemy permission to pick up their dead?

GLAUCON: No, by Zeus, they certainly should not.

SOCRATES: Moreover, we surely won't take weapons to the temples as offerings, and if we care anything about the goodwill of other Greeks, we especially won't do this with Greek weapons. On the contrary, we would **470a** even be afraid of polluting the temples if we brought them such things from our own race, unless, of course, the god ordains otherwise.

GLAUCON: That's absolutely right.

SOCRATES: What about ravaging Greek land and burning Greek houses? How will your soldiers behave toward their enemies?

GLAUCON: I would like to hear what *you* believe about that.

SOCRATES: Well, I believe they should do neither of these things, but destroy only the year's harvest. Do you want me to tell you why? **470b**

GLAUCON: Of course.

SOCRATES: It seems to me that just as we have the two names "war" and "faction," so there are also two things, and the names apply to differences between the two. The two I mean are, on the one hand, what is one's own and kin, and, on the other, what is foreign and strange. "Faction" applies to hostility toward one's own, "war" to hostility toward strangers.

GLAUCON: Yes, there is nothing wrong with that claim.

SOCRATES: Consider, then, whether this too is correct. I say that the Greek **470c** race, in relation to itself, is its own and kin, but, in relation to barbarians, is strange and foreign.

GLAUCON: That's right.

SOCRATES: When Greeks fight with barbarians, then, or barbarians with Greeks, we will say that that is warfare, that they are natural enemies, and that such hostilities should be called war. But when Greeks engage in such things with Greeks, we will say they are natural friends, that Greece is sick and divided into factions in such a situation, and that such hostilities **470d** should be called faction.

GLAUCON: I, for one, agree to think that way.

SOCRATES: Now, notice that whenever something of the sort that is currently called faction occurs and a city is divided, if each side devastates the land and burns the houses of the other, the faction is thought abominable and neither party is thought to love the city—otherwise they would never have dared to ravage their own nurse and mother. But it is thought reasonable for the ones who have proved stronger to carry off the weaker ones' crops, and to have the attitude of mind of people who will one day be **470e** reconciled and won't always be at war.

GLAUCON: That attitude of mind is far more civilized than the other.

SOCRATES: What about the city you are founding? Won't it be Greek?

GLAUCON: It will have to be.

SOCRATES: So won't its citizens be good and civilized people?

GLAUCON: Indeed, they will.

SOCRATES: Then won't they be lovers of Greeks? Won't they consider Greece as their own and share the same religious festivals as other Greeks?

GLAUCON: Yes, indeed.

471a SOCRATES: Then won't they regard their conflicts with Greeks—their own people—as faction, and not even use the name "war"?

GLAUCON: No, they won't use it.

SOCRATES: And so, they will quarrel with the aim of being reconciled, won't they?

GLAUCON: Of course.

SOCRATES: They will discipline their foes in a friendly spirit, then, and not punish them with enslavement and destruction, since they are discipliners, not enemies.

GLAUCON: That's right.

SOCRATES: As Greeks, then, they won't devastate Greece or burn its houses, nor will they agree that *all* the inhabitants in any city—men, women, and **471b** children—are their enemies, but only those few responsible for the conflict. For all these reasons, they won't be willing to devastate their country, since the majority of the inhabitants are their friends, nor destroy the houses, and they will pursue the conflict only to the point at which those responsible are compelled to pay the penalty by the innocent ones who are suffering painfully.

GLAUCON: I agree that this is how our citizens should treat their enemies, but they should treat barbarians the way Greeks currently treat each other.

471c SOCRATES: Then shall we also establish this law for the guardians, that they should neither ravage Greek land nor burn Greek houses?

GLAUCON: Yes, let's establish it. And let's assume that this law and its predecessors are right. But, Socrates, I think that if you are allowed to go on talking about this sort of thing, you will never remember the topic you set aside in order to say all this—namely, whether it is possible for this constitution to come into existence, and how it could ever do so. I agree that *if* it came into existence, everything would be lovely for the city that had it. I will even add some advantages that you have left out: they would **471d** fight excellently against their enemies because they would be least likely to desert each other. After all, they recognize each other as brothers, fathers, and sons, and call each other by those names. And if the women, too, joined in their campaigns, either stationed in the same ranks or in the rear, either to strike terror in the enemy or to provide support should the need ever arise, I know that this would make them quite unbeatable. And I also see all the good things they would have at home that you have omitted. Take it for granted that I agree that all these benefits, as well as innumerable 471e others, would result, *if* this constitution came into existence, and say no more about it. Instead, let's now try to convince ourselves of just this: that it is possible and how it is possible, and let's leave the rest aside.

SOCRATES: All of a sudden, you have practically assaulted my argument and **472a** lost all sympathy for my holding back. Perhaps you do not realize that just as I have barely escaped from the first two waves of objections, you are now bringing the greatest and most difficult of the three down upon me.[18] When you see and hear it, you will have complete sympathy and recognize that I had good reason after all for hesitating and for being afraid to state and try to examine so paradoxical an argument.

GLAUCON: The more you talk like that, the less we will let you get away without explaining how this constitution could come into existence. So 472b explain it, and do not delay any further.

SOCRATES: The first thing to recall, then, is that it was our inquiry into the nature of justice and injustice that brought us to this point.

GLAUCON: True. But what of it?

SOCRATES: Oh, nothing. However, if we discover the nature of justice, should we also expect the just man not to differ from justice itself in any way, but, on the contrary, to have entirely the same nature it does? Or will we be satisfied if he approximates as closely as possible to it and partakes in it far more than anyone else? 472c

GLAUCON: Yes, we will be satisfied with that.

SOCRATES: So, it was in order to have a model that we were inquiring into the nature of justice itself and of the completely just man, supposing he could exist, and what he would be like if he did; and similarly with injustice and the most unjust man. We thought that by seeing how they seemed to us to stand with regard to happiness and its opposite, we would also be compelled to agree about ourselves as well: that the one who was most like them would have a fate most like theirs. But we were not doing 472d this in order to demonstrate that it is possible for these men to exist.

GLAUCON: That's true.

SOCRATES: Do you think, then, that someone would be any less good a painter if he painted a model of what the most beautiful human being

---

[18] The third wave was proverbially the greatest.

would be like, and rendered everything in the picture perfectly well, but could not demonstrate that such a man could actually exist?

GLAUCON: No, by Zeus, I do not.

SOCRATES: What about our own case, then? Weren't we trying, as we put it, to produce a model in our discussion of a good city?

472e GLAUCON: Certainly.

SOCRATES: So, do you think that our discussion will be any less satisfactory if we cannot demonstrate that it is possible to found a city that is the same as the one we described in speech?

GLAUCON: Not at all.

SOCRATES: Then that is the truth of the matter. But if, in order to please you, we must do our best to demonstrate how, and under what condition, this would be most possible, you must again grant me the same points for the purposes of that demonstration.

GLAUCON: Which ones?

SOCRATES: Is it possible for anything to be carried out exactly as described
473a in speech, or is it natural for practice to have less of a grasp of truth than speech does, even if some people do not think so? Do you agree with this or not?

GLAUCON: I do.

SOCRATES: Then do not compel me to demonstrate it as coming about in practice exactly as we have described it in speech. Rather, if we are able to discover how a city that most closely approximates to what we have described could be founded, you must admit that we have discovered how
473b all you have prescribed could come about. Or wouldn't you be satisfied with that? *I* certainly would.

GLAUCON: Me, too.

SOCRATES: Then next, it seems, we should try to discover and show what is badly done in cities nowadays that prevents them from being managed our way, and what the smallest change would be that would enable a city to arrive at our sort of constitution—preferably one change; otherwise, two; otherwise, the fewest in number and the least extensive in effect.

473c GLAUCON: Absolutely.

SOCRATES: Well, there is one change we could point to that I think would accomplish this. It certainly is not small or easy, but it *is* possible.

GLAUCON: What is it?

SOCRATES: I am now about to confront what we likened to the greatest wave. Yet, it must be stated, even if it is going to drown me in a wave of outright ridicule and contempt, as it were. So listen to what I am about to say.

GLAUCON: Say it.

SOCRATES: Until philosophers rule as kings in their cities, or those who are nowadays called kings and leading men become genuine and adequate philosophers so that political power and philosophy become thoroughly blended together, while the numerous natures that now pursue either one exclusively are compelled not to do so, cities will have no rest from evils, my dear Glaucon, nor, I think, will the human race. And until that happens, the same constitution we have now described in our discussion will never be born to the extent that it can, or see the light of the sun. It is this claim that has made me hesitate to speak for so long. I saw how very unbelievable it would sound, since it is difficult to accept that there can be no happiness, either public or private, in any other way. 473d

473e

GLAUCON: Socrates, what a speech, what an argument you have let burst with! But now that you have uttered it, you must expect that a great many people—and not undistinguished ones either—will immediately throw off their cloaks and, stripped for action, snatch any available weapon and make a headlong rush at you, determined to do terrible things to you. So, if you do not defend yourself by argument and escape, you really will pay the penalty of general derision. **474a**

SOCRATES: But aren't *you* the one who is responsible for this happening to me?

GLAUCON: And I was right to do it. Still, I won't desert you. On the contrary, I will defend you in any way I can. And what I can do is provide good will and encouragement, and maybe give you more careful answers to your questions than someone else. So, with the promise of this sort of assistance, try to demonstrate to the unbelievers that things are as you claim. 474b

SOCRATES: I will have to, especially when you agree to be so great an ally! If we are going to escape from the people you mention, I think we need to define for them who the philosophers are that we dare to say should rule; so that once that is clear, one can defend oneself by showing that some people are fitted by nature to engage in philosophy *and* to take the lead in a city, while there are others who should not engage in it, but should follow a leader. 474c

GLAUCON: This would be a good time to define them.

SOCRATES: Come on, then, follow me on the path I am about to take, to see if it somehow leads to an adequate explanation.

GLAUCON: Lead on.

SOCRATES: Do I have to remind you, or do you recall, that when we say someone loves something, if the description is correct, it must be clear not just that he loves some part of it but not another; but, on the contrary, that he cherishes the whole of it?

GLAUCON: You will have to remind me, it seems. I do not recall the point at all.

474d   SOCRATES: I did not expect you to give that response, Glaucon. A passionate man should not forget that *all* boys in the bloom of youth somehow manage to sting and arouse a passionate lover of boys, and seem to merit his attention and passionate devotion. Isn't that the way you people behave to beautiful boys? One, because he is snub-nosed, you will praise as "cute;" another who is hook-nosed you will say is "regal;" while the one in the middle you say is "well proportioned." Dark ones look "manly," and pale

474e   ones are "children of the gods." As for the "honey-colored," do you think that this very term is anything but the euphemistic coinage of a lover who found it easy to tolerate a sallow complexion, provided it was accompanied

475a   by the bloom of youth? In a word, you people find any excuse, and use any expression, to avoid rejecting anyone whose flower is in full bloom.

GLAUCON: If you insist on taking *me* as your example of what passionate men do, I will go along with you . . . for the sake of argument!

SOCRATES: What about lovers of wine? Don't you observe them behaving in just the same way? Don't they find any excuse to indulge their passionate devotion to wine of any sort?

GLAUCON: They do, indeed.

SOCRATES: And you also observe, I imagine, that if honor-lovers cannot become generals, they serve as lieutenants, and if they cannot be honored by important people and dignitaries, they are satisfied with being honored by insignificant and inferior ones, since it is honor as a whole for which

475b   they have an appetite.

GLAUCON: Exactly.

SOCRATES: Then do you affirm this or not? When we say that someone has an appetite for something, are we to say that he has an appetite for everything of that kind, or for one part of it but not another?

GLAUCON: Everything.

SOCRATES: Then in the case of the philosopher, too, won't we say that he has an appetite for *wisdom*—not for one part and not another, but for all of it?

GLAUCON: True.

SOCRATES: So, if someone makes difficulties about what he learns, espe-

475c   cially if he is young and does not have a rational grasp of what is useful and what is not, we won't say that he is a lover of learning or a philosopher—any more than we would say that someone who is choosy about his food is famished, or has an appetite for food, or is a lover of food rather than a picky eater.

GLAUCON: And we would be right not to say it.

SOCRATES: But someone who is ready and willing to taste every kind of learning, who turns gladly to learning and is insatiable for it, *he* is the one we would be justified in calling a philosopher. Isn't that so?

GLAUCON: In that case, many strange people will be philosophers! I mean, 475d all the lovers of seeing are what they are, I imagine, because they take pleasure in learning things. And the lovers of listening are very strange people to include as philosophers: they would never willingly attend a serious discussion or spend their time that way; yet, just as if their ears were under contract to listen to every chorus, they run around to all the Dionysiac festivals, whether in cities or villages, and never miss one. Are we to say that these people—and others who are students of similar things or of petty crafts—are philosophers?   475e

SOCRATES: Not at all, but they are *like* philosophers.

GLAUCON: Who do you think, then, are the true ones?

SOCRATES: The lovers of seeing the truth.

GLAUCON: That, too, is no doubt correct, but what exactly do you mean by it?

SOCRATES: It would not be easy to explain to someone else. But you, I imagine, will agree to the following.

GLAUCON: What?

SOCRATES: That since beautiful is the opposite of ugly, they are two things. **476a**

GLAUCON: Of course.

SOCRATES: And since they are two things, each of them is also one?

GLAUCON: That's true too.

SOCRATES: And the same argument applies, then, to just and unjust, good and bad, and all the forms: each of them is itself one thing, but because they appear all over the place in partnership with actions and bodies, and with one another, each of them appears to be many things.

GLAUCON: That's right.

SOCRATES: Well, then, that is the basis of the distinction I draw: on one side are the lovers of seeing, the lovers of crafts, and the practical people you mentioned a moment ago; on the other, those we are arguing about, the only ones it is correct to call philosophers.   476b

GLAUCON: How do you mean?

SOCRATES: The lovers of listening and seeing are passionately devoted to beautiful sounds, colors, shapes, and everything fashioned out of such things. But their thought is unable to see the nature of the beautiful itself or to be passionately devoted to it.

GLAUCON: That's certainly true.

SOCRATES: On the other hand, won't those who *are* able to approach the beautiful itself, and see it by itself, be rare?

GLAUCON: Very.

476c SOCRATES: What about someone who believes in beautiful things but does not believe in the beautiful itself, and would not be able to follow anyone who tried to lead him to the knowledge of it? Do you think he is living in a dream, or is he awake? Just consider. Isn't it dreaming to think—whether asleep or awake—that a likeness is not a likeness, but rather the thing itself that it is like?

GLAUCON: I certainly think that someone who does that is dreaming.

SOCRATES: But what about someone who, to take the opposite case, does believe in the beautiful itself, is able to observe both it and the things that participate in it, and does not think that the participants are it, or that it is the participants—do you think he is living in a dream or is awake?

476d

GLAUCON: He is very much awake.

SOCRATES: So, because this person knows these things, we would be right to describe his thought as knowledge; but the other's we would be right to describe as belief, because he believes what he does?

GLAUCON: Certainly.

SOCRATES: What if the person we describe as believing but not knowing is angry with us and disputes the truth of what we say? Will we have any way of soothing and gently persuading him, while disguising the fact that he is not in a healthy state of mind?

476e

GLAUCON: We certainly need one, at any rate.

SOCRATES: Come on, then, consider what we will say to him. Or—once we have told him that nobody envies him any knowledge he may have— that, on the contrary, we would be delighted to discover that he knows something—do you want us to question him as follows? "Tell us this: does someone who knows know something or nothing?" You answer for him.

GLAUCON: I will answer that he knows something.

477a SOCRATES: Something that is or something that is not?

GLAUCON: That is. How could something that is not be known?

SOCRATES: We are adequately assured of this, then, and would remain so, no matter how many ways we examined it: what is completely is com- pletely an object of knowledge and what is in no way at all is an object of complete ignorance.

GLAUCON: Most adequately.

SOCRATES: Good. In that case, then, if anything is such as to be and also not to be, wouldn't it lie in between what purely is and what in no way is?

GLAUCON: Yes, in between them.

SOCRATES: Then, since knowledge deals with what is, ignorance must deal with what is not, while we must look in between knowledge and ignorance for what deals with what lies in between, if there *is* anything of that sort.   477b

GLAUCON: Yes.

SOCRATES: So, then, do we think there is such a thing as belief?

GLAUCON: Of course.

SOCRATES: Is it a different power from knowledge, or the same?

GLAUCON: A different one.

SOCRATES: So, belief has been assigned to deal with one thing, then, and knowledge with another, depending on what power each has.

GLAUCON: Right.

SOCRATES: Now, doesn't knowledge naturally deal with what is, to know how what is as it is? But first I think we should go through the following.

GLAUCON: What?

SOCRATES: We think powers are a type of thing that enables us—or any-   477c
thing else that has an ability—to do whatever we are able to do. Sight and hearing are examples of what I mean by powers, if you understand the kind of thing I am trying to describe.

GLAUCON: Yes, I do.

SOCRATES: Listen, then, to what I think about them. A power has no color for me to see, nor a shape, nor any feature of the sort that many other things have, and that I can consider in order to distinguish them for myself as different from one another. In the case of a power, I can consider only   477d
what it deals with and what it does, and it is on that basis that I come to call each the power it is: those assigned to deal with the same things and do the same, I call the same; those that deal with different things and do different things, I call different. What about you? What do you do?

GLAUCON: The same.

SOCRATES: Going back, then, to where we left off, my very good fellow: do you think knowledge is itself a power? Or to what type would you assign it?

GLAUCON: To that one. It is the most effective power of all.   477e

SOCRATES: What about belief? Shall we include it as a power or assign it to a different kind?

GLAUCON: Not at all. Belief is nothing other than the power that enables us to believe.

SOCRATES: But a moment ago you agreed that knowledge and belief are not the same.

GLAUCON: How could anyone with any sense think a fallible thing is the same as an infallible one?

SOCRATES: Fine. Then clearly we agree that belief is different from
478a knowledge.

GLAUCON: Yes, it is different.

SOCRATES: Each of them, then, since it has a different power, deals by
nature with something different?

GLAUCON: Necessarily.

SOCRATES: Surely knowledge deals with what is, to know what is as it is?

GLAUCON: Yes.

SOCRATES: Whereas belief, we say, believes?

GLAUCON: Yes.

SOCRATES: The very same thing that knowledge knows? Can the object
of knowledge and the object of belief be the same? Or is that impossible?

GLAUCON: It is impossible, given what we have agreed. If different powers
by nature deal with different things, and both opinion and knowledge are
478b powers but, as we claim, different ones, it follows from these that the object
of knowledge and the object of belief cannot be the same.

SOCRATES: Then if what is is the object of knowledge, mustn't the object
of belief be something other than what is?

GLAUCON: Yes, it must be something different.

SOCRATES: Does belief, then, believe what is not? Or is it impossible even
to believe what is not? Consider this: doesn't a believer take his belief to
deal with something? Or is it possible to believe, yet to believe nothing?

GLAUCON: No, it is impossible.

SOCRATES: In fact, there is some single thing that a believer believes?

GLAUCON: Yes.

SOCRATES: But surely what is not is most correctly characterized not as a
478c single thing, but as nothing?

GLAUCON: Of course.

SOCRATES: But we had to assign ignorance to what is not and knowledge
to what is?

GLAUCON: Correct.

SOCRATES: So belief neither believes what is nor what is not?

GLAUCON: No, it does not.

SOCRATES: Then belief cannot be either ignorance or knowledge?

GLAUCON: Apparently not.

SOCRATES: Well, then, does it lie beyond these two, surpassing knowledge
in clarity or ignorance in opacity?

GLAUCON: No, it does neither.

SOCRATES: Then does belief seem to you to be more opaque than knowledge but clearer than ignorance?

GLAUCON: Very much so.

SOCRATES: It lies within the boundaries determined by them?   478d

GLAUCON: Yes.

SOCRATES: So belief will lie in between the two?

GLAUCON: Absolutely.

SOCRATES: Now, didn't we say earlier that if something turned out both to be and not to be at the same time, it would lie in between what purely is and what in every way is not, and that neither knowledge nor ignorance would deal with it; but whatever it was again that turned out to lie in between ignorance and knowledge would?

GLAUCON: Correct.

SOCRATES: And now, what we are calling belief has turned out to lie in between them?

GLAUCON: It has.

SOCRATES: Apparently, then, it remains for us to find what partakes in both being and not being, and cannot correctly be called purely one or   478e
the other, so that if we find it, we can justifiably call it the object of belief, thereby assigning extremes to extremes and in-betweens to in-betweens. Isn't that so?

GLAUCON: It is.

SOCRATES: Now that all that has been established, I want him to tell me this—the excellent fellow who believes that there is no beautiful itself, no   **479a**
form of beauty itself that remains always the same in all respects, but who does believe that there are many beautiful things—I mean, that lover of seeing who cannot bear to hear anyone say that the beautiful is one thing, or the just, or any of the rest—I want him to answer this question: "My very good fellow," we will say, "of all the many beautiful things, is there one that won't also seem ugly? Or any just one that won't seem unjust? Or any pious one that won't seem impious?"

GLAUCON: There is not. On the contrary, it is inevitable that they would somehow seem both beautiful and ugly; and the same with the other things you asked about.   479b

SOCRATES: What about the many things that are doubles? Do they seem to be any the less halves than doubles?

GLAUCON: No.

SOCRATES: And again, will things that we say are great, small, light, or heavy be any more what we say they are than they will be the opposite?

GLAUCON: No, each of them is always both.

SOCRATES: Then is each of the many things any more what one says it is than it is not what one says it is?

479c GLAUCON: No, they are like those puzzles one hears at parties, or the children's riddle about the eunuch who threw something at a bat—the one about what he threw at it and what it was in.[19] For these things, too, are ambiguous, and one cannot understand them as fixedly being or fixedly not being, or as both, or as neither.

SOCRATES: Do you know what to do with them, then, or anywhere better to put them than in between being and not being? Surely they cannot be more opaque than what is not, by not-being more than it; nor clearer than what is, by *being* more than it.

479d GLAUCON: That's absolutely true.

SOCRATES: So, we have now discovered, it seems, that the masses' many conventional norms concerning beauty and the rest are somehow rolling around between what is not and what purely is.

GLAUCON: We have.

SOCRATES: And we agreed earlier that if anything turned out to be of that sort, it would have to be called an object of belief, not an object of knowledge—a wandering, in-between object grasped by the in-between power.

GLAUCON: We did.

479e SOCRATES: As for those, then, who look at many beautiful things but do not see the beautiful itself, and are incapable of following another who would lead them to it; or many just things but not the just itself, and similarly with all the rest—these people, we will say, have beliefs about all these things, but have no knowledge of what their beliefs are about.

GLAUCON: That is what we would have to say.

SOCRATES: On the other hand, what about those who in each case look at the things themselves that are always the same in every respect? Won't we say that they have knowledge, not mere belief?

GLAUCON: Once again, we would have to.

SOCRATES: Shall we say, then, that these people are passionately devoted to and love the things with which knowledge deals, as the others are devoted
480a to and love the things with which belief deals? We have not forgotten, have

---

[19] The riddle seems to have been this: a man who is not a man saw and did not see a bird that was not a bird in a tree (*xulon*) that was not a tree; he hit (*ballein*) and did not hit it with a stone that was not a stone. The answer is that a eunuch with bad eyesight saw a bat on a rafter, threw a pumice stone at it, and missed. "He saw a bird" is ambiguous between "he saw what was actually a bird" and "he saw what he took to be a bird," *xulon* means both "tree" and "rafter" or "roof tree," and *ballein* means both "to throw" and "to hit." The rest is obvious.

we, that the latter love and look at beautiful sounds, colors, and things of that sort, but cannot even bear the idea that the beautiful itself is a thing that is?

GLAUCON: No, we have not.

SOCRATES: Will we be striking a false note, then, if we call such people "philodoxers" (lovers of belief) rather than "philosophers" (lovers of wisdom or knowledge)? Will they be very angry with us if we call them that?

GLAUCON: Not if they take my advice. It is not in accord with divine law to be angry with the truth.

SOCRATES: So, those who in each case are passionately devoted to the thing itself are the ones we must call, not "philodoxers," but "philosophers"?

GLAUCON: Absolutely.

BOOK VI

SOCRATES' NARRATION CONTINUES:

SOCRATES: Who the philosophers are, then, Glaucon, and who they aren't   484a
has, through a somewhat lengthy argument and with much effort, somehow been made clear.

GLAUCON: That's probably because it could not easily have been done through a shorter one.

SOCRATES: I suppose not. Yet I, at least, think that the matter would have been made even clearer if we had had only that topic to discuss, and not the many others that remain for us to explore if we are to discover the difference between the just life and the unjust one.   484b

GLAUCON: What comes after this one, then?

SOCRATES: What else but the one that comes next? Since the philosophers are the ones who are able to grasp what is always the same in all respects, while those who cannot—those who wander among the many things that vary in every sort of way—are not philosophers, which of the two should be the leaders of a city?

GLAUCON: What would be a reasonable answer for us to give?

SOCRATES: Whichever of them seems capable of guarding a city's laws and practices should be established as guardians.

GLAUCON: That's right.

SOCRATES: So, is the answer to the following question clear: should a guardian who is going to keep watch over something be blind or keen-sighted?   484c

GLAUCON: Of course it is.

SOCRATES: Well, do you think there is any difference, then, between the blind and those who are really deprived of the knowledge of each thing

484d that is, and have no clear model of it in their souls—those who cannot look away, like painters, to what is most true, and cannot, by making constant reference to it and by studying it as exactly as possible, establish here on earth conventional norms concerning beautiful, just, or good things when they need to be established, or guard and preserve those that have been established?

GLAUCON: No, by Zeus, there is not much difference between them.

SOCRATES: Shall we appoint these blind people as our guardians, then, or those who know each thing that is, have no less experience than the others, and are not inferior to them in any other part of virtue?

GLAUCON: It would be absurd to choose anyone but philosophers, if indeed they are not inferior in these other things. For the very area in which they are superior is just about the greatest one.

485a SOCRATES: Shouldn't we explain, then, how the same men can have both sets of qualities?

GLAUCON: Certainly.

SOCRATES: Then, as we were saying at the beginning of this discussion, it is first necessary to understand the nature of philosophers. And I think that if we can agree sufficiently about that, we will also agree that the same people *can* have both qualities, and that they alone should be leaders in cities.

GLAUCON: How so?

485b SOCRATES: Let's agree that philosophic natures always love the sort of learning that makes clear to them some feature of the being that always is and does not wander around between coming-to-be and decaying.

GLAUCON: Yes, let's.

SOCRATES: And further, let's agree that they love all of it and are not willing to give up any part, whether great or small, significant or insignificant, just like the honor-lovers and passionate men we described before.

GLAUCON: That's right.

485c SOCRATES: Consider next whether there is a further feature they must have in their nature if they are going to be the way we described.

GLAUCON: What?

SOCRATES: Truthfulness; that is to say they must never willingly tolerate falsehood in any form. On the contrary, they must hate it and have a natural affection for the truth.

GLAUCON: They probably should have that feature.

SOCRATES: But it is not only *probable,* my friend; it is entirely necessary for a naturally passionate man to love everything akin to or related to the boys he loves.

GLAUCON: That's right.

SOCRATES: Well, could you find anything that is more intimately related to wisdom than truth?

GLAUCON: Of course not.

SOCRATES: Then is it possible for the same nature to be a philosopher (lover of wisdom) and a lover of falsehood?   485d

GLAUCON: Certainly not.

SOCRATES: So, right from childhood, a genuine lover of learning must strive above all for truth of every kind.

GLAUCON: Absolutely.

SOCRATES: But in addition, when someone's appetites are strongly inclined in one direction, we surely know that they become more weakly inclined in the others, just like a stream that has been partly diverted into another channel.

GLAUCON: Of course.

SOCRATES: Then when a person's desires flow toward learning and everything of that sort, they will be concerned, I imagine, with the pleasures that the soul experiences just by itself, and will be indifferent to those that come through the body—if indeed the person is not a counterfeit, but rather a true, philosopher.   485e

GLAUCON: That's entirely inevitable.

SOCRATES: A person like that will be temperate, then, and in no way a lover of money. After all, money and the big expenditures that go along with it are sought for the sake of things that other people may take seriously, but that he does not.

GLAUCON: That's right.

SOCRATES: And of course, there is also this to consider when you are going   486a
to judge whether a nature is philosophic or not.

GLAUCON: What?

SOCRATES: You should not overlook its sharing in illiberality; for surely petty-mindedness is altogether incompatible with that quality in a soul that is always reaching out to grasp all things as a whole, whether divine or human.

GLAUCON: That's absolutely true.

SOCRATES: And do you imagine that a thinker who is high-minded enough to look at all time and all being will consider human life to be a very great thing?

GLAUCON: He couldn't possibly.

SOCRATES: Then he won't consider death to be a terrible thing either, will he?   486b

GLAUCON: Not in the least.

SOCRATES: Then a cowardly and illiberal nature could not partake, apparently, in true philosophy.

GLAUCON: Not in my opinion.

SOCRATES: Well, then, is there any way that an orderly person, who is not money-loving, illiberal, a lying imposter, or a coward, could come to drive a hard bargain or be unjust?

GLAUCON: There is not.

SOCRATES: Moreover, when you are considering whether someone has a philosophic soul or not, you will consider whether he is just and gentle, right from the time he is young, or unsociable and savage.

GLAUCON: Of course.

486c SOCRATES: And you won't ignore this either, I imagine.

GLAUCON: What?

SOCRATES: Whether he is a slow learner or a fast one. Or do you expect someone to love something sufficiently well when it pains him to do it and a lot of effort brings only a small return?

GLAUCON: No, it could not happen.

SOCRATES: What if he could retain nothing of what he learned, because he was completely forgetful? Could he fail to be empty of knowledge?

GLAUCON: Of course not.

SOCRATES: Then if he is laboring in vain, don't you think that in the end he is bound to hate himself and what he is doing?

GLAUCON: Of course.

SOCRATES: So let's never include a person with a forgetful soul among those
486d who are sufficiently philosophical; the one we look for should be good at remembering.

GLAUCON: Absolutely.

SOCRATES: Moreover, we would deny that an unmusical and graceless nature is drawn to anything besides what is disproportionate.

GLAUCON: Of course.

SOCRATES: And do you think that truth is akin to what is disproportionate or to what is proportionate?

GLAUCON: To what is proportionate.

SOCRATES: Then, in addition to those other things, let's look for a mind that has a natural sense of proportion and grace, one whose innate disposition makes it easy to lead to the form of each thing which is.

GLAUCON: Indeed.

SOCRATES: Well, then, do you think the properties we have gone through 486e
aren't interconnected, or that any of them is in any way unnecessary to a
soul that is going to have a sufficiently complete grasp of what is?

GLAUCON: No, they are all absolutely necessary. 487a

SOCRATES: Is there any criticism you can find, then, of a pursuit that a person cannot practice adequately unless he is naturally good at remembering,
quick to learn, high-minded, graceful, and a friend and relative of truth,
justice, courage, and temperance?

GLAUCON: Not even Momus could criticize a pursuit like that.

SOCRATES: Well, then, when people of this sort are in perfect condition
because of their education and their stage of life, wouldn't you entrust the
city to them alone?

And Adeimantus replied: 487b

No one, Socrates, would be able to contradict these claims of yours. But all
the same, here is pretty much the experience people have on any occasion
on which they hear the sorts of things you are now saying: they think that
because they are inexperienced in asking and answering questions, they
are led astray a little bit by the argument at every question, and that when
these little bits are added together at the end of the discussion, a great false
step appears that is the opposite of what they said at the outset. Like the
unskilled, who are trapped by the clever checkers players in the end and
cannot make a move, they too are trapped in the end, and have nothing to 487c
say in this different kind of checkers, which is played not with pieces, but
with words. Yet they are not a bit more inclined to think that what you
claim is true. I say this in relation to the present case. You see, someone
might well say now that he is unable to find the words to oppose you as you
ask each of your questions. Yet, when it comes to facts rather than words,
he sees that of all those who take up philosophy—not those who merely
dabble in it while still young in order to complete their upbringing, and
then drop it, but those who continue in it for a longer time—the majority 487d
become cranks, not to say completely bad, while the ones who seem best
are rendered useless to the city because of the pursuit you recommend.

When I had heard him out, I said:

Do you think that what these people say is false?

ADEIMANTUS: I do not know. But I would be glad to hear what you think.

SOCRATES: You would hear that they seem to me to be telling the truth.

ADEIMANTUS: How, then, can it be right to say that there will be no end
to evils in our cities until philosophers—people we agree to be useless to 487e
cities—rule in them?

SOCRATES: The question you ask needs to be answered by means of an
image.

ADEIMANTUS: And you, of course, are not used to speaking in images!

SOCRATES: So! After landing me with a claim that is so difficult to establish, are you mocking me, too? Anyway, listen to my image, and you will appreciate all the more how I have to strain to make up images. What the best philosophers experience in relation to cities is so difficult to bear that there is no other single experience like it. On the contrary, one must construct one's image and one's defense of these philosophers from *many* sources, just as painters paint goat-stags by combining the features of different things.

Imagine, then, that the following sort of thing happens either on one ship or on many. The shipowner is taller and stronger than everyone else on board. But he is hard of hearing, he is a bit shortsighted, and his knowledge of seafaring is correspondingly deficient. The sailors are quarreling with one another about captaincy. Each of them thinks that he should captain the ship, even though he has not yet learned the craft and cannot name his teacher or a time when he was learning it. Indeed, they go further and claim that it cannot be taught at all, and are even ready to cut to pieces anyone who says it can. They are always crowding around the shipowner himself, pleading with him, and doing everything possible to get him to turn the rudder over to them. And sometimes, if they fail to persuade him and others succeed, they execute those others or throw them overboard. Then, having disabled their noble shipowner with mandragora[1] or drink or in some other way, they rule the ship, use up its cargo drinking and feasting, and make the sort of voyage you would expect of such people. In addition, they praise anyone who is clever at persuading or forcing the shipowner to let them rule, calling him a "sailor," a "skilled captain," and "an expert about ships" while dismissing anyone else as a good-for-nothing. They do not understand that a true captain must pay attention to the seasons of the year, the sky, the stars, the winds, and all that pertains to his craft if he is really going to be expert at ruling a ship. As for *how* he is going to become captain of the ship, whether people want him to or not, they do not think it possible to acquire the craft or practice of doing this at the same time as the craft of captaincy. When that is what is happening onboard ships, don't you think that a true captain would be sure to be called a "stargazer," a "useless babbler," and a "good-for-nothing" by those who sail in ships so governed?

ADEIMANTUS: I certainly do.

SOCRATES: I do not think you need to examine the image to see the resemblance to cities and how they're disposed toward true philosophers, but you already understand what I mean.

ADEIMANTUS: Indeed, I do.

488a

488b

488c

488d

488e

489a

---

[1] An intoxicant.

SOCRATES: First teach this image, then, to the person who is surprised that philosophers are not honored in cities, and try to persuade him that it would be far more surprising if they were honored.

489b

ADEIMANTUS: I will.

SOCRATES: Furthermore, try to persuade him that you are speaking the truth when you say that the best among the philosophers are useless to the masses. But tell him to blame their uselessness on those who do not make use of them, not on those good philosophers. You see, it is not natural for the captain to beg the sailors to be ruled by him, nor for the wise to knock at the doors of the rich. The man who came up with that bit of sophistry was lying.[2] What is truly natural is for the sick person, rich or poor, to go to doctors' doors, and for anyone who needs to be ruled to go to the doors of the one who can rule him. It is not for the ruler—if he is truly any use—to beg the subjects to accept his rule. Tell him he will make no mistake if he likens our present political rulers to the sailors we mentioned a moment ago, and those who are called useless stargazers by them to the true ship's captains.

489c

ADEIMANTUS: That's absolutely right.

SOCRATES: For those reasons, then, and in these circumstances, it is not easy for the best pursuit to be highly honored by those whose pursuits are its very opposites. But by far the greatest and most serious slander is brought on philosophy by those who claim to practice it—the ones about whom the prosecutor of philosophy declares, as you put it, that the majority of those who take it up are completely bad, while the best ones are useless. And I admitted that what you said was true, didn't I?[3]

489d

ADEIMANTUS: Yes.

SOCRATES: Haven't we now explained why the good ones are useless?

ADEIMANTUS: We certainly have.

SOCRATES: Do you next want us to discuss why it is inevitable that the greater number are bad, and try to show, if we can, that philosophy is not responsible for this either?

489e

ADEIMANTUS: Certainly.

SOCRATES: Then let's begin our dialogue by recalling the starting point of our description of the nature that someone must have if he is to become a fine and good person. First of all, if you remember, he was led by truth,[4]

490a

---

[2] Aristotle, *Rhetoric* 1391a, says that when Simonides was asked whether it was better to be rich or wise, he replied: "Rich—because the wise spend their time at the doors of the rich."

[3] 487d.

[4] 485c.

and he had to follow it wholeheartedly and unequivocally, on pain of being a lying imposter with no share at all in true philosophy.

ADEIMANTUS: That's what we said.

SOCRATES: Well, isn't that fact alone completely contrary to the belief currently held about him?

ADEIMANTUS: It certainly is.

SOCRATES: So, won't it be reasonable, then, for us to plead in his defense that a real lover of learning strive by nature for what is? He does not linger 490b over each of the many things that are believed to be, but keeps on going, without losing or lessening his passion, until he grasps what the nature of each thing itself is[5] with the element in his soul that is fitted to grasp a thing of that sort because of its kinship with it. Once he has drawn near to it, has intercourse with what really is, and has begotten understanding and truth, he knows, truly lives, is nourished, and—at that point, but not before—is relieved from his labor pains.

ADEIMANTUS: Nothing could be more reasonable.

SOCRATES: Well, then, will a person of that sort love falsehood or, in completely opposite fashion, will he hate it?

490c ADEIMANTUS: He will hate it.

SOCRATES: And if truth led the way, we would never say, I imagine, that a chorus of evils could follow it.

ADEIMANTUS: Of course not.

SOCRATES: On the contrary, it is followed by a healthy and just character, and the temperance that accompanies it.

ADEIMANTUS: That's right.

SOCRATES: What need is there, then, to go back to the beginning and compel the rest of the philosophic nature's chorus to line up all over again? You surely remember that courage, high-mindedness, ease in learning, and a good memory all belong to philosophers. Then you objected that anyone would be compelled to agree with what we are saying, but that if he left 490d the arguments aside and looked at the very people the argument is about, he would say that some of those he saw were useless, while the majority of them were thoroughly bad. Trying to discover the reason for this slander, we have arrived now at this question: why are the majority of them bad? And *that* is why we have again taken up the nature of the true philosophers and defined what it necessarily has to be.

ADEIMANTUS: That's right.

---

[5] Lit., "the what it is of the nature of each thing itself."

SOCRATES: What we now have to do is look at the ways this nature gets   490e
corrupted; how it gets completely destroyed in the majority of cases, while
a small number escape—the very ones that are called useless, rather than
bad. After that, we must next look at those who imitate this nature and
adopt its pursuit. We must see what natures the souls have that enter into   **491a**
a pursuit that is too valuable and too high for them—souls that, by often
striking false notes, give philosophy the reputation that you said it has with
everyone everywhere.

ADEIMANTUS: What sorts of corruption do you mean?

SOCRATES: I will try to explain them to you if I can. I imagine that everyone would agree with us about this: the sort of nature that possesses all
the qualities we prescribed just now for the person who is going to be a
complete philosopher, is seldom found among human beings, and there   491b
will be few who possess it. Or don't you think so?

ADEIMANTUS: I most certainly do.

SOCRATES: Consider, then, how many great sources of destruction there
are for these few.

ADEIMANTUS: What are they?

SOCRATES: The most surprising thing of all to hear is that each one of the
things we praised in that nature tends to corrupt the soul that has it and
drag it away from philosophy. I mean courage, temperance, and the other
things we mentioned.

ADEIMANTUS: That does sound strange.

SOCRATES: Furthermore, in addition to those, all so-called good things also   491c
corrupt it and drag it away—beauty, wealth, physical strength, powerful
family connections in the city, and all that goes along with these. You
understand the general pattern of things I mean?

ADEIMANTUS: I do, and I would be glad to acquire a more precise understanding of it.

SOCRATES: Grasp the general principle correctly and the matter will become
clear to you, and what I said about it before won't seem so strange.

ADEIMANTUS: What are you telling me to grasp?

SOCRATES: In the case of every seed or growing thing, whether plant or   491d
animal, we know that if it fails to get the food, climate, or location suitable
for it, then the more vigorous it is, the more it is deficient in the qualities
proper to it. For surely bad is more opposed to good than to not-good.

ADEIMANTUS: Of course.

SOCRATES: So, I suppose it is reasonable that the best nature comes off worse
than an inferior one from unsuitable nurture.

ADEIMANTUS: It is.

SOCRATES: Well, then, Adeimantus, won't we also say that if *souls* with
491e   the best natures get a bad education, they become exceptionally bad? Or
do you think that great injustices and unalloyed evil originate in an inferior nature, rather than in a vigorous one that has been corrupted by its
upbringing? Or that a weak nature is ever responsible for great good things
or great bad ones?

ADEIMANTUS: No, you are right.

492a   SOCRATES: Well, then, if the nature we proposed for the philosopher happens to receive the proper instruction, I imagine it will inevitably grow to
attain every virtue. But if it is not sown, planted, and grown in a suitable
environment, it will develop in entirely the opposite way, unless some
god comes to its aid. Or do you too believe, as the masses do, that some
young people are corrupted by sophists—that there are sophists, private
individuals, who corrupt them to a significant extent? Isn't it, rather, the
492b   very people who say this who are the greatest sophists of all, who educate
most effectively and produce young and old men and women of just the
sort they want?

ADEIMANTUS: When do they do that?

SOCRATES: When many of them sit together in assemblies, courts, theaters,
army camps, or any other gathering of a mass of people in public and, with
a loud uproar, object excessively to some of the things that are said or done,
then approve excessively of others, shouting and clapping; and when, in
492c   addition to these people themselves, the rocks and the surrounding space
itself echo and redouble the uproar of their praise or blame. In a situation
like that, how do you think—as the saying goes—a young man's heart is
affected?[6] How will whatever sort of private education he received hold
up for him, and not get swept away by such praise and blame, and go be
carried off by the flood wherever it goes, so that he will call the same
things beautiful or ugly as these people, practice what they practice, and
become like them?

492d   ADEIMANTUS: The compulsion to do so will be enormous, Socrates.

SOCRATES: And yet we have not mentioned the greatest compulsion of all.

ADEIMANTUS: What is that?

SOCRATES: It is what these educators and sophists impose by their actions if
their words fail to persuade. Or don't you know that they punish anyone
who is not persuaded, with disenfranchisement, fines, or death?

ADEIMANTUS: They most certainly do.

SOCRATES: What other sophist, then, or what sort of private conversations
do you think will oppose these and prove stronger?

---

[6] See Homer, *Iliad* xxiv.367.

ADEIMANTUS: None, I imagine.   492e

SOCRATES: No, indeed, even to try would be very foolish. You see, there is not now, never has been, nor ever will be, a character whose view of virtue goes contrary to the education these provide. I mean a human character, comrade—the divine, as the saying goes, is an exception to the rule. You may be sure that if anything is saved and turns out well in the political systems that exist now, you won't be mistaken in saying that divine   493a providence saved it.

ADEIMANTUS: That is what I think, too.

SOCRATES: Well, then, you should also agree to this.

ADEIMANTUS: What?

SOCRATES: None of those private wage-earners—the ones these people call sophists and consider to be their rivals in craft[7]—teaches anything other than the convictions the masses hold when they are assembled together, and this he calls wisdom. It is just as if someone were learning the passions and appetites of a huge, strong beast that he is rearing—how to approach   493b and handle it, when it is most difficult to deal with or most docile and what makes it so, what sounds it utters in either condition, and what tones of voice soothe or anger it. Having learned all this through associating and spending time with the beast, he calls this wisdom, gathers his information together as if it were a craft, and starts to teach it. Knowing nothing in reality about which of these convictions or appetites is fine or shameful, good or bad, just or unjust, he uses all these terms in conformity with the great   493c beast's beliefs—calling the things it enjoys good and the things that anger it bad. He has no other account to give of them, but calls everything he is compelled to do just and fine, never having seen how much the natures of compulsion and goodness really differ, and being unable to explain it to anyone. Don't you think, by Zeus, that someone like that would make a strange educator?

ADEIMANTUS: I do, indeed.

SOCRATES: Then does this person seem any different from the one who believes that wisdom is understanding the passions and pleasures of the   493d masses—multifarious people—assembled together, whether in regard to painting, music, or politics for that matter? For if a person associates with the masses and exhibits his poetry or some other piece of craftsmanship to them or his service to the city, and gives them mastery over him to any degree beyond what is unavoidable, he will be under Diomedean compulsion,[8] as it is called, to produce the things of which they approve.

---

[7] I.e., rivals in the craft of teaching virtue.

[8] An inescapable compulsion. The origin of the phrase is uncertain.

But that such things are truly good and beautiful—have you ever heard anyone presenting an argument for that conclusion that was not absolutely ridiculous?

493e ADEIMANTUS: No, and I do not suppose I ever will.

SOCRATES: So then, bearing all that in mind, recall our earlier question: can the majority in any way tolerate or accept that the beautiful itself (as opposed to the many beautiful things), or each thing itself (as opposed to 494a the corresponding many), exists?

ADEIMANTUS: Not in the least.

SOCRATES: It is impossible, then, for the majority to be philosophic.

ADEIMANTUS: It is impossible.

SOCRATES: And so, those who practice philosophy are inevitably disparaged by them?

ADEIMANTUS: Inevitably.

SOCRATES: And also by those private individuals who associate with the majority and want to please them.

ADEIMANTUS: Clearly.

SOCRATES: On the basis of these facts, then, do you see any way to preserve a philosophic nature and ensure that it will continue to practice philosophy and reach the end? Consider the question in light of what we said before. 494b We agreed that ease in learning, a good memory, courage, and high-mindedness belong to the philosophic nature.

ADEIMANTUS: Yes.

SOCRATES: Right from the start, then, won't someone like that be first among the children in everything, especially if his body's nature matches that of his soul?

ADEIMANTUS: Of course he will.

SOCRATES: So as he gets older, I imagine his family and fellow citizens will want to make use of him in connection with their own affairs.

ADEIMANTUS: Certainly.

SOCRATES: They will get down on their knees, begging favors from him 494c and honoring him, flattering ahead of time the power that is going to be his, so as to secure it for themselves.

ADEIMANTUS: That's usually what happens, at least.

SOCRATES: What do you think someone like that will do in such circumstances—especially if he happens to be from a great city where he is rich and noble, and if he is good-looking and tall as well? Won't he be filled with an impractical expectation and think himself capable of managing the 494d affairs, not only of the Greeks, but of the barbarians, too? And won't he exalt himself to great heights, as a result, and be brimming with pretension and empty, senseless pride?[9]

ADEIMANTUS: He certainly will.

SOCRATES: Now, suppose someone gently approaches a young man in that state of mind and tells him the truth: that he has no sense, although he needs it, and that it cannot be acquired unless he works like a slave to attain it. Do you think it will be easy for him to hear that message through the evils that surround him?

ADEIMANTUS: Far from it.

SOCRATES: And suppose that, because of his noble nature and his natural affinity for such arguments, he somehow sees the point and is turned around and drawn toward philosophy. What do we suppose those people   494e
will do if they believe that they are losing his services and companionship? Is there anything they won't do or say in his regard to prevent him from being persuaded? Or anything they won't do or say in regard to his persuader to prevent him from succeeding, whether it is in private plots or public court cases?[10]

ADEIMANTUS: There certainly is not.   **495a**

SOCRATES: Then is there any chance that such a person will practice philosophy?

ADEIMANTUS: None at all.

SOCRATES: Do you see, then, that we weren't wrong to say that when a philosophic nature is badly brought up, its very components—together with the other so-called goods, such as wealth and every provision of that sort—are somehow the cause of its falling away from the pursuit?

ADEIMANTUS: No, we were not. What we said was right.

SOCRATES: There you are, then, you amazing fellow! That is the extent of the sort of destruction and corruption that the nature best suited for the noblest pursuit undergoes. And such a nature is a rare occurrence anyway,   495b
we claim. Moreover, men who possess it are the ones that do the worst things to cities and individuals, and also—if they happen to be swept that way by the current—the greatest good. For a petty nature never does anything great, either to a private individual or a city.

ADEIMANTUS: That's very true.

SOCRATES: So when these men, for whom philosophy is most appropriate, fall away from her, they leave her desolate and unwed, and themselves lead

---

[9] Plato seems to have had Alcibiades in mind here and in what follows. See *Symposium* 215d–216d.

[10] The trial of Socrates in 399 BCE is the obvious case in point.

495c a life that is inappropriate and untrue. Then others, who are unworthy of her, come to her as to an orphan bereft of kinsmen, and shame her. They are the ones responsible for the reproaches that you say are cast upon philosophy by her detractors—that some of her consorts are useless, while the majority deserve many evils.

ADEIMANTUS: Yes, that is what they say.

SOCRATES: And it is a reasonable thing to say. For other worthless little men see that this position has become vacant, even though it is brimming
495d with fine accolades and pretensions, and—like prisoners escaping from jail who take refuge in a temple—leap gladly from their crafts to philosophy. These are the ones who are most sophisticated at their own petty craft. You see, at least in comparison to other crafts, and even in its present state, philosophy still has a grander reputation. And that is what many people are aiming at, people with defective natures, whose souls are as cramped and spoiled by their menial tasks as their bodies are warped by their crafts and
495e occupations. Isn't that inevitably what happens?

ADEIMANTUS: It certainly is.

SOCRATES: Do you think that they look any different than a little, bald-headed blacksmith who has come into some money and, newly released from debtor's prison, has taken a bath, put on a new cloak, got himself up as a bridegroom, and is about to marry the master's daughter because she is poor and abandoned?

496a ADEIMANTUS: They are no different at all.

SOCRATES: What sort of offspring are they likely to beget, then? Won't their children be wretched illegitimates?

ADEIMANTUS: Inevitably.

SOCRATES: What about when men who are unworthy of education approach philosophy and associate with her in a way unworthy of her? What kinds of thoughts and beliefs are we to say they beget? Won't they be what are truly and appropriately called sophisms, since they have nothing genuine or truly wise about them?

ADEIMANTUS: Absolutely.

SOCRATES: Then there remains, Adeimantus, only a very small group who
496b associate with philosophy in a way that is worthy of her: a noble and well brought-up character, perhaps, kept down by exile, who stays true to his nature and remains with philosophy because there is no one to corrupt him; or a great soul living in a small city, who disdains the city's affairs and looks beyond them. A very few might perhaps come to philosophy from other crafts that they rightly despise because they have good natures. And some might be held back by the bridle that restrains our friend Theages— you see, he meets all the other conditions needed to make him fall away

from philosophy, but his physical illness keeps him out of politics and pre-   496c
vents it. Finally, my own case is hardly worth mentioning—my daimonic
sign[11]—since I don't suppose it has happened to anyone else or to only a
few before. Now, those who have become members of this little group
have tasted how sweet and blessed a possession philosophy is. At the same
time, they have also seen the insanity of the masses and realized that there is
nothing healthy, so to speak, in public affairs, and that there is no ally with
whose aid the champion of justice can survive; that instead he would perish   496d
before he could profit either his city or his friends, and be useless both to
himself and to others—like a man who has fallen among wild animals and
is neither willing to join them in doing injustice nor sufficiently strong to
oppose the general savagery alone. Taking all this into his calculations, he
keeps quiet and does his own work, like someone who takes refuge under
a little wall from a storm of dust or hail driven by the wind. Seeing others
filled with lawlessness, the philosopher is satisfied if he can somehow lead
his present life pure of injustice and impious acts, and depart from it with   496e
good hope, blameless and content.

ADEIMANTUS: Well, that is no small thing for him to have accomplished
before departing.   497a

SOCRATES: But no very great one either, since he did not chance upon a
suitable constitution. In a suitable one, his own growth will be fuller and
he will save the community, as well as himself. Anyway, it seems to me
that we have now said enough about the slander brought against philosophy
and why it is unjust—unless, of course, you have got something to add.

ADEIMANTUS: I have nothing further to add on that issue. But which of our
present constitutions do you think is suitable for philosophy?

SOCRATES: None of them. But that is exactly my complaint. There is not   497b
one city today with a constitution worthy of the philosophic nature. That
is precisely why it is perverted and altered. It is like foreign seed sown in
alien ground: it tends to be overpowered and to fade away into the native
species. Similarly, the philosophic species does not maintain its own power
at present, but declines into a different character. But if it were to find the
best constitution, as it is itself the best, it would be clear that it is really   497c
divine and that other natures and pursuits are merely human. Obviously,
you are going to ask next what that constitution is.

ADEIMANTUS: You are wrong there. You see, I was not going to ask that,
but whether it was the constitution we described when we were founding
our city or a different one.

---

[11] See *Apology* 31c–32a.

SOCRATES: In all other respects, it is that one. But we said even then[12] that there must always be some people in the city who have a rational account of the constitution, the very same one that you, the lawgiver, also had when you made the laws.

497d

ADEIMANTUS: Yes, we did say that.

SOCRATES: But we did not explain it clearly enough, for fear of what our own objections have made clear: namely, that the demonstration of it would be long and difficult. Indeed, even what remains is not the easiest of all things to discuss.

ADEIMANTUS: What is that?

SOCRATES: How a city can engage in philosophy without being destroyed. You see, all great things are prone to fall and, as the saying goes, beautiful things are really difficult.

ADEIMANTUS: All the same, the demonstration won't be complete until this has been cleared up.

497e

SOCRATES: If anything prevents that, it won't be lack of willingness, but lack of ability. At any rate, you will see how passionate *I* am. Look now, in fact, at how passionately and recklessly I am going to argue that a city should practice philosophy in the opposite way to the present one.

ADEIMANTUS: How?

498a

SOCRATES: At present, those who take it up at all do so as young men, just out of childhood, who have yet to take up household management and moneymaking. Then, just when they reach the most difficult part they abandon it and are regarded as the most fully trained philosophers. By the most difficult part, I mean the one concerned with arguments.[13] In later life, if others are engaged in it and they are invited and deign to listen to them, they think they have done a lot, since they think this should only be a sideline. And, with a few exceptions, by the time they reach old age they are more thoroughly extinguished than the sun of Heraclitus, since they are never rekindled.[14]

498b

ADEIMANTUS: What should they do instead?

SOCRATES: Entirely the opposite. As young men and children, they should occupy themselves with an education and philosophy suitable to the young. Their bodies are blooming and growing into manhood at this time, and they should take very good care of them, so as to acquire a helper for philosophy. But as they grow older and their soul begins to reach maturity,

---

[12] 412a–b.

[13] I.e., dialectic.

[14] Heraclitus' sun was extinguished at night but rekindled the next morning.

they should make its exercises more rigorous. Then, when their strength begins to fail and they have retired from politics and military service, they should graze freely in the pastures of philosophy and do nothing else, except as a sideline—I mean those who are going to live happily and, when the end comes, crown the life they have lived with a fitting providence in that other place. 498c

ADEIMANTUS: You seem to be arguing with real passion, Socrates. But I am sure that most of your hearers will oppose you with even greater passion and won't be convinced in the least—beginning with Thrasymachus.

SOCRATES: Please do not try to raise a quarrel between me and Thrasymachus just as we have become friends—not that we were enemies before. You see, we won't relax our efforts until we convince him and the others—or at least do something that may benefit them in a later incarnation when, reborn, they happen upon these arguments again. 498d

ADEIMANTUS: You are talking about the short term, I see!

SOCRATES: It is certainly nothing compared to the whole of time! However, it is no wonder that the masses are not convinced by our arguments. I mean, they have never seen a *man* that matched our *plan*—though they have more often seen words purposely chosen to rhyme with one another than just happening to do so as in the present case. But a man who, as far as possible, matched and rhymed with virtue in word and deed, and wielded dynastic power in a city of the same type—that is something they have never seen even once. Or do you think they have? 498e

499a

ADEIMANTUS: No, definitely not.

SOCRATES: Nor, bless you, have they spent enough time listening to fine and free arguments that vigorously seek the truth in every way, so as to acquire knowledge and keep their distance from all the sophistries and eristic quibbles that—whether in public trials or private gatherings—strive for nothing except reputation and disputation.

ADEIMANTUS: No, they have not.

SOCRATES: It was for these reasons, and because we foresaw these difficulties, that we were afraid. All the same, we were compelled by the truth to say that no city, no constitution, and, indeed, no individual man will ever become perfect until some chance event compels those few philosophers who are not vicious (the ones who are now called useless) to take care of a city, whether they want to or not, and compels the city to obey them—or until a true passion for true philosophy flows by some divine inspiration into the sons of the men now wielding dynastic power or sovereignty, or into the men themselves. Now, it cannot be reasonably maintained, in my view, that either or both of these things is impossible. But if they were, we would be justly ridiculed for indulging in wishful thinking. Isn't that so? 499b

499c

ADEIMANTUS: It is.

SOCRATES: Then if, in the limitless past, some compulsion forced those who were foremost in philosophy to take charge of a city, or is doing so now in some barbaric place far beyond our ken, or will do so in the future, this is something we are prepared to fight about—our argument that the constitution we have described has existed, does exist, and will exist, at any rate, whenever it is that the muse of philosophy gains mastery of a city. It is not impossible for this to happen, so we are not speaking of impossibilities—that it is *difficult,* we agree ourselves.

ADEIMANTUS: *I* certainly think so.

SOCRATES: But the masses do not—is that what you are going to say?

ADEIMANTUS: They probably don't.

SOCRATES: Bless you, you should not make such a wholesale charge against the masses! They will surely come to hold a different belief if, instead of wanting to win a victory at their expense, you soothe them and try to remove their slanderous prejudice against the love of learning. You must show them what you mean by philosophers and define their nature and pursuit the way we did just now. Then they will realize you do not mean the same people they do. And if they once see it that way, even you will say that they will have a different opinion from the one you just attributed to them and will answer differently. Or do you think that anyone who is gentle and without malice is harsh to one who is not harsh, or malicious to one who is not malicious? I will anticipate you and say that I think a few people may have such a harsh character, but not the majority.

ADEIMANTUS: And I agree, of course.

SOCRATES: Then don't you also agree that the harshness of the masses toward philosophy is caused by those outsiders who do not belong and who have burst in like a band of revelers, abusing one another, indulging their love of quarreling, and always arguing about human beings—something that is least appropriate in philosophy?

ADEIMANTUS: I do, indeed.

SOCRATES: For surely, Adeimantus, someone whose mind is truly directed toward the things that are has not the leisure to look down at human affairs and be filled with malice and hatred as a result of entering into their disputes. Instead, as he looks at and contemplates things that are orderly and always the same, that neither do injustice to one another nor suffer it, being all in a rational order, he imitates them and tries to become as like them as he can. Or do you think there is any way to prevent someone from associating with something he admires without imitating it?

ADEIMANTUS: He can't possibly.

SOCRATES: Then the philosopher, by associating with what is orderly and divine, becomes as divine and orderly as a human being can. Though, mind you, there are always plenty of slanders around.   500d

ADEIMANTUS: Absolutely.

SOCRATES: And if he should come to be compelled to make a practice—in private and in public—of stamping what he sees there into the people's characters, instead of shaping only his own, do you think he will be a poor craftsman of temperance, justice, and the whole of popular virtue?

ADEIMANTUS: Not at all.

SOCRATES: And when the masses realize that what we are saying about him is true, will they be harsh with philosophers or mistrust us when we say that there is no way a city can ever find happiness unless its plan is drawn   500e
by painters who use the divine model?

ADEIMANTUS: They won't be harsh, if they do realize this. But what sort of drawing do you mean?   501a

SOCRATES: They would take the city and people's characters as their sketching slate, but first they would wipe it clean—which is not at all an easy thing to do. And you should be aware that this is an immediate difference between them and others—that they refuse to take either a private individual or a city in hand, or to write laws, unless they receive a clean slate or are allowed to clean it themselves.

ADEIMANTUS: And rightly so.

SOCRATES: And after that, don't you think they would draw the plan of the constitution?

ADEIMANTUS: Of course.

SOCRATES: And I suppose that, as they work, they would look often in each direction: on the one hand, toward what is in its nature just, beautiful,   501b
temperate, and all the rest; and, on the other, toward what they are trying to put into human beings, mixing and blending pursuits to produce a human likeness, based on the one that Homer too called divine and godly when it appeared among human beings.[15]

ADEIMANTUS: Right.

SOCRATES: They would erase one thing, I suppose, and draw in another,   501c
until they had made people's characters as dear to the gods as possible.

ADEIMANTUS: At any rate, the drawing would be most beautiful that way.

SOCRATES: Are we at all persuading the people you said were rushing to attack us, then, that the philosopher we were praising to them is really this

---

[15] See, e.g., *Iliad* i.131

sort of painter of constitutions? They were angry because we were entrusting cities to him; are they any calmer at hearing it now?

ADEIMANTUS: They will be much calmer, if they have any sense.

SOCRATES: After all, how could they possibly dispute it? Will they deny that philosophers are lovers both of what is and of the truth?

501d

ADEIMANTUS: That would be silly.

SOCRATES: Or that their nature, as we have described it, is akin to the best?

ADEIMANTUS: They cannot deny that either.

SOCRATES: Or that such a nature, when it happens to find appropriate pursuits, will not be as completely good and philosophic as any other? Or are they going to claim that the people we excluded are more so?

ADEIMANTUS: Certainly not.

501e

SOCRATES: Will they still be angry, then, when we say that until the philosopher class gains mastery of a city, there will be no respite from evils for either city or citizens, and the constitution we have been describing in our discussion will never be completed in practice?

ADEIMANTUS: They will probably be less so.

SOCRATES: If it is all right with you, then, let's not say that they will simply be less angry, but that they will become altogether gentle and persuaded; so that out of shame, if nothing else, they will agree.

502a

ADEIMANTUS: All right.

SOCRATES: So let's assume that they have been convinced of this. Will anyone contend, then, that there is no chance that the offspring of kings or men in power could be natural-born philosophers?

ADEIMANTUS: No one could.

SOCRATES: Could anyone claim that if such offspring are born, they must inevitably be corrupted? We agree ourselves that it is difficult for them to be saved. But that in the whole of time not one of them could be saved—could anyone contend that?

502b

ADEIMANTUS: Of course not.

SOCRATES: But surely the occurrence of one such individual is enough, provided his city obeys him, to bring to completion all the things that now seem so incredible.

ADEIMANTUS: Yes, one is enough.

SOCRATES: For I suppose that if a ruler established the laws and practices we have described, it is hardly impossible that the citizens would be willing to carry them out.

ADEIMANTUS: Not at all.

SOCRATES: Would it be either surprising or impossible, then, that others should think as we do?

ADEIMANTUS: I don't suppose so.   502c

SOCRATES: But I think our earlier discussion was sufficient to show that these arrangements are best, provided they are possible.

ADEIMANTUS: Indeed, it was.

SOCRATES: It seems, then, that the conclusion we have now reached about legislation is that the one we are describing is best, provided it is possible; and that while it is difficult for it to come about, it certainly is not impossible.

ADEIMANTUS: Yes, that is the conclusion we have reached.

SOCRATES: Now that this conclusion has, with much effort, been reached, we must next deal with the remaining issues—in what way, by means of what subjects and pursuits, the saviors of our constitution will come to   502d
exist, and at what ages they will take up each of them.

ADEIMANTUS: Yes, we must deal with that.

SOCRATES: I gained nothing by my cleverness, then, in omitting from our earlier discussion the troublesome topic of acquiring women, begetting children, and establishing rulers, because I knew the whole truth would provoke resentment and would be difficult to bring about. As it turned out, the need to discuss them arose anyway. Now, the subject of women   502e
and children has already been discussed. But that of the rulers has to be taken up again from the beginning. We said,[16] if you remember, that they must show themselves to be lovers of the city, when tested by pleasures and   **503a**
pains, by not abandoning this conviction through labors, fears, and all other adversities. Anyone who was incapable of doing so was to be rejected, while anyone who always came through pure—like gold tested in a fire—was to be made ruler and receive gifts and prizes, both while he lived and after his death. These were the sorts of things we were saying while our argument veiled its face and slipped by, for fear of stirring up the very problems that now confront us.

ADEIMANTUS: That's absolutely true. I do remember.   503b

SOCRATES: I was reluctant, my friend, to say the things we have now dared to say anyway. But now, let's also dare to say that we must establish philosophers as guardians in the most exact sense.

ADEIMANTUS: Let's do so.

SOCRATES: Bear in mind, then, that there will probably be only a few of them. You see, they have to have the nature we described, and its parts rarely consent to grow together in one person; rather, its many parts grow split off from one another.

---

[16] At 412b–414a.

ADEIMANTUS: How do you mean?

503c SOCRATES: Ease of learning, good memory, astuteness, and smartness, as you know, and all the other things that go along with them, such as youthful passion and high-mindedness, are rarely willing to grow together simultaneously with a disposition to live an orderly, quiet, and completely stable life. On the contrary, those who possess the former traits are carried by their quick wits wherever chance leads them, and have no stability at all.

ADEIMANTUS: That's true.

SOCRATES: Those with stable characters, on the other hand, who do not change easily, whom one would employ because of their greater reliability,
503d and who in battle are not easily moved by fears, act in the same way when it comes to their studies. They are hard to get moving and learn with difficulty, as if they are anesthetized, and are constantly falling asleep and yawning whenever they have to work hard at such things.

ADEIMANTUS: They are.

SOCRATES: Yet we say that someone must have a good and fine share of both characters, or he won't receive the truest education or honor, or be allowed to rule.

ADEIMANTUS: That's right.

SOCRATES: Then don't you think this will rarely occur?

ADEIMANTUS: Of course.

SOCRATES: He must be tested, then, in the labors, fears, and pleasures we
503e mentioned before. He must also be exercised in many other subjects, how-ever, which we did not mention but are adding now, to see whether his nature can endure the most important subjects or will shrink from them
504a like the cowards who shrink from the other tests.

ADEIMANTUS: It is certainly important to find that out. But what do you mean by the greatest subjects?

SOCRATES: Do you remember when we distinguished three kinds of things in the soul in order to help bring out what justice, temperance, courage, and wisdom each is?

ADEIMANTUS: If I didn't, I would not deserve to hear the rest.

SOCRATES: Do you also remember what preceded it?

ADEIMANTUS: No, what?

504b SOCRATES: We said, I believe, that in order to get the finest view of these matters, there is a longer road and if one travels it, they become clear, it was possible to give demonstrations that would be up to the standard of the previous discussion.[17] All of you said that was enough. The result was

---

[17] 435d.

that our subsequent discussion, as it seemed to me, was less than exact. But whether or not it satisfied all of you is for you to say.

ADEIMANTUS: I, at any rate, thought you gave us good measure. And so, apparently, did the others.

SOCRATES: No, my friend, any measure of such things that falls short in any way of what is, is not good measure at all, since nothing incomplete is a measure of anything. Some people, however, are occasionally of the opinion that an incomplete treatment is already adequate and that there is no need for further inquiry. 504c

ADEIMANTUS: Yes, a lot of people feel like that. Laziness is the cause.

SOCRATES: Well, that is a feeling that is least appropriate in a guardian of a city and its laws.

ADEIMANTUS: No doubt.

SOCRATES: He will have to take the longer road then, comrade, and put no less effort into learning than into physical training. For otherwise, as we were just saying, he will never pursue the greatest and most appropriate subject to the end. 504d

ADEIMANTUS: Why, aren't these virtues the greatest things? Is there something yet greater than justice and the other virtues we discussed?

SOCRATES: Not only is it greatest, but, even in the case of the virtues themselves, it is not enough to look at a mere sketch as we are doing now, while neglecting the most finished portrait. I mean, it is ridiculous, isn't it, to strain every nerve to attain the utmost exactness and clarity about other things of little value, while not treating the greatest things as meriting the most exactness? 504e

ADEIMANTUS: It certainly is. But do you think that anyone is going to let you off without asking you what you mean by this greatest subject, and what it is concerned with?

SOCRATES: No, I do not. And you may ask it, too. You have certainly heard the answer often, but now either you are not thinking or you intend to make trouble for me again by interrupting. And I suspect it is more the latter. You see, you have often heard it said that the form of the good is the greatest thing to learn about, and that it is by their relation to it that just things and the others become useful and beneficial. And now you must be pretty certain that that is what I am going to say, and, in addition, that we have no adequate knowledge of it. And if we do not know it, you know that even the fullest possible knowledge of other things is of no benefit to us, any more than if we acquire any possession without the good. Or do you think there is any benefit in possessing everything but the good? Or to know everything without knowing the good, thereby knowing nothing fine or good? 505a 505b

ADEIMANTUS: No, by Zeus, I do not.

SOCRATES: Furthermore, you also know that the masses believe pleasure to be the good, while the more refined believe it to be knowledge.

ADEIMANTUS: Of course.

SOCRATES: And, my friend, that those who believe this cannot show us what sort of knowledge it is, but in the end are compelled to say that it is knowledge of the good.

ADEIMANTUS: Which is completely ridiculous.

505c SOCRATES: How could it not be, when they blame us for not knowing the good and then turn around and talk to us as if we did know it? I mean, they say it is knowledge of the good—as if we understood what they mean when they utter the word "good."

ADEIMANTUS: That's absolutely true.

SOCRATES: What about those who define the good as pleasure? Are they any less full of confusion than the others? Or aren't even they compelled to admit that there are bad pleasures?

ADEIMANTUS: Most definitely.

SOCRATES: I suppose it follows, doesn't it, that they have to admit that the same things are both good and bad?

505d ADEIMANTUS: It certainly does.

SOCRATES: Isn't it clear, then, that there are lots of serious disagreements about the good?

ADEIMANTUS: Of course.

SOCRATES: Well, isn't it also clear that many people would choose things that are believed to be just or beautiful, even if they are not, and would act, acquire things, and form beliefs accordingly? Yet no one is satisfied to acquire things that are *believed* to be good. On the contrary, everyone seeks the things that *are* good. In this area, everyone disdains mere reputation.

ADEIMANTUS: Right.

SOCRATES: That, then, is what every soul pursues, and for its sake does
505e everything. The soul has a hunch that the good is something, but it is puzzled and cannot adequately grasp just what it is or acquire the sort of stable belief about it that it has about the other things, and so it misses the benefit, if any, that even those other things may give. Are we to accept
506a that even the best people in the city, to whom we entrust everything, must remain thus in the dark about something of this kind and importance?

ADEIMANTUS: That's the last thing we would do.

SOCRATES: Anyway, I imagine that just and beautiful things won't have acquired much of a guardian in someone who does not even know why they are good. And I have a hunch that no one will have adequate knowledge of them until he knows this.

ADEIMANTUS: That's a good hunch.

SOCRATES: But won't our constitution be perfectly ordered if such a guardian, one who knows these things, oversees it?   506b

ADEIMANTUS: It is bound to be. But you yourself, Socrates, do you say the good is knowledge or pleasure, or is it something else altogether?

SOCRATES: What a man! You made it good and clear long ago that other people's opinions about these matters would not satisfy you.

ADEIMANTUS: Well, Socrates, it does not seem right to me for you to be willing to state other people's convictions but not your own, when you have spent so much time occupied with these matters.   506c

SOCRATES: What? Do you think it is right to speak about things you do not know as if you do know them?

ADEIMANTUS: Not as if you know them, but you ought to be willing to state what you believe as what you believe.

SOCRATES: What? Haven't you noticed that beliefs without knowledge are all shameful and ugly things, since the best of them are blind? Do you think that those who have a true belief without understanding are any different from blind people who happen to travel the right road?

ADEIMANTUS: They are no different.

SOCRATES: Do you want to look at shameful, blind, and crooked things, then, when you might hear fine, illuminating ones from other people?

And Glaucon said:

By Zeus, Socrates, do not stop now, with the end in sight, so to speak!   506d
We will be satisfied if you discuss the good the way you discussed justice, temperance, and the rest.

SOCRATES: That, comrade, would well satisfy me too, but I am afraid that I won't be up to it and that I will disgrace myself and look ridiculous by trying. No, bless you, let's set aside what the good itself is for the time being. You see, even to arrive at my current beliefs about it seems beyond the range of our present discussion. But I am willing to tell you about what   506e
seems to be an offspring of the good and most like it, if that is agreeable to you; or otherwise to let the matter drop.

GLAUCON: Tell us, then. The story about the father remains a debt you will pay another time.

SOCRATES: I wish I could repay it, and you recover the debt, instead of just   507a
the interest. So here, then, is this child and offspring of the good itself. But

take care I do not somehow deceive you unintentionally by giving you an illegitimate account of the child.[18]

GLAUCON: We will take as much care as possible. So speak on.

SOCRATES: I will once I have come to an agreement with you and reminded you of things we have already said here as well as on many other occasions.

GLAUCON: Which things?

507b   SOCRATES: We say that there are many beautiful, many good, and many other such things, thereby distinguishing them in words.

GLAUCON: We do.

SOCRATES: We also say there is a beautiful itself and a good itself. And so, in the case of all the things that we then posited as many, we reverse ourselves and posit a single form belonging to each, since we suppose there is a single one, and call it what each is.

GLAUCON: That's true.

SOCRATES: And we say that the one class of things is visible but not intelligible, while the forms are intelligible but not visible.

GLAUCON: Absolutely.

507c   SOCRATES: With what of ours do we see visible things?

GLAUCON: With our sight.

SOCRATES: And don't we hear audible things with hearing and perceive all other perceptible things with our other senses?

GLAUCON: Of course.

SOCRATES: Have you ever thought about how lavish the craftsman of our senses was in making the power to see and be seen?

GLAUCON: No, not really.

SOCRATES: Well, think of it this way. Do hearing and sound need another kind of thing in order for the former to hear and the latter to be heard—a
507d   third thing in whose absence the one won't hear or the other be heard?

GLAUCON: No.

SOCRATES: And I think there cannot be many—not to say any—others that need such a thing. Or can you think of one?

GLAUCON: No, I cannot.

SOCRATES: Aren't you aware that sight and the visible realm have such a need?

GLAUCON: In what way?

---

[18] Throughout, Socrates is punning on the word *tokos,* which means either a child or the interest on capital.

SOCRATES: Surely sight may be present in the eyes and its possessor may try to use it, and colors may be present in things; but unless a third kind of thing is present, which is naturally adapted for this specific purpose, you know that sight will see nothing and the colors will remain unseen.   507e

GLAUCON: What kind of thing do you mean?

SOCRATES: The kind you call light.

GLAUCON: You are right.

SOCRATES: So it is no insignificant form of yoke, then, that yokes the sense of sight and the power to be seen. In fact, it is more honorable than any that   508a
yokes other yoked teams. Provided, of course, that light is not something without honor.

GLAUCON: And it is surely far from being without honor.

SOCRATES: Which of the gods in the heavens would you say is the controller of this—the one whose light makes our sight see best and visible things best seen?

GLAUCON: The very one you and others would name. I mean, it is clear that what you are asking about is the sun.[19]

SOCRATES: And isn't sight naturally related to that god in the following way?

GLAUCON: Which one?

SOCRATES: Neither sight itself nor that in which it comes to be—namely, the eye—is the sun.   508b

GLAUCON: No, it is not.

SOCRATES: But it is, I think, the most sunlike of the sense organs.

GLAUCON: By far the most.

SOCRATES: And doesn't it receive the power it has from the sun, just like an influx from an overflowing treasury?

GLAUCON: Certainly.

SOCRATES: The sun is not sight either; yet as its cause, isn't it seen by sight itself?

GLAUCON: It is.

SOCRATES: Let's say, then, that this is what I called the offspring of the good, which the good begot as its analogue. What the latter is in the intelligible realm in relation to understanding and intelligible things, the former is in   508c
the visible realm in relation to sight and visible things.

GLAUCON: How? Tell me more.

---

[19] Helios—the sun—was considered a god.

SOCRATES: You know that when our eyes no longer turn to things whose colors are illuminated by the light of day, but by the lights of night, they are dimmed and seem nearly blind, as if clear sight were no longer in them.

GLAUCON: Of course.

SOCRATES: Yet I suppose that whenever they are turned to things illuminated by the sun, they see clearly and sight is manifest in those very same eyes?

508d

GLAUCON: Indeed.

SOCRATES: Well, think about the soul in the same way. When it focuses on something that is illuminated both by truth and what is, it understands, knows, and manifestly possesses understanding. But when it focuses on what is mixed with obscurity, on what comes to be and passes away, it believes and is dimmed, changes its beliefs this way and that, and seems bereft of understanding.

GLAUCON: Yes, it does seem like that.

508e

SOCRATES: You must say, then, that what gives truth to the things known and the power to know to the knower is the form of the good. And as the cause of knowledge and truth, you must think of it as an object of knowledge. Both knowledge and truth are beautiful things. But if you are to think correctly, you must think of the good as other and more beautiful than they. In the visible realm, light and sight are rightly thought to be

509a

sunlike, but wrongly thought to be the sun. So, here it is right to think of knowledge and truth as goodlike, but wrong to think that either of them is the good—for the status of the good is yet more honorable.

GLAUCON: It is an incredibly beautiful thing you are talking about, if it provides both knowledge and truth but is itself superior to them in beauty. I mean, you surely do not think that *it* could be pleasure.

SOCRATES: No words of ill omen, please! Instead, examine our analogy in more detail.

GLAUCON: How?

509b

SOCRATES: The sun, I think you would say, not only gives visible things the power to be seen but also provides for their coming-to-be, growth, and nourishment—although it is not itself coming to be.

GLAUCON: I would.

SOCRATES: Therefore, you should also say that not only do the objects of knowledge owe their being known to the good, but their existence and being are also due to it; although the good is not being, but something yet beyond being, superior to it in rank and power.

And Glaucon quite ridiculously replied:

509c

By Apollo, what daimonic hyperbole!

SOCRATES: It is your own fault, you compelled me to tell my beliefs about it.

GLAUCON: And don't you stop, either—at least, not until you have finished discussing the good's similarity to the sun, if you are omitting anything.

SOCRATES: I am certainly omitting a lot.

GLAUCON: Well don't, not even the smallest detail.

SOCRATES: I think I will have to omit a fair amount. All the same, as far as is now possible, I won't purposely omit anything.

GLAUCON: Please don't.

SOCRATES: Then you should think, as we said, that there are these two 509d things, one sovereign of the intelligible kind and place, the other of the visible—I do not say "of the heavens," so as not to seem to you to be playing the sophist with the name.[20] In any case, do you understand these two kinds, visible and intelligible?

GLAUCON: I do.

SOCRATES: Represent them, then, by a line divided into two unequal sections. Then divide each section—that of the visible kind and that of the intelligible—in the same proportion as the line.[21] In terms now of relative clarity and opacity, you will have as one subsection of the visible, images. By images I mean, first, shadows, then reflections in bodies of water and 510a in all close-packed, smooth, and shiny materials, and everything of that sort. Do you understand?

GLAUCON: I do understand.

SOCRATES: Then, in the other subsection of the visible, put the originals of these images—that is, the animals around us, every plant, and the whole class of manufactured things.

GLAUCON: I will.

SOCRATES: Would you also be willing to say, then, that, as regards truth and untruth, the division is in this ratio: as what is believed is to what is known, so the likeness is to the thing it is like?

GLAUCON: Certainly.   510b

SOCRATES: Next, consider how the section of the intelligible is to be divided.

GLAUCON: How?

---

[20] The play seems to be on the similarity of sound between *orano* ("the heavens") and *orato* ("visible").

[21]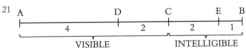

SOCRATES: As follows: in one subsection, the soul, using as images the things that were imitated before, is compelled to base its inquiry on hypotheses, proceeding not to a first principle, but to a conclusion. In the other subsection, by contrast, it makes its way to an unhypothetical first principle, proceeding from a hypothesis, but without the images used in the previous subsection, using forms themselves and making its methodical inquiry through them.

GLAUCON: I do not fully understand what you are saying.

510c

SOCRATES: Let's try again. You see, you will understand it more easily after this explanation. I think you know that students of geometry, calculation, and the like hypothesize the odd and the even, the various figures, the three kinds of angles, and other things akin to these in each of their methodical inquiries, regarding them as known. These they treat as hypotheses and do not think it necessary to give any account of them, either to themselves or to others, as if they were evident to everyone. And going from these first

510d

principles through the remaining steps, they arrive in full agreement at the point they set out to reach in their investigation.

GLAUCON: I certainly know that much.

SOCRATES: Then don't you also know that they use visible forms and make their arguments about them, although they are not thinking about them, but about those other things that they are like? They make their arguments with a view to the square itself and the diagonal itself, not the diagonal

510e

they draw, and similarly with the others. The very things they make and draw, of which shadows and reflections in water are images, they now in turn use as images in seeking to see those other things themselves that one

511a

cannot see except by means of thought.

GLAUCON: That's true.

SOCRATES: This, then, is the kind of thing that I said was intelligible. The soul is compelled to use hypotheses in the investigation of it, not traveling up to a first principle, since it cannot escape or get above its hypotheses, but using as images those very things of which images were made by the things below them, and which, by comparison to their images, were thought to be clear and to be honored as such.

GLAUCON: I understand that you mean what is dealt with in geometry and

511b

related crafts.

SOCRATES: Also understand, then, that by the other subsection of the intelligible I mean what reason itself grasps by the power of dialectical discussion, treating its hypotheses, not as first principles, but as genuine hypotheses (that is, stepping stones and links in a chain), in order to arrive at what is unhypothetical and the first principle of everything. Having grasped this principle, it reverses itself and, keeping hold of what follows from it, comes down to a conclusion, making no use of anything visible

at all, but only of forms themselves, moving on through forms to forms, 511c
and ending in forms.

GLAUCON: I understand, though not adequately—you see, in my opinion
you are speaking of an enormous task. You want to distinguish the part of
what is and is intelligible, the part looked at by the science of dialectical
discussion, as clearer than the part looked at by the so-called sciences—
those for which hypotheses are first principles. And although those who
look at the latter part are compelled to do so by means of thought rather
than sense perception, still, because they do not go back to a genuine
first principle in considering it, but proceed from hypotheses, you do not 511d
think that they have true understanding of them, even though—given
such a first principle—they are intelligible. And you seem to me to call
the state of mind of the geometers—and the others of that sort—thought
but not understanding; thought being intermediate between belief and ·
understanding.

SOCRATES: You have grasped my meaning most adequately. Join me, then,
in taking these four conditions in the soul as corresponding to the four
subsections of the line: understanding dealing with the highest, thought
dealing with the second; assign belief to the third, and imagination to the 511e
last. Arrange them in a proportion and consider that each shares in clarity
to the degree that the subsection it deals with shares in truth.

GLAUCON: I understand, agree, and arrange them as you say.

BOOK VII

SOCRATES' NARRATION CONTINUES:

SOCRATES: Next, then, compare the effect of education and that of the
lack of it on our nature to an experience like this. Imagine human beings **514a**
living in an underground, cavelike dwelling, with an entrance a long way
up that is open to the light and as wide as the cave itself. They have been
there since childhood, with their necks and legs fettered, so that they are
fixed in the same place, able to see only in front of them, because their 514b
fetter prevents them from turning their heads around. Light is provided
by a fire burning far above and behind them. Between the prisoners and
the fire, there is an elevated road stretching. Imagine that along this road a
low wall has been built—like the screen in front of people that is provided
by puppeteers, and above which they show their puppets.

GLAUCON: I am imagining it.

SOCRATES: Also imagine, then, that there are people alongside the wall 514c
carrying multifarious artifacts that project above it—statues of people and
other animals, made of stone, wood, and every material. And as you would **515a**
expect, some of the carriers are talking and some are silent.

GLAUCON: It is a strange image you are describing, and strange prisoners.

SOCRATES: They are like us. I mean, in the first place, do you think these prisoners have ever seen anything of themselves and one another besides the shadows that the fire casts on the wall of the cave in front of them?

GLAUCON: How could they, if they have to keep their heads motionless throughout life?

515b

SOCRATES: What about the things carried along the wall? Isn't the same true where they are concerned?

GLAUCON: Of course.

SOCRATES: And if they could engage in discussion with one another, don't you think they would assume that the words they used applied to the things they see passing in front of them?

GLAUCON: They would have to.

SOCRATES: What if their prison also had an echo from the wall facing them? When one of the carriers passing along the wall spoke, do you think they would believe that anything other than the shadow passing in front of them was speaking?

GLAUCON: I do not, by Zeus.

SOCRATES: All in all, then, what the prisoners would take for true reality is nothing other than the shadows of those artifacts.

515c

GLAUCON: That's entirely inevitable.

SOCRATES: Consider, then, what being released from their bonds and cured of their foolishness would naturally be like, if something like this should happen to them. When one was freed and suddenly compelled to stand up, turn his neck around, walk, and look up toward the light, he would be pained by doing all these things and be unable to see the things whose shadows he had seen before, because of the flashing lights. What do you think he would say if we told him that what he had seen before was silly nonsense, but that now—because he is a bit closer to what is, and is turned toward things that *are* more—he sees more correctly? And in particular, if we pointed to each of the things passing by and compelled him to answer what each of them is, don't you think he would be puzzled and believe that the things he saw earlier were more truly real than the ones he was being shown?

515d

GLAUCON: Much more so.

SOCRATES: And if he were compelled to look at the light itself, wouldn't his eyes be pained and wouldn't he turn around and flee toward the things he is able to see, and believe that they are really clearer than the ones he is being shown?

515e

GLAUCON: He would.

SOCRATES: And if someone dragged him by force away from there, along the rough, steep, upward path, and did not let him go until he had dragged him into the light of the sun, wouldn't he be pained and angry at being treated that way? And when he came into the light, wouldn't he have his eyes filled with sunlight and be unable to see a single one of the things now said to be truly real? **516a**

GLAUCON: No, he would not be able to—at least not right away.

SOCRATES: He would need time to get adjusted, I suppose, if he is going to see the things in the world above. At first, he would see shadows most easily, then images of men and other things in water, then the things themselves. From these, it would be easier for him to go on to look at the things in the sky and the sky itself at night, gazing at the light of the stars and the moon, than during the day, gazing at the sun and the light of the sun. **516b**

GLAUCON: Of course.

SOCRATES: Finally, I suppose, he would be able to see the sun—not reflections of it in water or some alien place, but the sun just by itself in its own place—and be able to look at it and see what it is like.

GLAUCON: Necessarily.

SOCRATES: After that, he would already be able to conclude about it that it provides the seasons and the years, governs everything in the visible world, and is in some way the cause of all the things that he and his fellows used to see. **516c**

GLAUCON: That would clearly be his next step.

SOCRATES: What about when he reminds himself of his first dwelling place, what passed for wisdom there, and his fellow prisoners? Don't you think he would count himself happy for the change and pity the others?

GLAUCON: Certainly.

SOCRATES: And if there had been honors, praises, or prizes among them for the one who was sharpest at identifying the shadows as they passed by; and was best able to remember which usually came earlier, which later, and which simultaneously; and who was thus best able to prophesize the future, do you think that our man would desire these rewards or envy those among the prisoners who were honored and held power? Or do you think he would feel with Homer that he would much prefer to "work the earth as a serf for another man, a man without possessions of his own,"[1] and go through any sufferings, rather than share their beliefs and live as they do? **516d**

GLAUCON: Yes, I think he would rather suffer anything than live like that. **516e**

---

[1] *Odyssey* xi.489–90. The shade of Achilles speaks these words to Odysseus, who is visiting Hades.

SOCRATES: Consider this too, then. If this man went back down into the cave and sat down in his same seat, wouldn't his eyes be filled with darkness, coming suddenly out of the sun like that?

GLAUCON: Certainly.

SOCRATES: Now, if he had to compete once again with the perpetual prisoners in recognizing the shadows, while his sight was still dim and before 517a his eyes had recovered, and if the time required for readjustment was not short, wouldn't he provoke ridicule? Wouldn't it be said of him that he had returned from his upward journey with his eyes ruined, and that it is not worthwhile even to try to travel upward? And as for anyone who tried to free the prisoners and lead them upward, if they could somehow get their hands on him, wouldn't they kill him?

GLAUCON: They certainly would.

SOCRATES: This image, my dear Glaucon, must be fitted together as a whole 517b with what we said before. The realm revealed through sight should be likened to the prison dwelling, and the light of the fire inside it to the sun's power. And if you think of the upward journey and the seeing of things above as the upward journey of the soul to the intelligible realm, you won't mistake my intention—since it is what you wanted to hear about. Only the god knows whether it is true. But this is how these phenomena seem to me: in the knowable realm, the last thing to be seen is the form of the good, and it is seen only with toil and trouble. Once one has seen it, however, one must infer that it is the cause of all that is correct and beautiful in anything, 517c that in the visible realm it produces both light and its source, and that in the intelligible realm it controls and provides truth and understanding; and that anyone who is to act sensibly in private or public must see it.

GLAUCON: I agree, so far as I am able.

SOCRATES: Come on, then, and join me in this further thought: you should not be surprised that the ones who get to this point are not willing to occupy themselves with human affairs, but that, on the contrary, their souls are always eager to spend their time above. I mean, that is surely what we 517d would expect, if indeed the image I described before is also accurate here.

GLAUCON: It is what we would expect.

SOCRATES: What about when someone, coming from looking at divine things, looks to the evils of human life? Do you think it is surprising that he behaves awkwardly and appears completely ridiculous, if—while his sight is still dim and he has not yet become accustomed to the darkness around him—he is compelled, either in the courts or elsewhere, to compete about the shadows of justice, or about the statues of which they are the shadows; and to dispute the way these things are understood by people who have 517e never seen justice itself?

GLAUCON: It is not surprising at all.

SOCRATES: On the contrary, anyone with any sense, at any rate, would remember that eyes may be confused in two ways and from two causes: 518a when they change from the light into the darkness, or from the darkness into the light. If he kept in mind that the same applies to the soul, then when he saw a soul disturbed and unable to see something, he would not laugh absurdly. Instead, he would see whether it had come from a brighter life and was dimmed through not having yet become accustomed to the dark, or from greater ignorance into greater light and was dazzled by the 518b increased brilliance. Then he would consider the first soul happy in its experience and life, and pity the latter. But even if he wanted to ridicule it, at least his ridiculing it would make him less ridiculous than ridiculing a soul that had come from the light above.

GLAUCON: That's an entirely reasonable claim.

SOCRATES: Then here is how we must think about these matters, if that is true: education is not what some people boastfully profess it to be. They say that they can pretty much put knowledge into souls that lack it, like 518c putting sight into blind eyes.

GLAUCON: Yes, they do say that.

SOCRATES: But here is what our present account shows about this power to learn that is present in everyone's soul, and the instrument with which each of us learns: just as an eye cannot be turned around from darkness to light except by turning the whole body, so this instrument must be turned around from what-comes-to-be together with the whole soul, until it is able to bear to look at what is and at the brightest thing that is—the one we call the good. Isn't that right? 518d

GLAUCON: Yes.

SOCRATES: Of this then—of this very turning around—there would be a craft concerned with how this instrument can be most easily and effectively turned around, not of putting sight into it. On the contrary, it takes for granted that sight is there, though not turned in the right way or looking where it should look, and contrives to redirect it appropriately.

GLAUCON: That's probably right.

SOCRATES: The other so-called virtues of the soul then, do seem to be closely akin to those of the body: they really are not present in it initially, but are added later by habit and practice. The virtue of wisdom, on the other hand, belongs above all, so it seems, to something more godlike, 518e which never loses its power, but is either useful and beneficial or useless and harmful, depending on the way it is led around. Or haven't you ever noticed in people who are said to be bad, but clever, how sharp the vision 519a of their little soul is and how sharply it distinguishes the things it is turned toward? This shows that its sight is not inferior, but is compelled to serve vice, so that the sharper it sees, the more evils it accomplishes.

GLAUCON: I certainly have.

SOCRATES: However, if this element of this sort of nature had been hammered at right from childhood, and struck free of the leaden weights, as it were, of kinship with becoming, which have been fastened to it by eating and other such pleasures and indulgences, which turn its soul's vision downward—if, I say, it got rid of these and turned toward truly real things, then the same element of the same people would see them most sharply, just as it now does the things it is now turned toward.

GLAUCON: That's probably right.

SOCRATES: Isn't it also probable, then—indeed, doesn't it follow necessarily from what was said before—that uneducated people who have no experience of true reality will never adequately govern a city, and neither will people who have been allowed to spend their whole lives in education. The former fail because they do not have a single goal in life at which all their actions, public and private, inevitably aim; the latter because they would refuse to act, thinking they had emigrated, while still alive, to the Isles of the Blessed.

GLAUCON: True.

SOCRATES: It is our task as founders, then, to compel the best natures to learn what was said before[2] to be the most important thing: namely, to see the good; to ascend that ascent. And when they have ascended and looked sufficiently, we must not allow them to do what they are allowed to do now.

GLAUCON: What's that, then?

SOCRATES: To stay there and refuse to go down again to the prisoners in the cave and share their labors and honors, whether the inferior ones or the more excellent ones.

GLAUCON: You mean we are to treat them unjustly, making them live a worse life when they could live a better one?

SOCRATES: You have forgotten again, my friend, that the law is not concerned with making any one class in the city do outstandingly well, but is contriving to produce this condition in the city as a whole, harmonizing the citizens together through both persuasion and compulsion, and making them share with each other the benefit they can confer on the community. It produces such men in the city, not in order to allow them to turn in whatever direction each one wants, but to make use of them to bind the city together.

---

[2] 505a–b.

GLAUCON: That's true. Yes, I had forgotten.

SOCRATES: Observe, then, Glaucon, that we won't be unjustly treating those who have become philosophers in our city, but that what we will say to them, when we compel them to take care of the others and guard them, will be just. We will say: "When people like you come to be in other cities, they are justified in not sharing in the others' labors. After all, they have grown there spontaneously, against the will of the constitution in each of them. And when something grows of its own accord and owes no debt for its upbringing, it has justice on its side when it is not keen to pay anyone for its upbringing. But both for your own sakes and for that of the rest of the city, we have bred you to be leaders and kings in the hive, so to speak. You are better and more completely educated than the others, and better able to share in both types of life. So each of you in turn must go down to live in the common dwelling place of the other citizens and grow accustomed to seeing in the dark. For when you are used to it, you will see infinitely better than the people there and know precisely what each image is, and also what it is an image of, because you have seen the truth about fine, just, and good things. So the city will be awake, governed by us and by you; not dreaming like the majority of cities nowadays, governed by men who fight against one another over shadows and form factions in order to rule—as if that were a great good. No, the truth of the matter is surely this: a city in which those who are going to rule are least eager to rule is necessarily best and freest from faction, whereas a city with the opposite kind of rulers is governed in the opposite way."

GLAUCON: Yes, indeed.

SOCRATES: Then do you think the people we have nurtured will disobey us when they hear these things, and be unwilling to share the labors of the city, each in turn, while living the greater part of their time with one another in the pure realm?

GLAUCON: No, they couldn't possibly. After all, we will be giving just orders to just people. However, each of them will certainly go to rule as to something compulsory, which is exactly the opposite of what is done by those who now rule in each city.

SOCRATES: That's right, comrade. If you can find a way of life that is better than ruling for those who are going to rule, your well-governed city will become a possibility. You see, in it alone the truly rich will rule—those who are rich not in gold, but in the wealth the happy must have: namely, a good and rational life. But if beggars—people hungry for private goods of their own—go into public life, thinking that the good is there for the seizing, then such a city is impossible. For when ruling is something fought over, such civil and domestic war destroys these men and the rest of the city as well.

GLAUCON: That's absolutely true.

521b   SOCRATES: Do you know of any other sort of life that looks down on political offices besides that of true philosophy?

GLAUCON: No, by Zeus, I do not.

SOCRATES: But surely it is those who are not lovers of ruling who must go do it. Otherwise, the rivaling lovers will fight over it.

GLAUCON: Of course.

SOCRATES: Who else, then, will you compel to go be guardians of the city if not those who know best what results in good government, and have different honors and a better life than the political?

GLAUCON: No one else.

521c   SOCRATES: Do you want us to consider now how such people will come to exist, and how we will lead them up to the light, like those who are said to have gone up from Hades to the gods?

GLAUCON: Yes, of course that's what I want.

SOCRATES: It seems, then, that this is not a matter of flipping a potsherd,[3] but of turning a soul from a day that is a kind of night in comparison to the true day—that ascent to what is, which we say is true philosophy.

GLAUCON: Yes, indeed.

SOCRATES: Then mustn't we try to discover what subjects have the power
521d   to bring this about?

GLAUCON: Of course.

SOCRATES: So what subject is it, Glaucon, that draws the soul from what is coming to be to what is? It occurs to me as I am speaking that we said, didn't we, that these people must be athletes of war when they are young?[4]

GLAUCON: Yes, we did say that.

SOCRATES: Then the subject we are looking for must also have this characteristic in addition to the former one.

GLAUCON: Which?

SOCRATES: It must not be useless to warlike men.

GLAUCON: If possible, it must not.

SOCRATES: Now, earlier they were educated by us in musical and physical training.

---

[3] A proverbial expression, referring to a children's game. The players were divided into two groups. A shell or potsherd—white on one side, black on the other—was thrown into space between them to the cry of "night or day?" Note the reference to night and day in what follows. According to whether white or black fell uppermost, one group ran away pursued by the other.

[4] 404a, 412b–417b.

GLAUCON: They were.

SOCRATES: And surely physical training is concerned with what-comes-to-   521e
be and dies, since it oversees the growth and decay of the body.

GLAUCON: Obviously.

SOCRATES: So it could not be the subject we are looking for.

GLAUCON: No, it could not.   522a

SOCRATES: Is it, then, the musical training we described before?

GLAUCON: But it is just the counterpart of physical training, if you remember. It educated the guardians through habits, conveying by harmony a
certain harmoniousness of temper, not knowledge; and by rhythm a certain rhythmical quality. Its stories, whether fictional or nearer the truth,
cultivated other habits akin to these. But as for a subject that leads to the
destination you have in mind, of the sort you are looking for now, there
was nothing of that in it.

SOCRATES: Your reminder is exactly to the point. It really does not have   522b
anything of that sort. You're a marvelous fellow, Glaucon, but what is there
that does? The crafts all seemed to be somehow menial.

GLAUCON: Of course. And yet, what subject is left that is separate from
musical and physical training, and from the crafts?

SOCRATES: Well, if we have nothing left beyond these, let's consider one of
those that touches all of them.

GLAUCON: Which?

SOCRATES: Why, for example, that common thing, the one that every type   522c
of craft, thought, and knowledge uses, and that is among the first things
everyone has to learn.

GLAUCON: Which one is that?

SOCRATES: That inconsequential matter of distinguishing the numbers one,
two, and three. In short, I mean number and calculation. Or isn't it true
that every type of craft and knowledge must share in them?

GLAUCON: Indeed it is.

SOCRATES: Then warfare must too.

GLAUCON: It must.

SOCRATES: In tragedies, at any rate, Palamedes is always showing up
Agamemnon as a totally ridiculous general. Haven't you noticed? He says   522d
that by inventing numbers he established how many troops there were
in the army at Ilium and counted their ships and everything else. The
implication is that they had not been counted before, and that Agamemnon
apparently did not even know how many feet he had, since he did not
know how to count. What kind of general do you think that made him?

GLAUCON: A very strange one, I'd say, if there is any truth in that.

522e   SOCRATES: Won't we posit this subject, then, as one a warrior is compelled
to learn so he can count and calculate?

GLAUCON: It is more essential than anything else—if, that is, he is going to
know anything at all about marshaling his troops—or if he is even going
to be human, for that matter.

SOCRATES: Then do you notice the same thing about this subject as I do?

GLAUCON: What?

SOCRATES: That in all likelihood it is one of the subjects we were looking
523a   for that naturally stimulate the understanding. But no one uses it correctly,
as something that really is fitted in every way to draw us toward being.

GLAUCON: How do you mean?

SOCRATES: I will try to make what I believe clear, at any rate. I will distinguish for myself the things that lead in the direction we mentioned from
those that do not. Then you must look at them along with me, and either
agree or disagree, so that we may see more clearly whether the distinction
is as I imagine.

GLAUCON: Show me the things you mean.

SOCRATES: All right, I will show you, if you can see that some sense-
perceptions do not summon the understanding to look into them, because
523b   the judgment of sense-perception is itself adequate; whereas others encourage it in every way to look into them, because sense-perception does not
produce a sound result.

GLAUCON: You are obviously referring to things appearing in the distance
and illusionist paintings.

SOCRATES: No, you are not quite getting what I mean.

GLAUCON: Then what do you mean?

SOCRATES: The ones that do not summon the understanding are all those
that do not at the same time result in an opposite sense-perception. But
523c   the ones that do I call *summoners*. That is when sense-perception does not
make one thing any more clear than its opposite, regardless of whether
what strikes the senses is close by or far away. What I mean will be clearer
if you look at it this way: these, we say, are three fingers—the smallest, the
second, and the middle finger.

GLAUCON: Of course.

SOCRATES: Assume that I am talking about them as being seen from close
by. Now consider this about them with me.

GLAUCON: What?

SOCRATES: It is obvious, surely, that each of them is equally a finger, and it
523d   makes no difference whether it is seen to be in the middle or at either end;
whether it is dark or pale, thick or thin, or anything else of that sort. You

see, in all these cases, the soul of most people is not compelled to ask the understanding what a finger is, since sight does not at any point suggest to it that a finger is at the same time the opposite of a finger.

GLAUCON: No, it does not.

SOCRATES: It is likely, then, that a perception of that sort would not summon or awaken the understanding.

GLAUCON: It is likely.

SOCRATES: Now, what about their greatness and smallness? Does sight 523e perceive them adequately? Does it make no difference to it whether one of them is in the middle or at the end? And is it the same with the sense of touch, as regards thickness and thinness, hardness and softness? What about the other senses, then—do they make such things sufficiently clear? Or doesn't each of them work as follows: in the first place, the sense that deals with hardness must also deal with softness; and it reports to the soul 524a that it perceives the same thing to be both hard and soft?

GLAUCON: That's right.

SOCRATES: In cases of this sort then, isn't the soul inevitably puzzled as to what this sense-perception means by hardness, if it says that the same thing is also soft; and in the case of the sense-perception of lightness and heaviness, what it means lightness and heaviness are, if what is heavy is light and what is light heavy?

GLAUCON: Yes, indeed, those are strange messages for the soul to receive 524b and do need to be examined.

SOCRATES: It is likely, then, that it is in cases of this sort that the soul, summoning calculation and understanding, first tries to determine whether each of the things reported to it is one or two.

GLAUCON: Of course.

SOCRATES: If there are obviously two, won't each of them be obviously one and distinct?

GLAUCON: Yes.

SOCRATES: If each of them is one, then, and both together are two, the soul will understand that the two are separate. I mean, it would not understand inseparable things as two, but as one. 524c

GLAUCON: That's right.

SOCRATES: But sight, we say, saw greatness and smallness, not as separate, but as mixed up together. Right?

GLAUCON: Yes.

SOCRATES: And to get clear about this, understanding was compelled to see greatness and smallness, too, not mixed up together, but distinguished—the opposite way from sight.

GLAUCON: True.

SOCRATES: Isn't it in cases like this that it first occurs to us to ask what greatness is, and smallness, too?

GLAUCON: Absolutely.

SOCRATES: Which is why we called one section the intelligible and the other the visible.

GLAUCON: Right.

524d SOCRATES: That, then, is what I was trying to express before when I said that some things summon thought, while others do not. I define summoners as those that strike the relevant sense at the same time as do their opposites. Those that do not do this, I said, do not wake up the understanding.

GLAUCON: I understand now, and I think you are right.

SOCRATES: Well then, to which of them does number, including the number one, belong?

GLAUCON: I do not know.

SOCRATES: Use what has already been said as an analogy. If the number one is adequately *seen* just by itself, or grasped by any of the other senses, then just as we were saying in the case of fingers, it would not draw the soul 524e toward being. But if something opposite to it is always seen at the same time, so that it no more appears to be one than the opposite of one, then there would be a need at that point for someone to decide the matter. And he would compel the soul within him to be puzzled, to inquire, to stir up the understanding within itself, and to ask what the number one itself is. 525a So, learning about the number one will be among the subjects that lead the soul and turn it around to look at what is.

GLAUCON: But surely the visual perception of it has just that feature, since we do see the same thing as one and as an unlimited number at the same time.

SOCRATES: Then if this is true of the number one, won't it also be true of all numbers?

GLAUCON: Of course.

SOCRATES: But now, calculation and arithmetic are wholly concerned with numbers.

GLAUCON: Right.

SOCRATES: Then they obviously lead toward truth.

GLAUCON: To an unnatural degree.

525b SOCRATES: Then they would belong, it seems, among the subjects we are seeking. I mean, a soldier must learn them in order to marshal his troops; and a philosopher, because it is necessary to be rising up out of becoming so as to grasp being, or he will never become able to calculate.

GLAUCON: That's right.

SOCRATES: And our guardian is, in fact, both a warrior and a philosopher.

GLAUCON: Of course.

SOCRATES: Then it would be appropriate, Glaucon, to prescribe this subject in our legislation and to persuade those who are going to take part in the 525c greatest things in the city to go in for calculation and take it up, not as laymen do, but staying with it until they reach the point at which they see the nature of the numbers by means of understanding itself; not like tradesmen and retailers, caring about it for the sake of buying and selling, but for the sake of war and for ease in turning the soul itself around from becoming to truth and being.

GLAUCON: Very well put.

SOCRATES: Moreover, it occurs to me now that the subject of calculation has been mentioned, how refined it is and in how many ways it is useful 525d for our purposes, provided you practice it for the sake of knowledge rather than trade.

GLAUCON: Which ways?

SOCRATES: Why, in the very one we were talking about just now. It gives the soul a strong lead upward and compels it to discuss the numbers themselves, never permitting anyone to propose for discussion numbers attached to visible or tangible bodies. I mean, you surely know what people who are clever in these matters are like. If, in the course of the argument, someone tries to divide the number one itself, they laugh and won't permit it. If *you* 525e divide it, they multiply it, taking care that the number one never appears to be, not one, but many parts.

GLAUCON: That's very true.

SOCRATES: Then what do you think would happen, Glaucon, if someone were to ask them: "What kind of numbers are you amazing fellows discuss- **526a** ing, where the number one is as you assume it to be, wholly equal in each and every case, without the least difference, and having no internal parts?" What do you think they would answer?

GLAUCON: I think they would answer that they are talking about those that are accessible only to thought and can be grasped in no other way.

SOCRATES: Do you see then, my friend, that this subject really does seem to be necessary to us, since it apparently compels the soul to use understanding 526b itself on the truth itself?

GLAUCON: It does so very strongly, in fact.

SOCRATES: Now, have you ever noticed that those who are naturally good at calculation are also naturally quick in all subjects, so to speak, and that those who are slow, if they are educated and exercised in it, even if they are benefited in no other way, nonetheless improve and become generally sharper than they were?

GLAUCON: That's right.

SOCRATES: Moreover, I do not think you will easily find many subjects that are harder to learn or practice than it.

GLAUCON: No indeed.

SOCRATES: For all these reasons, then, this subject is not to be neglected. On the contrary, the very best natures must be educated in it.

GLAUCON: I agree.

SOCRATES: Well, then, let's require that one. Second, let's consider whether the subject that follows after it is also appropriate for our purposes.

GLAUCON: Which one? Or do you mean geometry?

SOCRATES: That's it exactly.

GLAUCON: Insofar as it pertains to war, it is clearly appropriate. You see, when it comes to setting up camp, occupying a region, gathering and ordering troops, and all the other maneuvers armies make whether in battle itself or on the march, it makes all the difference whether someone is skilled in geometry or not.

SOCRATES: But still, for things like that, even a little bit of geometry—and of calculation—would suffice. What we need to consider is whether the greater and more advanced part of it tends to make it easier to see the form of the good. And that tendency, we say, is to be found in anything that compels the soul to turn itself around toward the region in which lies the happiest of the things that are; the one the soul must do everything possible to see.

GLAUCON: You are right.

SOCRATES: Therefore, if geometry compels one to look at being, it is appropriate; but if at becoming, it is inappropriate.

GLAUCON: Yes, that's what we are saying.

SOCRATES: Now, no one with even a little experience of geometry will dispute with us that this science is itself entirely the opposite of what is said about it in the accounts of its practitioners.

GLAUCON: How so?

SOCRATES: Well, they say completely ridiculous things about it because they are so hard up. I mean, they talk as if they were practical people who make all their arguments for the sake of action. They talk of squaring, applying, adding, and the like; whereas, in fact, the entire subject is practiced for the sake of acquiring knowledge.

GLAUCON: Absolutely.

SOCRATES: Mustn't we also agree on a further point?

GLAUCON: What?

SOCRATES: That it is knowledge of what always is, not of something that comes to be and passes away.

GLAUCON: That's easy to agree to, since geometry is knowledge of what always is.

SOCRATES: In that case, my noble fellow, it can draw the soul toward truth and produce philosophical thought by directing upward what we now wrongly direct downward.

GLAUCON: More than anything else.

SOCRATES: More than anything else, then, we must require the inhabitants of your beautiful city not to neglect geometry in any way, since even its byproducts are not insignificant. 527c

GLAUCON: What are they?

SOCRATES: The ones you mentioned that are concerned with war. And in addition, when it comes to being better able to pick up any subject, we surely know there is a world of difference between someone with a grasp of geometry and someone without one.

GLAUCON: Yes, by Zeus, a world of difference.

SOCRATES: Shall we prescribe it, then, as a second subject for the young?

GLAUCON: Let's.

SOCRATES: What about astronomy? Shall we make it the third? What do you think? 527d

GLAUCON: That's fine with me, at least. I mean, a better awareness of the seasons, months, and years is no less appropriate for a general than for a farmer or navigator.

SOCRATES: You are funny! You are like someone who is afraid that the masses will think he is prescribing useless subjects. It is no inconsequential task—indeed it is a very difficult one—to become persuaded that in everyone's soul there is an instrument that is purified and rekindled by such subjects when it has been blinded and destroyed by other pursuits—an 527e instrument that it is more important to preserve than 10,000 eyes, since only with it can the truth be seen. Those who share your belief that this is so will think you are speaking incredibly well, while those who are completely unaware of it will probably think you are talking nonsense, since they can see no other benefit worth mentioning in these subjects. So, decide right now which group you are engaging in discussion. Or is it neither of them, and are you making your arguments mostly for your 528a own sake—though you do not begrudge anyone else whatever profit he can get from them?

GLAUCON: That's what I prefer—to speak, question, and answer mostly for my own sake.

SOCRATES: Let's backtrack a bit. You see, we were wrong just now about the subject that comes after geometry.

GLAUCON: How so?

SOCRATES: After a plane surface, we went immediately to a solid that was revolving, without taking one just by itself. But the right way is to take up
528b the third dimension after the second. And it, I suppose, consists of cubes and of whatever shares in depth.

GLAUCON: Yes, you are right. But Socrates, that subject has not even been investigated yet.

SOCRATES: There are two reasons for that. Because no city values it, it is not vigorously investigated, due to its difficulty. And investigators need a director if they are to discover anything. Now, in the first place, such a director is difficult to find. Second, even if he could be found, as things
528c stand now, those who investigate it are too arrogant to obey him. But if an entire city served as his co-director and took the lead in valuing this subject, then they would obey him, and consistent and vigorous investigation would reveal the facts about it. For even now, when it is not valued by the masses and is hampered by investigators who lack any account of its usefulness—all the same, in spite of all these handicaps, the force of its appeal has caused it to be developed. So it would not be at all surprising if the facts about it were revealed in any case.

528d GLAUCON: Yes, indeed, it *is* an outstandingly appealing subject. But explain more clearly to me what you were saying just now. You took geometry, presumably, as dealing with plane surface.

SOCRATES: Yes.

GLAUCON: Then at first you put astronomy after it, but later you went back on that.

SOCRATES: Yes, the more I hurried to get through them all, the slower I went! You see, the subject dealing with the dimension of depth was next. But because of the ridiculous state of the methodical inquiry into it, I passed it by and spoke of astronomy—which deals with the motion of things having depth—after geometry.

GLAUCON: That's right.

528e SOCRATES: Let's then prescribe astronomy as the fourth subject, on the assumption that solid geometry, which we are now omitting, will be available if a city takes it up.

GLAUCON: That seems reasonable. And since you reproached me just now, Socrates, for praising astronomy in a vulgar manner, I will now praise it
529a your way. You see, I think it is clear to everyone that it compels the soul to look upward and leads it from things here to things there.

SOCRATES: It is clear to everyone except me, then, since that is not how I think of it.

GLAUCON: Then how do you think of it?

SOCRATES: As it is handled today by those who teach philosophy, it makes the soul look very much downward.

GLAUCON: How do you mean?

SOCRATES: In my opinion, your conception of "higher studies" is a good deal too generous! I mean, if someone were looking at something by leaning his head back and studying ornaments on a ceiling, it seems as though you would say that he is looking at them with his understanding, not with his eyes! Maybe you are right and I am foolish. You see, I just cannot conceive of any subject making the soul look upward except the one that is concerned with what is—and that is *invisible*. If anyone tries to learn something about perceptible things, whether by gaping upward or squinting downward, I would say that he never really learns—since there is no knowledge to be had of such things—and that his soul is not looking up but down, whether he does his learning lying on his back on land or on sea! 529b 529c

GLAUCON: A fair judgment! You are right to reproach me. But what did you mean, then, when you said that astronomy must be learned in a different way than people learn it at present, if it is going to be useful with regard to what we are talking about?

SOCRATES: It is like this: these ornaments in the heavens, since they are ornaments in something visible, may certainly be regarded as having the most beautiful and most exact motions that such things can have. But these fall far short of the true ones—those motions in which the things that are really fast or really slow, as measured in true numbers and as forming all the true geometrical figures, are moved relative to one another, and that move the things that are in them. And these, of course, must be grasped by reason and thought, not by sight. Don't you agree? 529d

GLAUCON: Of course.

SOCRATES: Therefore, we should use the ornaments in the heavens as models to help us study these other things. It is just as if someone chanced to find diagrams by Daedalus or some other craftsman or painter, which were very carefully drawn and worked out. I mean, anyone experienced in geometry who saw such things would consider them to be very beautifully executed, I suppose. But he would think it ridiculous to examine them seriously in order to find there the truth about equals, doubles, or any other ratio. 529e 530a

GLAUCON: How could it be anything but ridiculous?

SOCRATES: Don't you think, then, that a real astronomer will feel the same way when he looks at the motions of the stars? He will believe that the craftsman of the heavens arranged them and all that is in them in the most beautiful way possible for such things. But as for the ratio of night to day, of these to a month, of a month to a year, or of the motions of the stars to 530b them or to each other, don't you think he will consider it strange to believe that they are always the same and never deviate in the least, since they are connected to body and are visible things, or to seek by every means possible to grasp the truth about them?

GLAUCON: That's what I think—anyway, now that I hear it from you!

SOCRATES: Just as in geometry, then, it is by making use of problems that we will pursue astronomy too. We will leave the things in the heavens alone, if we are really going to participate in astronomy and make the naturally 530c wise element in the soul useful instead of useless.

GLAUCON: The task you are prescribing is a lot greater than anything now attempted in astronomy.

SOCRATES: And I suppose we will prescribe other subjects in the same way, if we are to be of any benefit as lawgivers. But can you in fact suggest any other appropriate subjects?

GLAUCON: Not at the moment, anyway.

SOCRATES: But motion, it seems to me, presents itself, not just in one form, but in several. A wise person could probably list them all, but there are two 530d that are evident even to us.

GLAUCON: What are they?

SOCRATES: Besides the one we have discussed, there is also its counterpart.

GLAUCON: What's that?

SOCRATES: It is probable that as the eyes fasten on astronomical motions, so the ears fasten on harmonic ones, and that these two sciences are somehow akin, as the Pythagoreans say. And we agree, Glaucon. Don't we?

GLAUCON: We do.

530e SOCRATES: Then, since the task is so huge, shouldn't we ask them their opinion and whether they have anything to add, all the while guarding our own requirement?

GLAUCON: What's that?

SOCRATES: That those we will be rearing should never attempt to learn anything incomplete, anything that does not always come out at the place all things should reach—the one we mentioned just now in the case of astronomy.[5] Or don't you know that people do something similar with 531a harmony, too? They measure audible concordances and sounds against one another, and so labor in vain, just like astronomers.

---

[5] 528d.

GLAUCON: Yes, by the gods, and pretty ridiculous they are, too. They talk about something they call a "dense interval" or quarter tone[6]—putting their ears to their instruments, like someone trying to overhear what the neighbors are saying. And some say they hear a tone in between, and that *it* is the shortest interval by which they must measure, while others argue that this tone sounds the same as a quarter tone. Both groups put ears before the understanding.

531b

SOCRATES: You mean those excellent fellows who vex their strings, torturing them and stretching them on pegs. I won't draw out the analogy by speaking of blows with the pick, or the charges laid against strings that are too responsive or too unresponsive. Instead, I will drop the analogy and say that I do not mean these people, but the ones we just said we were going to question about harmonics. You see, they do the same as the astronomers do. I mean, it is in these audible concordances that they search for numbers, but they do not ascend to problems or investigate which numbers are in concord and which are not, or what the explanation is in each case.

531c

GLAUCON: But that would be a daimonic task!

SOCRATES: Yet, it is useful in the search for the beautiful and the good! Pursued for any other purpose, though, it is useless.

GLAUCON: I suppose so.

SOCRATES: Moreover, I take it that if the methodical inquiry into all the subjects we have mentioned arrives at what they share in common with one another and what their affinities are, and draws conclusions about their kinship, it does contribute something to our goal and is not labor in vain; but that otherwise it is in vain.

531d

GLAUCON: I have the same hunch myself. But you are still talking about a very great task, Socrates.

SOCRATES: Do you mean the prelude, or what? Or don't you know that all these subjects are merely preludes to the theme itself that must be learned? I mean, you surely do not think that people who are clever in these matters are dialecticians.

GLAUCON: No, by Zeus, I do not. Although, I have met a few exceptions.

531e

SOCRATES: But did it ever seem to you that those who can neither give an account nor approve one know what any of the things are that we say they must know?

GLAUCON: Again, the answer is no.

SOCRATES: Then isn't this at last, Glaucon, the theme itself that dialectical discussion sings? It itself is intelligible. But the power of sight imitates it.

532a

---

[6] A dense interval is evidently the smallest difference in pitch that was recognized in ancient music.

We said that sight tries at last to look at the animals themselves, the stars themselves, and, in the end, at the sun itself.[7] In the same way, whenever someone tries, by means of dialectical discussion and without the aid of any sense-perceptions, to arrive through reason at the being of each thing itself, and does not give up until he grasps what good itself is with understanding

532b   itself, he reaches the end of the intelligible realm, just as the other reached the end of the visible one.

GLAUCON: Absolutely.

SOCRATES: Well, then, don't you call this journey dialectic?

GLAUCON: I do.

SOCRATES: Then the release from bonds and the turning around from shadows to statues and the light; and then the ascent out of the cave to the sun; and there the continuing inability to look directly at the animals, the

532c   plants, and the light of the sun, but instead at divine reflections in water and shadows of the things that are, and not, as before, merely at shadows of statues thrown by another source of light that, when judged in relation to the sun, is as shadowy as they—all this practice of the crafts we mentioned has the power to lead the best part of the soul upward until it sees the best among the things that are, just as before the clearest thing in the body was

532d   led to the brightest thing in the bodily and visible world.

GLAUCON: I accept that this is so. And yet, I think it is very difficult to accept; although—in another way—difficult not to accept! All the same, since the present occasion is not our only opportunity to hear these things, but we will get to return to them often in the future, let's assume that what you said about them just now is true and turn to the theme itself, and discuss it in the same way as we did the prelude. So, tell us then, in what way the power of dialectical discussion works, into what kinds it is divided, and what roads it follows. I mean, it is these, it seems, that would lead us

532e   at last to that place which is a rest from the road, so to speak, for the one who reaches it, and an end of his journey.

533a   SOCRATES: You won't be able to follow me any farther, my dear Glaucon—though not because of any lack of eagerness on my part. You would no longer see an image of what we are describing, but the truth itself as it seems to me, at least. Whether it is really so or not—that's not something on which it is any longer worth insisting. But that there is some such thing to be seen, *that* is something on which we must insist. Isn't that so?

GLAUCON: Of course.

---

[7] See 516a–b.

SOCRATES: And mustn't we also insist that the power of dialectical discussion could reveal it only to someone experienced in the subjects we described, and cannot do so in any other way?

GLAUCON: Yes, that is worth insisting on, too.

SOCRATES: At the very least, no one will dispute our claim by arguing that there is another road of inquiry that tries to acquire a methodical and wholly general grasp of what each thing itself is. By contrast, all the other 533b crafts are concerned with human beliefs and appetites, with growing or construction, or with the care of growing or constructed things. As for the rest, we described them as to some extent grasping what is—I mean, geometry and the subjects that follow it. For we saw that while they do dream about what is, they cannot see it while wide awake as long as they 533c make use of hypotheses that they leave undisturbed, and for which they cannot give any account. After all, when the first principle is unknown, and the conclusion and the steps in between are put together out of what is unknown, what mechanism could possibly turn any agreement reached in such cases into knowledge?

GLAUCON: None.

SOCRATES: Therefore, dialectic is the only method of inquiry that, doing away with hypotheses, journeys to the first principle itself in order to be made secure. And when the eye of the soul is really buried in a sort of barbaric bog, dialectic gently pulls it out and leads it upward, using the crafts 533d we described to help it and cooperate with it in turning the soul around. From force of habit, we have often called these branches of knowledge. But they need another name, since they are clearer than belief and darker than knowledge. We distinguished them by the term "thought" somewhere before.[8] But I don't suppose we will dispute about names, with matters as important as those before us to investigate.

GLAUCON: Of course not, just as long as they express the state of clarity 533e the soul possesses.

SOCRATES: It will be satisfactory, then, to do what we did before and call the first section knowledge, the second thought, the third opinion, and the fourth imagination. The last two together we call belief, the other 534a two, understanding. Belief is concerned with becoming; understanding with being. And as being is to becoming, so understanding is to belief; and as understanding is to belief, so knowledge is to belief and thought to imagination. But as for the ratios between the things these deal with, and the division of either the believable or the intelligible section into two, let's

---

[8] 511d–e.

pass them by, Glaucon, in case they involve us in discussions many times longer than the ones we have already gone through.

534b   GLAUCON: I agree with you about the rest of them, anyway, insofar as I am able to follow.

SOCRATES: So don't you, too, call someone a dialectician when he is able to grasp an account of the being of each thing? And when he cannot do so, won't you, too, say that to the extent that he cannot give an account of something either to himself or to another, to that extent he does not understand it?

GLAUCON: How could I not?

SOCRATES: Then the same applies to the good. Unless someone can give an account of the form of the good, distinguishing it from everything else, and 534c   can survive all examination as if in a battle, striving to examine things not in accordance with belief, but in accordance with being; and can journey through all that with his account still intact, you will say that he does not know the good itself or any other good whatsoever. And if he does manage to grasp some image of it, you will say that it is through belief, not knowledge, that he grasps it; that he is dreaming and asleep throughout his present life; and that, before he wakes up here, he will arrive in Hades 534d   and go to sleep forever.

GLAUCON: Yes, by Zeus, I will certainly say all that.

SOCRATES: Then as for those children of yours, the ones you are rearing and educating in your discussion, if you ever reared them in fact, I don't suppose that, while they are still as irrational as the proverbial lines,[9] you would allow them to rule in your city or control the greatest things.

GLAUCON: No, of course not.

SOCRATES: Won't you prescribe in your legislation, then, that they are to give the most attention to the education that will enable them to ask and 534e   answer questions most knowledgeably?

GLAUCON: I will prescribe it—together with you.

SOCRATES: Doesn't it seem to you, then, that dialectic is just like a capstone we have placed on top of the subjects, and that no other subject can rightly be placed above it, but that our account of the subjects has now come to 535a   an end?

GLAUCON: It does.

SOCRATES: Then it remains for you to deal with the distribution of these subjects: to whom we will assign them and in what way.

---

[9] A pun made possible by the fact that *alogon* can mean "irrational" (as applied to people) and "incommensurable" (as applied to lines in geometry).

GLAUCON: Clearly.

SOCRATES: Do you remember what sort of people we chose in our earlier selection of rulers?[10]

GLAUCON: How could I not?

SOCRATES: Well then, as regards the other requirements too, you must suppose that these same natures are to be chosen, since we have to select the most stable, the most courageous, and—as far as possible—the best-looking. In addition, we must look not only for people who have a noble and valiant character, but for those who also have natural qualities condu- 535b
cive to this education of ours.

GLAUCON: Which ones in particular?

SOCRATES: They must be keen on the subjects, bless you, and learn them without difficulty. For people's souls are much more likely to give up during strenuous studies than during physical training. The pain is more their own, you see, since it is peculiar to them and not shared with the body.

GLAUCON: That's true.

SOCRATES: We must also look for someone who has a good memory, is persistent, and is wholeheartedly in love with hard work. How else do you 535c
suppose he would be willing to carry out such hard physical labors and also complete so much learning and training?

GLAUCON: He would not, not unless his nature were an entirely good one.

SOCRATES: In any case, the mistake made at present—which, as we said before, explains why philosophy has fallen into dishonor—is that unworthy people take it up. For illegitimate people should not have taken it up, but genuine ones.

GLAUCON: How do you mean?

SOCRATES: In the first place, the one who takes it up must not be half-hearted in his love of hard work, with one half of him loving hard work 535d
and the other shirking it. That is what happens when someone is a lover of physical training and a lover of hunting and a lover of all kinds of hard bodily labor; yet is not a lover of learning, a lover of listening, or a keen investigator, but hates the work involved in all such things. And someone whose love of hard work tends in the opposite direction is also defective.

GLAUCON: That's absolutely true.

SOCRATES: Similarly with regard to truth, won't we say that a soul is maimed if it hates a voluntary lie, cannot endure to have one in itself, and 535e
is greatly angered when others lie; but is nonetheless content to accept an

---

[10] 412b–417b.

involuntary lie, does not get irritated when it is caught being ignorant, and bears its ignorance easily, wallowing in it like a pig?

536a GLAUCON: Absolutely.

SOCRATES: And with regard to temperance, courage, high-mindedness, and all the other parts of virtue, too, we must be especially on our guard to distinguish the illegitimate from the genuine. You see, when private individuals or cities do not know how to investigate all these things fully, they unwittingly employ defectives and illegitimates as their friends or rulers for whatever services they happen to need.

GLAUCON: Yes, that's just what happens.

536b SOCRATES: So we must take good care in all these matters, since, if we bring people who are sound of limb and mind to so important a subject, and train and educate them in it, justice itself will not find fault with us, and we will save both the city and its constitution. But if we bring people of a different sort to it, we will achieve precisely the opposite and let loose an even greater flood of ridicule upon philosophy as well.

GLAUCON: That would be a shame.

SOCRATES: It certainly would. But I seem to have made myself a little ridiculous just now.

GLAUCON: In what way?

536c SOCRATES: I forgot we were playing and spoke too vehemently. You see, while I was speaking I looked upon philosophy, and when I saw it undeservedly showered with abuse, I suppose I got irritated and, as if I were angry with those responsible, I said what I had to say in too serious a manner.

GLAUCON: Not too serious for me, by Zeus, as a member of the audience.

SOCRATES: But too serious for me as the speaker. In any case, let's not forget that in our earlier selection we chose older people, but here that is not permitted. You see, we must not believe Solon when he says that as someone 536d grows older, he is able to learn a lot. On the contrary, he is even less able to learn than to run. It is to young people that all great and frequent labors properly belong.

GLAUCON: Necessarily so.

SOCRATES: Well, then, calculation, geometry, and all the preparatory education that serves as preparation for dialectic must be offered to them in childhood—and not in the shape of compulsory instruction, either.

GLAUCON: Why's that?

536e SOCRATES: Because a free person should learn nothing slavishly. For while compulsory physical labors do no harm to the body, no compulsory instruction remains in the soul.

GLAUCON: That's true.

SOCRATES: Well, then, do not use compulsion, my very good man, to train the children in these subjects; use play instead. That way you will also be   537a able to see better what each of them is naturally suited for.

GLAUCON: What you say makes sense.

SOCRATES: Don't you remember that we also said that the children were to be led into war on horseback as observers, and that, wherever it is safe, they should be brought to the front and given a taste of blood, just like young dogs?

GLAUCON: I do remember.

SOCRATES: Those who always show the greatest facility in dealing with all these labors, studies, and fears must be enrolled in a unit.

GLAUCON: At what age?

SOCRATES: After they are released from compulsory physical training. For   537b during that period, whether it is two or three years, they are incapable of doing anything else, since weariness and sleep are enemies of learning. At the same time, one of the important tests of each of them is how he fares in physical training.

GLAUCON: It certainly is.

SOCRATES: Then, after that period, those selected from among the twenty-year-olds will receive greater honors than the others. Moreover, the subjects they learned in no particular order in their education as children, they   537c must now bring together into a unified vision of their kinship with one another and with the nature of what is.

GLAUCON: That, at any rate, is the only instruction that remains secure in those who receive it.

SOCRATES: It is also the greatest test of which nature is dialectical and which is not. For the person who can achieve a unified vision is dialectical, and the one who cannot isn't.

GLAUCON: I agree.

SOCRATES: Well, then, you will have to look out for those among them who most possess that quality; who are resolute in their studies and also resolute   537d in war and the other things conventionally expected of them. And when they have passed their thirtieth year, you will have to select them in turn from among those selected earlier and assign them yet greater honors, and test them by means of the power of dialectical discussion to see which of them can relinquish his eyes and other senses, and travel on in the company of truth to what itself is. And here, comrade, you have a task that needs a lot of safeguarding.

GLAUCON: How so?

537e   SOCRATES: Don't you realize the harm caused by dialectical discussion as it is currently practiced?

GLAUCON: What harm?

SOCRATES: Its practitioners are filled with lawlessness.

GLAUCON: They certainly are.

SOCRATES: Do you think it is at all surprising that this happens to them? Aren't you sympathetic?

GLAUCON: Why should I be?

538a   SOCRATES: It is like the case of a supposititious child brought up amid large wealth, a great and powerful family, and many flatterers, who finds out, when he has become a man, that he is not the child of his professed parents and that he cannot discover his real ones. Do you have any hunch as to what his attitude would be to the flatterers, and to his supposed parents, during the time when he did not know about the exchange, and, on the other hand, when he did know? Or would you rather hear my hunch?

GLAUCON: I would.

538b   SOCRATES: Well, then, my hunch is that he would be more likely to honor his father, his mother, and the rest of his supposed family than the flatterers, less likely to overlook any of their needs, less likely to treat them lawlessly in word or deed, and less likely to disobey them than the flatterers in any matters of importance, in the time when he did not know the truth.

GLAUCON: Probably so.

SOCRATES: But when he became aware of the truth, on the other hand, my hunch is that he would withdraw his honor and devotion from his family and increase them for the flatterers, whom he would obey far more than before, and he would begin to live the way they did, spend time with them 538c   openly, and—unless he was thoroughly good by nature—care nothing for that father of his or any of the rest of his supposed family.

GLAUCON: All that would probably happen as you say. But how is it like the case of those who take up argument?

SOCRATES: As follows. I take it we hold from childhood convictions about what things are just and fine; we are brought up with them as with our parents; we obey and honor them.

GLAUCON: Yes, we do.

538d   SOCRATES: And there are also other practices, opposite to those, which possess pleasures that flatter our soul and attract it to themselves, but which do not persuade people who are at all moderate—who continue to honor and obey the convictions of their fathers.

GLAUCON: That's right.

SOCRATES: What happens, then, when someone of that sort is met by the question, "What is the fine?" and, when he answers what he has heard from the traditional lawgiver, the argument refutes him; and by refuting him often and in many ways, reduces him to the belief that the fine is no more fine than shameful, and the same with the just, the good, and the things he honored most—what do you think he will do after that about honoring and obeying his earlier convictions?   538e

GLAUCON: It is inevitable that he won't honor or obey them in the same way.

SOCRATES: Then when he no longer regards them as honorable or as his own kin the way he did before, and cannot discover the true ones, will he be likely to adopt any other sort of life than the one that flatters him?   **539a**

GLAUCON: No, he won't.

SOCRATES: And so he will be taken, I suppose, to have changed from being law-abiding to being lawless.

GLAUCON: Inevitably.

SOCRATES: Isn't it likely, then, that this is what will happen to people who take up argument in that way, and, as I said just now, don't they deserve a lot of sympathy?

GLAUCON: Yes, and pity too.

SOCRATES: Then if you do not want your thirty-year-olds to be objects of such pity, won't you have to employ every sort of precaution when they take up argument?

GLAUCON: Yes, indeed.

SOCRATES: And isn't one very effective precaution not to let them taste argument while they are young? I mean, I don't suppose it has escaped your   539b notice that when young people get their first taste of argument, they misuse it as if it were playing a game, always using it for disputation. They imitate those who have refuted them by refuting others themselves, and, like puppies, enjoy dragging and tearing with argument anyone within reach.

GLAUCON: Excessively so.

SOCRATES: Then, when they have refuted many themselves and been refuted by many, they quickly fall into violently disbelieving everything   539c they believed before. And as a result of this, they themselves and the whole of philosophy as well are discredited in the eyes of others.

GLAUCON: That's absolutely true.

SOCRATES: But an older person would not be willing to take part in such madness. He will imitate someone who is willing to engage in dialectical discussion and look for the truth, rather than someone who plays at

disputation as a game. He will be more moderate himself and will bring
539d   honor, rather than discredit, to the practice.

GLAUCON: That's right.

SOCRATES: And wasn't everything we said before this also said as a precaution—that those with whom one takes part in arguments are to be orderly
and steady by nature, and not, as now, those, however unsuitable, who
chance to come along?

GLAUCON: Yes, it was.

SOCRATES: Is it enough, then, if someone devotes himself continuously and
strenuously to taking part in argument, doing nothing else, but training
in it just as he did in the physical training that is its counterpart, but for
539e   twice as many years?

GLAUCON: Do you mean six years or four?

SOCRATES: It does not matter. Make it five. You see, after that, you must
make them go down into the cave again, and compel them to take command in matters of war and the other offices suitable for young people, so
that they won't be inferior to the others in experience. And in these offices,
too, they must be tested to see whether they will remain steadfast when
540a   they are pulled in different directions, or give way.

GLAUCON: How much time do you assign to that?

SOCRATES: Fifteen years. Then, at the age of fifty, those who have survived
the tests and are entirely best in every practical task and every science must
be led at last to the end and compelled to lift up the radiant eye-beams of
their souls, and to look toward what itself provides light for everything.
And once they have seen the good itself, they must use it as their model and
put the city, its citizens, and themselves in order throughout the remainder
of their lives, each in turn. They will spend the greater part of their time
540b   doing philosophy, but, when his turn comes, each must labor in politics
and rule for the city's sake, not as something fine, but rather as something
compulsory. In that way, always having educated others like themselves
to take their place as guardians of the city, they will depart for the Isles of
the Blessed and dwell there. And the city will publicly establish memorials
540c   and sacrifices to them as daimons, if the Pythia agrees; but if not, as happy
and divine people.

GLAUCON: Like a sculptor, Socrates, you have produced thoroughly beautiful ruling men!

SOCRATES: And ruling women, too, Glaucon. You see, you must not think
that what I have said applies any more to men than it does to those women
of theirs who are born with the appropriate natures.

GLAUCON: That's right, if indeed they are to share everything equally with
the men, as we said.

SOCRATES: Well, then, do you agree that the things we have said about the city and its constitution are not altogether wishful thinking; that it is difficult for them to come about, but possible in a way, and in no way except the one we described: namely, when one or more true philosophers come to power in a city—people who think little of present honors, regarding them as illiberal and worthless, who prize what is right and the honors that come from it above everything, and who consider justice as the greatest and most compulsory thing, serving it and fostering it as they set their city in order?   540d

                                                      540e

GLAUCON: How will they do that?

SOCRATES: Everyone in the city who is over ten years old they will send into the country. They will take over the children, and far removed from current habits, which their parents possess, they will bring them up in their own ways and laws, which are the ones we described before. And with the city and constitution we were discussing thus established in the quickest and easiest way, it will itself be happy and bring the greatest benefit to the people among whom it comes to be.   541a

GLAUCON: That's by far the quickest and easiest way. And in my opinion, Socrates, you have well described how it would come into existence, if it ever did.   541b

SOCRATES: Haven't we said enough, then, about this city and the man who is like it? For surely it is clear what sort of person we will say he should be.

GLAUCON: Yes, it is clear. And as for your question, I think we have reached the end of this topic.

BOOK VIII

SOCRATES: All right. We are agreed, then, Glaucon, that if a city is going to be eminently well governed, women must be shared; children and their entire education must be shared; in both peace and war, pursuits must be shared; and their kings must be those among them who have proved best both in philosophy and where war is concerned.   543b

GLAUCON: We are agreed.

SOCRATES: Moreover, we also granted this: once the rulers are established, they will lead the soldiers and settle them in the kind of dwellings we described earlier, which are in no way private, but wholly shared. And surely we also came to an agreement, if you remember, about what sort of possessions they should have.

GLAUCON: Yes, I do remember. We thought that none of them should acquire any of the things that others now do; but that, as athletes of war

543c and guardians, they should receive their minimum yearly upkeep from the other citizens as a wage for their guardianship, and take care of themselves and the rest of the city.

SOCRATES: That's right. But since we have completed that discussion, let's recall the point at which we began the digression that brought us here, so that we can continue on the same path again.

GLAUCON: That is not difficult. You see, much the same as now, you were talking as if you had completed the description of the city. You were saying that you would class both the city you described and the man who is like it 543d as good, even though, as it seems, you had a still finer city and man to tell 544a us about. But in any case, you were saying that the others were defective, if it was correct. And you said, if I remember, that of the remaining kinds of constitution four were worth discussing, each with defects we should observe; and that we should do the same for the people like them in order to observe them all, come to an agreement about which man is best and which worst, and then determine whether the best is happiest and the worst most wretched, or whether it is otherwise. I was asking you which 544b four constitutions you had in mind, when Polemarchus and Adeimantus interrupted.[1] And that is when you took up the discussion that led here.

SOCRATES: That's absolutely right.

GLAUCON: Like a wrestler, then, give me the same hold again, and when I ask the same question, try to tell me what you were about to say before.

SOCRATES: If I can.

GLAUCON: In any case, I really want to hear for myself what four constitutions you meant.

SOCRATES: It won't be difficult for you to hear them. You see, the ones I 544c mean are the very ones that already have names: the one that is praised by "the many," your Cretan or Laconian [Spartan] constitution. The second— and second in the praise it receives—is called oligarchy, a constitution filled with a host of evils. Antagonistic to it, and next in order, is democracy. And "noble" tyranny, surpassing all of them, is the fourth and most extreme disease of cities. Can you think of another form of constitution—I mean, another distinct in form from these? For, no doubt, there are dynasties 544d and purchased kingships and other similar constitutions in between these, which one finds no less among barbarians than among Greeks.

GLAUCON: Many strange ones are certainly mentioned, at least.

SOCRATES: Are you aware, then, that there must be as many forms of human character as there are of constitutions? Or do you think constitutions arise

---

[1] 449b.

from oak or rock[2] and not from the characters of the people in the cities, which tip the scales, so to speak, and drag the rest along with them? 544e

GLAUCON: No, they could not possibly arise from anything other than that.

SOCRATES: So, if there are five of cities, there must also be five ways of arranging private individual souls.

GLAUCON: Of course.

SOCRATES: Now, we have already described the one who is like aristocracy, the one we rightly describe as good and just.

GLAUCON: Yes, we have described him. **545a**

SOCRATES: Mustn't we next describe the inferior ones—the victory-loving and honor-loving, which correspond to the Laconian constitution, followed by the oligarchic, democratic, and tyrannical—so that, having discovered the most unjust of all, we can oppose him to the most just and complete our investigation into how pure justice and pure injustice stand with regard to the happiness or wretchedness of the one who possesses them; and be persuaded either by Thrasymachus to practice injustice or by the argument 545b that is now coming to light to practice justice.

GLAUCON: That's exactly what we must do.

SOCRATES: Then just as we began by looking for the virtues of character in constitutions before looking for them in private individuals, thinking they would be clearer in the former, shouldn't we first examine the honor-loving constitution? I do not know another name that is commonly applied to it; it should be called either timocracy or timarchy. Then shouldn't we examine that sort of man by comparing him to it, and, after that, oligarchy and the oligarchic man, and democracy and the democratic man? Fourth, 545c having come to a city that is under a tyrant and having examined it, shouldn't we look into a tyrannical soul, and so try to become adequate judges of the topic we proposed for ourselves?

GLAUCON: That, at any rate, would be a reasonable way for us to go about observing and judging.

SOCRATES: Come on, then, let's try to describe how timocracy emerges from aristocracy. Or is it simply the case that, in all constitutions, change originates in the ruling element itself when faction breaks out within it; but 545d that if this group remains of one mind, then—however small it is—change is impossible?

GLAUCON: Yes, that's right.

SOCRATES: How, then, Glaucon, will our city be changed? How will faction arise, either between the auxiliaries and the rulers or within either

---

[2] Homer, *Odyssey* xix.163.

group? Or do you want us to be like Homer and pray to the Muses to tell
545e   us "how faction first broke out,"[3] and have them speak in tragic tones,
playing and jesting with us, as if we were children and they were speaking
in earnest?

GLAUCON: How do you mean?

546a   SOCRATES: Something like this: "It is difficult for a city constituted in this
way to change. However, since everything that comes-to-be must decay,
not even one so constituted will last forever. On the contrary, it, too,
must face dissolution. And this is how it will be dissolved: not only plants
that grow in the earth, but also animals that grow upon it, have periods
of fertility and infertility of both soul and bodies each time their cycles
complete a revolution. These cycles are short for what is short-lived and the
opposite for what is the opposite. However, even though they are wise, the
546b   people you have educated to be leaders in your city will, by using rational
calculation combined with sense-perception, nonetheless fail to ascertain
the periods of good fertility and of infertility for your species. Instead,
these will escape them, and so they will sometimes beget children when
they should not.

"Now, for the birth of a divine creature[4] there is a cycle comprehended
by a perfect number; while for a human being, it is the first number in
which are found increases involving both roots and powers, comprehend-
ing three intervals and four terms, of factors that cause likeness and unlike-
546c   ness, cause increase and decrease, and make all things mutually agreeable
and rational in their relations to one another. Of these factors, the base
ones—four in relation to three, together with five—give two harmonies
when thrice increased. One is a square, so many times a hundred. The
other is of equal length one way, but oblong. One of its sides are 100 squares
of the rational diameter of five each diminished by one, or alternatively
100 squares of the irrational diameter each diminished by two. The other
side are 100 cubes of three. This whole geometrical number controls better
and worse births.[5]

---

[3] Apparently an adaptation of *Iliad* xvi.112–13.

[4] The divine creature seems to be the world or universe. See *Timaeus* 30b–d,
32d, 34a–b. Plato does not specify its number.

[5] The human geometrical number is the product of 3, 4, and 5 "thrice increased":
if $(3 \times 4 \times 5) \times (3 \times 4 \times 5) = (3 \times 4 \times 5)^2$ is one increase, $(3 \times 4 \times 5) \times (3 \times 4 \times 5) \times$
$(3 \times 4 \times 5) \times (3 \times 4 \times 5) = (3 \times 4 \times 5)^4$ is three. This formula included "increases
involving both roots and powers": $(3 \times 4 \times 5)$ is a root; its indices are powers. It
"comprehends" three "intervals," symbolized by $\times$, and four "terms"—namely, the
roots. The resulting number, 12,960,000, can be represented geometrically as: (1) a
square whose sides are 3,600, or (2) an "oblong" or rectangle whose sides are 4,800 and
2,700. (1) is "so many times 100": 36 times. (2) is obtained as follows. The "rational

"And when, through ignorance of these, your guardians join brides   546d
and grooms at the wrong time, the children will be neither good-natured
nor fortunate. The older generation will choose the best of these children,
even though they do not deserve them. And when they in turn acquire
their fathers' powers, the first thing they will begin to neglect as guardians
will be us, by paying less attention to musical training than they should;
and the second is physical training. Hence your young people will become
more unmusical. And rulers chosen from among them won't be able to   546e
guard well the testing of Hesiod's and your own races—gold, silver, bronze, **547a**
and iron.[6] The intermixing of iron with silver and bronze with gold will
engender lack of likeness and unharmonious inequality, and these always
breed war and hostility wherever they arise. We must declare faction to be
'of this lineage,'[7] wherever and whenever it arises."

GLAUCON: And we will declare that they have answered correctly.

SOCRATES: They must. They are Muses, after all!

GLAUCON: What do the Muses say next?   547b

SOCRATES: When faction arose, each of these two races, the iron and the
bronze, pulled the constitution toward moneymaking and the acquisition
of land, houses, gold, and silver. The other two, by contrast, the gold and
silver races—since they are not poor, but naturally rich in their souls—led
toward virtue and the old political system. Striving and struggling with
one another, they compromised on a middle way: they distributed the land
and houses among themselves as private property; enslaved and held as serfs

---

diameter" of 5 is the nearest rational number to the real diameter of a square whose
sides are 5. This diameter = $\sqrt{5^2 + 5^2} = \sqrt{50} = 7$. Since the square of 7 is 49, we get
the longer side of the rectangle by diminishing 49 by 1 and multiplying the result by
100. This gives 4,800. The "irrational diameter" of 5 is $\sqrt{50}$. When squared (= 50),
diminished by 2 (= 48), and multiplied by 100, this, too, is 4,800. The short side,
"100 cubes of three," = 2,700. The significance of the number is more controversial.
The factors "that cause likeness and unlikeness, cause increase and decrease, and make
all things mutually agreeable and rational in their relations to one another" are probably the numbers, since odd numbers were thought to cause likeness and even ones
unlikeness. Of the numbers significant in human life, one is surely the 100 years of its
maximum span (615a–b). Another might be the number of days in the year (roughly
360), and a third might be the divisions of those days into smaller units determined
by the sun's place in the sky, since it is the sun that provides for "the coming-to-be,
growth, and nourishment" of all visible things (509b). Assuming that those units are
the 360 degrees of the sun's path around the earth, the number of moments in a human
life that have a potential effect on its coming-to-be, growth, and nourishment would
be $100 \times 360 \times 360$, or 12,960,000—Plato's human geometrical number.

[6] 414d–415c; Hesiod, *Works and Days* 109–202.

[7] Homer, *Iliad* vi.211.

547c   and servants those whom they had previously guarded as free friends and
providers of upkeep; and took responsibility themselves for making war
and for guarding against the ones they had enslaved.

GLAUCON: I think that is how the transformation begins.

SOCRATES: Wouldn't this constitution, then, be somehow in the middle
between aristocracy and oligarchy?

GLAUCON: Of course.

SOCRATES: Anyway, that is how the transformation occurs. But once transformed, how will it be managed? Or isn't it obvious that it will imitate
547d   the first constitution in some respects and oligarchy in others, since it is in
the middle between them; and that it will also have some features unique
to itself?

GLAUCON: That's right.

SOCRATES: In honoring the rulers, then, and in the fighting class's abstention
from farming, handicrafts, and other ways of making money, in providing
communal meals and being devoted to physical training and training for
war—in all such ways, won't the constitution be like the previous one?

GLAUCON: Yes.

547e   SOCRATES: But in its fear of appointing wise people as rulers, on the grounds
that men of that sort are no longer simple and earnest but mixed; in its
inclination toward spirited and simpler people, who are more naturally
548a   suited for war than peace; in its honoring the tricks and stratagems of war;
and spending all its time making war—in these respects, by contrast, isn't
it pretty much unique?

GLAUCON: Yes.

SOCRATES: Such men will have an appetite for money just like those in oligarchies, passionately adoring gold and silver in secret, owning storehouses
and private treasuries where they can deposit them and keep them hidden;
and they will have walls around their houses, real private nests, where they
548b   can spend lavishly on their women or on anyone else they please.

GLAUCON: That's absolutely true.

SOCRATES: They will be stingy with money, since they honor it and do not
possess it openly, but they will love to spend other people's money because
of their appetites. They will enjoy their pleasures in secret, running away
from the law like boys from their father, since they have not been educated
by persuasion but by force. This is because they have neglected the true
Muse, the companion of discussion and philosophy, and honored physical
548c   training more than musical training.

GLAUCON: The constitution you are describing is a thorough mixture of
good and bad.

SOCRATES: Yes, it is mixed. But because of its mastery by the spirited element, only one thing really stands out in it—the love of victories and honors.

GLAUCON: And very noticeable it is.

SOCRATES: That, then, is how this constitution would come to exist, and that is what it would be like. It is just an outline sketch of the constitution in words, not an exact account of it, since even from a sketch we will be   548d able to see the most just man and most unjust one. It would be an incredibly long task to discuss every constitution and every character without omitting any detail.

GLAUCON: Yes, that's right.

SOCRATES: Who, then, is the man corresponding to this constitution? How does he come to exist and what sort of man is he?

ADEIMANTUS: I think he would be very like Glaucon here, at least as far as the love of victory is concerned.

SOCRATES: Maybe in that respect, but in the following ones I do not think   548e his nature would be like that.

ADEIMANTUS: Which ones?

SOCRATES: He would have to be more stubborn and less well trained in music; a lover of music and of listening, yet not at all skilled in speaking; the sort of person who is harsh to slaves instead of looking down on them,   549a as an adequately educated person does; gentle to free people and very submissive to rulers; a lover of ruling and of honor, who does not base his claim to rule on his ability to speak or anything like that, but on his exploits in war and anything having to do with war; a lover of physical training and of hunting.

ADEIMANTUS: Yes, that is indeed the character belonging to this constitution.

SOCRATES: As regards money, too, wouldn't someone like that look down on it when he is young; but as he grows older, wouldn't he love it more   549b and more because he shares in the money-lover's nature and is not pure in his attitude to virtue, since he lacks the best guardian?

ADEIMANTUS: What's that?

SOCRATES: Reason mixed with musical training. You see, only it dwells within the person who possesses it as the lifelong preserver of his virtue.

ADEIMANTUS: Well put.

SOCRATES: That, then, is what a timocratic youth is like; he is like the corresponding city.

ADEIMANTUS: Yes, indeed.

SOCRATES: And he comes to exist in some such way as this: sometimes he is   549c the young son of a good father, who lives in a city that is not politically well governed; avoids honors, political office, lawsuits, and all such meddling in other people's affairs; and who is even willing to be put at a disadvantage so as to avoid trouble.

ADEIMANTUS: Yes, but how does he become timocratic?

SOCRATES: It first happens when he listens to his mother complaining that her man is not one of the rulers and that she is at a disadvantage among the other women as a result. Next, she sees that he is not very serious about money, either; does not fight or exchange insults in private lawsuits or in the public assembly, but takes easily everything of that sort; has a mind always absorbed in its own thoughts; and does not overvalue her or undervalue her either. As a result of all those things, she complains and tells her son that his father is unmanly and too easygoing, and makes a litany of the other sorts of things women love to recite on such occasions.

549d

ADEIMANTUS: Yes, indeed, it is just like them to have lots of such complaints.

549e

SOCRATES: You know, then, that the servants of such men—the ones thought to be loyal—also say similar things to the sons in private. If they see someone who owes the father money or has wronged him in some other way, whom he does not prosecute, they urge the son to punish all such people when he becomes a man, and be more of a man than his father. And when he goes out, the boy hears and sees other similar things: those who do their own work in the city are called fools and held to be of little account, while those who do not are honored and praised. When the young man hears and sees all this, then, and, on the other hand, also listens to what his father says, and sees his practices from close at hand and compares them with those of the others, he is pulled by both—his father nourishing the rational element in his soul and making it grow; the others nourishing the appetitive and spirited elements. And, because he is not a bad man by nature, but has kept bad company, he compromises on a middle way when he is pulled in these two directions, and surrenders the rule within him to the middle element—the victory-loving and spirited one—and becomes a proud and honor-loving man.

550a

550b

ADEIMANTUS: I think you have exactly described how such a man comes to exist.

SOCRATES: So, we now have the second constitution and the second man.

550c

ADEIMANTUS: We have.

SOCRATES: Next then, shall we, like Aeschylus, talk of "another man ordered like another city,"[8] or follow our plan and talk about the city first?

---

[8] The line does not occur in the extant plays, but it may be an adaptation of *Seven against Thebes* 451.

ADEIMANTUS: The latter, of course.

SOCRATES: And I suppose oligarchy would come next after such a constitution.

ADEIMANTUS: And what kind of political system do you mean by oligarchy?

SOCRATES: The constitution based on a property assessment, the one in which the rich rule and the poor man does not participate in ruling.

ADEIMANTUS: I understand. 550d

SOCRATES: So, mustn't we first describe how timarchy is transformed into oligarchy?

ADEIMANTUS: Yes.

SOCRATES: And surely the way it is transformed is clear even to the blind.

ADEIMANTUS: How?

SOCRATES: That storehouse filled with gold we mentioned,[9] which each possesses, destroys such a constitution. First, you see, the timocrats find ways of spending their money, then they alter the laws to allow them to do so, and then they and their women disobey the laws altogether.

ADEIMANTUS: Probably so.

SOCRATES: Next, I suppose, through one person seeing another and envying 550e him, they make the majority behave like themselves.

ADEIMANTUS: Probably so.

SOCRATES: After that then, they become further involved in moneymaking; and the more honorable they consider it, the less honorable they consider virtue. Or isn't virtue so opposed to wealth that if they were set on the scale of a balance, they would always incline in opposite directions?

ADEIMANTUS: It certainly is.

SOCRATES: So, when wealth and the wealthy are honored in a city, virtue **551a** and good people are honored less.

ADEIMANTUS: Clearly.

SOCRATES: And what is honored is always practiced, and what is not honored, neglected.

ADEIMANTUS: Yes.

SOCRATES: So, in the end, victory-loving and honor-loving men become lovers of making money and money-lovers, and they praise and admire the wealthy man and appoint him as ruler, and dishonor the poor one.

ADEIMANTUS: Of course.

SOCRATES: Isn't it then that they pass a law, which is a defining characteristic of an oligarchic constitution, establishing a wealth qualification—higher 551b

---

[9] 548a.

where it is more oligarchic, lower where it is less so—and proclaim that anyone whose property does not reach the stated assessment cannot participate in ruling? And they either put this through by force of arms, or else, without resorting to that, they use intimidation to establish this sort of constitution. Isn't that so?

ADEIMANTUS: It is.

SOCRATES: That, then, is, generally speaking, how it is established.

ADEIMANTUS: Yes, it is. But what is the constitution like? What are the defects we said it had?[10]

551c   SOCRATES: First of all, consider its defining characteristic. I mean, what would happen if ship captains were appointed like that, on the basis of property assessments, and a poor person was turned away even if he were a better captain?

ADEIMANTUS: People would make a very bad voyage!

SOCRATES: And doesn't the same apply to any other sort of rule whatsoever?

ADEIMANTUS: I suppose so.

SOCRATES: Except of a city? Or does it apply to that of a city, too?

ADEIMANTUS: It applies to it most of all, since it is the most difficult and greatest kind of rule there is.

551d   SOCRATES: That, then, is one major defect in oligarchy.

ADEIMANTUS: So it seems.

SOCRATES: And what about this one? Is it any smaller than the other?

ADEIMANTUS: Which?

SOCRATES: That a city of this sort is not one, but inevitably two—a city of the poor and one of the rich, living in the same place and always plotting against one another.

ADEIMANTUS: By Zeus, that's no smaller a defect.

SOCRATES: And this is hardly a good quality either: the likelihood of being unable to fight a war because of being compelled to arm and use the majority, or else, because of not using them, and so having to show up as true 551e   oligarchs[11] on the battlefield; and because, at the same time, the fact that they are money-lovers makes them unwilling to pay mercenaries.

ADEIMANTUS: That is not good.

SOCRATES: And what about what we condemned long ago[12]—the fact that in this constitution there is the meddling in other people's affairs

---

[10] 544c.

[11] I.e., as being few in number; *oligos* means few.

[12] 374b–c.

that occurs when the same people are farmers, moneymakers, and soldiers simultaneously? Or do you think it is right for things to be that way? **552a**

ADEIMANTUS: Not at all.

SOCRATES: Now, let's see whether it is the first to admit the greatest of all evils.

ADEIMANTUS: Which is?

SOCRATES: Allowing someone to sell all his possessions and someone else to buy them, and then allowing the seller to continue living in the city while not being any one of its parts—neither moneymaker nor craftsman, nor cavalryman, nor hoplite, but a poor person without means. 552b

ADEIMANTUS: It is the first.

SOCRATES: Anyway, this sort of thing certainly is not forbidden in oligarchies. I mean, if it were, some of their citizens would not be super rich and others totally impoverished.

ADEIMANTUS: That's right.

SOCRATES: Now, consider this: when a person like that was rich and spending his money, was he then of any greater use to the city in the ways we have just mentioned? Or did he merely seem to be one of the rulers, while in fact he was neither ruler nor subject of it, but only a squanderer of property?

ADEIMANTUS: That's right. He seemed to be a ruler but was nothing but a squanderer. 552c

SOCRATES: Do you want us to say of him, then, that as a drone existing in a cell is an affliction to the hive, so this person existing in a household is a drone and affliction to the city?

ADEIMANTUS: Yes, indeed, Socrates.

SOCRATES: And hasn't the god, Adeimantus, made all the winged drones stingless, as well as some of the footed ones, while other footed ones have terrible stings? And don't those who end up as beggars in old age come from among the stingless ones, while all those with stings are called evildoers? 552d

ADEIMANTUS: That's absolutely true.

SOCRATES: Clearly then, in any city where you see beggars, somewhere in the neighborhood there are thieves hidden, and pickpockets, temple robbers, and craftsmen of all such sorts of evil.

ADEIMANTUS: Clearly.

SOCRATES: What about oligarchic cities? Don't you see beggars in them?

ADEIMANTUS: Nearly everyone is one, apart from the rulers.

SOCRATES: Mustn't we suppose, then, that there are also many evildoers there with stings, whom the rulers forcibly keep in check by their cautiousness? 552e

ADEIMANTUS: We certainly must suppose it.

SOCRATES: And aren't we saying that the presence of such people is the result of lack of education, bad rearing, and a bad constitutional system?

ADEIMANTUS: We are.

SOCRATES: Well, then, that is roughly what the oligarchic city would be like. It would contain all these evils and probably others as well.

ADEIMANTUS: That's pretty much it.

553a   SOCRATES: Let's take it, then, that we have disposed of the constitution they call oligarchy, which gets its rulers on the basis of a property assessment. Next, let's consider how the person who is like it comes to exist, and what sort of person he is when he does.

ADEIMANTUS: Yes, let's.

SOCRATES: Doesn't the transformation from timocrat to oligarch mostly occur in this way?

ADEIMANTUS: Which?

SOCRATES: It happens when a son of his is born who begins by emulating his father and following in his footsteps, and then sees him suddenly crash-
553b   ing against the city as against a reef, and sees him and all his possessions spilling overboard. He had held a generalship or some other high office, was brought to court by sycophants, and was put to death or exiled, or was disenfranchised and had all his property confiscated.

ADEIMANTUS: Probably so.

SOCRATES: Anyway, my friend, after seeing and experiencing all that, and losing his property, the son is afraid, I imagine, and immediately throws the honor-loving and spirited element headlong from the throne in his own
553c   soul. And humbled by poverty, he turns greedily to moneymaking and, little by little, saving and working, he amasses property. Don't you think that someone like that will then establish the appetitive and moneymaking element on that throne, and make it a great king within himself, adorned with golden tiaras and collars and Persian swords?

ADEIMANTUS: I do.

SOCRATES: And I suppose he makes the rational and spirited elements sit
553d   on the ground beneath it, one on either side, and be slaves. He won't allow the first to calculate or consider anything except how a little money can be made into more; or the second to admire or honor anything except wealth and wealthy people, or to love being honored for anything besides the possession of wealth and whatever contributes to it.

ADEIMANTUS: There is no other way to turn an honor-loving young man
553e   into a money-loving one that is as swift and sure as that!

SOCRATES: Isn't this, then, the oligarchic person?

ADEIMANTUS: Well, he certainly developed from the sort of man who resembled the constitution from which oligarchy came.

SOCRATES: Then let's see whether he resembles it.   554a

ADEIMANTUS: Let's.

SOCRATES: Wouldn't he resemble it, primarily, by attaching the greatest importance to money?

ADEIMANTUS: Of course.

SOCRATES: And also by being a thrifty worker who satisfies only his necessary appetites and spends nothing on other things but enslaves his other appetites as pointless.

ADEIMANTUS: Yes, indeed.

SOCRATES: A pretty squalid fellow, at any rate, who tries to make a profit from everything: a treasury-builder—the sort the majority admire. Isn't that the sort of man who resembles this sort of constitution?   554b

ADEIMANTUS: *I* certainly think so. At any rate, money is honored more than anything else by both the city and the one who is like it.

SOCRATES: Because I don't suppose someone like that has paid any attention to education.

ADEIMANTUS: I don't think so. I mean, if he had, he would not have chosen a blind leader for his chorus and honored him most.[13]

SOCRATES: Well put! But consider this. Wouldn't we say that though the dronish appetites exist in him because of his lack of education, some of them beggars and others evildoers, they are forcibly kept in check by his general cautiousness?   554c

ADEIMANTUS: Certainly.

SOCRATES: Do you know, then, where you should look to see the evils such people do?

ADEIMANTUS: Where?

SOCRATES: Where they are guardians of orphans, or any other situation like that, where they have ample opportunity to do injustice.

ADEIMANTUS: True.

SOCRATES: So, doesn't that make it clear that in other contractual matters, where someone like that has a good reputation and is thought to be just, something good of his is forcibly holding in check the other bad appetites   554d within; not persuading them that they had better not, nor taming them by a word, but using compulsion and fear, because he is terrified of losing his other possessions?

---

[13] I.e., Plutus, the god of wealth, who is often represented as being blind.

ADEIMANTUS: Exactly.

SOCRATES: Yes, by Zeus, my friend, you will find that most of them, when they have other people's money to spend, have appetites in them akin to those of the drone.

ADEIMANTUS: Indeed, you certainly will!

SOCRATES: So, someone like that would not be entirely free from internal faction, and would not be a single person but somehow a twofold one, although his better appetites would generally master his worse appetites.

554e

ADEIMANTUS: That's right.

SOCRATES: Because of this, I suppose someone like that would be more respectable than many other people; but the true virtue of a single-minded and harmonious soul would somehow far escape him.

ADEIMANTUS: I suppose so.

SOCRATES: Furthermore, the thrifty man is a worthless individual contes-
555a tant in the city for any prize of victory or any of the other fine things the love of honor craves. He is unwilling to spend money for the sake of fame or other such results of competition, and, fearing to arouse his appetites for spending by allying them with love of victory, he fights in true oligarchic fashion, with only a few of his resources, and is mostly defeated, but remains rich!

ADEIMANTUS: Exactly.

SOCRATES: Are we still in any doubt, then, that, as regards resemblance, a
555b thrifty moneymaker corresponds to an oligarchic city?

ADEIMANTUS: Not at all.

SOCRATES: Then democracy, it seems, must be considered next—both the way it comes to exist and what it is like when it does—so that when we know the character of this sort of man, we can present him for judgment in turn.

ADEIMANTUS: At any rate, that would be consistent with what we have been doing.

SOCRATES: Well, then, isn't the change from an oligarchy to a democracy due in some way or other to the insatiable desire for the good set before it—the need to become as rich as possible?

ADEIMANTUS: How so?

555c SOCRATES: Since the rulers rule in it because they own a lot, I suppose they are not willing to enact laws to prevent young people who have become intemperate from spending and wasting their wealth, so that by buying and making loans on the property of such people, the rulers themselves can become even richer and more honored.

ADEIMANTUS: That's their primary goal, at any rate.

SOCRATES: So, isn't it clear by now that you cannot honor wealth in a city and maintain temperance in the citizens at the same time, but must inevitably neglect one or the other?   555d

ADEIMANTUS: That is pretty clear.

SOCRATES: The negligent encouragement of intemperance in oligarchies, then, sometimes reduces people who are not ill born to poverty.

ADEIMANTUS: Indeed, it does.

SOCRATES: And these people sit around in the city, I suppose, armed with stings or weapons—some of them in debt, some disenfranchised, some both—hating and plotting against those who have acquired their property, and all the others as well; passionately longing for revolution.   555e

ADEIMANTUS: That's right.

SOCRATES: These moneymakers, with their heads down, pretending not to see them, inject the poison of their money into any of the rest who do not resist, and, carrying away a multitude of offspring in interest from their principal, greatly increase the size of the drone and beggar class in the city.   556a

ADEIMANTUS: They certainly do increase it greatly.

SOCRATES: In any case, they are not willing to quench evil of this sort as it flares up, either by preventing a person from doing whatever he likes with his own property, or alternatively by passing this other law to do away with such abuses.

ADEIMANTUS: What law?

SOCRATES: The one that is next best and that compels the citizens to care about virtue. You see, if someone prescribed that most voluntary contracts be entered into at the lender's own risk, money would be less shamelessly   556b
pursued in the city and fewer of those evils we were mentioning just now would develop in it.

ADEIMANTUS: Far fewer.

SOCRATES: But as it is, and for all these reasons, the rulers in the city treat their subjects in the way we described. And as for themselves and those belonging to them, don't they bring up the young to be fond of luxury, incapable of effort either mental or physical, too soft to endure pleasures or pains, and lazy?   556c

ADEIMANTUS: Of course.

SOCRATES: And haven't they themselves neglected everything except making money and been no more concerned about virtue than poor people are?

ADEIMANTUS: Yes, they have.

SOCRATES: And when rulers and subjects, socialized in this way, meet on journeys or some other shared undertakings, whether in an embassy or a military campaign; or as shipmates or fellow soldiers; or when they watch

one another in dangerous situations—in these circumstances, don't you
556d   think the poor are in no way despised by the rich? On the contrary, don't
you think it is often the case that a poor man, lean and suntanned, is stationed in battle next to a rich one, reared in the shade and carrying a lot of
excess flesh, and sees him panting and completely at a loss? And don't you
think he believes that it is because of the cowardice of the poor that such
people are rich and that one poor man says to another when they meet in
556e   private: "These men are ours for the taking; they are good for nothing"?

ADEIMANTUS: I know very well they do.

SOCRATES: Well, just as a sick body needs only a slight shock from outside
to become ill and sometimes, even without external influence, becomes
divided into factions, itself against itself, doesn't a city in the same condition need only a small pretext—such as one side bringing in allies from an
oligarchy or the other from a democracy—to become ill and fight with
itself? And doesn't it sometimes become divided into factions even without
any external influence?

557a   ADEIMANTUS: Yes, violently so.

SOCRATES: Then democracy comes about, I suppose, when the poor are
victorious, kill or expel the others, and give the rest an equal share in the
constitution and the ruling offices, and the majority of offices in it are
assigned by lot.

ADEIMANTUS: Yes, that is how a democratic political system gets established, whether it comes to exist by force of arms or because intimidation
drives its opponents into exile.

SOCRATES: In what way, then, do these people live? What sort of constitu-
557b   tion do they have? For clearly the sort of man who is like it will turn out
to be democratic.

ADEIMANTUS: Clearly.

SOCRATES: Well, in the first place, aren't they free? And isn't the city full of
freedom and freedom of speech? And isn't there license in it to do whatever
one wants?

ADEIMANTUS: That's what they say, anyway.

SOCRATES: And where there is license, clearly each person would arrange
his own life in whatever way pleases him.

ADEIMANTUS: Clearly.

557c   SOCRATES: I imagine it is in this constitution, then, that multifarious people
come to exist.

ADEIMANTUS: Of course.

SOCRATES: It looks, then, as though it is the most beautiful of all the constitutions. For just like an embroidered cloak embroidered with every kind

of ornament, it is embroidered with every sort of character, and so would appear to be the most beautiful. And presumably, many people would behave like women and children looking at embroidered objects and actually judge it to be the most beautiful.

ADEIMANTUS: They certainly would.

SOCRATES: What is more, bless you, it is also a handy place in which to look for a constitution!

ADEIMANTUS: Why is that?   557d

SOCRATES: Because it contains all kinds of constitutions, as a result of its license. So whoever wants to organize a city, as we were doing just now, probably should go to a democracy and, as if he were in a supermarket of constitutions, pick out whatever pleases him and establish it.

ADEIMANTUS: He probably wouldn't be at a loss for examples, anyway!

SOCRATES: There is no compulsion to rule in this city, even if you are quali-   557e
fied to rule, or to be ruled if you do not want to be; or to be at war when the others are at war, or to keep the peace when the others are keeping it, if you do not want peace; or, even if there happens to be a law preventing you from ruling or from serving on a jury, to be any the less free to rule or serve on a jury—isn't that a heavenly and pleasant way to pass the time,   **558a**
while it lasts?

ADEIMANTUS: It probably is—while it lasts.

SOCRATES: And what about the calm of some of their condemned criminals? Isn't that a sophisticated quality? Or have you never seen people who have been condemned to death or exile in a constitution of this sort staying on all the same and living right in the middle of things, without anyone giving them a thought or staring at them, while they stroll around like a hero?

ADEIMANTUS: Yes, I have seen it a lot.

SOCRATES: And what about the city's tolerance, its complete lack of petty-mindedness, and its utter disregard for the things we took so seriously   558b
when we were founding the city—that unless someone had transcendent natural gifts, he would never become a good man if he did not play fine games right from early childhood and engage in practices that are all of that same sort? Isn't it magnificent how it tramples all that underfoot, gives no thought to what sort of practices someone went in for before he entered politics, and honors him if only he tells them he wishes the majority well?

ADEIMANTUS: That's true nobility!

SOCRATES: These, then, and others akin to them are the characteristics a   558c
democracy would possess. And it would, it seems, be a pleasant constitution—lacking rulers but not complexity, and assigning a sort of equality to equals and unequals alike.

ADEIMANTUS: Yes, that's well known!

SOCRATES: Look and see, then, what sort of private individual resembles it. Or should we first consider, as we did in the case of the constitution, how he comes to exist?

ADEIMANTUS: Yes.

558d SOCRATES: Well, doesn't it happen this way? Mightn't we suppose that our thrifty oligarchic man had a son brought up by his father with his father's traits of character?

ADEIMANTUS: Of course.

SOCRATES: Then he too would rule by force the pleasures that exist in him—the spendthrift ones that do not make money; the ones that are called unnecessary.

ADEIMANTUS: Clearly.

SOCRATES: In order not to have a discussion in the dark, would you like us first to define which appetites are necessary and which are not?

ADEIMANTUS: I would.

558e SOCRATES: Well, then, wouldn't those we cannot deny rightly be called necessary? And also those whose satisfaction benefits us? For we are by nature compelled to try to satisfy them both. Isn't that so?

ADEIMANTUS: Of course.

559a SOCRATES: So, we would be right to apply the term "necessary" to them?

ADEIMANTUS: We would be right.

SOCRATES: What about those someone could get rid of if he started practicing from childhood, those whose presence does no good but may even do the opposite? If we said that all of them were unnecessary, would we be right?

ADEIMANTUS: We would be right.

SOCRATES: Let's pick an example of each, so that we have a pattern to follow.

ADEIMANTUS: Yes, let's.

559b SOCRATES: Wouldn't the desire to eat to the point of health and well-being, and the desire for bread and relishes be necessary ones?

ADEIMANTUS: I suppose so.

SOCRATES: The desire for bread is surely necessary on both counts, in that it is beneficial and that unless it is satisfied, we die.

ADEIMANTUS: Yes.

SOCRATES: And so is the one for relishes, insofar as it is beneficial and conduces to well-being.

ADEIMANTUS: Indeed.

SOCRATES: What about an appetite that goes beyond these and seeks other sorts of foods; that, if it is restrained from childhood and educated, most people can hold in check; and that is harmful to the body or harmful to the soul's capacity for wisdom and temperance? Wouldn't it be correct to call it unnecessary?   559c

ADEIMANTUS: Entirely correct.

SOCRATES: Wouldn't we also say that the latter are spendthrift, then, whereas the former are moneymaking because they are useful where work is concerned?

ADEIMANTUS: Certainly.

SOCRATES: And won't we say the same about sexual appetites and the rest?

ADEIMANTUS: Yes.

SOCRATES: And didn't we say that the person we just now called a drone is full of such pleasures and appetites and is ruled by the unnecessary ones, while the one who is ruled by his necessary appetites is a thrifty oligarch?

ADEIMANTUS: Of course we did.

SOCRATES: Let's go back, then, and say how the democrat develops from   559d
the oligarch. It seems to me as if it mostly happens this way.

ADEIMANTUS: What way?

SOCRATES: When a young man who is reared in the uneducated and thrifty manner we described just now tastes the honey of the drones and associates with wild and terrible creatures who can provide multifarious pleasures of every degree of complexity and sort, that probably marks the beginning of his transformation from having an oligarchic constitution within him   559e
to having a democratic one.

ADEIMANTUS: It most certainly does.

SOCRATES: So, just as the city changed when one party received help from a like-minded alliance outside, doesn't the young man change in turn when external appetites of the same type and quality as it come to the aid of one of the parties within him?

ADEIMANTUS: Absolutely.

SOCRATES: And I suppose if a counter-alliance comes to the aid of the oligarchic party within him—whether from his father or from the rest of his family, who exhort and reproach him—then there is a faction and an   560a
opposing faction within him, and he battles against himself.

ADEIMANTUS: Of course.

SOCRATES: And sometimes, I suppose, the democratic party yields to the oligarchic, some of its appetites are overcome while others are expelled, and a kind of shame rises in the young man's soul and order is restored.

ADEIMANTUS: That does sometimes happen.

SOCRATES: Moreover, I suppose, as some appetites are expelled, others akin to them are being nurtured undetected because of the father's ignorance of upbringing, and become numerous and strong.

560b

ADEIMANTUS: At any rate, that's what usually happens.

SOCRATES: Then these desires draw him back to his old associates and, in secret intercourse, breed a multitude of others.

ADEIMANTUS: Of course.

SOCRATES: Finally, I suppose, they seize the citadel of the young man's soul, since they realize that it is empty of the fine studies and practices and the true arguments that are the best watchmen and guardians in the minds of men loved by the gods.

560c

ADEIMANTUS: By far the best.

SOCRATES: Then, I suppose, beliefs and arguments that are lying imposters rush up and occupy this same part of him in place of the others.

ADEIMANTUS: They do, indeed.

SOCRATES: Won't he then return to those Lotus-eaters and live with them openly? And if any help should come to the thrifty part of his soul from his relatives, don't those imposter arguments, having barred the gates of the royal wall within him, prevent the allied force itself from entering and even refusing to admit arguments of older, private individuals as ambassadors? Proving stronger in the battle, won't they call reverence foolishness and drive it out as a dishonored fugitive? And calling temperance cowardliness, won't they shower it with abuse and banish it? As for moderate and orderly expenditure, won't they persuade him that it is boorish and illiberal, and join with a multitude of useless appetites to drive it over the border?

560d

ADEIMANTUS: They will indeed.

560e

SOCRATES: And when they have somehow emptied and purged these from the soul of the one they are seizing hold of and initiating with solemn rites, they then immediately proceed to return arrogance, anarchy, extravagance, and shamelessness from exile in a blaze of torchlight, accompanied with a vast chorus of followers and crowned with garlands. They praise them and give them fine names, calling arrogance "good breeding," anarchy "freedom," extravagance "magnificence," and shamelessness "courage." Isn't it in some such way as this that a young person exchanges an upbringing among necessary appetites for the freeing and release of useless and unnecessary pleasures?

561a

ADEIMANTUS: Yes, that's clearly the way it happens.

SOCRATES: Then in his subsequent life, I suppose, someone like that spends no less money, effort, and time on the necessary pleasures than on the unnecessary pleasures. But if he is lucky and does not go beyond the limits in his bacchic frenzy, and if, as a result of his growing somewhat older,

the great tumult within him passes, he welcomes back some of the exiles 561b
and ceases to surrender himself completely to the newcomers. Then, putting all his pleasures on an equal footing, he lives, always surrendering rule over himself to whichever desire comes along, as if it were chosen by lot,[14] until it is satisfied; and after that to another, dishonoring none but satisfying all equally.

ADEIMANTUS: He does, indeed.

SOCRATES: And he does not accept or admit true reason into the guardhouse if someone tells him that some pleasures belong to fine and good appetites and others to bad ones, and that he must practice and honor the 561c
former and restrain and enslave the latter. On the contrary, he denies all this and declares that they are all alike and must be honored on an equal basis.

ADEIMANTUS: That's exactly what he feels and does.

SOCRATES: And so he lives from day to day, gratifying the appetite of the moment. Sometimes he drinks heavily while listening to the flute, while at others he drinks only water and is on a diet. Sometimes he goes in 561d
for physical training, while there are others when he is idle and neglects everything. Sometimes he spends his time engaged in what he takes to be philosophy. Often, though, he takes part in politics, leaping to his feet and saying and doing whatever happens to come into his mind. If he admires some military men, that is the direction in which he is carried; if some moneymakers, then in that different one. There is neither order nor necessity in his life, yet he calls it pleasant, free, and blessedly happy, and follows it throughout his entire life.

ADEIMANTUS: You have perfectly described the life of a man devoted to legal equality. 561e

SOCRATES: I certainly think he is a multifarious man and full of all sorts of characters, beautiful and complex, like the democratic city. Many men and women would envy his life because of the great number of examples of constitutions and characters it contains within it.

ADEIMANTUS: Yes, that's right.

SOCRATES: Well, then, will we set this man alongside democracy as the one 562a
who would rightly be called democratic?

ADEIMANTUS: We will.

SOCRATES: The finest constitution and the finest man remain for us to discuss: tyranny and the tyrant.

ADEIMANTUS: Absolutely.

SOCRATES: Come on, then; tell me, my dear comrade, how does tyranny come to exist? That it evolves from democracy, you see, is fairly clear.

---

[14] Many public officials in democratic Athens were elected by lot.

ADEIMANTUS: It is clear.

SOCRATES: So, isn't the way democracy evolves from oligarchy much the same as that in which tyranny evolves from democracy?

ADEIMANTUS: How do you mean?

562b SOCRATES: The good they proposed for themselves, and because of which oligarchy was established, was wealth, wasn't it?

ADEIMANTUS: Yes.

SOCRATES: And its insatiable desire for wealth and its neglect of other things for the sake of moneymaking was what destroyed it.

ADEIMANTUS: True.

SOCRATES: So, isn't democracy's insatiable desire for what it defines as the good also what destroys it?

ADEIMANTUS: What do you think it does define as the good?

SOCRATES: Freedom. For surely, in a democratic city, that is what you
562c would hear described as its finest possession, and as what makes it the only place worth living in for someone who is naturally free.

ADEIMANTUS: Yes, you often hear that said.

SOCRATES: As I was about to say, then, isn't it the insatiable desire for this good and the neglect of other things that changes this constitution and prepares it to need a dictatorship?

ADEIMANTUS: How does it do that?

562d SOCRATES: I suppose it is when a democratic city, athirst for freedom, happens to get bad cupbearers for its leaders and gets drunk by drinking more than it should of unmixed wine. Then, if the rulers are not very gentle and do not provide plenty of freedom, it punishes them and accuses them of being filthy oligarchs.

ADEIMANTUS: Yes, that is what it does.

SOCRATES: It showers with abuse those who obey the rulers as voluntary slaves and nonentities, but both in public and private it praises and honors rulers who are like subjects, and subjects who are like rulers. And isn't it inevitable in such a city that freedom should spread everywhere?

562e ADEIMANTUS: Of course.

SOCRATES: Yes, my friend, and so it is bound to make its way into private households until finally it breeds anarchy among the very animals.

ADEIMANTUS: What do you mean by that?

SOCRATES: For instance, a father gets into the habit of behaving like a child and fearing his son, and the son gets into the habit of behaving like a father, feeling neither shame nor fear in front of his parents—all in order to be
563a *free.* A resident alien feels himself equal to a citizen and a citizen to him, and a foreigner likewise.

ADEIMANTUS: Yes, those sorts of things do happen.

SOCRATES: They do—and so do other little things of the same sort. A teacher in such circumstances is afraid of his students and flatters them, while the students belittle their teachers and do the same to their tutors, too. In general, the young are the spitting images of their elders and compete with them in words and deeds, while the old stoop to the level of the young and are full of wit and indulgence, imitating the young for fear of being thought disagreeable and masterful. 563b

ADEIMANTUS: Absolutely.

SOCRATES: The ultimate freedom for the majority, my friend, comes about in such a city, when males and females bought as slaves are no less free than those who bought them. Then there is the case of women in relation to men, and men to women, and the extent of their legal equality and freedom—we almost forgot to mention that!

ADEIMANTUS: Are we not, with Aeschylus, going to "say whatever it was came to our lips just now?"[15] 563c

SOCRATES: Certainly. At any rate, I am going to say it. I mean, no one who had not experienced it would believe how much freer domestic animals are here than in any other city. Bitches follow the proverb exactly and become like their mistresses. Horses and donkeys are in the habit of proceeding with complete freedom and dignity, bumping into anyone they meet on the road who does not get out of their way. And everything else is full of freedom, too.

ADEIMANTUS: It is my own dream you are telling me. That often happens 563d
to me when I go to the country.

SOCRATES: Summing up all these things together, then, do you notice how sensitive they make the citizens' souls, so that if anyone tries to impose the least degree of slavery, they get irritated and cannot bear it? In the end, as I am sure you are aware, they take no notice of the laws—written or unwritten—in order to avoid having any master at all. 563e

ADEIMANTUS: I certainly am aware.

SOCRATES: This, my friend, is the fine and impetuous beginning from which tyranny seems to me to grow.

ADEIMANTUS: It is certainly impetuous. But what comes next?

SOCRATES: The same disease that developed in oligarchy and destroyed it also develops here—only more widespread and virulent because of the general permissiveness—and eventually enslaves democracy. In fact, excessive action in one direction usually sets up a great reaction in the opposite

---

[15] We no longer possess the play from which this fragment comes.

direction. This happens in seasons, in plants, in bodies, and particularly
564a in constitutions.

ADEIMANTUS: That's probably right.

SOCRATES: For extreme freedom probably cannot lead to anything but a
change to extreme slavery, whether in a private individual or a city.

ADEIMANTUS: No, it probably can't.

SOCRATES: Tyranny probably does not evolve from any constitution other
than democracy, then—the most severe and cruel slavery evolving from
what I suppose is the most eminent degree of freedom.

ADEIMANTUS: Yes, that's reasonable.

SOCRATES: But I think you were asking, not that, but rather what sort of
disease develops both in oligarchy and democracy alike, and enslaves the
564b latter.

ADEIMANTUS: That's true.

SOCRATES: Well, then, I meant that class of idle and extravagant men, with
the bravest as leaders and the more cowardly as followers. We compared
them to drones: the leaders to drones with stings, the followers to stingless
ones.

ADEIMANTUS: Rightly so.

SOCRATES: These two cause problems in any constitution in which they
564c arise, like phlegm and bile in the body. And it is against them that the
good doctor and lawgiver of a city must take no less advance precaution
than a wise beekeeper. He should preferably prevent them from arising at
all. But if they should happen to arise, he must cut them out, cells and all,
as quickly as possible.

ADEIMANTUS: Yes, by Zeus, and as thoroughly as possible.

SOCRATES: Then let's take up the question in this way, in order to see what
we want more distinctly.

ADEIMANTUS: In what way?

SOCRATES: Let's in our discussion divide a democratic city into three
parts—which is also how it is actually divided. One part is surely this class
564d of drones, which, because of the general permissiveness, grows in it no less
than in an oligarchy.

ADEIMANTUS: So it does.

SOCRATES: But it is much fiercer in it than in the other.

ADEIMANTUS: How so?

SOCRATES: There, because it is not honored but is excluded from the ranks
of the rulers, it does not get any exercise and does not become vigorous.
However, in a democracy, with few exceptions, it is surely the dominant
class. Its fiercest part does all the talking and acting, while the other one

settles near the speaker's platform. It buzzes and does not tolerate any dissent. As a result, this class is in charge of everything in such a constitu-   564e
tion—with a few exceptions.

ADEIMANTUS: That's right.

SOCRATES: Then, there is a second distinct class that is constantly emerging from the majority.

ADEIMANTUS: Which one?

SOCRATES: Surely, when everyone is trying to make money, the ones who are by nature most orderly generally become the wealthiest.

ADEIMANTUS: Probably so.

SOCRATES: Then that is where the most plentiful honey for the drones exists, I take it, and the easiest for them to extract.

ADEIMANTUS: How could anyone extract it from those who have very little?

SOCRATES: I suppose, then, that these rich people, as they are called, are fodder for the drones.

ADEIMANTUS: Pretty much.

SOCRATES: The people—those who work their own land, take no part in politics, and own few possessions—would be the third class. This is the   565a
largest and most powerful class in a democracy when it meets in assembly.

ADEIMANTUS: Yes, it is. But it is not willing to meet often, if it does not get a share of the honey.

SOCRATES: So, it always does get a share—one that allows the leaders, in taking the wealth of the rich and distributing it to the people, to keep the greatest share for themselves.

ADEIMANTUS: Yes, that is the sort of share they get.   565b

SOCRATES: Then I suppose that those whose wealth is taken away are compelled to defend themselves by speaking in the popular assembly and doing whatever else they can.

ADEIMANTUS: Of course.

SOCRATES: At which point—even if they have no appetite for revolution at all—they get accused by the others of plotting against the people and of being oligarchs.

ADEIMANTUS: They do.

SOCRATES: Finally, when they see the people—not intentionally, but through misapprehension and being misled by the accusers—trying to do   565c
injustice to them, then, whether they wish it or not, they really do become oligarchs—not from choice, though, but because the drone, by stinging them, engenders this evil.

ADEIMANTUS: Absolutely.

SOCRATES: Then there are impeachments, judgments, and trials on both sides.

ADEIMANTUS: Right.

SOCRATES: And don't the people always tend to set up one man as their special leader, nurturing him and making him great?

ADEIMANTUS: Yes.

565d SOCRATES: And it is clear that when a tyrant arises, the position of popular leader is the sole root from which he springs.

ADEIMANTUS: It is.

SOCRATES: What is the beginning, then, of the transformation from popular leader to tyrant? Isn't it clear that it happens when the popular leader begins to behave like the character in the story told about the temple of the Lycaean Zeus[16] in Arcadia?

ADEIMANTUS: What story?

SOCRATES: That whoever tastes the one piece of human innards cut up with those of all the other sacrificial victims inevitably becomes a wolf. Haven't
565e you heard that story?

ADEIMANTUS: I have.

SOCRATES: Isn't it the same, then, with a popular leader? Once he really takes over a docile mob, he does not restrain himself from shedding a fellow citizen's blood. But by leveling the usual false charges and bringing people into court, he commits murder. And by blotting out a man's life, his impious tongue and lips taste kindred blood. Then he banishes and kills and
566a drops hints about the cancellation of debts and the redistribution of land. And after that, isn't such a man inevitably fated either to be killed by his enemies or to be a tyrant, transformed from a man into a wolf?

ADEIMANTUS: Yes. That is the inevitable outcome.

SOCRATES: He is the one, then, who stirs up faction against the rich.

ADEIMANTUS: He is.

SOCRATES: And if he happens to be exiled but, despite his enemies, manages to return, doesn't he come back as a full-fledged tyrant?

ADEIMANTUS: Obviously.

SOCRATES: And if they are unable to expel him or put him to death by
566b accusing him before the city, they plot a violent death for him by covert means.

ADEIMANTUS: That's what tends to happen, anyway.

---

[16] Zeus the wolf-god.

SOCRATES: And everyone who has reached this stage soon discovers the famous tyrannical request—to ask the people to give him a bodyguard to keep their popular leader safe for them.

ADEIMANTUS: Right.

SOCRATES: And the people give it to him, I suppose, fearing for his safety but confident of their own.

ADEIMANTUS: Right.

SOCRATES: So, when a wealthy man sees this and is charged with being an enemy of the people because of his wealth, then, comrade, in the words of the oracle to Croesus, he "flees without delay to the banks of the many-pebbled Hermus, and is not ashamed at all of his cowardice."[17]   566c

ADEIMANTUS: He would certainly never get a second chance to be ashamed!

SOCRATES: If he is caught, I would imagine he is put to death.

ADEIMANTUS: Inevitably.

SOCRATES: As for this popular leader of ours, he clearly does not lie on the ground "mighty in his might,"[18] but, having brought down all those others, he stands in the chariot of the city as a complete tyrant instead of a popular leader.   566d

ADEIMANTUS: That's for sure.

SOCRATES: Shall we next describe the happiness of this man and of the city in which such a creature arises?

ADEIMANTUS: Yes, let's.

SOCRATES: To start with, in the early days of his reign, won't he greet everyone he meets with a smile, deny he is a tyrant, promise all sorts of things in private and in public, free the people from debt, redistribute the land to them and to his followers, and pretend to be gracious and gentle to all?   566e

ADEIMANTUS: Inevitably.

SOCRATES: But once he has dealt with his exiled enemies by making peace with some and destroying others, and all is calm on that front, his primary concern, I imagine, is to be constantly stirring up some war or other, so that the people will need a leader.

ADEIMANTUS: Very likely.

SOCRATES: And also, wouldn't you say, so that impoverished by war taxes, they will be compelled to concentrate on their daily needs and be less likely to plot against him?   567a

---

[17] The story of the Delphic oracle to Croesus is found in Herodotus, *Histories* i.55.

[18] See *Iliad* xvi.776.

ADEIMANTUS: Clearly.

SOCRATES: And in addition, I suppose, so that if there are some freethinking people he suspects of rejecting his rule, he can find pretexts for putting them at the mercy of the enemy and destroying them? For all these reasons, isn't a tyrant compelled to be always stirring up war?

ADEIMANTUS: He is.

SOCRATES: Don't all these actions tend to make him more hateful to the citizens?

ADEIMANTUS: Of course.

567b   SOCRATES: And don't some of those who helped establish his tyranny and hold positions of power within it, the ones who are bravest, speak freely to him and to each other, criticizing what is happening?

ADEIMANTUS: Probably.

SOCRATES: Then the tyrant will have to do away with all of them if he intends to rule, until he is left with no friend or enemy who is worth anything at all.

ADEIMANTUS: Obviously.

SOCRATES: He will have to keep a sharp lookout, then, for anyone who
567c   is brave, magnanimous, wise, or rich. He is so happy, you see, that he is compelled, whether he wants to or not, to be their enemy and plot against all of them until he has purged the city.

ADEIMANTUS: A fine purge that is!

SOCRATES: Yes. The opposite of the one doctors perform on our bodies. They draw off the worst and leave the best, whereas he does just the opposite!

ADEIMANTUS: Yet that's what he has to do, it seems, if he is to rule.

SOCRATES: It is a blessedly happy compulsion he is bound by, then, which
567d   requires him to live with inferior masses even though hated by them, or not live at all!

ADEIMANTUS: It is.

SOCRATES: And the more he makes the citizens hate him by doing those things, the larger and more trustworthy a bodyguard he will need, won't he?

ADEIMANTUS: Of course.

SOCRATES: And who will these trustworthy people be? And from where will he get them?

ADEIMANTUS: Lots of them will come swarming of their own accord, if he pays them wages.

SOCRATES: Drones again, by the dog![19] That is what I think you are talking about. Foreign, multifarious ones!   567e

ADEIMANTUS: Yes, you are right.

SOCRATES: What about the domestic ones? Wouldn't he be willing to deprive citizens of their slaves somehow, set them free, and enlist them in his bodyguard?

ADEIMANTUS: He certainly would, since they are the ones he can trust the most.

SOCRATES: What a blessedly happy thing this tyrant business is on your view, if these are the sorts of friends and trusted men he must employ after destroying his former ones!   **568a**

ADEIMANTUS: Nonetheless, they are the sorts he does employ.

SOCRATES: And these friends and new citizens admire and associate with him, whereas the good ones hate and avoid him?

ADEIMANTUS: Of course.

SOCRATES: It is no wonder, then, that tragedy seems to be something wholly wise, or that Euripides is outstanding in it.

ADEIMANTUS: Why is that?

SOCRATES: Because, among other things, he expressed the following shrewd thought: "tyrants are wise by associating with the wise." He meant evi-   568b dently that these associates of the tyrant are the wise ones.[20]

ADEIMANTUS: Yes. And he also praises tyranny as godlike, and lots of other things besides—and the other poets do, too.

SOCRATES: Then surely, since the tragic poets are so wise, they will forgive us and those with constitutions like ours if we do not admit them into our city, since they hymn the praises of tyranny.

ADEIMANTUS: For my part, I think they will forgive us—the more refined of them, anyway.   568c

SOCRATES: They can go around to all the other cities instead, I suppose, drawing large crowds and hiring actors with fine, loud, persuasive voices, and lead their constitutions to become tyrannies and democracies.

ADEIMANTUS: Yes, indeed.

SOCRATES: What's more, they are paid wages and honored for it, primarily—as one might expect—by tyrants and secondly by democracy. But the

---

[19] See 399e note.

[20] The fragment is from an unknown play. Euripides meant that tyrants gain wisdom from the wise people who, as Simonides said, "knock at the doors of the rich"(489b). Plato twists his words to mean that the drones and slaves, who are the tyrant's last resort, are wise, since they associate with him.

568d higher they go on the ascending scale of constitutions, the more their honor diminishes, as if unable to proceed for lack of breath.

ADEIMANTUS: Absolutely.

SOCRATES: But all that is a digression. Let's return to our tyrant's camp—the one that is beautiful, populous, complex, and never the same—and ask how he is going to maintain it.

ADEIMANTUS: If there are sacred treasuries in the city, he will obviously use them for as long as they last, as well as the property of those he has 568e destroyed, so the taxes he will require from the people will be smaller.

SOCRATES: What about when these resources give out?

ADEIMANTUS: Clearly, his father's estate will have to support him, his drinking companions, and his boyfriends and girlfriends, too.

SOCRATES: I understand. You mean the people who fathered the tyrant will have to support him and his friends.

ADEIMANTUS: They will have no choice.

SOCRATES: What if the people get irritated and say it is not just for a grown-up son to be supported by his father? On the contrary, the father should be 569a supported by his son. They did not father him and establish him in power, they say, so that, when he had become strong, they would be enslaved to their own slave and have to support him, his slaves, and other assorted rabble as well; but so that, with him as their popular leader, they would get free from the rule of the rich and the so-called fine and good people in the city. At that point, they order him and his friends to leave the city, as a father might drive a son and his troublesome drinking companions from his house. What do you think would happen then?

569b ADEIMANTUS: Then, by Zeus, the people will soon learn what kind of creature they have fathered, welcomed, and made strong, and that it is a case of the weaker trying to drive out the stronger.

SOCRATES: What do you mean? Will the tyrant dare to use force against his father or hit him if he does not obey?

ADEIMANTUS: Yes—once he has taken away his weapons.

SOCRATES: A tyrant is a parricide as you describe him, then, and a harsh nurse of old age; and we do now seem to have an acknowledged tyranny. And so the people, by trying to avoid the proverbial frying pan of enslave-569c ment to free men, have fallen into the fire of having slaves as their masters; and, in exchange for the excessive and inappropriate freedom they had before, have put upon themselves the harshest and most bitter slavery to slaves.

ADEIMANTUS: That's exactly what happens.

SOCRATES: Well, then, wouldn't we be justified in saying that we have adequately described how tyranny evolves from democracy, and what it is like once it has come to exist?

ADEIMANTUS: We would. Our description was entirely adequate.

BOOK IX

SOCRATES' NARRATION CONTINUES:

SOCRATES: The tyrannical man himself remains to be investigated: how he evolves from a democratic one, what he is like once he has come to exist, and whether the way he lives is wretched or blessedly happy.   571a

ADEIMANTUS: Yes, he still remains.

SOCRATES: Do you know what else I still miss?

ADEIMANTUS: What?

SOCRATES: I do not think we have adequately distinguished the nature and number of our appetites. And if that subject is not adequately dealt with, our investigation will lack clarity.

ADEIMANTUS: Well, isn't now as fine a time as any?   571b

SOCRATES: It certainly is. So, consider what I want to look at in them. It is this: among unnecessary pleasures and appetites, there are some that seem to me to be lawless. These are probably present in all of us, but they are held in check by the laws and by our better appetites allied with reason. In a few people they have been gotten rid of entirely or only a few weak ones remain, while in others they are stronger and more numerous.   571c

ADEIMANTUS: Which ones do you mean?

SOCRATES: The ones that wake up when we are asleep, whenever the rest of the soul—the rational, gentle, and ruling element—slumbers. Then the bestial and savage element, full of food or drink, comes alive, casts off sleep, and seeks to go and gratify its own characteristic instincts. You know it will dare to do anything in such a state, released and freed from all shame and wisdom. In fantasy, it does not shrink from trying to have sex with a   571d
mother or with anyone else—man, god, or beast. It will commit any foul murder, and there is no food it refuses to eat. In a word, it does not refrain from anything, no matter how foolish or shameful.

ADEIMANTUS: That's absolutely true.

SOCRATES: On the other hand, I suppose someone who keeps himself healthy and temperate will awaken his rational element before going to sleep and feast it on fine arguments and investigations, which he has brought to an agreed conclusion within himself. As for the appetitive element, he neither starves nor overfeeds it, so it will slumber and not disturb   571e

572a the best element with its pleasure or pain but will leave it alone, just by itself and pure, to investigate and reach out for the perception of something—whether past, present, or future—that it does not know. He soothes the spirited element in a similar way and does not get angry and fall asleep with his spirit still aroused. And when he has calmed these two elements and stimulated the third, in which wisdom resides, he takes his rest. You know this is the state in which he most readily grasps the truth and in which the visions appearing in his dreams are least lawless.

572b ADEIMANTUS: I completely agree.

SOCRATES: Well, we have been led a bit astray and said a bit too much. What we want to pay attention to is this: there are appetites of a terrible, savage, and lawless kind in everyone—even in those of us who seem to be entirely moderate. This surely becomes clear in sleep. Do you think I am talking sense? Do you agree with me?

ADEIMANTUS: Yes, I do agree.

SOCRATES: Now, recall what we said the democratic man is like.[1] He was
572c the result, we presumed, of a childhood upbringing by a thrifty father who honored only appetites that made money and despised the unnecessary ones whose objects are amusement and showing off. Isn't that right?

ADEIMANTUS: Yes.

SOCRATES: And by associating with more sophisticated men who are full of the appetites we just described, he starts to indulge in every kind of arrogance and adopt their kind of behavior, because of his hatred of his father's thrift. But, since he has a better nature than his corrupters, he is
572d pulled in both directions and settles in the middle between their two ways of life. And enjoying each in what he takes to be moderation, he lives a life that is neither illiberal nor lawless, transformed now from an oligarch to a democrat.

ADEIMANTUS: Yes, that was—and still is—our belief about someone like that.

SOCRATES: Suppose, then, that this man has now in turn become older and has a son who is also brought up in his father's way of life.

ADEIMANTUS: I will.

SOCRATES: Suppose, too, that the same things happen to him as happened to his father: he is led into all the kinds of lawlessness that those leading him
572e call total freedom. His father and the rest of his family come to the aid of the appetites that are in the middle, while the others help the opposite ones. And when these terrible enchanters and tyrant-makers have no hope of keeping hold of the young man in any other way, they contrive to implant

---

[1] 558c–562a.

a powerful passion in him as the popular leader of those idle and profligate appetites—a sort-of great, winged drone. Or do you think passion is ever **573a** anything else in such people?

ADEIMANTUS: I certainly do not think it is.

SOCRATES: And when the other appetites come buzzing around—filled with incense, perfumes, wreaths, wine, and all the other pleasures found in such company, they feed the drone, make it grow as large as possible, and plant the sting of longing in it. Then this popular leader of the soul adopts madness as its bodyguard and is stung to frenzy. If it finds any beliefs or **573b** appetites in the man that are regarded as good or are still moved by shame, it destroys them and throws them out, until it has purged him of temperance and filled him with imported madness.

ADEIMANTUS: You have perfectly described how a tyrannical man comes to exist.

SOCRATES: Is that, then, why Passion has long been called a tyrant?

ADEIMANTUS: Probably so.

SOCRATES: And hasn't a drunken man, my friend, something of a tyrannical cast of mind, too?   **573c**

ADEIMANTUS: He has.

SOCRATES: And of course someone who is mad and deranged attempts to rule not only human beings, but gods as well, and expects to be able to rule them.

ADEIMANTUS: Of course.

SOCRATES: A man becomes tyrannical in the precise sense, then, you marvelous fellow, when his nature or his practices or both together lead him to drunkenness, passion, and melancholia.

ADEIMANTUS: Absolutely.

SOCRATES: So, that, it seems, is how a tyrannical man comes to exist. Now, what is his life like?

ADEIMANTUS: Why don't *you* tell *me*, as askers of riddles usually do?   **573d**

SOCRATES: I will tell you. You see, I think someone in whom the tyrant of Passion dwells, and in whom it serves as captain of everything in the soul, next goes in for festivals, revelries, luxuries, girlfriends, and all that sort of thing.

ADEIMANTUS: Inevitably.

SOCRATES: And don't lots of terrible appetites sprout up each day and night beside it, creating needs for all sorts of things?

ADEIMANTUS: Indeed, they do.

SOCRATES: So, any income someone like that has is soon spent.

ADEIMANTUS: Of course.

SOCRATES: And the next thing, surely, is borrowing and expenditure of
573e   capital.

ADEIMANTUS: What else?

SOCRATES: And when everything is gone, won't the violent crowd of appetites that have nested within him inevitably shout in protest? And when
people of this sort are driven by the stings of these other appetites, but
particularly of Passion itself, which leads all the others as if they were its
bodyguard, stung to frenzy, don't they look to see who possesses anything
574a   that can be taken from him by deceit or force?

ADEIMANTUS: Certainly.

SOCRATES: He must take it from every source, then, or live in great suffering and pain.

ADEIMANTUS: He must.

SOCRATES: And just as the late-coming pleasures within him do better than
the older ones and steal away their satisfactions, won't he himself, young
as he is, think he deserves to do better than his father and mother? And if
he has spent his own share, won't he try to take some of his father's wealth
by converting it to his own use?

ADEIMANTUS: Of course.

SOCRATES: And if his parents resist him, won't he first try to steal it and
574b   deceive them?

ADEIMANTUS: Certainly.

SOCRATES: And if he cannot, won't he next try to seize it by force?

ADEIMANTUS: I suppose so.

SOCRATES: And if, you amazing man, the old man and woman stand their
ground and put up a fight, would he take care and be reluctant to act like
a tyrant?

ADEIMANTUS: I am not very optimistic about the parents of someone like
that!

SOCRATES: But in the name of Zeus, Adeimantus, do you really think that
574c   for the sake of his latest love, an unnecessary girlfriend, he would strike
his mother, who is his oldest and necessary friend? Or that for the sake
of his latest and unnecessary boyfriend, who is in the bloom of youth, he
would strike his aged and necessary father, the oldest of his friends, who is
no longer in the bloom of youth? Or that he would enslave his parents to
them, if he brought them into the same house?

ADEIMANTUS: Yes, by Zeus, he would.

SOCRATES: It seems to be a great blessing to produce a tyrannical son!

ADEIMANTUS: It certainly does!

SOCRATES: What happens to someone like that when the possessions of his 574d
father and mother give out and the swarm of pleasures now inside him has
grown dense? Won't he first try to break into someone's house or snatch
the cloak of someone walking late at night? Next, won't he try to clean out
some temple? And in the course of all that, his old childhood beliefs about
fine or shameful things—beliefs that are accounted just—are mastered by
the new ones that have been released from slavery and, as the bodyguard of
Passion, hold sway along with it. These are the ones that used to be freed
in sleep as a dream, when he himself, since he was still subject to the laws
and his father, had a democratic constitution within him. But under the 574e
tyranny of Passion, what he used to become occasionally in his dreams
he has now become permanently while awake, and so there is no terrible
murder, no food, and no act from which he will refrain. On the contrary, 575a
Passion lives like a tyrant within him in complete anarchy and lawlessness,
as his sole ruler, and drives him, as if he were a city, to dare anything that
will provide sustenance for itself and the unruly mob around it—some of
which have come in from the outside as a result of his bad associates, while
others have come from within, freed and let loose by his own bad habits.
Isn't this the life such a man leads?

ADEIMANTUS: It is.

SOCRATES: And if there are only a few men like that in a city, and the 575b
majority of the others are temperate, they emigrate in order to become the
bodyguard of some other tyrant or serve as paid auxiliaries if there happens
to be a war somewhere. But if they chance to live in a time of peace and
calm, they stay right there in the city and cause lots of little evils.

ADEIMANTUS: What sort of evils do you mean?

SOCRATES: They steal, break into houses, snatch purses, steal clothes, rob
temples, and kidnap people. Sometimes, if they are capable speakers, they
become sycophants and bear false witness and accept bribes.

ADEIMANTUS: You mean they are small evils—provided there are only a
few such people.

SOCRATES: Yes. After all, small evils are small by comparison to great ones. 575c
And when it comes to producing corruption and misery in a city, all these
evils together do not—as the saying goes—come within a mile of a tyrant.
But when you get a great number of these people and their followers in a
city, and they become aware of their numbers, they are the ones who—
together with the foolishness of the people—create the tyrant out of the
one among them who has in his soul the greatest and strongest tyrant of all.

ADEIMANTUS: Naturally, since he would be the most tyrannical. 575d

SOCRATES: That's if they submit willingly. But if the city doesn't put itself in
his hands, then just as he once chastised his mother and father, he will now

punish his fatherland in the same way, if he can, bringing in new friends and making and keeping his once beloved motherland—as the Cretans call it—or fatherland their slaves. And that is surely the end at which the appetites of a man like that aim.

ADEIMANTUS: It most certainly is.

SOCRATES: So, isn't this what such men are like in private life, before they start to rule? In the first place, don't they associate with flatterers who are ready to do anything to serve them? Or, if they need something from someone themselves, won't they grovel and willingly engage in any sort of posturing, the way slaves do? But once they get what they need, isn't it a different story altogether?

ADEIMANTUS: Yes, completely different.

SOCRATES: So, those with a tyrannical nature live their entire lives without ever being friends with anyone, always masters to one man or slaves to another, but never getting a taste of freedom or true friendship.

ADEIMANTUS: Exactly.

SOCRATES: Wouldn't we be right to call people like that untrustworthy?

ADEIMANTUS: Of course.

SOCRATES: And as unjust as anyone can be—assuming we were right in our earlier conclusions about what justice is like.

ADEIMANTUS: And we certainly were right.

SOCRATES: Let's sum up the worst type of man, then. He is surely the one who, when awake, is like the dreaming person we described earlier.[2]

ADEIMANTUS: Exactly.

SOCRATES: And he evolves from someone who, since he is by nature most tyrannical, achieves sole rule. And the longer he lives as tyrant, the more like that he becomes. "Inevitably," said Glaucon, taking over the argument.

SOCRATES: Well, then, won't the one who is plainly worst also be plainly most wretched? And the one who for the longest time is most a tyrant, won't he also be most wretched for the longest time, if truth be told? Though the views of the masses [the many] on the subject are naturally also many.

GLAUCON: All that, at any rate, must be true.

SOCRATES: Doesn't a tyrannical man correspond to and most resemble a city ruled by a tyrant, a democratic man a democratically ruled city, and similarly with the others?

GLAUCON: Of course.

---

[2] See 571c–d.

SOCRATES: And the comparison between city and city, as regards their virtue and happiness, isn't it the same as the comparison between man and man? 576d

GLAUCON: Certainly.

SOCRATES: As regards virtue, then, how does a city ruled by a tyrant compare to a city of the sort we described first that is ruled by a king?

GLAUCON: They are absolute opposites: one is the best, and the other is the worst.

SOCRATES: I won't ask you which is which, since it is obvious. But as regards happiness and wretchedness, is your judgment the same or different? And let's not become dazzled by looking at the tyrant—since he is just one man—or at the few who surround him. Instead, as is necessary, let's go in and study the city as a whole and, when we have gone down and looked into every corner, only then present what we believe. 576e

GLAUCON: That's a good suggestion. And it is clear to everyone that there is no city more wretched than a tyrannical one and none happier than one ruled by a king.

SOCRATES: Would it also be right, then, to suggest the same thing about the **577a** men—that the only fit judge of them is someone who can, in thought, go down into a man's character and discern it—not someone who sees it from the outside, the way a child does, and is dazzled by the façade that tyrants adopt for the outside world, but someone who discerns it adequately? And what if I were to assume that the person we must all listen to is the one who has this capacity to judge; who has lived in the same house as a tyrant and witnessed his behavior at home; who has seen how he deals with each member of his household, when he can best be observed stripped of his 577b tragic costume; and who has also seen how he deals with public dangers? Shouldn't we ask the one who has seen all that to tell us how the tyrant compares to the others with respect to happiness and wretchedness?

GLAUCON: That's also a very good suggestion.

SOCRATES: Then, in order to have someone to answer our questions, do you want us to pretend that we are among the ones who can make such a judgment, and that we have met tyrannical people already?

GLAUCON: I certainly do.

SOCRATES: Come on, then, and examine the matter like this for me. Bearing in mind the resemblance between the city and the man, examine each in turn and describe its condition. 577c

GLAUCON: What kinds of things do you want me to describe?

SOCRATES: Describe the city first. Would you say that a tyrannical city is free or enslaved?

GLAUCON: As enslaved as it is possible to be.

SOCRATES: Yet you can surely see masters and free people in it.

GLAUCON: I can certainly see a small group of people like that. But pretty much the whole population, and the best part of it, is shamefully and wretchedly enslaved.

577d   SOCRATES: If a man and his city are similar, then, mustn't the same structure exist in him, too? Mustn't his soul be full of slavery and illiberality, with those same parts of it enslaved, while a small part, the most wicked and most insane, is master?

GLAUCON: It must.

SOCRATES: Will you describe such a soul as enslaved, then, or as free?

GLAUCON: Enslaved, of course.

SOCRATES: And, to go back, isn't the enslaved, tyrannical city least able to do what it wishes?

GLAUCON: By far the least.

SOCRATES: So, a tyrannical soul will also least do what it wishes—I am
577e   talking about the soul as a whole—and will be full of disorder and regret, since it is always forcibly driven by a gadfly.

GLAUCON: Of course.

SOCRATES: Rich or poor? Which must a tyrannical city be?

GLAUCON: Poor.

578a   SOCRATES: So, a tyrannical soul, too, must always be poor and insatiable.

GLAUCON: It must.

SOCRATES: What about fear? Mustn't a city of this sort and a man of this sort be filled with it?

GLAUCON: They certainly must.

SOCRATES: And do you think you will find more wailing, groaning, lamenting, or painful suffering in any other city?

GLAUCON: No.

SOCRATES: What about in a man? Do you think such things are more common in anyone than in this tyrannical man, maddened by his appetites and passions?

GLAUCON: How could I?

SOCRATES: I imagine it is in view of all these things, then, as well as others
578b   like them, that you judged this city to be the most wretched of cities.

GLAUCON: And wasn't I right?

SOCRATES: Yes, of course. But how, again, do you describe the tyrannical man in view of these same things?

GLAUCON: He is by far the most wretched of them all.

SOCRATES: There your description is no longer right.

GLAUCON: How so?

SOCRATES: This man, I think, is not yet the most wretched.

GLAUCON: Then who is?

SOCRATES: Presumably, you will regard this next one as even more wretched.

GLAUCON: What one?

SOCRATES: The tyrannical man who does not live out his life as a private individual, but is unlucky, in that some misfortune gives him the opportunity of becoming an actual tyrant. 578c

GLAUCON: On the basis of what we have already said, I infer that what you are saying is true.

SOCRATES: Yes. But it is not good enough to believe these claims; one must carefully examine someone like that by means of argument. After all, the investigation concerns the greatest thing—a good life and a bad one.

GLAUCON: That's absolutely right.

SOCRATES: So, consider, then, whether there is anything in what I say. You see, I think we should investigate him on the basis of the following. 578d

GLAUCON: What?

SOCRATES: On the basis of each and every one of the wealthy private citizens in our cities who own many slaves. For they resemble a tyrant in ruling over many, although the number ruled by the tyrant is different.

GLAUCON: It is different.

SOCRATES: You know, then, that these people feel secure and do not fear their slaves.

GLAUCON: Of what have they to be afraid, after all?

SOCRATES: Nothing. But do you know why?

GLAUCON: Yes. Because the whole city is ready to defend each of its private citizens.

SOCRATES: That's right. But now, suppose some god were to lift one of these men, who has fifty or more slaves, out of the city, and put him down—with his wife, his children, his slaves, and his other property—in a deserted place, where no free men could come to his assistance? Can you imagine the sort and amount of fear he would feel that he and his wife and children would be killed by his slaves? 578e

GLAUCON: It would be huge, if you ask me.

SOCRATES: Wouldn't he at that point be compelled to start fawning on some of his slaves, promising them all sorts of things and setting them free—even though there was nothing he wanted to do less—and wouldn't he turn out to be a flatterer of slaves? 579a

GLAUCON: He would have to be. Otherwise, he would be killed.

SOCRATES: Now, suppose the god were to settle many other neighbors around him who would not tolerate anyone claiming to be master of another, but if they caught such a person, would inflict the most extreme punishments on him?

GLAUCON: I suppose he would be in even worse trouble, since he would 579b be surrounded by nothing but enemies.

SOCRATES: So, isn't this, then, the kind of prison in which the tyrant is held—the one whose nature we have described, filled with multifarious fears and passions? Though his soul is really greedy, he is the only one in the city who cannot go abroad or look at the sights at which other free people yearn to look. Instead, he is mostly stuck in house, living like a 579c woman, envying any other citizen who goes abroad and sees some good thing.

GLAUCON: Absolutely.

SOCRATES: Isn't such a harvest of evils, then, a measure of the difference between a tyrannical man who is badly governed politically on the inside— whom you judged just now to be most wretched—and one who does not live out his life as a private individual, but is compelled by some chance to become an actual tyrant and try to rule others, when he cannot even master himself? It is as if someone with a body that is sick and cannot master itself 579d were compelled, not to spend his life in private pursuits, but to compete and fight with other bodies.

GLAUCON: That's exactly what he is like. Your description is absolutely true, Socrates.

SOCRATES: And so, my dear Glaucon, isn't his condition completely wretched, and isn't the life of a tyrant even harsher than the one you judged to be harshest?

GLAUCON: It certainly is.

SOCRATES: So, in truth, then, and whatever some people may think, a real tyrant is really a slave to the worst sorts of fawning and slavery, and a flat- 579e terer of the worst kind of people. He is so far from satisfying his appetites in any way that he is in the greatest need of most things and truly poor—as is apparent if one knows how to look at a whole soul. He is full of fear throughout his life and overflowing with convulsions and pains, if in fact his condition is like that of the city he rules. And it is like it, isn't it?

GLAUCON: Yes, of course.

580a SOCRATES: And, in addition, shouldn't we also attribute to the man the qualities we mentioned earlier? We said that he is inevitably envious, untrustworthy, unjust, friendless, impious, and a host and nurse to every kind of vice; that ruling makes him even more so than before; and that, as a consequence, he is extremely unfortunate and goes on to make those near him so.

GLAUCON: No one with any sense could possibly contradict that.

SOCRATES: Come on, then, and tell me now at last, like the judge who makes the final decision,[3] who you believe is first in happiness and who second, and judge the others similarly, making five altogether—kingly, timocratic, oligarchic, democratic, tyrannical.

580b

GLAUCON: That's an easy judgment. You see, I rank them in the order of their appearance, just as if they were choruses, both in virtue and vice and in happiness and its opposite.

SOCRATES: Shall we, then, hire a herald, or shall I myself announce that the son of Ariston has given as his verdict that the best and most just is the most happy, and that he is the one who is most kingly and rules like a king over himself; whereas the worst and most unjust is the most wretched, and he, again, is the one who, because he is most tyrannical, is the greatest tyrant over himself and his city?

580c

GLAUCON: You have announced it!

SOCRATES: And shall I add that it holds whether or not their characters remain hidden from all human beings and gods?

GLAUCON: Do add it.

SOCRATES: Well, then, that is one of our demonstrations. But look at this second one and see if you think there is anything in it.

GLAUCON: What is it?

580d

SOCRATES: In just the way a city is divided into three classes, the soul of each person is also divided in three. That is the reason I think there is another demonstration.

GLAUCON: What is it?

SOCRATES: The following. It seems to me that the three also have three kinds of pleasure, one peculiar to each, and the same holds of appetites and kinds of rule.

GLAUCON: How do you mean?

SOCRATES: One element, we say, is that with which a person learns; another, that with which he feels anger. As for the third, because it is multiform, we had no one special name for it but named it after the greatest and strongest thing it has in it. I mean we called it the appetitive element because of the intensity of its appetites for food, drink, sex, and all the things that go

580e

---

[3] The reference is to the way plays were judged at dramatic festivals in Athens. A herald announced the results.

581a along with them. We also called it the money-loving element, because such appetites are most easily satisfied by means of money.

GLAUCON: And we were right.

SOCRATES: So, if we said its pleasure and love are for profit, wouldn't that best bring it together under one heading for the purposes of our argument and make clear to us what we mean when we speak of this part of the soul? And would we be right in calling it money-loving and profit-loving?

GLAUCON: I think so, anyway.

SOCRATES: What about the spirited element? Don't we say that its whole
581b aim is always mastery, victory, and high repute?

GLAUCON: Certainly.

SOCRATES: Then wouldn't it strike the right note for us to call it victory-loving and honor-loving?

GLAUCON: The absolutely right one.

SOCRATES: But surely it is clear to everyone that the element we learn with is always wholly straining to know where the truth lies, and that of the three it cares least for money and reputation.

GLAUCON: By far the least.

SOCRATES: Wouldn't it be appropriate, then, for us to call it learning-loving and philosophic?

GLAUCON: Of course.

581c SOCRATES: And doesn't it rule in some people's souls, while one of the others—whichever it happens to be—rules in other people's?

GLAUCON: Yes.

SOCRATES: And isn't that why we say there are three primary types of people, philosophic, victory-loving, and profit-loving?

GLAUCON: Absolutely.

SOCRATES: And also three kinds of pleasure, one assigned to each of them?

GLAUCON: Exactly.

SOCRATES: You realize, then, that if you chose to ask each of these three types of people in turn to tell you which of their lives is most pleasant, each would give the highest praise to his own? Won't the moneymaker say that,
581d compared to that of making a profit, the pleasures of being honored or of learning are worthless unless there is something in them that makes money?

GLAUCON: True.

SOCRATES: What about the honor-lover? Doesn't he think the pleasure of making money is vulgar, while the pleasure of learning—except to the extent that learning brings honor—is smoke and nonsense?

GLAUCON: He does.

SOCRATES: As for the philosopher, what do you suppose he thinks of the other pleasures in comparison to that of knowing where the truth lies and always enjoying some variety of it while he is learning? Won't he think they are far behind? And won't he call them really necessary, since he would 581e have no need for them if they were not necessary for life?

GLAUCON: He will. We can be sure of that.

SOCRATES: Since the pleasures of each kind and the lives themselves dispute with one another—not about which life is finer or more shameful or better or worse—but about which is more pleasant and less painful, how are we to know which of them is speaking the absolute truth? 582a

GLAUCON: I have no idea how to answer that.

SOCRATES: Consider the matter this way: how should we judge things if we want to judge them well? Isn't it by experience, knowledge, and argument? Or could someone have better criteria than these?

GLAUCON: No, of course not.

SOCRATES: Consider, then. Of the three types of men, which has most experience of the pleasures we mentioned? Do you think the profit-lover learns what the truth itself is like, or has more experience of the pleasure of knowing, than the philosopher does of making a profit? 582b

GLAUCON: There is a great difference between them. You see, the latter has to have tasted the other kinds of pleasure beginning from childhood. But it is not necessary for the profit-lover to taste or experience how sweet is the pleasure of learning the nature of the things that are—and even if he were eager to, he could not easily do so.

SOCRATES: So, the philosopher is far superior to the profit-lover in his experience of both kinds of pleasures.

GLAUCON: Very far superior. 582c

SOCRATES: What about compared to the honor-lover? Is he more inexperienced in the pleasure of being honored than the latter is in the pleasure of knowing?

GLAUCON: No. Honor comes to all of them, provided they accomplish their several aims. For the rich man, too, is honored by many people, as well as are the courageous and the wise ones. So, all have experienced what the pleasure of being honored is like. But the pleasure pertaining to the sight of what is cannot be tasted by anyone except the philosopher.

SOCRATES: So, as far as experience goes, then, he is the finest judge among the three types of men. 582d

GLAUCON: By far.

SOCRATES: And he alone will have gained his experience with the help of knowledge.

GLAUCON: Of course.

SOCRATES: Moreover, the tool that should be used to judge is not the tool of the profit-lover or the honor-lover, but of the philosopher.

GLAUCON: What one is that?

SOCRATES: Surely we said that judgment should be made by means of arguments. Didn't we?

GLAUCON: Yes.

SOCRATES: And arguments are, above all, his tool.

GLAUCON: Absolutely.

582e SOCRATES: If the things being judged were best judged by means of wealth and profit, the praise and criticism of the profit-lover would necessarily be closest to the truth.

GLAUCON: It would indeed.

SOCRATES: And if by means of honor, victory, and courage, wouldn't it be those of the honor-lover and victory-lover?

GLAUCON: Clearly.

SOCRATES: But since it is by means of experience, knowledge, and argument?

GLAUCON: The praise of the philosopher and argument-lover must be closest to the truth.

583a SOCRATES: So, of the three pleasures, then, the most pleasant would be that of the part of the soul with which we learn, and the one of us in whom it rules has the most pleasant life.

GLAUCON: How could it be otherwise? The knowledgeable person at least praises with authority when he praises his own life.

SOCRATES: What life and pleasure does the judge say are in second place?

GLAUCON: Clearly, those of the warrior and honor-lover, since they are closer to his own than those of the moneymaker.

SOCRATES: Then those of the profit-lover come last, apparently.

GLAUCON: Of course.

583b SOCRATES: Well, then, that makes two in a row. And twice the just person has defeated the unjust one. Now comes the third, which is dedicated in Olympic fashion to our savior, Olympian Zeus.[4] Observe, then, that the other pleasures—apart from that of the knowledgeable person—are neither entirely true nor pure. On the contrary, they are like some sort of illusionist painting, as I think I have heard some wise person say. Yet, if that were true, it would be the greatest and most decisive of the overthrows.

---

[4] The first toast at a banquet was to the Olympian Zeus, the third to our savior, Zeus. By combining both in a single form of address, Plato seems to be emphasizing the importance of this final proof.

GLAUCON: By far the greatest. But what exactly do you mean?

SOCRATES: I will find out, if you answer the questions while I ask them.   583c

GLAUCON: Start asking, then.

SOCRATES: Tell me, then, don't we say that pain is the opposite of pleasure?

GLAUCON: Yes.

SOCRATES: Isn't there also a state of feeling neither enjoyment nor pain?

GLAUCON: There is.

SOCRATES: Isn't it in the middle between these two, a sort of quiet state of the soul where they are concerned? Or wouldn't you describe it that way?

GLAUCON: I would.

SOCRATES: So then do you recall the sorts of things ill people say when they are ill?

GLAUCON: Which ones?

SOCRATES: That nothing is more pleasant than being healthy, but they had not realized it was most pleasant until they fell ill.   583d

GLAUCON: I do remember that.

SOCRATES: Don't you also hear people who are in great pain saying that nothing is more pleasant than the cessation of one's suffering?

GLAUCON: I do.

SOCRATES: And there are many similar circumstances, I presume, in which you see people in pain praising not enjoyment, but freedom from pain, and respite from that sort of thing, as most pleasant.

GLAUCON: Yes. For at such times, the respite presumably becomes pleasant enough to content them.

SOCRATES: And when someone ceases to enjoy something, this respite from pleasure will be painful.   583e

GLAUCON: Presumably.

SOCRATES: So, the quiet state we just now described as being in between the two will sometimes be both pain and pleasure.

GLAUCON: Apparently.

SOCRATES: And is it possible for what is neither to become both?

GLAUCON: Not in my view.

SOCRATES: Furthermore, when what is pleasant and what is painful arise in the soul, they are both a sort of motion, aren't they?

GLAUCON: Yes.

SOCRATES: And didn't we see just now that what is neither painful nor pleasant is a respite and in the middle between the two?   584a

GLAUCON: Yes, we did.

SOCRATES: How can it be right, then, to think that the absence of pain is pleasant or the absence of enjoyment painful?

GLAUCON: There's no way it can be.

SOCRATES: So, it is not right. But when the quiet state is next to what is painful, it appears pleasant; and when it is next to what is pleasant, it appears painful. And there is nothing sound in these illusions as far as the truth about pleasure is concerned. On the contrary, they are a sort of sorcery.

GLAUCON: That's what the argument suggests, at any rate.

SOCRATES: Well, then, take a look at pleasures that do not derive from pains, so that you won't be likely to think that, *in their case,* it is the nature of pleasure to be just the cessation of pain or of pain to be just the cessation of pleasure.

GLAUCON: Where am I to look? What pleasures do you mean?

SOCRATES: There are lots of others, but you might especially want to think about the pleasures of smell. You see, without being preceded by pain, they suddenly become incredibly intense. And when they cease, they leave no pain behind.

GLAUCON: That's absolutely true.

SOCRATES: So, let's not be persuaded that pure pleasure is relief from pain, or pure pain relief from pleasure.

GLAUCON: No, let's not.

SOCRATES: However, of the things called pleasures that reach the soul through the body, pretty much the greatest number—and the most intense ones, too—are of that kind: they are some sort of relief from pains.

GLAUCON: Yes, they are.

SOCRATES: And aren't those pleasures and pains of anticipation, which arise from the expectation of future pleasures or pains, of the same kind?

GLAUCON: They are.

SOCRATES: Do you know what they are like and what they most resemble?

GLAUCON: What?

SOCRATES: Do you think there is such a thing in the natural world as an up, a down, and a middle?

GLAUCON: I do.

SOCRATES: Don't you imagine, then, that if someone were brought from down below to the middle, he would think anything other than that he was moving upward? And if he stood at the middle and saw where he had come from, could he possibly think he was anywhere other than the upper region, since he hadn't seen the one that is truly up above?

GLAUCON: By Zeus, I do not see how he could think anything else.

SOCRATES: But if he were brought back again, wouldn't he think he was being brought down? And wouldn't he be thinking the truth?

GLAUCON: Of course.

SOCRATES: And wouldn't all this happen to him because he is inexperienced in what is truly and really up, middle, and down?

GLAUCON: Clearly.

SOCRATES: Would it surprise you, then, if those who are inexperienced in the truth have unsound beliefs about lots of other things as well— that they are so disposed toward pleasure, pain, and the middle state that, whenever they descend to the painful, they think the truth and really are in pain; but that, when they ascend from the painful to the middle state, 585a they firmly think they have reached fulfillment and pleasure? Like people who compare black to gray without having experienced white, don't they compare pain to painlessness while being inexperienced in pleasure, and so get deceived?

GLAUCON: No, by Zeus, it would not surprise me! In fact, I would be very surprised if it were not like that.

SOCRATES: Think of it this way, then: Aren't hunger, thirst, and the like some sort of emptiness related to the state of the body? 585b

GLAUCON: They are.

SOCRATES: And isn't foolishness and lack of knowledge, in turn, some sort of emptiness related to the state of the soul?

GLAUCON: It certainly is.

SOCRATES: Aren't people filled when they take in nourishment or gain understanding?

GLAUCON: Of course.

SOCRATES: Does the truer filling belong to what *is* less or to what *is* more?

GLAUCON: Clearly, it belongs to what is more.

SOCRATES: Which of the two types, then, partakes more of pure being? The sorts belonging to bread, drink, relishes, and nourishment in general? Or the kind belonging to true belief, knowledge, understanding, and, in sum, 585c to all of virtue? Judge it this way: what belongs to what is always the same, immortal, and true, is itself of that sort, and comes to be in something of that sort—it *is* more, don't you think, than what belongs to what is never the same and mortal, is itself of that kind, and comes to be in something of that kind?

GLAUCON: Far more. What belongs to what is always the same is far superior.

SOCRATES: And does the being of what is always the same partake any more of being than of knowledge?

GLAUCON: Not at all.

SOCRATES: What about of truth?

GLAUCON: Not of it, either.

SOCRATES: And if less of truth, less of being, too?

GLAUCON: Necessarily.

585d SOCRATES: Isn't it generally true that the types concerned with the care of the body partake less in truth and being than do those concerned with the care of the soul?

GLAUCON: Yes, much less.

SOCRATES: Don't you think the same holds of the body in comparison to the soul?

GLAUCON: I do.

SOCRATES: Then isn't what is filled with things that are more, and is itself more, more really filled than what is filled with things that are less, and is itself less?

GLAUCON: Of course.

585e SOCRATES: So, then, if being filled with what is appropriate to our nature is pleasant, what is more filled with things that *are* more is more really and truly caused to enjoy a more true pleasure; whereas what partakes of things that *are* less is less truly and surely filled and partakes of a less trustworthy and less true pleasure.

GLAUCON: That's absolutely inevitable.

586a SOCRATES: So, those who lack experience of knowledge or virtue, but are always occupied with feasts and the like, are brought down, apparently, and then back up to the middle state; and wander in this way throughout their lives, never reaching beyond this to what is truly higher up, never looking up at it or brought up to it, never filled with what really is, and never tasting any stable or pure pleasure. On the contrary, they are always looking downward like cattle and, with their heads bent over the earth or the dinner table, they feed, fatten, and fornicate. And, in order to do better than others in these things, they kick and butt with iron horns and 586b hooves, killing each other, because their desires are insatiable. For they aren't using things that *are* to fill the part of themselves that *is* a thing that is, and a leak-proof vessel.

GLAUCON: You have described the life of the masses, Socrates, just like an oracle!

SOCRATES: So, isn't it necessary, then, for these people to live with pleasures that are mixed with pains, mere phantoms and illusionist paintings of 586c true pleasures? And aren't they so colored by their juxtaposition with one another that they appear intense, beget mad passions for themselves in the

foolish, and are fought over—as Stesichorus tells us the phantom of Helen
was fought over at Troy—through ignorance of the truth?[5]

GLAUCON: Something like that must be what happens.

SOCRATES: Mustn't similar things happen to someone who succeeds in
satisfying the spirited element? Mustn't his love of honor be so colored by
envy, his love of victory by violence, and his spiritedness by peevishness,
that he pursues the satisfactions of honor, victory, and spiritedness without   586d
rational calculation or understanding?

GLAUCON: The same sorts of things must happen with regard to that element, too.

SOCRATES: Can't we confidently assert, then, that, even where the desires of
the profit-loving and honor-loving parts are concerned, those that follow
knowledge and argument, and pursue with their help the pleasures that
wisdom prescribes, will attain—to the degree that they can attain true
pleasure at all—the truest pleasures, because they follow truth, and those
that are most their own; if, indeed, what is the best for each thing is also   586e
what is most its own?

GLAUCON: But that, of course, is what is most its own.

SOCRATES: So, when the entire soul follows the philosophic element and
does not engage in faction, the result is that each element does its own
work and is just; and, in particular, each enjoys its own pleasures, the best
pleasures and—to the degree possible—the truest.   587a

GLAUCON: Absolutely.

SOCRATES: So, when one of the other parts gains mastery, the result is that
it cannot discover its own pleasure and compels the other parts to pursue
an alien, and not a true pleasure.

GLAUCON: Yes.

SOCRATES: And wouldn't what is most distant from philosophy and reason
be most likely to produce that result?

GLAUCON: By far.

SOCRATES: And isn't what is most distant from reason the very thing that
is most distant from law and order?

GLAUCON: Clearly.

SOCRATES: And wasn't it made evident that the passionate and tyrannical   587b
appetites are most distant?

---

5 According to the story, Stesichorus wrote a poem defaming Helen and was
punished by being struck with blindness. His sight was restored when he added a
verse to the poem in which he claimed that it was a phantom of Helen and not Helen
herself who was at Troy.

GLAUCON: By far the most.

SOCRATES: And the kingly and orderly ones least distant?

GLAUCON: Yes.

SOCRATES: Then the tyrant, I suppose, will be most distant from a true pleasure that is his own, while the king will be least distant.

GLAUCON: It is inevitable.

SOCRATES: And so, the tyrant will live most unpleasantly and the king most pleasantly.

GLAUCON: It is absolutely inevitable.

SOCRATES: Do you know, then, how much more unpleasant the tyrant's life is than the king's?

GLAUCON: Not unless you tell me.

SOCRATES: There are, it seems, three pleasures: one genuine and two illegitimate. The tyrant is at the extreme end of the illegitimate ones, since he
587c flees both law and reason and lives with a bodyguard of slavish pleasures. But it is not at all easy to say just how inferior he is—except perhaps as follows.

GLAUCON: How?

SOCRATES: The tyrant is somehow at a third remove from the oligarch, since the democrat was in the middle between them.[6]

GLAUCON: Yes.

SOCRATES: Won't he also live with a phantom of pleasure, then, that, as regards truth, is at a third remove from that other—if what we said before is true?

GLAUCON: He will.

SOCRATES: But the oligarch, in turn, is at a third remove from the king, if
587d we assume king and aristocrat to be the same.

GLAUCON: Yes, third.

SOCRATES: So a tyrant is removed from true pleasure by a numerical value of three times three.

GLAUCON: Apparently.

SOCRATES: So, on the basis of the size of this numerical value, it seems the phantom of the tyrant's pleasure is a plane figure.

GLAUCON: Exactly.

SOCRATES: On the basis of its square and cube, in that case, it becomes clear how far removed it is.

---

[6] Third because the Greeks always counted the first as well as the last member of a series. The day after tomorrow was the third day.

GLAUCON: Clear to someone skilled in calculation, anyway!

SOCRATES: Turning it the other way around, then, if someone wants to say how far the king is removed from the tyrant in terms of true pleasure, he will find, if he completes the calculation, that he lives 729 times more pleasantly, while the tyrant lives the same number of times more painfully.[7] 587e

GLAUCON: That's an extraordinary calculation of the difference between the two men—the just one and the unjust one—in terms of their pleasure 588a
and pain!

SOCRATES: And yet it is a number that is both true and appropriate to human lives—if indeed days, nights, months, and years are appropriate to them.

GLAUCON: And of course they are appropriate.

SOCRATES: If the victory of the good and just person over the bad and unjust one in terms of pleasure is as great as that, won't his victory in terms of its grace, beauty, and virtue be extraordinarily greater?

GLAUCON: Extraordinarily greater, indeed, by Zeus!

SOCRATES: All right, then. Since we have reached this point in the argument, let's return to the first things we mentioned that led us here. I think 588b
someone said that doing injustice profits a completely unjust person who is believed to be just. Wasn't that the claim?[8]

GLAUCON: Yes, it was.

SOCRATES: Let's discuss it with its proponent, then, since we have now agreed on the respective effects of doing unjust and doing just things.

GLAUCON: How?

SOCRATES: By fashioning an image of the soul in words, so that the one who said that will know what he was saying.

GLAUCON: What sort of image? 588c

SOCRATES: One of those creatures that ancient legends say used to exist. The Chimera, Scylla, Cerberus, and the numerous other cases where many different kinds are said to have grown together into one.

GLAUCON: Yes, they do describe such things.

SOCRATES: Well, then, fashion a single species of complex, many-headed beast, with a ring of tame and savage animal heads, all of which it can grow and change from within.

GLAUCON: That's a task for a clever fashioner of images! Still, since language is easier to fashion than wax and the like, consider the fashioning done. 588d

---

[7] Socrates' mathematics is difficult to follow.

[8] See 348b, 360c–361d, 392c.

SOCRATES: Now, fashion another single species—of lion—and a single one of human being. But make the first much the greatest and the second, second in size.

GLAUCON: That's easier—the fashioning is done.

SOCRATES: Now, join the three in one, so that they somehow grow together naturally.

GLAUCON: They are joined.

588e SOCRATES: Then fashion around the outside the image of one of them, that of the human being, so that to anyone who cannot see what is inside, but sees only the outer shell, it will look like a single creature, a human being.

GLAUCON: The surrounding shell has been fashioned.

SOCRATES: When someone claims, then, that it profits this human being to do injustice, but that doing what is just brings no advantage, let's tell him that he is saying nothing other than that it profits him to feed well and strengthen the multifarious beast, as well as the lion and everything that 589a pertains to the lion; to starve and weaken the human being, so that he is dragged along wherever either of the other two leads; and not to accustom the two to one another or make them friends, but leave them to bite and fight and devour one another.

GLAUCON: Yes, that's exactly what someone who praises doing injustice is saying.

SOCRATES: On the other hand, wouldn't someone who claims that what is just is profitable be saying we should do and say what will give the inner human being the greatest mastery over the human being, to get him to 589b take care of the many-headed beast like a farmer, feeding and domesticating the gentle heads and preventing the savage ones from growing; to make the lion's nature his ally; and to care for all in common, bringing them up in such a way that they will be friends with each other and with himself?

GLAUCON: Yes, that's exactly what someone who praises justice is saying.

SOCRATES: From every point of view, then, the one who praises what is just speaks truly while the one who praises what is unjust speaks falsely. 589c For whether we consider pleasure or good reputation or advantage, the one who praises the just tells the truth while the one who condemns it has nothing sound to say and condemns with no knowledge of what he is condemning.

GLAUCON: None at all, in my opinion.

SOCRATES: Then let's persuade him gently—after all, he is not getting it wrong intentionally—by questioning him as follows: "Bless you, but shouldn't we claim that this is also the basis of the conventional norms concerning what is fine and what is shameful: what is fine is what subordinates the beastlike elements in our nature to the human one—or better,

perhaps, to the divine, whereas what is shameful is what enslaves the tame   589d
element to the savage?" Will he agree, or what?

GLAUCON: He will if he takes my advice.

SOCRATES: Is there anyone, then, in light of this argument, who profits by
acquiring gold unjustly, if the result is something like this: in taking the
gold, he simultaneously enslaves the best element in himself to the most
wicked? If he got the gold by enslaving his son or daughter to savage and   589e
evil men, it would not profit him, no matter how much he got for doing
it. So, if he ruthlessly enslaves the most divine element in himself to the
most godless and polluted, how could he fail to be wretched, when he   **590a**
accepts golden gifts in return for a far more terrible destruction than that
of Eriphyle, who took the necklace in return for her husband's soul?[9]

GLAUCON: A much more terrible one. I will answer for him.

SOCRATES: And don't you think intemperance has long been condemned
for reasons of this sort; that it is because of vices like it that that terrible
creature, the great and multiform beast, is given more freedom than it
should be?

GLAUCON: Clearly.

SOCRATES: And aren't stubbornness and peevishness condemned because
they inharmoniously increase and stretch the lionlike and snakelike[10]
element?   590b

GLAUCON: Certainly.

SOCRATES: And aren't luxury and softness condemned for slackening and
loosening this same part, because that produces cowardice in it?

GLAUCON: Of course.

SOCRATES: And aren't flattery and illiberality condemned because they subject this same spirited element to the moblike beast, allow it to be showered
with abuse for the sake of money and the latter's insatiability, and habituate
it from youth to be an ape instead of a lion?

GLAUCON: Yes, indeed.

SOCRATES: Why do you think someone is reproached for menial work or   590c
handicraft? Or shall we say that it is for no other reason than because the
best element is naturally weak in him, so that it cannot rule the beasts
within him, but can only serve them and learn what flatters them?

---

[9] Eriphyle was bribed by Polynices to persuade her husband Amphiaraus to take
part in an attack on Thebes. Amphiaraus was killed, and Eriphyle was murdered by
her son in revenge. See *Odyssey* xi.326–27.

[10] The snakelike element hasn't been previously mentioned, although it may be
included in "everything that pertains to" the lion (588e).

GLAUCON: Apparently.

SOCRATES: In order to ensure, then, that someone like that is also ruled by something similar to what rules the best person, we say that he should be the slave of that best person who has the divine ruler within himself. It is not to harm the slave that we say he should be ruled, as Thrasymachus supposed was true of all subjects, but because it is better for everyone to be ruled by a divine and wise ruler—preferably one that is his own and that he has inside himself; otherwise one imposed on him from outside, so that we may all be as alike and as friendly as possible, because we are all captained by the same thing.

GLAUCON: Yes, that's right.

SOCRATES: This is clearly the aim of the law as well, which is the ally of everyone in the city. It is also our aim in ruling our children. We do not allow them to be free until we establish a constitution in them as in a city. That is to say, we take care of their best part with the similar one in ourselves and equip them with a guardian and ruler similar to our own to take our place. Only then do we set them free.

GLAUCON: Yes, that's clearly so.

SOCRATES: How, then, will we claim, Glaucon, and on the basis of what argument, that it profits someone to do injustice, or what is intemperate, or some shameful thing that will make him worse, even if it brings more money or power of some other sort?

GLAUCON: There's no way we can.

SOCRATES: Or how can we claim that it profits him to be undetected in his injustice and not pay the penalty? I mean, doesn't the one who remains undetected become even worse, while in the one who is discovered and punished, the bestial element is calmed and tamed and the gentle one freed? Doesn't his entire soul, when it returns to its best nature and acquires temperance and justice along with wisdom, achieve a condition that is as more honorable than that of a body when it acquires strength and beauty along with health, as a soul is more honorable than a body?

GLAUCON: Absolutely.

SOCRATES: Won't anyone with any sense, then, give everything he has to achieve it as long as he lives? First, won't he honor the studies that produce it and not honor the others?

GLAUCON: Clearly.

SOCRATES: Second, as regards the condition and nurture of his body, not only will he not give himself over to bestial and irrational pleasure, and live turned in that direction; but he won't make health his aim nor give precedence to the ways of becoming strong or healthy or beautiful, unless he is also going to become temperate as a result of them. On the contrary,

it is clear that he will always be tuning the harmony of his body for the   591d
sake of the concord of his soul.

GLAUCON: He certainly will, if indeed he is going to be truly musical.

SOCRATES: Won't he also keep order and concord in his acquisition of
money? He won't be dazzled, will he, by what the masses regard as blessed
happiness, and—by increasing the size of his wealth without limit—acquire
an unlimited number of evils?

GLAUCON: Not in my view.

SOCRATES: On the contrary, he will keep his eye fixed on the constitution   591e
[e] within him and guard against disturbing anything there either with too
much money or with too little. Captaining himself in that way, he will
increase and spend his wealth, as far as possible by reference to it.

GLAUCON: That's exactly what he will do.

SOCRATES: Where honors are concerned, too, he will keep his eye on the
same thing. He will willingly share in and taste those he believes will make   592a
him better. But those that might overthrow the established condition of
his soul, he will avoid, both in private and in public.

GLAUCON: So, he won't be willing to take part in politics, then, if that is
what he cares about.

SOCRATES: Yes, by the dog,[11] in his own city, he certainly will. But he may
not be willing to do so in his fatherland, barring some stroke of divine luck.

GLAUCON: I understand. You mean in the city we have just been founding
and describing; the one that exists in words, since I do not think it exists
anywhere on earth.

SOCRATES: But there may perhaps be a model of it in the heavens for anyone   592b
who wishes to look at it and to found himself on the basis of what he sees.
It makes no difference at all whether it exists anywhere or ever will. You
see, he would take part in the politics of it alone, and of no other.

GLAUCON: That's probably right.

BOOK X

SOCRATES' NARRATION CONTINUES:

SOCRATES: You know that there are many other things about our city that
make me think we were entirely right in founding it as we did, but I am   595a
particularly thinking of poetry when I say that.

GLAUCON: What about it?

---

[11] See 399e note.

SOCRATES: Our refusal to admit any of it that is imitative. Indeed, the need not to admit it seems even more evident, in my view, now that we have distinguished the elements in the soul from one another.

595b

GLAUCON: How do you mean?

SOCRATES: Between ourselves—for *you* won't denounce me to the tragic poets or any of the other imitative ones—I think all such poetry is likely to corrupt the mind of those of its hearers who do not have the knowledge of what it is really like as a drug to counteract it.

GLAUCON: What do you have in mind in saying that?

SOCRATES: I will have to tell you, even though a sort of reverential love I have had for Homer since childhood makes me hesitate to speak. You see,

595c

he seems to have been the first teacher and leader of all these fine tragedians. All the same, a man should not be honored more than the truth. So, as I say, I will have to tell you.

GLAUCON: Of course.

SOCRATES: Listen, then—or rather, answer my questions.

GLAUCON: Ask away.

SOCRATES: Could you tell me what imitation in general is? You see, I do not entirely understand what it is supposed to be.

GLAUCON: So is it likely that *I* will?

SOCRATES: There would be nothing strange in that, since there are many

596a

things the shortsighted see before the sharp-eyed!

GLAUCON: That's right. But with you present, I could not possibly be very eager to speak out even if there were something I saw. So, you will have to do the looking yourself.

SOCRATES: Do you want us to begin our inquiry with the following point, then, in accordance with our usual method? I mean, as you know, we usually posit some one particular form in connection with each set of many things to which we apply the same name. Or don't you understand?

GLAUCON: I do.

SOCRATES: Then in the present case, too, let's take any set of many things

596b

you like. For example, there are, if you like, many couches and tables.

GLAUCON: Of course.

SOCRATES: But the forms connected to these manufactured items are surely just two, one of a couch and one of a table.

GLAUCON: Yes.

SOCRATES: Don't we usually say, too, that the craftsman who makes each manufactured item looks toward the form when he makes the couches or the tables we use, and similarly with other things? For surely no craftsman makes the form itself—

GLAUCON: How could he?

SOCRATES: Well, now, see what you would call *this* craftsman?

GLAUCON: Which?   596c

SOCRATES: The one who makes everything each individual handicraftsman makes.

GLAUCON: That's an amazingly clever man you are talking about!

SOCRATES: Wait a minute and you will have even more reason to say that! You see, this same handicraftsman is able to make not only every manufactured item, but he also makes all the plants that grow from the earth, and produces all the animals, including himself; and, in addition, he produces earth and sky and gods and everything in the sky, and everything in Hades beneath the earth.

GLAUCON: You are talking about a wholly amazing sophist!   596d

SOCRATES: You do not believe me? Tell me, do you think such a craftsman is completely impossible? Or do you think there is a way in which a maker of all these things could exist, and a way in which he could not? Don't you see there is a certain way in which even you yourself could make all of them?

GLAUCON: What way is that?

SOCRATES: It is not difficult. On the contrary, it is a sort of craftsmanship that is widely available and quick—and quickest of all, I suppose, if you are willing to take a mirror and turn it around in all directions. That way you will quickly make the sun and the things in the sky; you will quickly 596e make the earth, yourself and the other animals, manufactured items, plants, and everything else that was mentioned just now.

GLAUCON: Yes, their appearances, but certainly not the things themselves as they truly are.

SOCRATES: Right! You attack the argument at just the right place. For I think the painter is also one of these craftsmen, isn't he?

GLAUCON: Of course.

SOCRATES: But you will say, I think, that he does not make the things he makes as they truly are—even though there is a certain way in which the painter also makes a couch. Isn't that right?

GLAUCON: Yes, he also makes the appearance of one.

SOCRATES: What about the couch-maker? Didn't you just say that he does not make the form—which we say is what a couch is—but only a particular **597a** couch?

GLAUCON: Yes, I did say that.

SOCRATES: Now, if he does not make what it is, he is not making what is, but something that is like what is, but is not. So, if someone were to say that the product of a couch-maker or any other handicraftsman completely is, he probably would not be speaking the truth?

GLAUCON: That, at any rate, is what those who occupy themselves with such arguments would think.

SOCRATES: So we should not be surprised if it also turns out to be somewhat dim in comparison to the truth.

GLAUCON: No, we should not.

597b   SOCRATES: Would you like us, then, to use these same examples to search for that imitator of ours and what he really is?

GLAUCON: I would, if you would.

SOCRATES: Well, then, we have these three sorts of couches. One, that is in nature, which I think we would say a god makes. Or is it someone else?

GLAUCON: No one, I suppose.

SOCRATES: One the carpenter makes.

GLAUCON: Yes.

SOCRATES: And one the painter makes. Isn't that so?

GLAUCON: It is.

SOCRATES: So painter, carpenter, and god—these three oversee three kinds of couches?

GLAUCON: Yes, three.

SOCRATES: Now, the god, either because he did not want to, or because it
597c   was somehow necessary for him not to make more than one that is in its nature a couch, made only the one that is what a couch itself is. Two or more of these have not been naturally developed by the god and never will be naturally developed.

GLAUCON: Why is that?

SOCRATES: Because, if he were to make only two, one would again come to light whose form they in turn would both possess, and *it* would be what a couch itself is, not the two.

GLAUCON: That's right.

SOCRATES: The god knew this, I suppose, and, wishing to be the real maker
597d   of the real couch and not just some particular maker of some particular couch, naturally developed the one that is in its nature unique.

GLAUCON: Probably so.

SOCRATES: Would you like us to call him its natural maker, then, or something like that?

GLAUCON: It would be right to do so, at any rate, since it is by nature that he has made it and all the others.

SOCRATES: What about the carpenter? Shouldn't we call him the craftsman who makes a couch?

GLAUCON: Yes.

SOCRATES: And should we call a painter, too, a craftsman and maker of such a thing?

GLAUCON: Certainly not.

SOCRATES: In that case, what is it you say he is, of a couch?

GLAUCON: In my view, the most reasonable thing to call him is this: he is   597e
an imitator of what the others are craftsmen of.

SOCRATES: All right. So the one whose product is three removed from the natural one, you call an imitator?

GLAUCON: Certainly.

SOCRATES: So the tragedian too, if indeed he is an imitator, will be someone who is by his nature third from king and truth, and so will all the other imitators.

GLAUCON: It looks that way.

SOCRATES: We are agreed about the imitator, then. Now, tell me this about   598a
the painter: in each case, do you think it is what each thing itself is in its nature that he is trying to imitate, or the products of the craftsmen?

GLAUCON: Those of the craftsmen.

SOCRATES: As they are, or as they appear to be? You have still to make that distinction.

GLAUCON: How do you mean?

SOCRATES: This: if you look at a couch from the side or the front or from anywhere else, does it differ in any way from itself? Or, while not differing at all, does it appear different? And similarly with the others?

GLAUCON: The latter. It appears different, but is not different at all.

SOCRATES: Then consider this very point: at what does painting aim in   598b
each case? To imitate what is as it is? Or what appears as it appears? Is it an imitation of an illusion, or of truth?

GLAUCON: Of an illusion.

SOCRATES: So, imitation is surely far removed from the truth. And the reason that it produces everything, it seems, is that it grasps only a small part of each thing—and that is an illusion. For example, the painter, we say, can paint us a cobbler, a carpenter, or any other craftsman, even though he knows nothing about these crafts. All the same, if he is a good painter,   598c
by painting a carpenter and displaying him at a distance, he might deceive children and foolish adults into thinking it truly is a carpenter.

GLAUCON: Of course.

SOCRATES: In fact, my friend, I imagine that what we must bear in mind in all these cases is this: when someone tells us he has met a human being who knows every craft as well as everything else anyone knows, and that

598d   there is nothing of which he does not have a more exact knowledge than anyone else, we should assume we are talking to a naïve fellow. He has been deceived, it seems, by an encounter with some sort of sorcerer or imitator, whom he therefore considers to be all-wise. But that is because of his own inability to distinguish between knowledge, lack of knowledge, and imitation.

GLAUCON: That's absolutely true.

SOCRATES: Well, then, we must next consider tragedy and its leader, Homer, since we hear from some that these men know every craft, everything rel-

598e   evant to human virtue and vice, and even all about divine matters. They claim, you see, that if a good poet is to write beautiful poetry about the things he writes about, he must have knowledge of them when he writes, or else he would be unable to. We should consider, then, whether those who tell us this have been deceived by their encounters with these imitators

599a   and do not realize, when they see their works, that they are three removes from what is, and are easy to produce without knowledge of the truth. For they produce illusions, not things that are. Or whether there is something in what they say, and good poets really do have knowledge of the things about which the masses think they speak so well.

GLAUCON: We certainly must consider that.

SOCRATES: Do you think, then, that if someone could make both what is imitated and its image, he would allow himself to take making images

599b   seriously, and put it at the forefront of his life as the best ability he had?

GLAUCON: No, I do not.

SOCRATES: But if he truly had knowledge of what he imitates, I suppose he would take deeds much more seriously than their imitations, would try to leave behind many beautiful deeds as his own memorials, and would be much more eager to be the subject of a eulogy than the author of one.

GLAUCON: I suppose so. I mean, these things certainly are not equal either in honor or in benefit.

SOCRATES: Let's not demand an account, then, of the other things from

599c   Homer or any other poet. Let's not ask if any of them is a doctor or only an imitator of what doctors say; or which people any of the poets, old or new, has reportedly made healthy, as Asclepius did; or which students of medicine he left behind, as Asclepius did his sons. And let's not ask them about the other crafts either, but leave them aside. When it comes, however, to the greatest and most beautiful things of which Homer under-takes to speak—warfare, generalship, city government, and a person's

education—surely, it is fair to question him as follows: "My dear Homer,   599d
if you are not third removed from the truth about virtue, and are not the
sort of craftsman of an image, which is what we defined an imitator to be,
but if you are even in second place and capable of knowing what practices
make people better or worse in private or in public life, tell us which cities
are better governed because of you, as the Lacedaemonians are because of
Lycurgus, and as many others—great and small—are because of many other
men. What city gives you credit for having proved to be a good lawgiver   599e
who benefited it? Italy and Sicily give it to Charondas, and we give it to
Solon. Who gives it to you?" Will he be able to name one?

GLAUCON: I suppose not. At any rate, none is mentioned even by the
Homeridae[1] themselves.

SOCRATES: Then is any war in Homer's time remembered that was well
fought because of his leadership or advice?   **600a**

GLAUCON: None at all.

SOCRATES: Then as you would expect in the case of a man wise in deeds,
are we told of his many ingenious inventions in the crafts or other activities,
as we are about Thales of Miletus and Anacharsis the Scythian?

GLAUCON: There's nothing of that sort.

SOCRATES: Then if there is nothing of a public nature, is Homer said to
have been a leader, during his own lifetime, in the education of people who
loved associating with him and passed on a Homeric way of life to those
who came later? Is he like Pythagoras, who was himself particularly loved   600b
for this reason, and whose followers even today still seem to be conspicuous
for a way of life they call Pythagorean?

GLAUCON: Again, we are told nothing of this kind. Indeed, Socrates,
Creophylus, the companion of Homer, would presumably seem even more
ridiculous than his name[2] suggests as an example of such education, if
the story told about Homer is true. You see, we are told that while he was
alive, Creophylus completely neglected him.   600c

SOCRATES: Yes, we are told that. But, Glaucon, if Homer had really been
able to educate people and make them better, if he had been able, not
to imitate such matters but to know about them, wouldn't he have had
many companions who honored and loved him? Protagoras of Abdera,
Prodicus of Ceos, and a great many others are able to convince anyone
who associates with them in private that he wouldn't be able to manage   600d

---

[1] The rhapsodes and poets who recited and expounded Homer throughout the
Greek world.

[2] It derives from two words, *kreas* (meat) and *phylon* (race or kind). A modern
equivalent might be "meathead."

his household or city unless they themselves supervised his education, and they are so intensely loved because of this wisdom of theirs that their disciples do everything except carry them around on their shoulders. Are we to believe, then, that if Homer had been able to help people become virtuous, his companions would have allowed either him or Hesiod to wander around as rhapsodes, and wouldn't have clung far tighter to them than to gold and compelled them to come home and live with them? And if persuasion failed, wouldn't they have followed them wherever they went until they had received sufficient education?

GLAUCON: I think what you say is entirely true, Socrates.

SOCRATES: Are we to conclude, then, that all poets, beginning with Homer, imitate images of virtue and of all the other things they write about, and have no grasp of the truth? Although, as we were saying just now, a painter will make what seems to be a shoemaker to those who know as little about shoemaking as he does himself, but who look at things in terms of their colors and shapes.

GLAUCON: That's right.

SOCRATES: Similarly, I suppose, we will say that the poet uses words and phrases to paint colored pictures of each of the crafts, even though he knows only how to imitate them; so that others like himself, who look at things in terms of words, will think he speaks extremely well about shoemaking or generalship or anything else, provided he speaks with meter, rhythm, and harmony. That is how great a natural spell these things cast. For if a poet's works are stripped of their musical colorings and spoken just by themselves, I think you know what they look like. You have surely seen them.

GLAUCON: I certainly have.

SOCRATES: Don't they resemble the faces of those who are young but not really beautiful, after the bloom of youth has left them?

GLAUCON: Absolutely.

SOCRATES: Come on, then, consider this: the maker of an image—the imitator—knows nothing, we say, about what is, but only about what appears. Isn't that so?

GLAUCON: Yes.

SOCRATES: Then let's not leave the story half-told. Let's look at the whole thing.

GLAUCON: Go on.

SOCRATES: A painter, we say, will paint reins and a bit?

GLAUCON: Yes.

SOCRATES: But it is the saddler and the blacksmith who make them?

GLAUCON: Of course.

SOCRATES: Does the painter know what the reins and bit should be like, then? Or do not even their makers—the saddler and the blacksmith—know this, but only the one who knows how to use them, the horseman?

GLAUCON: That's absolutely true.

SOCRATES: So, won't we say that the same holds for everything?

GLAUCON: What?

SOCRATES: That for each thing there are these three crafts: one that will use, one that will make, one that will imitate?   601d

GLAUCON: Yes.

SOCRATES: Then aren't the virtue, goodness, and correctness of each manufactured item, living creature, and activity related to nothing but the use for which each is made or naturally developed?

GLAUCON: They are.

SOCRATES: So it is entirely necessary, then, that the user of each thing has the most experience of it, and that he inform the maker about what the good and bad points are in the actual use of the thing he uses. For example, it is the flute player, I take it, who informs the flute-maker about which flutes respond well in actual playing, and prescribes how they should be   601e made, while the maker obeys him.

GLAUCON: Of course.

SOCRATES: Doesn't the one who knows give information, then, about good and bad flutes, whereas the other, by relying on him, makes them?

GLAUCON: Yes.

SOCRATES: So, as regards the same manufactured item, its maker—through associating with the one who knows and having to listen to the one who knows—has correct belief about its good and bad qualities, while its user   602a has knowledge.

GLAUCON: Exactly.

SOCRATES: What about the imitator? Will he, on the basis of using the things he paints, have knowledge of whether they are good and correct or not? Or will he have correct belief through having to associate with the one who knows and being told how he should paint them?

GLAUCON: Neither.

SOCRATES: So an imitator has neither knowledge nor correct belief about whether the things he makes are good or bad.

GLAUCON: Apparently not.

SOCRATES: How well situated the poetic imitator is, then, in relation to wisdom about the subjects of his poems!

GLAUCON: He isn't really.

SOCRATES: And yet he will go on imitating all the same, even though he
602b　does not know in what way each thing is good or bad. On the contrary,
whatever appears good to the masses who know nothing—that, it seems,
is what he will imitate.

GLAUCON: What else?

SOCRATES: Apparently, then, we are fairly well agreed on the following:
that the imitator knows nothing worth mentioning about the things he
imitates, but that imitation is a kind of game, not something to be taken
seriously; and that tragic poets, whether in iambic or epic verse, are as
imitative as they could possibly be.

GLAUCON: Absolutely.

SOCRATES: In the name of Zeus, then, this business of imitation is con-
602c　cerned with what is third removed from the truth. Isn't that right?

GLAUCON: Yes.

SOCRATES: Now, then, on which of the elements in a human being does
it have its effect?

GLAUCON: What sort of element do you mean?

SOCRATES: This sort: the same object, viewed from nearby, does not appear
the same size, I presume, as when viewed from a distance.

GLAUCON: No, it does not.

SOCRATES: And the same things appear bent and straight when seen in
water or out of it, or concave and convex because sight is misled by colors;
602d　and every other similar sort of confusion is clearly present in our soul. It
is because it exploits this weakness in our nature that illusionist painting
is nothing short of sorcery, and neither are jugglery or many other similar
sorts of trickery.

GLAUCON: True.

SOCRATES: And haven't measuring, counting, and weighing proved to be
most welcome assistants in these cases, ensuring that what appears greater
or smaller or more numerous or heavier does not rule within us, but rather
what has calculated or measured or even weighed?

GLAUCON: Of course.

602e　SOCRATES: And that is the task of the soul's rational element?

GLAUCON: Yes, of it.

SOCRATES: But quite often, when it has measured and indicates that some
things are greater or smaller than others, or the same size, the opposite
simultaneously appears to it to hold it of these same things.

GLAUCON: Yes.

SOCRATES: And didn't we say that it is impossible for the same thing to believe opposites about the same thing at the same time?[3]

GLAUCON: Yes, and we were right to say it.

SOCRATES: So, the element in the soul that believes contrary to the measurements and the one that believes in accord with the measurements could not be the same.   603a

GLAUCON: No, they could not.

SOCRATES: But the one that puts its trust in measurement and calculation would be the best element in the soul.

GLAUCON: Of course.

SOCRATES: So the one that opposes it would be one of the inferior parts in us.

GLAUCON: Necessarily.

SOCRATES: That, then, was what I wanted to get agreement about when I said that painting—and imitation as a whole—are far from the truth when they produce their work; and moreover that imitation really consorts with an element in us that is far from wisdom, and that nothing healthy or true   603b
can come from their relationship or friendship.

GLAUCON: That's absolutely right.

SOCRATES: So, imitation is an inferior thing that consorts with another inferior thing to produce inferior offspring.

GLAUCON: So it seems.

SOCRATES: Does this apply only to the imitation that is visible, or also to the one that is audible—the one we call poetry?

GLAUCON: It probably applies to that as well.

SOCRATES: Well, let's not rely solely on a probable analogy with painting. Instead, let's also go directly again to the very element in our mind with   603c
which poetic imitation consorts and see whether it is inferior or excellent.

GLAUCON: Yes, we should.

SOCRATES: Then let's put it as follows. Imitative poetry, we say, imitates human beings acting under compulsion or voluntarily, who, as a result of these actions, believe they are doing either well or badly, and so experience either pain or enjoyment in all these situations. Does it imitate anything apart from these?

GLAUCON: Not a thing.

SOCRATES: So, is a human being of one mind in all these circumstances then? Or, just as in the case of visible representation, where he was split

---

[3] 436b–c.

603d into factions and had opposite beliefs in him about the same things at the same time, is he also split into factions and at war with himself in matters of action? But I am reminded that there is really no need now for us to reach agreement on this question. You see, in our earlier arguments, we were sufficiently agreed about all that when we said that our soul is filled with myriad opposites of that sort at the same time.[4]

GLAUCON: And rightly so.

SOCRATES: Yes, it *was* right. But we omitted something then that I now
603e think we must discuss.

GLAUCON: What's that?

SOCRATES: When a good man suffers some stroke of bad luck, such as the loss of a son or something else he values very highly, we also said in our earlier arguments, as you know, that he will bear it more easily than others.[5]

GLAUCON: We certainly did.

SOCRATES: Now, let's consider this: will he not grieve at all? Or, since that is impossible, will he be somehow measured in the face of pain?

GLAUCON: The latter is probably closer to the truth.

SOCRATES: Now, tell me this about him: do you think he will be more
604a likely to fight and resist pain when he is seen by his equals, or when he is just by himself in a solitary place?

GLAUCON: He's sure to fight it far more when he is being seen.

SOCRATES: But when he is alone, I imagine, he will venture to say many things he would be ashamed if someone else heard, and to do many things he would not want anyone else to see him doing.

GLAUCON: That's right.

SOCRATES: And isn't it reason and law that tell him to resist, while what urges him to give in to the pains is the feeling itself?

GLAUCON: True.

604b SOCRATES: And when there are opposite impulses in a human being in relation to the same thing at the same time, we say that there must be two elements in him.

GLAUCON: Of course.

SOCRATES: Isn't one part ready to be persuaded to follow the law, wherever the law leads?

GLAUCON: Can you explain how?

SOCRATES: The law says, as you know, that it is best to keep as quiet as possible in misfortunes and not get irritated, since what is really good or

---

[4] 439c–441c.

[5] 387d–e.

bad in such things is not clear. There is nothing to be gained by taking them hard, nor is any aspect of human affairs worth getting very serious about. And the very thing whose aid we need as quickly as possible in such circumstances is the one our grieving hinders.   604c

GLAUCON: Which do you mean?

SOCRATES: The capacity to deliberate about what has happened and, as with the fall of the dice, to arrange our affairs, given what has befallen us, in whatever way reason determines would be best. Instead of acting like children who have fallen over, and who hold on to the hurt part and spend their time wailing, we should always accustom our souls to turn as quickly   604d as possible to curing and raising up the part that has suffered a fall and is sick, so as to banish lamentation by means of medicine.

GLAUCON: That would be the most correct way to deal with bad luck, anyway.

SOCRATES: So it is the best element, we say, that is willing to follow this rational calculation.

GLAUCON: Clearly.

SOCRATES: As for the part that leads us to recollections of our suffering and to lamentations, and is insatiable for these things, won't we say that it is the element that lacks reason, is idle, and is a friend of cowardice?

GLAUCON: We certainly will.

SOCRATES: Now, this element—the one that gets irritated—admits of much complex imitation; whereas the wise and quiet character, which always   604e remains pretty much selfsame, is neither easy to imitate nor easy to understand when imitated—especially not at a festival where multifarious people are gathered together in theaters. For the experience being imitated is alien to them.

GLAUCON: Absolutely.   605a

SOCRATES: The imitative poet, then, clearly does not naturally relate to this best element in the soul, and his wisdom is not directed to pleasing it—not if he is going to attain a good reputation with the masses—but to the irritable and complex character, because it is easy to imitate.

GLAUCON: Clearly.

SOCRATES: So, it would at last be right to take him and place him beside the painter as his counterpart. For he is like the latter in producing things that are inferior as regards truth, and is also similar to him in associating with the other element in souls, not with the best one. So, we would also at last be justified in not admitting him into a city that is to be well governed.   605b You see, he arouses and nourishes this element in the soul and, by making it strong, destroys the rational one—just as someone in a city who makes wicked people strong, by handing the city over to them, ruins the better ones. Similarly, we will say an imitative poet produces a bad constitution in the soul of each individual by making images that are very far removed from the truth and by gratifying the element in it that lacks understanding and cannot distinguish greater from smaller, but believes the same things to be now large, now small.

GLAUCON: He does, indeed.

SOCRATES: But we haven't yet brought our chief charge against imitation. For its power to corrupt all but a very few *good* people is surely an altogether terrible one.

GLAUCON: It certainly is, if it really can do that.

SOCRATES: Listen and consider. When even the best of us hear Homer, or some other tragic poet, imitating one of the heroes in a state of grief and making a long speech of lamentation, or even chanting and beating his breast, you know we enjoy it and give ourselves over to it. We suffer along with the hero and take his sufferings seriously. And we praise the one who affects us most in this way as a good poet.

GLAUCON: Of course I know.

SOCRATES: But when one of us suffers a personal loss, you also realize we do the opposite: we pride ourselves if we are able to keep quiet and endure it, in the belief that that is what a *man* does, whereas what we praised before is what a woman does.

GLAUCON: I do realize that.

SOCRATES: Is praise of that sort rightly bestowed, then? Is it right to look at the sort of man we would be, not honored, but rather ashamed to resemble, and instead of being disgusted by what we see to enjoy and praise it?

GLAUCON: No, by Zeus, that does not seem reasonable.

SOCRATES: Yes, it does. At least, it does if you look at it in the following way.

GLAUCON: How?

SOCRATES: If you reflect as follows: what is forcibly kept in check in our personal misfortunes and has an insatiable hunger for weeping and lamenting—since that is what it has a natural appetite for—is the very element that gets satisfaction and enjoyment from the poets. Second, our naturally best element, since it has not been adequately educated by reason or habit, relaxes its guard over the lamenting one, since it is watching the sufferings of somebody else and thinks there is no shame involved for it in praising and pitying another purportedly good man who grieves excessively. On the contrary, it thinks that to be a clear profit—I mean the pleasure it gets. And it would not want to be deprived of it by despising the whole poem. You see, I think only a few people are able to calculate that the enjoyment of other people's sufferings is inevitably transferred to one's own, since, when pity is nourished and strengthened by the former, it is not easily suppressed in the case of one's own sufferings.

GLAUCON: That's absolutely true.   606c

SOCRATES: Doesn't the same argument also apply to humor? You see, if there are jokes you would be ashamed to tell yourself, but that you very much enjoy when you hear them imitated in a comedy or even in private, and that you don't hate as something bad, aren't you doing the same as with the things you pity? For the element in you that wanted to tell the jokes, but which you held back by means of reason because you were afraid of being reputed a buffoon, you now release; and having made it strong in that way, you have been led unawares into becoming a comedian in your own life.

GLAUCON: Exactly.

SOCRATES: And in the case of sexual desires, anger, and all the appetites,   606d
pains, and pleasures in the soul, which we say accompany every action of ours, the effect of poetic imitation on us is the same. I mean, it nurtures and waters them when they should be dried up, and establishes them as rulers in us when—if we are to be become better and happier rather than worse and more wretched—they should be ruled.

GLAUCON: I cannot disagree with you.

SOCRATES: In that case, Glaucon, when you meet admirers of Homer—who   606e
tell us that this is the poet who educated Greece, and that for the management of human affairs and education in them, one should take up his works and learn them and live guided by this poet in the arrangement of one's whole life—you should befriend and welcome them, since they are the best they are capable of being. And you should agree that Homer is   607a
the most poetic of the tragedians and the first among them. Nonetheless, be aware that hymns to the gods and eulogies of good people are the only poetry we can admit into our city. For if you admit the honeyed Muse, whether in lyric or epic poetry, pleasure and pain will be kings in your city instead of law and the thing that has always been generally believed to be best—reason.

GLAUCON: That's absolutely true.

SOCRATES: Let that, then, be our defense for our return to the topic of   607b
poetry, which shows that, given her nature, we were right to banish her from the city earlier, since our argument compelled us. But let's also tell her—in case we are charged with some harshness and boorishness—that there is an ancient quarrel between poetry and philosophy. For such expressions as "the bitch yelping at its master" and "howling," and "great in the empty eloquence of fools," and "control by a mob of the omni-wise," and   607c
"the subtle thinkers who are beggars all," and countless others are signs of

this old opposition.[6] All the same, let it be said that, if the imitative poetry that aims at pleasure has any argument to show it should have a place in a well-governed city, we would gladly welcome it back, since we are well aware of being charmed by it ourselves. Still, it is not pious to betray what one believes to be the truth. What about you, my friend; aren't you also charmed by it, especially when it is through Homer that you look at it?

607d

GLAUCON: Very.

SOCRATES: Isn't it just, then, for her to reenter in that way, when she has defended herself in lyric or some other meter?

GLAUCON: Yes, indeed.

SOCRATES: Then we will surely allow her defenders—the ones who are not poets themselves, but lovers of poetry—to argue without meter on her behalf, showing that she gives not only pleasure but also benefit both to constitutions and to human life. Indeed, we will listen to them graciously, since we would certainly profit if poetry were shown to be not only pleas-

607e

ant but also beneficial.

GLAUCON: How could we fail to profit?

SOCRATES: But if it is not, my dear comrade, we will behave like men who have fallen in love. If they do not believe their passion is beneficial, hard though it is, they nonetheless stay away. And we too, because of the passion for this sort of poetry implanted in us by our upbringing in those

608a

fine constitutions, are well disposed to have her appear in the best and truest light. But as long as she is not able to produce such a defense, then whenever we listen to her, we will chant to ourselves the argument we just now put forward as a counter-charm to prevent us from slipping back into the childish passion that the masses have. For we have come to see that such poetry is not to be taken seriously, as a serious undertaking that grasps truth; but that anyone who listens to it should be careful, if he is

608b

concerned about the constitution within him, and should believe what we have said about poetry.

GLAUCON: I completely agree.

SOCRATES: It is a great struggle, my dear Glaucon, greater than people think, to become good rather than bad. So, we must not be tempted by honor, money, or any sort of office whatever—not even by poetry!—into thinking that it is worthwhile to neglect justice and the rest of virtue.

GLAUCON: I agree with you on the basis of what we have said. And so, I

608c

think, would anyone else.

SOCRATES: And yet the greatest rewards of virtue, and the prizes proposed for it, have not been discussed.

---

[6] The sources of these quotations are unknown.

GLAUCON: You must have something incredibly great in mind, if it is greater than those already mentioned!

SOCRATES: In a short period of time, could anything really great come to pass? I mean, the entire period from childhood to old age is surely short when compared to the whole of time.

GLAUCON: It's a mere nothing.

SOCRATES: Well, then, do you think an immortal thing should be seriously concerned with that period rather than the whole of time?

GLAUCON: I suppose not, but what exactly do you have in mind by that?   608d

SOCRATES: Haven't you realized that our souls are immortal and never destroyed?

He looked at me and said in amazement:

No, by Zeus, I have not. But are you really in a position to assert that?

SOCRATES: I certainly ought to be, and I think you are, too. There is nothing difficult about it.

GLAUCON: There is for me. So I would be glad to hear from you about this non-difficult topic!

SOCRATES: Listen then.

GLAUCON: All you have to do is speak!

SOCRATES: Do you think there is a good and a bad?

GLAUCON: I do.   608e

SOCRATES: And do you think about them the same way I do?

GLAUCON: What way?

SOCRATES: What destroys and corrupts coincides entirely with the bad, while what preserves and benefits coincides entirely with the good.

GLAUCON: I do.

SOCRATES: And do you think there is a good and a bad for each thing, such as ophthalmia for the eyes, sickness for the whole body, blight for grain,   609a
rot for wood, rust for iron and bronze, and, as I say, a natural badness and sickness for nearly everything?

GLAUCON: I certainly do.

SOCRATES: And when one of them attaches itself to something, doesn't it make the thing to which it attaches itself deficient? And in the end, doesn't it break it down completely and destroy it?

GLAUCON: Of course.

SOCRATES: So the badness natural to each thing—the deficiency peculiar to each—destroys it, but if that does not destroy it, there is nothing else left to destroy it. For obviously the good will never destroy anything, and   609b
again what is neither good nor bad won't either.

GLAUCON: How could it?

SOCRATES: So if we discover something, the badness of which causes it to deteriorate but cannot break it down and destroy it, won't we immediately know that something with such a nature cannot be destroyed after all?

GLAUCON: That seems reasonable.

SOCRATES: Well, then, what about the soul? Isn't there something that makes it bad?

GLAUCON: Certainly. All the things we were discussing earlier: injustice, intemperance, cowardice, and ignorance.

609c   SOCRATES: Do any of these break it down and destroy it? Think about it, so we are not deceived into believing that when an unjust and foolish person is caught, he is destroyed by injustice, which is a deficiency in a soul. Instead, let's proceed this way: just as the body's deficiency, which is disease, wastes and destroys a body, and brings it to the point of not being a body at all, so all the things we mentioned just now reach the point of not being when
609d   their own peculiar badness attaches itself to them, is present in them, and destroys them. Isn't that so?

GLAUCON: Yes.

SOCRATES: Come on, then, and look at the soul in the same way. When injustice and the rest of vices are present in it, does their presence in it and attachment to it corrupt and wither it until they bring it to the point of death and separate it from the body?

GLAUCON: No, they never do that.

SOCRATES: But surely it is unreasonable to suppose that a thing is destroyed by something else's deficiency and not by its own?

GLAUCON: It is unreasonable.

609e   SOCRATES: Think about it, Glaucon. We do not even believe that a body would be destroyed by the deficiency belonging to foods, whether it is staleness, rottenness, or anything else. But if the foods' own deficiency induces bodily deterioration, we will say the body was destroyed *through* them *by* its own badness, which is disease. But we will never admit that
610a   the body is destroyed *by* the deficiency belonging to foods—since they and the body are different things—except when external badness induces the natural badness.

GLAUCON: That's absolutely right.

SOCRATES: By the same argument, then, if the body's deficiency does not induce a soul's own deficiency in a soul, we will never admit that a soul is destroyed by external badness in the absence of its own peculiar deficiency—one thing by another's badness.

GLAUCON: Yes, that's reasonable.

SOCRATES: Well, then, let's refute these arguments and show that what we said was not right. Or, so long as they remain unrefuted, let's never say that the soul even comes close to being destroyed by a fever or any other 610b disease, or by killing for that matter—not even if one were to cut the entire body up into the very smallest pieces—until someone demonstrates to us that these conditions of the body make the soul itself more unjust and more impious. But when an external badness is present, while its own particular badness is absent, let's not allow anyone to say that a soul or anything else whatever is destroyed.   610c

GLAUCON: But you may be sure no one will ever prove that the souls of the dying are made more unjust by death!

SOCRATES: But suppose someone dares to come to grips with our argument and—simply in order to avoid having to agree that our souls are immortal—dares to say that a dying man does become worse and more unjust. We are sure to reply that if what he says is true, injustice must be as deadly as a disease to those who have it, and that those who catch it must die because of its own deadly nature—with the worst cases dying quickly and the less 610d serious ones more slowly—and not as now in fact happens, where the unjust are put to death because of their injustice by others who inflict the penalty.

GLAUCON: By Zeus, injustice won't seem so altogether terrible if it will be deadly to the person who contracts it, since then it would be an *escape* from evils! But I am more inclined to think that it will be shown to be entirely the opposite—something that kills others if it can, but makes its possessor 610e very lively indeed—and not just lively, but positively sleepless! That's how far it is, in my view, from being deadly.

SOCRATES: You are right. After all, if its own deficiency—its own badness—is not enough to kill and destroy the soul, an evil designed for the destruction of something else will hardly destroy the soul, or anything else except what it is designed to destroy.

GLAUCON: "Hardly" is right, it seems.

SOCRATES: Then when something is not destroyed by a single bad thing—whether its own or an external one—clearly it must always exist. And if it **611a** always exists, it is immortal.

GLAUCON: It must be.

SOCRATES: Well, then, let's assume it to be so. And if it is so, you realize that the same ones will always exist. I mean, they surely could not become fewer in number if none is destroyed, or more numerous either. For if anything immortal is increased, you know that the increase would have to come from the mortal, and then everything would end up being immortal.

GLAUCON: True.

SOCRATES: Then we must not think such a thing—for our argument does
611b   not allow it. And we must not think, either, that the soul in its truest nature
is full of complexity and dissimilarity and conflict with itself.

GLAUCON: How do you mean?

SOCRATES: It is not easy for something to be immortal when it is composed
of many elements and is not composed in the most beautiful way—which
is how the soul now seemed to us.

GLAUCON: It probably isn't.

SOCRATES: Yet both our recent arguments and others as well compel us to
accept that the soul *is* immortal. But what it is like in truth, seen as it should
be, not maimed by its partnership with the body and other bad things,
611c   which is how we see it now, what it is like when it has become pure—*that*
we can adequately see only by means of rational calculation. And you will
find it to be a much more beautiful thing than we thought and get a much
clearer view of all the cases of justice and injustice and of all the other
things that we have so far discussed. So far, what we have said about the
soul is true of it as it appears at present. But the condition we have seen
it in is like that of all the sea god Glaucus, whose original nature cannot
easily be made out by those who catch glimpses of him, because some of
611d   the original parts of his body have been broken off, others have been worn
away and altogether mutilated by the waves, and other things—shells,
seaweeds, and rocks—have grown into him, so that he looks more like any
wild beast than what he naturally was. Such, too, is the condition of the
soul when we see it beset by myriad bad things. But, Glaucon, we should
be looking in another direction.

GLAUCON: Where?

SOCRATES: To its love of wisdom. We must keep in mind what it grasps
and the kinds of things with which it longs to associate, because it is akin
611e   to what is divine and immortal and what always exists, and what it would
become if it followed this longing with its whole being and if that impulse
lifted it out of the sea in which it now is, and struck off the rocks and shells
612a   that, because it now feasts on earth, have grown around it in a wild, earthy,
and stony profusion as a result of those so-called happy feastings. And then
you would see its true nature, whether multiform or uniform, or somehow
some other way. But we have given a pretty good account now, I think, of
what its condition is and what form it takes in human life.

GLAUCON: We certainly have.

SOCRATES: In the course of our discussion, then, did we respond to the
other points, without having to invoke the wages and reputations of justice,
612b   as you all said Homer and Hesiod did? Instead, haven't we found that justice
itself is the best thing for the soul itself, and that the soul should do what
is just, whether it has Gyges' ring or not, or even the cap of Hades as well.

GLAUCON: That's absolutely true. We have.

SOCRATES: So, Glaucon, isn't it now at last unobjectionable, in addition, also to give back to justice and the rest of virtue both the kind and quantity of wages they bring to the soul, both from human beings and from gods, both during life and after death? 612c

GLAUCON: Certainly.

SOCRATES: Then will you give *me* back what you borrowed from me in the course of the discussion?

GLAUCON: What in particular?

SOCRATES: I granted you that the just man should seem unjust and the unjust one just. For you thought that even if it would be impossible for these things to remain hidden from both gods and human beings, all the same, it had to be granted for the sake of argument, so that justice itself could be judged in relation to injustice itself.[7] Don't you remember? 612d

GLAUCON: *I* would be unjust if I didn't!

SOCRATES: Well, then, since they have now been judged, I ask on behalf of justice for a return of the reputation it in fact has among gods and human beings; and that we agree that it does indeed have such a reputation, and so may carry off the prizes it gains for someone by making him seem just; since we have already seen that it does give the good things that come from being just, and does not deceive those who really possess it.

GLAUCON: That's a just request. 612e

SOCRATES: Then won't you first give this back, that it certainly does not remain hidden from the gods what each of the two is like?

GLAUCON: We will.

SOCRATES: But if it does not remain hidden, one would be loved by the gods and one hated, as we agreed at the beginning.[8]

GLAUCON: That's right.

SOCRATES: And won't we also agree that everything that comes to the one who is loved by gods—insofar as it comes from the gods themselves—is the best possible, unless it is some unavoidable bad thing due to him for 613a an earlier mistake?

GLAUCON: Certainly.

SOCRATES: Similarly, we must suppose that if a just man falls into poverty or disease or some of the other things that seem bad, it will end well for him during his lifetime or even in death. For surely the gods at least will

---

[7] See 360e–361d, 367b–e.

[8] 352a–b, 363a–e.

never neglect anyone who eagerly wishes to become just and, by practicing
613b   virtue, to make himself as much like a god as a human being can.

GLAUCON: It is certainly reasonable to think that a man of that sort won't
be neglected by one who is like him.

SOCRATES: And mustn't we think the opposite of the unjust one?

GLAUCON: Definitely.

SOCRATES: Those, then, are the sorts of prizes that come from the gods to
the just man.

GLAUCON: That's certainly what I believe.

SOCRATES: What about from human beings? What does a just man get from
them? If we are to assert what is really the case, isn't it this? Aren't clever
but unjust men precisely like runners who run well on the first leg but not
on the return one?[9] They leap away sharply at first, but in the end they
become ridiculous and, heads drooping, run off the field uncrowned. True
613c   runners, on the other hand, make it to the end, collect the prizes, and are
crowned as victors. And isn't it also generally what happens to just people?
Toward the end of each course of action and association and of life as a
whole, don't they enjoy a good reputation and collect the prizes that come
from human beings?

GLAUCON: Of course.

SOCRATES: Will you then allow me to say about them what *you* said about
613d   the unjust?[10] For I will claim that it is the just who, when they are old
enough, hold the ruling offices in their city if they choose, marry from
whatever family they choose, and give their children in marriage to whomever they please. Indeed, all the things that you said about the others, I
now say about these. As for the unjust, the majority of them, even if they
remain hidden when they are young, are caught by the end of the race
and ridiculed, and, by the time they get old, have become wretched and
are showered with abuse by foreigners and citizens, beaten with whips,
and made to suffer those punishments you rightly described as crude, such
613e   as racking and burning. Imagine I have claimed that they suffer all such
things. Well, as I say, see if you will stand for it.

GLAUCON: Of course I will. What you say is right.

SOCRATES: Well, then, while the just man is alive, these are the sorts of
614a   prizes, wages, and gifts he receives from gods and human beings, in addition to those good things that justice itself provides.

GLAUCON: Fine and secure ones they are, too!

---

[9] The race is a sprint from one end of the stadium to the other and back.

[10] 361d–362c.

SOCRATES: Well, they are nothing in number or size compared to those that await each man after death. We must hear about them, too, so that, by hearing them, each of these men may get back in full what he is owed by the argument.

GLAUCON: Please describe them, then, since there are not many things it would be more pleasant to hear.   614b

SOCRATES: Well, it is not an Alcinous-story I am going to tell you, but that of a brave man called Er, the son of Armenias, by race a Pamphylian.[11] Once upon a time, he was killed in battle. On the tenth day, when the rest of the dead were picked up, they were already putrefying, but he was picked up still quite sound. When he had been taken home and was lying on the pyre before his funeral on the twelfth day, he revived and, after reviving, told what he had seen in the other world.

He said that when his soul had departed, it traveled together with many others and came to a daimonic place, where there were two adjacent open-   614c
ings in the earth and two in the heavens above and opposite them. Judges were seated between these. And, when they had made their judgments, they told the just to go to the right up through the heavens, with signs of the judgments attached to their fronts. But the unjust they told to travel to the left and down. And they too had on their backs signs of all their deeds. When he himself came forward, they said that he was to be a messenger   614d
to human beings to tell them about the things happening there, and they told him to listen to and look at everything in the place.

Through one of the openings in the heavens and one in the earth, he saw souls departing after judgment had been passed on them. Through the other two, they were arriving. From the one in the earth they came up parched and dusty, while from the one in the heavens they came down pure. And the ones that had just arrived seemed to have come from a long   614e
journey, and went off gladly to the meadow, like a crowd going to a festival, and set up camp there. Those that knew one another exchanged greetings and those coming up from the earth asked the others about the things up there, while those from the heavens asked about the others' experiences. They told their stories to one another, the former weeping and lamenting   615a
as they recollected all they had suffered and seen on their journey below the earth—which lasted a thousand years—and the ones from the heavens tell-ing, in turn, about their happy experiences and the inconceivably beautiful sights they had seen.To tell it all, Glaucon, would take a long time. But the gist, he said, was this: for all the unjust things they had done and for all the people they had wronged, they had paid the penalty for every one in turn,

---

[11] Books ix–xi of the *Odyssey* were traditionally referred to as *Alkinou apologoi,* the tales of Alcinous. Included among them is the story of Odysseus' descent into Hades.

ten times over for each. That is to say, they paid for each injustice once in every hundred years of their journey, so that, on the assumption that a hundred years is roughly the length of a human life, they paid a tenfold penalty for each injustice. For example, if some of them had caused many deaths or had betrayed cities or armies and reduced them to slavery, or had taken part in other evildoing, they would receive ten times the pain for each of them. On the other hand, if they had done good deeds and become just and pious, they received commensurate awards.

He said some other things about the stillborn and those who lived for only a short time, but they are not worth recounting. And he told of even greater wages for impiety or piety toward gods or parents, and for murder. He said he was there, you see, when someone asked where the great Ardiaius was. This Ardiaius had been a tyrant in a city in Pamphylia just a thousand years before that, and was said to have killed his aged father and older brother and committed many other impious deeds as well. He said the one who was asked responded: "He has not come here and never will. For in fact this, too, was one of the terrible sights we saw. When we were near the mouth, about to come up after all our sufferings were over, we suddenly saw Ardiaius together with some others, almost all of whom were tyrants—although there were also some private individuals among them who had committed great crimes. They thought that they were about to go up, but the mouth would not let them through. Instead, it roared whenever one of these incurably bad people, or anyone else who had not paid a sufficient penalty, tried to go up. At that location, there were savage men, all fiery to look at, standing by, paying attention to the sound, who grabbed some of these people and led them away. But in the case of Ardiaius and others, they bound their feet, hands, and neck and threw them down and flayed them. They dragged them along the road outside, lacerating them on thorn bushes. They explained to those who were passing by at the time why they were being dragged away, and said that they were to be thrown into Tartarus. He said that of the many and multifarious fears they experienced there, the greatest each of them had was that the sound would be heard as he came up, and that each was very pleased when it was silent as he went up. Such then were the penalties and punishments, and the rewards that were their counterparts.

When each group had spent seven days in the meadow, on the eighth they had to move on from there and continue their journey. In four days, they came to a place where they could see stretching from above, through the whole heavens and earth, a straight beam of light, like a column, very closely resembling a rainbow, but brighter and more pure. They reached the beam after traveling another day's journey. And there, in the middle of the light, they saw stretching from the heavens the ends of its bonds—for this light is what binds the heavens, like the cables underneath a trireme,

615b

615c

615d

615e

616a

616b

616c

thus holding the entire revolving thing together. From those ends hangs the spindle of Necessity, by means of which all the revolving things are turned. Its shaft and hook were adamant, while its whorl[12] was adamant mixed with materials of other kinds. The nature of the whorl was as follows. Its shape was like the ones here on Earth, but from Er's description, we must think of it as being like this: in one great whorl, hollow and scooped out, lay another just like it, only smaller, that fitted into it exactly, the way nested bowls fit together; and similarly a third and a fourth, and four others. For there were eight whorls altogether, lying inside one another, with their rims appearing as circles from above, while from the back they formed one continuous whorl around the shaft, which is driven right through the center of the eighth.

    Now, the first or outermost whorl had the broadest circular rim, that of the sixth was second, third was that of the fourth, fourth that of the eighth, fifth that of the seventh, sixth that of the fifth, seventh that of the third, and eighth that of the second. That of the greatest was spangled; that of the seventh was brightest; that of the eighth took its color from the seventh's shining on it; that of the second and fifth were very similar to one another, being yellower than the rest; the third was the whitest in color; the fourth was reddish; and the sixth was second in whiteness.

    The spindle as a whole revolved at the same speed, but within the revolving whole the seven inner circles gently revolved in the opposite direction to the whole. Of these, the eighth moved fastest; second, and at the same speed as one another, were the seventh, sixth, and fifth; third, it seemed to them, in the speed of its counter-revolution, was the fourth; fourth was the third; and fifth the second.[13]

616d

616e

617a

617b

---

12 The circular weight that twirls a spindle in weaving.

13 Plato's description of the beam of light and the spindle is difficult. He compares the light to the ropes that bind a trireme together. These ropes seem to have girded the trireme from stem to stern and to have entered it at both places. Within the trireme, they were connected to some sort of twisting device that allowed them to be tightened when the water caused them to stretch and become slack. The spindle of Necessity seems to be just such a twisting device. Hence, the extremities of the light's bonds must enter into the universe just as the ropes enter the trireme, and the spindle must be attached to these extremities, so that its spinning tightens the light and holds the universe together. The light is thus like two rainbows around the universe (or the whorl of the spindle), whose ends enter the universe and are attached to the spindle. The upper half of the whorl of the spindle consists of concentric hemispheres that fit into one another, with their lips or rims fitting together in a single plane. The outer hemisphere is that of the fixed stars; the second is the orbit of Saturn; the third of Jupiter; the fourth of Mars; the fifth of Mercury; the sixth of Venus; the seventh of the sun; and the eighth of the moon. The earth is in the center. The hemispheres are

The spindle revolved on the lap of Necessity. On top of each of its circles stood a Siren, who was carried around by its rotation, emitting a single sound, one single note. And from all eight in concord, a single harmony was produced. And there were three other women seated around it equidistant from one another, each on a throne. They were the daughters of Necessity, the Fates, dressed in white with garlands on their heads—Lachesis, Clotho, and Atropos—and they sang to the accompaniment of the Sirens' harmony, Lachesis singing of the past, Clotho of the present, and Atropos of the future. Clotho, using her right hand, touched the outer circumference of the spindle and helped it turn, pausing from time to time; Atropos, with her left, did the same to the inner ones; and Lachesis used each hand in turn to touch both.

When the souls arrived, they had to go straight to Lachesis. A sort of spokesman first arranged them in ranks; then, taking lots and models of lives from the lap of Lachesis, he mounted a high platform, and said:

"The word of Lachesis, maiden daughter of Necessity! Ephemeral souls. The beginning of another death-bringing cycle for mortal-kind! Your daimon will not be assigned to you by lot; you will choose him. The one who has the first lot will be the first to choose a life to which he will be bound by necessity. Virtue has no master: as he honors or dishonors it, so shall each of you have more or less of it. Responsibility lies with the chooser; the god is blameless."

After saying that, the spokesman threw the lots out among them all, and each picked up the one that fell next to him—except for Er, who was not allowed. And to the one who picked it up, it was clear what number he had drawn. After that again the spokesman placed the models of lives on the ground before them—many more of them than those who were present. They were multifarious: all animal lives were there, as well as all human lives. There were tyrannies among them, some life-long, others ending halfway through in poverty, exile, and beggary. There were lives of famous men—some famous for the beauty of their appearance or for their other strengths or athletic prowess, others for their nobility and the virtues of their ancestors, and also some infamous in these respects—and similarly for women. But the structure of the soul was not included, because with the choice of a different life it would inevitably become different. But all the other qualities were mixed with each other and with wealth or poverty, sickness or health, or the states in between.

Here, it seems, my dear Glaucon, a human being faces the greatest danger of all, and because of that each must, to the neglect of all other

transparent and the width of their rims is the distance of the heavenly bodies from one another.

subjects, take care above all else to be a seeker and student of that subject which will enable him to learn and discover who will give him the ability and the knowledge to distinguish a good life from a bad, so that he will always and in any circumstances choose the better one from among those that are possible. He must calculate the effect of all the things we have mentioned just now, both jointly and severally, on the virtue of a life, so as to know what the good and bad things are that beauty does when it is mixed with wealth or poverty and this or that state of the soul; what high and low birth, private lives and ruling offices, physical strength and weak- 618d nesses, ease and difficulties in learning, and all the things that are either naturally part of the soul or can be acquired by it do, when they are mixed with one another. On the basis of all that he will be able, by considering the nature of the soul, to reason out which life is better and which worse and choose accordingly, calling worse the one that will lead the soul to 618e become more unjust, and better the one that leads it to become more just. Everything else he will ignore. For we have seen that this is the best way to choose, whether in life or death.

Holding this belief with adamantine determination, he must go down **619a** to Hades, so that even there he won't be dazzled[14] by wealth and other such evils, and won't rush into tyrannies or other similar practices and so commit irreparable evils, and suffer even greater ones; but instead will know to choose the middle life in such circumstances, and avoid either of the extremes, both in this life, so far as is possible, and in the whole of the life to come. For this is how a human being becomes happiest. 619b

At that point our messenger from the other world also reported that the spokesman said this: "Even for the one who comes last, if he chooses wisely and lives earnestly, there is a satisfactory life available, not a bad one. Let not the first to choose be careless, nor the last discouraged."

When the spokesman had told them that, Er said, the one who drew the first lot came up and immediately chose the greatest tyranny. In his foolishness and greed, you see, he chose it without adequately examining everything, and did not notice that it involved being fated to eat his own 619c children, among other evils. When he examined the life at leisure, how- ever, he beat his breast and bemoaned his choice, ignoring the warning of the spokesman. For he did not blame himself for these evils, but chance, daimons, and everything except himself. He was one of those who had come down from the heavens, having lived his previous life in an orderly constitution, sharing in virtue through habit but without philosophy. 619d

Generally speaking, not the least number of the people caught out in this way were souls who came from the heavens, and so were untrained

---

[14] See 364d, 576d.

in sufferings. The majority of those from the earth, on the other hand, because they had suffered themselves and had seen others doing so, were in no rush to make their choices. Because of that, and also because of the chance of the lottery, there was an exchange of evils and goods for most of the souls. Yet, if a person, whenever he came to the life that is here, always

619e practiced philosophy in a sound manner, and if the fall of the lot did not put his choice of life among the last, it is likely, from what was reported by Er about the next world, that not only will he be happy here, but also that his journey from here to there and back again will not be underground and rough, but smooth and through the heavens.

He said it was a sight worth seeing how the various souls chose their

620a lives, since seeing it caused pity, ridicule, and surprise. For the most part, their choice reflected the character of their former life. He saw the soul that had once belonged to Orpheus, he said, choosing a swan's life: he hated the female sex because of his death at their hands, and so was unwilling to be conceived in a woman and born.[15] He saw the soul of Thamyris choosing a nightingale's life, a swan changing to the choice of a human life, and other musical animals doing the same. The twentieth soul chose

620b the life of a lion. It was that of Ajax, son of Telamon, who avoided human life because he remembered the judgment about the armor.[16] The next was that of Agamemnon, which also hated the human race on account of what it suffered, and so changed to the life of an eagle. Allotted a place in the middle, the soul of Atalanta, when it saw the great honors of a male athlete, unable to pass them by, chose his life. After her, he saw the soul of Epeius,

620c son of Panopeus, taking on the nature of a craftswoman. Further on, among the last, he saw the soul of the ridiculous Thersites clothing itself as an ape.

Now it chanced that Odysseus' soul drew the last lot of all, and came to make its choice. Remembering its former sufferings, it rejected love of honor, and went around for a long time looking for the life of a private individual who did his own work, and with difficulty it found one lying off somewhere neglected by the others. When it saw it, it said that it would

620d have done the same even if it had drawn the first-place lot, and chose it gladly. Similarly, souls went from the other animals into human beings, or into one another; the unjust changing into savage animals, the just into tame ones; and every sort of mixture occurred.

---

[15] According to one myth, Orpheus was killed and dismembered by Thracian women, or Maenads.

[16] Ajax thought that he deserved to be awarded the armor of the dead Achilles, but instead it was awarded to Odysseus. Ajax was maddened by this injustice and later killed himself because of the terrible things he had done while mad.

When all the souls had chosen lives, in the same allotted order they went forward to Lachesis. She assigned to each the daimon it had chosen, as guardian of its life and fulfiller of its choices. This daimon first led the soul 620e under the hand of Clotho as it turned the revolving spindle, thus ratifying the allotted fate it had chosen. After receiving her touch, he led the soul to the spinning of Atropos, to make the spun fate irreversible. Then, without turning around, it went under the throne of Necessity. When it had passed through that, and when the others had also passed through, they all traveled 621a to the plain of Lethe, through burning and choking and terrible heat, for it was empty of trees and earthly vegetation. They camped, since evening was coming on, beside the river of forgetfulness, whose water no vessel can hold. All of them had to drink a certain measure of this water. But those not saved by wisdom drank more than the measure. And as each of them drank, he forgot everything. When they were asleep and midnight came, 621b there was a clap of thunder and an earthquake, and they were suddenly carried away from there, this way and that, up to their births, like shooting stars. But Er himself was prevented from drinking the water. Yet how or where he had come back to his body, he did not know, but suddenly recovering his sight he now saw himself lying on the pyre at dawn.

And so, Glaucon, his story was saved and not lost; and it would save us, too, 621c if we were persuaded by it, since we would safely cross the river Lethe with our souls undefiled. But if we are persuaded by me, we will believe that the soul is immortal and able to endure every evil and also every good, and always hold to the upward path, practicing justice with wisdom every way we can, so that we will be friends to ourselves and to the gods, both while we remain here on Earth and when we receive the rewards of justice, and go around like victors in the games collecting prizes; and so both in this 621d life and on the thousand-year journey we have described, we will fare well.

Select Bibliography

Annas, Julia. *An Introduction to Plato's Republic*. Oxford: Clarendon Press, 1981.

Dover, K. J. *Greek Homosexuality*. Cambridge, Mass.: Harvard University Press, 1978.

Evans, J. D. G. *A Plato Primer*. Ithaca: Cornell University Press, 2010.

Ferrari, G. R. F. *Listening to the Cicadas: A Study of Plato's Phaedrus*. Cambridge: Cambridge University Press, 1987.

————, ed. *The Cambridge Companion to Plato's Republic*. Cambridge: Cambridge University Press, 2007.

Fine, Gail, ed. *Plato 1: Metaphysics and Epistemology*. Oxford: Oxford University Press, 1999.

————. *Plato 2: Ethics, Politics, Religion, and the Soul*. Oxford: Oxford University Press, 1999.

————. *The Oxford Handbook of Plato*. Oxford: Oxford University Press, 2008.

Irwin, Terence. *Plato's Ethics*. New York: Oxford University Press, 1995.

Kraut, Richard, ed. *The Cambridge Companion to Plato*. Cambridge: Cambridge University Press, 1992.

Murdoch, Iris. *The Fire and the Sun: Why Plato Banished the Artists*. Oxford: Oxford University Press, 1977.

Reeve, C. D. C. *Socrates in the Apology: An Essay on Plato's Apology of Socrates*. Indianapolis: Hackett, 1989.

————. *Philosopher-Kings: The Argument of Plato's Republic*. Indianapolis: Hackett, 2006.

Schofield, Malcolm. *Plato: Political Philosophy*. Oxford: Oxford University Press, 2006.

Scott, Dominic. *Plato's Meno*. Cambridge: Cambridge University Press, 2006.

Sheffield, Frisbee C. C. *Plato's Symposium: The Ethics of Desire*. Oxford: Oxford University Press, 2006.